Ideas That Created the Future

Ideas That Created the Future

Classic Papers of Computer Science

edited by Harry R. Lewis

The MIT Press
Cambridge, Massachusetts
London, England

This book was set in New Times Roman by the editor using LaTeX. Printed and bound in the United States of America.

Library of Congress Cataloging-in-Publication Data

Names: Lewis, Harry R., editor.
Title: Ideas that created the future : classic papers of computer science /
    edited by Harry R. Lewis.
Description: Cambridge, Massachusetts : The MIT Press, [2021] | Includes
    bibliographical references and index.
Identifiers: LCCN 2020018950 | ISBN 9780262045308 (paperback)
Subjects: LCSH: Computer science.
Classification: LCC QA76 .I34 2020 | DDC 004–dc23
LC record available at https://lccn.loc.gov/2020018950

10   9   8   7   6   5   4   3

To those quirky and skeptical teachers who took me new places:
Phil Bridgess, Jim Maguire, Van Elliott, Desmond O'Grady,
Sheila Greibach, Tom Cheatham, Ivan Sutherland, and Burt Dreben

"I can tell your future. Nothing easier. ... But who can tell your past? ... What did it mean? What was it trying to say to you?"
—Thornton Wilder, *The Skin of Our Teeth*

Contents

Preface

This volume tells the story of computer science in the words that created the field. The collection came into being for two reasons. First, to relieve 21st-century readers of the misimpression that the established conventions of the field were handed down to contemporary culture in finished form. Computer science has a rich family history that should be known to students and practitioners of the field. And second, to help readers see how important new ideas come to be, how tentative, clumsy baby steps become graceful, progressive strides—or sometimes go nowhere for years and then are taken up again after a long delay. The field is still young and dynamic; anyone looking around it today might see some novelty that will be tomorrow's canon, hardly recognizable in its infancy.

To tell this story I have selected, with considerable anxiety, 46 papers from the earliest times to 1980, and have introduced each with a brief context-setting essay. Each of these papers made a memorable contribution to the field. Many others might have been selected in addition to or instead of these, and the 1980 cut-off date is arbitrary—though it does represent a moment when the field became so diversified as to defy summation in a small collection like this one.

This book is an educational volume documenting the origins of the field, and neither a critical edition of the papers nor a history of the field. The Introduction sets the papers in their historical context, but for those seeking a more thorough and nuanced account of historical developments, Priestley (2011) successfully avoids both over-reliance on self-interested recollections of the principals and *post hoc ergo propter hoc* fallacies. For the early history of computing *machines*, the reader is referred to Pratt (1987) and Jones (2016).

This volume is suitable for a one-semester course aimed at graduate students or advanced undergraduates, and has been used for that purpose at both Harvard and MIT. It can also serve as a guided tour for a curious professional. Among the factors considered when selecting and editing papers were these:

1. Many papers are heavily excerpted, both to focus on the key contributions and to omit technical details no longer of great interest. For example, I have omitted the ugly details of Turing's code for his universal machine. Omitted text is indicated throughout by use of an

ellipsis (...). Needless to say, readers hungry for more detail should track down the full papers. Each chapter begins with the bibliographic reference for the paper, though the year in the bibliographic citation may not match the year included with the title, since some papers were presented orally first or revised after their first publication. Moreover, the invention or discovery documented in the paper may have occurred earlier than the publication date.

2. I preferred short and readable papers to long or difficult papers, no matter how important.

3. I included only papers, not book extracts (with the exception of Boole's *The Laws of Thought* and the title essay from Brooks's collection *The Mythical Man-Month*).

4. I did not attempt to condense the defining reports for major programming languages such as FORTRAN, COBOL, or ALGOL, important though they were to the development of the field.

5. Important early efforts to systematize the field are also omitted, for example *Curriculum 68* (Atchison et al., 1968) and the history of programming languages by Jean Sammet (1972).

6. The page count of authors included cannot be taken as a measure of their importance as computer scientists of the period. Donald Knuth would be under-represented by that standard and Edsger Dijkstra perhaps over-represented; great names such as Backus, Chomsky, Church, Floyd, Gray, Kleene, Newell, Lamport, Lampson, Rabin, Scott, and Tarjan are missing entirely. Apologies to anyone whose favorite paper or scientist did not make it in!

And a few purely editorial details.

· All references have been moved to a common bibliography at the end of the book, and Chicago style citations are used throughout. Any document cited in the original paper but not cited within the excerpted part of the text of a paper has not been included in the bibliography.

· Typographical errors in the original papers have been corrected, and punctuation has generally been standardized.

· Section and figure numbering has been made uniform. §33.7 is section 7 (or perhaps the seventh unnumbered section) of the original paper that appears here as chapter 33.

· The original numbering of theorems and lemmas has generally been retained.

· Footnotes have been omitted or incorporated as parentheses in the running text.

· In a few places, I have included editorial comments using the form "[EDITOR: The comment]."

For their careful proofreading I am grateful to the students of Harvard CS191 in 2019 and MIT 6.S897 in 2020. Brian Sapozhnikov and Adham Meguid were especially eagle-eyed. Thanks also to Peter Denning, Bill Gasarch, Warren Goldfarb, Matthew Lena, Maryanthe Malliaris, Tasha Schoenstein, Lloyd Strickland, Sherry Turkle, and Joel Wachman for their helpful comments and corrections. Of course, any remaining errors are solely my responsibility.

Harry Lewis
July 2020

Introduction: The Roots and Growth of Computer Science

THE first computing was numerical calculation; piles of *calculi* (pebbles) were tools of early accountants. Later notational and mechanical inventions were put to use by observers of the skies and by engineers of military and naval adventures. The demand for calculation intensified as the physical world was subjected to human understanding and control, especially during the Enlightenment, and later in wartime.

But the intellectual roots of computer science are not merely bookkeeping, astronomy, and ballistics. Computer science is the child of logic, the mathematical sciences, and the human imagination. Because of its mixed intellectual parentage and its only indirect connection to the natural world, the field struggled for legitimacy through much of the twentieth century. By the time computational phenomena became ubiquitously significant in science, engineering, and economics, as well as in mathematics, the energy had drained from the semantic wars about whether computer science, or any other "science of the artificial" (Simon, 1996), could legitimately be called a "science." That the field became accepted as a science is to the credit of mid-twentieth century education pioneers who designed the first courses and curricula for colleges and universities, often against resistance from the departments of mathematics or engineering from which it was emerging. We cannot tell their story here, but it is fair to note that this retelling of the genesis of the field might have been very different had the educational systematizers organized the field differently.

Logic lurked in the family tree since ancient times, making only clumsy and episodic contact with calculation until, in the mid-nineteenth century, it became a tool of metamathematics. Algorithms were reified in the first decades of the twentieth century as part of the program of metamathematicians to determine what mathematics can be known to be true. And scientific and business calculation, which had stimulated a long series of incremental improvements in mechanical calculator design, got an important boost from the unique demands placed on physics and engineering during World War II.

All along the way a hubristic idea kept nosing its way into the serious work: might human beings breathe life into the machines they were building? As computer science matured, that mythic vision wound around the mathematics of computation in a tightening gyre, portending fusion in a singularity. With continued improvements in the quality of synthetic vision, speech, and dexterity, the debate continues about the consequences for individuals and societies.

To be sure, the birthdate of computer science is arbitrary. We leave to the field's prehistory works such as the *Arithmetic* of Diophantus in the third century (Diophantus, 1910) and the *Algebra* of al-Kwarizmi in the ninth century (al Khwārizmī, 1915), intellectually remarkable though both are. (Diophantus does make a cameo appearance in chapter 5 of this volume, for having studied numerical questions which, once generalized, turned out to be recursively unsolvable.)

But we have to start with Aristotle, who gave us the notion that propositions can include variables representing properties (chapter 1). Such a proposition might be true regardless of the instantiation of the variables, or might be true only sometimes, or never. Such logical analysis has a specific relevance to computer science. What makes a digital computer "general-purpose" is that the same binary logic elements can signify different things at different times. A storage register that signifies time of day when it is used in one program may at the next instant signify street address in a different program. To Aristotle we owe the realization that fixed rules of logic can apply to different phenomena—that logic provides a general framework for reasoning.

Early in the seventeenth century Kepler formulated mathematical laws for the trajectories of the planets, Descartes reduced geometry to algebra, and Pascal characterized fluids in mathematical terms. Since observable physical phenomena were being described by mathematical formulas, the ancient problems of calculating areas and volumes of curved shapes assumed greater practical importance, all the more so because, with advances in optics, celestial measurements became more precise. The advances in the mathematics of continuous quantities laid the groundwork for the nearly simultaneous invention of the calculus of infinitesimals by Isaac Newton in England and by Gottfried Leibniz on the Continent.

Leibniz was a skilled calculator. Pascal had developed an ingenious mechanical adding machine, having observed his father's labors with accounting for tax collections; Leibniz extended the device to carry out multiplications and divisions—thus building one of the first nested-loop calculating engines (but see page 62). Leibniz understood and wrote about the merits of binary notation long before its utility was seen by others; even the pioneer Howard Hathaway Aiken, working more than 250 years later, gave up decimal arithmetic only reluctantly. Most importantly, in addition to inventing the calculus of infinitesimals, Leibniz conceived of a calculus of ideas. Chapter 2 is only one of many utopian visions about rationalizing human affairs, and Leibniz did not get very far toward executing his plan. He was aware that in the thirteenth century, Ramon Llull had built a machine to perform certain syllogistic inferences, and Leibniz notes that once his calculus is complete, humankind "will have an instrument which will serve to exalt reason no less than the Telescope serves to perfect vision." The logical atoms on which his calculus would operate reappear almost two centuries later in the work of George Boole (see below) and have become the base facts of logic programming languages such as Prolog and Datalog.

Charles Babbage's design for his Analytical Engine (chapter 3) might have marked the arrival of the age of computers, as the device would have been both programmable and adaptable. But Babbage could not get it built. He kept running out of money, in spite of pleas that the machine was *almost* done—in 1835, Babbage (1989, p. 245) wrote, "the greatest difficulties of the invention have already been surmounted, and that the plans will be finished in a few months"—and was important to the national defense—"the control of the Analytical Engine over all the great Astronomical questions on which the safety of the Navy so much depends can scarcely fail to impart to the subject an interest in the mind of Her Majesty," he wrote to Prince Albert (Babbage, 1843). Nonetheless, Babbage's apprentice Ada Lovelace was able to grasp a variety of recognizably modern programming concepts by reasoning about this never-functional machine.

George Boole (1854, here chapter 4) had a different agenda. About 25 years Babbage's junior and not university-educated, Boole did cross paths with Babbage at least once, but his own goal was to bring Aristotle up to date, to capture the rules of human reason in mathematical form. His work on logic was the more innovative for being out of the mainstream, and its influence on computing was limited—until the 1930s, when Claude Shannon made it an essential tool for designing digital circuits.

By the turn of the twentieth century logicians were using the methods of mathematics itself to mathematize the idea of proof and were seeking to complete Leibniz's logical agenda. David Hilbert's grand challenge, his Entscheidungsproblem—to determine whether formalized mathematical statements could be proved—was posed crisply only some years after his famous 1900 address to the International Congress of Mathematicians, excerpted here as chapter 5. But "Mathematical Problems" both foreshadows mechanized logic with its appeal to finitary methods and conveys a Leibnizian optimism that if the world's mathematicians work hard enough, their house will be put in order.

It was not to be, at least not as Hilbert had imagined it. First Gödel, then Church, and then Turing (1936, here chapter 6) illuminated a metamathematical world that could not have been imagined before the twentieth century. Though each had a significant impact on computer science, Turing's contribution was the most important, because (a) it convincingly formalized the idea of a computing machine, and thus the idea that it was possible to prove things about them; (b) it persuasively reified computational universality and showed that devices made of simple components could achieve it; as well as (c) combining (a) and (b) with irrefutable logic to prove that there were limits to the computable.

Turing's demolition of Hilbert's Entscheidungsproblem is the exclamation point of his paper. An important technical trick in the middle of the proof uses the data storage unit of an automaton to store the programs of other automata. To complete his argument, Turing then reached back to Cantor's 1891 diagonalization argument—originally devised for the very different purpose of showing the uncountability of the reals (Cantor, 1996). A decade later, Eckert and Mauchly incorporated a similar stored-program idea into a modification of their ENIAC computer, though they did so for purely practical reasons, uninfluenced by Turing's theoretical work—storing the program in vacuum tube memory sped up the machine and made the program easier to change (Priestley, 2011, p. 125). When John von Neumann teamed up with Eckert and Mauchly in 1945 to design the EDVAC, a successor machine to the ENIAC, it fell to him to write the design notes (chapter 10), and the stored-program design has ever since been known, too generously, as the "von Neumann architecture." The same idea was used in the Manchester "Baby" about the same time and Turing's ACE soon after. In his proposal Turing (1945, page 3) cites the EDVAC report, but the stored program seems to have been one of those scientific ideas that emerge almost simultaneously in more than one place when the time is ripe.

But back to the 1930s. While Turing was moving to Princeton to further his studies of logic, the applied mathematician Howard Hathaway Aiken (Aiken et al., 1964, here chapter 7) was working at Harvard on the old problem of numerical computing, on which not much progress had been made since Leibniz. Aiken designed the massive, electromechanical Mark I to print tables of the values of mathematical functions—some of them, like the Bessel functions, straight out of the eighteenth century tradition of mathematical analysis, and some of them, ballistic trajectories for example, to meet the demands of modern warfare. His project wound up in a dispute with his partner, IBM, over whose machine it really was—a question akin to the one about Babbage: Does the glory go to the designer of a computer or to the people who build it and get it running?

Aiken was not alone in thinking about automatic calculation in the late 1930s. Konrad Zuse was working on his own electromechanical calculators in Berlin, and John Vincent Atanasoff was developing an electronic machine in Iowa, all independently—though Eckert and Mauchly, working for the Army at the University of Pennsylvania, certainly knew about Atanasoff's work, a circumstance that later resulted in bitter patent litigation.

As computing was making small hatching sounds in several separate places, telephony was exploding everywhere. There was more than one way to wire several switches together to produce the same functional result, and clever engineers mastered the art of shrinking the required hardware. When Claude Shannon (1938, here chapter 8) started working on these problems as an MIT graduate student, he realized that Boole's *Laws of Thought*, which he knew from an undergraduate philosophy course, were also the laws of circuits. Once a circuit had been translated into boolean logic, the logic formula could be simplified and then translated back into a more economical circuit. These methods assumed great importance for the design of digital computers, and are still in use to this day.

Binary representation has many advantages for electrical processing. Not only can boolean logic be used to manipulate complicated expressions, but it is easier to restore a degraded signal to its true value if there are only two possible values, one voltage to represent 0 and the other to represent 1. With the binary system firmly accepted, the mechanization of logic accelerated during the 1940s. The Eckert–Mauchly–von Neumann team used binary in their design for the EDVAC (von Neumann, 1993, here chapter 10), and carried out some of the earliest analysis of algorithms for binary arithmetic. Shannon published a second landmark paper, tying communications engineering to binary data representation, and defining "bit" along the way (Shannon, 1948, here chapter 12). And Hamming (1950, here chapter 13) presented a general method for adding extra bits to binary data so that errors could be detected and, under some circumstances, corrected after data was garbled in transit.

Important as they were, all these developments were to some degree incremental. The stored program architecture had many parents and ancestors, and Shannon gives due credit for his work to Nyquist and other communications engineers of the day. The work of neuroscientist Warren McCulloch and self-taught logician Walter Pitts (McCulloch and Pitts, 1943, here chapter 9) was altogether different. Nothing like it had ever been published before. A robust Renaissance literature likened the human body to assemblies of levers, and in the nineteenth century the analogy expanded to connect the energy usage of the body to that of the steam engine. The notion that thinking was a form of calculation precedes Leibniz, going back at least to Thomas Hobbes (1655, p. 2): "by 'reasoning,' I mean computation" (*per ratiocinationem autem intelligo computationem*). But to explain the brain itself as a specific kind of mechanism was a new thing, and it was even more audacious to connect the all-or-nothing firing of neurons to the switching of electric circuits and thereby to the elaborate logical calculus of Whitehead and Russell (1910). McCulloch and Pitts did not merely toy with this analogy; they declared the mysteries of the human mind solved—except for details to be worked out later. Their work was the only one cited in von Neumann's first draft report on computer design (chapter 10). Nerve nets evolved into an important computing model, though the details of the McCulloch–Pitts work have mostly been supplanted. The crucial reboot of a more realistic neural model was the paper of Frank Rosenblatt (1958a, here chapter 18) on perceptrons, though nerve nets today have a life in computer science theory largely divorced from their neuroanatomical origins.

The reciprocal idea, that machines could be made to act like human beings, runs very deep in mythology. In the *Iliad*, Homer described servant automata of the divine blacksmith Hephaestus: "He set the bellows away from the fire . . . , took up a heavy stick in his hand, and went to the doorway limping. And in support of their master moved his attendants. These are golden, and in appearance like living young women. There is intelligence in their hearts, and there is speech in them and strength, and from the immortal gods they have learned how to do things. These stirred nimbly in support of their master" (Homer, 1962, 18.412ff.). Already in the eighth century BCE, this passage described several subfields of artificial intelligence: general intelligence, learning, speech, dexterity. Boole seems to have discussed Babbage's "thinking engine" with him during their one known meeting in 1862, though Lady Lovelace had cautioned against expecting the Analytical Engine to be capable of original thought. But the cat was out of the bag; soon after, Samuel Butler, in "Darwin among the machines," anticipated that machines could evolve to become intelligent (Butler, 1863, originally published anonymously).

By the late 1940s, Turing was in a position to combine what he knew about computers (not just the theory—he had been designing and building computing machines) with the centuries-old speculations about thinking machines and the modern British practice of analytic philosophy. The result was "Computing machinery and intelligence" (Turing, 1950, here chapter 14), in which Turing imagined, as a thought-experiment alternative to the metaphysical thinking computer, a machine that could successfully fool a human interrogator into believing that the machine was human. Turing's dispassionate dissection of the counter-arguments (including Lady Lovelace's) has stimulated debate and response ever since.

Starting in 1964, Joseph Weizenbaum (1966, here chapter 27) wrote a very primitive program that held content-free chats with humans, simply pasting words the human had used into syntactically correct positions in the computer's responses. Weizenbaum saw the program, which he dubbed ELIZA, as a technical demonstration about limited language processing. It was not intended for significant conversation, but the willingness of people to engage with it as they would with fellow humans raised significant ethical questions about human–computer interactions. Norbert Wiener (1960, here chapter 19) had already challenged computer professionals to consider the ethical implications of their work while contemplating the implications of automation and the skill of game-playing computers—the consequences, that is, of thoughtlessly assigning to computers decisions that should be retained by humans.

The 1950s were something of a Cambrian era in computer design. The detailed EDVAC design document opened the floodgates for variations and improvements, and for experiments with new storage and switching elements, in both the academy and the for-profit sector. Maurice Wilkes's 1952 invention of microcode (Wilkes, 1981, here chapter 15) is included as an example of the emergence of an important idea in simple form in response to immediate needs: it was just getting too tiresome to keep rewiring computers as improvements were made to the instruction set. The dramatic increase in the number of logic components resulting from transistorization and then integrated circuits set in motion the crazy exponential growth named after Gordon Moore (1965, here chapter 25) in a magazine article with a cartoon depiction of a home computer well before anyone was imagining what use such a device could have.

Grace Hopper recognized, before it was apparent to others, that hardware would soon become the cheapest part of a computer system, because the computer was a one-time purchase but new software investments could go on forever (Hopper, 1952, here chapter 16). Moreover, she understood that higher-level languages were not merely a convenience but a necessity, since no one with a code base could afford to rewrite it from scratch every time a new computer was acquired.

FORTRAN, ALGOL, and COBOL all emerged during the 1950s, COBOL thanks to Hopper, who recognized the importance of business computing. We cannot here do justice to any of these programming languages or their creators, except to John McCarthy for daring to adapt Alonzo Church's lambda-calculus, developed to put the Entscheidungsproblem to rest, as a functional programming language (McCarthy, 1960, here chapter 21). In doing so he connected the logical tradition directly to the art of computer programming: if viewing computation as symbol manipulation was key to understanding the limits of the computable, why not take symbol manipulation as primitive in a practical programming language? McCarthy also brought the recursive style of function definition, which had been established in the metamathematics of the early twentieth century and systematized by Rósza Péter (1951), convincingly into the center of computer programming.

The influence of Alonzo Church cannot be overstated. His PhD students at Princeton included Turing, Michael Rabin, and Dana Scott; McCarthy, who was also a PhD student at Princeton in the Church era, is responsible for the founding of artificial intelligence, for the first time-sharing system (Corbató et al., 1962, here chapter 23), and for symbolic and functional programming.

The engineering of computer systems as assistants to human memory and thought, not just calculation, can be traced to the publication by Vannevar Bush (1945a, here chapter 11), in a popular magazine, of the article "As We May Think." He tried to imagine how human thought might be assisted by technology in the future, but did not have any clear notion that a computer would be helpful. Over the next decade large, clunky computers began to appear, and visionaries began to imagine ways in which human beings might someday work more gracefully with them. J. C. R. Licklider (1960, here chapter 20) imagined cooperation between humans and computers, and Doug Engelbart (1962, here chapter 22) worked to make it real. Ivan Sutherland (1963, here chapter 24) dramatically launched the field of computer graphics with his PhD thesis at MIT, where Bush had imagined a thought assistant almost twenty years earlier.

The study of formal, mathematical, abstract methods to describe and analyze computations has many threads. There had been better and worse paper and pencil algorithms for centuries, and the descriptions of mechanical programmable calculators by Lovelace and Aiken suggest making certain programming choices to improve performance or accuracy. Graph algorithms were studied as part of operations research during the World War II years, and evolved into a major subfield of computer science. Kruskal (1956, here chapter 17) presented the minimum spanning tree algorithm now learned by virtually every student of computer science, and Edmonds (1965) talked explicitly about algorithmic efficiency while discussing maximum matching.

The field of algorithms and their efficiency grew organically as computers forced precise articulation and programming presented new challenges. On the positive side, Volker Strassen discovered stunningly original algorithms for the old problems of matrix multiplication and inversion (Strassen, 1969, here chapter 30) and Edsger Dijkstra (1965, here chapter 26) provably solved a tricky problem in concurrency control. On the negative side, Stephen Cook (1971b, here chapter 34) adapted Turing's proof that programs could be described by logical formulas to the concrete case of $\mathcal{NP}$ and propositional logic, thereby posing the as yet unsolved $\mathcal{P} = \mathcal{NP}$ problem; and Richard Karp (1972, here chapter 36) showed that a great variety of known problems exhibiting combinatorial explosion were essentially variations on the same problem. Knuth (1976, here chapter 43) proposed the notation that is now almost universally accepted for comparing the computational complexity of algorithms—and also, in an equally delightful note (Knuth, 1974b), proposed the terminology for $\mathcal{P}$ and $\mathcal{NP}$ on which the scientific community has agreed.

As the abstraction of algorithms proceeded, so did the impetus to treat actual programs more formally and abstractly, even if that meant giving up the full expressive power of programming languages. So Dijkstra (1968a, here chapter 29) proposed getting rid of branches and jumps entirely, a radical proposal that is now generally accepted; Hoare (1969, here chapter 31) proposed treating programs like logic formulas, subject to formal verification; and DeMillo et al.

(1979, here chapter 44) pushed back forcefully against the verification agenda. Also Liskov and Zilles (1974, here chapter 39) proposed applying the same abstraction standards to data that had been accepted as appropriate for control, initiating a trend that culminated in object-oriented programming.

A line connects the earliest time-sharing operating system, by Corbató et al. (1962, here chapter 23), to the "THE" multiprogramming system of Dijkstra (1968b, here chapter 28) and UNIX (Ritchie and Thompson, 1974, here chapter 37), which now exists in many variants.

Such large software systems became increasingly cumbersome to write and to get working. In the 1960s and 1970s, some multimillion-dollar projects cost millions more to fix shortly after release, or had to be junked entirely. Software engineering emerged as a practitioner's art, the subject of two classic treatments in particular: Royce (1970, here chapter 33) and Brooks (1995, originally published in 1975, here chapter 40). Every programmer should read both.

Large data sets likewise required new methods. Codd (1970, here chapter 32) defined the relational model, which is conceptually elegant but required software sophistication to become practical. It is now at the core of the data management industry. Retrieval from large text databases is now taken for granted as an aspect of Web search, but it is an old information retrieval problem. Karen Spärck Jones (1972, here chapter 35) discovered useful principles for relevance of terms, balancing frequency in a document (which tends to suggest relevance) against frequency in the entire corpus (which suggests that a word is not distinctive and hence not a useful indexing key).

Networking exploded in the 1970s. Cerf and Kahn (1974, here chapter 38) lay out the internet protocols, little changed today from their original description, and Metcalfe and Boggs (1976, here chapter 41) describe the Ethernet protocols for local area networks. The acceptance of these two protocols as nonproprietary standards has made it possible for computers everywhere to communicate with each other.

Ubiquitous interconnection required better secrecy. Encryption was an old technology for conveying messages in secret between two parties, but traditional methods were of limited use on the internet because the encryption/decryption key would have to be shared through the same insecure channel as the message. Diffie and Hellman (1976a, here chapter 42) stunned the community by proposing a solution (which, it turned out, had been partially anticipated by Ralph Merkle and by members of GCHQ, the British intelligence service). Rivest et al. (1978, here chapter 45) supplied the crucial enabling mathematics; their algorithm is widely used today, even though its security rests on unproven foundations. The current explosion of interest in quantum computing is in no small part due to the possibility that quantum computers could be used to break the RSA codes (Shor, 1999). Shamir (1979, here chapter 46), the last paper in this volume, is a gem on sharing secrets in a way that requires a certain level of cooperation for recovery; it is a problem that can be stated without reference to computers and uses only high school mathematics to solve, and yet makes sense only in the computer age.

1 Prior Analytics (∼350 BCE)

Aristotle

Some ideas in computer science are so familiar that it is hard to remember that they were once new. The idea of logic is one. Calculating methods from the ancient world had limited influence on the design of today's computers, but the principles of two-valued logic underpin digital computing.

Computers are general-purpose. Most chess-playing computers or inventory-keeping computers are just generic computers that can be used for games or for business. A bit that one day indicates whether the knight on square f3 is white or black might the next day indicate whether this book is in stock. The logical rules embedded in the computer's hardware can be used for manipulating both kinds of information. These abstract ideas of things, properties, and logical rules for reasoning about them did not always exist. These were Aristotle's ideas, and they were necessary first steps toward computations about things and their properties.

Aristotle (384–322 BCE) was the great systematizer. In many works, mostly lost, he analyzed and categorized everything imaginable. His *Prior Analytics* presented the world's first system of logic. Its purpose is to infer conclusions from premises in a way that depends only on the form of the argument, not on the persuasiveness of the speaker or on anything not mentioned in the premises. Aristotle's explanation of a logical deduction is the root of all modern logic.

Aristotle's technical vocabulary makes for difficult reading. Fortunately, the archaic details are not important to us. He works with the idea of a *predicate*, a property that a thing may or may not have. This gave rise to the modern idea of a thing being a member of a set, the set of all things having that property. Aristotle's notion of "belonging" can be understood as the subset relation. For example, to say that property A belongs to none of the Bs is to say that no member of the set B is a member of A, that is, that B is disjoint from A. So the example "if A is predicated of every B and B of every C, it is necessary for A to be predicated of every C" is a statement of the transitivity of the superset relation: If $A \supseteq B$ and $B \supseteq C$, then $A \supseteq C$. Aristotle had no such notation at his disposal, but those who formalized logic and set theory stood on his shoulders.

There had been convincing mathematical arguments before Aristotle, but Aristotle was the first to abstract the form of such arguments from their content. In doing so, he showed how to reason mechanically, by matching propositions to general templates and inferring the conclusions that necessarily followed. Aristotle neither designed nor built logical calculating machines, but his vocabulary hints that he was describing a computational process. The word translated here as

Reprinted from Aristotle (1989), with permission from Hackett Publishing Company, Inc.

"deduction" is συλλογισμός, which means a "reckoning up" or "computation." "Syllogism," the English rendition of Aristotle's term, now means something narrower, the particular forms of deduction that Aristotle explains in this work.

Aristotle also exhibits a method for showing that certain purported forms of inference are *not* universally valid, by the use of counterexamples. He invites the reader to draw a general inference from the premises $A \supseteq B$ and $B \cap C = \emptyset$. In fact, no necessary conclusion about the relation of A and C can be inferred from these two premises. For if we take A = animals, B = horses, and C = men, then the premises are satisfied (horses are animals, but no horse is a man), and $A \supseteq C$ (men are animals); but if A = animals, B = men, and C = stones, then again the premises are satisfied (men are animals, but no man is a stone), but A is disjoint from C (no stone is an animal). (In a modern argument, we would have to finish by noting that C cannot simultaneously be a subset of and disjoint from A, as long as C is nonempty.) This is the method used to this day to refute conjectures and to prove the independence of hypotheses.

W E must first state what our inquiry is about and what its object is, saying that it is about demonstration and that its object is demonstrative science. Next, we must determine what a premise is, what a term is, and what a deduction is, and what sort of deduction is complete and what sort incomplete; and after these things, what it is for something to be or not be in something as a whole, and what we mean by "to be predicated of every" or "predicated of none."

A *premise*, then, is a sentence affirming or denying something about something. This sentence may be universal, particular, or indeterminate. I call belonging "to every" or "to none" universal; I call belonging "to some," "not to some," or "not to every," particular, and I call belonging or not belonging (without a universal or particular) indeterminate (as, for example, "the science of contraries is the same" or "pleasure is not a good").

A demonstrative premise is different from a dialectical one in that a demonstrative premise is the taking of one or the other part of a contradiction (for someone who is demonstrating does not ask for premises but takes them), whereas a dialectical premise is the asking of a contradiction. However, this will make no difference as to whether a deduction comes about for either man, for both the one who demonstrates and the one who asks deduce by taking something either to belong or not to belong with respect to something. Consequently, a deductive premise without qualification will be either the affirmation or the denial of one thing about another, in the way that this has been explained. It will be demonstrative if it is true and has been obtained by means of the initial assumptions; a dialectical premise, on the other hand, is the posing of a contradiction as a question (when one is getting answers) and the taking of something apparent and accepted (when one is deducing), as was explained in the *Topics*.

What a premise is, then, and how deductive, demonstrative, and dialectical premises differ, will be explained more precisely in what follows; let the distinctions just made be sufficient for our present needs.

I call that a *term* into which a premise may be broken up, i.e., both that which is predicated and that of which it is predicated (whether or not "is" or "is not" is added or divides them).

A *deduction* is a discourse in which, certain things having been supposed, something different from the things supposed results of necessity because these things are so. By "because these things are so," I mean "resulting through them," and by "resulting through them" I mean "needing no further term from outside in order for the necessity to come about."

I call a deduction *complete* if it stands in need of nothing else besides the things taken in order for the necessity to be evident; I call it *incomplete* if it still needs either one or several additional things which are necessary because of the terms assumed, but yet were not taken by means of premises.

For one thing to be in another as a whole is the same as for one thing to be predicated of every one of another. We use the expression "predicated of every" when none of the subject can be taken of which the other term cannot be said, and we use "predicated of none" likewise.

Now, every premise expresses either belonging, or belonging of necessity, or being possible to belong; and some of these, for each prefix respectively, are affirmative and others negative; and of the affirmative and negative premises, in turn, some are universal, some are in part, and some indeterminate.

It is necessary for a universal privative premise of belonging to convert with respect to its terms. For instance, if no pleasure is a good, neither will any good be a pleasure. And the positive premise necessarily converts, though not universally but in part. For instance, if every pleasure is a good, then some good will be a pleasure. Among the particular premises, the affirmative must convert partially (for if some pleasure is a good, then some good will be a pleasure), but the privative premise need not (for it is not the case that if man does not belong to some animal, then animal will not belong to some man).

First, then, let premise *AB* be universally privative. Now, if *A* belongs to none of the *B*s, then neither will *B* belong to any of the *A*s. For if it does belong to some (for instance to *C*), it will not be true that *A* belongs to none of the *B*s, since *C* is one of the *B*s. And if *A* belongs to every *B*, then *B* will belong to some *A*. For if it belongs to none, neither will *A* belong to any *B*; but it was assumed to belong to every one. And similarly if the premise is particular: if *A* belongs to some of the *B*s, then necessarily *B* belongs to some of the *A*s. (For if it belongs to none, then neither will *A* belong to any of the *B*s.) But if *A* does not belong to some *B*, it is not necessary for *B* also not to belong to some *A* (for example if *B* is animal and *A* man: for man does not belong to every animal, but animal belongs to every man). . . .

Having made these determinations, let us now say through what premises, when, and how every deduction comes about. (We will need to discuss demonstration later. Deduction should be discussed before demonstration because deduction is more universal: a demonstration is a kind of deduction, but not every deduction is a demonstration.)

Whenever, then, three terms are so related to each other that the last is in the middle as a whole and the middle is either in or not in the first as a whole, it is necessary for there to be a complete deduction of the extremes. (I call that the *middle* which both is itself in another and has another in it—this is also middle in position—and call both that which is itself in another and that which has another in it *extremes*.) For if *A* is predicated of every *B* and *B* of every *C*, it is necessary for *A* to be predicated of every *C* (for it was stated earlier what we mean by "of every"). Similarly, if *A* is predicated of no *B* and *B* of every *C*, it is necessary that *A* will belong to no *C*. However, if the first extreme follows all the middle and the middle belongs to none of the last, there will not be a deduction of the extremes, for nothing necessary results in virtue of these things being so. For it is possible for the first extreme to belong to all as well as to none of the last. Consequently, neither a particular nor a universal conclusion becomes necessary; and, since nothing is necessary because of these, there will not be a deduction. Terms for belonging to every are animal, man, horse; for belonging to none, animal, man, stone. Nor when neither the first belongs to any of the middle nor the middle to any of the last: there will not be a deduction in this way either. Terms for belonging are science, line, medicine; for not belonging, science, line, unit.

Thus, it is clear when there will and when there will not be a deduction in this figure if the terms are universal; and it is also clear both that if there is a deduction, then the terms must necessarily be related as we have said, and that if they are related in this way, then there will be a deduction.

If one of the terms is universal and the other is particular in relation to the remaining term, then when the universal is put in relation to the major extreme (whether this is positive or privative) and the particular is put in relation to the minor extreme (which is positive), then there will necessarily be a complete deduction; when, however, the universal is put in relation to the minor extreme, or when the terms are related in any other way, this is impossible. (I call that extreme the "major" which the middle is in and that extreme the "minor" which is under the middle.) For let *A* belong to every *B* and *B* to some *C*. Then, if to be predicated of every is what was said in the beginning, it is necessary for *A* to belong to some *C*. And if *A* belongs to no *B* and *B* to some *C*, then it is necessary for *A* not to belong to some *C*. (For it has also been defined what we mean by "predicated of no" so that there will be a complete deduction.) Similarly also if *BC* should be indeterminate, provided it is positive (for it will be the same deduction whether an indeterminate premise or a particular one is taken). ...

2 The True Method (1677)

Gottfried Wilhelm Leibniz

Gottfried Wilhelm Leibniz (1646–1716) was a polymath—a philosopher of great breadth and a legal and political thinker, as well as a profound and prolific mathematician. He would be in the running for the title of first computer scientist. Pascal might be considered for his adding machine, and others before and after, but Leibniz built a nested-loop calculator that could both multiply and divide (see page 62). More remarkably, he invented binary arithmetic (Figure 2.1) and designed a binary calculator (which was never built).

Leibniz shares credit with Isaac Newton for discovering what was then called the calculus of infinitesimals. Today the calculus is so identified with mathematics that we no longer hear the reference to the calculations that were its original motivations—for example, how to find the area of a figure by adding up the areas of thin slices. Leibniz's notation dx for an infinitesimal change in x survives to this day, because the notation makes it easy to state plug-and-chug rules

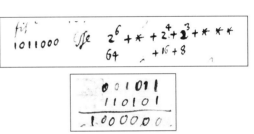

Figure 2.1: Binary to decimal conversion and a binary sum, from Leibniz's *De progressione dyadica* (1679).

that are almost inexpressible in Newton's dot notation. For example, the identity $\frac{dy}{dx} = \frac{dy}{du} \cdot \frac{du}{dx}$ is very awkward to state using Newton's notation $\dot{y}$ for the derivative of y.

Leibniz recognized how good notation can contribute to clear thought. He had been introduced to Aristotle at age 14, and as part of his education wrote a thesis on the use of a systematized logic in legal reasoning (Leibniz, 1666). He developed formal notations for logical reasoning, an early form of mathematical logic (Struik, 1969, page 123). His effort to capture reasoning in a logical system with formal rules evolved into a grand plan to unify all of human knowledge in a system that would settle all disputes; the facts, once established, would then yield incontestable answers. All of human reasoning would be reduced to plugging and chugging, and the result would be an unequivocally better world. Leibniz's famous optimism—his confidence that the world we live in was the best of all possible worlds—thus melded with an early techno-utopianism.

Even as he was recognized for his mathematical contributions, he was ridiculed for his optimism. In 1759 Voltaire caricatured him as Dr. Pangloss in *Candide*. Today his dream of a perfect world through logic and mechanized reasoning seems naïve and a poor fit for the theological framework on which he stretched it. And yet his imagined logical reductionism reappears regularly—recognizably in McCulloch and Pitts (1943, here page 83) and Bush (1945a, here page 114), and generally in every automated decision support system.

—◦•◦⟋❀⟍◦•◦—

S INCE happiness consists in contentment, and since enduring contentment depends on the assurance we have of the future—assurance based on the knowledge we should have of the nature of God and the soul—it follows that knowledge is necessary for true happiness.

But knowledge depends upon demonstration, and the invention of demonstrations by a *certain method*, which is not known to everyone. For although every man is capable of judging a demonstration (since it would not deserve this name if all those who consider it attentively were not convinced and persuaded by it), nevertheless not every man is capable of devising demonstrations on his own initiative, nor to propose them clearly once they are found, for want of leisure or method.

The true method taken in all of its extent is to my mind a thing hitherto quite unknown, and has not been practised except in mathematics. It is still very imperfect with regard to mathematics itself, as I had the good fortune to show to some (who are considered today to be among the foremost mathematicians of the century) by means of surprising proofs. And I expect to offer some examples of it, which will be perhaps not unworthy of posterity.

Yet if the method of mathematicians has not been sufficient to discover all that could be wished from them, it has at least been able to save them from mistakes, and if they have not said everything they ought to say, they have also said nothing they ought not to say.

If those who have cultivated the other sciences had imitated the mathematicians at least on this point, we would be very happy, and we would have long since had a secure metaphysics, as well as the morals which depend upon it, since metaphysics contains knowledge of God and the soul, knowledge which should govern our life.

Moreover, we would have the science of motion, which is the key to physics and, consequently, to medicine. It is true I believe we are now in a state to aspire to it, and some of my first thoughts, because of their wonderful simplicity, have been received with such applause by the most learned of our time that I believe we now have only to perform certain experiments properly designed and considered (rather than by chance and by trial and error, as commonly happens) in order to erect thereupon the bastion of a certain and demonstrative physics.

Now, the reason the art of demonstration has been until now found only in mathematics has not been properly fathomed by anyone, for if the cause of the difficulty had been known, the remedy would have long since been discovered. The reason is that mathematics carries its own test with it. For when I am presented with a false theorem, I do not need to examine it or even to know the demonstration, since I shall discover its falsity a posteriori by an easy experiment, which costs nothing but ink and paper, that is, by calculation, which will reveal the error, no matter how small it is. If it were as easy in other matters to verify reasoning by experiments then there would not be such differing opinions. But the trouble is that experiments in physics are difficult and have a high cost, and in metaphysics they are impossible unless God, for our sake, performs a miracle to make remote immaterial things known to us.

This difficulty is not insurmountable, although at first it seems to us that it is. But those who will want to consider what I am going to say about it will soon change their mind. It must be noted, then, that the tests or experiments performed in mathematics to guard against false reasoning (as are, for example, the test of casting out nines, the calculation of Ludolph of Cologne concerning the size of the circle, tables of sines or others) are not made on the thing itself, but on the characters we have substituted in place of the thing. [EDITOR: "Casting out nines" is to test whether a number is divisible by 9 by repeatedly adding up its digits. Aristotle had approximated the value of π by calculating the area of a regular 96-sided polygon; Ludolph (1540–1610) used a 2^{62}-sided polygon instead, thus calculating π to 35 decimal places, an effort that took years (Ludolph van Ceulen, 1596).] For to take a calculation of numbers, for example if 1677 times 365 makes 612,105, it would never have been done if one had to make 365 heaps and put 1677 small stones in each one and then at length count them all in order to know if the aforementioned number is found. That is why we are content to do it with characters on paper, by means of the test of nines or some other. Likewise, when someone proposes a supposedly exact quadrature of the circle, we do not need to make a material circle and tie a thread around it in order to see whether the length of this thread or the circumference to the diameter has the proportion proposed; that would be difficult, for even if the error is a thousandth (or less) part of the diameter, a large circle constructed with a great deal of accuracy would be required. Yet we nonetheless refute this false quadrature by experiment and by the calculation or test in numbers. But this test is performed only on paper, and consequently on the characters which represent the thing, and not on the thing itself.

This consideration is fundamental in this matter, and although many very able people, especially in our century, have claimed to give us demonstrations regarding physics, metaphysics, morals, and even in politics, jurisprudence, and medicine, nevertheless either they have been mistaken (because all the steps are slippery and it is difficult not to fall unless guided by some directions), or even if they did hit upon them, they have been unable to make their arguments accepted universally (because there has not yet been a way to examine arguments by some easy tests of which everyone is capable).

From this it is clear that, if we could find characters or signs appropriate for expressing all our thoughts as clearly and exactly as arithmetic expresses numbers or geometric analysis expresses lines, we could accomplish in all matters, *insofar as they are amenable to reasoning*, everything that can be done in arithmetic and geometry.

For all inquiries that depend upon reasoning would be performed by the transposition of these characters and by a kind of calculation, which would make the invention of beautiful things quite easy. For we would not have to rack our brains as much as we are forced to do today, and nevertheless we would be sure of being able to accomplish everything feasible, *in accordance with the given facts.*

Moreover, everyone would be made to agree on what had been found or concluded, since it would be easy to verify the calculation either by repeating it or by trying some tests similar to that of casting out nines in arithmetic. And if someone were to doubt what I had done, I would say to him, "Let us calculate, Sir," and thus taking up pen and ink we should soon settle the matter.

I always add: *insofar as can be done by reasoning, in accordance with the given facts.* For although certain experiments are always needed to serve as a basis for reasoning, nevertheless, once these experiments are given, we would draw from them everything that anyone else could possibly draw from them, and would even discover the experiments which remain to be per- formed for the clarification of all remaining doubts. That would be an admirable help, even in politics and medicine, for reasoning about the given symptoms and circumstances in a steady and perfect way. For even though there will not be enough given circumstances to form an infallible judgement, we shall always be able to determine what is most probable *from the given facts.* And that is all reason can do.

Now the characters that will express all our thoughts will form a new language which can be written and spoken; this language will be very difficult to construct but very easy to learn. It will be quickly accepted by everyone on account of its great use and its surprising facility, and it will serve wonderfully for communication among many peoples, which will help make it accepted. Those who will write in this language will not make mistakes, provided they avoid the errors of calculation, barbarisms, solecisms, and other mistakes of grammar and construction. Moreover, this language will possess a wonderful property, namely that of silencing the ignorant. For one will be unable to speak or write in this language except about what he understands, or if one tries to do so, one of two things will happen: either the vanity of what is advanced will be obvious to everyone, or it will be learned by writing or speaking. Just as indeed those who calculate learn by writing and those who speak sometimes encounter success they did not imagine, *with the tongue running ahead of the mind.* This will happen especially in our language because of its exactness. So much so that there will be no equivocations or amphibolies, and everything that will be said intelligibly in it will be said with propriety.

I dare say that this is the highest effort of the human mind, and when the project is accomplished it will merely be up to men to be happy since they will have an instrument which will serve to exalt reason no less than the telescope serves to perfect vision.

It is one of my ambitions to finish this project if God grants me the time. I owe it only to myself, and I had the first thought about it at the age of eighteen, as I evidenced a little later in a printed discourse (Leibniz, 1666). And as I am certain there is no invention which comes close to this one, I believe there is nothing so capable of immortalizing the name of the inventor. But I have much stronger reasons for thinking about it, for the religion I follow closely assures me that the love of God consists in an ardent desire to procure the general good, and reason teaches me that there is nothing which contributes more to the general good of all men than what perfects reason.

3 Sketch of the Analytical Engine (1843)

L. F. Menabrea,
with Notes by the Translator, Ada Augusta, Countess of Lovelace

The Analytical Engine of Charles Babbage (1791–1871) was the first device that could reasonably be called a computer rather than a calculator, so Babbage's assistant Ada Lovelace was among the first computer programmers. This chapter documents many other firsts—including the first computer system pitched as almost operational that never worked properly.

Babbage was an eminent British academic, Lucasian Professor of Mathematics at the University of Cambridge—a post held by Isaac Newton and Stephen Hawking, among others. His "Difference Engine" was a system of gears and wheels that could be used to calculate the values of polynomials, and hence approximations to a variety of mathematical functions, based on the principle of accumulating differences. The simplest example arises from the identity $\sum_{i=0}^{n}(2i + 1) = (n + 1)^2$, so that the sequence of perfect squares can be produced by repeatedly adding successive odd numbers, that is, numbers that start at 1 and differ by 2. In the mid-1830s Babbage conceived of the Analytical Engine, a device that was capable of much more—more, indeed, than Babbage imagined.

Ada Augusta (1815–1852) was the daughter of the romantic poet Lord Byron, who abandoned the family shortly after her birth and decamped to Greece, where he died eight years later. Ada's embittered mother, determined that Ada would not herself become a silly romantic, provided her the best mathematical education available to women. Ada apprenticed herself to Babbage, and after becoming familiar with his calculating machines, began to imagine the Analytical Engine's possibilities. The device was to be constructed on the model of a Jacquard loom, which used punched cards to control the pattern it would weave. Babbage and Ada Augusta realized that the control mechanism was so general that the Analytical Engine could effect calculations of almost unlimited sophistication.

Could—if it could be built at all. Alas, the precision of machining available in the day was inadequate to construct a workable Analytical Engine at the scale described in this document. The Analytical Engine was never operational as planned. (Construction of the full-scale Difference Engine was suspended when Babbage's attention turned to the Analytical Engine. A version was finally completed using machining techniques developed during the work on the failed Analytical Engine.)

Reprinted from Menabrea (1843).

Babbage lectured in Italy on his Analytical Engine in 1840. Luigi Federico Menabrea (1809–1896) was an Italian engineer who heard the lectures and wrote them up, and Ada (by then married to the Count of Lovelace, and therefore named Ada Augusta Lovelace) translated and annotated Menabrea's write-up. The number of now-familiar programming concepts it mentions is quite staggering: compilation (Figure 3.1 on page 14 is effectively an assembly-language compilation of an algebraic expression); step counting (page 21); loops controlled by an integer index (page 24); conditional branches and nested loops (page 23); accounting for code size (page 25); exception handling (page 14); mechanical solution of linear systems (page 24); the dichotomy between data and code (page 12); nonnumeric computing (pages 17 and 23); the underestimation of the difficulties of programming (page 15); and the repeated hints of an undiscovered ontology of computations.

Ada Lovelace died at age 36 of uterine cancer and the blood-letting done to treat it. Though Babbage later imagined machines that could win at board games and the automation of other activities, his inventions were largely forgotten until the digital revolution. Howard Aiken knew of Babbage's work and considered himself Babbage's heir, but his appreciation probably came only after he had undertaken the design of his automatic calculator. Babbage and Lovelace trod the spectacular wilderness of the field, but the shortcomings of their technology and the passage of time largely obliterated the path they blazed until others began to follow it again.

3.1   Babbage's Analytical Engine ...

THE much-admired machine of Pascal is now simply an object of curiosity, which, whilst it displays the powerful intellect of its inventor, is yet of little utility in itself. Its powers extended no further than the execution of the first four operations of arithmetic, and indeed were in reality confined to that of the first two, since multiplication and division were the result of a series of additions and subtractions. The chief drawback hitherto on most of such machines is, that they require the continual intervention of a human agent to regulate their movements, and thence arises a source of errors; so that, if their use has not become general for large numerical calculations, it is because they have not in fact resolved the double problem which the question presents, that of *correctness* in the results, united with *economy* of time.

Struck with similar reflections, Mr. Babbage has devoted some years to the realization of a gigantic idea. He proposed to himself nothing less than the construction of a machine capable of executing not merely arithmetical calculations, but even all those of analysis, if their laws are known. The imagination is at first astounded at the idea of such an undertaking; but the more calm reflection we bestow on it, the less impossible does success appear, and it is felt that it may depend on the discovery of some principle so general, that, if applied to machinery, the latter may be capable of mechanically translating the operations which may be indicated to it by algebraical notation. ...

When analysis is employed for the solution of any problem, there are usually two classes of operations to execute: first, the numerical calculation of the various coefficients; and secondly, their distribution in relation to the quantities affected by them. If, for example, we have to obtain the product of two binomials $(a + bx)(m + nx)$, the result will be represented by $am + (an + bm)x + bnx^2$, in which expression we must first calculate am, an, bm, bn; then take the sum of $an + bm$; and lastly, respectively distribute the coefficients thus obtained amongst the powers of the variable. In order to reproduce these operations by means of a machine, the latter must therefore possess two distinct sets of powers: first, that of executing numerical calculations; secondly, that of rightly distributing the values so obtained.

But if human intervention were necessary for directing each of these partial operations, nothing would be gained under the heads of correctness and economy of time; the machine must therefore have the additional requisite of executing by itself all the successive operations required for the solution of a problem proposed to it, when once the *primitive numerical data* for this same problem have been introduced. Therefore, since, from the moment that the nature of the calculation to be executed or of the problem to be resolved have been indicated to it, the machine is, by its own intrinsic power, of itself to go through all the intermediate operations which lead to the proposed result, it must exclude all methods of trial and guess-work, and can only admit the direct processes of calculation.

It is necessarily thus; for the machine is not a thinking being, but simply an automaton which acts according to the laws imposed upon it. This being fundamental, one of the earliest researches its author had to undertake, was that of finding means for effecting the division of one number by another without using the method of guessing indicated by the usual rules of arithmetic. The difficulties of effecting this combination were far from being among the least; but upon it depended the success of every other. Under the impossibility of my here explaining the process through which this end is attained, we must limit ourselves to admitting that the first four operations of arithmetic, that is addition, subtraction, multiplication and division, can be performed in a direct manner through the intervention of the machine. This granted, the machine is thence capable of performing every species of numerical calculation, for all such calculations ultimately resolve themselves into the four operations we have just named. To conceive how the machine can now go through its functions according to the laws laid down, we will begin by giving an idea of the manner in which it materially represents numbers.

Let us conceive a pile or vertical column consisting of an indefinite number of circular discs, all pierced through their centres by a common axis, around which each of them can take an independent rotatory movement. If round the edge of each of these discs are written the ten figures which constitute our numerical alphabet, we may then, by arranging a series of these figures in the same vertical line, express in this manner any number whatever. It is sufficient for this purpose that the first disc represent units, the second tens, the third hundreds, and so on. When two numbers have been thus written on two distinct columns, we may propose to combine them arithmetically with each other, and to obtain the result on a third column. In general, if we have a series of columns consisting of discs, which columns we will designate as V_0, V_1, V_2, V_3, V_4, &c., we may require, for instance, to divide the number written on the column V_1 by that on the column V_4, and to obtain the result on the column V_7. To effect this operation, we must impart to the machine two distinct arrangements; through the first it is prepared for executing a *division*, and through the second the columns it is to operate on are indicated to it, and also the column on which the result is to be represented. If this division is to be followed, for example, by the addition of two numbers taken on other columns, the two original arrangements of the machine must be simultaneously altered. If, on the contrary, a series of operations of the same nature is to be gone through, then the first of the original arrangements will remain, and the second alone must be altered. Therefore, the arrangements that may be communicated to the various parts of the machine may be distinguished into two principal classes:

First, that relative to the *Operations.*

Secondly, that relative to the *Variables.*

By this latter we mean that which indicates the columns to be operated on. As for the operations themselves, they are executed by a special apparatus, which is designated by the name of *mill*, and which itself contains a certain number of columns, similar to those of the Variables. When two numbers are to be combined together, the machine commences by effacing them from the columns where they are written, that is, it places *zero* on every disc of the two vertical lines on which the numbers were represented; and it transfers the numbers to the mill. There, the apparatus having been disposed suitably for the required operation, this latter is effected, and, when completed, the result itself is transferred to the column of Variables which shall have been indicated. Thus the mill is that portion of the machine which works, and the columns of Variables constitute that where the results are represented and arranged. After the preceding explanations, we may perceive that all fractional and irrational results will be represented in decimal fractions. Supposing each column to have forty discs, this extension will be sufficient for all degrees of approximation generally required.

It will now be inquired how the machine can of itself, and without having recourse to the hand of man, assume the successive dispositions suited to the operations. The solution of this problem has been taken from Jacquard's apparatus, used for the manufacture of brocaded stuffs, in the following manner:—

Two species of threads are usually distinguished in woven stuffs; one is the *warp* or longitudinal thread, the other the *woof* or transverse thread, which is conveyed by the instrument called the shuttle, and which crosses the longitudinal thread or warp. When a brocaded stuff is required, it is necessary in turn to prevent certain threads from crossing the woof, and this according to a succession which is determined by the nature of the design that is to be reproduced. Formerly this process was lengthy and difficult, and it was requisite that the workman, by attending to the design which he was to copy, should himself regulate the movements the threads were to take. Thence arose the high price of this description of stuffs, especially if threads of various colours entered into the fabric. To simplify this manufacture, Jacquard devised the plan of connecting each group of threads that were to act together, with a distinct lever belonging exclusively to that group. All these levers terminate in rods, which are united together in one bundle, having usually the form of a parallelopiped with a rectangular base. The rods are cylindrical, and are separated from each other by small intervals. The process of raising the threads is thus resolved into that of moving these various lever-arms in the requisite order. To effect this, a rectangular sheet of pasteboard is taken, somewhat larger in size than a section of the bundle of lever-arms. If this sheet be applied to the base of the bundle, and an advancing motion be then communicated to the pasteboard, this latter will move with it all the rods of the bundle, and consequently the threads that are connected with each of them. But if the pasteboard, instead of being plain, were pierced with holes corresponding to the extremities of the levers which meet it, then, since each of the levers would pass through the pasteboard during the motion of the latter, they would all remain in their places. We thus see that it is easy so to determine the position of the holes in the pasteboard, that, at any given moment, there shall be a certain number of levers, and consequently of parcels of threads, raised, while the rest remain where they were. Supposing this process is successively repeated according to a law indicated by the pattern to be executed, we perceive that this pattern may be reproduced on the stuff. For this purpose we need merely compose a series of cards according to the law required, and arrange them in suitable order one after the other; then, by causing them to pass over a polygonal beam which is so connected as to turn a new face for every stroke of the shuttle, which face shall then be impelled parallelly to itself against the bundle of lever-arms, the operation of raising the threads will be regularly performed. Thus we see that brocaded tissues may be manufactured with a precision and rapidity formerly difficult to obtain.

Arrangements analogous to those just described have been introduced into the Analytical Engine. It contains two principal species of cards: first, Operation cards, by means of which the parts of the machine are so disposed as to execute any determinate series of operations, such as additions, subtractions, multiplications, and divisions; secondly, cards of the Variables, which indicate to the machine the columns on which the results are to be represented. The cards, when put in motion, successively arrange the various portions of the machine according to the nature of the processes that are to be effected, and the machine at the same time executes these processes by means of the various pieces of mechanism of which it is constituted.

In order more perfectly to conceive the thing, let us select as an example the resolution of two equations of the first degree with two unknown quantities. Let the following be the two equations, in which x and y are the unknown quantities:—

$$\begin{cases} mx + ny = d \\ m'x + n'y = d'. \end{cases}$$

We deduce $x = \frac{dn' - d'n}{n'm - nm'}$, and for y an analogous expression. Let us continue to represent by V_0, V_1, V_2, &c. the different columns which contain the numbers, and let us suppose that the first eight columns have been chosen for expressing on them the numbers represented by m, n, d, m',

n', d', n and n', which implies that $V_0 = m$, $V_1 = n$, $V_2 = d$, $V_3 = m'$, $V_4 = n'$, $V_5 = d'$, $V_6 = n$, $V_7 = n'$.

The series of operations commanded by the cards, and the results obtained, may be represented in Figure 3.1.

Number of the operations	Operation-cards — Symbols indicating the nature of the operations	Cards of the variables — Columns on which operations are to be performed	Cards of the variables — Columns which receive results of operations	Progress of the operations
1	$\times$	$V_2 \times V_4 =$	$V_8 \ldots\ldots$	$= dn'$
2	$\times$	$V_5 \times V_1 =$	$V_9 \ldots\ldots$	$= d'n$
3	$\times$	$V_4 \times V_0 =$	$V_{10} \ldots\ldots$	$= n'm$
4	$\times$	$V_1 \times V_3 =$	$V_{11} \ldots\ldots$	$= nm'$
5	$-$	$V_8 - V_9 =$	$V_{12} \ldots\ldots$	$= dn' - d'n$
6	$-$	$V_{10} - V_{11} =$	$V_{13} \ldots\ldots$	$= n'm - mn'$
7	$\div$	$\dfrac{V_{12}}{V_{13}} =$	$V_{14} \ldots\ldots$	$= x = \frac{dn' - d'n}{n'm - nm'}$

Figure 3.1

... We may deduce the following important consequence from these explanations, viz. that since the cards only indicate the nature of the operations to be performed, and the columns of Variables with which they are to be executed, these cards will themselves possess all the generality of analysis, of which they are in fact merely a translation. We shall now further examine some of the difficulties which the machine must surmount, if its assimilation to analysis is to be complete. There are certain functions which necessarily change in nature when they pass through zero or infinity, or whose values cannot be admitted when they pass these limits. When such cases present themselves, the machine is able, by means of a bell, to give notice that the passage through zero or infinity is taking place, and it then stops until the attendant has again set it in action for whatever process it may next be desired that it shall perform. If this process has been foreseen, then the machine, instead of ringing, will so dispose itself as to present the new cards which have relation to the operation that is to succeed the passage through zero and infinity. These new cards may follow the first, but may only come into play contingently upon one or other of the two circumstances just mentioned taking place.

Let us consider a term of the form ab^n; since the cards are but a translation of the analytical formula, their number in this particular case must be the same, whatever be the value of n; that is to say, whatever be the number of multiplications required for elevating b to the nth power (we are supposing for the moment that n is a whole number). Now, since the exponent n indicates that b is to be multiplied n times by itself, and all these operations are of the same nature, it will be sufficient to employ one single operation-card, viz. that which orders the multiplication. ...

Resuming what we have explained concerning the Analytical Engine, we may conclude that it is based on two principles: the first consisting in the fact that every arithmetical calculation ultimately depends on four principal operations—addition, subtraction, multiplication, and division; the second, in the possibility of reducing every analytical calculation to that of the coefficients for the several terms of a series. If this last principle be true, all the operations of analysis come within the domain of the engine. To take another point of view: the use of the cards offers a generality equal to that of algebraical formulæ, since such a formula simply indicates the nature and order of the operations requisite for arriving at a certain definite result, and similarly the cards merely command the engine to perform these same operations; but in order that the mechanisms may be able to act to any purpose, the numerical data of the problem must in every particular case be introduced. Thus the same series of cards will serve for all questions whose sameness of nature is such as to require nothing altered excepting the numerical data. In this light the cards are merely a translation of algebraical formulæ, or, to express it better, another form of analytical notation.

Since the engine has a mode of acting peculiar to itself, it will in every particular case be necessary to arrange the series of calculations conformably to the means which the machine possesses; for such or such a process which might be very easy for a calculator may be long and complicated for the engine, and *vice versa*.

Considered under the most general point of view, the essential object of the machine being to calculate, according to the laws dictated to it, the values of numerical coefficients which it is then to distribute appropriately on the columns which represent the variables, it follows that the interpretation of formulæ and of results is beyond its province, unless indeed this very interpretation be itself susceptible of expression by means of the symbols which the machine employs. Thus, although it is not itself the being that reflects, it may yet be considered as the being which executes the conceptions of intelligence. The cards receive the impress of these conceptions, and transmit to the various trains of mechanism composing the engine the orders necessary for their action. When once the engine shall have been constructed, the difficulty will be reduced to the making out of the cards; but as these are merely the translation of algebraical formulæ, it will, by means of some simple notations, be easy to consign the execution of them to a workman. Thus the whole intellectual labour will be limited to the preparation of the formulæ, which must be adapted for calculation by the engine.

Now, admitting that such an engine can be constructed, it may be inquired: what will be its utility? To recapitulate; it will afford the following advantages:—First, rigid accuracy. We know that numerical calculations are generally the stumbling-block to the solution of problems, since errors easily creep into them, and it is by no means always easy to detect these errors. Now the engine, by the very nature of its mode of acting, which requires no human intervention during the course of its operations, presents every species of security under the head of correctness:

besides, it carries with it its own check; for at the end of every operation it prints off, not only the results, but likewise the numerical data of the question; so that it is easy to verify whether the question has been correctly proposed. Secondly, economy of time: to convince ourselves of this, we need only recollect that the multiplication of two numbers, consisting each of twenty figures, requires at the very utmost three minutes. Likewise, when a long series of identical computations is to be performed, such as those required for the formation of numerical tables, the machine can be brought into play so as to give several results at the same time, which will greatly abridge the whole amount of the processes. Thirdly, economy of intelligence: a simple arithmetical computation requires to be performed by a person possessing some capacity; and when we pass to more complicated calculations, and wish to use algebraical formulæ in particular cases, knowledge must be possessed which presupposes preliminary mathematical studies of some extent. Now the engine, from its capability of performing by itself all these purely material operations, spares intellectual labour, which may be more profitably employed. Thus the engine may be considered as a real manufactory of figures, which will lend its aid to those many useful sciences and arts that depend on numbers. Again, who can foresee the consequences of such an invention? In truth, how many precious observations remain practically barren for the progress of the sciences, because there are not powers sufficient for computing the results! And what discouragement does the perspective of a long and arid computation cast into the mind of a man of genius, who demands time exclusively for meditation, and who beholds it snatched from him by the material routine of operations! Yet it is by the laborious route of analysis that he must reach truth; but he cannot pursue this unless guided by numbers; for without numbers it is not given us to raise the veil which envelopes the mysteries of nature. Thus the idea of constructing an apparatus capable of aiding human weakness in such researches, is a conception which, being realized, would mark a glorious epoch in the history of the sciences. The plans have been arranged for all the various parts, and for all the wheel-work, which compose this immense apparatus, and their action studied; but these have not yet been fully combined together in the drawings and mechanical notation. The confidence which the genius of Mr. Babbage must inspire, affords legitimate ground for hope that this enterprise will be crowned with success; and while we render homage to the intelligence which directs it, let us breathe aspirations for the accomplishment of such an undertaking.

3.2   Note A by the Translator

The particular function whose integral the Difference Engine was constructed to tabulate, is $\Delta^7 u_z = 0$. The purpose which that engine has been specially intended and adapted to fulfil, is the computation of nautical and astronomical tables. The integral of $\Delta^7 u_z = 0$ being

$$u_z = a + bx + cx^2 + dx^3 + ex^4 + fx^5 + gx^6,$$

the constants a, b, c, &c. are represented on the seven columns of discs, of which the engine consists. It can therefore tabulate *accurately* and to an *unlimited extent*, all series whose general term is comprised in the above formula; and it can also tabulate *approximatively* between *intervals of greater or less extent*, all other series which are capable of tabulation by the Method of Differences.

The Analytical Engine, on the contrary, is not merely adapted for *tabulating* the results of one particular function and of no other, but for *developing and tabulating* any function whatever. In fact the engine may be described as being the material expression of any indefinite function of any degree of generality and complexity, such as for instance, $F(x, y, z, \log x, \sin y, x^p, \&c.)$, which is, it will be observed, a function of all other possible functions of any number of quantities.

In this, which we may call the *neutral* or *zero* state of the engine, it is ready to receive at any moment, by means of cards constituting a portion of its mechanism (and applied on the principle of those used in the Jacquard-loom), the impress of whatever *special* function we may desire to develop or to tabulate. These cards contain within themselves (in a manner explained in the Memoir itself) the law of development of the particular function that may be under consideration, and they compel the mechanism to act accordingly in a certain corresponding order. One of the simplest cases would be for example, to suppose that $F(x, y, z, \&c.\&c.)$ is the particular function $\Delta^n u_z = 0$ which the Difference Engine tabulates for values of n only up to 7. In this case the cards would order the mechanism to go through that succession of operations which would tabulate

$$u_z = a + bx + cx^2 + \cdots + mx^{n-1}$$

where n might be any number whatever.

These cards, however, have nothing to do with the regulation of the particular *numerical* data. They merely determine the *operations* to be effected, which operations may of course be performed on an infinite variety of particular numerical values, and do not bring out any definite numerical results unless the numerical data of the problem have been impressed on the requisite portions of the train of mechanism. In the above example, the first essential step towards an arithmetical result would be the substitution of specific numbers for n, and for the other primitive quantities which enter into the function. . . .

The operating mechanism can even be thrown into action independently of any object to operate upon (although of course no *result* could then be developed). Again, it might act upon other things besides *number*, were objects found whose mutual fundamental relations could be expressed by those of the abstract science of operations, and which should be also susceptible of adaptations to the action of the operating notation and mechanism of the engine. Supposing, for instance, that the fundamental relations of pitched sounds in the science of harmony and of musical composition were susceptible of such expression and adaptations, the engine might compose elaborate and scientific pieces of music of any degree of complexity or extent. . . .

The distinctive characteristic of the Analytical Engine, and that which has rendered it possible to endow mechanism with such extensive faculties as bid fair to make this engine the executive right-hand of abstract algebra, is the introduction into it of the principle which Jacquard devised for regulating, by means of punched cards, the most complicated patterns in the fabrication of brocaded stuffs. It is in this that the distinction between the two engines lies. Nothing of the sort exists in the Difference Engine. We may say most aptly, that the Analytical Engine *weaves algebraical patterns* just as the Jacquard-loom weaves flowers and leaves. Here, it seems to us, resides much more of originality than the Difference Engine can be fairly entitled to claim. We do not wish to deny to this latter all such claims. We believe that it is the only proposal or attempt ever made to construct a calculating machine *founded on the principle of successive orders of differences*, and capable of *printing off its own results*; and that this engine surpasses its predecessors, both in the extent of the calculations which it can perform, in the facility, certainty and accuracy with which it can effect them, and in the absence of all necessity for the intervention of human intelligence *during the performance of its calculations*. Its nature is, however, limited to the strictly arithmetical, and it is far from being the first or only scheme for constructing *arithmetical* calculating machines with more or less of success.

The bounds of *arithmetic* were however outstepped the moment the idea of applying the cards had occurred; and the Analytical Engine does not occupy common ground with mere "calculating machines." It holds a position wholly its own; and the considerations it suggests are most interesting in their nature. In enabling mechanism to combine together *general* symbols in successions of unlimited variety and extent, a uniting link is established between the operations of matter and the abstract mental processes of the *most abstract* branch of mathematical science. A new, a vast, and a powerful language is developed for the future use of analysis, in which to wield its truths so that these may become of more speedy and accurate practical application for the purposes of mankind than the means hitherto in our possession have rendered possible. Thus not only the mental and the material, but the theoretical and the practical in the mathematical world, are brought into more intimate and effective connexion with each other. We are not aware of its being on record that anything partaking in the nature of what is so well designated the *Analytical* Engine has been hitherto proposed, or even thought of, as a practical possibility, any more than the idea of a thinking or of a reasoning machine. ...

Those who incline to very strictly utilitarian views may perhaps feel that the peculiar powers of the Analytical Engine bear upon questions of abstract and speculative science, rather than upon those involving every-day and ordinary human interests. These persons being likely to possess but little sympathy, or possibly acquaintance, with any branches of science which they do not find to be *useful* (according to *their* definition of that word), may conceive that the undertaking of that engine, now that the other one is already in progress, would be a barren and unproductive laying out of yet more money and labour; in fact, a work of supererogation. Even in the utilitarian aspect, however, we do not doubt that very valuable practical results would be developed by the extended faculties of the Analytical Engine; some of which results we think we could now hint at, had we the space; and others, which it may not yet be possible to foresee, but which would be brought forth by the daily increasing requirements of science, and by a more intimate practical acquaintance with the powers of the engine, were it in actual existence. ...   A. A. L.

3.3   Note B by the Translator

That portion of the Analytical Engine here alluded to is called the storehouse. It contains an indefinite number of the columns of discs described by M. Menabrea. The reader may picture to himself a pile of rather large draughtsmen heaped perpendicularly one above another to a considerable height, each counter having the digits from 0 to 9 inscribed on its *edge* at equal intervals; and if he then conceives that the counters do not actually lie one upon another so as to be in contact, but are fixed at small intervals of vertical distance on a common axis which passes perpendicularly through their centres, and around which each disc can *revolve horizontally* so that any required digit amongst those inscribed on its margin can be brought into view, he will have a good idea of one of these columns. The lowest of the discs on any column belongs to the units, the next above to the tens, the next above this to the hundreds, and so on. Thus, if we wished to inscribe 1345 on a column of the engine, it would stand thus:—

$$1$$
$$3$$
$$4$$
$$5$$

In the Difference Engine there are seven of these columns placed side by side in a row, and the working mechanism extends behind them: the general form of the whole mass of machinery is that of a quadrangular prism (more or less approaching to the cube); the results always appearing on that perpendicular face of the engine which contains the columns of discs, opposite to which face a spectator may place himself. In the Analytical Engine there would be many more of these columns, probably at least two hundred. The precise form and arrangement which the whole mass of its mechanism will assume is not yet finally determined.

We may conveniently represent the columns of discs on paper in a diagram like Figure 3.2.

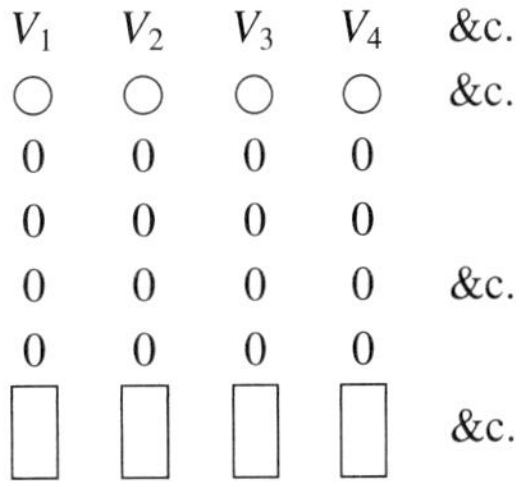

The *V*'s are for the purpose of convenient reference to any column, either in writing or speaking, and are consequently numbered. The reason why the letter *V* is chosen for the purpose in preference to any other letter, is because these columns are designated (as the reader will find in proceeding with the Memoir) the *Variables*, and sometimes the *Variable columns*, or the *columns of Variables*. The origin of this appellation is, that the values on the columns are destined to change, that is to

Figure 3.2

vary, in every conceivable manner. But it is necessary to guard against the natural misapprehension that the columns are only intended to receive the values of the *variables* in an analytical

formula, and not of the *constants*. The columns are called Variables on a ground wholly uncon-
nected with the *analytical* distinction between constants and variables. In order to prevent the
possibility of confusion, we have, both in the translation and in the notes, written Variable with a
capital letter when we use the word to signify a *column of the engine*, and variable with a small
letter when we mean the *variable of a formula*. Similarly, *Variable-cards* signify any cards that
belong to a column of the engine.

To return to the explanation of the diagram: each circle at the top is intended to contain the
algebraic sign + or −, either of which can be substituted for the other, according as the number
represented on the column below is positive or negative. In a similar manner any other purely
symbolical results of algebraical processes might be made to appear in these circles. In Note A,
the practicability of developing *symbolical* with no less ease than *numerical* results has been
touched on. The zeros beneath the *symbolic* circles represent each of them a disc, supposed to
have the digit 0 presented in front. Only four tiers of zeros have been figured in the diagram, but
these may be considered as representing thirty or forty, or any number of tiers of discs that may
be required. Since each disc can present any digit, and each circle any sign, the discs of every
column may be so adjusted as to express any positive or negative number whatever within the
limits of the machine; which limits depend on the *perpendicular* extent of the mechanism, that
is, on the number of discs to a column.

Each of the squares below the zeros is intended for the inscription of any *general* symbol
or combination of symbols we please; it being understood that the number represented on the
column immediately above is the numerical value of that symbol, or combination of symbols.
Let us, for instance, represent the three quantities a, n, x, and let us further suppose that $a = 5$,
$n = 7$, $x = 98$. We should have Figure 3.3.

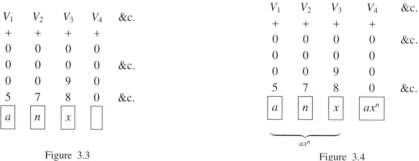

Figure 3.3   Figure 3.4

We may now combine these symbols in a variety of ways, so as to form any required function
or functions of them, and we may then inscribe each such function below brackets, every bracket
uniting together those quantities (and those only) which enter into the function inscribed below
it. We must also, when we have decided on the particular function whose numerical value we

desire to calculate, assign another column to the right-hand for receiving the *results*, and must inscribe the function in the square below this column. In the above instance we might have any one of the following functions:—

ax^n, x^{an}, $a \cdot n \cdot x$, $\frac{a}{n}x$, $a + n + x$, &c. &c.

Let us select the first. It would stand as follows, previous to calculation (Figure 3.4). The data being given, we must now put into the engine the cards proper for directing the operations in the case of the particular function chosen. These operations would in this instance be,—

First, six multiplications in order to get x^n ($= 98^7$ for the above particular data).

Secondly, one multiplication in order then to get $a \cdot x^n$ ($= 5 \cdot 98^7$).

In all, seven multiplications to complete the whole process. We may thus represent them:—

$(\times, \times, \times, \times, \times, \times, \times)$, or 7 ($\times$).

The multiplications would, however, at successive stages in the solution of the problem, operate on pairs of numbers, derived from *different* columns. In other words, the *same operation* would be performed on different *subjects of operation*. And here again is an illustration of the remarks made in the preceding Note on the independent manner in which the engine directs its *operations*. In determining the value of ax^n, the *operations are homogeneous*, but are distributed amongst different *subjects of operation*, at successive stages of the computation. It is by means of certain punched cards, belonging to the Variables themselves, that the action of the operations is so *distributed* as to suit each particular function. The *Operation-cards* merely determine the succession of operations in a general manner. They in fact throw all that portion of the mechanism included in the *mill* into a series of different *states*, which we may call the *adding state*, or the *multiplying state*, &c. respectively. In each of these states the mechanism is ready to act in the way peculiar to that state, on any pair of numbers which may be permitted to come within its sphere of action. Only *one* of these operating states of the mill can exist at a time; and the nature of the mechanism is also such that only *one pair of numbers* can be received and acted on at a time. Now, in order to secure that the mill shall receive a constant supply of the proper pairs of numbers in succession, and that it shall also rightly locate the result of an operation performed upon any pair, each Variable has cards of its own belonging to it. It has, first, a class of cards whose business it is to *allow* the number on the Variable to pass into the mill, there to be operated upon. These cards may be called the *Supplying-cards*. They furnish the mill with its proper food. Each Variable has, secondly, another class of cards, whose office it is to allow the Variable to *receive* a number *from* the mill. These cards may be called the *Receiving-cards*. They regulate the location of results, whether temporary or ultimate results. The Variable-cards in general (including both the preceding classes) might, it appears to us, be even more appropriately designated the Distributive-cards, since it is through their means that the action of the operations, and the results of this action, are rightly *distributed*.

There are *two varieties* of the *Supplying* Variable-cards, respectively adapted for fulfilling two distinct subsidiary purposes: but as these modifications do not bear upon the present subject, we shall notice them in another place.

In the above case of ax^n, the Operation-cards merely order seven multiplications, that is, they order the mill to be in the *multiplying state* seven successive times (without any reference to the particular columns whose numbers are to be acted upon). The proper Distributive Variable-cards step in at each successive multiplication, and cause the distributions requisite for the particular case (Figure 3.5).

For	x^{an}	The operations would be			$34\,(\times)$
$\cdots$	$a \cdot n \cdot x$	$\cdots$	$\cdots$	$\cdots$	$(\times, \times)$ or $2\,(\times)$
$\cdots$	$\frac{a}{n} \cdot x$	$\cdots$	$\cdots$	$\cdots$	$(\div, \times)$
$\cdots$	$a + n + x$	$\cdots$	$\cdots$	$\cdots$	$(+, +)$ or $2\,(+)$

Figure 3.5

The engine might be made to calculate all these in succession. Having completed ax^n, the function x^{an} might be written under the brackets instead of ax^n, and a new calculation commenced (the appropriate Operation and Variable-cards for the new function of course coming into play). The results would then appear on V_5. So on for any number of different functions of the quantities a, n, x. Each *result* might either permanently remain on its column during the succeeding calculations, so that when all the functions had been computed, their values would simultaneously exist on V_4, V_5, V_6, &c.; or each result might (after being printed off, or used in any specified manner) be effaced, to make way for its successor. The square under V_4 ought, for the latter arrangement, to have the functions ax^n, x^{an}, anx, &c. successively inscribed in it. . . .

The further we analyse the manner in which such an engine performs its processes and attains its results, the more we perceive how distinctly it places in a true and just light the mutual relations and connexion of the various steps of mathematical analysis; how clearly it separates those things which are in reality distinct and independent, and unites those which are mutually dependent.   A. A. L.

3.4   Note C by the Translator

Those who may desire to study the principles of the Jacquard-loom in the most effectual manner, viz. that of practical observation, have only to step into the Adelaide Gallery or the Polytechnic Institution. In each of these valuable repositories of scientific *illustration*, a weaver is constantly working at a Jacquard-loom, and is ready to give any information that may be desired as to the construction and modes of acting of his apparatus. The volume on the manufacture of silk, in Lardner's Cyclopædia, contains a chapter on the Jacquard-loom, which may also be consulted with advantage.

The mode of application of the cards, as hitherto used in the art of weaving, was not found, however, to be sufficiently powerful for all the simplifications which it was desirable to attain in such varied and complicated processes as those required in order to fulfil the purposes of an Analytical Engine. A method was devised of what was technically designated *backing* the cards in certain groups according to certain laws. The object of this extension is to secure the possibility of bringing any particular card or set of cards into use *any number of times successively* in the solution of one problem. Whether this power shall be taken advantage of or not, in each particular instance, will depend on the nature of the operations which the problem under consideration may require. The process is alluded to by M. Menabrea, and it is a very important simplification. It has been proposed to use it for the reciprocal benefit of that art, which, while it has itself no apparent connexion with the domains of abstract science, has yet proved so valuable to the latter, in suggesting the principles which, in their new and singular field of application, seem likely to place *algebraical* combinations not less completely within the province of mechanism, than are all those varied intricacies of which *intersecting threads* are susceptible. By the introduction of the system of *backing* into the Jacquard-loom itself, patterns which should possess symmetry, and follow regular laws of any extent, might be woven by means of comparatively few cards.

   Those who understand the mechanism of this loom will perceive that the above improvement is easily effected in practice, by causing the prism over which the train of pattern-cards is suspended to revolve *backwards* instead of *forwards*, at pleasure, under the requisite circumstances; until, by so doing, any particular card, or set of cards, that has done duty once, and passed on in the ordinary regular succession, is brought back to the position it occupied just before it was used the preceding time. The prism then resumes its *forward* rotation, and thus brings the card or set of cards in question into play a second time. This process may obviously be repeated any number of times.   A. A. L.

. . .

3.6   Note E by the Translator . . .

Many persons who are not conversant with mathematical studies, imagine that because the business of the engine is to give its results in *numerical notation*, the *nature of its processes* must consequently be *arithmetical* and *numerical*, rather than *algebraical* and *analytical*. This is an error. The engine can arrange and combine its numerical quantities exactly as if they were *letters* or any other *general* symbols; and in fact it might bring out its results in algebraical *notation*, were provisions made accordingly. It might develop three sets of results simultaneously, viz. *symbolic* results (as already alluded to in Notes A and B), *numerical* results (its chief and primary object); and *algebraical* results in *literal* notation.

   . . . A *cycle* of operations . . . must be understood to signify any *set of operations* which is repeated *more than once*. It is equally a cycle, whether it be repeated *twice* only, or an indefinite number of times; for it is the fact of a *repetition occurring at all* that constitutes it such. In many cases of analysis there is a *recurring group* of one or more *cycles*; that is, a *cycle of a cycle*, or a *cycle of cycles*. . . .   A. A. L.

3.7   Note F by the Translator

There is in existence a beautiful woven portrait of Jacquard, in the fabrication of which 24,000 cards were required.

The power of *repeating* the cards, alluded to by M. Menabrea, and more fully explained in Note C, reduces to an immense extent the number of cards required. It is obvious that this mechanical improvement is especially applicable wherever *cycles* occur in the mathematical operations, and that, in preparing data for calculations by the engine, it is desirable to arrange the order and combination of the processes with a view to obtain them as much as possible *symmetrically* and in cycles, in order that the mechanical advantages of the *backing* system may be applied to the utmost. It is here interesting to observe the manner in which the value of an *analytical* resource is *met* and *enhanced* by an ingenious *mechanical* contrivance. We see in it an instance of one of those mutual *adjustments* between the purely mathematical and the mechanical departments, mentioned in Note A, as being a main and essential condition of success in the invention of a calculating engine. The nature of the resources afforded by such adjustments would be of two principal kinds. In some cases, a difficulty (perhaps in itself insurmountable) in the one department would be overcome by facilities in the other; and sometimes (as in the present case) a strong point in the one would be rendered still stronger and more available by combination with a corresponding strong point in the other.

As a mere example of the degree to which the combined systems of cycles and of backing can diminish the *number* of cards requisite, we shall choose a case which places it in strong evidence, and which has likewise the advantage of being a perfectly different *kind* of problem from those that are mentioned in any of the other Notes. Suppose it be required to eliminate nine variables from ten simple equations of the form—

$$ax_0 + bx_1 + cx_2 + dx_3 + \cdots = p$$
$$a'x_0 + b'x_1 + c'x_2 + d'x_3 + \cdots = p'$$
$$\text{\&c.} \qquad \text{\&c.} \qquad \text{\&c.} \qquad \text{\&c.}$$

We should explain, before proceeding, that it is not our object to consider this problem with reference to the actual arrangement of the data on the Variables of the engine, but simply as an abstract question of the *nature* and *number* of the *operations* required to be performed during its complete solution.

The first step would be the elimination of the first unknown quantity x_0 between the first two equations. This would be obtained by the form—

$$(a'a - aa')x_0 + (a'b - ab')x_1 + (a'c - ac')x_2+$$
$$+(a'd - ad')x_3 + \cdots\cdots\cdots\cdots\cdots\cdots = a'p - ap',$$

for which the operations $10\ (\times, \times, -)$ would be needed. The second step would be the elimination of x_0 between the second and third equations, for which the operations would be precisely the same. We should then have had altogether the following operations:—

$$10(\times, \times, -), 10(\times, \times, -) = 20(\times, \times, -).$$

Continuing in the same manner, the total number of operations for the complete elimination of x_0 between all the successive pairs of equations would be—

$$9 \cdot 10(\times, \times, -) = 90(\times, \times, -).$$

We should then be left with nine simple equations of nine variables from which to eliminate the next variable x_1, for which the total of the processes would be

$$8 \cdot 9(\times, \times, -) = 72(\times, \times, -).$$

We should then be left with eight simple equations of eight variables from which to eliminate x_2, for which the processes would be—

$$7 \cdot 8(\times, \times, -) = 56(\times, \times, -)$$

and so on. The total operations for the elimination of all the variables would thus be—

$$9 \cdot 10 + 8 \cdot 9 + 7 \cdot 8 + 6 \cdot 7 + 5 \cdot 6 + 4 \cdot 5 + 3 \cdot 4 + 2 \cdot 3 + 1 \cdot 2 = 330.$$

So that *three* Operation-cards would perform the office of 330 such cards.

If we take n simple equations containing $n - 1$ variables, n being a number unlimited in magnitude, the case becomes still more obvious, as the same three cards might then take the place of thousands or millions of cards.

We shall now draw further attention to the fact, already noticed, of its being by no means necessary that a formula proposed for solution should ever have been actually worked out, as a condition for enabling the engine to solve it. Provided we know the *series of operations* to be gone through, that is sufficient. In the foregoing instance this will be obvious enough on a slight consideration. And it is a circumstance which deserves particular notice, since herein may reside a latent value of such an engine almost incalculable in its possible ultimate results. We already know that there are functions whose numerical value it is of importance for the purposes both of abstract and of practical science to ascertain, but whose determination requires processes so lengthy and so complicated, that, although it is possible to arrive at them through great expenditure of time, labour and money, it is yet on these accounts practically almost unattainable; and we can conceive there being some results which it may be *absolutely impossible* in practice to attain with any accuracy, and whose precise determination it may prove highly important for some of the future wants of science, in its manifold, complicated and rapidly-developing fields of inquiry, to arrive at.

Without, however, stepping into the region of conjecture, we will mention a particular problem which occurs to us at this moment as being an apt illustration of the use to which such an engine may be turned for determining that which human brains find it difficult or impossible to work out unerringly. In the solution of the famous problem of the Three Bodies, there are, out of about 295 coefficients of lunar perturbations given by M. Clausen (Astro^e. Nachrichten, No. 406) as the result of the calculations by Burg, of two by Damoiseau, and of one by Burckhardt, fourteen coefficients that differ in the nature of their algebraic sign; and out of the remainder there are only

101 (or about one-third) that agree precisely both in signs and in amount. These discordances, which are generally small in individual magnitude, may arise either from an erroneous determination of the abstract coefficients in the development of the problem, or from discrepancies in the data deduced from observation, or from both causes combined. The former is the most ordinary source of error in astronomical computations, and this the engine would entirely obviate.

We might even invent laws for series of formulæ in an arbitrary manner, and set the engine to work upon them, and thus deduce numerical results which we might not otherwise have thought of obtaining; but this would hardly perhaps in any instance be productive of any great practical utility, or calculated to rank higher than as a philosophical amusement.   A. A. L.

3.8   Note G by the Translator

It is desirable to guard against the possibility of exaggerated ideas that might arise as to the powers of the Analytical Engine. In considering any new subject, there is frequently a tendency, first, to *overrate* what we find to be already interesting or remarkable; and, secondly, by a sort of natural reaction, to *undervalue* the true state of the case, when we do discover that our notions have surpassed those that were really tenable.

The Analytical Engine has no pretensions whatever to *originate* anything. It can do whatever we *know how to order it* to perform. It can *follow* analysis; but it has no power of *anticipating* any analytical relations or truths. Its province is to assist us in making available what we are already acquainted with. This it is calculated to effect primarily and chiefly of course, through its executive faculties; but it is likely to exert an *indirect* and reciprocal influence on science itself in another manner. For, in so distributing and combining the truths and the formulæ of analysis, that they may become most easily and rapidly amenable to the mechanical combinations of the engine, the relations and the nature of many subjects in that science are necessarily thrown into new lights, and more profoundly investigated. This is a decidedly indirect, and a somewhat *speculative*, consequence of such an invention. It is however pretty evident, on general principles, that in devising for mathematical truths a new form in which to record and throw themselves out for actual use, views are likely to be induced, which should again react on the more theoretical phase of the subject. There are in all extensions of human power, or additions to human knowledge, various *collateral* influences, besides the main and primary object attained. ...   A. A. L.

4 An Investigation of the Laws of Thought on Which Are Founded the Mathematical Theories of Logic and Probabilities (1854)

George Boole

When George Boole (1815–1864) was a student two millennia after Aristotle, the *Prior Analytics* was still a standard logic text. Astonishing advances in continuous mathematics had been made in the eighteenth century. The orbits of the planets and the behavior of other objects in motion could now be accurately—if tediously—determined by calculation. Yet in spite of Leibniz's vision of a calculus of ideas to match his calculus of infinitesimals, and his tentative start at developing formal rules of reasoning, logic was barely more systematic than it had been in ancient times. Boole realized that logic was a branch of mathematics, and as such was subject to rules that could be the basis for calculations about propositions. His goal was "to give expression in this treatise to the fundamental laws of reasoning in the symbolical language of a Calculus" (§4.1).

The mathematician George Peacock, a member of a Cambridge intellectual circle that included Charles Babbage, foreshadowed Boole when, in his *Treatise on Algebra* (Peacock, 1830), he propounded a view of algebra as "the science of general reasoning by symbolical language." Yet the publication of Boole's *Laws of Thought* marked a crucial moment in the development of computer science. His reduction of logic to an algebra of true and false variables influenced other contemporary logicians, including Augustus De Morgan (remembered today for his laws) and John Venn (remembered for his diagrams). A few years after publication of *The Laws of Thought*, Boole's countryman William Jevons (1835–1882) built a "logic piano" for doing calculations with the truth-values of propositions. It wasn't a useful device, being restricted to four propositions, but it was the first mechanization of what we now know as boolean logic.

Boole's conception of logical algebra in fact extends beyond boolean logic to what we would now call naïve set theory and probability theory. On page 30, Boole explains his word "class" to mean what we now call a set, and explicitly states the possibility that a class might be empty, a singleton, or the entire universe. Boole articulates that a variable x can be treated indifferently as a proposition stating that an individual has a given property, or as a class of entities having that property. He then goes on to use "+" for union, "−" for difference, and "×" or juxtaposition for intersection, and to derive the commutative and distributive laws, and to infer the duality or dichotomy principle (nothing can belong to a set and to its complement) algebraically from idempotency (the intersection of a set with itself is the same set). The book is laid out as a

Reprinted from Boole (1854).

series of definitions, propositions, and "rules," all designed to instruct in algebraic manipulation of logical formulas (and, later in the work, of probabilities).

George Boole was a largely self-taught mathematician, the son of an English shoemaker and the beneficiary of only primary education. He managed to publish serious mathematical research in his twenties while supporting himself as a schoolmaster. He won a professorship a decade later at the new Queen's College at Cork in Ireland, one of three colleges Queen Victoria had simultaneously endowed "for the advancement of learning in Ireland" (the other two were in Belfast and Galway). It was from this perch, away from the great mathematical centers of Oxford and Cambridge, that Boole wrote his unique opus, from which we include a small selection.

In these pages Boole patiently explains some of the rules and methods of propositional logic, including the commutative law. It all seems quite routine to us now, so used are we to the then-novel idea that true and false can be manipulated algebraically. Almost a century later, Claude Shannon incorporated Boole's ideas wholesale into the emerging world of digital circuitry (chapter 8). Our selection closes with the idea of a truth-function and the insight that such a function can be decomposed into subfunctions by fixing the value of one variable to be true or false. Boole likened this process to a Taylor series expansion of a differentiable function.

Boole died at age 49 of an infection contracted while walking three miles to his lecture in the cold Irish rain (MacHale, 2014).

—◦◦⨌◦◦—

4.1   Nature and Design of This Work

THE design of the following treatise is to investigate the fundamental laws of those operations of the mind by which reasoning is performed; to give expression to them in the symbolical language of a Calculus, and upon this foundation to establish the science of Logic and construct its method; to make that method itself the basis of a general method for the application of the mathematical doctrine of Probabilities; and, finally, to collect from the various elements of truth brought to view in the course of these inquiries some probable intimations concerning the nature and constitution of the human mind. ...

4.2   Of Signs in General, and of the Signs Appropriate to the Science of Logic in Particular; Also of the Laws to Which That Class of Signs Are Subject

4.2.1   That Language is an instrument of human reason, and not merely a medium for the expression of thought, is a truth generally admitted. It is proposed in this chapter to inquire what it is that renders Language thus subservient to the most important of our intellectual faculties. In the various steps of this inquiry we shall be led to consider the constitution of Language, considered as a system adapted to an end or purpose; to investigate its elements; to seek to determine their mutual relation and dependence; and to inquire in what manner they contribute to the attainment of the end to which, as co-ordinate parts of a system, they have respect. ...

4.2.2   The elements of which all language consists are signs or symbols. Words are signs. Sometimes they are said to represent things; sometimes the operations by which the mind combines together the simple notions of things into complex conceptions; sometimes they express the relations of action, passion, or mere quality, which we perceive to exist among the objects of our experience; sometimes the emotions of the perceiving mind. But words, although in this and in other ways they fulfil the office of signs, or representative symbols, are not the only signs which we are capable of employing. Arbitrary marks, which speak only to the eye, and arbitrary sounds or actions, which address themselves to some other sense, are equally of the nature of signs, provided that their representative office is defined and understood. In the mathematical sciences, letters, and the symbols $+$, $-$, $=$, &c., are used as signs, although the term "sign" is applied to the latter class of symbols, which represent operations or relations, rather than to the former, which represent the elements of number and quantity. As the real import of a sign does not in any way depend upon its particular form or expression, so neither do the laws which determine its use. In the present treatise, however, it is with written signs that we have to do, and it is with reference to these exclusively that the term "sign" will be employed.

The essential properties of signs are enumerated in the following definition.

Definition.—A sign is an arbitrary mark, having a fixed interpretation, and susceptible of combination with other signs in subjection to fixed laws dependent upon their mutual interpretation.

. . .

4.2.4   The analysis and classification of those signs by which the operations of reasoning are conducted will be considered in the following Proposition:

All the operations of Language, as an instrument of reasoning, may be conducted by a system of signs composed of the following elements, viz.:

1st. *Literal symbols, as x, y, &c., representing things as subjects of our conceptions.*

2nd. *Signs of operation, as $+$, $-$, $\times$, standing for those operations of the mind by which the conceptions of things are combined or resolved so as to form new conceptions involving the same elements.*

3rd. *The sign of identity, $=$.*

And these symbols of Logic are in their use subject to definite laws, partly agreeing with and partly differing from the laws of the corresponding symbols in the science of Algebra.

Let it be assumed as a criterion of the true elements of rational discourse, that they should be susceptible of combination in the simplest forms and by the simplest laws, and thus combining should generate all other known and conceivable forms of language; and adopting this principle, let the following classification be considered.

4.2.5   CLASS I.   *Appellative or descriptive signs, expressing either the name of a thing, or some quality or circumstance belonging to it.*

To this class we may obviously refer the substantive proper or common, and the adjective. These may indeed be regarded as differing only in this respect, that the former expresses the substantive existence of the individual thing or things to which it refers; the latter implies that existence. If we attach to the adjective the universally understood subject "being" or "thing," it becomes virtually a substantive, and may for all the essential purposes of reasoning be replaced by the substantive. Whether or not, in every particular of the mental regard, it is the same thing to say, "Water is a fluid thing," as to say, "Water is fluid"; it is at least equivalent in the expression of the processes of reasoning.

It is clear also, that to the above class we must refer any sign which may conventionally be used to express some circumstance or relation, the detailed exposition of which would involve the use of many signs. The epithets of poetic diction are very frequently of this kind. They are usually compounded adjectives, singly fulfilling the office of a many-worded description. Homer's "deep-eddying ocean" embodies a virtual description in the single word βαϑυδίνης. And conventionally any other description addressed either to the imagination or to the intellect might equally be represented by a single sign, the use of which would in all essential points be subject to the same laws as the use of the adjective "good" or "great." Combined with the subject "thing," such a sign would virtually become a substantive; and by a single substantive the combined meaning both of thing and quality might be expressed.

4.2.6   Now, as it has been defined that a sign is an arbitrary mark, it is permissible to replace all signs of the species above described by letters. Let us then agree to represent the class of individuals to which a particular name or description is applicable, by a single letter, as x. If the name is "men," for instance, let x represent "all men," or the class "men." By a class is usually meant a collection of individuals, to each of which a particular name or description may be applied; but in this work the meaning of the term will be extended so as to include the case in which but a single individual exists, answering to the required name or description, as well as the cases denoted by the terms "nothing" and "universe," which as "classes" should be understood to comprise respectively "no beings," "all beings." Again, if an adjective, as "good," is employed as a term of description, let us represent by a letter, as y, all things to which the description "good" is applicable, i.e. "all good things," or the class "good things." Let it further be agreed, that by the combination xy shall be represented that class of things to which the names or descriptions represented by x and y are simultaneously applicable. Thus, if x alone stands for "white things," and y for "sheep," let xy stand for "white sheep"; and in like manner, if z stand for "horned things," and x and y retain their previous interpretations, let zxy represent "horned white sheep," i.e. that collection of things to which the name "sheep," and the descriptions "white" and "horned" are together applicable.

Let us now consider the laws to which the symbols x, y, &c., used in the above sense, are subject.

4.2.7   First, it is evident, that according to the above combinations, the order in which two symbols are written is indifferent. The expressions xy and yx equally represent that class of things to the several members of which the names or descriptions x and y are together applicable. Hence we have,

$$xy = yx. \tag{4.1}$$

In the case of *x* representing white things, and *y* sheep, either of the members of this equation will represent the class of "white sheep." There may be a difference as to the order in which the conception is formed, but there is none as to the individual things which are comprehended under it. In like manner, if *x* represent "estuaries," and *y* "rivers," the expressions *xy* and *yx* will indifferently represent "rivers that are estuaries," or "estuaries that are rivers," the combination in this case being in ordinary language that of two substantives, instead of that of a substantive and an adjective as in the previous instance.

Let there be a third symbol, as *z*, representing that class of things to which the term "navigable" is applicable, and any one of the following expressions, *zxy*, *zyx*, *xyz*, &c., will represent the class of "navigable rivers that are estuaries."

If one of the descriptive terms should have some implied reference to another, it is only necessary to include that reference expressly in its stated meaning, in order to render the above remarks still applicable. Thus, if *x* represent "wise" and *y* "counsellor," we shall have to define whether *x* implies wisdom in the absolute sense, or only the wisdom of counsel. With such definition the law *xy* = *yx* continues to be valid.

We are permitted, therefore, to employ the symbols x, y, z, &c., in the place of the substantives, adjectives, and descriptive phrases subject to the rule of interpretation, that any expression in which several of these symbols are written together shall represent all the objects or individuals to which their several meanings are together applicable, and to the law that the order in which the symbols succeed each other is indifferent.

As the rule of interpretation has been sufficiently exemplified, I shall deem it unnecessary always to express the subject "things" in defining the interpretation of a symbol used for an adjective. When I say, let *x* represent "good," it will be understood that *x* only represents "good" when a subject for that quality is supplied by another symbol, and that, used alone, its interpretation will be "good things."

4.2.8   Concerning the law above determined, the following observations, which will also be more or less appropriate to certain other laws to be deduced hereafter, may be added.

First, I would remark, that this law is a law of thought, and not, properly speaking, a law of things. Difference in the order of the qualities or attributes of an object, apart from all questions of causation, is a difference in conception merely. The law (4.1) expresses as a general truth, that the same thing may be conceived in different ways, and states the nature of that difference; and it does no more than this.

Secondly, as a law of thought, it is actually developed in a law of Language, the product and the instrument of thought. Though the tendency of prose writing is toward uniformity, yet even there the order of sequence of adjectives absolute in their meaning, and applied to the same subject, is indifferent, but poetic diction borrows much of its rich diversity from the extension of the same lawful freedom to the substantive also. The language of Milton is peculiarly distinguished by this species of variety. Not only does the substantive often precede the adjectives by which it is qualified, but it is frequently placed in their midst. In the first few lines of the invocation to Light, we meet with such examples as the following:

"*Offspring of heaven first-born.*"
"The rising world of *waters dark and deep.*"
"Bright effluence of *bright essence increate.*"

Now these inverted forms are not simply the fruits of a poetic license. They are the natural expressions of a freedom sanctioned by the intimate laws of thought, but for reasons of convenience not exercised in the ordinary use of language.

Thirdly, the law expressed by (4.1) may be characterized by saying that the literal symbols x, y, z, are *commutative, like the symbols of Algebra.* In saying this, it is not affirmed that the process of multiplication in Algebra, of which the fundamental law is expressed by the equation $xy = yx$, possesses in itself any analogy with that process of logical combination which xy has been made to represent above; but only that if the arithmetical and the logical process are expressed in the same manner, their symbolical expressions will be subject to the same formal law. The evidence of that subjection is in the two cases quite distinct.

4.2.9   As the combination of two literal symbols in the form xy expresses the whole of that class of objects to which the names or qualities represented by x and y are together applicable, it follows that if the two symbols have exactly the same signification, their combination expresses no more than either of the symbols taken alone would do. In such case we should therefore have $xy = x$. As y is, however, supposed to have the same meaning as x, we may replace it in the above equation by x, and we thus get $xx = x$. Now in common Algebra the combination xx is more briefly represented by x^2. Let us adopt the same principle of notation here; for the mode of expressing a particular succession of mental operations is a thing in itself quite as arbitrary as the mode of expressing a single idea or operation. In accordance with this notation, then, the above equation assumes the form

$$x^2 = x, \tag{4.2}$$

and is, in fact, the expression of a second general law of those symbols by which names, qualities, or descriptions, are symbolically represented.

The reader must bear in mind that although the symbols x and y in the examples previously formed received significations distinct from each other, nothing prevents us from attributing to them precisely the same signification. It is evident that the more nearly their actual significations approach to each other, the more nearly does the class of things denoted by the combination xy approach to identity with the class denoted by x, as well as with that denoted by y. The case supposed in the demonstration of the equation (4.2) is that of *absolute* identity of meaning. The law which it expresses is practically exemplified in language. To say "good, good," in relation to any subject, though a cumbrous and useless pleonasm, is the same as to say "good." Thus "good, good" men, is equivalent to "good" men. Such repetitions of words are indeed sometimes employed to heighten a quality or strengthen an affirmation. But this effect is merely secondary and conventional; it is not founded in the intrinsic relations of language and thought. Most of the operations which we observe in nature, or perform ourselves, are of such a kind that their effect is augmented by repetition, and this circumstance prepares us to expect the same thing in language, and even to use repetition when we design to speak with emphasis. But neither in strict reasoning nor in exact discourse is there any just ground for such a practice.

4.2.10   We pass now to the consideration of another class of the signs of speech, and of the laws connected with their use.

4.2.11   CLASS II.   *Signs of those mental operations whereby we collect parts into a whole, or separate a whole into its parts.*

We are not only capable of entertaining the conceptions of objects, as characterized by names, qualities, or circumstances, applicable to each individual of the group under consideration, but also of forming the aggregate conception of a group of objects consisting of partial groups, each of which is separately named or described. For this purpose we use the conjunctions "and," "or," &c. "Trees and minerals," "barren mountains, or fertile vales," are examples of this kind. In strictness, the words "and," "or," interposed between the terms descriptive of two or more classes of objects, imply that those classes are quite distinct, so that no member of one is found in another. In this and in all other respects the words "and" "or" are analogous with the sign + in algebra, and their laws are identical. Thus the expression "men and women" is, conventional meanings set aside, equivalent with the expression "women and men." Let x represent "men," y, "women"; and let + stand for "and" and "or," then we have $x+y = y+x$, an equation which would equally hold true if x and y represented numbers, and + were the sign of arithmetical addition.

Let the symbol z stand for the adjective "European," then since it is, in effect, the same thing to say "European men and women," as to say "European men and European women," we have

$$z(x + y) = zx + zy. \tag{4.3}$$

And this equation also would be equally true were x, y, and z symbols of number, and were the juxtaposition of two literal symbols to represent their algebraic product, just as in the logical signification previously given, it represents the class of objects to which both the epithets conjoined belong.

The above are the laws which govern the use of the sign +, here used to denote the positive operation of aggregating parts into a whole. But the very idea of an operation effecting some positive change seems to suggest to us the idea of an opposite or negative operation, having the effect of undoing what the former one has done. Thus we cannot conceive it possible to collect parts into a whole, and not conceive it also possible to separate a part from a whole. This operation we express in common language by the sign *except*, as, "All men *except* Asiatics," "All states *except* those which are monarchical." Here it is implied that the things excepted form a part of the things from which they are excepted. As we have expressed the operation of aggregation by the sign +, so we may express the negative operation above described by – minus. Thus if x be taken to represent men, and y, Asiatics, i.e. Asiatic men, then the conception of "All men except

Asiatics" will be expressed by $x - y$. And if we represent by x, "states," and by y the descriptive property "having a monarchical form," then the conception of "All states except those which are monarchical" will be expressed by $x - xy$.

As it is indifferent for all the *essential* purposes of reasoning whether we express excepted cases first or last in the order of speech, it is also indifferent in what order we write any series of terms, some of which are affected by the sign $-$. Thus we have, as in the common algebra,

$$x - y = -y + x.$$

Still representing by x the class "men," and by y "Asiatics," let z represent the adjective "white." Now to apply the adjective "white" to the collection of men expressed by the phrase "Men except Asiatics," is the same as to say, "White men, except white Asiatics." Hence we have

$$z(x - y) = zx - zy. \tag{4.4}$$

This is also in accordance with the laws of ordinary algebra.

The equations (4.3) and (4.4) may be considered as exemplification of a single general law, which may be stated by saying, *that the literal symbols, x, y, z, &c. are distributive in their operation.* The general fact which that law expresses is this, viz.: If any quality or circumstance is ascribed to all the members of a group, formed either by aggregation or exclusion of partial groups, the resulting conception is the same as if the quality or circumstance were first ascribed to each member of the partial groups, and the aggregation or exclusion effected afterwards. That which is ascribed to the members of the whole is ascribed to the members of all its parts, howsoever those parts are connected together.

4.2.12   CLASS III.   *Signs by which relation is expressed, and by which we form propositions.*

Though all verbs may with propriety be referred to this class, it is sufficient for the purposes of Logic to consider it as including only the substantive verb *is* or *are*, since every other verb may be resolved into this element, and one of the signs included under Class I. For as those signs are used to express quality or circumstance of every kind, they may be employed to express the active or passive relation of the subject of the verb, considered with reference either to past, to present, or to future time. Thus the Proposition, "Cæsar conquered the Gauls," may be resolved into "Cæsar is he who conquered the Gauls." The ground of this analysis I conceive to be the following:—Unless we understand what is meant by having conquered the Gauls, i.e. by the expression "One who conquered the Gauls," we cannot understand the sentence in question. It is, therefore, truly an element of that sentence; another element is "Cæsar," and there is yet another required, the copula is to show the connexion of these two. I do not, however, affirm that there is no other mode than the above of contemplating the relation expressed by the proposition, "Cæsar conquered the Gauls"; but only that the analysis here given is a correct one for the particular point of view which has been taken, and that it suffices for the purposes of logical deduction. It may be remarked that the passive and future participles of the Greek language imply the existence of the principle which has been asserted, viz.: that the sign *is* or *are* may be regarded as an element of every personal verb.

4.2.13   The above sign, *is* or *are* may be expressed by the symbol =. The laws, or as would usually be said, the axioms which the symbol introduces, are next to be considered. Let us take the Proposition, "The stars are the suns and the planets," and let us represent stars by x, suns by y, and planets by z; we have then

$$x = y + z. \tag{4.5}$$

Now if it be true that the stars are the suns and the planets, it will follow that the stars, except the planets, are suns. This would give the equation $x - z = y$, which must therefore be a deduction from (4.5). Thus a term z has been removed from one side of an equation to the other by changing its sign. This is in accordance with the algebraic rule of transposition.

But instead of dwelling upon particular cases, we may at once affirm the general axioms:—

1st. If equal things are added to equal things, the wholes are equal.

2nd. If equal things are taken from equal things, the remainders are equal.

And it hence appears that we may add or subtract equations, and employ the rule of transposition above given just as in common algebra.

Again: If two classes of things, x and y, be identical, that is, if all the members of the one are members of the other, then those members of the one class which possess a given property z will be identical with those members of the other which possess the same property z. Hence if we have the equation $x = y$; then whatever class or property z may represent, we have also $zx = zy$.

This is formally the same as the algebraic law:—If both members of an equation are multiplied by the same quantity, the products are equal.

In like manner it may be shown that if the corresponding members of two equations are multiplied together, the resulting equation is true.

4.2.14   Here, however, the analogy of the present system with that of algebra, as commonly stated, appears to stop. Suppose it true that those members of a class x which possess a certain property z are identical with those members of a class y which possess the same property z, it does not follow that the members of the class x universally are identical with the members of the class y. Hence it cannot be inferred from the equation $zx = zy$, that the equation $x = y$ is also true. In other words, the axiom of algebraists, that both sides of an equation may be divided by the same quantity, has no formal equivalent here. I say no *formal equivalent*, because, in accordance with the general spirit of these inquiries, it is not even sought to determine whether the mental operation which is represented by removing a logical symbol, z, from a combination zx, is in itself analogous with the operation of division in Arithmetic. That mental operation is indeed identical with what is commonly termed Abstraction, and it will hereafter appear that its laws are dependent upon the laws already deduced in this chapter. What has now been shown is, that there does not exist among those laws anything analogous in form with a commonly received axiom of Algebra.

But a little consideration will show that even in common algebra that axiom does not possess the generality of those other axioms which have been considered. The deduction of the equation $x = y$ from the equation $zx = zy$ is only valid when it is known that z is not equal to 0. If then the value $z = 0$ is supposed to be admissible in the algebraic system, the axiom above stated ceases to be applicable, and the analogy before exemplified remains at least unbroken.

4.2.15   However, it is not with the symbols of quantity generally that it is of any importance, except as a matter of speculation, to trace such affinities. We have seen (§4.2.9) that the symbols of Logic are subject to the special law, $x^2 = x$. Now of the symbols of Number there are but two, viz. 0 and 1, which are subject to the same formal law. We know that $0^2 = 0$, and that $1^2 = 1$; and the equation $x^2 = x$, considered as algebraic, has no other roots than 0 and 1. Hence, instead of determining the measure of formal agreement of the symbols of Logic with those of Number generally, it is more immediately suggested to us to compare them with symbols of quantity *admitting only of the values* 0 *and* 1. Let us conceive, then, of an Algebra in which the symbols x, y, z, etc. admit indifferently of the values 0 and 1, and of these values alone. The laws, the axioms, and the processes, of such an Algebra will be identical in their whole extent with the laws, the axioms, and the processes of an Algebra of Logic. Difference of interpretation will alone divide them. Upon this principle the method of the following work is established.

4.2.16   It now remains to show that those constituent parts of ordinary language which have not been considered in the previous sections of this chapter are either resolvable into the same elements as those which have been considered, or are subsidiary to those elements by contributing to their more precise definition.

The substantive, the adjective, and the verb, together with the particles *and*, *except*, we have already considered. The pronoun may be regarded as a particular form of the substantive or the adjective. The adverb modifies the meaning of the verb, but does not affect its nature. Prepositions contribute to the expression of circumstance or relation, and thus tend to give precision and detail to the meaning of the literal symbols. The conjunctions *if*, *either*, *or*, are used chiefly in the expression of relation among propositions, and it will hereafter be shown that the same relations can be completely expressed by elementary symbols analogous in interpretation, and identical in form and law with the symbols whose use and meaning have been explained in this chapter. As to any remaining elements of speech, it will, upon examination, be found that they are used either to give a more definite significance to the terms of discourse, and thus enter into the interpretation of the literal symbols already considered, or to express some emotion or state of feeling accompanying the utterance of a proposition, and thus do not belong to the province of the understanding, with which alone our present concern lies. Experience of its use will testify to the sufficiency of the classification which has been adopted.

4.3   Derivation of the Laws of the Symbols of Logic from the Laws of the Operations of the Human Mind . . .

4.3.12   The remainder of this chapter will be occupied with questions relating to that law of thought whose expression is $x^2 = x$ (§4.2.9), a law which, as has been implied (§4.2.15), forms the characteristic distinction of the operations of the mind in its ordinary discourse and reasoning, as compared with its operations when occupied with the general algebra of quantity. An important part of the following inquiry will consist in proving that the symbols 0 and 1 occupy a place, and are susceptible of an interpretation, among the symbols of Logic; and it may first be necessary to show how particular symbols, such as the above, may with propriety and advantage be employed in the representation of distinct systems of thought.

   The ground of this propriety cannot consist in any community of interpretation. For in systems of thought so truly distinct as those of Logic and Arithmetic (I use the latter term in its widest sense as the science of Number), there is, properly speaking, no community of subject. The one of them is conversant with the very conceptions of things, the other takes account solely of their numerical relations. But inasmuch as the forms and methods of any system of reasoning depend immediately upon the laws to which the symbols are subject, and only mediately, through the above link of connexion, upon their interpretation, there may be both propriety and advantage in employing the same symbols in different systems of thought, provided that such interpretations can be assigned to them as shall render their formal laws identical, and their use consistent. The ground of that employment will not then be community of interpretation, but the community of the formal laws, to which in their respective systems they are subject. Nor must that community of formal laws be established upon any other ground than that of a careful observation and comparison of those results which are seen to flow independently from the interpretations of the systems under consideration.

   These observations will explain the process of inquiry adopted in the following Proposition. The literal symbols of Logic are universally subject to the law whose expression is $x^2 = x$. Of the symbols of Number there are two only, 0 and 1, which satisfy this law. But each of these symbols is also subject to a law peculiar to itself in the system of numerical magnitude, and this suggests the inquiry, what interpretations must be given to the literal symbols of Logic, in order that the same peculiar and formal laws may be realized in the logical system also.

4.3.13   *To determine the logical value and significance of the symbols 0 and 1.*   The symbol 0, as used in Algebra, satisfies the following formal law,

$$0 \times y = 0, \text{ or } 0y = 0, \tag{4.6}$$

whatever *number* y may represent. That this formal law may be obeyed in the system of Logic, we must assign to the symbol 0 such an interpretation that the class represented by 0y may be identical with the class represented by 0, whatever the class y may be. A little consideration will show that this condition is satisfied if the symbol 0 represent Nothing. In accordance with a previous definition, we may term Nothing a class. In fact, Nothing and Universe are the two limits of class extension, for they are the limits of the possible interpretations of general names, none of which can relate to fewer individuals than are comprised in Nothing, or to more than are comprised in the Universe.

Now whatever the class y may be, the individuals which are common to it and to the class "Nothing" are identical with those comprised in the class "Nothing," for they are none. And thus by assigning to 0 the interpretation Nothing, the law (4.6) is satisfied; and it is not otherwise satisfied consistently with the perfectly general character of the class y.

Secondly, the symbol 1 satisfies in the system of Number the following law, viz.,

$$1 \times y = y, \text{ or } 1y = y,$$

whatever number y may represent. And this formal equation being assumed as equally valid in the system of this work, in which 1 and y represent classes, it appears that the symbol 1 must represent such a class that all the individuals which are found in *any* proposed class y are also all the individuals $1y$ that are common to that class y and the class represented by 1. A little consideration will here show that the class represented by 1 must be "the Universe," since this is the only class in which are found all the individuals that exist in any class. Hence the respective interpretations of the symbols 0 and 1 in the system of Logic are *Nothing* and *Universe*.

4.3.14   As with the idea of any class of objects as "men," there is suggested to the mind the idea of the contrary class of beings which are not men; and as the whole Universe is made up of these two classes together, since of every individual which it comprehends we may affirm either that it is a man, or that it is not a man, it becomes important to inquire how such contrary names are to be expressed. Such is the object of the following Proposition.

If x represent any class of objects, then will $1 - x$ represent the contrary or supplementary class of objects., i.e. the class including all objects which are not comprehended in the class x.

For greater distinctness of conception let x represent the class men, and let us express, according to the last Proposition, the Universe by 1; now if from the conception of the Universe, as consisting of "men" and "not-men," we exclude the conception of "men," the resulting conception is that of the contrary class, "not-men." Hence the class "not-men" will be represented by $1 - x$. And, in general, whatever class of objects is represented by the symbol x, the contrary class will be expressed by $1 - x$.

4.3.15   Although the following Proposition belongs in strictness to a future chapter of this work, devoted to the subject of *maxims* or *necessary truths*, yet, on account of the great importance of that law of thought to which it relates, it has been thought proper to introduce it here.

That axiom of metaphysicians which is termed the principle of contradiction, and which affirms that it is impossible for any being to possess a quality, and at the same time not to possess it, is a consequence of the fundamental law of thought, whose expression is $x^2 = x$.

Let us write this equation in the form $x - x^2 = 0$, whence we have

$$x(1 - x) = 0; \tag{4.7}$$

both these transformations being justified by the axiomatic laws of combination and transposition (§4.2.13). Let us, for simplicity of conception, give to the symbol x the particular interpretation of *men*, then $1 - x$ will represent the class of "not-men" (§4.3.14). Now the formal product of the expressions of two classes represents that class of individuals which is common to them both (§4.2.9). Hence $x(1 - x)$ will represent the class whose members are at once "men," and "not men," and the equation (4.7) thus express the principle, *that a class whose members are at the same time men and not men does not exist.* In other words, that *it is impossible for the same individual to be at the same time a man and not a man.* Now let the meaning of the symbol x be extended from the representing of "men," to that of any class of beings characterized by the possession of any quality whatever; and the equation (4.7) thus will then express that it is impossible for a being to possess a quality and not to possess that quality at the same time. But this is identically that "principle of contradiction" which Aristotle has described as the fundamental axiom of all philosophy. "It is impossible that the same quality should both belong and not belong to the same thing. ... This is the most certain of all principles. ... Wherefore they who demonstrate refer to this as an ultimate opinion. For it is by nature the source of all the other axioms."

The above interpretation has been introduced not on account of its immediate value in the present system, but as an illustration of a significant fact in the philosophy of the intellectual powers, viz., that what has been commonly regarded as the fundamental axiom of metaphysics is but the consequence of a law of thought, mathematical in its form. I desire to direct attention also to the circumstance that the equation (4.7) thus in which that fundamental law of thought is expressed is an equation of the second degree. ...

4.3.16 The law of thought expressed by the equation (4.7) thus will, for reasons which are made apparent by the above discussion, be occasionally referred to as the "law of duality."

4.4 Of the Division of Propositions into the Two Classes of "Primary" and "Secondary," of the Characteristic Properties of Those Classes, and of the Laws of the Expression of Primary Propositions

4.4.1 The laws of those mental operations which are concerned in the processes of Conception or Imagination having been investigated, and the corresponding laws of the symbols by which they are represented explained, we are led to consider the practical application of the results obtained: first, in the expression of the complex terms of propositions; secondly, in the expression of propositions; and lastly, in the construction of a general method of deductive analysis. In the present chapter we shall be chiefly concerned with the first of these objects, as an introduction to which it is necessary to establish the following Proposition:

All logical propositions may be considered as belonging to one or the other of two great classes, to which the respective names of "Primary" or "Concrete Propositions," and "Secondary" or "Abstract Propositions," may be given.

Every assertion that we make may be referred to one or the other of the two following kinds. Either it expresses a relation among *things*, or it expresses, or is equivalent to the expression of, a relation among *propositions*. An assertion respecting the properties of things, or the phænomena which they manifest, or the circumstances in which they are placed, is, properly speaking, the assertion of a relation among things. To say that "snow is white," is for the ends of logic equivalent to saying, that "snow is a white thing." An assertion respecting facts or events, their mutual connexion and dependence, is, for the same ends, generally equivalent to the assertion, that such and such propositions concerning those events have a certain relation to each other as respects their mutual truth or falsehood. The former class of propositions, relating to *things*, I call "Primary"; the latter class, relating to *propositions*, I call "Secondary." The distinction is in practice nearly but not quite co-extensive with the common logical distinction of propositions as categorical or hypothetical.

For instance, the propositions, "The sun shines," "The earth is warmed," are primary; the proposition, "If the sun shines the earth is warmed," is secondary. To say, "The sun shines," is to say, "The sun is that which shines," and it expresses a relation between two classes of things, viz., "the sun" and "things which shine." The secondary proposition, however, given above, expresses a relation of dependence between the two primary propositions, "The sun shines," and "The earth is warmed." I do not hereby affirm that the relation between these propositions is, like that which exists between the facts which they express, a relation of causality, but only that the relation among the propositions so implies, and is so implied by, the relation among the facts, that it may for the ends of logic be used as a fit representative of that relation.

4.4.2   If instead of the proposition, "The sun shines," we say, "It is true that the sun shines," we then speak not directly of things, but of a proposition concerning things, viz., of the proposition, "The sun shines." And, therefore, the proposition in which we thus speak is a secondary one. Every primary proposition may thus give rise to a secondary proposition, viz., to that secondary proposition which asserts its truth, or declares its falsehood.

It will usually happen, that the particles *if*, *either*, *or*, will indicate that a proposition is secondary; but they do not necessarily imply that such is the case. The proposition, "Animals are either rational or irrational," is primary. It cannot be resolved into "Either animals are rational or animals are irrational," and it does not therefore express a relation of dependence between the two propositions connected together in the latter disjunctive sentence. The particles, *either*, *or*, are in fact no *criterion* of the nature of propositions, although it happens that they are more frequently found in secondary propositions. Even the conjunction *if* may be found in primary propositions. "Men are, if wise, then temperate," is an example of the kind. It cannot be resolved into "If all men are wise, then all men are temperate."

4.4.3   As it is not my design to discuss the merits or defects of the ordinary division of propositions, I shall simply remark here, that the principle upon which the present classification is founded is clear and definite in its application, that it involves a real and fundamental distinction in propositions, and that it is of essential importance to the development of a general method of reasoning. Nor does the fact that a primary proposition may be put into a form in which it becomes secondary at all conflict with the views here maintained. For in the case thus supposed, it is not of the things connected together in the primary proposition that any direct account is taken, but only of the proposition itself considered as *true* or as *false*.

4.4.4   In the expression both of primary and of secondary propositions, the same symbols, subject, as it will appear, to the same laws, will be employed in this work. The difference between the two cases is a difference not of form but of interpretation. In both cases the actual relation which it is the object of the proposition to express will be denoted by the sign =. In the expression of primary propositions, the members thus connected will usually represent the "terms" of a proposition, or, as they are more particularly designated, its subject and predicate.

4.4.5   *To deduce a general method, founded upon the enumeration of possible varieties, for the expression of any class or collection of things, which may constitute a "term" of a Primary Proposition.*

First, If the class or collection of things to be expressed is defined only by names or qualities common to all the individuals of which it consists, its expression will consist of a single term, in which the symbols expressive of those names or qualities will be combined without any connecting sign, as if by the algebraic process of multiplication. Thus, if x represent opaque substances, y polished substances, z stones, we shall have,

$xyz = $ opaque polished stones;

$xy(1 - z) = $ opaque polished substances which are not stones;

$x(1 - y)(1 - z) = $ opaque substances which are not polished, and are not stones;

and so on for any other combination. Let it be observed, that each of these expressions satisfies the same law of duality, as the individual symbols which it contains. Thus,

$$xyz \times xyz = xyz;$$
$$xy(1 - z) \times xy(1 - z) = xy(1 - z);$$

and so on. Any such term as the above we shall designate as a "class term," because it expresses a class of things by means of the common properties or names of the individual members of such class.

Secondly, If we speak of a collection of things, different portions of which are defined by different properties, names, or attributes, the expressions for those different portions must be separately formed, and then connected by the sign +. But if the collection of which we desire to speak has been formed by excluding from some wider collection a defined portion of its members, the sign − must be prefixed to the symbolical expression of the excluded portion. Respecting the use of these symbols some further observations may be added.

4.4.6   Speaking generally, the symbol + is the equivalent of the conjunctions "and," "or," and the symbol −, the equivalent of the preposition "except." Of the conjunctions "and" and "or," the former is usually employed when the collection to be described forms the subject, the latter when it forms the predicate, of a proposition. "The scholar *and* the man of the world desire happiness," may be taken as an illustration of one of these cases. "Things possessing utility are *either* productive of pleasure *or* preventive of pain," may exemplify the other. Now whenever an expression involving these particles presents itself in a primary proposition, it becomes very important to know whether the groups or classes separated in thought by them are intended to be quite distinct from each other and mutually exclusive, or not. Does the expression, "Scholars and men of the world," include or exclude those who are both? Does the expression, "Either productive of pleasure or preventive of pain," include or exclude things which possess both these qualities? I apprehend that in strictness of meaning the conjunctions "and," "or," do possess the power of separation or exclusion here referred to; that the formula, "All *x*'s are either *y*'s or *z*'s," rigorously interpreted, means, "All *x*'s are either *y*'s, but not *z*'s," or, "*z*'s but not *y*'s." But it must at the same time be admitted, that the *jus et norma loquendi* seems rather to favour an opposite interpretation. The expression, "Either *y*'s or *z*'s," would generally be understood to include things that are *y*'s and *z*'s at the same time, together with things which come under the one, but not the other. Remembering, however, that the symbol + does possess the separating power which has been the subject of discussion, we must resolve any disjunctive expression which may come before us into elements really separated in thought, and then connect their respective expressions by the symbol +.

And thus, according to the meaning implied, the expression, "Things which are either *x*'s or *y*'s," will have two different symbolical equivalents. If we mean, "Things which are *x*'s, but not *y*'s, or *y*'s, but not *x*'s," the expression will be $x(1 - y) + y(1 - x)$; the symbol *x* standing for *x*'s, *y* for *y*'s. If, however, we mean, "Things which are either *x*'s, or, if not *x*'s, then *y*'s," the expression will be $x + y(1 - x)$. This expression supposes the admissibility of things which are both *x*'s and *y*'s at the same time. It might more fully be expressed in the form $xy + x(1 - y) + y(1 - x)$; but this expression, on addition of the two first terms, only reproduces the former one.

Let it be observed that the expressions above given satisfy the fundamental law of duality. Thus we have

$$\{x(1 - y) + y(1 - x)\}^2 = x(1 - y) + y(1 - x),$$
$$\{x + y(1 - x)\}^2 = x + y(1 - x).$$

It will be seen hereafter, that this is but a particular manifestation of a general law of expressions representing "classes or collections of things." [EDITOR: Original has $\{x + (1 - x)\}^2 = x + y(1 - x)$ for the second equation, apparently in error.]

4.4.7   The results of these investigations may be embodied in the following rule of expression.

RULE.—*Express simple names or qualities by the symbols x, y, z, &c., their contraries by* $1 - x$, $1 - y$, $1 - z$, *&c.; classes of things defined by common names or qualities, by connecting the corresponding symbols as in multiplication; collections of things, consisting of portions different from each other, by connecting the expressions of those portions by the sign +. In particular, let the expression, "Either x's or y's," be expressed by* $x(1 - y) + y(1 - x)$, *when the classes denoted by x and y are exclusive, by* $x + y(1 - x)$ *when they are not exclusive. Similarly let the expression, "Either x's, or y's, or z's," be expressed by* $x(1 - y)(1 - z) + y(1 - x)(1 - z) + z(1 - x)(1 - y)$, *when the* *classes denoted by x, y, and z, are designed to be mutually exclusive, by* $x+y(1-x)+z(1-x)(1-y)$, *when they are not meant to be exclusive, and so on.*

4.4.8   On this rule of expression is founded the converse rule of interpretation. Both these will be exemplified with, perhaps, sufficient fulness in the following instances. Omitting for brevity the universal subject "things," or "beings," let us assume $x =$ hard, $y =$ elastic, $z =$ metals; and we shall have the following results:

"Non-elastic metals," will be expressed by $z(1 - y)$;
"Elastic substances with non-elastic metals," by $y + z(1 - y)$;
"Hard substances, except metals," by $x - z$;
"Metallic substances, except those which are neither hard nor elastic," by
$z - z(1 - x)(1 - y)$, or by $z\{1 - (1 - x)(1 - y)\}$.

In the last example, what we had really to express was "Metals, except not hard, not elastic, metals." Conjunctions used between adjectives are usually superfluous, and, therefore, must not be expressed symbolically.

Thus, "Metals hard and elastic," is equivalent to "Hard elastic metals," and expressed by xyz.

Take next the expression, "Hard substances, except those which are metallic and non-elastic, and those which are elastic and non-metallic." Here the word *those* means hard substances, so that the expression really means, *Hard substances except hard substances, metallic, non-elastic, and hard substances non-metallic, elastic*; the word *except* extending to both the classes which follow it. The complete expression is $x - \{xz(1 - y) + xy(1 - z)\}$; or, $x - xz(1 - y) - xy(1 - z)$.

4.5   Of the Fundamental Principles of Symbolical Reasoning, and of the Expansion or Development of Expressions Involving Logical Symbols . . .

4.5.8   *Definition.*—Any algebraic expression involving a symbol x is termed a function of x, and may be represented under the abbreviated general form $f(x)$. Any expression involving two symbols, x and y, is similarly termed a function of x and y, and may be represented under the general form $f(x, y)$, and so on for any other case. . . .

4.5.9   *Definition.*—Any function $f(x)$, in which x is a logical symbol, or a symbol of quantity susceptible only of the values 0 and 1, is said to be developed, when it is reduced to the form $ax + b(1 - x)$, a and b being so determined as to make the result equivalent to the function from which it was derived.

This definition assumes, that it is possible to represent any function $f(x)$ in the form supposed. The assumption is vindicated in the following Proposition.

4.5.10   ***To develop any function f(x) in which x is a logical symbol.***   By the principle which has been asserted in this chapter, it is lawful to treat x as a quantitative symbol, susceptible only of the values 0 and 1.

Assume then, $f(x) = ax + b(1 - x)$, and making $x = 1$, we have $f(1) = a$. Again, in the same equation making $x = 0$, we have $f(0) = b$. Hence the values of a and b are determined, and substituting them in the first equation, we have

$$f(x) = f(1)x + f(0)(1 - x);$$

as the development sought. The second member of the equation adequately represents the function $f(x)$, whatever the form of that function may be. ...

5 Mathematical Problems (1900)

David Hilbert

Nothing is more important to the progress of science than knowing what question to ask. The great German mathematician David Hilbert (1862–1943) of the University of Göttingen used the occasion of the International Congress of Mathematicians at the turn of the twentieth century to characterize mathematical problems and their solutions generally, and to challenge his colleagues with a list of 23 unsolved problems. Several problems were solved quickly, but the tenth problem took seventy years to resolve, and the resolution came in a form—a demonstration of recursive unsolvability—that Hilbert could not have articulated in 1900. The eighth problem, the Riemann hypothesis, is still unresolved; the status of other more ambiguously worded problems is arguable.

In the year 2000, the Clay Mathematics Institute updated Hilbert's list with a list of seven Millennium Prize problems, offering a $1 million dollar reward for the solution of each (Clay Mathematics Institute, 2000). To date, only one—the Poincaré conjecture—has been solved. The Riemann hypothesis is on the Millennium list; so is the $\mathcal{P} = \mathcal{NP}$ problem (chapter 34).

No precise notion of an algorithm was known in 1900, much less of recursive unsolvability. And yet Hilbert's address is full of hints of things to come: his references to processes with a "finite number of steps," and to "the impossibility of the solution under the given hypotheses, or in the sense contemplated"—for which he gives as an example the ancient proof of the irrationality of $\sqrt{2}$. In the late nineteenth century, the logical revolution foreshadowed by Boole developed into the field of metamathematics, the program to construct solid mathematical foundations for the conduct of mathematics itself. Gottlob Frege (1879) provided the first rigorous axiomatization of modern logic with the publication of *Begriffsschrift*, and Whitehead and Russell (1910) published the first part of their massive *Principia Mathematica*, an attempt to completely formalize all of mathematics. Leibniz's dream seemed within reach.

Yet as the attempts to formalize mathematics became more robust, several inconsistencies and paradoxes emerged. Hilbert, troubled by the shaky ground on which his optimism was founded, challenged the mathematical community to "dispose of the foundational questions in mathematics as such once and for all" (Hilbert, 1928; Van Heijenoort, 1967). This challenge became known as Hilbert's program, and only once the challenge was posed was it possible to imagine that it might not be achievable.

Reprinted from Hilbert (1902).

In Hilbert's 1900 address, there is not much thinking about such an impossibility. The tone is uplifting and encouraging. Every problem can be solved, one way or another. There is no *ignorabimus* (literally, no "we shall not know"—that is, no giving up on finding the answer).

In fact this spirit informed much of human culture at the time. The turn of the twentieth century was a moment of general positivity in the world. Wars were limited and of manageable scale. The Industrial Revolution had brought prosperity and progress, at least to the Western world. Fifty million people visited the *Exposition Universelle* (World Fair) in Paris to see first-hand the wonders of the modern world. Romantic, swirly artworks in the *art nouveau* ("new art") style spoke to the general feelings that life was gentle, beautiful, flourishing organically, and could only get better.

We excerpt the prefatory remarks of Hilbert's address. Of the 23 problems, we include only the second and the tenth. The tenth is the problem of determining whether a diophantine equation is solvable over the integers. These are equations of the form $p(x_1, \ldots, x_k) = 0$, where p is a polynomial in which the terms are integer constants multiplied by products of the variables raised to integer powers—for example, $17x_1x_2^2 - 13x_1^2x_2 + 3x_1 + 11 = 0$. The requirement that the values of $x_1, \ldots, x_k$ be integers turns what looks like an algebraic problem into a combinatorial problem. The decades-long efforts of Martin Davis, Hilary Putnam, Julia Robinson, and Yuri Matiyasevich eventually demonstrated the unsolvability of the general problem of determining whether such an equation has a solution, with Matiyasevich contributing the number-theoretic *coup de grâce* in 1970 (Matiyasevich, 1993).

Fifteen years after Hilbert's address, Europe was in the depths of a bloody, seemingly senseless and endless war. Literature turned ironic and cynical; dark and violent themes emerged in the visual arts. As though reflecting the pessimistic shift, between the two World Wars Gödel and Turing demonstrated the unexpected consequences of formalizing symbolically the idea of a finite process of discrete steps. Formal systems themselves have their limits, it seemed.

Hilbert's health declined during the 1920s, and the great school of mathematicians that had grown around him at Göttingen was all but dissolved when the Nazis purged it of Jewish professors. Hilbert's gravestone bears (in German) his brave words, "We must know. We shall know." He had said this in 1930, on the day before Kurt Gödel announced a result in a line of inquiry stimulated by Hilbert's second problem, about the independence and consistency of axioms. Gödel proved that in any recursively axiomatizable consistent logical system strong enough to axiomatize basic arithmetic, some true propositions could not be proved—thus confounding any attempt at a simple answer to the question of what can be known.

And yet, in closing one door, Gödel and Turing opened countless others. Gödel's proof that mathematics can never be a single closed system also meant that its possibilities are limitless. Turing, in defining what an algorithm is in order to prove what algorithms cannot do, opened the study of algorithms to scientific analysis, both theoretical and practical, and ushered in the computational world of today.

WHO of us would not be glad to lift the veil behind which the future lies hidden; to cast a glance at the next advances of our science and at the secrets of its development during future centuries? What particular goals will there be toward which the leading mathematical spirits of coming generations will strive? What new methods and new facts in the wide and rich field of mathematical thought will the new centuries disclose?

History teaches the continuity of the development of science. We know that every age has its own problems, which the following age either solves or casts aside as profitless and replaces by new ones. If we would obtain an idea of the probable development of mathematical knowledge in the immediate future, we must let the unsettled questions pass before our minds and look over the problems which the science of today sets and whose solution we expect from the future. To such a review of problems the present day, lying at the meeting of the centuries, seems to me well adapted. For the close of a great epoch not only invites us to look back into the past but also directs our thoughts to the unknown future.

The deep significance of certain problems for the advance of mathematical science in general and the important role which they play in the work of the individual investigator are not to be denied. As long as a branch of science offers an abundance of problems, so long is it alive; a lack of problems foreshadows extinction or the cessation of independent development. Just as every human undertaking pursues certain objects, so also mathematical research requires its problems. It is by the solution of problems that the investigator tests the temper of his steel; he finds new methods and new outlooks, and gains a wider and freer horizon.

It is difficult and often impossible to judge the value of a problem correctly in advance; for the final award depends upon the gain which science obtains from the problem. Nevertheless we can ask whether there are general criteria which mark a good mathematical problem. An old French mathematician said: "A mathematical theory is not to be considered complete until you have made it so clear that you can explain it to the first man whom you meet on the street." This clearness and ease of comprehension, here insisted on for a mathematical theory, I should still more demand for a mathematical problem if it is to be perfect; for what is clear and easily comprehended attracts, the complicated repels us.

Moreover a mathematical problem should be difficult in order to entice us, yet not completely inaccessible, lest it mock at our efforts. It should be to us a guide post on the mazy paths to hidden truths, and ultimately a reminder of our pleasure in the successful solution. The mathematicians of past centuries were accustomed to devote themselves to the solution of difficult particular problems with passionate zeal. They knew the value of difficult problems. I remind you only of the "problem of the line of quickest descent," proposed by John Bernoulli. Experience teaches, explains Bernoulli in the public announcement of this problem, that lofty minds are led to strive for the advance of science by nothing more than by laying before them difficult and at the same time useful problems, and he therefore hopes to earn the thanks of the mathematical world by following the example of men like Mersenne, Pascal, Fermat, Viviani and others and laying before the distinguished analysts of his time a problem by which, as a touchstone, they may test

the value of their methods and measure their strength. The calculus of variations owes its origin
to this problem of Bernoulli and to similar problems.

Fermat had asserted, as is well known, that the diophantine equation

$$x^n + y^n = z^n$$

(x, y and z integers) is unsolvable—except in certain self-evident cases. The attempt to prove
this impossibility offers a striking example of the inspiring effect which such a very special
and apparently unimportant problem may have upon science. For Kummer, incited by Fermat's
problem, was led to the introduction of ideal numbers and to the discovery of the law of the
unique decomposition of the numbers of a circular field into ideal prime factors—a law which
today, in its generalization to any algebraic field by Dedekind and Kronecker, stands at the center
of the modern theory of numbers and whose significance extends far beyond the boundaries of
number theory into the realm of algebra and the theory of functions.

To speak of a very different region of research, I remind you of the problem of three bodies.
The fruitful methods and the far-reaching principles which Poincaré has brought into celestial
mechanics and which are today recognized and applied in practical astronomy are due to the
circumstance that he undertook to treat anew that difficult problem and to approach nearer a
solution.

The two last mentioned problems—that of Fermat and the problem of the three bodies—seem
to us almost like opposite poles—the former a free invention of pure reason, belonging to the
region of abstract number theory, the latter forced upon us by astronomy and necessary to an
understanding of the simplest fundamental phenomena of nature.

But it often happens also that the same special problem finds application in the most unlike
branches of mathematical knowledge. So, for example, the problem of the shortest line plays a
chief and historically important part in the foundations of geometry, in the theory of curved lines
and surfaces, in mechanics and in the calculus of variations. And how convincingly has F. Klein,
in his work on the icosahedron, pictured the significance which attaches to the problem of the
regular polyhedra in elementary geometry, in group theory, in the theory of equations and in that
of linear differential equations. ...

It remains to discuss briefly what general requirements may be justly laid down for the solution
of a mathematical problem. I should say first of all, this: that it shall be possible to establish the
correctness of the solution by means of a finite number of steps based upon a finite number of
hypotheses which are implied in the statement of the problem and which must always be exactly
formulated. This requirement of logical deduction by means of a finite number of processes
is simply the requirement of rigor in reasoning. Indeed the requirement of rigor, which has
become proverbial in mathematics, corresponds to a universal philosophical necessity of our
understanding; and, on the other hand, only by satisfying this requirement do the thought content
and the suggestiveness of the problem attain their full effect. A new problem, especially when
it comes from the world of outer experience, is like a young twig, which thrives and bears fruit

only when it is grafted carefully and in accordance with strict horticultural rules upon the old stem, the established achievements of our mathematical science. . . .

Some remarks upon the difficulties which mathematical problems may offer, and the means of surmounting them, may be in place here.

If we do not succeed in solving a mathematical problem, the reason frequently consists in our failure to recognize the more general standpoint from which the problem before us appears only as a single link in a chain of related problems. After finding this standpoint, not only is this problem frequently more accessible to our investigation, but at the same time we come into possession of a method which is applicable also to related problems. The introduction of complex paths of integration by Cauchy and of the notion of the IDEALS in number theory by Kummer may serve as examples. This way for finding general methods is certainly the most practicable and the most certain; for he who seeks for methods without having a definite problem in mind seeks for the most part in vain.

In dealing with mathematical problems, specialization plays, as I believe, a still more important part than generalization. Perhaps in most cases where we seek in vain the answer to a question, the cause of the failure lies in the fact that problems simpler and easier than the one in hand have been either not at all or incompletely solved. All depends, then, on finding out these easier problems, and on solving them by means of devices as perfect as possible and of concepts capable of generalization. This rule is one of the most important levers for overcoming mathematical difficulties and it seems to me that it is used almost always, though perhaps unconsciously.

Occasionally it happens that we seek the solution under insufficient hypotheses or in an incorrect sense, and for this reason do not succeed. The problem then arises: to show the impossibility of the solution under the given hypotheses, or in the sense contemplated. Such proofs of impossibility were effected by the ancients, for instance when they showed that the ratio of the hypotenuse to the side of an isosceles right triangle is irrational. In later mathematics, the question as to the impossibility of certain solutions plays a preeminent part, and we perceive in this way that old and difficult problems, such as the proof of the axiom of parallels, the squaring of the circle, or the solution of equations of the fifth degree by radicals have finally found fully satisfactory and rigorous solutions, although in another sense than that originally intended. It is probably this important fact along with other philosophical reasons that gives rise to the conviction (which every mathematician shares, but which no one has as yet supported by a proof) that every definite mathematical problem must necessarily be susceptible of an exact settlement, either in the form of an actual answer to the question asked, or by the proof of the impossibility of its solution and therewith the necessary failure of all attempts. Take any definite unsolved problem, such as the question as to the irrationality of the Euler-Mascheroni constant C, or the existence of an infinite number of prime numbers of the form $2^n + 1$. However unapproachable these problems may seem to us and however helpless we stand before them, we have, nevertheless, the firm conviction that their solution must follow by a finite number of purely logical processes.

Is this axiom of the solvability of every problem a peculiarity characteristic of mathematical thought alone, or is it possibly a general law inherent in the nature of the mind, that all questions which it asks must be answerable? For in other sciences also one meets old problems which have been settled in a manner most satisfactory and most useful to science by the proof of their impossibility. I instance the problem of perpetual motion. After seeking in vain for the construction of a perpetual motion machine, the relations were investigated which must subsist between the forces of nature if such a machine is to be impossible; and this inverted question led to the discovery of the law of the conservation of energy, which, again, explained the impossibility of perpetual motion in the sense originally intended.

This conviction of the solvability of every mathematical problem is a powerful incentive to the worker. We hear within us the perpetual call: There is the problem. Seek its solution. You can find it by pure reason, for in mathematics there is no *ignorabimus*. ...

2. The Compatibility of the Arithmetical Axioms

When we are engaged in investigating the foundations of a science, we must set up a system of axioms which contains an exact and complete description of the relations subsisting between the elementary ideas of that science. The axioms so set up are at the same time the definitions of those elementary ideas; and no statement within the realm of the science whose foundation we are testing is held to be correct unless it can be derived from those axioms by means of a finite number of logical steps. Upon closer consideration the question arises: *Whether, in any way, certain statements of single axioms depend upon one another, and whether the axioms may not therefore contain certain parts in common, which must be isolated if one wishes to arrive at a system of axioms that shall be altogether independent of one another.*

But above all I wish to designate the following as the most important among the numerous questions which can be asked with regard to the axioms: *To prove that they are not contradictory, that is, that a finite number of logical steps based upon them can never lead to contradictory results.* ...

10. Determination of the Solvability of a Diophantine Equation

Given a diophantine equation with any number of unknown quantities and with rational integral numerical coefficients: *To devise a process according to which it can be determined by a finite number of operations whether the equation is solvable in rational integers.* ...

6 On Computable Numbers, with an Application to the Entscheidungsproblem (1936)

Alan Mathison Turing

"Entscheidungsproblem" is German for "decision problem," and with the definite article refers to the problem of determining whether an arbitrary mathematical proposition is provable. In 1928, the logical foundations of mathematics had been firmly enough established that David Hilbert and his student Wilhelm Ackermann could stipulate that the axiomatic system in question was the predicate calculus (referred to here as the "functional calculus K"). The hunt was on to find a procedure that would, in effect, answer all mathematical questions and complete Hilbert's program. Various researchers offered decision procedures for fragments of the predicate calculus, but there was at first no serious work toward an impossibility proof—in part because the notion of a "decision procedure" was merely intuitive. Imagining that no procedure might exist required that the class of all procedures be circumscribed.

In 1930 Kurt Gödel announced his groundbreaking negative result (Gödel, 1931), that in any system like that of *Principia Mathematica* (Whitehead and Russell, 1910) or the predicate calculus, some propositions were neither provable nor disprovable (unless the system itself is inconsistent, in which case everything is provable). To do this, Gödel exploited a version of the diagonalization argument that Cantor had used in 1891 to prove that the real numbers were not countable (not "enumerable," to follow Turing's usage). Gödel's other innovation was to encode a finite string of symbols (a formula of the predicate calculus, for example) as a positive integer, using a product of the first k primes for a string of length k and making the exponent of the kth prime a digit encoding the kth symbol of the string.

Gödel's result was stunning, but it did not settle the Entscheidungsproblem. (Though as Turing explains on page 60, had Gödel proved the opposite of what he did prove, he would have settled the Entscheidungsproblem in the positive.) In rapid succession, Alonzo Church and Turing formalized the notion of an "algorithm" in very different but equivalent ways, Church (1936b) first via the lambda-calculus, and Turing shortly after via what are now called Turing machines. Both are credited with showing the unsolvability of the Entscheidungsproblem.

Each author was faced with the dual tasks of proving his theorem, and of convincing his readers that his class of computational procedures was large enough to encompass all imaginable computational processes. Because of the abstruseness of the lambda-calculus, Church's paper was unpersuasive on the latter point—even though the lambda-calculus would later become the basis for functional programming (chapter 21).

Reprinted from Turing (1936), with permission from the London Mathematical Society.

Thus Turing's machines had to be simple enough to admit a proof of what they could not do, and yet demonstrably powerful enough to carry out anything that a reasonable person would call a computation. We include parts of both arguments, but we omit all the code. It turned out that the write-a-symbol-in-a-box-and-move-to-an-adjacent-box reductionism of Turing's machines had been anticipated by the mathematician Emil Post, who, however, did not take the further steps needed to carry out the proof. Post's work, which refers to Church (1936b) but was unpublished at the time, appears in Davis (1965, pp. 289–291).

It will be helpful to gloss Turing's language. His machines (he used the term "computer" only to refer to a human being carrying out a computation) are designed simply to start up on blank tape and go to work. They print 0s and 1s (what he calls "figures"), perhaps interspersed with other symbols. The possibly infinite series of figures is to be read with a decimal point at the beginning, and so represents a real number between 0 and 1. Some such real numbers are computable, and some are not (because the number of machines is countable but the number of reals in [0,1] is not). It is easy to see a computable number as a way of representing a computable set of nonnegative integers (calculating the ith bit of a real number in [0, 1] is equivalent to determining whether the integer i is or is not in the set corresponding to that real number), or a computable function from integers to integers using a different coding system, etc.

What Turing calls an m-configuration would today be called a state of the machine, and is generally denoted using a variant on the letter q. A "configuration," by contrast, consists of both the state and the scanned symbol, that is, everything that determines the next move, and a "complete configuration" includes also the full contents of the tape and the location of the scanning head—everything there is to say about the machine at a particular moment of its operation.

A "circular" machine is one that prints only finitely many figures, and a "circle-free" machine is one that prints an infinite series of figures.

Turing's "universal" machine is one that can simulate any other. To provide a machine as input to the universal machine, Turing needed an encoding of arbitrary machines over a fixed alphabet. He represented state q_i as DA^i and symbol S_j by DC^j. The concatenation of the quadruples thus encoded was a string Turing called the "standard description" (S.D), the first clear instantiation of a stored program: the general purpose memory could be used to store a program, so there was no essential difference between program and data. Replacing the few individual symbols in this universal code by decimal digits, Turing derived a numerical value for each machine, what he called its "description number" or D.N—a different technique for encoding strings as numbers than the one Gödel had devised. From the existence of the universal machine Turing is able to show by diagonalization that no machine can reliably distinguish circular from circle-free machines. In a couple of further steps, the unsolvability of the Entscheidungsproblem followed. (We omit most of the construction representing a machine computation in a logical formula—the details were flawed and later corrected [Turing, 1938].)

The life of Alan Mathison Turing (1912–1954) is well documented in the biography by Andrew Hodges (1983), on which the film *The Imitation Game* is based. Turing wrote this paper two years after receiving first class honours in mathemactics from Cambridge, and then studied for his PhD under Church at Princeton. His mathematical career was diverted in support of the codebreaking effort during World War II. Outed as a homosexual, he lost his security clearance and was arrested. Having accepted chemical castration as an alternative to imprisonment, he died of cyanide poisoning—apparently by suicide, though some have noted evidence that the death might have been accidental. Only 41 years old at the time of his death, he was "a giant of logic lost to the irrational," as science writer Chet Raymo (1996) put it. Queen Elizabeth posthumously pardoned Turing in 2014, wiping his indecency conviction from the record, and in 2019 the Bank of England announced that his image would appear on the 50 banknote.

———————— ∞◦◯◦∞ ————————

THE "computable" numbers may be described briefly as the real numbers whose expressions as a decimal are calculable by finite means. Although the subject of this paper is ostensibly the computable numbers, it is almost equally easy to define and investigate computable functions of an integral variable or a real or computable variable, computable predicates, and so forth. The fundamental problems involved are, however, the same in each case, and I have chosen the computable numbers for explicit treatment as involving the least cumbrous technique. I hope shortly to give an account of the relations of the computable numbers, functions, and so forth to one another. This will include a development of the theory of functions of a real variable expressed in terms of computable numbers. According to my definition, a number is computable if its decimal can be written down by a machine.

In §§6.9, 6.10 I give some arguments with the intention of showing that the computable numbers include all numbers which could naturally be regarded as computable. In particular, I show that certain large classes of numbers are computable. They include, for instance, the real parts of all algebraic numbers, the real parts of the zeros of the Bessel functions, the numbers π, e, etc. The computable numbers do not, however, include all definable numbers, and an example is given of a definable number which is not computable.

Although the class of computable numbers is so great, and in many ways similar to the class of real numbers, it is nevertheless enumerable. In §6.8 I examine certain arguments which would seem to prove the contrary. By the correct application of one of these arguments, conclusions are reached which are superficially similar to those of Gödel (1931). These results have valuable applications. In particular, it is shown (§6.11) that the Hilbertian Entscheidungsproblem can have no solution.

In a recent paper Alonzo Church (1936b) has introduced an idea of "effective calculability," which is equivalent to my "computability," but is very differently defined. Church also reaches similar conclusions about the Entscheidungsproblem (Church, 1936a). The proof of equivalence between "computability" and "effective calculability" is outlined in an appendix to the present paper. [EDITOR: Appendix omitted here.]

6.1   Computing Machines

We have said that the computable numbers are those whose decimals are calculable by finite means. This requires rather more explicit definition. No real attempt will be made to justify the definitions given until we reach §6.9. For the present I shall only say that the justification lies in the fact that the human memory is necessarily limited.

We may compare a man in the process of computing a real number to a machine which is only capable of a finite number of conditions $q_1, q_2, \ldots, q_R$ which will be called "*m*-configurations." The machine is supplied with a "tape" (the analogue of paper) running through it, and divided into sections (called "squares") each capable of bearing a "symbol." At any moment there is just one square, say the rth bearing the symbol $\mathfrak{S}(r)$ which is "in the machine." We may call this square the "scanned square." The symbol on the scanned square may be called the "scanned symbol." The "scanned symbol" is the only one of which the machine is, so to speak, "directly aware." However, by altering its *m*-configuration the machine can effectively remember some of the symbols which it has "seen" (scanned) previously. The possible behaviour of the machine at any moment is determined by the *m*-configuration q_n and the scanned symbol $\mathfrak{S}(r)$. This pair q_n, $\mathfrak{S}(r)$ will be called the "configuration": thus the configuration determines the possible behaviour of the machine. In some of the configurations in which the scanned square is blank (i.e. bears no symbol) the machine writes down a new symbol on the scanned square: in other configurations it erases the scanned symbol. The machine may also change the square which is being scanned, but only by shifting it one place to right or left. In addition to any of these operations the *m*-configuration may be changed. Some of the symbols written down will form the sequence of figures which is the decimal of the real number which is being computed. The others are just rough notes to "assist the memory." It will only be these rough notes which will be liable to erasure.

It is my contention that these operations include all those which are used in the computation of a number. The defence of this contention will be easier when the theory of the machines is familiar to the reader. In the next section I therefore proceed with the development of the theory and assume that it is understood what is meant by "machine," "tape," "scanned," etc.

6.2   Definitions

6.2.1   Automatic machines   If at each stage the motion of a machine (in the sense of §6.1) is completely determined by the configuration, we shall call the machine an "automatic machine" (or *a*-machine).

For some purposes we might use machines (choice machines or *c*-machines) whose motion is only partially determined by the configuration (hence the use of the word "possible" in §6.1). When such a machine reaches one of these ambiguous configurations, it cannot go on until some arbitrary choice has been made by an external operator. This would be the case if we were using machines to deal with axiomatic systems. In this paper I deal only with automatic machines, and will therefore often omit the prefix *a*-.

6.2.2   Computing machines   If an *a*-machine prints two kinds of symbols, of which the first kind (called figures) consists entirely of 0 and 1 (the others being called symbols of the second kind), then the machine will be called a computing machine. If the machine is supplied with a blank tape and set in motion, starting from the correct initial *m*-configuration, the subsequence of the symbols printed by it which are of the first kind will be called the *sequence computed by the machine*. The real number whose expression as a binary decimal is obtained by prefacing this sequence by a decimal point is called the *number computed by the machine*.

At any stage of the motion of the machine, the number of the scanned square, the complete sequence of all symbols on the tape, and the *m*-configuration will be said to describe the *complete configuration* at that stage. The changes of the machine and tape between successive complete configurations will be called the *moves* of the machine.

6.2.3   Circular and circle-free machines   If a computing machine never writes down more than a finite number of symbols of the first kind, it will be called *circular*. Otherwise it is said to be *circle-free*.

A machine will be circular if it reaches a configuration from which there is no possible move, or if it goes on moving, and possibly printing symbols of the second kind, but cannot print any more symbols of the first kind. The significance of the term "circular" will be explained in §6.8.

6.2.4   Computable sequences and numbers   A sequence is said to be computable if it can be computed by a circle-free machine. A number is computable if it differs by an integer from the number computed by a circle-free machine.

We shall avoid confusion by speaking more often of computable sequences than of computable numbers.

6.3   Examples of Computing Machines

... "R" means "the machine moves so that it scans the square immediately on the right of the one it was scanning previously. Similarly for "L." "E" means "the scanned symbol is erased" and "P" stands for "prints." ... [EDITOR: encoding and programming details omitted.]

6.4   Abbreviated tables ...

6.5   Enumeration of Computable Sequences

... Let us write down all expressions so formed from the table for the machine and separate them by semi-colons. In this way we obtain a complete description of the machine. In this description we shall replace q_i by the letter "D" followed by the letter "A" repeated *i* times, and S_j by "D" followed by "C" repeated *j* times. This new description of the machine may be called the standard description (S.D). It is made up entirely from the letters "A", "C", "D", "L", "R", "N", and from ";".

If finally we replace "A" by "1", "C" by "2", "D" by "3", "L" by "4", "R" by "5", "N" by "6", and ";" by "7", we shall have a description of the machine in the form of an arabic numeral. The integer represented by this numeral may be called a description number (D.N) of the machine.

The D.N determine the S.D and the structure of the machine uniquely. The machine whose D.N is n may be described as $M(n)$.

To each computable sequence there corresponds at least one description number, while to no description number does there correspond more than one computable sequence. The computable sequences and numbers are therefore enumerable. ...

A description number is 31332531173113353111731113322531111731111335317, and so is 31332531173113353111731113322531111731111335317317323253117.

A number which is a description number of a circle-free machine will be called a *satisfactory* number. In §6.8 it is shown that there can be no general process for determining whether a given number is satisfactory or not.

6.6   The Universal Computing Machine

It is possible to invent a single machine which can be used to compute any computable sequence. If this machine U is supplied with a tape on the beginning of which is written the S.D of some computing machine M, then U will compute the same sequence as M. ...

6.7   Detailed description of the Universal Machine ...

6.8   Application of the Diagonal Process

It may be thought that arguments which prove that the real numbers are not enumerable would also prove that the computable numbers and sequences cannot be enumerable (Hobson, 1921, pp. 87–88). It might, for instance, be thought that the limit of a sequence of computable numbers must be computable. This is clearly only true if the sequence of computable numbers is defined by some rule.

Or we might apply the diagonal process. "If the computable sequences are enumerable, let a_n be the nth computable sequence, and let $\phi_n(m)$ be the mth figure in a_n. Let β be the sequence with $1 - \phi_n(n)$ as its nth figure. Since β is computable, there exists a number K such that $1 - \phi_n(n) = \phi_K(n)$ all n. Putting $n = K$, we have $1 = 2\phi_K(K)$, i.e. 1 is even. This is impossible. The computable sequences are therefore not enumerable."

The fallacy in this argument lies in the assumption that β is computable. It would be true if we could enumerate the computable sequences by finite means, but the problem of enumerating computable sequences is equivalent to the problem of finding out whether a given number is the D.N of a circle-free machine, and we have no general process for doing this in a finite number of steps. In fact, by applying the diagonal process argument correctly, we can show that there cannot be any such general process.

The simplest and most direct proof of this is by showing that, if this general process exists, then there is a machine which computes β. This proof, although perfectly sound, has the disadvantage that it may leave the reader with a feeling that "there must be something wrong." The proof which I shall give has not this disadvantage, and gives a certain insight into the significance of the idea "circle-free." It depends not on constructing β, but on constructing β', whose n^{th} figure is $\phi_n(n)$.

Let us suppose that there is such a process; that is to say, that we can invent a machine $\mathcal{D}$ which, when supplied with the S.D of any computing machine $\mathcal{M}$ will test this S.D and if $\mathcal{M}$ is circular will mark the S.D with the symbol "u" and if it is circle-free will mark it with "s." By combining the machines $\mathcal{D}$ and $\mathcal{U}$ we could construct a machine $\mathcal{H}$ to compute the sequence β'. ...

The machine $\mathcal{H}$ has its motion divided into sections. In the first $N - 1$ sections, among other things, the integers 1, 2, ..., $N - 1$ have been written down and tested by the machine $\mathcal{D}$. A certain number, say $R(N - 1)$, of them have been found to be the D.N's of circle-free machines. In the Nth section the machine $\mathcal{D}$ tests the number N. If N is satisfactory, i.e., if it is the D.N of a circle-free machine, then $R(N) = 1 + R(N - 1)$ and the first $R(N)$ figures of the sequence of which a D.N is N are calculated. The $R(N)^{\text{th}}$ figure of this sequence is written down as one of the figures of the sequence β' computed by $\mathcal{H}$. If N is not satisfactory, then $R(N) = R(N - 1)$ and the machine goes on to the $(N + 1)^{\text{th}}$ section of its motion.

From the construction of $\mathcal{H}$ we can see that $\mathcal{H}$ is circle-free. Each section of the motion of $\mathcal{H}$ comes to an end after a finite number of steps. For, by our assumption about $\mathcal{D}$, the decision as to whether N is satisfactory is reached in a finite number of steps. If N is not satisfactory, then the Nth section is finished. If N is satisfactory, this means that the machine $\mathcal{M}(N)$ whose D.N is N is circle-free, and therefore its $R(N)^{\text{th}}$ figure can be calculated in a finite number of steps. When this figure has been calculated and written down as the $R(N)^{\text{th}}$ figure of β' the Nth section is finished. Hence $\mathcal{H}$ is circle-free.

Now let K be the D.N of $\mathcal{H}$. What does $\mathcal{H}$ do in the Kth section of its motion? It must test whether K is satisfactory, giving a verdict "s" or "u." Since K is the D.N of $\mathcal{H}$ and since $\mathcal{H}$ is circle-free, the verdict cannot be "u." On the other hand the verdict cannot be "s." For if it were, then in the Kth section of its motion $\mathcal{H}$ would be bound to compute the first $R(K - 1) + 1 = R(K)$ figures of the sequence computed by the machine with K as its D.N and to write down the $R(K)^{\text{th}}$ as a figure of the sequence computed by $\mathcal{H}$. The computation of the first $R(K) - 1$ figures would be carried out all right, but the instructions for calculating the $R(K)^{\text{th}}$ would amount to "calculate the first $R(K)$ figures computed by $\mathcal{H}$ and write down the $R(K)^{\text{th}}$." This $R(K)^{\text{th}}$ figure would never be found. I.e., $\mathcal{H}$ is circular, contrary both to what we have found in the last paragraph and to the verdict "s." Thus both verdicts are impossible and we conclude that there can be no machine $\mathcal{D}$.

We can show further that *there can be no machine $\mathcal{E}$ which, when supplied with the S.D of an arbitrary machine $\mathcal{M}$, will determine whether $\mathcal{M}$ ever prints a given symbol (0 say).* ...

6.9   The Extent of the Computable Numbers

No attempt has yet been made to show that the "computable" numbers include all numbers which would naturally be regarded as computable. All arguments which can be given are bound to be, fundamentally, appeals to intuition, and for this reason rather unsatisfactory mathematically. The real question at issue is "What are the possible processes which can be carried out in computing a number?"

The arguments which I shall use are of three kinds.

(a) A direct appeal to intuition.

(b) A proof of the equivalence of two definitions (in case the new definition has a greater intuitive appeal).

(c) Giving examples of large classes of numbers which are computable.

Once it is granted that computable numbers are all "computable," several other propositions of the same character follow. In particular, it follows that, if there is a general process for determining whether a formula of the Hilbert function calculus is provable, then the determination can be carried out by a machine.

I. [Type (a)]. This argument is only an elaboration of the ideas of §6.1.

Computing is normally done by writing certain symbols on paper. We may suppose this paper is divided into squares like a child's arithmetic book. In elementary arithmetic the two-dimensional character of the paper is sometimes used. But such a use is always avoidable, and I think that it will be agreed that the two-dimensional character of paper is no essential of computation. I assume then that the computation is carried out on one-dimensional paper, i.e. on a tape divided into squares. I shall also suppose that the number of symbols which may be printed is finite. If we were to allow an infinity of symbols, then there would be symbols differing to an arbitrarily small extent. The effect of this restriction of the number of symbols is not very serious. It is always possible to use sequences of symbols in the place of single symbols. Thus an Arabic numeral such as 17 or 999999999999999 is normally treated as a single symbol. Similarly in any European language words are treated as single symbols (Chinese, however, attempts to have an enumerable infinity of symbols). The differences from our point of view between the single and compound symbols is that the compound symbols, if they are too lengthy, cannot be observed at one glance. This is in accordance with experience. We cannot tell at a glance whether 9999999999999999 and 999999999999999 are the same.

The behaviour of the computer at any moment is determined by the symbols which he is observing, and his "state of mind" at that moment. [EDITOR: Here a "computer" is a person who is performing computations.] We may suppose that there is a bound B to the number of symbols or squares which the computer can observe at one moment. If he wishes to observe more, he must use successive observations. We will also suppose that the number of states of mind which need be taken into account is finite. The reasons for this are of the same character as those which restrict the number of symbols. If we admitted an infinity of states of mind, some of them will be "arbitrarily close" and will be confused. Again, the restriction is not one which seriously affects computation, since the use of more complicated states of mind can be avoided by writing more symbols on the tape.

Let us imagine the operations performed by the computer to be split up into "simple operations" which are so elementary that it is not easy to imagine them further divided. Every such operation consists of some change of the physical system consisting of the computer and his tape. We know the state of the system if we know the sequence of symbols on the tape, which of these are observed by the computer (possibly with a special order), and the state of mind of the computer.

We may suppose that in a simple operation not more than one symbol is altered. Any other changes can be split up into simple changes of this kind. The situation in regard to the squares whose symbols may be altered in this way is the same as in regard to the observed squares. We may, therefore, without loss of generality, assume that the squares whose symbols are changed are always "observed" squares.

Besides these changes of symbols, the simple operations must include changes of distribution of observed squares. The new observed squares must be immediately recognisable by the computer. I think it is reasonable to suppose that they can only be squares whose distance from the closest of the immediately previously observed squares does not exceed a certain fixed amount. Let us say that each of the new observed squares is within L squares of an immediately previously observed square.

In connection with "immediate recognisability," it may be thought that there are other kinds of square which are immediately recognisable. In particular, squares marked by special symbols might be taken as immediately recognisable. Now if these squares are marked only by single symbols there can be only a finite number of them, and we should not upset our theory by adjoining these marked squares to the observed squares. If, on the other hand, they are marked by a sequence of symbols, we cannot regard the process of recognition as a simple process. This is a fundamental point and should be illustrated. In most mathematical papers the equations and theorems are numbered. Normally the numbers do not go beyond (say) 1000. It is, therefore, possible to recognise a theorem at a glance by its number. But if the paper was very long, we might reach Theorem 157767733443477; then, further on in the paper, we might find "... hence (applying Theorem 157767733443477) we have ...." In order to make sure which was the relevant theorem we should have to compare the two numbers figure by figure, possibly ticking the figures off in pencil to make sure of their not being counted twice. If in spite of this it is still thought that there are other "immediately recognisable" squares, it does not upset my contention so long as these squares can be found by some process of which my type of machine is capable. ...

The simple operations must therefore include:

(a) Changes of the symbol on one of the observed squares.

(b) Changes of one of the squares observed to another square within L squares of one of the previously observed squares.

It may be that some of these changes necessarily involve a change of state of mind. The most general single operation must therefore be taken to be one of the following:

(A) A possible change (a) of symbol together with a possible change of state of mind.

(B) A possible change (b) of observed squares, together with a possible change of state of mind.

The operation actually performed is determined, as has been suggested ..., by the state of mind of the computer and the observed symbols. In particular, they determine the state of mind of the computer after the operation is carried out.

We may now construct a machine to do the work of this computer. To each state of mind of the computer corresponds an "*m*-configuration" of the machine. The machine scans *B* squares corresponding to the *B* squares observed by the computer. In any move the machine can change a symbol on a scanned square or can change any one of the scanned squares to another square distant not more than *L* squares from one of the other scanned squares. The move which is done, and the succeeding configuration, are determined by the scanned symbol and the *m*-configuration. The machines just described do not differ very essentially from computing machines as defined in §6.2, and corresponding to any machine of this type a computing machine can be constructed to compute the same sequence, that is to say the sequence computed by the computer. ...

6.10   Examples of Large Classes of Numbers Which are Computable ...

6.11   Application to the Entscheidungsproblem

The results of §6.8 have some important applications. In particular, they can be used to show that the Hilbert Entscheidungsproblem can have no solution. ...

I propose, therefore, to show that there can be no general process for determining whether a given formula $\mathfrak{A}$ of the functional calculus *K* is provable, i.e. that there can be no machine which, supplied with any one $\mathfrak{A}$ of these formulae, will eventually say whether $\mathfrak{A}$ is provable.

It should perhaps be remarked that what I shall prove is quite different from the well-known results of Gödel. Gödel has shown that (in the formalism of *Principia Mathematica*) there are propositions $\mathfrak{A}$ such that neither $\mathfrak{A}$ nor $-\mathfrak{A}$ is provable. As a consequence of this, it is shown that no proof of consistency of *Principia Mathematica* (or of *K*) can be given within that formalism. On the other hand, I shall show that there is no general method which tells whether a given formula $\mathfrak{A}$ is provable in *K*, or, what comes to the same, whether the system consisting of *K* with $-\mathfrak{A}$ adjoined as an extra axiom is consistent.

If the negation of what Gödel has shown had been proved, i.e. if, for each $\mathfrak{A}$, either $\mathfrak{A}$ or $-\mathfrak{A}$ is provable, then we should have an immediate solution of the Entscheidungsproblem. For we can invent a machine $\mathcal{K}$ which will prove consecutively all provable formulae. Sooner or later $\mathcal{K}$ will reach either $\mathfrak{A}$ or $-\mathfrak{A}$. If it reaches $\mathfrak{A}$, then we know that $\mathfrak{A}$ is provable. If it reaches $-\mathfrak{A}$, then, since *K* is consistent (Hilbert and Ackermann, p. 65), we know that $\mathfrak{A}$ is not provable.

Owing to the absence of integers in *K* the proofs appear somewhat lengthy. The underlying ideas are quite straightforward.

Corresponding to each computing machine $\mathcal{M}$ we construct a formula $\mathrm{Un}(\mathcal{M})$ and we show that, if there is a general method for determining whether $\mathrm{Un}(\mathcal{M})$ is provable, then there is a general method for determining whether $\mathcal{M}$ ever prints 0.

The interpretations of the propositional functions involved are as follows:

$R_S(x, y)$ is to be interpreted as "in the complete configuration x (of $\mathcal{M}$) the symbol on the square y is S." $I(x, y)$ is to be interpreted as "in the complete configuration x the square y is scanned." $K_{q_m}(x)$ is to be interpreted as "in the complete configuration x the *m*-configuration is q_m." $F(x, y)$ is to be interpreted as "y is the immediate successor of x." ...

7 A Proposed Automatic Calculating Machine (1937)

Howard Hathaway Aiken

Well into the twentieth century, books of the values of mathematical functions, ten-place logarithms for example, were on the desk of every practicing physical scientist and engineer. Slide rules were useful aids but of limited precision. Electromechanical desk calculators were important machines for the practice of both business and science, but the work of their human operators (mostly women known as "computers") was tedious in the extreme.

Howard Hathaway Aiken (1900–1973) was a physics professor at Harvard who attained the rank of Commander in the U.S. Naval Reserve. He became a graduate student at Harvard at the age of 33 after working as an engineer for Westinghouse and other companies in the electric industries. In the course of grinding out approximate solutions to equations he needed for his thesis, Aiken tired of doing calculations with the available mechanical calculators and numerical tables. Babbage's gears and wheels came to his attention and served as an inspiration, though only after he had begun to design his own automatic calculator (Cohen, 1999, p. 67). He seems to have been unaware of the details of Babbage's design and of Lady Lovelace's explanation of how it would be programmed, and there is no evidence that he knew anything of Alan Turing's groundbreaking mathematical work of 1936 or the cryptologic machinery Turing designed during World War II.

This selection is the proposal Aiken submitted for industrial support in constructing the largest electromechanical machine that had ever been built. The Automatic Sequence Controlled Calculator, later dubbed the Mark I, was developed with the assistance of IBM and put into service in 1944. Part of it remains on display at Harvard. Originally some 50 feet long, 8 feet high, and 3 feet deep, weighing nearly 5 tons, it was a marvel of 530 miles of wire, thousands of electromagnetic relays for switches, decimal dials to hold numerical constants, and decimal counters for intermediate storage. Input was punched on card stock; output was printed on an electric typewriter. For decades I walked past this machine almost daily. To pause and examine it is to puzzle over a set of evolutionary dead ends, from the number system to the wiring. The parts are connected by sturdy bell wire, with insulation in unfaded yellow, blue, and red. But rather than bundling different colors together as in modern ribbon cables, so the ends of the same wire could be matched up easily, all the yellow wires in the Mark I are bundled together, as are all the blue and all the red. The bundles are massive, several inches thick, and it is hard today to imagine what purpose the color variation was supposed to serve.

Reprinted from Aiken et al. (1964), with permission from the Harvard University Archives.

Most importantly, the Mark I's program was punched into a loop of tape made from the paper stock used for IBM cards. So the machine was designed for repetitive operations, such as summing the terms of a series, but was incapable of executing a recursive algorithm, nested loop, or even, as originally built, a conditional branch. Even in Aiken's later machines (the Mark IV was the last), there was no concept of a stored program. So while the Mark I was certainly programmable—in the sense that some researchers could prepare new programs while others were using the machine to do useful work—it enjoyed nothing of what we know as software. Aiken's commitment to what came to be known as the "Harvard architecture"—data and programs in separate kinds of storage—left Aiken's machines in an intellectual sidetrack. The action moved to other universities and to corporations, and Aiken retired from Harvard at the age of 60.

The Mark I was noisy and clunky, but it worked. Addition or subtraction of 23 decimal digits took 0.3 sec.; multiplication, up to 6 sec.; division, up to 15.6 sec.; $\log x$, e^x, or $\sin x$, a minute or more. These speeds were sufficient for the numerical solution of a dozen simultaneous linear equations, an application for which Harvard economist Wassily Leontief used the machine while developing his input–output theory. And Aiken got the last laugh. Most working computers today are in embedded systems, their programs frozen in firmware that cannot accidentally be altered as the machine is running, just like the Mark I's tape loop.

━━━━━━━━━━━━◦◦◦◦◦━━━━━━━━━━━━

T HE desire to economize time and mental effort in arithmetical computations, and to eliminate human liability to error, is probably as old as the science of arithmetic itself. This desire has led to the design and construction of a variety of aids to calculation, beginning with groups of small objects, such as pebbles, first used loosely, later as counters on ruled boards, and later still as beads mounted on wires fixed in a frame, as in the abacus. This instrument was probably invented by the Semitic races and later adopted in India, whence it spread westward throughout Europe and eastward to China and Japan.

After the development of the abacus, no further advances were made until John Napier devised his numbering rods, or Napier's Bones, in 1617. Various forms of the Bones appeared, some approaching the beginning of mechanical computation, but it was not until 1642 that Blaise Pascal gave us the first mechanical calculating machine in the sense that the term is used today. The application of his machine was restricted to addition and subtraction, but in 1666 Samuel Morland adapted it to multiplication by repeated additions. [EDITOR: Described in Morland (1673)]

The next advance was made by Leibniz who conceived a multiplying machine in 1671 and finished its construction in 1694. [EDITOR: In fact, it was working by 1674 and still works today.] In the process of designing this machine Leibniz invented two important devices which still occur as components of modern calculating machines today: the stepped reckoner, and the pin wheel.

Meanwhile, following the invention of logarithms by Napier, the slide rule was being developed by Oughtred, John Brown, Coggeshall, Everard, and others. Owing to its low cost and ease of construction, the slide rule received wide recognition from scientific men as early as 1700. Further development has continued up to the present time, with ever increasing application to the solution of scientific problems requiring an accuracy of not more than three or four significant figures, and when the total bulk of the computation is not too great. Particularly in engineering design has the slide rule proved to be an invaluable instrument.

Though the slide rule was widely accepted, at no time, however, did it act as a deterrent to the development of the more precise methods of mechanical computation. Thus we find the names of some of the greatest mathematicians and physicists of all time associated with the development of calculating machinery. Naturally enough, in an effort to devise means of scientific advancement, these men considered mechanical calculation largely from their own point of view. A notable exception was Pascal who invented his calculating machine for the purpose of assisting his father in computations with sums of money. Despite this widespread scientific interest, the development of modern calculating machinery proceeded slowly until the growth of commercial enterprises and the increasing complexity of accounting made mechanical computation an economic necessity. Thus the ideas of the physicists and mathematicians, who foresaw the possibilities and gave the fundamentals, have been turned to excellent purposes, but differing greatly from those for which they were originally intended.

Few calculating machines have been designed strictly for application to scientific investigations, the notable exceptions being those of Charles Babbage and others who followed him. In 1812 Babbage conceived the idea of a calculating machine of a higher type than those previously constructed, to be used for calculating and printing tables of mathematical functions. This machine worked by the method of differences, and was known as a difference engine. Babbage's first model was made in 1822, and in 1823 the construction of the machine was begun with the aid of a grant from the British Government. The construction was continued until 1833 when state aid was withdrawn after an expenditure of nearly 20 000. At present the machine is in the collection of the Science Museum, South Kensington. ...

Since the time of Babbage, the development of calculating machinery has continued at an increasing rate. Key-driven calculators designed for single arithmetical operations such as addition, subtraction, multiplication, and division, have been brought to a high degree of perfection. In large commercial enterprises, however, the volume of accounting work is so great that these machines are no longer adequate in scope.

Hollerith, therefore, returned to the punched card first employed in calculating machinery by Babbage and with it laid the groundwork for the development of tabulating, counting, sorting, and arithmetical machinery such as is now widely utilized in industry. The development of electrical apparatus and technique found application in these machines as manufactured by the International Business Machines Company, until today many of the things Babbage wished to accomplish are being done daily in the accounting offices of industrial enterprises all over the world.

As previously stated, these machines are all designed with a view to special applications to accounting. In every case they are concerned with the four fundamental operations of arithmetic, and not with operations of algebraic character. Their existence, however, makes possible the construction of an automatic calculating machine specially designed for the purposes of the mathematical sciences.

7.1   The Need for More Powerful Calculating Methods in the Mathematical and Physical Sciences

It has already been indicated that the need for mechanical assistance in computation has been felt from the beginning of science, but at present this need is greater than ever before. The intensive development of the mathematical and physical sciences in recent years has included the definition of many new and useful functions, nearly all of which are defined by infinite series or other infinite processes. Most of these are inadequately tabulated and their application to scientific problems is thereby retarded.

The increased accuracy of physical measurement has made necessary more accurate computation in physical theory, and experience has shown that small differences between computed theoretical and experimental results may lead to the discovery of a new physical effect, sometimes of the greatest scientific and industrial importance.

Many of the most recent scientific developments, including such devices as the thermionic vacuum tube, are based on nonlinear effects. Only too often the differential equations designed to represent these physical effects correspond to no previously studied forms, and thus defy all methods available for their integration. The only methods of solution available in such cases are expansions in infinite series and numerical integration. Both these methods involve enormous amounts of computational labor.

The present development of theoretical physics through wave mechanics is based entirely on mathematical concepts and clearly indicates that the future of the physical sciences rests in mathematical reasoning directed by experiment. At present there exist problems beyond our ability to solve, not because of theoretical difficulties, but because of insufficient means of mechanical computation.

In some fields of investigation in the physical sciences as, for instance, in the study of the ionosphere, the mathematical expressions required to represent the phenomena are too long and complicated to write in several lines across a printed page, yet the numerical investigation of such expressions is an absolute necessity to our study of the physics of the upper atmosphere, and on this type of research rests the future of radio communication and television.

These are but a few examples of the computational difficulties with which the physical and mathematical sciences are faced, and to these may be added many others taken from astronomy, the theory of relativity, and even the rapidly growing science of mathematical economy. All these computational difficulties can be removed by the design of suitable automatic calculating machinery.

7.2   Points of Difference between Punched Card Accounting Machinery and Calculating Machinery as Required in the Sciences

The features to be incorporated in calculating machinery specially designed for rapid work on scientific problems, and not to be found in calculating machines as manufactured for accounting purposes, are the following:

1. Ordinary accounting machines are concerned almost entirely with problems of positive numbers, while machines designed for mathematical purposes must be able to handle both positive and negative quantities.

2. For mathematical purposes, calculating machinery should be able to supply and utilize a wide variety of transcendental functions, as the trigonometric functions; elliptic, Bessel, and probability functions; and many others. Fortunately, not all these functions occur in a single computation; therefore a means of changing from one function to another may be designed and the proper flexibility provided.

3. Most of the computations of mathematics, as the calculation of a function by series, the evaluation of a formula, the solution of a differential equation by numerical integration, etc., consist of repetitive processes. Once a process is established it may continue indefinitely until the range of the independent variables is covered, and usually the range of the independent variables may be covered by successive equal steps. For this reason calculating machinery designed for application to the mathematical sciences should be fully automatic in its operation once a process is established.

4. Existing calculating machinery is capable of calculating $\phi(x)$ as a function of x by steps. Thus, if x is defined in the interval $a < x < b$ and $\phi(x)$ is obtained from x by a series of arithmetical operations, the existing procedure is to compute step (1) for all values of x in the interval $a < x < b$. Then step (2) is accomplished for all values of the result of step (1), and so on until $\phi(x)$ is reached. This process, however, is the reverse of that required in many mathematical operations. Calculating machinery designed for application to the mathematical sciences should be capable of computing lines instead of columns, for very often, as in the numerical solution of a differential equation, the computation of the second value in the computed table of a function depends on the preceding value or values.

Fundamentally, these four features are all that are required to convert existing punched-card calculating machines such as those manufactured by the International Business Machines Company into machines specially adapted to scientific purposes. Because of the greater complexity of scientific problems as compared to accounting problems, the number of arithmetical elements involved would have to be greatly increased.

7.3   Mathematical Operations Which Should Be Included

The mathematical operations which should be included in an automatic calculating machine are:

1. The fundamental operations of arithmetic: addition, subtraction, multiplication, and division

2. Positive and negative numbers
3. Parentheses and brackets: $(\ ) + (\ )$, $[(\ ) + (\ )] \cdot [(\ ) + (\ )]$, etc.
4. Powers of numbers: integral, fractional
5. Logarithms: base 10 and all other bases by multiplication
6. Antilogarithms or exponential functions: base 10 and other bases
7. Trigonometric functions
8. Antitrigonometric functions
9. Hyperbolic functions
10. Antihyperbolic functions
11. Superior transcendentals: probability integral, elliptic function, and Bessel function
    With the aid of these functions, the processes to be carried out should be:
12. Evaluation of formulae and tabulation of results
13. Computation of series
14. Solution of ordinary differential equations of the first and second order
15. Numerical integration of empirical data
16. Numerical differentiation of empirical data

7.4   The Mathematical Means of Accomplishing the Operations

The following mathematical processes may be made the basis of design of an automatic calculating machine:

1. The fundamental arithmetical operations require no comment, as they are already available, save that all the other operations must eventually be reduced to these in order that a mechanical device may be utilized.

2. Fortunately the algebra of positive and negative signs is extremely simple. In any case only two possibilities are offered. Later on it will be shown that these signs may be treated as numbers for the purposes of mechanical calculation.

3. The use of parentheses and brackets in writing a formula requires that the computation must proceed piecewise. Thus, a portion of the result is obtained and must be held pending the determination of some other portion, and so on. This means that a calculating machine must be equipped with means of temporarily storing numbers until they are required for further use. Such means are available in counters.

4. Integral powers of numbers may be obtained by successive multiplication, and fractional powers by the method of iteration. Thus, if it is required to find $5^{1/3}$,

$$y = f(x) = x^3 - 5$$

and

$$x_n = x_{n-1} - \frac{f(x_{n-1})}{f'(x_{n-1})}$$

$$x_n = x_{n-1} - \frac{x_{n-1}^3 - 5}{3x_{n-1}^2}$$

or

$$x_n = \frac{2}{3}x_{n-1} + \frac{5}{3x_{n-1}^2}.$$

Let

$$x_0 = 2$$
$$x_1 = \frac{4}{3} + \frac{5}{12} = \frac{21}{12}$$
$$x_2 = \frac{42}{36} + \frac{5 \times 144}{3 \times 441} = 1.166 + 0.544$$
$$= 1.710 \tag{7.1}$$

which is the cube root of 5 to four significant figures. In general the rth root of θ is given by the iteration of the expression

$$x_n = \left(1 - \frac{1}{r}\right)x_{n-1} + \frac{\theta}{rx_{n-1}^{r-1}}.$$

Finally, if r is not an integer, recourse may be had to the mechanical table of logarithms later to be described. ...

16. The numerical integration of empirical data may be carried out by the rules of Simpson, Weddle, Gauss, and others. All these rules involve sums of successive values of y multiplied by specified numerical coefficients. Hence the only new mechanical component involved is a means of mechanically introducing a list of numbers. Means of accomplishing this will be discussed later.

17. Numerical differentiation of empirical data is best accomplished by means of a difference formula. Most experimental observations are of such an accuracy that fifth differences may be neglected by taking observations sufficiently close together. If, then, all differences above the fifth may be neglected, the process of numerical differentiation may be carried out by a fifth difference engine such as originally designed by Babbage. Such a device can, however, be assembled from standard addition-subtraction machines with but a few changes. The differentiating apparatus would also be applicable to many other problems. In fact, most of the problems already discussed may under certain circumstances be solved by application of difference formulae.

7.5   Mechanical Considerations

In the last section it was shown that even complicated mathematical operations may be reduced to a repetitive process involving the fundamental rules of arithmetic. At present the calculating machines of the International Business Machines Company are capable of carrying out such operations as:

$$A + B = F$$
$$A - B = F$$
$$AB + C = F$$
$$AB + C + D = F \tag{7.2}$$
$$A + B + C = F$$
$$A - B - C = F$$
$$A + B - C = F$$

In these equations A, B, C, D are tabulations of numbers on punched cards, and F, the result, is also obtained through punched cards. The F cards may then be put through another machine and printed or utilized as A, B, $\ldots$, cards in another computation.

Changing a given machine from any of the operations (7.2) to any other is accomplished by means of electrical wiring on a plug board. In the hands of a skilled operator such changes can be made in a few minutes.

No further effort will be made here to describe the mechanism of the IBM machines. Suffice it to say that all the operations described in the last section can be accomplished by these existing machines when equipped with suitable controls, and assembled in sufficient number. The whole problem of design of an automatic calculating machine suitable for mathematical operations is thus reduced to a problem of suitable control design, and even this problem has been solved for simple arithmetical operations.

The main features of the specialized controls are machine switching and replacement of the punched cards by continuous perforated tapes. In order that the switching sequence can be changed quickly to any possible sequence, the switching mechanism should itself utilize a paper tape control in which mathematical formulae may be represented by suitable disposed perforations.

7.6   Present Conceptions of the Apparatus

At present the automatic calculator is visualized as a switchboard on which are mounted various pieces of calculating machine apparatus. Each panel of the switchboard is given over to definite mathematical operations.

The following is a rough outline of the apparatus required:

1. IBM machines utilize two electric potentials: 120 volts ac for motor operation, and 32 volts
   dc for relay operation, etc. A main power supply panel would have to be provided including control for a 110-volt-ac/32-volt-dc motor generator and adequate fuse protection for all
   circuits.

2. Master control panel: The purpose of this control is to route the flow of numbers through
   the machines and to start operation. The processes involved are: (a) Deliver the number in
   position (x) to position (y); and (b) start the operation for which position (y) is intended.
   The master control must itself be subject to interlocking to prevent the attempt to remove a
   number before its value is determined, or to begin a second operation in position (y) before
   a previous operation is finished.

   It would be desirable to have four such master controls, each capable of controlling the entire machine or any of its parts. Thus, for complicated problems the entire resources could
   be thrown together; for simpler problems fewer resources are required and several problems
   could be in progress at the same time.

3. The progress of the independent variable in any calculation would go forward by equal steps
   subject to manual readjustment for change in the increment. The easiest way to obtain such
   an arithmetical sequence is to supply a first value, x_0, to an adding machine, together with
   an increment Δx. Then successive additions of Δx will give the sequence desired.

   There should be four such independent variable devices in order to (a) calculate formulae
   involving four variables; and (b) operate four master controls independently.

4. Certain constants: many mathematical formulae involve certain constants such as e, π,
   $\log_{10} e$, and so forth. These constants should be permanently installed and available at all
   times.

5. Mathematical formulae nearly always involve constant quantities. In the computation of
   a formula as a function of an independent variable these constants are used over and over
   again. Hence the machine should be supplied with 24 adjustable number positions for these
   constants.

6. In the evaluation of infinite series the number 24 might be greatly exceeded. To take care of
   this case it should be possible to introduce specific values by means of a perforated tape, the
   successive values being supplied by moving the tape ahead one position. Two such devices
   should be supplied.

7. The introduction of empirical data for nonrepetitive operations can be accomplished best by
   standard punched-card magazine feed. One such device should be supplied.

8. At various stages of a computation involving parentheses and brackets it may be necessary to
   hold a part of the result pending the computation of some other part. If results are held in the
   calculating units, these elements are not available for carrying out succeeding steps. Therefore it is necessary that numbers may be removed from the calculating units and temporarily
   stored in storage positions. Twelve such positions should be available.

9. The fundamental operations of arithmetic may be carried on three machines: addition and subtraction, multiplication, and division. Four units of each should be supplied in addition to those directly associated with the transcendental functions.

10. The permanently installed mathematical functions should include: logarithms, antilogarithms, sines, cosines, inverse sines, and inverse tangents.

11. Two units for MacLauren series expansion of other functions as needed.

12. In order to carry out the process of differentiation and integration on empirical data, adding and subtracting accumulators should be provided sufficient to compute out to fifth differences.

13. All results should be printed, punched in paper tapes, or in cards, at will. Final results would be printed. Intermediate results would be punched in preparation for further calculations.

It is believed that the apparatus just enumerated, controlled by automatic switching, should care for most of the problems encountered.

	Products Per Hour
2×8	1500
3×8	1285
4×8	1125
5×8	1000
6×8	900
7×8	818
8×8	750

Figure 7.1: Expected multiplication speed

7.7   Probable Speed of Computation

An idea of the speed attained by the IBM machines can be had from the following tabulation of multiplication in which 2×8 refers to the multiplication of an 8 significant figure number by a 2 significant figure number, zeros not counted (Figure 7.1).

In the computation of 10 place logarithms the average speed would be about 90 per hour. If all the 10-place logarithms of the natural numbers from 1000 to 100,000 were required, the time of computation would be approximately 1100 hours, or 50 days, allowing no time for addition or printing. This is justified since these operations are extremely rapid and can be carried out during the multiplying time.

7.8   Suggested Accuracy

Ten significant figures have been used in the above examples. If all numbers were to be given to this accuracy it would be necessary to provide 23 number positions on most of the computing components, 10 to the left of the decimal point, 12 to the right, and one for plus and minus. Of the twelve to the right, two would be guard places and thrown away.

7.9   Ease of Publication of Results

As already mentioned, all computed results would be printed in tabular form. By means of photolithography these results could be printed directly without type setting or proof reading. Not only does this indicate a great saving in the publishing of mathematical functions, but it also eliminates many possibilities of error.

8 A Symbolic Analysis of Relay and Switching Circuits (1938)

Claude Shannon

Electric wires connected by switches either conduct electricity or don't, depending on the interconnection pattern and the settings of the switches. As early as 1886, the philosopher Charles Sanders Peirce had recognized the relation of logical connectives to series and parallel electric circuits. But it was Claude Shannon (1916–2001) who exploited the electric interpretation of Boole's laws of thought. Shannon had tinkered with electric circuits while growing up in rural northern Michigan and had built a barbed wire telegraph to a friend's house. By the 1930s the radio and telephone industries were flourishing, and Shannon studied electrical engineering at the University of Michigan. He encountered Boole's writings in a philosophy class, and as an MIT graduate student he made the connection between the two binary-valued systems—thus giving birth to a profoundly elegant methodology for managing complex circuit design problems.

Today we take it for granted that the intended behavior of a circuit can be described mathematically, and that the resulting formulas can be manipulated using mathematical rules and then "compiled" into hardware. Shannon, in his Master's thesis, was the first to do it. This selection is an excerpt from a paper that became part of that thesis; it has had immense impact on circuit design ever since. It deals with the analysis and synthesis of electrical circuits, some far more complicated than the simple ones in our brief selection. In a passage we do not include, Shannon's paper goes on to prove upper and lower bounds on the size of circuits for certain boolean functions under particular restrictions about the form of those circuits, thus foreshadowing the rich and important field of circuit complexity.

8.1 Introduction

IN the control and protective circuits of complex electrical systems it is frequently necessary to make intricate interconnections of relay contacts and switches. Examples of these circuits occur in automatic telephone exchanges, industrial motor-control equipment, and in almost any circuits designed to perform complex operations automatically. In this paper a mathematical analysis of certain of the properties of such networks will be made. Particular attention will be given to the problem of network synthesis. Given certain characteristics, it is required to find a circuit incorporating these characteristics. The solution of this type of problem is not unique

Reprinted from Shannon (1938), with permission from the Massachusetts Institute of Technology.

and methods of finding those particular circuits requiring the least number of relay contacts and switch blades will be studied. Methods will also be described for finding any number of circuits equivalent to a given circuit in all operating characteristics. It will be shown that several of the well-known theorems on impedance networks have roughly analogous theorems in relay circuits. Notable among these are the delta-wye and star-mesh transformations, and the duality theorem.

The method of attack on these problems may be described briefly as follows: any circuit is represented by a set of equations, the terms of the equations corresponding to the various relays and switches in the circuit. A calculus is developed for manipulating these equations by simple mathematical processes, most of which are similar to ordinary algebraic algorithms. This calculus is shown to be exactly analogous to the calculus of propositions used in the symbolic study of logic. For the synthesis problem the desired characteristics are first written as a system of equations, and the equations are then manipulated into the form representing the simplest circuit. The circuit may then be immediately drawn from the equations. By this method it is always possible to find the simplest circuit containing only series and parallel connections, and in some cases the simplest circuit containing any type of connection.

Our notation is taken chiefly from symbolic logic. Of the many systems in common use we have chosen the one which seems simplest and most suggestive for our interpretation. Some or our phraseology, such as node, mesh, delta, wye, etc., is borrowed from ordinary network theory for simple concepts in switching circuits.

8.2   Series-Parallel Two-Terminal Circuits: Definitions and Postulates

We shall limit our treatment of circuits containing only relay contacts and switches, and therefore at any given time the circuit between any two terminals must be either open (infinite impedance) or closed (zero impedance). Let us associate a symbol X_{ab} or more simply X, with the terminals a and b. This variable, a function of time, will be called the hindrance of the two-terminal circuit $a - b$. The symbol 0 (zero) will be used to represent the hindrance of a closed circuit, and the symbol 1 (unity) to represent the hindrance of an open circuit. Thus when the circuit $a - b$ is open $X_{ab} = 1$ and when closed $X_{ab} = 0$. Two hindrances X_{ab} and X_{cd} will be said to be equal if whenever the circuit $a - b$ is open, the circuit $c - d$ is open, and whenever $a - b$ is closed, $c - d$ is closed. Now let the symbol + (plus) be defined to mean the series connection of the two-terminal circuits whose hindrances are added together. Thus $X_{ab} + X_{cd}$ is the hindrance of the circuit $a - d$ when b and c are connected together. Similarly the product of two hindrances $X_{ab} \cdot X_{cd}$, or more briefly $X_{ab}X_{cd}$ will be defined to mean the hindrance of the circuit formed by connecting the circuits $a - b$ and $c - d$ in parallel. A relay contact or switch will be represented in a circuit by the symbol in Figure 8.1, the letter being the corresponding hindrance function. Figure 8.2 shows the interpretation of the plus sign and Figure 8.3 the multiplication sign. This choice of symbols makes the manipulation of hindrances very similar to ordinary numerical algebra.

It is evident that with the above definitions, the following postulates will hold:

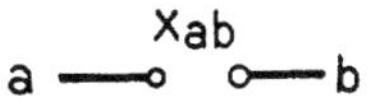

Figure 8.1: Symbol for hindrance function

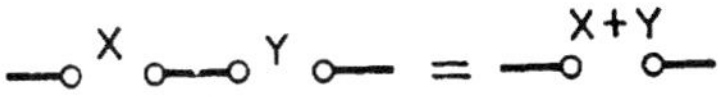

Figure 8.2: Interpretation of addition

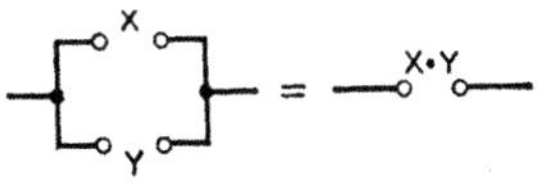

Figure 8.3: Interpretation of multiplication

Postulates

1.	*a.*	$0 \cdot 0 = 0$	A closed circuit in parallel with a closed circuit is a closed circuit.
	b.	$1 + 1 = 1$	An open circuit in series with an open circuit is an open circuit.
2.	*a.*	$1+0 = 0+1 = 1$	An open circuit in series with a closed circuit in either order (i.e., whether the open circuit is to the right or left of the closed circuit) is an open circuit.
	b.	$0 \cdot 1 = 1 \cdot 0 = 0$	A closed circuit in parallel with an open circuit in either order is a closed circuit.
3.	*a.*	$0 + 0 = 0$	A closed circuit in series with a closed circuit is a closed circuit.
	b.	$1 \cdot 1 = 1$	An open circuit in parallel with an open circuit is an open circuit.
4.			At any given time either $X = 0$ or $X = 1$.

These are sufficient to develop all the theorems which will be used in connection with circuits containing only series and parallel connections. The postulates are arranged in pairs to emphasize a duality relationship between the operations of addition and multiplication and the quantities zero and one. Thus if in any of the *a* postulates the zero's are replaced by one's and the multiplications by additions and vice versa, the corresponding *b* postulate will result. This fact is of great importance. It gives each theorem a dual theorem, it being necessary to prove only one to establish both. The only one of these postulates which differs from ordinary algebra is 1*b*. However, this enables great simplifications in the manipulation of these symbols.

8.2.1   Theorems   In this section a number of theorems governing the combination of hindrances will be given. Inasmuch as any of the theorems may be proved by a very simple process, the proofs will not be given except for an illustrative example. The method of proof is that of "perfect induction," i.e., the verification of the theorem for all possible cases. Since by Postulate 4 each variable is limited to the values 0 and 1, this is a simple matter. Some of the theorems may be proved more elegantly by recourse to previous theorems, but the method of perfect induction is so universal that it is probably to be preferred.

$$X + Y = Y + X, \tag{8.1a}$$

$$XY = YX, \tag{8.1b}$$

$$X + (Y + Z) = (X + Y) + Z, \tag{8.2a}$$

$$X(YZ) = (XY)Z, \tag{8.2b}$$

$$X(Y + Z) = XY + XZ, \tag{8.3a}$$

$$X + YZ = (X + Y)(X + Z), \tag{8.3b}$$

$$1 \cdot X = X, \tag{8.4a}$$

$$0 + X = X, \tag{8.4b}$$

$$1 + X = 1, \tag{8.5a}$$

$$0 \cdot X = 0. \tag{8.5b}$$

For example, to prove Theorem 8.4a, note that X is either 0 or 1. If it is 0, the theorem follows from Postulate 2b: if 1, it follows from Postulate 3b. Theorem 8.4b now follows by the duality principle, replacing the 1 by 0 and the $\cdot$ by +.

Due to the associative laws (8.2a and 8.2b) parentheses may be omitted in a sum or product of several terms without ambiguity. The Σ and Π symbols will be used as in ordinary algebra.

The distributive law (8.3a) makes it possible to "multiply out" products and to factor sums. The dual of this theorem, (8.3b), however, is not true in numerical algebra.

We shall now define a new operation to be called negation. The negative of a hindrance X will be written X' and is defined to be a variable which is equal to 1 when X equals 0 and equal to 0 when X equals 1. If X is the hindrance of the make contacts of a relay, then X' is the hindrance of the break contacts of the same relay. The definition of the negative of a hindrance gives the following theorems:

$$X + X' = 1, \tag{8.6a}$$

$$XX' = 0, \tag{8.6b}$$

$$0' = 1, \tag{8.7a}$$

$$1' = 0, \tag{8.7b}$$

$$(X')' = X. \tag{8.8}$$

8.2.2   Analogue with the calculus of propositions   We are now in a position to demonstrate the equivalence of this calculus with certain elementary parts of the calculus of propositions. The algebra of logic, originated by George Boole, is a symbolic method of investigating logical relationships. The symbols of boolean algebra admit of two logical interpretations. If interpreted in terms of classes, the variables are not limited to the two possible values 0 and 1. This interpretation is known as the algebra of classes. If, however, the terms are taken to represent propositions, we have the calculus of propositions in which variables are limited to the values 0 and 1, as are the hindrance functions above. Usually the two subjects are developed simultaneously from the same set of postulates, except for the addition in the case of the calculus of propositions of a postulate equivalent to Postulate 4 above. E. V. Huntington gives the following set of postulates for symbolic logic:

1. The class K contains at least two distinct elements.
2. If a and b are in the class K then $a + b$ is in the class K.
3. $a + b = b + a$.
4. $(a + b) + c = a + (b + c)$.
5. $a + a = a$.
6. $ab + ab' = a$ where ab is defined as $(a' + b')'$.

If we let the class K be the class consisting of the two elements 0 and 1, then these postulates follow from those given in the first section. Also Postulates 1, 2, and 3 given there can be deduced from Huntington's postulates. Adding 4 and restricting our discussion to the calculus of propositions, it is evident that a perfect analogy exists between the calculus for switching circuits and this branch of symbolic logic. The two interpretations of the symbols are shown in Figure 8.4.

Symbol	Interpretation in Relay Circuits	Interpretation in the Calculus of Propositions
X	The circuit X	The proposition X
0	The circuit is closed	The proposition is false
1	The circuit is open	The proposition is true
$X + Y$	The series connection of circuits X and Y	The proposition which is true if either X or Y is true
XY	The parallel connection of circuits X and Y	The proposition which is true if both X and Y are true
X'	The circuit which is open when X is closed and closed when X is open	The contradictory of proposition X
=	The circuits open and close simultaneously	Each proposition implies the other

Figure 8.4: Analogue between the calculus of propositions and the symbolic relay analysis

Due to this analogy any theorem of the calculus of propositions is also a true theorem if interpreted in terms of relay circuits. The remaining theorems in this section are taken directly from this field.

De Morgan's theorem:

$$(X + Y + Z + \dots)' = X' \cdot Y' \cdot Z' \cdot \dots \tag{8.9a}$$

$$(X \cdot Y \cdot Z \cdot \dots)' = X' + Y' + Z' + \dots . \tag{8.9b}$$

This theorem gives the negative of a sum or product in terms of the negatives of the summands or factors. It may be easily verified for two terms by substituting all possible values and then extended to any number n of variables by mathematical induction.

A function of certain variables X_1, X_2, ..., X_n is any expression formed from the variables with the operations of addition, multiplication, and negation. The notation $f(X_1, X_2, \dots, X_n)$ will be used to represent a function. Thus we might have $f(X, Y, Z) = XY + X'(Y' + Z')$. In infinitesimal calculus it is shown that any function (providing it is continuous and all derivatives are continuous) may be expanded in a Taylor series. A somewhat similar expansion is possible in the calculus of propositions. To develop the series expansion of functions first note the following equations: [EDITOR: Cf. Boole, page 44]

$$f(X_1, X_2, \dots, X_n) = X_1 \cdot f(1, X_2, \dots, X_n) + X_1' \cdot f(0, X_2, \dots, X_n) \tag{8.10a}$$

$$f(X_1, X_2, \dots, X_n) = [f(0, X_2, \dots, X_n) + X_1] \cdot [f(1, X2, \dots, X_n) + X_1']. \tag{8.10b}$$

These reduce to identities if we let X_1 equal either 0 or 1. In these equations the function f is said to be expanded about X_1. The coefficients of X_1 and X_1' in (8.10a) are functions of the $(n-1)$ variables $X_2, \dots, X_n$ and may thus be expanded about any of these variables in the same manner. The additive terms in (8.10b) also may be expanded in this manner. Expanding about X_2 we have:

$$f(X_1, \dots, X_n) = X_1 X_2 f(1, 1, X_3, \dots, X_n) + X_1 X_2' f(1, 0, X_3, \dots, X_n) +$$
$$X_1' X_2 f(0, 1, X_3, \dots, X_n) + X_1' X_2' f(0, 0, X_3, \dots, X_n) \tag{8.11a}$$

$$f(X_1, \dots, X_n) = [X_1 + X_2 + f(0, 0, X_3, \dots, X_n)] \cdot [X_1 + X_2' + f(0, 1, X_3, \dots, X_n)] \cdot$$
$$[X_1' + X_2 + f(1, 0, X_3, \dots, X_n)] \cdot [X_1' + X_2' + f(1, 1, X_3, \dots, X_n)]. \tag{8.11b}$$

Continuing this process n times we will arrive at the complete series expansion having the form:

$$f(X_1, \dots, X_n) = f(1, 1, 1, \dots, 1) X_1 X_2 \dots X_n + f(0, 1, 1, \dots, 1) X_1' X_2 \dots X_n + \cdots \tag{8.12a}$$
$$+ f(0, 0, 0, \dots, 0) X_1' X_2' \dots X_n',$$

$$f(X_1, \dots, X_n) = [X_1 + X_2 + \cdots X_n + f(0, 0, 0, \dots, 0)] \cdot \cdots \tag{8.12b}$$
$$\cdot [X_1' + X_2' + \cdots + X_n' + f(1, 1, 1, \dots, 1)].$$

By (8.12a), f is equal to the sum of the products formed by permuting primes on the terms of $X_1, X_2, \dots, X_n$ in all possible ways and giving each product a coefficient equal to the value of the function when that product is 1. Similarly for (8.12b).

As an application of the series expansion it should be noted that if we wish to find a circuit representing any given function we can always expand the function by either (8.10a) or (8.10b) in such a way that any given variable appears at most twice, once as a make contact and once as a break contact. This is shown in Figure 8.5. Similarly by (8.11a) and (8.11b) any other variable need appear no more than four times (two make and two break contacts), etc.

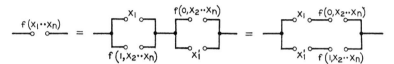

Figure 8.5: Expansion about one variable

A generalization of De Morgan's theorem is represented symbolically in the following equation:

$$f(X_1, X_2, \ldots, X_n, +, \cdot)' = f(X_1', X_2', \ldots, X_n', \cdot, +). \qquad (8.13)$$

By this we mean that the negative of any function may be obtained by replacing each variable by its negative and interchanging the $+$ and $\cdot$ symbols. Explicit and implicit parentheses will, of course, remain in the same places. For example, the negative of $X + Y(Z + WX')$ will be $X'[Y' + Z'(W' + X)]$.

Some other theorems useful in simplifying expressions are given below:

$$X = X + X = X + X + X = \text{ etc.,} \qquad (8.14a)$$

$$X = X \cdot X = X \cdot X \cdot X = \text{ etc.,} \qquad (8.14b)$$

$$X + XY = X, \qquad (8.15a)$$

$$X(X + Y) = X, \qquad (8.15b)$$

$$XY + X'Z = XY + X'Z + YZ, \qquad (8.16a)$$

$$(X + Y)(X' + Z) = (X + Y)(X' + Z)(Y + Z), \qquad (8.16b)$$

$$Xf(X, Y, Z, \ldots) = Xf(1, Y, Z, \ldots), \qquad (8.17a)$$

$$X + f(X, Y, Z, \ldots) = X + f(0, Y, Z, \ldots), \qquad (8.17b)$$

$$X'f(X, Y, Z, \ldots) = X'f(0, Y, Z, \ldots), \qquad (8.18a)$$

$$X' + f(X, Y, Z, \ldots) = X' + f(1, Y, Z, \ldots). \qquad (8.18b)$$

All of these theorems may be proved by the method of perfect induction.

Any expression formed with the operations of addition, multiplication, and negation represents explicitly a circuit containing only series and parallel connections. Such a circuit will be called a series-parallel circuit. Each letter in an expression of this sort represents a make or break relay contact, or a switch blade and contact. To find the circuit requiring the least number of contacts, it is therefore necessary to manipulate the expression into the form in which the least number of letters appear. The theorems given above are always sufficient to do this. A little practice in the manipulation of these symbols is all that is required. Fortunately most of the theorems are exactly the same as those of numerical algebra—the associative, commutative, and distributive laws of algebra hold here. The writer has found (8.3), (8.6), (8.9), (8.14), (8.15), (8.16a), (8.17), and (8.18) to be especially useful in the simplification of complex expressions. Frequently a function may be written in several ways, each requiring the same minimum number of elements. In such a case the choice of circuit may be made arbitrarily from among these, or from other considerations.

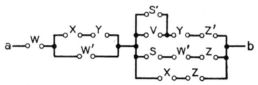

Figure 8.6: Circuit to be simplified

As an example of the simplification of expressions consider the circuit shown in Figure 8.6. The hindrance function X_{ab} for this circuit will be:

$$X_{ab} = W + W'(X + Y) + (X + Z)(S + W' + Z)(Z' + Y + S'V)$$
$$= W + X + Y + (X + Z)(S + 1 + Z)(Z' + Y + S'V)$$
$$= W + X + Y + Z(Z' + S'V).$$

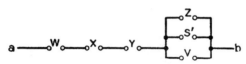

Figure 8.7: Simplification of Figure 8.6

These reductions were made with (8.17b) using first W, then X and Y as the "X" of (8.17b). Now multiplying out:

$$X_{ab} = W + X + Y + ZZ' + ZS'V$$
$$= W + X + Y + ZS'V.$$

The circuit corresponding to this expression is shown in Figure 8.7. Note the large reduction in the number of elements. ...

9

A Logical Calculus of the Ideas Immanent in Nervous Activity (1943)

Warren McCulloch and Walter Pitts

This is a strange and wonderful paper, technically convoluted and hubristically prophetic, an admixture of wet neuroscience and austere mathematical abstraction unlike anything written before. It is complex in its notation and extravagant in its pretensions. Its goal is nothing less than to reduce the functioning of the human brain to mathematical logic, and thereby to explain thought, memory, and mind. In all its immodesty and naïveté, it is the bubbling source of ideas that have nourished computer science for decades.

The authors picture a neural network consisting of two kinds of neurons. Some receive inputs from no other neurons; they are the bearers of sensory data and are referred to as "peripheral afferents." The others are switches, and can be in one of two states, either firing or not. A global clock synchronizes the system, and the state of each neuron at time $t + 1$ depends on the states of its inputs at time t. The inputs to a neuron are from peripheral afferents or from the outputs ("efferents") of other neurons; the junction points, where the inputs arrive at a neuron, are synapses. A McCulloch–Pitts neuron i has a threshold θ_i; neuron i fires if more than θ_i of its inputs fire—except that the neuron also has an inhibitory input, and will not fire if the inhibitory input is activated. In their drawings of neurons (Figure 9.1 on page 86), the excitatory inputs are on the slanted sides of the triangular diagram, the inhibitory input is at the point on the left, and the output or efferent comes from the vertical side on the right.

In short, this paper models the brain and all its functions as a digital system. The neurons of Figure 9.1 are gates in what would today be called a threshold logic. The authors' goal is to determine what kinds of computations such a network can carry out. They do this by associating with each neuron i a predicate $N_i(t)$ that is true if neuron i is firing at time t. With this background, it is worth working through some of the diagrams and formulas of Figure 9.1 before beginning to read the paper. (The single dots and vertical double dots are an alternative to parentheses; they tend to push formulas apart, two dots more strongly than one. A single dot can also denote conjunction. So the first line of part (e) corresponds to $N_3(t) \equiv [N_1(t-1) \vee (N_2(t-3) \wedge \sim N_2(t-2))]$, where $\sim$ stands for "not," $\vee$ for "or," and $\wedge$ for "and.")

The specific technical accomplishment of the paper is to prove that the set of predicates computable by neural nets is exactly the same as the set of predicates expressible in a certain very expressive logic. Particular attention is given to networks with feedback, in which the output of one neuron, after affecting a series of other neurons, loops back as an input to the original neuron.

Reprinted from McCulloch and Pitts (1943), with permission from Springer.

Such cycles of activity, the authors suggest, explain memory. So given a complete account of the network, they reasoned, "for prognosis, history is never necessary" (page 88). The brain is what we would now call a deterministic finite-state machine: its future is completely determined by its present state and its inputs going forward.

The paper's formulas are ridden with errors and infelicities—"S" names the successor function, but boldface "S" is an unrelated variable standing for "sentence." Stephen Cole Kleene simplified the model and used it in 1951 as the basis for his formalization of finite automata and regular expressions. Readers who find "A Logical Calculus" tough going should be reassured by Kleene's take on it: "The present article is partly an exposition of the McCulloch–Pitts results; but we found the part of their paper which treats of arbitrary nerve nets obscure .... " (Kleene, 1951).

It soon became evident that the digital contraption McCulloch and Pitts described was a poor model for the brain. The discovery that "what the frog's eye tells the frog's brain" (Lettvin et al., 1959) was not a bitmap seemed to shatter Pitts's hope of making logical sense of the world. And yet McCulloch and Pitts had given birth not just to finite automata theory but to the sprawling field of neural computing. Their audacity paid off—just not in the way they had hoped.

"A Logical Calculus" is the product of an extraordinary and tragic partnership. Warren McCulloch (1898–1969) was a neuroscientist who longed to understand the mind scientifically. A member of a successful family of lawyers and engineers, McCulloch was skeptical of the Freudian theories that dominated mid-twentieth century psychology. He had encountered the logic of Whitehead and Russell's *Principia Mathematica* but could not marry it to his understanding of neural anatomy and function. Walter Pitts (1923–1969), the son of an abusive working-class father in Detroit, found shelter as a boy in a public library. He became remarkably learned through solitary study, and in particular read the *Principia* at the age of 12 and entered into a correspondence about it with Bertrand Russell. A few years later, hearing that Russell was lecturing at the University of Chicago, he ran away from home, never to return. He hung around the University, where he met McCulloch. (You would not be wrong to think of *Good Will Hunting*.) McCulloch, 42 at the time and a professor, and Pitts, a homeless 18-year-old runaway, had both read Leibniz and were determined to develop a Leibnizian calculus of thought with a sound mathematical and neuroanatomical basis. This paper is the upshot. For the first time, McCulloch later declared, "we know how we know." In the last section, it proposes that mental functioning having been explained, mental disorders would in the future be understood as specific neural net malfunctions.

Pitts, alas, himself fell prey to mental illness. Both he and McCulloch wound up at MIT—Pitts, though he had never attended high school, as a graduate student for the pioneering cybernetician Norbert Wiener (the author of chapter 19). A fracture in the personal relationship between the three men sent Pitts into a spiral of depression and alcoholism from which he died at age 46. McCulloch, 25 years his senior, died a few months later (Gefter, 2015).

9.0 Abstract

BECAUSE of the "all-or-none" character of nervous activity, neural events and the relations among them can be treated by means of propositional logic. It is found that the behavior of every net can be described in these terms, with the addition of more complicated logical means for nets containing circles; and that for any logical expression satisfying certain conditions, one can find a net behaving in the fashion it describes. It is shown that many particular choices among possible neurophysiological assumptions are equivalent, in the sense that for every net behaving under one assumption, there exists another net which behaves under the other and gives the same results, although perhaps not in the same time. Various applications of the calculus are discussed.

9.1 Introduction

Theoretical neurophysiology rests on certain cardinal assumptions. The nervous system is a net of neurons, each having a soma and an axon. Their adjunctions, or synapses, are always between the axon of one neuron and the soma of another. At any instant a neuron has some threshold, which excitation must exceed to initiate an impulse. This, except for the fact and the time of its occurrence, is determined by the neuron, not by the excitation. From the point of excitation the impulse is propagated to all parts of the neuron. The velocity along the axon varies directly with its diameter, from < 1 ms^{-1} in thin axons, which are usually short, to > 150 ms^{-1} in thick axons, which are usually long. The time for axonal conduction is consequently of little importance in determining the time of arrival of impulses at points unequally remote from the same source. Excitation across synapses occurs predominantly from axonal terminations to somata. It is still a moot point whether this depends upon irreciprocity of individual synapses or merely upon prevalent anatomical configurations. To suppose the latter requires no hypothesis *ad hoc* and explains known exceptions, but any assumption as to cause is compatible with the calculus to come. No case is known in which excitation through a single synapse has elicited a nervous impulse in any neuron, whereas any neuron may be excited by impulses arriving at a sufficient number of neighboring synapses within the period of latent addition, which lasts < 0.25 ms. Observed temporal summation of impulses at greater intervals is impossible for single neurons and empirically depends upon structural properties of the net. Between the arrival of impulses upon a neuron and its own propagated impulse there is a synaptic delay of > 0.5 ms. During the first part of the nervous impulse the neuron is absolutely refractory to any stimulation. Thereafter its excitability returns rapidly, in some cases reaching a value above normal from which it sinks again to a subnormal value, whence it returns slowly to normal. Frequent activity augments this subnormality. Such specificity as is possessed by nervous impulses depends solely upon their time and place and not on any other specificity of nervous energies. Of late only inhibition has been seriously adduced to contravene this thesis. Inhibition is the termination or prevention of the activity of one group of neurons by concurrent or antecedent activity of a second group. Until recently this could be explained on the supposition that previous activity of neurons of the second group might so raise the thresholds of internuncial neurons that they could no longer be excited by neurons of the first group, whereas the impulses of the first group must sum with the impulses of these internuncials to excite the now inhibited neurons. Today, some inhibitions have been shown to consume < 1 ms. This excludes internuncials and requires synapses through which impulses inhibit that neuron which is being stimulated by impulses through other synapses. As yet experiment has not shown whether the refractoriness is relative or absolute. We will assume the latter and demonstrate that the difference is immaterial to our argument. Either variety of refractoriness can be accounted for in either of two ways. The "inhibitory synapse" may be of such a kind as to produce a substance which raises the threshold of the neuron, or it may be so placed that the local disturbance produced by its excitation opposes the alteration induced by the otherwise excitatory synapses. Inasmuch as position is already known to have such effects in the cases of electrical stimulation, the first hypothesis is to be excluded unless and until it be substantiated, for the second involves no new hypothesis. We have, then, two explanations of inhibition based on the same general premises, differing only in the assumed nervous nets and, consequently, in the time required for inhibition. Hereafter we shall refer to such nervous nets as *equivalent in the extended sense*. Since we are concerned with properties of nets which are invariant under equivalence, we may make the physical assumptions which are most convenient for the calculus.

Many years ago one of us, by considerations impertinent to this argument, was led to conceive of the response of any neuron as factually equivalent to a proposition which proposed its adequate stimulus. He therefore attempted to record the behavior of complicated nets in the notation of the symbolic logic of propositions. The "all-or-none" law of nervous activity is sufficient to insure that the activity of any neuron may be represented as a proposition. Physiological relations existing among nervous activities correspond, of course, to relations among the propositions; and the utility of the representation depends upon the identity of these relations with those of the logic of propositions. To each reaction of any neuron there is a corresponding assertion of a simple proposition. This, in turn, implies either some other simple proposition or the disjunction of the conjunction, with or without negation, of similar propositions, according to the configuration of the synapses upon and the threshold of the neuron in question. Two difficulties appeared. The first concerns facilitation and extinction, in which antecedent activity temporarily alters responsiveness to subsequent stimulation of one and the same part of the net. The second concerns learning, in which activities concurrent at some previous time have altered the net permanently, so that a stimulus which would previously have been inadequate is now adequate. But for nets undergoing both alterations, we can substitute equivalent fictitious nets composed of neurons whose connections and thresholds are unaltered. But one point must be made clear: neither of us conceives the formal equivalence to be a factual explanation. *Per contra!*—we regard facilitation and extinction as dependent upon continuous changes in threshold related to electrical and chemical variables, such as after-potentials and ionic concentrations; and learning as an enduring change which can survive sleep, anaesthesia, convulsions and coma. The importance of the formal equivalence lies in this: that the alterations actually underlying facilitation, extinction and learning in no way affect the conclusions which follow from the formal treatment of the activity of nervous nets, and the relations of the corresponding propositions remain those of the logic of propositions.

The nervous system contains many circular paths, whose activity so regenerates the excitation of any participant neuron that reference to time past becomes indefinite, although it still implies that afferent activity has realized one of a certain class of configurations over time. Precise specification of these implications by means of recursive functions, and determination of those that can be embodied in the activity of nervous nets, completes the theory.

9.2   The Theory: Nets without Circles

We shall make the following physical assumptions for our calculus.

1. The activity of the neuron is an "all-or-none" process.

2. A certain fixed number of synapses must be excited within the period of latent addition in order to excite a neuron at any time, and this number is independent of previous activity and position on the neuron.

3. The only significant delay within the nervous system is synaptic delay.

4. The activity of any inhibitory synapse absolutely prevents excitation of the neuron at that time.

5. The structure of the net does not change with time.

To present the theory, the most appropriate symbolism is that of Language II of Carnap (1937), augmented with various notations drawn from Whitehead and Russell (1910), including the *Principia* conventions for dots. Typographical necessity, however, will compel us to use the upright "*E*" for the existential operator instead of the inverted, and an arrow ($\rightarrow$) for implication instead of the horseshoe. We shall also use the Carnap syntactical notations, but print them in boldface rather than German type; and we shall introduce a functor S, whose value for a property P is the property which holds of a number when P holds of its predecessor; it is defined by "$S(P)(t) \; . \equiv . \; P(x) \; . \; t = x'$" [EDITOR: speculatively corrected from the original]; the brackets around its argument will often be omitted, in which case this is understood to be the nearest predicate-expression [Pr] on the right. Moreover, we shall write $S^2 Pr$ for $S(S(Pr))$, etc.

The neurons of a given net N may be assigned designations "c_1," "c_2," ..., "c_n." This done, we shall denote the property of a number, that a neuron c_i fires at a time which is that number of synaptic delays from the origin of time, by "N" with the numeral i as subscript, so that $N_i(t)$ asserts that c_i fires at the time t. N_i is called the *action* of c_i. We shall sometimes regard the subscripted numeral of "N" as if it belonged to the object-language, and were in a place for a functoral argument, so that it might be replaced by a number-variable [z] and quantified; this enables us to abbreviate long but finite disjunctions and conjunctions by the use of an operator. We shall employ this locution quite generally for sequences of Pr; it may be secured formally by an obvious disjunctive definition. The predicates "N_1," "N_2," ..., comprise the syntactical class "N."

Let us define the *peripheral afferents* of N as the neurons of N with no axons synapsing upon them. Let N_1, ..., N_p denote the actions of such neurons and N_{p+1}, N_{p+2}, ..., N_n those of the rest. Then a *solution* of N will be a class of sentences of the form $S_i : N_{p+1}(z_1) \cdot \equiv \cdot$ $Pr_i(N_1, N_2, \ldots, N_p, z_1)$, where Pr_i contains no free variable save z_1 and no descriptive symbols save the N in the argument [Arg], and possibly some constant sentences [sa]; and such that each S_i is true of N. Conversely, given a $Pr_1({}^1p_1^1, {}^1p_2^1, \ldots, {}^1p_p^1, z_1, s)$, containing no free variable save those in its Arg, we shall say that it is *realizable in the narrow sense* if there exists a net N and a series of N_i in it such that $N_1(z_1) \cdot \equiv \cdot Pr_1(N_1, N_2, \ldots, z_1, sa_1)$ is true of it, where sa_1 has the form $N(0)$. We shall call it *realizable in the extended sense*, or simply *realizable*, if for some n, $S^n(Pr_1)(p_1, \ldots, p_p, z_1, s)$ is realizable in the above sense. c_{pi} is here the realizing neuron. We shall say of two laws of nervous excitation which are such that every S which is realizable in either sense upon one supposition is also realizable, perhaps by a different net, upon the other, that they are equivalent assumptions, in that sense.

The following theorems about realizability all refer to the extended sense. In some cases, sharper theorems about narrow realizability can be obtained; but in addition to greater complication in statement this were of little practical value, since our present neurophysiological knowledge determines the law of excitation only to extended equivalence, and the more precise theorems differ according to which possible assumption we make. Our less precise theorems, however, are invariant under equivalence, and are still sufficient for all purposes in which the exact time for impulses to pass through the whole net is not crucial.

Our central problems may now be stated exactly: first, to find an effective method of obtaining a set of computable S constituting a solution of any given net; and second, to characterize the class of realizable S in an effective fashion. Materially stated, the problems are to calculate the behavior of any net, and to find a net which will behave in a specified way, when such a net exists.

A net will be called *cyclic* if it contains a circle, i.e. if there exists a chain $c_i, c_{i+1}, \ldots$ of neurons on it, each member of the chain synapsing upon the next, with the same beginning and end. If a set of its neurons $c_1, c_2, \ldots, c_p$ is such that its removal from N leaves it without circles, and no smaller class of neurons has this property, the set is called a *cyclic* set, and its cardinality is the *order* of N. In an important sense, as we shall see, the order of a net is an index of the complexity of its behaviour. In particular, nets of zero order have especially simple properties; we shall discuss them first.

Let us define a *temporal propositional expression* (a *TPE*), designating a temporal propositional function (*TPF*), by the following recursion.

1. A ${}^1p^1[z_1]$ is a *TPE*, where p_1 is a predicate-variable.
2. If S_1 and S_2 are *TPE* containing the same free individual variable, so are $SS_1, S_1 \vee S_2, S_1 \cdot S_2$, and $S_1 \cdot {\sim}S_2$.
3. Nothing else is a *TPE*.

THEOREM 1. *Every net of order 0 can be solved in terms of temporal propositional expressions.*

Let c_i be any neuron of N with a threshold $\theta_i > 0$, and let $c_{i1}, c_{i2}, \ldots, c_{ip}$ have respectively n_{i1}, $n_{i2}, \ldots, n_{ip}$ excitatory synapses upon it. Let $c_{j1}, c_{j2}, \ldots, c_{jq}$ have inhibitory synapses upon it. Let κ_i be the set of the subclasses of $\{n_{i1}, n_{i2}, \ldots, n_{ip}\}$ such that the sum of their members exceeds θ_i.

We shall then be able to write, in accordance with the assumptions mentioned above:

$$N_i(z_1) \; . \; \equiv \; . \; S \left\{ \prod_{m=1}^{q} \sim N_{jm}(z_1) \; . \; \sum_{\alpha \in \kappa_i} \prod_{s \in \alpha} N_{is}(z_1) \right\}, \tag{9.1}$$

where the "$\sum$" and "$\prod$" are syntactical symbols for disjunctions and conjunctions which are finite in each case. Since an expression of this form can be written for each c_i which is not a peripheral afferent, we can, by substituting the corresponding expression in (9.1) for each N_{jm} or N_{is} whose neuron is not a peripheral afferent, and repeating the process on the result, ultimately come to an expression for N_i in terms solely of peripherally afferent N, since $\mathcal{N}$ is without circles. Moreover, this expression will be a *TPE*, since obviously (9.1) is; and it follows immediately from the definition that the result of substituting a *TPE* for a constituent $p(z)$ in a *TPE* is also one.

THEOREM 2. *Every* TPE *is realizable by a net of order zero.*

   The functor S obviously commutes with disjunction, conjunction, and negation. It is obvious that the result of substituting any S_i, realizable in the narrow sense (i.n.s.), for the $p(z)$ in a realizable expression S_1 is itself realizable i.n.s.; one constructs the realizing net by replacing the peripheral afferents in the net for S_1 by the realizing neurons in the nets for the S_i. The one neuron net realizes $p_1(z_1)$ i.n.s., and Figure 9.1a shows a net that realizes $S p_1(z_1)$ and hence $S S_2$, i.n.s., if S_2 can be realized i.n.s. Now if S_2 and S_3 are realizable then $S^m S_2$ and $S^n S_3$ are realizable i.n.s., for suitable m and n. Hence so are $S^{m+n} S_2$ and $S^{m+n} S_3$. Now the nets of Figures 9.1b–d respectively realize $S(p_1(z_1) \vee p_2(z_1))$, $S(p_1(z_1) \; . \; p_2(z_1))$, and $S(p_1(z_1) \; . \; \sim p_2(z_1))$ i.n.s. Hence $S^{m+n+1}(S_1 \vee S_2)$, $S^{m+n+1}(S_1 \; . \; S_2)$, and $S^{m+n+1}(S_1 \; . \; \sim S_2)$ are realizable i.n.s. Therefore $S_1 \vee S_2$, $S_1 \; . \; S_2$, $S_1 \; . \; \sim S_2$ are realizable if S_1 and S_2 are. By complete induction, all *TPE* are realizable. In this way all nets may be regarded as built out of the fundamental elements of Figures 9.1a–d, precisely as the temporal propositional expressions are generated out of the operations of precession, disjunction, conjunction, and conjoined negation. In particular, corresponding to any description of state, or distribution of the values true and false for the actions of all the neurons of a net save that which makes them all false, a single neuron is constructible whose firing is a necessary and sufficient condition for the validity of that description. Moreover, there is always an indefinite number of topologically different nets realizing any *TPE*. ...

   The phenomena of learning, which are of a character persisting over most physiological changes in nervous activity, seem to require the possibility of permanent alterations in the structure of nets. The simplest such alteration is the formation of new synapses or equivalent local depressions of threshold. We suppose that some axonal terminations cannot at first excite the succeeding neuron; but if at any time the neuron fires, and the axonal terminations are simultaneously excited, they become synapses of the ordinary kind, henceforth capable of exciting the neuron. The loss of an inhibitory synapse gives an entirely equivalent result. We shall then have

THEOREM 7. *Alterable synapses can be replaced by circles.*

   This is accomplished by the method of Figure 9.1i. It is also to be remarked that a neuron which becomes and remains spontaneously active can likewise be replaced by a circle, which

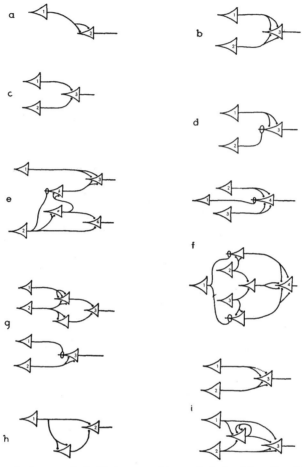

Figure 9.1: The neuron c_i is always marked with the numeral i upon the body of the cell, and the corresponding action is denoted by "N" with i as subscript, as in the text.

(a) $N_2(t) \ . \equiv . \ N_1(t-1)$

(b) $N_3(t) \ . \equiv . \ N_1(t-1) \vee N_2(t-1)$

(c) $N_3(t) \ . \equiv . \ N_1(t-1) \ . \ N_2(t-1)$

(d) $N_3(t) \ . \equiv . \ N_1(t-1) \ . \sim N_2(t-1)$

(e) $N_3(t) : \equiv : N_1(t-1) \ . \vee . \ N_2(t-3) \ . \sim N_2(t-2)$

$\quad\ N_4(t) \ . \equiv . \ N_2(t-2) \ . \ N_2(t-1)$

(f) $N_4(t) : \equiv : \sim N_1(t-1) \ . \ N_2(t-1) \vee N_3(t-1)$

$\quad\ N_4(t) : \equiv : \sim N_1(t-2) \ . \ N_2(t-2) \vee N_3(t-2) \ . \vee . \ N_1(t-2) \ . \ N_2(t-2) \ . \ N_3(t-2)$

(g) $N_3(t) \ . \equiv . \ N_2(t-2) \ . \sim N_1(t-3)$

(h) $N_2(t) \ . \equiv . \ N_1(t-1) \ . \ N_1(t-2)$

(i) $N_3(t) : \equiv : N_2(t-1) \ . \vee . \ N_1(t-1) \ . \ (Ex)t-1 \ . \ N_1(x) \ . \ N_2(x)$

is set into activity by a peripheral afferent when the activity commences, and inhibited by one when it ceases. [EDITOR: In Figure 9.1, the expression for top part of (f) has been corrected and the expression for top part of (i) is missing in the original. Part (g) is mysterious—the bottom diagram is a version of (d), but the expression for (g) matches neither part of the diagram for (g).]

9.3   The Theory: Nets with Circles

The treatment of nets which do not satisfy our previous assumption of freedom from circles is very much more difficult than that case. This is largely a consequence of the possibility that activity may be set up in a circuit and continue reverberating around it for an indefinite period of time, so that the realizable *Pr* may involve reference to past events of an indefinite degree of remoteness. ...[EDITOR: The expression $(Ex)t - 1 \cdot N_1(x) \cdot N_2(x)$ (in part (i) of Figure 9.1) means that there was a point x in time, no later than time $t - 1$, when $N_1(x)$ and $N_2(x)$ were both true. The unlabeled neuron—which feeds back on itself—will keep firing indefinitely.]

One more thing is to be remarked in conclusion. It is easily shown: first, that every net, if furnished with a tape, scanners connected to afferents, and suitable efferents to perform the necessary motor-operations, can compute only such numbers as can a Turing machine; second, that each of the latter numbers can be computed by such a net; and that nets with circles can be computed by such a net; and that nets with circles can compute, without scanners and a tape, some of the numbers the machine can, but no others, and not all of them. This is of interest as affording a psychological justification of the Turing definition of computability and its equivalents, Church's λ-definability and Kleene's primitive recursiveness: if any number can be computed by an organism, it is computable by these definitions, and conversely.

9.4   Consequences

Causality, which requires description of states and a law of necessary connection relating them, has appeared in several forms in several sciences, but never, except in statistics, has it been as irreciprocal as in this theory. Specification for any one time of afferent stimulation and of the activity of all constituent neurons, each an "all-or-none" affair, determines the state. Specification of the nervous net provides the law of necessary connection whereby one can compute from the description of any state that of the succeeding state, but the inclusion of disjunctive relations prevents complete determination of the one before. Moreover, the regenerative activity of constituent circles renders reference indefinite as to time past. Thus our knowledge of the world, including ourselves, is incomplete as to space and indefinite as to time. This ignorance, implicit in all our brains, is the counterpart of the abstraction which renders our knowledge useful. The role of brains in determining the epistemic relations of our theories to our observations and of these to the facts is all too clear, for it is apparent that every idea and every sensation is realized by activity within that net, and by no such activity are the actual afferents fully determined.

There is no theory we may hold and no observation we can make that will retain so much as its old defective reference to the facts if the net be altered. Tinitus, paraesthesias, hallucinations, delusions, confusions and disorientation intervene. Thus empiry confirms that if our nets are undefined, our facts are undefined, and to the "real" we can attribute not so much as one quality or "form." With determination of the net, the unknowable object of knowledge, the "thing in itself," ceases to be unknowable.

To psychology, however defined, specification of the net would contribute all that could be achieved in that field—even if the analysis were pushed to ultimate psychic units or "psychons," for a psychon can be no less than the activity of a single neuron. Since that activity is inherently propositional, all psychic events have an intentional, or "semiotic," character. The "all-or-none" law of these activities, and the conformity of their relations to those of the logic of propositions, insure that the relations of psychons are those of the two-valued logic of propositions. Thus in psychology, introspective, behavioristic or physiological, the fundamental relations are those of two-valued logic.

Hence arise constructional solutions of holistic problems involving the differentiated continuum of sense awareness and the normative, perfective and resolvent properties of perception and execution. From the irreciprocity of causality it follows that even if the net be known, though we may predict future from present activities, we can deduce neither afferent from central, nor central from efferent, nor past from present activities—conclusions which are reinforced by the contradictory testimony of eye-witnesses, by the difficulty of diagnosing differentially the organically diseased, the hysteric and the malingerer, and by comparing one's own memories or recollections with his contemporaneous records. Moreover, systems which so respond to the difference between afferents to a regenerative net and certain activity within that net, as to reduce the difference, exhibit purposive behavior; and organisms are known to possess many such systems, subserving homeostasis, appetition and attention. Thus both the formal and the final aspects of that activity which we are wont to call *mental* are rigorously deducible from present neurophysiology. The psychiatrist may take comfort from the obvious conclusion concerning causality—that, for prognosis, history is never necessary. He can take little from the equally valid conclusion that his observables are explicable only in terms of nervous activities which, until recently, have been beyond his ken. The crux of this ignorance is that inference from any sample of overt behavior to nervous nets is not unique, whereas, of imaginable nets, only one in fact exists, and may, at any moment, exhibit some unpredictable activity. Certainly for the psychiatrist it is more to the point that in such systems "Mind" no longer "goes more ghostly than a ghost." Instead, diseased mentality can be understood without loss of scope or rigor, in the scientific terms of neurophysiology. For neurology, the theory sharpens the distinction between nets necessary or merely sufficient for given activities, and so clarifies the relations of disturbed structure to disturbed function. In its own domain the difference between equivalent nets and nets equivalent in the narrow sense indicates the appropriate use and importance of temporal studies of nervous activity: and to mathematical biophysics the theory contributes a tool for rigorous symbolic treatment of known nets and an easy method of constructing hypothetical nets of required properties.

10 First Draft of a Report on the EDVAC (1945)

John von Neumann

The so-called "von Neumann architecture" described but not named in this report has the logical structure of the "universal computing machine" described by Turing (1936, here chapter 6), though the similarity seems to be something of a coincidence (see page xviii). The same memory that holds the data on which a program operates holds the program itself (pages 94, 104). Alan Turing cites this report but not his own theoretical work in his plan for an Automatic Calculating Engine (Turing, 1945).

In 1944 Arthur Burks (1915–2008) and Herman Goldstine (1913–2004) were two members of the team led by Presper Eckert and John Mauchly designing an electronic computer known as the EDVAC at the Moore School of the University of Pennsylvania—the successor to the Eckert–Mauchly ENIAC that was already grinding out ballistics calculations for the U.S. Army. After Goldstine happened to meet the eminent mathematician John von Neumann (1903–1957) and told him about the EDVAC project, von Neumann joined the group. John von Neumann wrote up the design in this memo, which Goldstine typed and released in 1945, listing only von Neumann as author. That was regrettable: the document was von Neumann's, but the design was the group's, and the stored program was already part of the ENIAC (though in that machine, the program resided in read-only memory).

Figure 10.1 shows the cover page of the typescript, which is very rough. Where possible, we have supplied section cross-references that in the original were left to be filled in later. A revised report (Burks et al., 1947) was issued in 1946 under the name "Preliminary discussion of the logical design of an electronic computing instrument," adding Goldstine and Burks as co-authors.

These reports set the direction for computer design that would eventually make the software industry possible, since programs could be processed and loaded into memory like any other kind of data. The reports analyze the device into memory and control units ("organs") using binary notation, and the later "Preliminary discussion" adds explanations of memory addresses ("location-numbers"), registers of various kinds, floating-point representation, and use of the first six letters of the Roman alphabet as hexadecimal digits. But in the short run, the reports' failure to acknowledge the contributions of others caused resentment among the founding members of the design team—in particular Mauchly, who had authored the proposal under which the EDVAC and its predecessor machine the ENIAC had been funded and designed. After the war,

Reprinted from von Neumann (1993), with permission from the Institute for Electrical and Electronics Engineers.

Mauchly and Eckert broke off to start a computer business, in 1947 filing patents that were ultimately invalidated because of the prior release of this report. (The subsequent history of the Eckert–Mauchly Computer Corporation is sketched on page 169.) Burks and Goldstine pursued academic careers, joining von Neumann at Princeton.

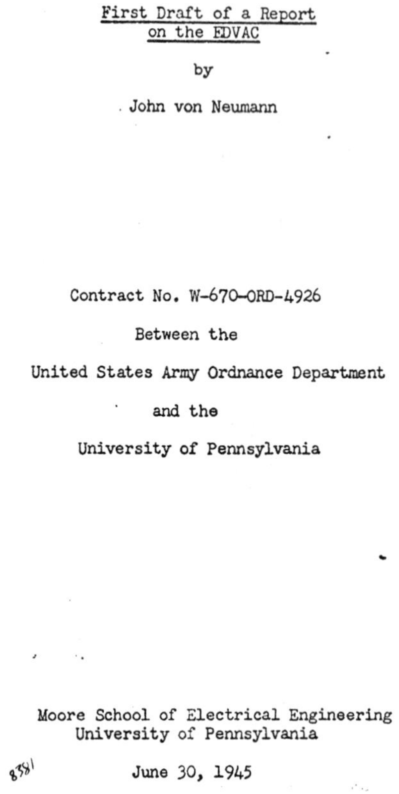

First Draft of a Report
on the EDVAC

by

John von Neumann

Contract No. W-670-ORD-4926

Between the

United States Army Ordnance Department

and the

University of Pennsylvania

Moore School of Electrical Engineering
University of Pennsylvania

June 30, 1945

Figure 10.1: Title page of "First draft" typescript

By the time von Neumann joined the EDVAC team, he was already one of the most accomplished mathematicians in the world, having made contributions to a great variety of mathematical fields, to mathematical economics, and to quantum mechanics. Born and educated in Hungary, he moved to Berlin in 1930 to be part of the circle surrounding David Hilbert (see chapter 5). He emigrated to the US before the outbreak of the Second World War and was an important contributor to the Manhattan Project, which designed the atomic bomb. He witnessed the work of hundreds of human "computers" using individual mechanical calculators to solve the equations he had worked out in the design of a fission bomb, and though he could not discuss that classified work with the groups he worked with at the Moore School or at Princeton, it provided motivation for his work developing high-speed automatic computers.

Some of the terminology of the "First draft" is confusingly implementation-specific. The memory was in the form of a delay line, organized in what we would today call 32-bit words—von Neumann called them "minor cycles." One of the 32 bits was a flag to indicate whether the word represented a number or an instruction ("order"). Numbers used another bit for the sign, with the remaining bits representing a binary fraction between −1 and 1. 32 minor cycles constituted a "major cycle" or delay line organ (DLA). The full memory comprised 256 DLAs, so to specify, for example, the address of a number in memory required 8 bits to identify the DLA and 5 more bits to single out the minor cycle.

To achieve a level of design abstraction, the "First draft" posits a bistable "element" that might have a variety of physical realizations. In §10.4.2, von Neumann cites McCulloch and Pitts at some length, but he does not mention Turing. In an omitted section, the report goes on to note that "an element which stimulates itself will hold a stimulus indefinitely," exactly as "A Logical Calculus" had said of neurons (page 87). And von Neumann's use of circuitry synchronized by a clock is reminiscent of the discrete time variable McCulloch and Pitts imposed on neuronal circuits to subject their behavior to logical analysis. In fact the analogy between a vacuum tube and a neuron is not heavily used in the design, though it was of interest to von Neumann in his speculations about the computational power of the brain, and the EDVAC's program was stored in fast memory, rather than on cards or tape as in Aiken's Mark I, simply so that successive instructions could be accessed at electronic speeds.

The discussion of neuronal computing in this "First draft" disappeared in the "Preliminary discussion," but von Neumann never lost interest in the idea of the brain as a computer and was still working on it at the time of his death from cancer at age 53. *The Computer and the Brain* (von Neumann, 2000) was published posthumously.

———————◦◦◯◦◦———————

10.1   Definitions

10.1.1   The considerations which follow deal with the structure of a *very high speed automatic digital computing system*, and in particular with its *logical control*. Before going into specific details, some general explanatory remarks regarding these concepts may be appropriate.

10.1.2   An *automatic computing system* is a (usually highly composite) device, which can carry out instructions to perform calculations of a considerable order of complexity—e.g. to solve a non-linear partial differential equation in 2 or 3 independent variables numerically.

The instructions which govern this operation must be given to the device in absolutely exhaustive detail. They include all numerical information which is required to solve the problem under consideration: Initial and boundary values of the dependent variables, values of fixed parameters (constants), tables of fixed functions which occur in the statement of the problem. These instructions must be given in some form which the device can sense: Punched into a system of punchcards or on teletype tape, magnetically impressed on steel tape or wire, photographically impressed on motion picture film, wired into one or more fixed or exchangeable plugboards— this list being by no means necessarily complete. All these procedures require the use of some code to express the logical and the algebraical definition of the problem under consideration, as well as the necessary numerical material (cf. above).

Once these instructions are given to the device, it must be able to carry them out completely and without any need for further intelligent human intervention. At the end of the required operations the device must record the results again in one of the forms referred to above. The results are numerical data; they are a specified part of the numerical material produced by the device in the process of carrying out the instructions referred to above.

10.1.3   It is worth noting, however, that the device will in general produce essentially more numerical material (in order to reach the results) than the (final) results mentioned. Thus only a fraction of its numerical output will have to be recorded as indicated in §10.1.2, the remainder will only circulate in the interior of the device, and never be recorded for human sensing. This point will receive closer consideration subsequently . . . .

10.1.4   The remarks of §10.1.2 on the desired automatic functioning of the device must, of course, assume that it functions faultlessly. Malfunctioning of any device has, however, always a finite probability—and for a complicated device and a long sequence of operations it may not be possible to keep this probability negligible. Any error may vitiate the entire output of the device. For the recognition and correction of such malfunctions intelligent human intervention will in general be necessary.

However, it may be possible to avoid even these phenomena to some extent. The device may recognize the most frequent malfunctions automatically, indicate their presence and location by externally visible signs, and then stop.   Under certain conditions it might even carry out the necessary correction automatically and continue (cf. §10.3.3).

10.2   Main Subdivision of the System

10.2.1   In analyzing the functioning of the contemplated device, certain classificatory distinctions suggest themselves immediately.

10.2.2   First: Since the device is primarily a computer, it will have to perform the elementary operations of arithmetics most frequently. These are addition, subtraction, multiplication and division: $+, -, \times, \div$. It is therefore reasonable that it should contain specialized organs for just these operations.

It must be observed, however, that while this principle as such is probably sound, the specific way in which it is realized requires close scrutiny. Even the above list of operations: $+, -, \times, \div$, is not beyond doubt. It may be extended to include such operation as $\sqrt{\ }$, $\sqrt[3]{\ }$ sgn, $|\ |$, also $\log_{10}$, $\log_2$, ln, sin and their inverses, etc. One might also consider restricting it, e.g. omitting $\div$ and even $\times$. One might also consider more elastic arrangements. For some operations radically different procedures are conceivable, e.g. using successive approximation methods or function tables. ... At any rate a *central arithmetical* part of the device will probably have to exist, and this constitutes *the first specific part: CA.*

10.2.3   Second: The logical control of the device, that is the proper sequencing of its operations, can be most efficiently carried out by a central control organ. If the device is to be *elastic*, that is as nearly as possible *all purpose*, then a distinction must be made between the specific instructions given for and defining a particular problem, and the general control organs which see to it that these instructions—no matter what they are—are carried out. The former must be stored in some way—in existing devices this is done as indicated in §10.1.2—the latter are represented by definite operating parts of the device. By the *central control* we mean this latter function only, and the organs which perform it form *the second specific part: CC.*

10.2.4   Third: Any device which is to carry out long and complicated sequences of operations (specifically of calculations) must have a considerable memory.   At least the four following phases of its operation require a memory:

(a) Even in the process of carrying out a multiplication or a division, a series of intermediate (partial) results must be remembered. This applies to a lesser extent even to additions and subtractions (when a carry digit may have to be carried over several positions), and to a greater extent to $\sqrt{}$, $\sqrt[3]{}$, if these operations are wanted. ...

(b) The instructions which govern a complicated problem may constitute a considerable material, particularly so, if the code is circumstantial (which it is in most arrangements). This material must be remembered.

(c) In many problems specific functions play an essential role. They are usually given in form of a table. Indeed in some cases this is the way in which they are given by experience (e.g. the equation of state of a substance in many hydrodynamical problems), in other cases they may be given by analytical expressions, but it may nevertheless be simpler and quicker to obtain their values from a fixed tabulation, than to compute them anew (on the basis of the analytical definition) whenever a value is required. It is usually convenient to have tables of a moderate number of entries only (100–200) and to use interpolation. Linear and even quadratic interpolation will not be sufficient in most cases, so it is best to count on a standard of cubic or biquadratic (or even higher order) interpolation ....

Some of the functions mentioned in the course of §10.2.2 may be handled in this way: $\log_{10}$, $\log_2$, ln, sin and their inverses, possibly also $\sqrt{}$, $\sqrt[3]{}$. Even the reciprocal might be treated in this manner, thereby reducing ÷ to ×.

(d) For partial differential equations the initial conditions and the boundary conditions may constitute an extensive numerical material, which must be remembered throughout a given problem.

(e) For partial differential equations of the hyperbolic or parabolic type, integrated along a variable t, the (intermediate) results belonging to the cycle t must be remembered for the calculation of the cycle $t + dt$. This material is much of the type (d), except that it is not put into the device by human operators, but produced (and probably subsequently again removed and replaced by the corresponding data for $t + dt$) by the device itself, in the course of its automatic operation.

(f) For total differential equations (d), (e) apply too, but they require smaller memory capacities. Further memory requirements of the type (d) are required in problems which depend on given constants, fixed parameters, etc.

(g) Problems which are solved by successive approximations (e.g. partial differential equations of the elliptic type, treated by relaxation methods) require a memory of the type (e): The (intermediate) results of each approximation must be remembered, while those of the next one are being computed.

(h) Sorting problems and certain statistical experiments (for which a very high speed device offers an interesting opportunity) require a memory for the material which is being treated.

10.2.5 To sum up the third remark: The device requires a considerable memory. While it appeared that various parts of this memory have to perform functions which differ somewhat in their nature and considerably in their purpose, it is nevertheless tempting to treat the entire memory as one organ, and to have its parts even as interchangeable as possible for the various functions enumerated above. This point will be considered in detail ....

At any rate the total *memory* constitutes *the third specific part of the device: M.*

10.2.6   The three specific parts CA, CC (together C) and M correspond to the *associative* neurons in the human nervous system. It remains to discuss the equivalents of the *sensory* or *afferent* and the *motor* or *efferent* neurons. These are the *input* and the *output* organs of the device, and we shall now consider them briefly.

In other words: All transfers of numerical (or other) information between the parts C and M of the device must be effected by the mechanisms contained in these parts. There remains, however, the necessity of getting the original definitory information from outside into the device, and also of getting the final information, the results, from the device into the outside.

By the outside we mean media of the type described in §10.1.2: Here information can be produced more or less directly by human action (typing, punching, photographing light impulses produced by keys of the same type, magnetizing metal tape or wire in some analogous manner, etc.), it can be statically stored, and finally sensed more or less directly by human organs.

The device must be endowed with the ability to maintain the input and output (sensory and motor) contact with some specific medium of this type (cf. §10.1.2): That medium will be called the *outside recording medium of the device:* R. Now we have:

10.2.7   Fourth: The device must have organs to transfer (numerical or other) information from R into its specific parts, C and M. These organs form its *input*, the *fourth specific part: I.* It will be seen that it is best to make all transfers from R (by I) into M, and never directly into C (cf. §10.14.1).

10.2.8   Fifth: The device must have organs to transfer (presumably only numerical information) from its specific parts C and M into R. These organs form its output, the fifth specific part: O. It will be seen that it is again best to make all transfers from M (by O) into R, and never directly from C, (cf. §10.14.1).

10.2.9   The output information, which goes into R, represents, of course, the final results of the operation of the device on the problem under consideration. These must be distinguished from the intermediate results, discussed e.g. in §10.2.4, (e)–(g), which remain inside M. At this point an important question arises: Quite apart from its attribute of more or less direct accessibility to human action and perception R has also the properties of a memory. Indeed, it is the natural medium for long time storage of all the information obtained by the automatic device on various problems. Why is it then necessary to provide for another type of memory within the device M? Could not all, or at least some functions of M—preferably those which involve great bulks of information—be taken over by R?

Inspection of the typical functions of M, as enumerated in §10.2.4, (a)–(h), shows this: It would be convenient to shift (a) (the short-duration memory required while an arithmetical operation is being carried out) outside the device, i.e. from M into R. (Actually (a) will be inside the device, but in CA rather than in M. . . .) All existing devices, even the existing desk computing machines, use the equivalent of M at this point. However (b) (logical instructions) might be sensed from outside, i.e. by I from R, and the same goes for (c) (function tables) and (e), (g) (intermediate results). The latter may be conveyed by O to R when the device produces them, and sensed by I from R when it needs them. The same is true to some extent of (d) (initial conditions and parameters) and possibly even of (f) (intermediate results from a total differential equation). As to (h) (sorting and statistics), the situation is somewhat ambiguous: In many cases the possibility of using M accelerates matters decisively, but suitable blending of the use of M with a longer range use of R may be feasible without serious loss of speed and increase the amount of material that can be handled considerably.

Indeed, all existing (fully or partially automatic) computing devices use R—as a stack of punchcards or a length of teletype tape—for all these purposes (excepting (a), as pointed out above). Nevertheless it will appear that a really high speed device would be very limited in its usefulness unless it can rely on M, rather than on R, for all the purposes enumerated in §10.2.4, (a)–(h), with certain limitations in the case of (e), (g), (h) . . . .

10.3   Procedure of Discussion

10.3.1   The classification of §10.2 being completed, it is now possible to take up the five specific parts into which the device was seen to be subdivided, and to discuss them one by one. Such a discussion must bring out the features required for each one of these parts in itself, as well as in their relations to each other. It must also determine the specific procedures to be used in dealing with numbers from the point of view of the device, in carrying out arithmetical operations, and providing for the general logical control. All questions of timing and of speed, and of the relative importance of various factors, must be settled within the framework of these considerations.

10.3.2   The ideal procedure would be, to take up the five specific parts in some definite order, to treat each one of them exhaustively, and go on to the next one only after the predecessor is completely disposed of. However, this seems hardly feasible. The desirable features of the various parts, and the decisions based on them, emerge only after a somewhat zigzagging discussion. It is therefore necessary to take up one part first, pass after an incomplete discussion to a second part, return after an equally incomplete discussion of the latter with the combined results to the first part, extend the discussion of the first part without yet concluding it, then possibly go on to a third part, etc. Furthermore, these discussions of specific parts will be mixed with discussions of general principles, of arithmetical procedures, of the elements to be used, etc.

In the course of such a discussion the desired features and the arrangements which seem best suited to secure them will crystallize gradually until the device and its control assume a fairly definite shape. As emphasized before, this applies to the physical device as well as to the arithmetical and logical arrangements which govern its functioning.

10.3.3   In the course of this discussion the viewpoints of §10.1.4, concerned with the detection, location, and under certain conditions even correction, of malfunctions must also receive some consideration. That is, attention must be given to facilities for checking errors. We will not be able to do anything like full justice to this important subject, but we will try to consider it at least cursorily whenever this seems essential . . . .

10.4   Elements, Synchronism, Neuron Analogy

10.4.1   We begin the discussion with some general remarks:

Every digital computing device contains certain relay like *elements*, with discrete equilibria. Such an element has two or more distinct states in which it can exist indefinitely. These may be perfect equilibria, in each of which the element will remain without any outside support, while appropriate outside stimuli will transfer it from one equilibrium into another. Or, alternatively, there may be two states, one of which is an equilibrium which exists when there is no outside support, while the other depends for its existence upon the presence of an outside stimulus. The relay action manifests itself in the omission of stimuli by the element whenever it has itself received a stimulus of the type indicated above. The emitted stimuli must be of the same kind as the received one, that is, they must be able to stimulate other elements. There must, however, be no energy relation between the received and the emitted stimuli, that is, an element which has received one stimulus, must be able to emit several of the same intensity. In other words: Being a relay, the element must receive its energy supply from another source than the incoming stimulus.

In existing digital computing devices various mechanical or electrical devices have been used as elements: Wheels, which can be locked into any one of ten (or more) significant positions, and which on moving from one position to another transmit electric pulses that may cause other similar wheels to move; single or combined telegraph relays, actuated by an electromagnet and opening or closing electric circuits; combinations of these two elements;—and finally there exists the plausible and tempting possibility of using vacuum tubes, the grid acting as a valve for the cathode-plate circuit. In the last mentioned case the grid may also be replaced by deflecting organs, i.e. the vacuum tube by a cathode ray tube—but it is likely that for some time to come the greater availability and various electrical advantages of the vacuum tubes proper will keep the first procedure in the foreground.

Any such device may time itself autonomously, by the successive reaction times of its elements. In this case all stimuli must ultimately originate in the input. Alternatively, they may have their timing impressed by a fixed clock, which provides certain stimuli that are necessary for its functioning at definite periodically recurrent moments. This clock may be a rotating axis in a mechanical or a mixed, mechanico-electrical device; and it may be an electrical oscillator (possibly crystal controlled) in a purely electrical device. If reliance is to be placed on synchronisms of several distinct sequences of operations performed simultaneously by the device, the clock impressed timing is obviously preferable. We will use the term *element* in the above defined technical sense, and call the device *synchronous* or *asynchronous*, according to whether its timing is impressed by a clock or autonomous, as described above.

10.4.2   It is worth mentioning, that the neurons of the higher animals are definitely elements in the above sense. They have all-or-none character, that is two states: Quiescent and excited. They fulfill the requirements of §10.4.1 with an interesting variant: An excited neuron emits the standard stimulus along many lines (axons). Such a line can, however, be connected in two different ways to the next neuron: First: In an *excitatory synapse*, so that the stimulus causes the excitation of the neuron. Second: In an *inhibitory synapse*, so that the stimulus absolutely prevents the excitation of the neuron by any stimulus on any other (excitatory) synapse. The neuron also has a definite reaction time, between the reception of a stimulus and the emission of the stimuli caused by it, the *synaptic delay*.

Following McCulloch and Pitts (1943, here chapter 9) we ignore the more complicated aspects of neuron functioning: Thresholds, temporal summation, relative inhibition, changes of the threshold by after-effects of stimulation beyond the synaptic delay, etc. It is, however, convenient to consider occasionally neurons with fixed thresholds 2 and 3, that is, neurons which can be excited only by (simultaneous) stimuli on 2 or 3 excitatory synapses (and none on an inhibitory synapse). ...

It is easily seen that these simplified neuron functions can be imitated by telegraph relays or by vacuum tubes. Although the nervous system is presumably asynchronous (for the synaptic delays), precise synaptic delays can be obtained by using synchronous setups. ...

10.4.3   It is clear that a very high speed computing device should ideally have vacuum tube elements. Vacuum tube aggregates like counters and scalers have been used and found reliable at reaction times (synaptic delays) as short as a microsecond (= 10^{-6} seconds), this is a performance which no other device can approximate. Indeed: Purely mechanical devices may be entirely disregarded and practical telegraph relay reaction times are of the order of 10 milliseconds (= 10^{-2} seconds) or more. It is interesting to note that the synaptic time of a human neuron is of the order of a millisecond (= 10^{-3} seconds).

In the considerations which follow we will assume accordingly, that the device has vacuum tubes as elements. We will also try to make all estimates of numbers of tubes involved, timing, etc., on the basis that the types of tubes used are the conventional and commercially available ones. That is, that no tubes of unusual complexity or with fundamentally new functions are to be used. The possibilities for the use of new types of tubes will actually become clearer and more definite after a thorough analysis with the conventional types (or some equivalent elements ...) has been carried out.

Finally, it will appear that a synchronous device has considerable advantages ....

10.5   Principles Governing the Arithmetical Operations

10.5.1   Let us now consider certain functions of the first specific part: The central arithmetical part CA.

The element in the sense of §10.4.3, the vacuum tube used as a current valve or *gate*, is an all-or-none device, or at least it approximates one: According to whether the grid bias is above or below cut-off, it will pass current or not. It is true that it needs definite potentials on all its electrodes in order to maintain either state, but there are combinations of vacuum tubes which have perfect equilibria: Several states in each of which the combination can exist indefinitely, without any outside support, while appropriate outside stimuli (electric pulses) will transfer it from one equilibrium into another. These are the so called trigger circuits, the basic one having two equilibria and containing two triodes or one pentode. The trigger circuits with more than two equilibria are disproportionately more involved.

Thus, whether the tubes are used as gates or as triggers, the all-or-none, two equilibrium, arrangements are the simplest ones. Since these tube arrangements are to handle numbers by means of their digits, it is natural to use a system of arithmetic in which the digits are also two valued. This suggests the use of the binary system.

The analogs of human neurons, discussed in §§10.4.2–10.4.3, are equally all-or-none elements. It will appear that they are quite useful for all preliminary, orienting, considerations of vacuum tube systems (cf. §§10.6.1–10.6.2). It is therefore satisfactory that here too the natural arithmetical system to handle is the binary one.

10.5.2   A consistent use of the binary system is also likely to simplify the operations of multiplication and division considerably. Specifically it does away with the decimal multiplication table, or with the alternative double procedure of building up the multiples of each multiplier or quotient digit by additions first, and then combining these (according to positional value) by a second sequence of additions or subtractions. In other words: Binary arithmetics has a simpler and more one-piece logical structure than any other, particularly than the decimal one.

It must be remembered, of course, that the numerical material which is directly in human use, is likely to have to be expressed in the decimal system. Hence, the notations used in R should be decimal. But it is nevertheless preferable to use strictly binary procedures in CA, and also in whatever numerical material may enter into the central control CC. Hence M should store binary material only.

This necessitates incorporating decimal-binary and binary-decimal conversion facilities into I and O. Since these conversions require a good deal of arithmetical manipulating, it is most economical to use CA, and hence for coordinating purposes also CC, in connection with I and O. The use of CA implies, however, that all arithmetics used in both conversions must be strictly binary. . . .

10.5.3   At this point there arises another question of principle. In all existing devices where the element is not a vacuum tube the reaction time of the element is sufficiently long to make a certain telescoping of the steps involved in addition, subtraction, and still more in multiplication and division, desirable. To take a specific case consider binary multiplication. A reasonable precision for many differential equation problems is given by carrying 8 significant decimal digits, that is by keeping the relative rounding-off errors below 10^{-8}. This corresponds to 2^{-27} in the binary system, that is to carrying 27 significant binary digits. Hence a multiplication consists of pairing each one of 27 multiplicand digits with each one of 27 multiplier digits, and forming product digits 0 and 1 accordingly, and then positioning and combining them. These are essentially $27^2 = 729$ steps, and the operations of collecting and combining may about double their number. So 1000–1500 steps are essentially right.

It is natural to observe that in the decimal system a considerably smaller number of steps obtains $8^2 = 64$ steps, possibly doubled, that is about 100 steps. However, this low number is purchased at the price of using a multiplication table or otherwise increasing or complicating the equipment. At this price the procedure can be shortened by more direct binary artifices, too, which will be considered presently. For this reason it seems not necessary to discuss the decimal procedure separately.

10.5.4   As pointed out before, 1000–1500 successive steps per multiplication would make any non vacuum tube device unacceptably slow. All such devices, excepting some of the latest special relays, have reaction times of more than 10 milliseconds, and these newest relays (which may have reaction times down to 5 milliseconds) have not been in use very long. This would give an extreme minimum of 10–15 seconds per (8 decimal digit) multiplication, whereas this time is 10 seconds for fast modern desk computing machines, and 6 seconds for the standard IBM multipliers. (For the significance of these durations, as well as of those of possible vacuum tube devices, when applied to typical problems, cf. . . . .)

The logical procedure to avoid these long durations, consists of *telescoping operations*, that is of carrying out simultaneously as many as possible. The complexities of carrying prevent even such simple operations as addition or subtraction to be carried out at once. In division the calculation of a digit cannot even begin unless all digits to its left are already known. Nevertheless considerable simultaneisations are possible: In addition or subtraction all pairs of corresponding digits can be combined at once, all first carry digits can be applied together in the next step, etc. In multiplication all the partial products of the form (multiplicand) × (multiplier digit) can be formed and positioned simultaneously—in the binary system such a partial product is zero or the multiplicand, hence this is only a matter of positioning. In both addition and multiplication the above mentioned accelerated forms of addition and subtraction can be used. Also, in multiplication the partial products can be summed up quickly by adding the first pair together simultaneously with the second pair, the third pair, etc.; then adding the first pair of pair sums together simultaneously with the second one, the third one, etc.; and so on until all terms are collected. (Since $27 \leq 2^5$, this allows to collect 27 partial sums—assuming a 27 binary digit multiplier—in 5 addition times. This scheme is due to H. Aiken.)

Such accelerating, telescoping procedures are being used in all existing devices. (The use of the decimal system, with or without further telescoping artifices is also of this type, as pointed out at the end of §10.5.3. It is actually somewhat less efficient than purely dyadic procedures. The arguments of §§10.5.1–10.5.2 speak against considering it here.) However, they save time only at exactly the rate at which they multiply the necessary equipment, that is the number of elements in the device: Clearly if a duration is halved by systematically carrying out two additions at once, double adding equipment will be required (even assuming that it can be used without disproportionate control facilities and fully efficiently), etc.

This way of gaining time by increasing equipment is fully justified in non vacuum tube element devices, where gaining time is of the essence, and extensive engineering experience is available regarding the handling of involved devices containing many elements. A really all-purpose automatic digital computing system constructed along these lines must, according to all available experience, contain over 10,000 elements.

10.5.5   For a vacuum tube element device on the other hand, it would seem that the opposite procedure holds more promise.

As pointed out in §10.4.3, the reaction time of a not too complicated vacuum tube device can be made as short as one microsecond. Now at this rate even the unmanipulated duration of the multiplication, obtained in §10.5.3 is acceptable: 1000–1500 reaction times amount to 1–1.5 milliseconds, and this is so much faster than any conceivable non vacuum tube device, that it actually produces a serious problem of keeping the device balanced, that is to keep the necessarily human supervision beyond its input and output ends in step with its operations. . . .

Regarding other arithmetical operations this can be said: Addition and subtraction are clearly much faster than multiplication. On a basis of 27 binary digits (cf. §10.5.3) and taking carrying into consideration, each should take at most twice 27 steps, that is about 30–50 steps or reaction times. This amounts to .03–.05 milliseconds. Division takes, in this scheme where shortcuts and telescoping have not been attempted in multiplying and the binary system is being used, about the same number of steps as multiplication. . . . Square rooting is usually, and in this scheme too, not essentially longer than dividing.

10.5.6   Accelerating these arithmetical operations does therefore not seem necessary—at least not until we have become thoroughly and practically familiar with the use of very high speed devices of this kind, and also properly understood and started to exploit the entirely new possibilities for numerical treatment of complicated problems which they open up. Furthermore it seems questionable whether the method of acceleration by telescoping processes at the price of multiplying the number of elements required would in this situation achieve its purpose at all: The more complicated the vacuum tube equipment—that is, the greater the number of elements required—the wider the tolerances must be. Consequently any increase in this direction will also necessitate working with longer reaction times than the above mentioned one of one microsecond. The precise quantitative effects of this factor are hard to estimate in a general way—but they are certainly much more important for vacuum tube elements than for telegraph relay ones.

Thus it seems worthwhile to consider the following viewpoint: The device should be as simple as possible, that is, contain as few elements as possible. This can be achieved by never performing two operations simultaneously, if this would cause a significant increase in the number of elements required. The result will be that the device will work more reliably and the vacuum tubes can be driven to shorter reaction times than otherwise.

10.5.7   The point to which the application of this principle can be profitably pushed will, of course, depend on the actual physical characteristics of the available vacuum tube elements. It may be, that the optimum is not at a 100% application of this principle and that some compromise will be found to be optimal. However, this will always depend on the momentary state of the vacuum tube technique, clearly the faster the tubes are which will function reliably in this situation, the stronger the case is for uncompromising application of this principle. It would seem that already with the present technical possibilities the optimum is rather nearly at this uncompromising solution.

It is also worth emphasizing that up to now all thinking about high speed digital computing devices has tended in the opposite direction: Towards acceleration by telescoping processes at the price of multiplying the number of elements required. It would therefore seem to be more instructive to try to think out as completely as possible the opposite viewpoint: That of absolutely refraining from the procedure mentioned above, that is of carrying out consistently the principle formulated in §10.5.6.

We will therefore proceed in this direction. ...

10.6   E-Elements

10.6.1   The considerations of §10.5 have defined the main principles for the treatment of CA. We continue now on this basis, with somewhat more specific and technical detail.

In order to do this it is necessary to use some schematic picture for the functioning of the standard element of the device: Indeed, the decisions regarding the arithmetical and the logical control procedures of the device, as well as its other functions, can only be made on the basis of some assumptions about the functioning of the elements.

The ideal procedure would be to treat the elements as what they are intended to be: as vacuum tubes. However, this would necessitate a detailed analysis of specific radio engineering questions at this early stage of the discussion, when too many alternatives are still open to be treated all exhaustively and in detail. Also, the numerous alternative possibilities for arranging arithmetical procedures, logical control, etc., would superpose on the equally numerous possibilities for the choice of types and sizes of vacuum tubes and other circuit elements from the point of view of practical performance, etc. All this would produce an involved and opaque situation in which the preliminary orientation which we are now attempting would be hardly possible.

In order to avoid this we will base our considerations on a hypothetical element, which functions essentially like a vacuum tube—e.g. like a triode with an appropriate associated RLC-circuit— but which can be discussed as an isolated entity, without going into detailed radio frequency electromagnetic considerations. We re-emphasize: This simplification is only temporary, only a transient standpoint, to make the present preliminary discussion possible. After the conclusions of the preliminary discussion the elements will have to be reconsidered in their true electromagnetic nature. But at that time the decisions of the preliminary discussion will be available, and the corresponding alternatives accordingly eliminated.

10.6.2   The analogs of human neurons, discussed in §§10.4.2–10.4.3 and again referred to at the end of §10.5.1, seem to provide elements of just the kind postulated at the end of §10.6.1. We propose to use them accordingly for the purpose described there: as the constituent elements of the device, for the duration of the preliminary discussion. We must therefore give a precise account of the properties which we postulate for these elements.

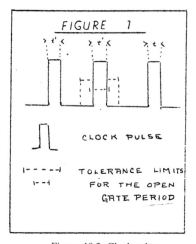

Figure 10.2: Clock pulses

The element which we will discuss, to be called an *E-element*, will be represented to be a circle O, which receives the excitatory and inhibitory stimuli, and emits its own stimuli along a line attached to it: O—. This axis may branch: O—⌐, O—⌐. The emission along it follows the original stimulation by a *synaptic delay*, which we can assume to be a fixed time, the same for all E-elements, to be denoted by *t*. We propose to neglect the other delays (due to conduction of the stimuli along the lines) aside of *t*. We will mark the presence of the delay *t* by an arrow on the line: O—>—, O—>—<. This will also serve to identify the origin and the direction of the line.

10.6.3   At this point the following observation is necessary. In the human nervous system the conduction times along the lines (axons) can be longer than the synaptic delays, hence our above procedure of neglecting them aside of *t* would be unsound. In the actually intended vacuum tube interpretation, however, this procedure is justified: *t* is to be about a microsecond, an electromagnetic impulse travels in this time 300 meters, and as the lines are likely to be short compared to this, the conduction times may indeed be neglected. (It would take an ultra high frequency device—$t = 10^{-8}$ seconds or less—to vitiate this argument.)

Another point of essential divergence between the human nervous system and our intended application consists in our use of a well-defined dispersionless synaptic delay *t*, common to all E-elements. (The emphasis is on the exclusion of a dispersion. We will actually use E-elements with a synaptic delay 2*t*, ...) We propose to use the delays *t* as absolute units of time which can be relied upon to synchronize the functions of various parts of the device. The advantages of such an arrangement are immediately plausible, specific technical reasons will appear in [EDITOR: sentence ends here].

In order to achieve this, it is necessary to conceive the device as synchronous in the sense of §10.4.1. The central clock is best thought of as an electrical oscillator, which emits in every period *t* a short, standard pulse of a length *t′* of about $\frac{1}{5}t-\frac{1}{2}t$. The stimuli emitted nominally by an E-element are actually pulses of the clock, for which the pulse acts as a gate. There is clearly a wide tolerance for the period during which the gate must be kept open, to pass the clock-pulse without distortion. Cf. Figure 10.2. Thus the opening of the gate can be controlled by any electric delay device with a mean delay time t, but considerable permissible dispersion. Nevertheless, the effective synaptic delay will be t with the full precision of the clock, and the stimulus is completely renewed and synchronized after each step. ...

10.12   Capacity of the Memory M, General Principles

10.12.1   We consider next the third specific part: the memory M. ...

10.12.2   Preceding this discussion, however, we must consider the capacity which we desire in M. It is the number of stimuli which this organ can remember, or more precisely, the number of occasions for which it can remember whether or not a stimulus was present. The presence or absence of a stimulus (at a given occasion, i.e. on a given line in a given moment) can be used to express the value 1 or 0 for a binary digit (in a given position). Hence the capacity of a memory is the number of binary digits (the values of) which it can retain. In other words:

The *(capacity) unit of memory* is the ability to retain the value of one binary digit.

We can now express the "cost" of various types of information in these memory units.

Let us consider first the memory capacity required to store a standard (real) number. As indicated ..., we shall fix the size of such a number at 30 binary digits (at least for most uses ...). This keeps the relative rounding-off errors below 2^{-30}, which corresponds to 10^{-9}, i.e. to carrying 9 significant decimal digits. Thus a standard number corresponds to 30 memory units. To this must be added one unit for its sign ... and it is advisable to add a further unit in lieu of a symbol which characterizes it as a number (to distinguish it from an order, cf. §10.14). In this way we arrive at $32 = 2^6$ units per number.

The fact that a number requires 32 memory units, makes it advisable to subdivide the entire memory in this way: First, obviously, into units, second into groups of 32 units, to be called *minor cycles*. ... Each standard (real) number accordingly occupies precisely one minor cycle. It simplifies the organization of the entire memory, and various synchronization problems of the device along with it, if all other constants of the memory are also made to fit into this subdivision into minor cycles. ...

10.14   CC and M

10.14.1   Our next aim is to go deeper into the analysis of CC. Such an analysis, however, is dependent upon a precise knowledge of the system of orders used in controlling the device, since the function of CC is to receive these orders, to interpret them, and then either to carry them out, or to stimulate properly those organs which will carry them out. It is therefore our immediate task to provide a list of the orders which control the device, i.e. to describe the *code* to be used in the device, and to define the mathematical and logical meaning and the operational significance of its *code words*.

Before we can formulate this code, we must go through some general considerations concerning the functions of CC and its relation to M.

The orders which are received by CC come from M, i.e. from the same place where the numerical material is stored. (Cf. §10.2.4 ....) The content of M consists of minor cycles ..., hence by the above each minor cycle must contain a distinguishing mark which indicates whether it is a standard number or an order.

The orders which CC receives fall naturally into these four classes: (a) orders for CC to instruct CA to carry out one of its ten specific operations ...; (b) orders for CC to cause the transfer of a standard number from one place to another; (c) orders for CC to transfer its own connection with M to a different point in M, with the purpose of getting its next order from there; (d) orders controlling the operation of the input and the output of the device (i.e. I of §10.2.7 and O of §10.2.8).

Let us now consider these classes (a)–(d) separately. We cannot at this time add anything to the statements ... concerning (a) .... The discussion of (d) is also better delayed .... We propose, however, to discuss (b) and (c) now.

10.14.2   *Ad* (b): These transfers can occur within M, or within CA, or between M and CA. The first kind can always be replaced by two operations of the last kind, i.e. all transfers within M can be routed through CA. We propose to do this, since this is in accord with the general principle of §10.5.6 ..., and in this way we eliminate all transfers of the first kind. Transfers of the second kind are obviously handled by the operating controls of CA. Hence those of the last kind alone remain. They fall obviously into two classes: Transfers from M to CA and transfers from CA to M. We may break up accordingly (b) into (b′) and (b″), corresponding to these two operations.

10.14.3   *Ad* (c): In principle CC should be instructed, after each order, where to find the next order that it is to carry out. We saw, however, that this is undesirable per se, and that it should be reserved for exceptional occasions, while as a normal routine CC should obey the orders in the temporal sequence, in which they naturally appear at the output of the DLA organ to which CC is connected (cf. the corresponding discussion for the iconoscope memory ...). There must, however, be orders available, which may be used at the exceptional occasions referred to, to instruct CC to transfer its connection to any other desired point in M. This is primarily a transfer of this connection to a different DLA organ (i.e. a delay line organ ...). Since, however, the connection actually wanted must be with a definite minor cycle, the order in question must consist of two instructions: First, the connection of CC is to be transferred to a definite DLA organ. Second, CC is to wait there until a definite r-period, the one in which the desired minor cycle appears at the output of this DLA, and CC is to accept an order at this time only.

Apart from this, such a transfer order might provide that, after receiving and carrying out the order in the desired minor cycle, CC should return its connection to the DLA organ which contains the minor cycle that follows upon the one containing the transfer order, wait until this minor cycle appears at the output, and then continue to accept orders from there on in the natural temporal sequence. Alternatively, after receiving and carrying out the order in the desired minor cycle, CC should continue with that connection, and accept orders from there on in the natural temporal sequence. It is convenient to call a transfer of the first type a *transient* one, and one of the second type a *permanent* one.

It is clear that permanent transfers are frequently needed, hence the second type is certainly necessary. Transient transfers are undoubtedly required in connection with transferring standard numbers (orders (c') and (c''), cf. the end of §10.14.2 ...). It seems very doubtful whether they are ever needed in true orders, particularly since such orders constitute only a small part of the contents of M ..., and a transient transfer order can always be expressed by two permanent transfer orders. We will therefore make all transfers permanent, except those connected with transferring standard numbers, as indicated above. ...

10.15 The Code

10.15.1 The considerations of §10.14 provide the basis for a complete classification of the contents of M, i.e. they enumerate a system of successive disjunctions which give together this classification. This classification will put us into the position to formulate the code which effects the logical control of CC, and hence of the entire device.

Let us therefore restate the pertinent definitions and disjunctions.

The contents of M are the memory units, each one being characterized by the presence or absence of a stimulus. It can be used to represent accordingly the binary digit 1 or 0, and we will at any rate designate its content by the binary digit $i = 1$ or 0 to which it corresponds in this manner. ... These units are grouped together to form 32-unit minor cycles, and these minor cycles are the entities which will acquire direct significance in the code which we will introduce. ... We denote the binary digits which make up the 32 units of a minor cycle, in their natural temporal sequence, by $i_0, i_1, i_2, \ldots, i_{31}$. The minor cycles with these units may be written $I = (i_0, i_1, i_2, \ldots, i_{31}) = (i_v)$.

Minor cycles fall into two classes: *Standard numbers* and *orders*. (Cf. ... §10.14.1.) These two categories should be distinguished from each other by their respective first units ... i.e. by the value of i_0. We agree accordingly that $i_0 = 0$ is to designate a standard number, and $i_0 = 1$ an order.

10.15.2 The remaining 31 units of a standard number express its binary digits and its sign. It is in the nature of all arithmetical operations, specifically because of the role of carry digits, that the binary digits of the numbers which enter into them must be fed in from right to left, i.e. those with the lowest positional values first. (This is so because the digits appear in a temporal succession and not simultaneously.... The details are most simply evident in the discussion of the adder ....) The sign plays the role of the digit farthest left, i.e. of the highest positional value .... Hence it comes last, i.e. $i_{31} = 0$ designates the + sign and $i_{31} = 1$ the − sign. Finally ... the binary point follows immediately after the sign digit, and the number ξ thus represented must be moved mod 2 into the interval −1, 1. That is $\xi = i_{31}i_{30}i_{29} \ldots i_1 = \sum_{v=1}^{31} i_v 2^{v-31} \pmod 2$, $-1 \leq \xi < 1$.

10.15.3   The remaining 31 units of an order, on the other hand, must express the nature of this order. The orders were classified in §10.14.1 into four classes (a)–(d), and these were subdivided further .... [EDITOR: Figure 10.3 shows the orders in tabular form.]

Table.

(I) Type.	(II) Meaning.	(III) Short Symbol	(IV) Code Symbol
			Minor cycle $I = (i_\gamma) = (i_0 i_1 i_2 \text{---} i_{31})$
Standard number or Order (γ)	Storage for the number defined by $\xi = i_{31}$. $i_{30}\, i_{29} \text{---} i_1 = \sum_{v}^{i_1} i_v 2^{31-v} \pmod 2)_1 - 1 \leq \xi < 1.$ i_{31} is the sign: 0 for +, i for -. If CC is connected to this minor cycle, then it operates as an order, causing the transfer of into I_{ca}. This does not apply however if this minor cycle follows immediately upon an order $w \rightarrow A$ or $wh \longrightarrow A.$	$N\xi$	$i_0 = 0$
Order (α) +(δ)	Order to carry out the operation w in CA and to dispose of the result. w is from the list of 11.4. These are the operations of 11.4, with their current numbers w and their symbols w:	$w \rightarrow up$ or $wh \rightarrow up$	$i_1 = 1$
Order (α) +(ϵ)		$w \rightarrow f$ or $wh \rightarrow f$	
Order (α) +(δ)		$w \rightarrow A$ or $wh \rightarrow A$	
Order (α)	h means that the result is to be held in O_{ca}. $\rightarrow up$ means, that the result is to be transferred into the minor cycle ρ in the major cycle u; $\rightarrow f$, that it is to be transferred into the minor cycle immediately following upon the order; $\rightarrow A$, that it is to be transferred into I_{ca}; no $\rightarrow$, that no disposal is wanted (apart from h).	wh	
Order (δ)	Order to transfer the number in the minor cycle in the major cycle u into I_{ca}.	$A \leftarrow up$	
Order	Order to connect CC with the minor cycle in the major cycle μ.	$C \leftarrow up$	

Table embedded within Order rows:

w.decimal	w.binary	w	w.decimal	w.binary	w
0	0000	+	5	0101	i
1	0001	−	6	0110	j
2	0010	x	7	0111	s
3	0011	/	8	1000	db
4	0100	√	9	1001	bd

Figure 10.3: First draft EDVAC "orders" (instructions)

11 As We May Think (1945)

Vannevar Bush

While teaching engineering at MIT, Vannevar Bush (1890–1974) built an analog computer called a *differential analyzer* for solving differential equations. It was a clumsy device by modern standards, mostly mechanical with a few electrical components, but it worked. Bush hired Claude Shannon as a research assistant in 1936 to run the device, an experience that got Shannon thinking systematically about switching circuits and led to his famous Master's thesis (chapter 8). Bush turned to thinking about information storage and retrieval. Influenced by the recently expanded commercial use of microfilm (the *New York Times* began publishing in microform in 1935), Bush imagined the device he describes in this prophetic 1945 article as a *memex*. Microfilm had similarly inspired science fiction writer H. G. Wells (1938). "There is no practical obstacle whatever now," he wrote, "to the creation of an efficient index to all human knowledge, ideas and achievements, to the creation, that is, of a complete planetary memory for all mankind. ... The whole human memory can be, and probably in a short time will be, made accessible to every individual."

Bush, by contrast, was writing as an engineer, and not just any engineer. He had served as Director of the Office of Scientific Research and Development during World War II, marshaling the American scientific community's efforts to aid the war effort. He was well aware, for example, of Aiken's Mark I at Harvard and of the difficult computations done as part of the Manhattan Project to design an atomic weapon. This article appeared about the same time as Bush submitted to President Truman "Science, the Endless Frontier" (Bush, 1945c), a report on the future of science that led to the creation of the National Science Foundation. Bush published this piece in the *Atlantic*—and soon after in abbreviated and dramatically illustrated form in *Life* (Bush, 1945b)—as part of his effort to increase public support for scientific research.

Bush here asks what science can contribute to the peaceful future of humankind, and offers in response a vision of instantaneous, ubiquitous, associative information retrieval. The storage media available at the time could not support such an achievement—the article is fascinating just for its review of the available computing and storage technologies and the projections for their improvement—but his functional vision has inspired many an electronic system since then.

———◦◦◦———

Reprinted from Bush (1945a), with permission from Tribune Content Agency—*The Atlantic*.

Tᴴɪs has not been a scientist's war; it has been a war in which all have had a part. The scientists, burying their old professional competition in the demand of a common cause, have shared greatly and learned much. It has been exhilarating to work in effective partnership. Now, for many, this appears to be approaching an end. What are the scientists to do next? For the biologists, and particularly for the medical scientists, there can be little indecision, for their war has hardly required them to leave the old paths. Many indeed have been able to carry on their war research in their familiar peacetime laboratories. Their objectives remain much the same.

It is the physicists who have been thrown most violently off stride, who have left academic pursuits for the making of strange destructive gadgets, who have had to devise new methods for their unanticipated assignments. They have done their part on the devices that made it possible to turn back the enemy, have worked in combined effort with the physicists of our allies. They have felt within themselves the stir of achievement. They have been part of a great team. Now, as peace approaches, one asks where they will find objectives worthy of their best.

11.1

Of what lasting benefit has been man's use of science and of the new instruments which his research brought into existence? First, they have increased his control of his material environment. They have improved his food, his clothing, his shelter; they have increased his security and released him partly from the bondage of bare existence. They have given him increased knowledge of his own biological processes so that he has had a progressive freedom from disease and an increased span of life. They are illuminating the interactions of his physiological and psychological functions, giving the promise of an improved mental health. Science has provided the swiftest communication between individuals; it has provided a record of ideas and has enabled man to manipulate and to make extracts from that record so that knowledge evolves and endures throughout the life of a race rather than that of an individual. There is a growing mountain of research. But there is increased evidence that we are being bogged down today as specialization extends. The investigator is staggered by the findings and conclusions of thousands of other workers—conclusions which he cannot find time to grasp, much less to remember, as they appear. Yet specialization becomes increasingly necessary for progress, and the effort to bridge between disciplines is correspondingly superficial.

Professionally our methods of transmitting and reviewing the results of research are generations old and by now are totally inadequate for their purpose. If the aggregate time spent in writing scholarly works and in reading them could be evaluated, the ratio between these amounts of time might well be startling. Those who conscientiously attempt to keep abreast of current thought, even in restricted fields, by close and continuous reading might well shy away from an examination calculated to show how much of the previous month's efforts could be produced on call. Mendel's concept of the laws of genetics was lost to the world for a generation because his publication did not reach the few who were capable of grasping and extending it; and this sort of catastrophe is undoubtedly being repeated all about us, as truly significant attainments become lost in the mass of the inconsequential.

The difficulty seems to be, not so much that we publish unduly in view of the extent and variety of present day interests, but rather that publication has been extended far beyond our present ability to make real use of the record. The summation of human experience is being expanded at a prodigious rate, and the means we use for threading through the consequent maze to the momentarily important item is the same as was used in the days of square-rigged ships. But there are signs of a change as new and powerful instrumentalities come into use. Photocells capable of seeing things in a physical sense, advanced photography which can record what is seen or even what is not, thermionic tubes capable of controlling potent forces under the guidance of less power than a mosquito uses to vibrate his wings, cathode ray tubes rendering visible an occurrence so brief that by comparison a microsecond is a long time, relay combinations which will carry out involved sequences of movements more reliably than any human operator and thousands of times as fast—there are plenty of mechanical aids with which to effect a transformation in scientific records.

Two centuries ago Leibniz invented a calculating machine which embodied most of the essential features of recent keyboard devices, but it could not then come into use. The economics of the situation were against it: the labor involved in constructing it, before the days of mass production, exceeded the labor to be saved by its use, since all it could accomplish could be duplicated by sufficient use of pencil and paper. Moreover, it would have been subject to frequent breakdown, so that it could not have been depended upon; for at that time and long after, complexity and unreliability were synonymous.

Babbage, even with remarkably generous support for his time, could not produce his great arithmetical machine. His idea was sound enough, but construction and maintenance costs were then too heavy. Had a Pharaoh been given detailed and explicit designs of an automobile, and had he understood them completely, it would have taxed the resources of his kingdom to have fashioned the thousands of parts for a single car, and that car would have broken down on the first trip to Giza.

Machines with interchangeable parts can now be constructed with great economy of effort. In spite of much complexity, they perform reliably. Witness the humble typewriter, or the movie camera, or the automobile. Electrical contacts have ceased to stick when thoroughly understood. Note the automatic telephone exchange, which has hundreds of thousands of such contacts, and yet is reliable. A spider web of metal, sealed in a thin glass container, a wire heated to brilliant glow, in short, the thermionic tube of radio sets, is made by the hundred million, tossed about in packages, plugged into sockets—and it works! Its gossamer parts, the precise location and alignment involved in its construction, would have occupied a master craftsman of the guild for months; now it is built for thirty cents. The world has arrived at an age of cheap complex devices of great reliability; and something is bound to come of it.

11.2

A record if it is to be useful to science, must be continuously extended, it must be stored, and above all it must be consulted. Today we make the record conventionally by writing and photography, followed by printing; but we also record on film, on wax disks, and on magnetic wires. Even if utterly new recording procedures do not appear, these present ones are certainly in the process of modification and extension.

Certainly progress in photography is not going to stop.

Faster material and lenses, more automatic cameras, finer-grained sensitive compounds to allow an extension of the minicamera idea, are all imminent. Let us project this trend ahead to a logical, if not inevitable, outcome. The camera hound of the future wears on his forehead a lump a little larger than a walnut. It takes pictures 3 millimeters square, later to be projected or enlarged, which after all involves only a factor of 10 beyond present practice. The lens is of universal focus, down to any distance accommodated by the unaided eye, simply because it is of short focal length. There is a built-in photocell on the walnut such as we now have on at least one camera, which automatically adjusts exposure for a wide range of illumination. There is film in the walnut for a hundred exposures, and the spring for operating its shutter and shifting its film is wound once for all when the film clip is inserted. It produces its result in full color. It may well be stereoscopic, and record with two spaced glass eyes, for striking improvements in stereoscopic technique are just around the corner.

The cord which trips its shutter may reach down a man's sleeve within easy reach of his fingers. A quick squeeze, and the picture is taken. On a pair of ordinary glasses is a square of fine lines near the top of one lens, where it is out of the way of ordinary vision. When an object appears in that square, it is lined up for its picture. As the scientist of the future moves about the laboratory or the field, every time he looks at something worthy of the record, he trips the shutter and in it goes, without even an audible click. Is this all fantastic? The only fantastic thing about it is the idea of making as many pictures as would result from its use.

Will there be dry photography? It is already here in two forms. When Brady made his Civil War pictures, the plate had to be wet at the time of exposure. Now it has to be wet during development instead. In the future perhaps it need not be wetted at all. There have long been films impregnated with diazo dyes which form a picture without development, so that it is already there as soon as the camera has been operated. An exposure to ammonia gas destroys the unexposed dye, and the picture can then be taken out into the light and examined. The process is now slow, but someone may speed it up, and it has no grain difficulties such as now keep photographic researchers busy. Often it would be advantageous to be able to snap the camera and to look at the picture immediately.

Another process now in use is also slow, and more or less clumsy. For fifty years impregnated papers have been used which turn dark at every point where an electrical contact touches them, by reason of the chemical change thus produced in an iodine compound included in the paper. They have been used to make records, for a pointer moving across them can leave a trail behind.

If the electrical potential on the pointer is varied as it moves, the line becomes light or dark in accordance with the potential.

This scheme is now used in facsimile transmission. The pointer draws a set of closely spaced lines across the paper one after another. As it moves, its potential is varied in accordance with a varying current received over wires from a distant station, where these variations are produced by a photocell which is similarly scanning a picture. At every instant the darkness of the line being drawn is made equal to the darkness of the point on the picture being observed by the photocell. Thus, when the whole picture has been covered, a replica appears at the receiving end. . . .

Like dry photography, microphotography still has a long way to go. . . . Assume a linear ratio of 100 for future use. Consider film of the same thickness as paper, although thinner film will certainly be usable. Even under these conditions there would be a total factor of 10,000 between the bulk of the ordinary record on books, and its microfilm replica. The *Encyclopedia Britannica* could be reduced to the volume of a matchbox. A library of a million volumes could be compressed into one end of a desk. If the human race has produced since the invention of movable type a total record, in the form of magazines, newspapers, books, tracts, advertising blurbs, correspondence, having a volume corresponding to a billion books, the whole affair, assembled and compressed, could be lugged off in a moving van. Mere compression, of course, is not enough; one needs not only to make and store a record but also be able to consult it, and this aspect of the matter comes later. Even the modern great library is not generally consulted; it is nibbled at by a few.

Compression is important, however, when it comes to costs. The material for the microfilm Britannica would cost a nickel, and it could be mailed anywhere for a cent. What would it cost to print a million copies? To print a sheet of newspaper, in a large edition, costs a small fraction of a cent. The entire material of the Britannica in reduced microfilm form would go on a sheet eight and one-half by eleven inches. Once it is available, with the photographic reproduction methods of the future, duplicates in large quantities could probably be turned out for a cent apiece beyond the cost of materials. The preparation of the original copy? That introduces the next aspect of the subject.

11.3

To make the record, we now push a pencil or tap a typewriter. Then comes the process of digestion and correction, followed by an intricate process of typesetting, printing, and distribution. To consider the first stage of the procedure, will the author of the future cease writing by hand or typewriter and talk directly to the record? He does so indirectly, by talking to a stenographer or a wax cylinder; but the elements are all present if he wishes to have his talk directly produce a typed record. All he needs to do is to take advantage of existing mechanisms and to alter his language.

At a recent World Fair a machine called a Voder was shown. A girl stroked its keys and it emitted recognizable speech. No human vocal chords entered into the procedure at any point; the keys simply combined some electrically produced vibrations and passed these on to a loud-speaker. In the Bell Laboratories there is the converse of this machine, called a Vocoder. The loudspeaker is replaced by a microphone, which picks up sound. Speak to it, and the corresponding keys move. This may be one element of the postulated system.

The other element is found in the stenotype, that somewhat disconcerting device encountered usually at public meetings. A girl strokes its keys languidly and looks about the room and sometimes at the speaker with a disquieting gaze. From it emerges a typed strip which records in a phonetically simplified language a record of what the speaker is supposed to have said. Later this strip is retyped into ordinary language, for in its nascent form it is intelligible only to the initiated. Combine these two elements, let the Vocoder run the stenotype, and the result is a machine which types when talked to.

Our present languages are not especially adapted to this sort of mechanization, it is true. It is strange that the inventors of universal languages have not seized upon the idea of producing one which better fitted the technique for transmitting and recording speech. Mechanization may yet force the issue, especially in the scientific field; whereupon scientific jargon would become still less intelligible to the layman.

One can now picture a future investigator in his laboratory. His hands are free, and he is not anchored. As he moves about and observes, he photographs and comments. Time is automatically recorded to tie the two records together. If he goes into the field, he may be connected by radio to his recorder. As he ponders over his notes in the evening, he again talks his comments into the record. His typed record, as well as his photographs, may both be in miniature, so that he projects them for examination.

Much needs to occur, however, between the collection of data and observations, the extraction of parallel material from the existing record, and the final insertion of new material into the general body of the common record. For mature thought there is no mechanical substitute. But creative thought and essentially repetitive thought are very different things. For the latter there are, and may be, powerful mechanical aids.

Adding a column of figures is a repetitive thought process, and it was long ago properly relegated to the machine. True, the machine is sometimes controlled by a keyboard, and thought of a sort enters in reading the figures and poking the corresponding keys, but even this is avoidable. Machines have been made which will read typed figures by photocells and then depress the corresponding keys; these are combinations of photocells for scanning the type, electric circuits for sorting the consequent variations, and relay circuits for interpreting the result into the action of solenoids to pull the keys down.

All this complication is needed because of the clumsy way in which we have learned to write figures. If we recorded them positionally, simply by the configuration of a set of dots on a card, the automatic reading mechanism would become comparatively simple. In fact if the dots are holes, we have the punched-card machine long ago produced by Hollerith for the purposes of the census, and now used throughout business. Some types of complex businesses could hardly operate without these machines.

Adding is only one operation. To perform arithmetical computation involves also subtraction, multiplication, and division, and in addition some method for temporary storage of results, removal from storage for further manipulation, and recording of final results by printing. Machines for these purposes are now of two types: keyboard machines for accounting and the like, manually controlled for the insertion of data, and usually automatically controlled as far as the sequence of operations is concerned; and punched-card machines in which separate operations are usually delegated to a series of machines, and the cards then transferred bodily from one to another. Both forms are very useful; but as far as complex computations are concerned, both are still in embryo.

Rapid electrical counting appeared soon after the physicists found it desirable to count cosmic rays. For their own purposes the physicists promptly constructed thermionic-tube equipment capable of counting electrical impulses at the rate of 100,000 a second. The advanced arithmetical machines of the future will be electrical in nature, and they will perform at 100 times present speeds, or more.

Moreover, they will be far more versatile than present commercial machines, so that they may readily be adapted for a wide variety of operations. They will be controlled by a control card or film, they will select their own data and manipulate it in accordance with the instructions thus inserted, they will perform complex arithmetical computations at exceedingly high speeds, and they will record results in such form as to be readily available for distribution or for later further manipulation. Such machines will have enormous appetites. One of them will take instructions and data from a whole roomful of girls armed with simple key board punches, and will deliver sheets of computed results every few minutes. There will always be plenty of things to compute in the detailed affairs of millions of people doing complicated things.

11.4

The repetitive processes of thought are not confined however, to matters of arithmetic and statistics. In fact, every time one combines and records facts in accordance with established logical processes, the creative aspect of thinking is concerned only with the selection of the data and the process to be employed and the manipulation thereafter is repetitive in nature and hence a fit matter to be relegated to the machine. Not so much has been done along these lines, beyond the bounds of arithmetic, as might be done, primarily because of the economics of the situation. The needs of business and the extensive market obviously waiting, assured the advent of mass-produced arithmetical machines just as soon as production methods were sufficiently advanced.

With machines for advanced analysis no such situation existed; for there was and is no extensive market; the users of advanced methods of manipulating data are a very small part of the population. There are, however, machines for solving differential equations—and functional and integral equations, for that matter. There are many special machines, such as the harmonic synthesizer which predicts the tides. There will be many more, appearing certainly first in the hands of the scientist and in small numbers.

If scientific reasoning were limited to the logical processes of arithmetic, we should not get far in our understanding of the physical world. One might as well attempt to grasp the game of poker entirely by the use of the mathematics of probability. The abacus, with its beads strung on parallel wires, led the Arabs to positional numeration and the concept of zero many centuries before the rest of the world; and it was a useful tool—so useful that it still exists.

It is a far cry from the abacus to the modern keyboard accounting machine. It will be an equal step to the arithmetical machine of the future. But even this new machine will not take the scientist where he needs to go. Relief must be secured from laborious detailed manipulation of higher mathematics as well, if the users of it are to free their brains for something more than repetitive detailed transformations in accordance with established rules. A mathematician is not a man who can readily manipulate figures; often he cannot. He is not even a man who can readily perform the transformations of equations by the use of calculus. He is primarily an individual who is skilled in the use of symbolic logic on a high plane, and especially he is a man of intuitive judgment in the choice of the manipulative processes he employs.

All else he should be able to turn over to his mechanism, just as confidently as he turns over the propelling of his car to the intricate mechanism under the hood. Only then will mathematics be practically effective in bringing the growing knowledge of atomistics to the useful solution of the advanced problems of chemistry, metallurgy, and biology. For this reason there still come more machines to handle advanced mathematics for the scientist. Some of them will be sufficiently bizarre to suit the most fastidious connoisseur of the present artifacts of civilization.

11.5

The scientist, however, is not the only person who manipulates data and examines the world about him by the use of logical processes, although he sometimes preserves this appearance by adopting into the fold anyone who becomes logical, much in the manner in which a British labor leader is elevated to knighthood. Whenever logical processes of thought are employed—that is, whenever thought for a time runs along an accepted groove—there is an opportunity for the machine. Formal logic used to be a keen instrument in the hands of the teacher in his trying of students' souls. It is readily possible to construct a machine which will manipulate premises in accordance with formal logic, simply by the clever use of relay circuits.

Put a set of premises into such a device and turn the crank, and it will readily pass out conclusion after conclusion, all in accordance with logical law, and with no more slips than would be expected of a keyboard adding machine. [EDITOR: Compare to page 8.]

Logic can become enormously difficult, and it would undoubtedly be well to produce more assurance in its use. The machines for higher analysis have usually been equation solvers. Ideas are beginning to appear for equation transformers, which will rearrange the relationship expressed by an equation in accordance with strict and rather advanced logic. Progress is inhibited by the exceedingly crude way in which mathematicians express their relationships. They employ a symbolism which grew like Topsy and has little consistency; a strange fact in that most logical field.

A new symbolism, probably positional, must apparently precede the reduction of mathematical transformations to machine processes. Then, on beyond the strict logic of the mathematician, lies the application of logic in everyday affairs. We may some day click off arguments on a machine with the same assurance that we now enter sales on a cash register. But the machine of logic will not look like a cash register, even of the streamlined model.

So much for the manipulation of ideas and their insertion into the record. Thus far we seem to be worse off than before—for we can enormously extend the record; yet even in its present bulk we can hardly consult it. This is a much larger matter than merely the extraction of data for the purposes of scientific research; it involves the entire process by which man profits by his inheritance of acquired knowledge. The prime action of use is selection, and here we are halting indeed. There may be millions of fine thoughts, and the account of the experience on which they are based, all encased within stone walls of acceptable architectural form; but if the scholar can get at only one a week by diligent search, his syntheses are not likely to keep up with the current scene.

Selection, in this broad sense, is a stone adze in the hands of a cabinetmaker. Yet, in a narrow sense and in other areas, something has already been done mechanically on selection. The personnel officer of a factory drops a stack of a few thousand employee cards into a selecting machine, sets a code in accordance with an established convention, and produces in a short time a list of all employees who live in Trenton and know Spanish. Even such devices are much too slow when it comes, for example, to matching a set of fingerprints with one of five million on file. Selection devices of this sort will soon be speeded up from their present rate of reviewing data at a few hundred a minute. By the use of photocells and microfilm they will survey items at the rate of a thousand a second, and will print out duplicates of those selected.

This process, however, is simple selection: it proceeds by examining in turn every one of a large set of items, and by picking out those which have certain specified characteristics. There is another form of selection best illustrated by the automatic telephone exchange. You dial a number and the machine selects and connects just one of a million possible stations. It does not run over them all. It pays attention only to a class given by a first digit, then only to a subclass of this given by the second digit, and so on; and thus proceeds rapidly and almost unerringly to the selected station. It requires a few seconds to make the selection, although the process could be speeded up if increased speed were economically warranted. If necessary, it could be made extremely fast by substituting thermionic-tube switching for mechanical switching, so that the full selection could be made in one one-hundredth of a second. No one would wish to spend the money necessary to make this change in the telephone system, but the general idea is applicable elsewhere.

Take the prosaic problem of the great department store. Every time a charge sale is made, there are a number of things to be done. The inventory needs to be revised, the salesman needs to be given credit for the sale, the general accounts need an entry, and, most important, the customer needs to be charged. A central records device has been developed in which much of this work is done conveniently. The salesman places on a stand the customer's identification card, his own card, and the card taken from the article sold—all punched cards. When he pulls a lever, contacts are made through the holes, machinery at a central point makes the necessary computations and entries, and the proper receipt is printed for the salesman to pass to the customer.

But there may be ten thousand charge customers doing business with the store, and before the full operation can be completed someone has to select the right card and insert it at the central office. Now rapid selection can slide just the proper card into position in an instant or two, and return it afterward. Another difficulty occurs, however. Someone must read a total on the card, so that the machine can add its computed item to it. Conceivably the cards might be of the dry photography type I have described. Existing totals could then be read by photocell, and the new total entered by an electron beam.

The cards may be in miniature, so that they occupy little space. They must move quickly. They need not be transferred far, but merely into position so that the photocell and recorder can operate on them. Positional dots can enter the data. At the end of the month a machine can readily be made to read these and to print an ordinary bill. With tube selection, in which no mechanical parts are involved in the switches, little time need be occupied in bringing the correct card into use—a second should suffice for the entire operation. The whole record on the card may be made by magnetic dots on a steel sheet if desired, instead of dots to be observed optically, following the scheme by which Poulsen long ago put speech on a magnetic wire. This method has the advantage of simplicity and ease of erasure. By using photography, however one can arrange to project the record in enlarged form and at a distance by using the process common in television equipment.

One can consider rapid selection of this form, and distant projection for other purposes. To be able to key one sheet of a million before an operator in a second or two, with the possibility of then adding notes thereto, is suggestive in many ways. It might even be of use in libraries, but that is another story. At any rate, there are now some interesting combinations possible. One might, for example, speak to a microphone, in the manner described in connection with the speech controlled typewriter, and thus make his selections. It would certainly beat the usual file clerk.

11.6

The real heart of the matter of selection, however, goes deeper than a lag in the adoption of mechanisms by libraries, or a lack of development of devices for their use. Our ineptitude in getting at the record is largely caused by the artificiality of systems of indexing. When data of any sort are placed in storage, they are filed alphabetically or numerically, and information is found (when it is) by tracing it down from subclass to subclass. It can be in only one place, unless duplicates are used; one has to have rules as to which path will locate it, and the rules are cumbersome. Having found one item, moreover, one has to emerge from the system and re-enter on a new path.

The human mind does not work that way. It operates by association. With one item in its grasp, it snaps instantly to the next that is suggested by the association of thoughts, in accordance with some intricate web of trails carried by the cells of the brain. It has other characteristics, of course; trails that are not frequently followed are prone to fade, items are not fully permanent, memory is transitory. Yet the speed of action, the intricacy of trails, the detail of mental pictures, is awe-inspiring beyond all else in nature.

Man cannot hope fully to duplicate this mental process artificially, but he certainly ought to be able to learn from it. In minor ways he may even improve, for his records have relative permanency. The first idea, however, to be drawn from the analogy concerns selection. Selection by association, rather than indexing, may yet be mechanized. One cannot hope thus to equal the speed and flexibility with which the mind follows an associative trail, but it should be possible to beat the mind decisively in regard to the permanence and clarity of the items resurrected from storage.

Consider a future device for individual use, which is a sort of mechanized private file and library. It needs a name, and, to coin one at random, "memex" will do. A memex is a device in which an individual stores all his books, records, and communications, and which is mechanized so that it may be consulted with exceeding speed and flexibility. It is an enlarged intimate supplement to his memory.

It consists of a desk, and while it can presumably be operated from a distance, it is primarily the piece of furniture at which he works. On the top are slanting translucent screens, on which material can be projected for convenient reading. There is a keyboard, and sets of buttons and levers. Otherwise it looks like an ordinary desk.

In one end is the stored material. The matter of bulk is well taken care of by improved microfilm. Only a small part of the interior of the memex is devoted to storage, the rest to mechanism. Yet if the user inserted 5000 pages of material a day it would take him hundreds of years to fill the repository, so he can be profligate and enter material freely.

Most of the memex contents are purchased on microfilm ready for insertion. Books of all sorts, pictures, current periodicals, newspapers, are thus obtained and dropped into place. Business correspondence takes the same path. And there is provision for direct entry. On the top of the memex is a transparent platen. On this are placed longhand notes, photographs, memoranda, all sorts of things. When one is in place, the depression of a lever causes it to be photographed onto the next blank space in a section of the memex film, dry photography being employed. There is, of course, provision for consultation of the record by the usual scheme of indexing. If the user wishes to consult a certain book, he taps its code on the keyboard, and the title page of the book promptly appears before him, projected onto one of his viewing positions. Frequently-used codes are mnemonic, so that he seldom consults his code book; but when he does, a single tap of a key projects it for his use. Moreover, he has supplemental levers. On deflecting one of these levers to the right he runs through the book before him, each page in turn being projected at a speed which just allows a recognizing glance at each. If he deflects it further to the right, he steps through the book 10 pages at a time; still further at 100 pages at a time. Deflection to the left gives him the same control backwards.

A special button transfers him immediately to the first page of the index. Any given book of his library can thus be called up and consulted with far greater facility than if it were taken from a shelf. As he has several projection positions, he can leave one item in position while he calls up another. He can add marginal notes and comments, taking advantage of one possible type of dry photography, and it could even be arranged so that he can do this by a stylus scheme, such as is now employed in the telautograph seen in railroad waiting rooms, just as though he had the physical page before him.

11.7

All this is conventional, except for the projection forward of present-day mechanisms and gadgetry. It affords an immediate step, however, to associative indexing, the basic idea of which is a provision whereby any item may be caused at will to select immediately and automatically another. This is the essential feature of the memex. The process of tying two items together is the important thing.

When the user is building a trail, he names it, inserts the name in his code book, and taps it out on his keyboard. Before him are the two items to be joined, projected onto adjacent viewing positions. At the bottom of each there are a number of blank code spaces, and a pointer is set to indicate one of these on each item. The user taps a single key, and the items are permanently joined. In each code space appears the code word. Out of view, but also in the code space, is inserted a set of dots for photocell viewing; and on each item these dots by their positions designate the index number of the other item.

Thereafter, at any time, when one of these items is in view, the other can be instantly recalled merely by tapping a button below the corresponding code space. Moreover, when numerous items have been thus joined together to form a trail, they can be reviewed in turn, rapidly or slowly, by deflecting a lever like that used for turning the pages of a book. It is exactly as though the physical items had been gathered together from widely separated sources and bound together to form a new book. It is more than this, for any item can be joined into numerous trails.

The owner of the memex, let us say, is interested in the origin and properties of the bow and arrow. Specifically he is studying why the short Turkish bow was apparently superior to the English long bow in the skirmishes of the Crusades. He has dozens of possibly pertinent books and articles in his memex. First he runs through an encyclopedia, finds an interesting but sketchy article, leaves it projected. Next, in a history, he finds another pertinent item, and ties the two together. Thus he goes, building a trail of many items. Occasionally he inserts a comment of his own, either linking it into the main trail or joining it by a side trail to a particular item. When it becomes evident that the elastic properties of available materials had a great deal to do with the bow, he branches off on a side trail which takes him through textbooks on elasticity and tables of physical constants. He inserts a page of longhand analysis of his own. Thus he builds a trail of his interest through the maze of materials available to him.

And his trails do not fade. Several years later, his talk with a friend turns to the queer ways in which a people resist innovations, even of vital interest. He has an example, in the fact that the outraged Europeans still failed to adopt the Turkish bow. In fact he has a trail on it. A touch brings up the code book. Tapping a few keys projects the head of the trail. A lever runs through it at will, stopping at interesting items, going off on side excursions. It is an interesting trail, pertinent to the discussion. So he sets a reproducer in action, photographs the whole trail out, and passes it to his friend for insertion in his own memex, there to be linked into the more general trail.

11.8

Wholly new forms of encyclopedias will appear, ready made with a mesh of associative trails running through them, ready to be dropped into the memex and there amplified. The lawyer has at his touch the associated opinions and decisions of his whole experience, and of the experience of friends and authorities. The patent attorney has on call the millions of issued patents, with familiar trails to every point of his client's interest. The physician, puzzled by a patient's reactions, strikes the trail established in studying an earlier similar case, and runs rapidly through analogous case histories, with side references to the classics for the pertinent anatomy and histology. The chemist, struggling with the synthesis of an organic compound, has all the chemical literature before him in his laboratory, with trails following the analogies of compounds, and side trails to their physical and chemical behavior.

The historian, with a vast chronological account of a people, parallels it with a skip trail which stops only on the salient items, and can follow at any time contemporary trails which lead him all over civilization at a particular epoch. There is a new profession of trail blazers, those who find delight in the task of establishing useful trails through the enormous mass of the common record. The inheritance from the master becomes, not only his additions to the world's record, but for his disciples the entire scaffolding by which they were erected.

Thus science may implement the ways in which man produces, stores, and consults the record of the race. It might be striking to outline the instrumentalities of the future more spectacularly, rather than to stick closely to methods and elements now known and undergoing rapid development, as has been done here. Technical difficulties of all sorts have been ignored, certainly, but also ignored are means as yet unknown which may come any day to accelerate technical progress as violently as did the advent of the thermionic tube. In order that the picture may not be too commonplace, by reason of sticking to present-day patterns, it may be well to mention one such possibility, not to prophesy but merely to suggest, for prophecy based on extension of the known has substance, while prophecy founded on the unknown is only a doubly involved guess.

All our steps in creating or absorbing material of the record proceed through one of the senses—the tactile when we touch keys, the oral when we speak or listen, the visual when we read. Is it not possible that some day the path may be established more directly? We know that when the eye sees, all the consequent information is transmitted to the brain by means of electrical vibrations in the channel of the optic nerve. This is an exact analogy with the electrical vibrations which occur in the cable of a television set: they convey the picture from the photocells which see it to the radio transmitter from which it is broadcast. We know further that if we can approach that cable with the proper instruments, we do not need to touch it; we can pick up those vibrations by electrical induction and thus discover and reproduce the scene which is being transmitted, just as a telephone wire may be tapped for its message. The impulses which flow in the arm nerves of a typist convey to her fingers the translated information which reaches her eye or ear, in order that the fingers may be caused to strike the proper keys. Might not these currents be intercepted, either in the original form in which information is conveyed to the brain, or in the marvelously metamorphosed form in which they then proceed to the hand?

By bone conduction we already introduce sounds: into the nerve channels of the deaf in order that they may hear. Is it not possible that we may learn to introduce them without the present cumbersomeness of first transforming electrical vibrations to mechanical ones, which the human mechanism promptly transforms back to the electrical form? With a couple of electrodes on the skull the encephalograph now produces pen-and-ink traces which bear some relation to the electrical phenomena going on in the brain itself. True, the record is unintelligible, except as it points out certain gross misfunctioning of the cerebral mechanism; but who would now place bounds on where such a thing may lead?

In the outside world, all forms of intelligence whether of sound or sight, have been reduced to the form of varying currents in an electric circuit in order that they may be transmitted. Inside the human frame exactly the same sort of process occurs. Must we always transform to mechanical movements in order to proceed from one electrical phenomenon to another? It is a suggestive thought, but it hardly warrants prediction without losing touch with reality and immediateness.

Presumably man's spirit should be elevated if he can better review his shady past and analyze more completely and objectively his present problems. He has built a civilization so complex that he needs to mechanize his records more fully if he is to push his experiment to its logical conclusion and not merely become bogged down part way there by overtaxing his limited memory. His excursions may be more enjoyable if he can reacquire the privilege of forgetting the manifold things he does not need to have immediately at hand, with some assurance that he can find them again if they prove important.

The applications of science have built man a well-supplied house, and are teaching him to live healthily therein. They have enabled him to throw masses of people against one another with cruel weapons. They may yet allow him truly to encompass the great record and to grow in the wisdom of race experience. He may perish in conflict before he learns to wield that record for his true good. Yet, in the application of science to the needs and desires of man, it would seem to be a singularly unfortunate stage at which to terminate the process, or to lose hope as to the outcome.

12 A Mathematical Theory of Communication (1948)

Claude Shannon

After writing his important Master's thesis (chapter 8), Claude Shannon developed an algebra for computations in Mendelian genetics, submitting it as his PhD dissertation in 1940. He then moved to Bell Labs and, in this paper, invented information theory. The advantages of binary notation were already known; the EDVAC team had settled on binary for all internal storage and arithmetic. The "First Draft" states unequivocally, "The *(capacity) unit of memory* is the ability to retain the value of one binary digit" (page 103 of this volume). Shannon famously dubs that unit the "bit," though attributes the coinage to mathematician John Tukey. Shannon then pursues the question of how to encode long messages with a relatively small number of bits when not all messages may be possible or equally likely. This work is the basis not only for the theory of data compression and its limits (Huffman codes, for example [Huffman, 1952]) but for the important theory of reconstruction of messages when their bits may be corrupted in transit from source to destination (see chapter 13). The term "entropy," now in common usage, is here borrowed from statistical physics to represent a measure of the information content of a source.

Shannon later published a third masterpiece, "Communication Theory of Secrecy Systems" (Shannon, 1949), which laid out some of the principles of cryptography from an information-theoretic viewpoint. It was based on classified work he had done under a contract between Bell Labs and the U.S. military. Shannon returned to MIT as a professor in 1958 and long remained the playful tinkerer. He juggled, rode a unicycle, and sometimes did both simultaneously. He built a machine that juggled and programmed a mechanical mouse to learn its path out of a maze.

He eventually became less prolific mathematically and stopped publishing and teaching, finally dying in 2001 of Alzheimer's disease at the age of 84.

12.0 Introduction

THE recent development of various methods of modulation such as PCM and PPM which exchange bandwidth for signal-to-noise ratio has intensified the interest in a general theory of communication. [EDITOR: Pulse Code Modulation and Pulse Position Modulation.] A basis for such a theory is contained in the important papers of Nyquist (1924, 1928) and Hartley (1928) on this subject. In the present paper we will extend the theory to include a number of new factors,

Reprinted from Shannon (1948), with permission from Nokia Bell Labs.

in particular the effect of noise in the channel, and the savings possible due to the statistical structure of the original message and due to the nature of the final destination of the information.

The fundamental problem of communication is that of reproducing at one point either exactly or approximately a message selected at another point. Frequently the messages have meaning; that is they refer to or are correlated according to some system with certain physical or conceptual entities. These semantic aspects of communication are irrelevant to the engineering problem. The significant aspect is that the actual message is one *selected from a set* of possible messages. The system must be designed to operate for each possible selection, not just the one which will actually be chosen since this is unknown at the time of design.

If the number of messages in the set is finite then this number or any monotonic function of this number can be regarded as a measure of the information produced when one message is chosen from the set, all choices being equally likely. As was pointed out by Hartley the most natural choice is the logarithmic function. Although this definition must be generalized considerably when we consider the influence of the statistics of the message and when we have a continuous range of messages, we will in all cases use an essentially logarithmic measure.

The logarithmic measure is more convenient for various reasons:

1. It is practically more useful. Parameters of engineering importance such as time, bandwidth, number of relays, etc., tend to vary linearly with the logarithm of the number of possibilities. For example, adding one relay to a group doubles the number of possible states of the relays. It adds 1 to the base 2 logarithm of this number. Doubling the time roughly squares the number of possible messages, or doubles the logarithm, etc.

2. It is nearer to our intuitive feeling as to the proper measure. This is closely related to (1) since we intuitively measure entities by linear comparison with common standards. One feels, for example, that two punched cards should have twice the capacity of one for information storage, and two identical channels twice the capacity of one for transmitting information.

3. It is mathematically more suitable. Many of the limiting operations are simple in terms of the logarithm but would require clumsy restatement in terms of the number of possibilities.

The choice of a logarithmic base corresponds to the choice of a unit for measuring information. If the base 2 is used the resulting units may be called binary digits, or more briefly *bits*, a word suggested by J. W. Tukey. A device with two stable positions, such as a relay or a flip-flop circuit, can store one bit of information. N such devices can store N bits, since the total number of possible states is 2^N and $\log_2 2^N = N$. If the base 10 is used the units may be called decimal digits. Since

$$\log_2 M = \log_{10} M / \log_{10} 2$$
$$= 3.32 \log_{10} M,$$

a decimal digit is about $3\frac{1}{3}$ bits. A digit wheel on a desk computing machine has ten stable positions and therefore has a storage capacity of one decimal digit. In analytical work where

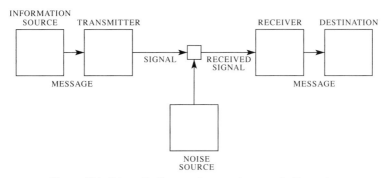

Figure 12.1: Schematic diagram of a general communication system.

integration and differentiation are involved the base e is sometimes useful. The resulting units of information will be called natural units. Change from the base a to base b merely requires multiplication by $\log_b a$.

By a communication system we will mean a system of the type indicated schematically in Figure 12.1. It consists of essentially five parts:

1. An *information source* which produces a message or sequence of messages to be communicated to the receiving terminal. The message may be of various types: (a) A sequence of letters as in a telegraph of teletype system; (b) A single function of time $f(t)$ as in radio or telephony; (c) A function of time and other variables as in black and white television—here the message may be thought of as a function $f(x, y, t)$ of two space coordinates and time, the light intensity at point (x, y) and time t on a pickup tube plate; (d) Two or more functions of time, say $f(t)$, $g(t)$, $h(t)$—this is the case in "three-dimensional" sound transmission or if the system is intended to service several individual channels in multiplex; (e) Several functions of several variables—in color television the message consists of three functions $f(x, y, t)$, $g(x, y, t)$, $h(x, y, t)$ defined in a three-dimensional continuum—we may also think of these three functions as components of a vector field defined in the region—similarly, several black and white television sources would produce "messages" consisting of a number of functions of three variables; (f) Various combinations also occur, for example in television with an associated audio channel.

2. A *transmitter* which operates on the message in some way to produce a signal suitable for transmission over the channel. In telephony this operation consists merely of changing sound pressure into a proportional electrical current. In telegraphy we have an encoding operation which produces a sequence of dots, dashes and spaces on the channel corresponding to the message. In a multiplex PCM system the different speech functions must be sampled, compressed, quantized and encoded, and finally interleaved properly to construct the signal. Vocoder systems, television and frequency modulation are other examples of complex operations applied to the message to obtain the signal.

3. The *channel* is merely the medium used to transmit the signal from transmitter to receiver. It may be a pair of wires, a coaxial cable, a band of radio frequencies, a beam of light, etc.

4. The *receiver* ordinarily performs the inverse operation of that done by the transmitter, reconstructing the message from the signal.

5. The *destination* is the person (or thing) for whom the message is intended.

We wish to consider certain general problems involving communication systems. To do this it is first necessary to represent the various elements involved as mathematical entities, suitably idealized from their physical counterparts. We may roughly classify communication systems into three main categories: discrete, continuous and mixed. By a discrete system we will mean one in which both the message and the signal are a sequence of discrete symbols. A typical case is telegraphy where the message is a sequence of letters and the signal a sequence of dots, dashes and spaces. A continuous system is one in which the message and signal are both treated as continuous functions, e.g., radio or television. A mixed system is one in which both discrete and continuous variables appear, e.g., PCM transmission of speech.

We first consider the discrete case. This case has applications not only in communication theory, but also in the theory of computing machines, the design of telephone exchanges and other fields. In addition the discrete case forms a foundation for the continuous and mixed cases which will be treated in the second half of the paper.

12.1   The Discrete Noiseless Channel

Teletype and telegraphy are two simple examples of a discrete channel for transmitting information. Generally, a discrete channel will mean a system whereby a sequence of choices from a finite set of elementary symbols $S_1, \ldots, S_n$ can be transmitted from one point to another. Each of the symbols S_i is assumed to have a certain duration in time t_i seconds (not necessarily the same for different S_i, for example the dots and dashes in telegraphy). It is not required that all possible sequences of the S_i be capable of transmission on the system; certain sequences only may be allowed. These will be possible signals for the channel. Thus in telegraphy suppose the symbols are: (1) A dot, consisting of line closure for a unit of time and then line open for a unit of time; (2) A dash, consisting of three time units of closure and one unit open; (3) A letter space consisting of, say, three units of line open; (4) A word space of six units of line open. We might place the restriction on allowable sequences that no spaces follow each other (for if two letter spaces are adjacent, it is identical with a word space). The question we now consider is how one can measure the capacity of such a channel to transmit information.

In the teletype case where all symbols are of the same duration, and any sequence of the 32 symbols is allowed the answer is easy. Each symbol represents five bits of information. If the system transmits n symbols per second it is natural to say that the channel has a capacity of $5n$ bits per second. This does not mean that the teletype channel will always be transmitting information at this rate—this is the maximum possible rate and whether or not the actual rate reaches this maximum depends on the source of information which feeds the channel, as will appear later. In the more general case with different lengths of symbols and constraints on the allowed sequences, we make the following definition:

Definition: The capacity C of a discrete channel is given by

$$C = \lim_{T \to \infty} \frac{\log N(T)}{T}$$

where $N(T)$ is the number of allowed signals of duration T.

It is easily seen that in the teletype case this reduces to the previous result. It can be shown that the limit in question will exist as a finite number in most cases of interest. Suppose all sequences of the symbols $S_1, \ldots, S_n$ are allowed and these symbols have durations $t_1, \ldots, t_n$. What is the channel capacity? If $N(t)$ represents the number of sequences of duration t we have

$$N(t) = N(t - t_1) + N(t - t_2) + \cdots + N(t - t_n).$$

The total number is equal to the sum of the numbers of sequences ending in $S_1, S_2, \ldots, S_n$ and these are $N(t - t_1)$, $N(t - t_2)$, $\ldots$, $N(t - t_n)$, respectively. According to a well-known result in finite differences, $N(t)$ is then asymptotic for large t to X_0^t where X_0 is the largest real solution of the characteristic equation $X^{-t_1} + X^{-t_2} + \cdots + X^{-t_n} = 1$, and therefore $C = \log X_0$.

In case there are restrictions on allowed sequences we may still often obtain a difference equation of this type and find C from the characteristic equation. In the telegraphy case mentioned above

$$N(t) = N(t - 2) + N(t - 4) + N(t - 5) + N(t - 7) + N(t - 8) + N(t - 10)$$

as we see by counting sequences of symbols according to the last or next to the last symbol occurring. Hence C is $-\log \mu_0$ where μ_0 is the positive root of $1 = \mu^2 + \mu^4 + \mu^5 + \mu^7 + \mu^8 + \mu^{10}$. Solving this we find $C = 0.539$.

A very general type of restriction which may be placed on allowed sequences is the following: We imagine a number of possible states $a_1, a_2, \ldots, a_m$. For each state only certain symbols from the set $S_1, \ldots, S_n$ can be transmitted (different subsets for the different states). When one of these has been transmitted the state changes to a new state depending both on the old state and the particular symbol transmitted. The telegraph case is a simple example of this. There are two states depending on whether or not a space was the last symbol transmitted. If so, then only a dot or a dash can be sent next and the state always changes. If not, any symbol can be transmitted and the state changes if a space is sent, otherwise it remains the same. The conditions can be indicated in a linear graph as shown in Figure 12.2. The junction points correspond to the states and the lines indicate the symbols possible in a state and the resulting state. In Appendix 1 [EDITOR: omitted] it is shown that if the conditions on allowed sequences can be described in this form C will exist and can be calculated in accordance with the following result:

Theorem 1: Let $b_{ij}^{(s)}$ be the duration of the sth symbol which is allowable in state i and leads to state j. Then the channel capacity C is equal to $\log W$ where W is the largest real root of the *determinant equation:*

$$\left| \sum_s W^{-b_{ij}^{(s)}} - \delta_{ij} \right| = 0$$

where $\delta_{ij} = 1$ if $i = j$ and is zero otherwise.

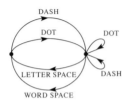

DASH

DOT   DOT

LETTER SPACE   DASH

WORD SPACE

Figure 12.2: Graphical representation of the constraints on telegraph symbols.

For example, in the telegraph case (Figure 12.2) the determinant is:

$$\left| \begin{array}{cc} -1 & (W^{-1} + W^{-4}) \\ (W^{-3} + W^{-6}) & (W^{-2} + W^{-4} - 1) \end{array} \right| = 0.$$

On expansion this leads to the equation given above for this case.

12.2   The Discrete Source of Information

We have seen that under very general conditions the logarithm of the number of possible signals in a discrete channel increases linearly with time. The capacity to transmit information can be specified by giving this rate of increase, the number of bits per second required to specify the particular signal used. We now consider the information source. How is an information source to be described mathematically, and how much information in bits per second is produced in a given source? The main point at issue is the effect of statistical knowledge about the source in reducing the required capacity of the channel, by the use of proper encoding of the information. In telegraphy, for example, the messages to be transmitted consist of sequences of letters. These sequences, however, are not completely random. In general, they form sentences and have the statistical structure of, say, English. The letter E occurs more frequently than Q, the sequence TH more frequently than XP, etc. The existence of this structure allows one to make a saving in time (or channel capacity) by properly encoding the message sequences into signal sequences. This is already done to a limited extent in telegraphy by using the shortest channel symbol, a dot, for the most common English letter E; while the infrequent letters, Q, X, Z are represented by longer sequences of dots and dashes. This idea is carried still further in certain commercial codes where common words and phrases are represented by four- or five-letter code groups with a considerable saving in average time. The standardized greeting and anniversary telegrams now in use extend this to the point of encoding a sentence or two into a relatively short sequence of numbers.

We can think of a discrete source as generating the message, symbol by symbol. It will choose successive symbols according to certain probabilities depending, in general, on preceding choices as well as the particular symbols in question. A physical system, or a mathematical model of a system which produces such a sequence of symbols governed by a set of probabilities, is known as a stochastic process (see, for example, Chandrasekhar [1943]). We may consider a discrete source, therefore, to be represented by a stochastic process. Conversely, any stochastic process which produces a discrete sequence of symbols chosen from a finite set may be considered a discrete source. This will include such cases as:

1. Natural written languages such as English, German, Chinese.
2. Continuous information sources that have been rendered discrete by some quantizing process. For example, the quantized speech from a PCM transmitter, or a quantized television signal.
3. Mathematical cases where we merely define abstractly a stochastic process which generates a sequence of symbols. The following are examples of this last type of source.

(A) Suppose we have five letters A, B, C, D, E which are chosen each with probability .2, successive choices being independent. This would lead to a sequence of which the following is a typical example.

B D C B C E C C C A D C B D D A A E C E E A

A B B D A E E C A C E E B A E E C B C E A D.

This was constructed with the use of a table of random numbers (Kendall, 1939).

(B) Using the same five letters let the probabilities be .4, .1, .2, .2, .1, respectively, with successive choices independent. A typical message from this source is then:

A A A C D C B D C E A A D A D A C E D A

E A D C A B E D A D D C E C A A A A A D.

(C) A more complicated structure is obtained if successive symbols are not chosen independently but their probabilities depend on preceding letters. In the simplest case of this type a choice depends only on the preceding letter and not on ones before that. The statistical structure can then be described by a set of transition probabilities $p_i(j)$, the probability that letter i is followed by letter j. The indices i and j range over all the possible symbols. A second equivalent way of specifying the structure is to give the "digram" probabilities $p(i, j)$, i.e., the relative frequency of the digram i j. The letter frequencies $p(i)$ (the probability of letter i), the transition probabilities $p_i(j)$ and the digram probabilities $p(i, j)$ are related by the following formulas:

$$p(i) = \sum_j p(i, j) = \sum_j p(j, i) = \sum_j p(j)p_j(i)$$

$$p(i, j) = p(i)p_i(j)$$

$$\sum_j p_i(j) = \sum_i p(i) = \sum_{i,j} p(i, j) = 1.$$

As a specific example suppose there are three letters A, B, C with the probability tables:

$p_i(j)$	j				i	$p(i)$		$p(i,j)$	j		
	A	B	C		A	$\frac{9}{27}$			A	B	C
A	0	$\frac{4}{5}$	$\frac{1}{5}$		B	$\frac{16}{27}$		A	0	$\frac{4}{15}$	$\frac{1}{15}$
i B	$\frac{1}{2}$	$\frac{1}{2}$	0		C	$\frac{2}{27}$		i B	$\frac{8}{27}$	$\frac{8}{27}$	0
C	$\frac{1}{2}$	$\frac{2}{5}$	$\frac{1}{10}$					C	$\frac{1}{27}$	$\frac{4}{135}$	$\frac{1}{135}$

A typical message from this source is the following:

A B B A B A B A B A B A B A B B B A B B B B B A B A B A B A B A B B B A C
A C A B B A B B B B B A B B A B A C B B B A B A.

The next increase in complexity would involve trigram frequencies but no more. The choice of a letter would depend on the preceding two letters but not on the message before that point. A set of trigram frequencies $p(i, j, k)$ or equivalently a set of transition probabilities $p_{ij}(k)$ would be required. Continuing in this way one obtains successively more complicated stochastic processes. In the general n-gram case a set of n-gram probabilities $p(i_1, i_2, \ldots, i_n)$ or of transition probabilities $p_{i_1, i_2, \ldots, i_{n-1}}(i_n)$ is required to specify the statistical structure.

(D)   Stochastic processes can also be defined which produce a text consisting of a sequence of n "words." Suppose there are five letters A, B, C, D, E and 16 "words" in the language with associated probabilities:

.10 A	.16 BEBE	.11 CABED	.04 DEB
.04 ADEB	.04 BED	.05 CEED	.15 DEED
.05 ADEE	.02 BEED	.08 DAB	.01 EAB
.01 BADD	.05 CA	.04 DAD	.05 EE

Suppose successive "words" are chosen independently and are separated by a space. A typical message might be:

DAB EE A BEBE DEED DEB ADEE ADEE EE DEB BEBE BEBE BEBE ADEE BED
DEED DEED CEED ADEE A DEED DEED BEBE CABED BEBE BED DAB DEED
ADEB.

If all the words are of finite length this process is equivalent to one of the preceding type, but the description may be simpler in terms of the word structure and probabilities. We may also generalize here and introduce transition probabilities between words, etc.

These artificial languages are useful in constructing simple problems and examples to illustrate various possibilities. We can also approximate to a natural language by means of a series of simple artificial languages. The zero-order approximation is obtained by choosing all letters with the same probability and independently. The first-order approximation is obtained by choosing successive letters independently but each letter having the same probability that it has in the natural language. (Letter, digram, and trigram frequencies are given in Pratt [1939]. Word frequencies are tabulated in Dewey [1923].) Thus, in the first-order approximation to English, E is chosen with probability .12 (its frequency in normal English) and W with probability .02, but there is no influence between adjacent letters and no tendency to form the preferred digrams such as TH, ED, etc. In the second-order approximation, digram structure is introduced. After a letter is chosen, the next one is chosen in accordance with the frequencies with which the various letters follow the first one. This requires a table of digram frequencies $p_i(j)$. In the third-order approximation, trigram structure is introduced. Each letter is chosen with probabilities which depend on the preceding two letters.

12.3   The Series of Approximations to English

To give a visual idea of how this series of processes approaches a language, typical sequences in the approximations to English have been constructed and are given below. In all cases we have assumed a 27-symbol "alphabet," the 26 letters and a space.

1. Zero-order approximation (symbols independent and equiprobable).
    XFOML RXKHRJFFJUJ ZLPWCFWKCYJ FFJEYVKCQSGHYD
    QPAAMKBZAACIBZLHJQD.
2. First-order approximation (symbols independent but with frequencies of English text).
    OCRO HLI RGWR NMIELWIS EU LL NBNESEBYA TH EEI ALHENHTTPA
    OOBTTVA NAH BRL.
3. Second-order approximation (digram structure as in English).
    ON IE ANTSOUTINYS ARE T INCTORE ST BE S DEAMY ACHIN D ILONASIVE
    TUCOOWE AT TEASONARE FUSO TIZIN ANDY TOBE SEACE CTISBE.
4. Third-order approximation (trigram structure as in English).
    IN NO IST LAT WHEY CRATICT FROURE BIRS GROCID PONDENOME OF
    DEMONSTURES OF THE REPTAGIN IS REGOACTIONA OF CRE.
5. First-order word approximation. Rather than continue with tetragram, . . . , n-gram structure it is easier and better to jump at this point to word units. Here words are chosen independently but with their appropriate frequencies (Dewey, 1923).
    REPRESENTING AND SPEEDILY IS AN GOOD APT OR COME CAN DIFFERENT
    NATURAL HERE HE THE A IN CAME THE TO OF TO EXPERT GRAY COME TO
    FURNISHES THE LINE MESSAGE HAD BE THESE.
6. Second-order word approximation. The word transition probabilities are correct but no further structure is included.
    THE HEAD AND IN FRONTAL ATTACK ON AN ENGLISH WRITER THAT THE
    CHARACTER OF THIS POINT IS THEREFORE ANOTHER METHOD FOR THE
    LETTERS THAT THE TIME OF WHO EVER TOLD THE PROBLEM FOR AN
    UNEXPECTED.

The resemblance to ordinary English text increases quite noticeably at each of the above steps. Note that these samples have reasonably good structure out to about twice the range that is taken into account in their construction. Thus in (3) the statistical process insures reasonable text for two-letter sequences, but four-letter sequences from the sample can usually be fitted into good sentences. In (6) sequences of four or more words can easily be placed in sentences without unusual or strained constructions. The particular sequence of ten words "attack on an English writer that the character of this" is not at all unreasonable. It appears then that a sufficiently complex stochastic process will give a satisfactory representation of a discrete source.

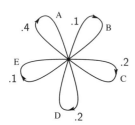

Figure 12.3: A graph corresponding to the source in example B.

The first two samples were constructed by the use of a book of random numbers in conjunction with (for example 2) a table of letter frequencies. This method might have been continued for (3), (4) and (5), since digram, trigram and word frequency tables are available, but a simpler equivalent method was used. To construct (3) for example, one opens a book at random and selects a letter at random on the page. This letter is recorded. The book is then opened to another page and one reads until this letter is encountered. The succeeding letter is then recorded. Turning to another page this second letter is searched for and the succeeding letter recorded, etc. A similar process was used for (4), (5) and (6). It would be interesting if further approximations could be constructed, but the labor involved becomes enormous at the next stage.

12.4   Graphical Representation of a Markoff Process

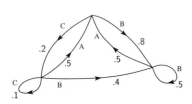

Figure 12.4: A graph corresponding to the source in example C.

Stochastic processes of the type described above are known mathematically as discrete Markoff processes and have been extensively studied in the literature (for a detailed treatment, see Frechet [1938]). The general case can be described as follows: There exist a finite number of possible "states" of a system; S_1, S_2, $\ldots$, S_n. In addition there is a set of transition probabilities, $p_i(j)$, the probability that if the system is in state S_i it will next go to state S_j. To make this Markoff process into an information source we need only assume that a letter is produced for each transition from one state to another. The states will correspond to the "residue of influence" from preceding letters.

The situation can be represented graphically as shown in Figures 12.3, 12.4 and 12.5. The "states" are the junction points in the graph and the probabilities and letters produced for a transition are given beside the corresponding line. Figure 12.3 is for the example B in §12.2, while Figure 12.4 corresponds to the example C. In Figure 12.3, there is only one state since successive letters are independent. In Figure 12.4 there are as many states as letters. If a trigram example were constructed there would be at most n^2 states corresponding to the possible pairs of letters preceding the one being chosen. Figure 12.5 is a graph for the case of word structure in example D. Here S corresponds to the "space" symbol. ...

12.6 Choice, Uncertainty, and Entropy

We have represented a discrete information source as a Markoff process. Can we define a quantity which will measure, in some sense, how much information is "produced" by such a process, or better, at what rate information is produced?

Suppose we have a set of possible events whose probabilities of occurrence are $p_1, p_2, \ldots, p_n$. These probabilities are known but that is all we know concerning which event will occur. Can we find a measure of how much "choice" is involved in the selection of the event or of how uncertain we are of the outcome?

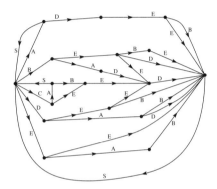

Figure 12.5: A graph corresponding to the source in example D.

If there is such a measure, say $H(p_1, p_2, \ldots, p_n)$, it is reasonable to require of it the following properties:

1. H should be continuous in the p_i.
2. If all the p_i are equal, $p_i = \frac{1}{n}$, then H should be a monotonic increasing function of n. With equally likely events there is more choice, or uncertainty, when there are more possible events.
3. If a choice be broken down into two successive choices, the original H should be the weighted sum of the individual values of H. The meaning of this is illustrated in Figure 12.6. At the left we have three possibilities $p_1 = \frac{1}{2}$, $p_2 = \frac{1}{3}$, $p_3 = \frac{1}{6}$. On the right we first choose between two possibilities each with probability $\frac{1}{2}$, and if the second occurs make another choice with probabilities $\frac{2}{3}$, $\frac{1}{3}$. The final results have the same probabilities as before. We require, in this special case, that

$$H\left(\frac{1}{2}, \frac{1}{3}, \frac{1}{6}\right) = H\left(\frac{1}{2}, \frac{1}{2}\right) + \frac{1}{2}H\left(\frac{2}{3}, \frac{1}{3}\right).$$

The coefficient $\frac{1}{2}$ is because this second choice only occurs half the time.

In Appendix 2 [EDITOR: omitted], the following result is established:

Theorem 2: The only H satisfying the three above assumptions is of the form:

$$H = -K \sum_{i=1}^{n} p_i \log p_i$$

where K is a positive constant.

This theorem, and the assumptions required for its proof, are in no way necessary for the present theory. It is given chiefly to lend a certain plausibility to some of our later definitions. The real justification of these definitions, however, will reside in their implications.

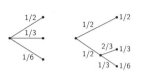

Figure 12.6: Decomposition of a choice from three possibilities.

Quantities of the form $H = -\sum p_i \log p_i$ (the constant K merely amounts to a choice of a unit of measure) play a central role in information theory as measures of information, choice and uncertainty. The form of H will be recognized as that of entropy as defined in certain formulations of statistical mechanics where p_i is the probability of a system being in cell i of its phase space. H is then, for example, the H in Boltzmann's famous H theorem. We shall call $H = -\sum p_i \log p_i$ the entropy of the set of probabilities $p_1, \ldots, p_n$. If x is a chance variable we will write $H(x)$ for its entropy; thus x is not an argument of a function but a label for a number, to differentiate it from $H(y)$ say, the entropy of the chance variable y.

The entropy in the case of two possibilities with probabilities p and $q = 1 - p$, namely

$$H = -(p \log p + q \log q)$$

is plotted in Figure 12.7 as a function of p.

The quantity H has a number of interesting properties which further substantiate it as a reasonable measure of choice or information.

1. $H = 0$ if and only if all the p_i but one are zero, this one having the value unity. Thus only when we are certain of the outcome does H vanish. Otherwise H is positive.

2. For a given n, H is a maximum and equal to $\log n$ when all the p_i are equal (i.e., $\frac{1}{n}$). This is also intuitively the most uncertain situation.

3. Suppose there are two events, x and y, in question with m possibilities for the first and n for the second. Let $p(i, j)$ be the probability of the joint occurrence of i for the first and j for the second. The entropy of the joint event is

$$H(x, y) = -\sum_{i,j} p(i, j) \log p(i, j)$$

while

$$H(x) = -\sum_{i,j} p(i, j) \log \sum_{j} p(i, j)$$
$$H(y) = -\sum_{i,j} p(i, j) \log \sum_{i} p(i, j).$$

It is easily shown that $H(x, y) \leq H(x) + H(y)$, with equality only if the events are independent (i.e., $p(i, j) = p(i)p(j)$). The uncertainty of a joint event is less than or equal to the sum of the individual uncertainties.

4. Any change toward equalization of the probabilities p_1, p_2, ..., p_n increases H. Thus if $p_1 < p_2$ and we increase p_1, decreasing p_2 an equal amount so that p_1 and p_2 are more nearly equal, then H increases. More generally, if we perform any "averaging" operation on the p_i of the form

$$p_i' = \sum_j a_{ij} p_j$$

where $\sum_i a_{ij} = \sum_j a_{ij} = 1$, and all $a_{ij} \geq 0$, then H increases (except in the special case where this transformation amounts to no more than a permutation of the p_j with H of course remaining the same).

5. Suppose there are two chance events x and y as in 3, not necessarily independent. For any particular value i that x can assume there is a conditional probability $p_i(j)$ that y has the value j. This is given by

$$p_i(j) = \frac{p(i, j)}{\sum_j p(i, j)}.$$

We define the *conditional entropy* of y, $H_x(y)$ as the average of the entropy of y for each value of x, weighted according to the probability of getting that particular x. That is

$$H_x(y) = -\sum_{i,j} p(i, j) \log p_i(j).$$

This quantity measures how uncertain we are of y on the average when we know x. Substituting the value of $p_i(j)$ we obtain

$$H_x(y) = -\sum_{i,j} p(i, j) \log p(i, j) + \sum_{i,j} p(i, j) \log \sum_j p(i, j)$$

$$= H(x, y) - H(x)$$

or $H(x, y) = H(x) + H_x(y)$. The uncertainty (or entropy) of the joint event x, y is the uncertainty of x plus the uncertainty of y when x is known.

6. From 3 and 5 we have $H(x) + H(y) \geq H(x, y) = H(x) + H_x(y)$. Hence $H(y) \geq H_x(y)$. The uncertainty of y is never increased by knowledge of x. It will be decreased unless x and y are independent events, in which case it is not changed.

12.7   The Entropy of an Information Source

Consider a discrete source of the finite state type considered above. For each possible state i there will be a set of probabilities $p_i(j)$ of producing the various possible symbols j. Thus there is an entropy H_i for each state. The entropy of the source will be defined as the average of these

H_i weighted in accordance with the probability of occurrence of the states in question:

$$H = \sum_i P_i H_i$$

$$= - \sum_{i,j} P_i p_i(j) \log p_i(j).$$

This is the entropy of the source per symbol of text. If the Markoff process is proceeding at a definite time rate there is also an entropy per second $H' = \sum_i f_i H_i$, where f_i is the average frequency (occurrences per second) of state i. Clearly $H' = mH$ where m is the average number of symbols produced per second. H or H' measures the amount of information generated by the source per symbol or per second. If the logarithmic base is 2, they will represent bits per symbol or per second.

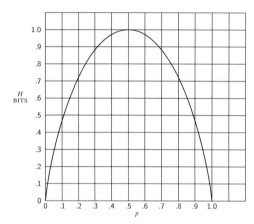

Figure 12.7: Entropy in the case of two possibilities with probabilities p and $(1 - p)$.

If successive symbols are independent then H is simply $-\sum p_i \log p_i$ where p_i is the probability of symbol i. Suppose in this case we consider a long message of N symbols. It will contain with high probability about $p_1 N$ occurrences of the first symbol, $p_2 N$ occurrences of the second, etc. Hence the probability of this particular message will be roughly

$$p \doteq p_1^{p_1 N} p_2^{p_2 N} \cdots p_n^{p_n N}$$

or

$$\log p \doteq N \sum_i p_i \log p_i$$

$$\log p \doteq -NH$$

$$H \doteq \frac{\log 1/p}{N}.$$

H is thus approximately the logarithm of the reciprocal probability of a typical long sequence divided by the number of symbols in the sequence. The same result holds for any source. . . .

13 Error Detecting and Error Correcting Codes (1950)

R. W. Hamming

We take it for granted today that if a number is stored in computer memory and then retrieved, the number that comes out of memory is the same as the number that went in. If the value of π is stored, then when a program uses that value it will be 3.14159 every time, never 3.24159 or 3.14158. Similarly, no program meant to access memory location 2468 will ever access location 2478 instead. Computers malfunction, to be sure, because of programming errors, short circuits, and bad input data. But the bits themselves are reliably correct, even if transmitted halfway around the world or from a probe in deep space, and even though the physical stuff in which they are stored and moved is continuous, imperfect, and subject to the laws of statistical physics. When data does become garbled, our computers tend to tell us so.

It was not always so.

Because the relays and gears of early mechanical calculating equipment were so unreliable, some of those devices used parity codes to detect when a bit was in error. If there were four data bits, for example, a fifth bit would be the mod 2 sum of the other four, that is, 0 if there were an even number of 1s among the four data bits and 1 if there were an odd number of 1s among the four data bits.

Richard Hamming (1915–1998) worked with John von Neumann on the Manhattan Project before joining Bell Telephone Labs as a mathematician in 1946. There he shared an office with Claude Shannon and began to marry the computing experience he had gained at Los Alamos with the emerging science of information theory. The biography accompanying his Turing Award describes what happened in 1947 that caused him to open up an entirely new field.

> One Friday, while working for Bell Laboratories, he set their pre-computer calculating machines to solving a complex problem and expected the result to be waiting for him when he began work on the following Monday. But when he arrived on Monday, he found that an error had occurred early on in the calculations and the relay-based calculators had been unable to proceed. (ACM, 1968)

A parity check had failed and the entire calculation simply stopped. Hamming, by training a mathematician who had appreciatively read Boole's *Laws of Thought*, realized that if a computer could figure out that there was a mistake, a computer might also be able to figure out where the mistake was, and correct it. Thus was born the idea of an error correcting code, which in the case

Reprinted from Hamming (1950), with permission from Nokia Bell Labs.

of a four-bit datum requires three more bits. (In fact, the "First Draft" EDVAC report, page 92 of this volume, had already observed that while hardware errors were inevitable, some might be corrected automatically.)

In this paper Hamming first improvises a specific single-error-correcting code and then establishes a general theory. He defines the distance between two bit vectors as the number of positions in which they differ, a measure now universally known as the *Hamming distance*. Two bit vectors that cannot be confused with one another by a one-bit error are at distance at least 2 from each other. So finding an n-bit code, like a simple parity code, that identifies one-bit errors is equivalent to finding a set of points in $\{0, 1\}^n$, called codewords, in which no two points have distance less than 2 between them. If the minimum distance between codewords is 3, the code can correct single-bit errors, since any bit vector can be at distance 1 from only one codeword. Designing codes thus becomes a problem of packing non-overlapping spheres (points of constant distance from a given point) in $\{0, 1\}^n$.

The field exploded after the publication of Hamming's paper. The physical size of bits in modern storage devices is so small, and their number so large, that errors at the bit level are inevitable. Computers achieve macroscopic perfection today by including carefully designed redundancy at the microscopic level, invisible to users, by methods built on those Hamming first developed.

Richard Hamming made many other contributions to communications theory, and in 1976 transitioned to academia. He was a proponent of improved teaching of mathematics until months before his death at the age of 82.

13.1   Introduction

THE author was led to the study given in this paper from a consideration of large scale computing machines in which a large number of operations must be performed without a single error in the end result. This problem of "doing things right" on a large scale is not essentially new; in a telephone central office, for example, a very large number of operations are performed while the errors leading to wrong numbers are kept well under control, though they have not been completely eliminated. This has been achieved, in part, through the use of self-checking circuits. The occasional failure that escapes routine checking is still detected by the customer and will, if it persists, result in customer complaint. While if it is transient it will produce only occasional wrong numbers. At the same time the rest of the central office functions satisfactorily. In a digital computer, on the other hand, a single failure usually means the complete failure, in the sense that if it is detected no more computing can be done until the failure is located and corrected, while if it escapes detection then it invalidates all subsequent operations of the machine. Put in other words, in a telephone central office there are a number of parallel paths which are more or less independent of each other; in a digital machine there is usually a single long path which passes through the same piece of equipment many, many times before the answer is obtained.

In transmitting information from one place to another digital machines use codes which are simply sets of symbols to which meanings or values are attached. Examples of codes which were designed to detect isolated errors are numerous; among them are the highly developed 2 out of 5 codes used extensively in common control switching systems and in the Bell Relay Computers (Alt, 1948a,b), the 3 out of 5 code used for radio telegraphy (Sparks and Kreer, 1947, especially page 417), and the word count sent at the end of telegrams.

In some situations self checking is not enough. For example, in the Model 5 Relay Computers built by Bell Telephone Laboratories for the Aberdeen Proving Grounds, observations in the early period indicated about two or three relay failures per day in the 8900 relays of the two computers, representing about one failure per two to three million relay operations. The self-checking feature meant that these failures did not introduce undetected errors. Since the machines were run on an unattended basis over nights and week-ends. However, the errors meant that frequently the computations came to a halt although often the machines took up new problems. The present trend is toward electronic speeds in digital computers where the basic elements are somewhat more reliable per operation than relays. However, the incidence of isolated failures, even when detected, may seriously interfere with the normal use of such machines. Thus it appears desirable to examine the next step beyond error detection, namely error correction.

We shall assume that the transmitting equipment handles information in the binary form of a sequence of 0s and 1s. This assumption is made both for mathematical convenience and because the binary system is the natural form for representing the open and closed relays, flip-flop circuits, dots and dashes, and perforated tapes that are used in many forms of communication. Thus each code symbol will be represented by a sequence of 0s and 1s.

The codes used in this paper are called *systematic* codes. Systematic codes may be defined as codes in which each code symbol has exactly n binary digits, where m digits are associated with the information while the other $k = n - m$ digits are used for error detection and correction. This produces a *redundancy* R defined as the ratio of the number of binary digits used to the minimum number necessary to convey the same information, that is,

$$R = n/m.$$

This serves to measure the efficiency of the code as far as the transmission of information is concerned, and is the only aspect of the problem discussed in any detail here. The redundancy may be said to lower the effective channel capacity for sending information.

The need for error correction having assumed importance only recently, very little is known about the economics of the matter. It is clear that in such codes there will be extra equipment for encoding and correcting errors as well as the lowered effective channel capacity referred to above. Because of these considerations applications of these codes may be expected to occur first only under extreme conditions. Some typical situations seem to be:

a. unattended operation over long periods of time with the minimum of standby equipment.

b. extremely large and tightly interrelated systems where a single failure incapacitates the entire installation.

c. signaling in the presence of noise where it is either impossible or uneconomical to reduce the effect of the noise on the signal.

These situations are occurring more and more often. The first two are particularly true of large scale digital computing machines, while the third occurs, among other places, in "jamming" situations.

   The principles for designing error detecting and correcting codes in the cases most likely to be applied first are given in this paper. Circuits for implementing these principles may be designed by the application of well-known techniques, but the problem is not discussed here. Part I of the paper shows how to construct special minimum redundancy codes in the following cases:

a. single error detecting codes

b. single error correcting codes

c. single error correcting plus double error detecting codes.

Part II discusses the general theory of such codes and proves that under the assumptions made the codes of Part I are the "best" possible.

PART I: SPECIAL CODES

13.2   Single Error Detecting Codes

We may construct a single error detecting code having n binary digits in the following manner: In the first $n - 1$ positions we put $n - 1$ digits of information. In the nth position we place either 0 or 1, so that the entire n positions have an even number of 1s. This is clearly a single error detecting code since any single error in transmission would leave an odd number of 1s in a code symbol.

   The redundancy of these codes is, since $m = n - 1$,

$$R = \frac{n}{n-1} = 1 + \frac{1}{n-1}.$$

It might appear that to gain a low redundancy we should let n become very large. However, by increasing n, the probability of at least one error in a symbol increases; and the risk of a double error, which would pass undetected, also increases. For example, if $p \ll 1$ is the probability of any error, then for n so large as $1/p$, the probability of a correct symbol is approximately $1/e = 0.3679\ldots$, while a double error has probability $1/2e = 0.1839\ldots$.

   The type of check used above to determine whether or not the symbol has any single error will be used throughout the paper and will be called a *parity check*. The above was an *even* parity check; had we used an odd number of 1s to determine the setting of the check position it would have been an odd parity check. Furthermore, a parity check need not always involve all the positions of the symbol but may be a check over selected positions only.

13.3   Single Error Correcting Codes

To construct a single error correcting code we first assign m of the n available positions as information positions. We shall regard the m as fixed, but the specific positions are left to a later determination. We next assign the k remaining positions as check positions. The values in these k positions are to be determined in the encoding process by even parity checks over selected information positions.

Let us imagine for the moment that we have received a code symbol, with or without an error. Let us apply the k parity checks in order, and for each time the parity check assigns the value observed in its check position we write a 0, while for each time the assigned and observed values disagree we write a 1. When written from right to left in a line this sequence of k 0s and 1s (to be distinguished from the values assigned by the parity checks) may be regarded as a binary number and will be called the checking number. We shall require that this checking number give the position of any single error, with the zero value meaning no error in the symbol. Thus the check number must describe $m + k + 1$ different things, so that $2^k \geq m + k + 1$ is a condition on k. Writing $n = m + k$ we find

$$2^m \leq \frac{2^n}{n+1}.$$

Using this inequality we may calculate Figure 13.1, which gives the maximum m for a given n, or, what is the same thing, the minimum n for a given m.

n	m	Corresponding k
1	0	1
2	0	2
3	1	2
4	1	3
5	2	3
6	3	3
7	4	3
8	4	4
9	5	4
10	6	4
11	7	4
12	8	4
13	9	4
14	10	4
15	11	4
16	11	5
etc.		

Figure 13.1

We now determine the positions over which each of the various parity checks is to be applied. The checking number is obtained digit by digit, from right to left, by applying the parity checks in order and writing down the corresponding 0 or 1 as the case may be. Since the checking number is to give the position of any error in a code symbol, any position which has a 1 on the right of its binary representation must cause the first check to fail. Examining the binary form of the various integers we find

$$1 = \quad 1$$
$$3 = \quad 11$$
$$5 = \quad 101$$
$$7 = \quad 111$$
$$9 = 1001$$

etc.

have a 1 on the extreme right. Thus the first parity check must use positions $1, 3, 5, 7, 9, \dots$.

In an exactly similar fashion we find that the second parity check must use those positions which have 1s for the second digit from the right of their binary representation,

$$2 = \quad 10$$
$$3 = \quad 11$$
$$6 = \quad 110$$
$$7 = \quad 111$$
$$10 = 1010$$
$$11 = 1011$$

etc.,

the third parity check

$$4 = \quad 100$$
$$5 = \quad 101$$
$$6 = \quad 110$$
$$7 = \quad 111$$
$$12 = \quad 1100$$
$$13 = \quad 1101$$
$$14 = \quad 1110$$
$$15 = \quad 1111$$
$$20 = 10100$$

etc.

It remains to decide for each parity check which positions are to contain information and which the check. The choice of the positions $1, 2, 4, 8, \dots$ for check positions, as given in the following table, has the advantage of making the setting of the check positions independent of each other. All other positions are information positions. Thus we obtain Figure 13.2.

Check Number	Check Position	Positions Checked
1	1	1, 3, 5, 7, 9, 11, 13, 15, 17, …
2	2	2, 3, 6, 7, 10, 11, 14, 15, 18, …
3	4	4, 5, 6, 7, 12, 13, 14, 15, 20, …
4	8	8, 9, 10, 11, 12, 13, 14, 15, 24, …
⋮	⋮	⋮

Figure 13.2

As an illustration of the above theory we apply it to the case of a seven-position code. From Figure 13.1 we find for $n = 7$, $m = 4$ and $k = 3$. From Figure 13.2 we find that the first parity check involves positions 1, 3, 5, 7 and is used to determine the value in the first position; the second parity check, positions 2, 3, 6, 7, and determines the value in the second position; and the third parity check. positions 4, 5, 6, 7, and determines the value in position four. This leaves positions 3, 5, 6, 7 as information positions. The results of writing down all possible binary numbers using positions 3, 5, 6, 7, and then calculating the values in the check positions 1, 2, 4, are shown in Figure 13.3.

Thus a seven-position single error correcting code admits of 16 code symbols. There are, of course, $2^7 - 16 = 112$ meaningless symbols. In some applications it may be desirable to drop the first symbol from the code to avoid the all zero combination as either a code symbol or a code symbol plus a single error, since this might be confused with no message. This would still leave 15 useful code symbols.

As an illustration of how this code "works" let us take the symbol 0 1 1 1 1 0 0 corresponding to the decimal value 12 and change the 1 in the fifth position to a 0. We now examine the new symbol 0 1 1 1 0 0 0 by the methods of this section to see how the error is located. From Figure 13.2 the first parity check is over positions 1, 3, 5, 7 and predicts a 1 for the first position while we find a 0 there; hence we write a 1. The second parity check is over positions 2, 3, 6, 7 and predicts the second position correctly: hence we write a 0 to the left of the 1, obtaining 0 1. The third parity check is over positions 4, 5, 6, 7 and predicts wrongly: hence we write a 1 to the left of the 0 1, obtaining 1 0 1. This sequence of 0s and 1s regarded as a binary number is the number 5; hence the error is in the fifth position. The correct symbol is therefore obtained by changing the 0 in the fifth position to a 1.

13.4   Single Error Correcting Plus Double Error Detecting Codes

To construct a single error correcting plus double error detecting code we begin with a single error correcting code. To this code we add one more position for checking all the previous positions, using an even parity check. To see the operation of this code we have to examine a number of cases:

1. No errors. All parity checks, including the last, are satisfied.

Position							Decimal Value of Symbol
1	2	3	4	5	6	7	
0	0	0	0	0	0	0	0
1	1	0	1	0	0	1	1
0	1	0	1	0	1	0	2
1	0	0	0	0	1	1	3
1	0	0	1	1	0	0	4
0	1	0	0	1	0	1	5
1	1	0	0	1	1	0	6
0	0	0	1	1	1	1	7
1	1	1	0	0	0	0	8
0	0	1	1	0	0	1	9
1	0	1	1	0	1	0	10
0	1	1	0	0	1	1	11
0	1	1	1	1	0	0	12
1	0	1	0	1	0	1	13
0	0	1	0	1	1	0	14
1	1	1	1	1	1	1	15

Figure 13.3

2. Single error. The last parity check fails in all such situations whether the error be in the information, the original check positions, or the last check position. The original checking number gives the position of the error, where now the zero value means the last check position.

3. Two errors. In all such situations the last parity check is satisfied, and the checking number indicates some kind of error.

As an illustration let us construct an eight-position code from the previous seven-position code. To do this we add an eighth position which is chosen so that there are an even number of 1s in the eight positions. Thus we add an eighth column to Figure 13.3 (see Figure 13.4).

PART II. GENERAL THEORY

13.5   A Geometric Model

When examining various problems connected with error detecting and correcting codes it is often convenient to introduce a geometric model. The model used here consists in identifying the various sequences of 0s and 1s which are the symbols of a code with vertices of a unit *n*-

dimensional cube. The code points, labelled x, y, z, ..., form a subset of the set of all vertices of the cube. Into this space of 2^n points we introduce a *distance*, or, as it is usually called, a *metric*, $D(x, y)$. The definition of the metric is based on the observation that a single error in a code point changes one coordinate, two errors, two coordinates, and in general d errors produce a difference in d coordinates. Thus we define the distance $D(x, y)$ between two points x and y as the number of coordinates for which x and y are different. This is the same as the least number of edges which must be traversed in going from x to y. This distance function satisfies the usual three conditions for a metric, namely,

$$D(x, y) = 0 \text{ if and only if } x = y$$

$$D(x, y) = D(y, x) > 0 \text{ if } x \neq y$$

$$D(x, y) + D(y, z) \geq D(x, z) \text{ (triangle inequality)}.$$

As an example we note that each of the following code points in the three-dimensional cube is two units away from the others: $0\,0\,1$; $0\,1\,0$; $1\,0\,0$; $1\,1\,1$. To continue the geometric language, a sphere of radius r about a point x is defined as all points which are at a distance r from the point x. Thus, in the above example, the first three code points are on a sphere of radius 2 about the point $(1, 1, 1)$. In fact, in this example any one code point may be chosen as the center and the other three will lie on the surface of a sphere of radius 2.

If all the code points are at a distance of at least 2 from each other, then it follows that any single error will carry a code point over to a point that is not a code point, and hence is a meaningless symbol. This in turn means that any single error is detectable. If the minimum distance between code points is at least three units then any single error will leave the point nearer to the correct code point than to any other code point, and this means that any single error will be correctable. This type of information is summarized in Figure 13.5.

Conversely, it is evident that, if we are to effect the detection and correction listed, then all the distances between code points must equal or exceed the minimum distance listed. Thus the problem of finding suitable codes is the same as that of finding subsets of points in the space which maintain at least the minimum distance condition. The special codes in §§13.2, 13.3, and 13.4 were merely descriptions of how to choose a particular subset of points for minimum distances 2, 3, and 4 respectively.

It should perhaps be noted that, at a given minimum distance, some of the correctability may be exchanged for more detectability. For example, a subset with minimum distance 5 may be used for:

0
0
1
1
1
1
0
0
1
1
0
0
0
0
1
1

Figure 13.4

a. double error correction (with, of course, double error detection)

b. single error correction plus triple error detection

c. quadruple error detection.

Returning for the moment to the particular codes constructed in Part I we note that any interchanges of positions in a code do not change the code in any essential way. Neither does interchanging the 0s and 1s in any position, a process usually called complementing. This idea is made more precise in the following definition:

Minimum Distance	Meaning
1	uniqueness
2	single error detection
3	single error correction
4	single error correction plus double error detection
5	double error correction
	etc.

Figure 13.5

Definition. Two codes are said to be *equivalent* to each other if, by a finite number of the following operations, one can be transformed into the other:

1. The interchange of any two positions in the code symbols.

2. The complementing of the values in any position in the code symbols.

This is a formal equivalence relation ($\sim$) since $A \sim A$; $A \sim B$ implies $B \sim A$; and $A \sim B$, $B \sim C$ implies $A \sim C$. Thus we can reduce the study of a class of codes to the study of typical members of each equivalence class. In terms of the geometric model, equivalence transformations amount to rotations and reflections of the unit cube.

13.6   Single Error Detecting Codes

The problem studied in this section is that of packing the maximum number of points in a unit n-dimensional cube such that no two points are closer than 2 units from each other. We shall show that, as in §13.2, 2^{n-1} points can be so packed, and, further, that any such optimal packing is equivalent to that used in §13.2.

To prove these statements we first observe that the vertices of the n-dimensional cube are composed of those of two $(n - 1)$-dimensional cubes. Let A be the maximum number of points packed in the original cube. Then one of the two $(n - 1)$-dimensional cubes has at least $A/2$ points. This cube being again decomposed into two lower dimensional cubes, we find that one of them has at least $A/2^2$ points. Continuing in this way we come to a two-dimensional cube having $A/2^{n-2}$ points. We now observe that a square can have at most two points separated by at least two units; hence the original n-dimensional cube had at most 2^{n-1} points not less than two units apart.

To prove the equivalence of any two optimal packings we note that, if the packing is optimal, then each of the two sub-cubes has half the points. Calling this the first coordinate we see that half the points have a 0 and half have a 1. The next subdivision will again divide these into two equal groups having 0s and 1s respectively. After $(n - 1)$ such stages we have, upon reorderinng the assigned values if there be any, exactly the first $n - 1$ positions of the code devised in §13.2. To each sequence of the first $n - 1$ coordinates there exist $n - 1$ other sequences which differ from it by one co-ordinate. Once we fix the nth coordinate of some one point, say the origin which has all 0s, then to maintain the known minimum distance of two units between code points the nth coordinate is uniquely determined for all other code points. Thus the last coordinate is determined within a complementation so that any optimal code is equivalent to that given in §13.2.

It is interesting to note that in these two proofs we have used only the assumption that the code symbols are all of length n.

13.7   Single Error Correcting Codes

It has probably been noted by the reader that, in the particular codes of Part I, a distinction was made between information and check positions, while, in the geometric model, there is no real distinction between the various coordinates. To bring the two treatments more in line with each other we re-define a *systematic* code as a code whose symbol lengths are all equal and

1. The positions checked are independent of the information contained in the symbol.
2. The checks are independent of each other.
3. We use parity checks.

This is equivalent to the earlier definition. To show this we form a matrix whose i^{th} row has 1s in the positions of the ith parity check and 0s elsewhere. By assumption 1 the matrix is fixed and does not change from code symbol to code symbol. From 2 the rank of the matrix is k. This in turn means that the system can be solved for k of the positions expressed in terms of the other $n - k$ positions. Assumption 3 indicates that in this solving we use the arithmetic in which $1 + 1 = 0$.

There exist non-systematic codes, but so far none have been found which for a given n and minimum distance d have more code symbols than a systematic code. ...

Turning to the main problem of this section we find from Figure 13.5 that a single error correcting code has code points at least three units from each other. Thus each point may be surrounded by a sphere of radius 1 with no two spheres having a point in common. Each sphere has a center point and n points on its surface, a total of $n + 1$ points. Thus the space of 2^n points can have at most:

$$\frac{2^n}{n + 1}$$

spheres. This is exactly the bound we found before in §13.3.

While we have shown that the specific single error correcting code constructed in §13.3 is of minimum redundancy, we cannot show that all optimal codes are equivalent, since the following trivial example shows that this is not so. For $n = 4$ we find from Figure 13.1 that $m = 1$ and $k = 3$. Thus there are at most two code symbols in a four-position code. The following two optical codes are clearly not equivalent:

$$\begin{matrix} 0000 \\ 1111 \end{matrix} \quad \text{and} \quad \begin{matrix} 0000 \\ 0111 \end{matrix}.$$

13.8   Single Error Correcting plus Double Error Detecting Codes

In this section we shall prove that the codes constructed in §13.4 are of minimum redundancy. We have already shown in §13.4 how for a minimum redundancy code of $n-1$ dimensions with a minimum distance of 3, we can construct an n dimensional code having the same number of code symbols but with a minimum distance of 4. If this were not of minimum redundancy there would exist a code having more code symbols but with the same n and the same minimum distance 4 between them. Taking this code we remove the last coordinate. This reduces the dimension from n to $n-1$ and the minimum distance between code symbols by, at most, one unit, while leaving the number of code symbols the same. This contradicts the assumption that the code we began our construction with was of minimum redundancy. Thus the codes of §13.4 are of minimum redundancy.

This is a special case of the following general theorem: To any minimum redundancy code of N points in $n-1$ dimensions and having a minimum distance of $2k-1$ there corresponds a minimum redundancy code of N points in n dimensions having a minimum distance of $2k$, and conversely. To construct the n dimensional code from the $n-1$ dimensional code we simply add a single n^{th} coordinate which is fixed by an even parity check over the n positions. This also increases the minimum distance by 1 for the following reason: Any two points which, in the $n-1$ dimensional code, were at a distance $2k-1$ from each other had an odd number of differences between their coordinates. Thus the parity check was set oppositely for the two points, increasing the distance between them to $2k$. The additional co-ordinate could not decrease any distances, so that all points in the code are now at a minimum distance of $2k$. To go in the reverse direction we simply drop one coordinate from the n dimensional code. This reduces the minimum distance of $2k$ to $2k-1$ while leaving N the same. It is clear that if one code is of minimum redundancy then the other is too. ...

14 Computing Machinery and Intelligence (1950)

Alan Mathison Turing

Alan Turing started intermittent work with British intelligence on codebreaking not long after publication of "On Computable Numbers" (see chapter 6 for more on Turing's life). After the UK declared war on Germany, he began full time work at Bletchley Park, the wartime center of British intelligence. There he led an ultimately successful effort to crack the Enigma code that was being used for communications between the German command and ships and troops. Like all Bletchley Park work, it remained classified and unpublished for decades, but a consensus now exists that Turing's work was essential to the war effort and may have shortened the war significantly. Indeed, Britain recognized him for his service in 1946.

Drawing on his wartime experience and at about the same time as the Moore School group was at work designing the EDVAC, Turing began the design at Cambridge of an "Automatic Calculating Engine," dubbed the ACE. Though it would eventually become a proper stored-program computer, its construction was tied up in red tape because of the overlap with secret research, and Turing left the project. He moved instead to the University of Manchester and became active in the design of the Mark 1 (discussed further in chapter 15—a different machine from Aiken's Mark I at Harvard). While at Manchester he began to imagine what computers might someday be able to do. This remarkable paper caused the "Turing test" to enter popular parlance—even though, as Turing makes clear in the introduction, his "imitation game" is not a test of whether machines can think (a question Turing describes as "meaningless") but instead a scientifically tractable substitute question. Weizenbaum's ELIZA program (chapter 27) seduced people so readily as to challenge the appropriateness of the Turing test; the philosopher John Searle (1980) advanced a more nuanced argument against it. The paper's arguments are still debated today (see Shieber [2004] for a thorough account).

Turing is remembered not only for his mathematical work but for the breadth of his curiosity. *Mind*, where this paper was originally published, is an important philosophy journal; the paper is here reprinted in full, except for a section describing the universality of mathematical automata. In Turing's last years he turned to mathematical biology, which had long fascinated him.

Reprinted from Turing (1950), with permission from Oxford University Press.

14.1   The Imitation Game

I propose to consider the question, "Can machines think?" This should begin with definitions of the meaning of the terms "machine" and "think." The definitions might be framed so as to reflect so far as possible the normal use of the words, but this attitude is dangerous. If the meaning of the words "machine" and "think" are to be found by examining how they are commonly used it is difficult to escape the conclusion that the meaning and the answer to the question, "Can machines think?" is to be sought in a statistical survey such as a Gallup poll. But this is absurd. Instead of attempting such a definition I shall replace the question by another, which is closely related to it and is expressed in relatively unambiguous words.

The new form of the problem can be described in terms of a game which we call the "imitation game." It is played with three people, a man (A), a woman (B), and an interrogator (C) who may be of either sex. The interrogator stays in a room apart from the other two. The object of the game for the interrogator is to determine which of the other two is the man and which is the woman. He knows them by labels X and Y, and at the end of the game he says either "X is A and Y is B" or "X is B and Y is A." The interrogator is allowed to put questions to A and B thus:
C: Will X please tell me the length of his or her hair?

Now suppose X is actually A, then A must answer. It is A's object in the game to try and cause C to make the wrong identification. His answer might therefore be:
"My hair is shingled, and the longest strands are about nine inches long."

In order that tones of voice may not help the interrogator the answers should be written, or better still, typewritten. The ideal arrangement is to have a teleprinter communicating between the two rooms. Alternatively the question and answers can be repeated by an intermediary. The object of the game for the third player (B) is to help the interrogator. The best strategy for her is probably to give truthful answers. She can add such things as "I am the woman, don't listen to him!" to her answers, but it will avail nothing as the man can make similar remarks.

We now ask the question, "What will happen when a machine takes the part of A in this game?" Will the interrogator decide wrongly as often when the game is played like this as he does when the game is played between a man and a woman? These questions replace our original, "Can machines think?"

14.2   Critique of the New Problem

As well as asking, "What is the answer to this new form of the question," one may ask, "Is this new question a worthy one to investigate?" This latter question we investigate without further ado, thereby cutting short an infinite regress.

The new problem has the advantage of drawing a fairly sharp line between the physical and the intellectual capacities of a man. No engineer or chemist claims to be able to produce a material which is indistinguishable from the human skin. It is possible that at some time this might be done, but even supposing this invention available we should feel there was little point in trying to make a "thinking machine" more human by dressing it up in such artificial flesh. The form in

which we have set the problem reflects this fact in the condition which prevents the interrogator
from seeing or touching the other competitors, or hearing their voices. Some other advantages of
the proposed criterion may be shown up by specimen questions and answers. Thus:

Q: Please write me a sonnet on the subject of the Forth Bridge.

A: Count me out on this one. I never could write poetry.

Q: Add 34957 to 70764.

A: (Pause about 30 seconds and then give as answer) 105621.

Q: Do you play chess?

A: Yes.

Q: I have K at my K1, and no other pieces. You have only K at K6 and R at R1. It is your move.
What do you play?

A: (After a pause of 15 seconds) R-R8 mate.

The question and answer method seems to be suitable for introducing almost any one of the
fields of human endeavour that we wish to include. We do not wish to penalise the machine for
its inability to shine in beauty competitions, nor to penalise a man for losing in a race against
an aeroplane. The conditions of our game make these disabilities irrelevant. The "witnesses"
can brag, if they consider it advisable, as much as they please about their charms, strength or
heroism, but the interrogator cannot demand practical demonstrations.

The game may perhaps be criticised on the ground that the odds are weighted too heavily
against the machine. If the man were to try and pretend to be the machine he would clearly make
a very poor showing. He would be given away at once by slowness and inaccuracy in arithmetic.
May not machines carry out something which ought to be described as thinking but which is very
different from what a man does? This objection is a very strong one, but at least we can say that
if, nevertheless, a machine can be constructed to play the imitation game satisfactorily, we need
not be troubled by this objection.

It might be urged that when playing the "imitation game" the best strategy for the machine
may possibly be something other than imitation of the behaviour of a man. This may be, but I
think it is unlikely that there is any great effect of this kind. In any case there is no intention to
investigate here the theory of the game, and it will be assumed that the best strategy is to try to
provide answers that would naturally be given by a man.

14.3   The Machines Concerned in the Game

The question which we put in §14.1 will not be quite definite until we have specified what we
mean by the word "machine." It is natural that we should wish to permit every kind of engineering
technique to be used in our machines. We also wish to allow the possibility that an engineer
or team of engineers may construct a machine which works, but whose manner of operation
cannot be satisfactorily described by its constructors because they have applied a method which
is largely experimental. Finally, we wish to exclude from the machines men born in the usual
manner. It is difficult to frame the definitions so as to satisfy these three conditions. One might

for instance insist that the team of engineers should be all of one sex, but this would not really be satisfactory, for it is probably possible to rear a complete individual from a single cell of the skin (say) of a man. To do so would be a feat of biological technique deserving of the very highest praise, but we would not be inclined to regard it as a case of "constructing a thinking machine." This prompts us to abandon the requirement that every kind of technique should be permitted. We are the more ready to do so in view of the fact that the present interest in "thinking machines" has been aroused by a particular kind of machine, usually called an "electronic computer" or "digital computer." Following this suggestion we only permit digital computers to take part in our game.

This restriction appears at first sight to be a very drastic one. I shall attempt to show that it is not so in reality. To do this necessitates a short account of the nature and properties of these computers. It may also be said that this identification of machines with digital computers, like our criterion for "thinking," will only be unsatisfactory if (contrary to my belief), it turns out that digital computers are unable to give a good showing in the game.

There are already a number of digital computers in working order, and it may be asked, "Why not try the experiment straight away? It would be easy to satisfy the conditions of the game. A number of interrogators could be used, and statistics compiled to show how often the right identification was given." The short answer is that we are not asking whether all digital computers would do well in the game nor whether the computers at present available would do well, but whether there are imaginable computers which would do well. But this is only the short answer. We shall see this question in a different light later.

14.4   Digital Computers

The idea behind digital computers may be explained by saying that these machines are intended to carry out any operations which could be done by a human computer. The human computer is supposed to be following fixed rules; he has no authority to deviate from them in any detail. We may suppose that these rules are supplied in a book, which is altered whenever he is put on to a new job. He has also an unlimited supply of paper on which he does his calculations. He may also do his multiplications and additions on a "desk machine," but this is not important. ...

The idea of a digital computer is an old one. Charles Babbage, Lucasian Professor of Mathematics at Cambridge from 1828 to 1839, planned such a machine, called the Analytical Engine, but it was never completed. Although Babbage had all the essential ideas, his machine was not at that time such a very attractive prospect. The speed which would have been available would be definitely faster than a human computer but something like 100 times slower than the Manchester machine, itself one of the slower of the modern machines. The storage was to be purely mechanical, using wheels and cards.

The fact that Babbage's Analytical Engine was to be entirely mechanical will help us to rid ourselves of a superstition. Importance is often attached to the fact that modern digital computers are electrical, and that the nervous system also is electrical. Since Babbage's machine was not electrical, and since all digital computers are in a sense equivalent, we see that this use of electricity cannot be of theoretical importance. Of course electricity usually comes in where fast signalling is concerned, so that it is not surprising that we find it in both these connections. In the nervous system chemical phenomena are at least as important as electrical. In certain computers the storage system is mainly acoustic. The feature of using electricity is thus seen to be only a very superficial similarity. If we wish to find such similarities we should look rather for mathematical analogies of function.

14.5   Universality of Digital Computers

The digital computers considered in the last section may be classified amongst the "discrete-state machines." These are the machines which move by sudden jumps or clicks from one quite definite state to another. These states are sufficiently different for the possibility of confusion between them to be ignored. Strictly speaking there are no such machines. Everything really moves continuously. But there are many kinds of machine which can profitably be *thought of* as being discrete-state machines. For instance in considering the switches for a lighting system it is a convenient fiction that each switch must be definitely on or definitely off. There must be intermediate positions, but for most purposes we can forget about them. ... [EDITOR: Argument for universality omitted]

This special property of digital computers, that they can mimic any discrete-state machine, is described by saying that they are universal machines. The existence of machines with this property has the important consequence that, considerations of speed apart, it is unnecessary to design various new machines to do various computing processes. They can all be done with one digital computer, suitably programmed for each case. It will be seen that as a consequence of this all digital computers are in a sense equivalent.

We may now consider again the point raised at the end of §14.3. It was suggested tentatively that the question, "Can machines think?" should be replaced by "Are there imaginable digital computers which would do well in the imitation game?" If we wish we can make this superficially more general and ask "Are there discrete-state machines which would do well?" But in view of the universality property we see that either of these questions is equivalent to this, "Let us fix our attention on one particular digital computer C. Is it true that by modifying this computer to have an adequate storage, suitably increasing its speed of action, and providing it with an appropriate programme, C can be made to play satisfactorily the part of A in the imitation game, the part of B being taken by a man?"

14.6   Contrary Views on the Main Question

We may now consider the ground to have been cleared and we are ready to proceed to the debate on our question, "Can machines think?" and the variant of it quoted at the end of the last section. We cannot altogether abandon the original form of the problem, for opinions will differ as to the appropriateness of the substitution and we must at least listen to what has to be said in this connexion. It will simplify matters for the reader if I explain first my own beliefs in the matter.

Consider first the more accurate form of the question. I believe that in about fifty years' time it will be possible to programme computers, with a storage capacity of about 10^9, to make them play the imitation game so well that an average interrogator will not have more than 70 per cent chance of making the right identification after five minutes of questioning. The original question, "Can machines think?" I believe to be too meaningless to deserve discussion. Nevertheless I believe that at the end of the century the use of words and general educated opinion will have altered so much that one will be able to speak of machines thinking without expecting to be contradicted. I believe further that no useful purpose is served by concealing these beliefs. The popular view that scientists proceed inexorably from well-established fact to well-established fact, never being influenced by any improved conjecture, is quite mistaken. Provided it is made clear which are proved facts and which are conjectures, no harm can result. Conjectures are of great importance since they suggest useful lines of research.

I now proceed to consider opinions opposed to my own.

14.6.1   The theological objection   Thinking is a function of man's immortal soul. God has given an immortal soul to every man and woman, but not to any other animal or to machines. Hence no animal or machine can think.

I am unable to accept any part of this, but will attempt to reply in theological terms. I should find the argument more convincing if animals were classed with men, for there is a greater difference, to my mind, between the typical animate and the inanimate than there is between man and the other animals. The arbitrary character of the orthodox view becomes clearer if we consider how it might appear to a member of some other religious community. How do Christians regard the Moslem view that women have no souls? [EDITOR: Smith and Haddad (1975, footnote 2) address the source of this misconception about Islam.] But let us leave this point aside and return to the main argument. It appears to me that the argument quoted above implies a serious restriction of the omnipotence of the Almighty. It is admitted that there are certain things that He cannot do such as making one equal to two, but should we not believe that He has freedom to confer a soul on an elephant if He sees fit? We might expect that He would only exercise this power in conjunction with a mutation which provided the elephant with an appropriately improved brain to minister to the needs of this sort. An argument of exactly similar form may be made for the case of machines. It may seem different because it is more difficult to "swallow." But this really only means that we think it would be less likely that He would consider the circumstances suitable for conferring a soul. The circumstances in question are discussed in the rest of this paper. In attempting to construct such machines we should not be irreverently usurping His power of creating souls, any more than we are in the procreation of children: rather we are, in either case, instruments of His will providing mansions for the souls that He creates.

However, this is mere speculation. I am not very impressed with theological arguments whatever they may be used to support. Such arguments have often been found unsatisfactory in the past. In the time of Galileo it was argued that the texts, "And the sun stood still ... and hasted not to go down about a whole day" (Joshua 10:13) and "He laid the foundations of the earth, that it should not move at any time" (Psalm 105:5) were an adequate refutation of the Copernican theory. With our present knowledge such an argument appears futile. When that knowledge was not available it made a quite different impression.

14.6.2   The "heads in the sand" objection   "The consequences of machines thinking would be too dreadful. Let us hope and believe that they cannot do so."

This argument is seldom expressed quite so openly as in the form above. But it affects most of us who think about it at all. We like to believe that Man is in some subtle way superior to the rest of creation. It is best if he can be shown to be necessarily superior, for then there is no danger of him losing his commanding position. The popularity of the theological argument is clearly connected with this feeling. It is likely to be quite strong in intellectual people, since they value the power of thinking more highly than others, and are more inclined to base their belief in the superiority of Man on this power.

I do not think that this argument is sufficiently substantial to require refutation. Consolation would be more appropriate: perhaps this should be sought in the transmigration of souls.

14.6.3   The mathematical objection   There are a number of results of mathematical logic which can be used to show that there are limitations to the powers of discrete-state machines. The best known of these results is known as Gödel's theorem (Gödel, 1931) and shows that in any sufficiently powerful logical system statements can be formulated which can neither be proved nor disproved within the system, unless possibly the system itself is inconsistent. There are other, in some respects similar, results due to Church (1936b), Kleene (1935a,b), Rosser, and Turing (1936, here chapter 6). The latter result is the most convenient to consider, since it refers directly to machines, whereas the others can only be used in a comparatively indirect argument: for instance if Gödel's theorem is to be used we need in addition to have some means of describing logical systems in terms of machines, and machines in terms of logical systems. The result in question refers to a type of machine which is essentially a digital computer with an infinite capacity. It states that there are certain things that such a machine cannot do. If it is rigged up to give answers to questions as in the imitation game, there will be some questions to which it will either give a wrong answer, or fail to give an answer at all however much time is allowed for a reply. There may, of course, be many such questions, and questions which cannot be answered by one machine may be satisfactorily answered by another. We are of course supposing for the present that the questions are of the kind to which an answer "Yes" or "No" is appropriate, rather than questions such as "What do you think of Picasso?" The questions that we know the machines must fail on are of this type, "Consider the machine specified as follows .... Will this machine ever answer 'Yes' to any question?" The dots are to be replaced by a description of some machine in a standard form, which could be something like that used in §14.5. When the machine described bears a certain comparatively simple relation to the machine which is under interrogation, it can be shown that the answer is either wrong or not forthcoming. This is the mathematical result: it is argued that it proves a disability of machines to which the human intellect is not subject.

The short answer to this argument is that although it is established that there are limitations to the powers of any particular machine, it has only been stated, without any sort of proof, that no such limitations apply to the human intellect. But I do not think this view can be dismissed quite so lightly. Whenever one of these machines is asked the appropriate critical question, and gives a definite answer, we know that this answer must be wrong, and this gives us a certain feeling of superiority. Is this feeling illusory? It is no doubt quite genuine, but I do not think too much importance should be attached to it. We too often give wrong answers to questions ourselves to be justified in being very pleased at such evidence of fallibility on the part of the machines. Further, our superiority can only be felt on such an occasion in relation to the one machine over which we have scored our petty triumph. There would be no question of triumphing simultaneously over all machines. In short, then, there might be men cleverer than any given machine, but then again there might be other machines cleverer again, and so on.

Those who hold to the mathematical argument would, I think, mostly be willing to accept the imitation game as a basis for discussion. Those who believe in the two previous objections would probably not be interested in any criteria.

14.6.4   The argument from consciousness   This argument is very well expressed in Jefferson (1949), from which I quote. "Not until a machine can write a sonnet or compose a concerto because of thoughts and emotions felt, and not by the chance fall of symbols, could we agree that machine equals brain—that is, not only write it but know that it had written it. No mechanism could feel (and not merely artificially signal, an easy contrivance) pleasure at its successes, grief when its valves fuse, be warmed by flattery, be made miserable by its mistakes, be charmed by sex, be angry or depressed when it cannot get what it wants."

This argument appears to be a denial of the validity of our test. According to the most extreme form of this view the only way by which one could be sure that a machine thinks is to *be* the machine and to feel oneself thinking. One could then describe these feelings to the world, but of course no one would be justified in taking any notice. Likewise according to this view the only way to know that a *man* thinks is to be that particular man. It is in fact the solipsist point of view. It may be the most logical view to hold but it makes communication of ideas difficult. A is liable to believe "A thinks but B does not" whilst B believes "B thinks but A does not." Instead of arguing continually over this point it is usual to have the polite convention that everyone thinks.

I am sure that Professor Jefferson does not wish to adopt the extreme and solipsist point of view. Probably he would be quite willing to accept the imitation game as a test. The game (with the player B omitted) is frequently used in practice under the name of *viva voce* to discover whether some one really understands something or has "learnt it parrot fashion." Let us listen in to a part of such a *viva voce*:

Interrogator: In the first line of your sonnet which reads "Shall I compare thee to a summer's day," would not "a spring day" do as well or better?

Witness: It wouldn't scan.

Interrogator: How about "a winter's day"? That would scan all right.

Witness: Yes, but nobody wants to be compared to a winter's day.

Interrogator: Would you say Mr. Pickwick reminded you of Christmas?

Witness: In a way.

Interrogator: Yet Christmas is a winter's day, and I do not think Mr. Pickwick would mind the comparison.

Witness: I don't think you're serious. By a winter's day one means a typical winter's day, rather than a special one like Christmas.

And so on. What would Professor Jefferson say if the sonnet-writing machine was able to answer like this in the *viva voce*? I do not know whether he would regard the machine as "merely artificially signalling" these answers, but if the answers were as satisfactory and sustained as in the above passage I do not think he would describe it as "an easy contrivance." This phrase is, I think, intended to cover such devices as the inclusion in the machine of a record of someone reading a sonnet, with appropriate switching to turn it on from time to time.

In short then, I think that most of those who support the argument from consciousness could be persuaded to abandon it rather than be forced into the solipsist position. They will then probably be willing to accept our test.

I do not wish to give the impression that I think there is no mystery about consciousness. There is, for instance, something of a paradox connected with any attempt to localise it. But I do not think these mysteries necessarily need to be solved before we can answer the question with which we are concerned in this paper.

14.6.5   Arguments from various disabilities   These arguments take the form, "I grant you that you can make machines do all the things you have mentioned but you will never be able to make one to do X." Numerous features X are suggested in this connexion. I offer a selection:

Be kind, resourceful, beautiful, friendly, have initiative, have a sense of humour, tell right from wrong, make mistakes, fall in love, enjoy strawberries and cream, make some one fall in love with it, learn from experience, use words properly, be the subject of its own thought, have as much diversity of behaviour as a man, do something really new.

No support is usually offered for these statements. I believe they are mostly founded on the principle of scientific induction. A man has seen thousands of machines in his lifetime. From what he sees of them he draws a number of general conclusions. They are ugly, each is designed for a very limited purpose, when required for a minutely different purpose they are useless, the variety of behaviour of any one of them is very small, etc., etc. Naturally he concludes that these are necessary properties of machines in general. Many of these limitations are associated with the very small storage capacity of most machines. (I am assuming that the idea of storage capacity is extended in some way to cover machines other than discrete-state machines. The exact definition does not matter as no mathematical accuracy is claimed in the present discussion.) A few years ago, when very little had been heard of digital computers, it was possible to elicit much incredulity concerning them, if one mentioned their properties without describing their construction. That was presumably due to a similar application of the principle of scientific induction.

These applications of the principle are of course largely unconscious. When a burnt child fears the fire and shows that he fears it by avoiding it, I should say that he was applying scientific induction. (I could of course also describe his behaviour in many other ways.) The works and customs of mankind do not seem to be very suitable material to which to apply scientific induction. A very large part of space-time must be investigated, if reliable results are to be obtained. Otherwise we may (as most English children do) decide that everybody speaks English, and that it is silly to learn French.

There are, however, special remarks to be made about many of the disabilities that have been mentioned. The inability to enjoy strawberries and cream may have struck the reader as frivolous. Possibly a machine might be made to enjoy this delicious dish, but any attempt to make one do so would be idiotic. What is important about this disability is that it contributes to some of the other disabilities, e.g., to the difficulty of the same kind of friendliness occurring between man and machine as between white man and white man, or between black man and black man.

The claim that "machines cannot make mistakes" seems a curious one. One is tempted to retort, "Are they any the worse for that?" But let us adopt a more sympathetic attitude, and try to see what is really meant. I think this criticism can be explained in terms of the imitation game. It is claimed that the interrogator could distinguish the machine from the man simply by setting them a number of problems in arithmetic. The machine would be unmasked because of its deadly accuracy. The reply to this is simple. The machine (programmed for playing the game) would not attempt to give the right answers to the arithmetic problems. It would deliberately introduce mistakes in a manner calculated to confuse the interrogator. A mechanical fault would probably show itself through an unsuitable decision as to what sort of a mistake to make in the arithmetic. Even this interpretation of the criticism is not sufficiently sympathetic. But we cannot afford the space to go into it much further. It seems to me that this criticism depends on a confusion between two kinds of mistake. We may call them "errors of functioning" and "errors of conclusion." Errors of functioning are due to some mechanical or electrical fault which causes the machine to behave otherwise than it was designed to do. In philosophical discussions one likes to ignore the possibility of such errors; one is therefore discussing "abstract machines." These abstract machines are mathematical fictions rather than physical objects. By definition they are incapable of errors of functioning. In this sense we can truly say that "machines can never make mistakes." Errors of conclusion can only arise when some meaning is attached to the output signals from the machine. The machine might, for instance, type out mathematical equations, or sentences in English. When a false proposition is typed we say that the machine has committed an error of conclusion. There is clearly no reason at all for saying that a machine cannot make this kind of mistake. It might do nothing but type out repeatedly "$0 = 1$." To take a less perverse example, it might have some method for drawing conclusions by scientific induction. We must expect such a method to lead occasionally to erroneous results.

The claim that a machine cannot be the subject of its own thought can of course only be answered if it can be shown that the machine has some thought with some subject matter. Nevertheless, "the subject matter of a machine's operations" does seem to mean something, at least to the people who deal with it. If, for instance, the machine was trying to find a solution of the equation $x^2 - 40x - 11 = 0$ one would be tempted to describe this equation as part of the machine's subject matter at that moment. In this sort of sense a machine undoubtedly can be its own subject matter. It may be used to help in making up its own programmes, or to predict the effect of alterations in its own structure. By observing the results of its own behaviour it can modify its own programmes so as to achieve some purpose more effectively. These are possibilities of the near future, rather than Utopian dreams.

The criticism that a machine cannot have much diversity of behaviour is just a way of saying that it cannot have much storage capacity. Until fairly recently a storage capacity of even a thousand digits was very rare.

The criticisms that we are considering here are often disguised forms of the argument from consciousness. Usually if one maintains that a machine can do one of these things, and describes the kind of method that the machine could use, one will not make much of an impression. It is thought that the method (whatever it may be, for it must be mechanical) is really rather base. Compare the parentheses in Jefferson's statement quoted on page 154 [EDITOR: of this volume].

14.6.6   Lady Lovelace's objection   Our most detailed information of Babbage's Analytical Engine comes from a memoir by *Lady Lovelace*. In it she states [EDITOR: page 26 of this volume], "The Analytical Engine has no pretensions to *originate* anything. It can do *whatever we know how to order it* to perform" (her italics). This statement is quoted by Hartree (1949) who adds: "This does not imply that it may not be possible to construct electronic equipment which will 'think for itself,' or in which, in biological terms, one could set up a conditioned reflex, which would serve as a basis for 'learning.' Whether this is possible in principle or not is a stimulating and exciting question, suggested by some of these recent developments. But it did not seem that the machines constructed or projected at the time had this property."

I am in thorough agreement with Hartree over this. It will be noticed that he does not assert that the machines in question had not got the property, but rather that the evidence available to Lady Lovelace did not encourage her to believe that they had it. It is quite possible that the machines in question had in a sense got this property. For suppose that some discrete-state machine has the property. The Analytical Engine was a universal digital computer, so that, if its storage capacity and speed were adequate, it could by suitable programming be made to mimic the machine in question. Probably this argument did not occur to the Countess or to Babbage. In any case there was no obligation on them to claim all that could be claimed.

This whole question will be considered again under the heading of learning machines.

A variant of Lady Lovelace's objection states that a machine can "never do anything really new." This may be parried for a moment with the saw, "There is nothing new under the sun." Who can be certain that "original work" that he has done was not simply the growth of the seed planted in him by teaching, or the effect of following well-known general principles. A better variant of the objection says that a machine can never "take us by surprise." This statement is a more direct challenge and can be met directly. Machines take me by surprise with great frequency. This is largely because I do not do sufficient calculation to decide what to expect them to do, or rather because, although I do a calculation, I do it in a hurried, slipshod fashion, taking risks. Perhaps I say to myself, "I suppose the voltage here ought to be the same as there: anyway let's assume it is." Naturally I am often wrong, and the result is a surprise for me for by the time the experiment is done these assumptions have been forgotten. These admissions lay me open to lectures on the subject of my vicious ways, but do not throw any doubt on my credibility when I testify to the surprises I experience.

I do not expect this reply to silence my critic. He will probably say that such surprises are due to some creative mental act on my part, and reflect no credit on the machine. This leads us back to the argument from consciousness, and far from the idea of surprise. It is a line of argument we must consider closed, but it is perhaps worth remarking that the appreciation of something as surprising requires as much of a "creative mental act" whether the surprising event originates from a man, a book, a machine or anything else.

The view that machines cannot give rise to surprises is due, I believe, to a fallacy to which philosophers and mathematicians are particularly subject. This is the assumption that as soon as a fact is presented to a mind all consequences of that fact spring into the mind simultaneously with it. It is a very useful assumption under many circumstances, but one too easily forgets that it is false. A natural consequence of doing so is that one then assumes that there is no virtue in the mere working out of consequences from data and general principles.

14.6.7   Argument from continuity in the nervous system   The nervous system is certainly not a discrete-state machine. A small error in the information about the size of a nervous impulse impinging on a neuron, may make a large difference to the size of the outgoing impulse. It may be argued that, this being so, one cannot expect to be able to mimic the behaviour of the nervous system with a discrete-state system.

It is true that a discrete-state machine must be different from a continuous machine. But if we adhere to the conditions of the imitation game, the interrogator will not be able to take any advantage of this difference. The situation can be made clearer if we consider some other simpler continuous machine. A differential analyser will do very well. (A differential analyser is a certain kind of machine not of the discrete-state type used for some kinds of calculation.) Some of these provide their answers in a typed form, and so are suitable for taking part in the game. It would not be possible for a digital computer to predict exactly what answers the differential analyser would give to a problem, but it would be quite capable of giving the right sort of answer. For instance, if asked to give the value of π (actually about 3.1416) it would be reasonable to choose at random between the values 3.12, 3.13, 3.14, 3.15, 3.16 with the probabilities of 0.05, 0.15, 0.55, 0.19, 0.06 (say). Under these circumstances it would be very difficult for the interrogator to distinguish the differential analyser from the digital computer.

14.6.8   The argument from informality of behaviour   It is not possible to produce a set of rules purporting to describe what a man should do in every conceivable set of circumstances.

One might for instance have a rule that one is to stop when one sees a red traffic light, and to go if one sees a green one, but what if by some fault both appear together? One may perhaps decide that it is safest to stop. But some further difficulty may well arise from this decision later. To attempt to provide rules of conduct to cover every eventuality, even those arising from traffic lights, appears to be impossible. With all this I agree.

From this it is argued that we cannot be machines. I shall try to reproduce the argument, but I fear I shall hardly do it justice. It seems to run something like this. "If each man had a definite set of rules of conduct by which he regulated his life he would be no better than a machine. But there are no such rules, so men cannot be machines." The undistributed middle is glaring. I do not think the argument is ever put quite like this, but I believe this is the argument used nevertheless. There may however be a certain confusion between "rules of conduct" and "laws of behaviour" to cloud the issue. By "rules of conduct" I mean precepts such as "Stop if you see red lights," on which one can act, and of which one can be conscious. By "laws of behaviour" I mean laws of nature as applied to a man's body such as "if you pinch him he will squeak." If we substitute "laws of behaviour which regulate his life" for "laws of conduct by which he regulates his life" in the argument quoted the undistributed middle is no longer insuperable. For we believe that it is not only true that being regulated by laws of behaviour implies being some sort of machine (though not necessarily a discrete-state machine), but that conversely being such a machine implies being regulated by such laws. However, we cannot so easily convince ourselves of the absence of complete laws of behaviour as of complete rules of conduct. The only way we know of for finding such laws is scientific observation, and we certainly know of no circumstances under which we could say, "We have searched enough. There are no such laws."

We can demonstrate more forcibly that any such statement would be unjustified. For suppose we could be sure of finding such laws if they existed. Then given a discrete-state machine it should certainly be possible to discover by observation sufficient about it to predict its future behaviour, and this within a reasonable time, say a thousand years. But this does not seem to be the case. I have set up on the Manchester computer a small programme using only 1,000 units of storage, whereby the machine supplied with one sixteen-figure number replies with another within two seconds. I would defy anyone to learn from these replies sufficient about the programme to be able to predict any replies to untried values.

14.6.9   The argument from extrasensory perception   I assume that the reader is familiar with the idea of extrasensory perception, and the meaning of the four items of it, viz., telepathy, clairvoyance, precognition and psychokinesis. These disturbing phenomena seem to deny all our usual scientific ideas. How we should like to discredit them! Unfortunately the statistical evidence, at least for telepathy, is overwhelming. It is very difficult to rearrange one's ideas so as to fit these new facts in. Once one has accepted them it does not seem a very big step to believe in ghosts and bogies. The idea that our bodies move simply according to the known laws of physics, together with some others not yet discovered but somewhat similar, would be one of the first to go. This argument is to my mind quite a strong one. One can say in reply that many scientific theories seem to remain workable in practice, in spite of clashing with E.S.P.; that in fact one can get along very nicely if one forgets about it. This is rather cold comfort, and one fears that thinking is just the kind of phenomenon where E.S.P. may be especially relevant.

A more specific argument based on E.S.P. might run as follows: "Let us play the imitation game, using as witnesses a man who is good as a telepathic receiver, and a digital computer. The interrogator can ask such questions as 'What suit does the card in my right hand belong to?' The man by telepathy or clairvoyance gives the right answer 130 times out of 400 cards. The machine can only guess at random, and perhaps gets 104 right, so the interrogator makes the right identification." There is an interesting possibility which opens here. Suppose the digital computer contains a random number generator. Then it will be natural to use this to decide what answer to give. But then the random number generator will be subject to the psychokinetic powers of the interrogator. Perhaps this psychokinesis might cause the machine to guess right more often than would be expected on a probability calculation, so that the interrogator might still be unable to make the right identification. On the other hand, he might be able to guess right without any questioning, by clairvoyance. With E.S.P. anything may happen.

If telepathy is admitted it will be necessary to tighten our test up. The situation could be regarded as analogous to that which would occur if the interrogator were talking to himself and one of the competitors was listening with his ear to the wall. To put the competitors into a "telepathy-proof room" would satisfy all requirements.

14.7   Learning Machines

The reader will have anticipated that I have no very convincing arguments of a positive nature to support my views. If I had I should not have taken such pains to point out the fallacies in contrary views. Such evidence as I have I shall now give.

Let us return for a moment to Lady Lovelace's objection, which stated that the machine can only do what we tell it to do. One could say that a man can "inject" an idea into the machine, and that it will respond to a certain extent and then drop into quiescence, like a piano string struck by a hammer. Another simile would be an atomic pile of less than critical size: an injected idea is to correspond to a neutron entering the pile from without. Each such neutron will cause a certain disturbance which eventually dies away. If, however, the size of the pile is sufficiently increased, the disturbance caused by such an incoming neutron will very likely go on and on increasing until the whole pile is destroyed. Is there a corresponding phenomenon for minds, and is there one for machines? There does seem to be one for the human mind. The majority of them seem to be "subcritical," i.e., to correspond in this analogy to piles of subcritical size. An idea presented to such a mind will on average give rise to less than one idea in reply. A smallish proportion are supercritical. An idea presented to such a mind that may give rise to a whole "theory" consisting of secondary, tertiary and more remote ideas. Animals minds seem to be very definitely subcritical. Adhering to this analogy we ask, "Can a machine be made to be supercritical?"

The "skin-of-an-onion" analogy is also helpful. In considering the functions of the mind or the brain we find certain operations which we can explain in purely mechanical terms. This we say does not correspond to the real mind: it is a sort of skin which we must strip off if we are to find the real mind. But then in what remains we find a further skin to be stripped off, and so on. Proceeding in this way do we ever come to the "real" mind, or do we eventually come to the skin which has nothing in it? In the latter case the whole mind is mechanical. (It would not be a discrete-state machine however. We have discussed this.)

These last two paragraphs do not claim to be convincing arguments. They should rather be described as "recitations tending to produce belief."

The only really satisfactory support that can be given for the view expressed at the beginning of §14.6, will be that provided by waiting for the end of the century and then doing the experiment described. But what can we say in the meantime? What steps should be taken now if the experiment is to be successful?

As I have explained, the problem is mainly one of programming. Advances in engineering will have to be made too, but it seems unlikely that these will not be adequate for the requirements. Estimates of the storage capacity of the brain vary from 10^{10} to 10^{15} binary digits. I incline to the lower values and believe that only a very small fraction is used for the higher types of thinking. Most of it is probably used for the retention of visual impressions, I should be surprised if more than 10^9 was required for satisfactory playing of the imitation game, at any rate against a blind man. (Note: The capacity of the Encyclopaedia Britannica, 11th edition, is 2×10^9.) A storage capacity of 10^7, would be a very practicable possibility even by present techniques. It is probably not necessary to increase the speed of operations of the machines at all. Parts of modern machines which can be regarded as analogs of nerve cells work about a thousand times faster than the latter. This should provide a "margin of safety" which could cover losses of speed arising in many ways. Our problem then is to find out how to programme these machines to play the game. At my present rate of working I produce about a thousand digits of programme a day, so that about sixty workers, working steadily through the fifty years might accomplish the job, if nothing went into the wastepaper basket. Some more expeditious method seems desirable.

In the process of trying to imitate an adult human mind we are bound to think a good deal about the process which has brought it to the state that it is in. We may notice three components.

(a) The initial state of the mind, say at birth,
(b) The education to which it has been subjected,
(c) Other experience, not to be described as education, to which it has been subjected.

Instead of trying to produce a programme to simulate the adult mind, why not rather try to produce one which simulates the child's? If this were then subjected to an appropriate course of education one would obtain the adult brain. Presumably the child brain is something like a notebook as one buys it from the stationer's. Rather little mechanism, and lots of blank sheets. (Mechanism and writing are from our point of view almost synonymous.) Our hope is that there is so little mechanism in the child brain that something like it can be easily programmed. The amount of work in the education we can assume, as a first approximation, to be much the same as for the human child.

We have thus divided our problem into two parts. The child programme and the education process. These two remain very closely connected. We cannot expect to find a good child machine at the first attempt. One must experiment with teaching one such machine and see how well it learns. One can then try another and see if it is better or worse. There is an obvious connection between this process and evolution, by the identifications

Structure of the child machine = hereditary material

Changes of the child machine = mutation

Judgment of the experimenter = natural selection

[EDITOR: The sides of the third equation have been swapped from their positions in the original paper, so that all the evolutionary terms are on the right.] One may hope, however, that this process will be more expeditious than evolution. The survival of the fittest is a slow method for measuring advantages. The experimenter, by the exercise of intelligence, should be able to speed it up. Equally important is the fact that he is not restricted to random mutations. If he can trace a cause for some weakness he can probably think of the kind of mutation which will improve it.

It will not be possible to apply exactly the same teaching process to the machine as to a normal child. It will not, for instance, be provided with legs, so that it could not be asked to go out and fill the coal scuttle. Possibly it might not have eyes. But however well these deficiencies might be overcome by clever engineering, one could not send the creature to school without the other children making excessive fun of it. It must be given some tuition. We need not be too concerned about the legs, eyes, etc. The example of Miss Helen Keller shows that education can take place provided that communication in both directions between teacher and pupil can take place by some means or other. We normally associate punishments and rewards with the teaching process. Some simple child machines can be constructed or programmed on this sort of principle. The machine has to be so constructed that events which shortly preceded the occurrence of a punishment signal are unlikely to be repeated, whereas a reward signal increased the probability of repetition of the events which led up to it. These definitions do not presuppose any feelings on the part of the machine, I have done some experiments with one such child machine, and succeeded in teaching it a few things, but the teaching method was too unorthodox for the experiment to be considered really successful.

The use of punishments and rewards can at best be a part of the teaching process. Roughly speaking, if the teacher has no other means of communicating to the pupil, the amount of information which can reach him does not exceed the total number of rewards and punishments applied. By the time a child has learnt to repeat "Casabianca" he would probably feel very sore indeed, if the text could only be discovered by a "Twenty Questions" technique, every "NO" taking the form of a blow. It is necessary therefore to have some other "unemotional" channels of communication. If these are available it is possible to teach a machine by punishments and rewards to obey orders given in some language, e.g., a symbolic language. These orders are to be transmitted through the "unemotional" channels. The use of this language will diminish greatly the number of punishments and rewards required.

Opinions may vary as to the complexity which is suitable in the child machine. One might try to make it as simple as possible consistently with the general principles. Alternatively one might have a complete system of logical inference "built in." In the latter case the store would be largely occupied with definitions and propositions. The propositions would have various kinds of status, e.g., well-established facts, conjectures, mathematically proved theorems, statements given by an authority, expressions having the logical form of proposition but not belief-value. Certain propositions may be described as "imperatives." The machine should be so constructed that as soon as an imperative is classed as "well established" the appropriate action automatically takes place. To illustrate this, suppose the teacher says to the machine, "Do your homework now." This may cause "Teacher says 'Do your homework now'" to be included amongst the well-established facts. Another such fact might be, "Everything that teacher says is true." Combining these may eventually lead to the imperative, "Do your homework now," being included amongst the well-established facts, and this, by the construction of the machine, will mean that the homework actually gets started, but the effect is very satisfactory. The processes of inference used by the machine need not be such as would satisfy the most exacting logicians. There might for instance be no hierarchy of types. But this need not mean that type fallacies will occur, any more than we are bound to fall over unfenced cliffs. Suitable imperatives (expressed within the systems, not forming part of the rules of the system) such as "Do not use a class unless it is a subclass of one which has been mentioned by teacher" can have a similar effect to "Do not go too near the edge."

The imperatives that can be obeyed by a machine that has no limbs are bound to be of a rather intellectual character, as in the example (doing homework) given above. Important amongst such imperatives will be ones which regulate the order in which the rules of the logical system concerned are to be applied. For at each stage when one is using a logical system, there is a very large number of alternative steps, any of which one is permitted to apply, so far as obedience to the rules of the logical system is concerned. These choices make the difference between a brilliant and a footling reasoner, not the difference between a sound and a fallacious one. Propositions leading to imperatives of this kind might be "When Socrates is mentioned, use the syllogism in Barbara" or "If one method has been proved to be quicker than another, do not use the slower method." Some of these may be "given by authority," but others may be produced by the machine itself, e.g. by scientific induction. The idea of a learning machine may appear paradoxical to some readers. How can the rules of operation of the machine change? They should describe completely how the machine will react whatever its history might be, whatever changes it might undergo. The rules are thus quite time-invariant. This is quite true. The explanation of the paradox is that the rules which get changed in the learning process are of a rather less pretentious kind, claiming only an ephemeral validity. The reader may draw a parallel with the Constitution of the United States.

An important feature of a learning machine is that its teacher will often be very largely ignorant of quite what is going on inside, although he may still be able to some extent to predict his pupil's behavior. This should apply most strongly to the later education of a machine arising from a child machine of well-tried design (or programme). This is in clear contrast with normal procedure when using a machine to do computations one's object is then to have a clear mental picture of the state of the machine at each moment in the computation. This object can only be achieved with a struggle. The view that "the machine can only do what we know how to order it to do," appears strange in face of this. Most of the programmes which we can put into the machine will result in its doing something that we cannot make sense of at all, or which we regard as completely random behaviour. Intelligent behaviour presumably consists in a departure from the completely disciplined behaviour involved in computation, but a rather slight one, which does not give rise to random behaviour, or to pointless repetitive loops. Another important result of preparing our machine for its part in the imitation game by a process of teaching and learning is that "human fallibility" is likely to be omitted in a rather natural way, i.e., without special "coaching." (The reader should reconcile this with the point of view on page 156.) Processes that are learnt do not produce a hundred per cent certainty of result; if they did they could not be unlearnt.

It is probably wise to include a random element in a learning machine. A random element is rather useful when we are searching for a solution of some problem. Suppose for instance we wanted to find a number between 50 and 200 which was equal to the square of the sum of its digits, we might start at 51 then try 52 and go on until we got a number that worked. Alternatively we might choose numbers at random until we got a good one. This method has the advantage that it is unnecessary to keep track of the values that have been tried, but the disadvantage that one may try the same one twice, but this is not very important if there are several solutions. The systematic method has the disadvantage that there may be an enormous block without any solutions in the region which has to be investigated first. Now the learning process may be regarded as a search for a form of behaviour which will satisfy the teacher (or some other criterion). Since there is probably a very large number of satisfactory solutions the random method seems to be better than the systematic. It should be noticed that it is used in the analogous process of evolution. But there the systematic method is not possible. How could one keep track of the different genetical combinations that had been tried, so as to avoid trying them again?

We may hope that machines will eventually compete with men in all purely intellectual fields. But which are the best ones to start with? Even this is a difficult decision. Many people think that a very abstract activity, like the playing of chess, would be best. It can also be maintained that it is best to provide the machine with the best sense organs that money can buy, and then teach it to understand and speak English. This process could follow the normal teaching of a child. Things would be pointed out and named, etc. Again I do not know what the right answer is, but I think both approaches should be tried.

We can only see a short distance ahead, but we can see plenty there that needs to be done.

15 The Best Way to Design an Automatic Calculating Machine (1951)

Maurice Wilkes

In 1946, Maurice Wilkes (1913–2010), then head of the Mathematics Laboratory at the University of Cambridge in England, attended a summer school taught at the Moore School of the University of Pennsylvania and learned about the EDVAC of Burks, Goldstine, von Neumann, et al. On the return voyage, he began the design of a machine he dubbed the Electronic Delay Storage Automatic Calculator, or EDSAC. By 1949, when the EDSAC was up and running, a stored-program computer called the Mark 1 was already operational in England at the University of Manchester—a project mentioned both by Wilkes in this piece and by Turing in chapter 14 (pages 150 and 159). The Manchester Mark 1 served more as an experimental prototype than as a computational workhorse (a follow-on machine was put into commercial production in 1951 as the Ferranti Mark 1).

The EDSAC, by contrast, was soon being used to capacity as a resource to the Cambridge scientific community, and Wilkes began work on a successor machine. As he designed the data formats and instruction set, he came to the crucial realization that it would be far easier to design a more primitive micro-instruction set for such micro-operations as shifting bits within a register or moving bits between registers, and then to implement the actual machine instructions as micro-programs of those micro-instructions—"giving the control unit the full flexibility of a programmed computer in miniature," as he later put it (Wilkes, 1986). At the end of this article he even imagines that programmers might some day be able to choose their own instruction sets.

Microcode was indeed quickly recognized as the "best way" to design a computer. Later in the 1950s, IBM adopted microcode for the design of its System/360 line of computers, greatly easing the task of debugging and even field modifying the design of complex operations such as multiplication. The idea of flexible, hierarchical, updatable design is behind the ubiquitous use of firmware in modern systems.

Wilkes went on to a distinguished career as a professor at Cambridge and authored one of the earliest textbooks on computer programming. He received the Turing Award in 1967 for his many contributions to the field.

———————◦◦◖◗◦◦———————

Reprinted from Wilkes (1981), with permission from Elsevier.

. . .

I think that most people will agree that the first consideration for a designer at the present time is how he is to achieve the maximum degree of reliability in his machine. Amongst other things the reliability of the machine will depend on the following:

(a) The amount of equipment it contains.

(b) Its complexity.

(c) The degree of repetition of units.

By the complexity of a machine I mean the extent to which cross-connections between the various units obscure their logical interrelation. A machine is easier to repair if it consists of a number of units connected together in a simple way without cross-connections between them; it is also easier to construct since different people can work on the different units without getting in each other's way.

As regards repetition I think everyone would prefer to have in a particular part of the machine a group of five identical units rather than a group of five different units. Most people would prefer to have six identical units rather than five different units. How far one ought to be prepared to go in the direction of accepting a greater quantity of equipment in order to achieve repetition is a matter of opinion. The matter may be put as follows. Suppose that it is regarded as being equally desirable to have a particular part of the machine composed of a group of n different units, or composed of a group of kn identical units, all the units being of similar size. What is the value of k? My conjecture is that $k > 2$. I should say that I am thinking of a machine which has about 10 groups of units and that n is approximately equal to 10.

The remarks I have just made are of general application. I will now try to be more specific. If one builds a parallel machine one has a good example, in the arithmetical unit, of a piece of equipment consisting of identical units repeated many times. Such an arithmetical unit is, however, much larger than that in a serial machine. On the other hand I think it is true to say that the control in a parallel machine is simpler than in a serial machine. I am using the word *control* here in a very general sense to include everything that does not appertain to the store proper (i.e., it includes the access circuits) or to the registers and adders in the arithmetical unit. . . .

We are thus led to think of an arithmetical unit composed of a number of standard units each containing four flip-flops (one belonging to each of four registers) together with an adder. Gates would be provided to make possible the transfer of numbers from one register to another, through the adder when necessary. These transfers would be effected by pulsing one or more of a set of wires emerging from the arithmetical unit.

It is also necessary to have registers in the control of a machine. These, with the names given to them respectively in the Manchester machine and in the EDSAC, are as follows:

Register for holding the address of the next order due to be executed (control, or sequence control tank).

Register holding order at present being executed (current instruction register, or order tank).

Register for counting the number of steps in a multiplication or shifting operation (not needed with the fast multiplier on the Manchester machine, timing control tank in the EDSAC).

In addition the Manchester machine has a number of B registers.

If one B register is considered to be sufficient the parallel machine we are considering can use the same unit (containing 4 flip-flops and 1 adder) for the control registers as for arithmetical registers. In this way an extreme degree of repetition can be achieved.

It remains to consider the control proper, that is, the part of the machine which supplies the pulses for operating the gates associated with the arithmetical and control registers. The designer of this part of a machine usually proceeds in an *ad hoc* manner, drawing block diagrams until he sees an arrangement which satisfies his requirements and appears to be reasonably economical. I would like to suggest a way in which the control can be made systematic, and therefore less complex.

Each operation called for by an order in the order code of the machine involves a sequence of steps which may include transfers from the store to control or arithmetical registers, or *vice versa*, and transfers from one register to another. Each of these steps is achieved by pulsing certain of the wires associated with the control and arithmetical registers, and I will refer to it as a "micro-operation." Each true machine operation is thus made up of a sequence of "micro-programme" of micro-operations.

Figure 15.1 shows the way in which pulses for performing the micro-operations may be generated. The timing pulse which initiates a micro-operation enters the decoding tree and is routed to one of the outputs according to the number set on the register R. It passes into the rectifier matrix A and gives rise to pulses on certain of the output wires of this matrix according to the arrangement of the rectifiers. These pulses operate the gates associated with the control and arithmetical registers, and cause the correct micro-operation to be performed. The pulse from the decoding tree also passes into matrix B and gives rise to pulses on certain of the output wires of this matrix. These pulses are conducted, via a short delay line, to the register R and cause the number set up on it to be changed. The result is that the next initiating pulse to enter the decoding tree will emerge from a different outlet and will consequently cause a different micro-operation to be performed. It will thus be seen that each row of rectifiers in matrix A corresponds to one of the micro-orders in the sequence required to perform a machine operation.

The system as described would enable a fixed cycle of operations only to be performed. Its utility can be greatly extended by making some of the micro-orders conditional in the sense that they are followed by one of two alternative micro-orders according to the state of the machine. This can be done by making the output of the decoding tree branch before it enters matrix B. The direction the pulse takes at the branch is controlled by the potential on a wire coming from another part of the machine; for example, it might come from the sign flip-flop of the accumulator. The bottom row of matrix A in Figure 15.1 corresponds to a conditional micro-order. The matrix A contains sequences of micro-orders for performing all the basic operations in the order code of the machine. All that is necessary to perform a particular operation is that "micro-control" shall be switched to the first micro-order in the appropriate sequence. This is done by causing the function digits of the order to be set up on the first four or five flip-flops of the register *R*, zero being set on the others.

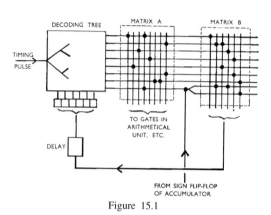

Figure 15.1

A control system designed in this way is certainly very logical in structure but two comments, slightly contradictory in their implications, might be made. In the first place it might be said that there is nothing very new about the arrangement since it makes use of flip-flops, gates, and mixing diodes which are the elements out of which any control is built. With this criticism I would agree. In fact, the controls of various machines now in existence or being constructed could no doubt be drawn in some way closely resembling Figure 15.1. The other objection is that the scheme appears to be rather extravagant in equipment. This I

think is not true, particularly if some departures from the precise form of Figure 15.1 are allowed. I think that by starting with a logical layout one is likely to arrive at a final arrangement which is both logical and economical. Moreover, one is able to see at each stage what one is sacrificing in the way of logical layout in order to achieve economy and vice versa. In order to get some idea of the number of micro-orders required I have constructed a micro-programme for a simple machine with the following orders: add, subtract, multiply (two orders, one for the multiplier, one for the multiplicand), right and left shift (any number of places), transfer from the accumulator to the store, conditional operation depending on the sign of the number in the accumulator, conditional operation depending on the sign of the number in the B register (one B register is assumed), transfer from the store to the B register, input, and output. The micro-programme also provides for the preliminary extraction of the order from the store (Stage 1 in EDSAC terminology). Only 40 micro-orders are required to perform all these operations.

The considerations involved in drawing-up a micro-programme resemble those involved in drawing-up an ordinary programme. The final details of the control are thus settled by a systematic process instead of by the usual *ad hoc* procedures based on the use of block diagrams. Of course, sound engineering would be necessary to produce designs for the decoding tree and the matrices which could be used for any desired micro-programme by arranging the rectifiers suitably in the matrices. One important advantage of this method of designing the control is that the order code need not be decided on finally until a late stage in the construction of the machine; it would even be possible to change it after the machine had been put into operation simply by rewiring the matrices.

16 The Education of a Computer (1952)

Grace Murray Hopper

Grace Murray Hopper (1906–1992) had a remarkable professional career, duly honored today both in the name of the national meeting of women computer scientists (the annual Grace Murray Hopper Conference) and in the name of a U.S. Naval warship (the USS Hopper, a guided missile destroyer). In 1934 she received a PhD in mathematics from Yale, and until the start of World War II was a mathematics professor at Vassar, where she had earned her undergraduate degree. Starting around 1940 she tried to join the Navy, but was rejected as too old. In 1943 she finally was accepted into the Naval Reserve in spite of being underweight at 120 pounds. She was assigned to Howard Aiken's Computation Lab at Harvard, where she programmed the Mark I and its successor machine the Mark II. She famously taped into a log book a moth that had caused a relay to malfunction. Her ironic notation "First actual case of a bug being found," acknowledges that she didn't coin the term "bug," which was already engineering jargon for a machine error. More importantly, she recognized, as Aiken did, that the future of computing would be as much in business data processing as in scientific calculation.

In 1949 Hopper joined the Eckert–Mauchly Computer Corporation, which was commercializing the design that had come out of the Moore School (see page 90). That company was bought by Remington Rand, Hopper's affiliation as listed in this paper; the company's machine was called the UNIVAC. (After further mergers and acquisitions the company became UNISYS.)

In the 1940s there were no higher level languages, no parsers, and hardly even a usable symbolic representation for machine code. There were no compilers and no debugging tools. The entire process of translating an algorithm into running code was done by hand, using paper and pencil until the very last step of inputting the program. Hopper here signals the beginning of the process of computers assisting programmers. The paper includes allusions not only to "compilers" (including what today would be called linking loaders and code relocation) but symbolic programming (she anticipates that computers will compute symbolic derivatives); code optimization trade-offs; global program analysis ("sweeping the computer information once to examine its structure"); macro-assembly language (referred to here as a "multiple-address code"); formal specifications of subroutines; hierarchical program structure; the redirection of attention from the kinds of numerical algorithms that had been so important during wartime toward commercial applications; and the recognition that the cost of software would in the long run vastly exceed the cost of hardware.

Reprinted from Hopper (1952), with permission from the Association for Computing Machinery.

All these elements are in this paper, but they are not described straightforwardly. The paper is elaborately anthropomorphic. It is hard to tell at each stage of expansion and generalization where the line between human and machine is supposed to lie, because Hopper is anticipating that the line would shift over time—the computer's "education" would advance. Within a couple of years she had become the head of "automatic programming" at Remington Rand, leading the development of the early programming languages ARITH-MATIC and MATH-MATIC (Ash et al., 1957), which seem to correspond roughly to the Type A and Type B routines of this paper.

Those languages were specific to the UNIVAC. But Hopper went on to be the determined force behind the development and standardization of COBOL (a COmmon Business Oriented Language), in the face of skepticism that computers could be made to handle data manipulations paraphrased in English-like vocabulary, and that the gains in programming efficiency from using such languages would far outweigh any loss in execution speed. She had a reputation as a stubborn, contrarian thinker throughout her life, using vivid metaphors to make her points. She brought "nanoseconds" to pass out in public talks in the form of foot-long segments of copper wire, and displayed a backwards-running clock with a mirror-image dial behind her desk to make the point that conventions are made to be broken.

Hopper had a distinguished career in the Navy, attaining the rank of Rear Admiral. I have a personal memory of her, one that suggests the obstacles that stood in the way of her career at every step. When she returned to Harvard in uniform in the 1970s, decades after her Mark I work there as a novice reservist, she was in a foul mood. The cabin crew of the airplane on which she had flown to Boston had treated the diminutive, gray-haired lady in the Navy admiral's uniform with great deference—as a retired stewardess!

—◦◦◦◦◦◦—

WHILE the materialization is new, the idea of mechanizing mathematical thinking is not new. Its lineage starts with the abacus and descends through Pascal, Leibniz, and Babbage. More immediately, the ideas here presented originate from Howard H. Aiken of Harvard University, John W. Mauchly of Eckert–Mauchly and M. V. Wilkes of the University of Cambridge. From Aiken came, in 1946, the idea of a library of routines described in the Mark I manual, and the concepts embodied in the Mark III coding machine, from Mauchly, the basic principles of the "short-order code" and suggestions, criticisms, and untiring patience in listening to these present attempts; from Wilkes, the greatest help of all, a book on the subject. For those of their ideas which are included herein, I most earnestly express my debt and my appreciation.

16.1   Introduction

To start at the beginning, Figure 16.1 represents the configuration of the elements required by an operation: input to the operations; controls, even if they be only start and stop; previously prepared tools supplied to the operation; and output of products, which may, in turn, become the

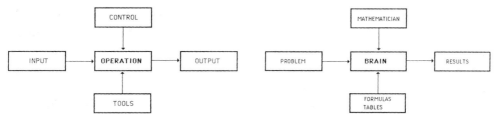

Figure 16.1: An operation   Figure 16.2: Solution of problem

input of another operation. This is the basic element of a production line; input of raw materials, controlled by human beings, possibly through instruments; supplied with machine tools; the operation produces an automobile, a rail, or a can of tomatoes.

The armed services, government, and industry are interested not only in creating new operations to produce new results, but also increasing the efficiency of old operations. A very old operation, Figure 16.2, is the solution of a mathematical problem. It fits the operational configuration: input of mathematical data; control by the mathematician; supplied with memory, formulas, tables, pencil, and paper; the brain carries on the arithmetic, and produces results.

It is the current aim to replace, as far as possible, the human brain by an electronic digital computer. That such computers themselves fit this configuration may be seen in Figure 16.3. (With your permission, I shall use UNIVAC as synonymous with electronic digital computer; primarily because I think that way, but also because it is convenient.)

Adding together the configurations of the human being and the electronic computer, Figure 16.4 shows the solution of a problem in two levels of operation. The arithmetical

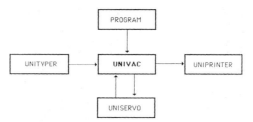

Figure 16.3: The UNIVAC system. [EDITOR: UNITYPER was a typewriter input device, UNISERVO a magnetic tape drive.]

chore has been removed from the mathematician, who has become a programmer, and this duty assigned to the UNIVAC. The programmer has been supplied with a "code" into which he translates his instructions to the computer. The "standard knowledge" designed into the UNIVAC by its engineers, consists of its elementary arithmetic and logic.

This situation remains static until the novelty of inventing programs wears off and degenerates into the dull labor of writing and checking programs. This duty now looms as an imposition on the human brain. Also, with the computer paid for, the cost of programming and the time consumed, comes to the notice of vice-presidents and project directors. Common sense dictates the insertion of a third level of operation, Figure 16.5.

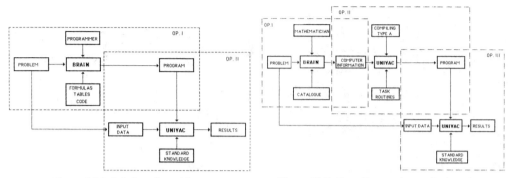

Figure 16.4: Solution of a problem.   Figure 16.5: Compiling routines and subroutines.

The programmer may return to being a mathematician. He is supplied with a catalogue of subroutines. No longer does he need to have available formulas or tables of elementary functions. He does not even need to know the particular instruction code used by the computer. He needs only to be able to use the catalogue to supply information to the computer about his problem. The UNIVAC, on the basis of the information supplied by the mathematician, under the control of a "compiling routine of type A," using subroutines and its own instruction code, produces a program. This program, in turn directs the UNIVAC through the computation on the input data and the desired results are produced. A major reduction in time consumed and in sources of error has been made. If the library is well-stocked, programming has been reduced to a matter of hours, rather than weeks. The program is no longer subject either to errors of transcription or of untested routines.

Specifications for computer information, a catalogue, compiling routines, and subroutines will be given after adding another level to the block diagram. As Figure 16.5 stands the mathematician must still perform all mathematical operations, relegating to the UNIVAC programming and computational operations. However, the computer information delivered by the mathematician no longer deals with numerical quantities as such. It treats of variables and constants in symbolic form together with operations upon them. The insertion of a fourth level of operation is now possible, Figure 16.6. Suppose, for example, the mathematician wishes to evaluate a function and its first *n* derivatives. He sends the information defining the function itself to the UNIVAC. Under control of a "compiling routine of type B," in this case a differentiator, using task routines, the UNIVAC delivers the information necessary to program the computation of the function and its derivatives. From the formula for the function, the UNIVAC derives the formulas of the successive derivatives. This information processed under a compiling routine of Type A yields a program to direct the computation.

Expansion makes this procedure look, and seem, long and complicated. It is not. Reducing again to the two-component system, the mathematician and the computer, Figure 16.7 presents a more accurate picture of the computing system.

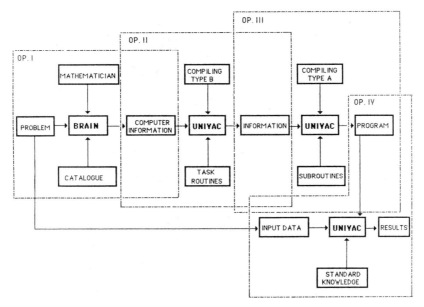

Figure 16.6: Compiling Type B and task routines.

Presuming that code, program, input data, and results are familiar terms, it remains to define and specify the forms of information and routines acceptable to this system. These include catalogue; computer information; subroutine; compiling routines; type A and B; and task routines.

As soon as the purpose is stated to make use of subroutines, two methods arise. In one, the program refers to an immediately available subroutine, uses it, and continues computation. For a limited number of subroutines, this method is feasible and useful. Such a system has been developed under the nickname of the "short-order code" by members of the staff of the Computational Analysis Laboratory [EDITOR: at Eckert–Mauchly Computer Corporation].

The second method not only looks up the subroutine, but translates it, properly adjusted, into a program. Thus, the completed program may be run as a unit whenever desired, and may itself be placed in the library as a more advanced subroutine.

16.2   Catalogue and Computer Information

Each problem must be reduced to the level of the available subroutines. Suppose a simple problem, to compute $y = e^{-x^2} \sin cx$, using elementary subroutines. Each step of the formula falls into the operational pattern, Figure 16.8; that is, $u = x^2; U = e^{-u}; v = cx; V = \sin v; y = UV$. As presented in Figure 16.9, however, this information is not yet sufficiently standardized to be acceptable to a compiling routine. Several problems must be considered and procedures defined. [EDITOR: Hopper here follows the footsteps of Lovelace—compare to Figure 3.1 on page 14.]

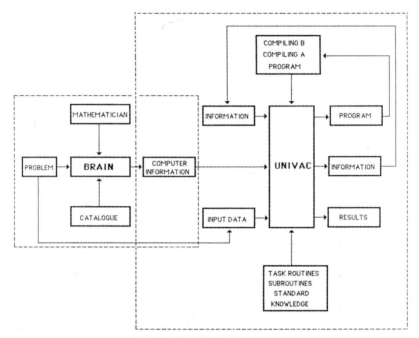

Figure 16.7: Computing system.

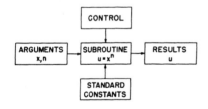

Figure 16.8: Operation

The operations are numbered in normal sequence and this number becomes part of the computer information. Thus when it is desired to change the normal sequence, the alternate destination is readily identified. The compiling routine translates these operation numbers into instructions in the coded program. Two fundamental situations arise, the alternate destination either precedes the operation under consideration or follows it, by-passing several intermediate operations. In both cases, it is necessary only to have the compiling routine remember where it has placed each subroutine or that a transfer of control to operation k has been indicated. In any event the mathematician need only state, "go to operation k," and the compiling routine does the rest.

The symbols to be used for the arguments and results, as well as for the operations, are of next concern. One mathematician might write $y = e^{-x^2} \sin cx$, and another $u = e^{-v^2} \sin gv$. The obvious solution proves best. Make a list of arguments and results and number them. (This amounts to writing all constants and variables as x_i.) The order is immaterial, so that forgotten quantities can be added at the end (Figure 16.10).

$y = e^{-x^2} \sin cx$				
Operation number	Operation	Arguments	Results	Control
0	TRANSFER b0i	$0, 0.01, 0.99, 2, 5$ $I(1, 2, 3, 4, 5)$	$x, \Delta x, L_x, n, c$ $1, 2, 3, 10, 6$	
1	x^n apn	x, n $1, 10$	$u = x^2$ 4	
2	e^{-u} x-e	u 4	$U = e^{-u}$ 5	
3	$c\otimes$ amc	c, x $6, 1$	$v = cx$ 7	
4	$\sin v$ ts0	v 7	$V = \sin v$ 8	
5	$\otimes$ am0	U, V $5, 8$	$y = UV$ 9	
6	EDIT yrs	x, y $1, 9$	$\bar{x}, \bar{y}$ O (1, 2)	
7	$\oplus \to L$ aaL	$x, \Delta x, L_x$ $1, 2, 3$	$x + \Delta x \to x$ 1	$x < L_x \to 1, x \geq L_x \to 8$ 8, 1
8	STOP ust			

1	x	x_1
2	Δx	x_2
3	L_x	x_3
4	u	x_4
5	U	x_5
6	c	x_6
7	v	x_7
8	V	x_8
9	y	x_9
10	n	x_{10}

Figure 16.9: Example [EDITOR: aaL = "add to a limit" (Ash et al., 1957, page 86).]

Figure 16.10: Variable table for Figure 16.9

As symbols for the operations and subroutines, a system of "call-numbers" is used. These alphabetic characters represent the class of subroutines. Following Dr. Wilkes' example, these symbols are partially phonetic; that is, a = arithmetic, t = trigonometric, and x = exponential; amc = arithmetic, multiplication by a constant; x-e = e^{-U}; ts0 = trigonometric, sine. Placed with the call-numbers, n, f, or s, indicates normal, floating, or stated (fixed) decimal point. Other letters and digits indicate radians or degrees for angles, complex numbers, etc. These call-numbers are listed in the catalogue together with the order in which arguments, controls, and results are to be stated. ...

16.3   Subroutines

Each subroutine in the library is expressed in coding relative to its entrance line considered as 001. They are, in general, programmed and coded for maximum accuracy and minimum computing time. They may store within themselves constants peculiar to themselves. They may also make use of certain "permanent constants" read in with every program. These permanent constants occupy a reserved section of the memory and are called for by alphabetic memory locations, a trick, at present peculiar to UNIVAC. Thus, these addresses are not modified in the course of positioning the subroutine in a program. They include such quantities as $1/2\pi$, $\pi/4$, $\log_{10} e$, ± 0, .2, .5, and the like.

Each subroutine is preceded by certain information, matching and supplementing that supplied by the mathematician:

1. call-number;

2. arguments, the destination of the arguments within the subroutine, expressed in the relative coding of the subroutines;

3. non-modification indicators locating constants embedded in the subroutine which are not to be altered;

4. results, the positions of the results within the subroutine, expressed in relative coding.

Each subroutine is arranged in a standard pattern.

Entrance line – The first line of a subroutine is its entrance line, thus in relative coding it is number one. It is the first line of the subroutine transferred to a program, and it contains an instruction transferring control to the first action line.

Exit lines – The second line of a subroutine is its normal exit line. This contains an instruction transferring control to the line following the last line of the subroutine. Unless an alternate transfer of control is desired, all exits from the subroutine are referred to the normal exit line. Alternate exit lines, involving transfers of control from the usual sequence follow the normal exit line in a predetermined order as listed in the catalogue.

Arguments – The exit lines are followed by spaces reserved for the arguments arranged in predetermined order.

Results – The results, also in specified order, follow the arguments.

Constants – The results are followed, when possible, by any arbitrary constants peculiar to the subroutine. When the subroutine has been compounded from other subroutines groups of constants may also appear embedded in the subroutine. These are cared for by the non-modification information.

The *first action line* appears next in the subroutine. Its position in the relative coding is defined by the entrance line. No instruction line may precede this line.

The sequence assigned to the entrance and exit lines, arguments, results, and constants is arbitrary. It is convenient. All that is required is that a sequence be established and that the computer recognize this sequence.

For convenience in manipulation, a certain number of elementary subroutines have been combined to form a sub-library. . . . As subroutines are added to extend the library, it becomes more useful and programming time is further reduced.

Indeed, the day may come when the elementary subroutines are rarely used and the computer information will contain but seven or eight items calling into play powerful subroutines.

16.4   Construction of Subroutines

It is not necessary, nor is it advisable that the inexperienced programmer tamper with the coding within a subroutine. It is usually minimum latency coding using every trick and device known to the experienced programmer. It has been tested by operation on the computer. . . .

Compiling Routines Type A are designed to select and arrange subroutines according to information supplied by the mathematician or by the computer. Basically, there is but one Type A routine. However since the UNIVAC code contains instructions transferring two neighboring quantities simultaneously, a second compiling routine has been designed to care for floating decimal, complex number, and double precision programs. For each operation listed by the mathematician a type A routine will perform the following services:

1. locate the subroutine indicated by the call-number;
2. from the computer and subroutine information combined with its record of the program fabricate and enter in the program the instructions transferring the arguments from working storage to the subroutines;
3. adjust the entrance and normal exit lines to the position of the subroutine in the program and enter them in the program;
4. according to the control information supplied by the programmer adjust alternate exit lines and enter them in the program (this process involves reference to the record);
5. according to the control information supplied with previous operations adjust auxiliary entrance lines and enter them in the program;
6. modify all addresses in the subroutine instructions and enter these instructions in the program;
7. according to information supplied by the subroutine, leave unaltered all constants embedded in the subroutine and transfer them to the program;
8. from the computer and the subroutine information fabricate and enter in the program the instructions transferring the results to [EDITOR: text missing, perhaps "working storage"].
9. maintain and produce a record of the program including the call-number of each subroutine and the position of its entrance line in the program.

The compiling routines also contain certain instructions concerning input tapes, tape library, and program tapes peculiar to the UNIVAC. All counting operations such as allocation of temporary storage and program space, and control of input and output are carried on steadily by the compiling routine. Stated bluntly the compiling routine is the programmer and performs all those services necessary to the production of a finished program.

Compiling Routines of Type B will for each operation, by means of "task routines," replace or supplement the given computer information with new information. Thus, compiling routine B-1 will, for each operation, copy the information concerning that operation and call in the corresponding task routine. The task routine will generate the formula, and derive the information necessary to compute the derivative of the operation. Compiling routine B-1 then records this information in a form suitable for submission to a Type A routine.

Since information may be re-submitted to a type B routine, it is obvious that in order to obtain a program to compute $f(x)$ and its first n derivatives only the information defining $f(x)$ and the value of n need be given. The formulas for the derivatives of $f(x)$ will be derived by repeated applications of B-1 and programmed by a type A routine.

It is here that the question can best be answered concerning a liking for or an aversion to subroutines. Since the use of subroutines in this fashion increases the abilities of the computer, the question becomes meaningless and transforms into a question of how to produce better subroutines faster. However, balancing the advantages and disadvantages of using subroutines, among the advantages are

1. relegation of mechanical jobs such as memory allocation, address modification, and transcription to the UNIVAC;
2. removal of error sources such as programming errors and transcription errors;
3. conservation of programming time;
4. ability to operate on operations;
5. duplication of effort is avoided, since each program in turn may become a subroutine.

Only two disadvantages are immediately evident. Because of standardization, a small amount of time is lost in performing duplicate data transfers which could be eliminated in a tailor-made routine. In base load problems, this could become serious. Even in this case however, it is worthwhile to have UNIVAC produce the original program and then eliminate such duplication before rerunning the problem. The second disadvantage should not long remain serious. It is the fact that, if a desired subroutine does not exist, it must be programmed and added to the library. This will be most likely to occur in the case of input and output editing routines until a large variety is accumulated. This situation also emphasizes the need for the greatest generality in the construction of subroutines.

Several directions of future developments in this field can be pointed out. . . .

More type A compiling routines will be devised: those handling commercial rather than mathematical programs; some special purpose compiling routines such as a routine which will compute approximate magnitudes as it proceeds and select sub-routines accordingly. Compiling routines must be informed of the average time required for each sub-routine so that they can supply estimates of running time with each program. For example, if both $\sin\theta$ and $\cos\theta$ are called for in a single routine, they will be computed more rapidly simultaneously. This will involve sweeping the computer information once to examine its structure.

Type B routines at present include linear operators. More type B routines must be designed. It can scarcely be denied that type C and D routines will be found to exist adding higher levels of operation. Work is already in progress to produce the formulas developed by type B routines in algebraic form in addition to producing their computational programs.

Thus by considering the professional programmer (not the mathematician), as an integral part of the computer, it is evident that the memory of the programmer and all information and data to which he can refer is available to the computer subject only to translation into suitable language. And it is further evident that the computer is fully capable of remembering and acting upon any instructions once presented to it by the programmer.

With some specialized knowledge of more advanced topics, UNIVAC at present has a well grounded mathematical education fully equivalent to that of a college sophomore, and it does not forget and does not make mistakes. It is hoped that its undergraduate course will be completed shortly and it will be accepted as a candidate for a graduate degree.

17 On the Shortest Spanning Subtree of a Graph and the Traveling Salesman Problem (1956)

Joseph B. Kruskal, Jr.

This paper by mathematician Joseph Kruskal (1928–2010) marks an early step along a path from operations research—a field that had flourished during the 1940s in response to the need to solve a variety of commercial, military, and logistical problems—to computer science, which some define as the study of algorithms. The particular algorithm presented here as Construction A, now known as Kruskal's algorithm, finds the minimum-cost spanning tree in an undirected graph by growing a forest, adding edges one by one from shortest to longest, not including any edge that would create a cycle. Borůvka (1926), to which the paper refers in its first sentence, is probably the first published algorithm for this problem, dating from a time before the basic vocabulary of graph theory had been formalized. In that paper, the Czech mathematician Otakar Borůvka had solved the problem of finding the most efficient electrical network for Moravia, a region of what is now the Czech Republic.

To contemporary readers, Kruskal's presentation is remarkable for its lucidity—the description and proof of the algorithm are as spare and elegant as in any more recent treatment—and for the complete absence of any analysis. Kruskal describes his algorithm as "practical" without suggesting what that might mean in terms of runtime or any other specific form of complexity, or even what parameters most seriously affect the algorithm's behavior.

Deconstructing that term "practical" recapitulates the remarkable history of algorithm analysis. It would take another decade before Edmonds and Cobham would characterize polynomial running time as a rough proxy for the intuitive notion of practicality (see page 333). But then Donald Knuth raised the bar for finer-grained algorithm analysis (see chapter 43). Taking into account the time required to retrieve the edges in order using naïve methods, the time complexity of Kruskal's algorithm is $O(m \log n)$, where m is the number of edges and n is the number of vertices. But that is not the end of the story. Knuth's student Robert Tarjan (1975) developed a remarkable analysis of a known simple algorithm for keeping track of sets and their unions. Using those data structures, the complexity of Kruskal's algorithm turns out to be $O(m\alpha(n))$ under certain commonly satisfied assumptions. Here $\alpha(n)$ is the inverse of Ackermann's function—an unbounded function that grows so slowly that $\alpha(n) < 5$ for all n less than the number of particles in the universe. For all intents and purposes, the running time of a good implementation of Kruskal's algorithm grows in simple proportion to the number of edges.

Reprinted from Kruskal (1956), with permission from the American Mathematical Society.

Kruskal notes the elegant similarity between the minimum spanning tree problem and the traveling salesman problem, without making any progress toward an efficient solution of the latter. The dramatic difference between these problems would not be clarified until the early 1970s, when Karp showed that the traveling salesman problem is $\mathcal{NP}$-complete. (UNDIRECTED HAMILTON CIRCUIT, page 354, is a special case of the traveling salesman problem in which distances between adjacent vertices are all 1.)

The other leading algorithm for finding the minimum spanning tree is known as Prim's algorithm in honor of its publication by Robert Clay Prim (1957)—in fact it is a special case of Kruskal's Construction B in which the set he refers to as V includes only one vertex. This algorithm grows a single tree by adding edges adjacent to the existing tree, starting with the shortest (and not including edges that would create a cycle)—like Construction A, an example of what is now known as a greedy strategy. Prim's algorithm was rediscovered by Edsger Dijkstra (1959) in the course of developing his algorithm for the shortest paths problem, though in fact Prim, Kruskal Construction B, and Dijkstra were all anticipated by the much earlier work of another Czech, Vojtěch Jarník (1930). (Kruskal also includes a third greedy algorithm A' that has no common name.) The transitive closure algorithm of Warshall (1962) and the all-pairs shortest path algorithm of Floyd (1962) are both examples of dynamic programming, marking another step along the path from operations research to computer science.

Joseph Kruskal was a member of a remarkable mathematical family. His father, a Jewish immigrant from the Baltics to New York in 1892, became a successful furrier; his mother was a pioneer in introducing origami to America. Joseph's oldest brother, William, became a professor of statistics at the University of Chicago, and a second brother, Martin David, was a professor of astrophysical sciences and applied mathematics at Princeton. His nephew Clyde Kruskal is a professor of computer science at the University of Maryland. Joseph wrote this paper while he was a graduate student at Princeton, where he received his PhD in 1954, and it was published while he was working at Princeton under the auspices of the U.S. Office of Naval Research. In 1959 he joined Bell Labs, where he spent most of his career. He did important work in statistics and statistical linguistics as well as in the field we now know as computer science.

SEVERAL years ago a typewritten translation (of obscure origin) of Borůvka (1926) raised some interest. This paper is devoted to the following theorem: If a (finite) connected graph has a positive real number attached to each edge (the *length* of the edge), and if these lengths are all distinct, then among the spanning trees (German: Gerüst) of the graph there is only one, the sum of whose edges is a minimum; that is, the shortest spanning tree of the graph is unique. (A subgraph spans a graph if it contains all the vertices of the graph. Actually in Borůvka [1926] this theorem is stated and proved in terms of the "matrix of lengths" of the graph, that is, the matrix $\|a_{ij}\|$ where a_{ij} is the length of the edge connecting vertices i and j. Of course, it is assumed that $a_{ij} = a_{ji}$ and that $a_{ii} = 0$ for all i and j.)

The proof in Borůvka (1926) is based on a not unreasonable method of constructing a spanning subtree of minimum length. It is in this construction that the interest largely lies, for it is a solution to a problem (Problem 1 below) which on the surface is closely related to one version (Problem 2 below) of the well-known traveling salesman problem.

PROBLEM 1. Give a practical method for constructing a spanning subtree of minimum length.

PROBLEM 2. Give a practical method for constructing an unbranched spanning subtree of minimum length.

The construction given in Borůvka (1926) is unnecessarily elaborate. In the present paper I give several simpler constructions which solve Problem 1, and I show how one of these constructions may be used to prove the theorem of Borůvka (1926). Probably it is true that any construction which solves Problem 1 may be used to prove this theorem.

First I would like to point out that there is no loss of generality in assuming that the given connected graph G is complete, that is, that every pair of vertices is connected by an edge. For if any edge of G is "missing," an edge of great length may be inserted, and this does not alter the graph in any way which is relevant to the present purposes. Also, it is possible and intuitively appealing to think of missing edges as edges of infinite length.

CONSTRUCTION A. Perform the following step as many times as possible: Among the edges of G not yet chosen, choose the shortest edge which does not form any loops with those edges already chosen. Clearly the set of edges eventually chosen must form a spanning tree of G, and in fact it forms a shortest spanning tree.

CONSTRUCTION B. Let V be an arbitrary but fixed (nonempty) subset of the vertices of G. Then perform the following step as many times as possible: Among the edges of G which are not yet chosen but which are connected either to a vertex of V or to an edge already chosen, pick the shortest edge which does not form any loops with the edges already chosen. Clearly the set of edges eventually chosen forms a spanning tree of G, and in fact it forms a shortest spanning tree. In case V is the set of all vertices of G, then Construction B reduces to Construction A.

CONSTRUCTION A'. This method is in some sense dual to A. Perform the following step as many times as possible: Among the edges not yet chosen, choose the longest edge whose removal will not disconnect them. Clearly the set of edges not eventually chosen forms a spanning tree of G, and in fact it forms a shortest spanning tree. It is not clear to me whether Construction B in general has a dual analogous to this.

Before showing how Construction A may be used to prove the theorem of Borůvka (1926), I find it convenient to combine into a theorem a number of elementary facts of graph theory. The reader should have no trouble convincing himself that these are true. For aesthetic reasons, I state considerably more than I need.

PRELIMINARY THEOREM. *If G is a connected graph with n vertices, and T is a subgraph of G, then the following conditions are all equivalent:*

(a) T is a spanning tree of G;

(b) T is a maximal forest in G;

(c) T is a minimal connected spanning graph of G;

(d) T is a forest with n − 1 edges;

(e) T is a connected spanning graph with n − 1 edges.

(A graph is "maximal" if it is not contained in any larger graph of the same sort; it is "minimal" if it does not contain any smaller graph of the same sort. A "forest" is a graph which does not have any loops.) The theorem to be proved states that if the edges of G all have distinct lengths, then T is unique, where T is any shortest spanning tree of G. Clearly T may be redefined as any shortest forest with $n − 1$ edges.

In Construction A, let the edges chosen be called $a_1, \ldots, a_{n-1}$ in the order chosen. Let A_i be the forest consisting of edges a_1 through a_i. It will be proved that $T = A_{n-1}$. From the hypothesis that the edges of G have distinct lengths, it is easily seen that Construction A proceeds in a unique manner. Thus the A_i are unique, and hence also T.

It remains to prove that $T = A_{n-1}$. If $T \neq A_{n-1}$, let a_i be the first edge of A_{n-1} which is not in T. Then $a_1, \ldots, a_{i-1}$ are in T. $T \cup a_i$ must have exactly one loop, which must contain a_i. This loop must also contain some edge e which is not in A_{n-1}. Then $T \cup a_i - e$ is a forest with $n − 1$ edges.

As $A_{i-1} \cup e$ is contained in the last named forest, it is a forest, so from Construction A,

$$\text{length}(e) > \text{length}(a_i).$$

But then $T \cup a_i - e$ is shorter than T. This contradicts the definition of T, and hence proves indirectly that $T = A_{n-1}$.

18 The Perceptron: A Probabilistic Model for Information Storage and Organization (1958)

Frank Rosenblatt

The "perceptron" of Frank Rosenblatt (1928–1971) is at once a dramatic early step toward artificial intelligence, a temporary casualty of intellectual rivalry, and a case study in the faddishness of scientific research trends. Educated at Cornell as a psychologist, Rosenblatt began developing an artificial perceptual mechanism when he joined Cornell's Aeronautical Laboratory after receiving his PhD in 1956. There he had access to what then counted as a large computer, the IBM 704. His first cut at a perceptron, in 1957, was an early experiment in training an artificial pattern-recognition system to improve its performance through reinforcement learning. This 1958 paper describes his refined model, complete with various tunable parameters and mathematics commonly used to describe physical systems. Rosenblatt pursued this line of research and other dramatically different experiments in neuroscience as a psychology professor until his death in a boating accident on his forty-third birthday.

Rosenblatt was ahead of his time, and the line of descent from his invention to today's trained neural nets is anything but direct. In 1969 Marvin Minsky, a founding father of artificial intelligence at MIT, and Seymour Papert, his psychologist colleague there, published *Perceptrons* (Minsky and Papert, 1969), which studied the power of a restricted "one-layer" version of Rosenblatt's model. *Perceptrons* correctly showed the limitations of one-layer nets. As a scientific matter, that should not have been enough to sidetrack research on the full perceptron model, but it seems to have had that effect, perhaps because it was published at a moment of frustratingly slow progress in producing nontrivial experimental results in artificial intelligence. Minsky (who had been one grade behind Rosenblatt at Bronx High School of Science) and his MIT colleagues (some soon to depart for Stanford) were championing a different approach to AI, through logic and other symbolic systems rather than through mimicking the architecture of the human brain.

Rosenblatt's early research came out of mothballs in the 1980s, when computers began to be powerful enough to simulate multi-layer nets and to train them on sizable data sets. As a result neural computing models are now of great interest to researchers in artificial intelligence.

Reprinted from Rosenblatt (1958a).

I F we are eventually to understand the capability of higher organisms for perceptual recognition, generalization, recall, and thinking, we must first have answers to three fundamental questions:

1. How is information about the physical world sensed, or detected, by the biological system?
2. In what form is information stored, or remembered?
3. How does information contained in storage, or in memory, influence recognition and behavior?

The first of these questions is in the province of sensory physiology, and is the only one for which appreciable understanding has been achieved. This article will be concerned primarily with the second and third questions, which are still subject to a vast amount of speculation, and where the few relevant facts currently supplied by neurophysiology have not yet been integrated into an acceptable theory.

With regard to the second question, two alternative positions have been maintained. The first suggests that storage of sensory information is in the form of coded representations or images, with some sort of one-to-one mapping between the sensory stimulus and the stored pattern. According to this hypothesis, if one understood the code or "wiring diagram" of the nervous system, one should, in principle, be able to discover exactly what an organism remembers by reconstructing the original sensory patterns from the "memory traces" which they have left, much as we might develop a photographic negative, or translate the pattern of electrical charges in the "memory" of a digital computer. This hypothesis is appealing in its simplicity and ready intelligibility, and a large family of theoretical brain models has been developed around the idea of a coded, representational memory (Culbertson, 1950, 1956; Köhler, 1951; Rashevsky, 1938). The alternative approach, which stems from the tradition of British empiricism, hazards the guess that the images of stimuli may never really be recorded at all, and that the central nervous system simply acts as an intricate switching network, where retention takes the form of new connections, or pathways, between centers of activity. In many of the more recent developments of this position (Hebb's "cell assembly," and Hull's "cortical anticipatory goal response," for example) the "responses" which are associated to stimuli may be entirely contained within the CNS itself. In this case the response represents an "idea" rather than an action. The important feature of this approach is that there is never any simple mapping of the stimulus into memory, according to some code which would permit its later reconstruction. Whatever information is retained must somehow be stored as a *preference for a particular response;* i.e., the information is contained in *connections* or *associations* rather than topographic representations. (The term *response*, for the remainder of this presentation, should be understood to mean any distinguishable state of the organism, which may or may not involve externally detectable muscular activity. The activation of some nucleus of cells in the central nervous system, for example, can constitute a response, according to this definition.)

Corresponding to these two positions on the method of information retention, there exist two hypotheses with regard to the third question, the manner in which stored information exerts its influence on current activity. The "coded memory theorists" are forced to conclude that recognition of any stimulus involves the matching or systematic comparison of the contents of storage with incoming sensory patterns, in order to determine whether the current stimulus has been seen before, and to determine the appropriate response from the organism. The theorists in the empiricist tradition, on the other hand, have essentially combined the answer to the third question with their answer to the second: since the stored information takes the form of new connections, or transmission channels in the nervous system (or the creation of conditions which are functionally equivalent to new connections), it follows that the new stimuli will make use of these new pathways which have been created, automatically activating the appropriate response without requiring any separate process for their recognition or identification.

The theory to be presented here takes the empiricist, or "connectionist" position with regard to these questions. The theory has been developed for a hypothetical nervous system, or machine, called a *perceptron*. The perceptron is designed to illustrate some of the fundamental properties of intelligent systems in general, without becoming too deeply enmeshed in the special, and frequently unknown, conditions which hold for particular biological organisms. The analogy between the perceptron and biological systems should be readily apparent to the reader.

During the last few decades, the development of symbolic logic, digital computers, and switching theory has impressed many theorists with the functional similarity between a neuron and the simple on-off units of which computers are constructed, and has provided the analytical methods necessary for representing highly complex logical functions in terms of such elements. The result has been a profusion of brain models which amount simply to logical contrivances for performing particular algorithms (representing "recall," stimulus comparison, transformation, and various kinds of analysis) in response to sequences of stimuli—e.g., Rashevsky (1938); McCulloch (1951); McCulloch and Pitts (1943); Culbertson (1950); Kleene (1951); Minsky (1956). A relatively small number of theorists, like Ashby (1952), von Neumann (1951), and von Neumann (1956), have been concerned with the problems of how an imperfect neural network, containing many random connections, can be made to perform reliably those functions which might be represented by idealized wiring diagrams. Unfortunately, the language of symbolic logic and boolean algebra is less well suited for such investigations. The need for a suitable language for the mathematical analysis of events in systems where only the gross organization can be characterized, and the precise structure is unknown, has led the author to formulate the current model in terms of probability theory rather than symbolic logic.

The theorists referred to above were chiefly concerned with the question of how such functions as perception and recall might be achieved by a deterministic physical system of any sort, rather than how this is actually done by the brain. The models which have been produced all fail in some important respects (absence of equipotentiality, lack of neuroeconomy, excessive specificity of connections and synchronization requirements, unrealistic specificity of stimuli sufficient for cell firing, postulation of variables or functional features with no known neurological correlates, etc.) to correspond to a biological system. The proponents of this line of approach have maintained that, once it has been shown how a physical system of any variety might be made to perceive and recognize stimuli, or perform other brainlike functions, it would require only a refinement or modification of existing principles to understand the working of a more realistic nervous system, and to eliminate the shortcomings mentioned above. The writer takes the position, on the other hand, that these shortcomings are such that a mere refinement or improvement of the principles already suggested can never account for biological intelligence; a *difference in principle* is clearly indicated. The theory of statistical separability (Rosenblatt, 1958b), which is to be summarized here, appears to offer a solution in principle to all of these difficulties.

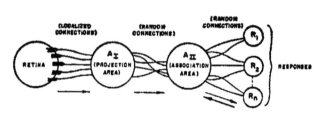

Figure 18.1: Organization of a perceptron.

Those theorists—Hebb (1949); Milner (1957); Eccles (1953); Hayek (1952)—who have been more directly concerned with the biological nervous system and its activity in a natural environment, rather than with formally analogous machines, have generally been less exact in their formulations and far from rigorous in their analysis, so that it is frequently hard to assess whether or not the systems that they describe could actually work in a realistic nervous system, and what the necessary and sufficient conditions might be. Here again, the lack of an analytic language comparable in proficiency to the boolean algebra of the network analysts has been one of the main obstacles. The contributions of this group should perhaps be considered as suggestions of what to look for and investigate, rather than as finished theoretical systems in their own right. Seen from this viewpoint, the most suggestive work, from the standpoint of the following theory, is that of Hebb and Hayek.

   The position, elaborated by Hebb (1949); Hayek (1952); Uttley (1956); Ashby (1952), in particular, upon which the theory of the perceptron is based, can be summarized by the following assumptions:

1. The physical connections of the nervous system which are involved in learning and recognition are not identical from one organism to another. At birth, the construction of the most important networks is largely random, subject to a minimum number of genetic constraints.

2. The original system of connected cells is capable of a certain amount of plasticity; after a period of neural activity, the probability that a stimulus applied to one set of cells will cause a response in some other set is likely to change, due to some relatively long-lasting changes in the neurons themselves.

3. Through exposure to a large sample of stimuli, those which are most "similar" (in some sense which must be defined in terms of the particular physical system) will tend to form pathways to the same sets of responding cells. Those which are markedly "dissimilar" will tend to develop connections to different sets of responding cells.

4. The application of positive and/or negative reinforcement (or stimuli which serve this function) may facilitate or hinder whatever formation of connections is currently in progress.

5. *Similarity*, in such a system, is represented at some level of the nervous system by a tendency of similar stimuli to activate the same sets of cells. Similarity is not a necessary attribute of particular formal or geometrical classes of stimuli, but depends on the physical organization of the perceiving system, an organization which evolves through interaction with a given environment. The structure of the system, as well as the ecology of the stimulus-environment, will affect, and will largely determine, the classes of "things" into which the perceptual world is divided.

18.1   The Organization of a Perceptron

The organization of a typical photo-perceptron (a perceptron responding to optical patterns as stimuli) is shown in Figure 18.1. The rules of its organization are as follows:

1. Stimuli impinge on a retina of sensory units (S-points), which are assumed to respond on an all-or-nothing basis, in some models, or with a pulse amplitude or frequency proportional to the stimulus intensity, in other models. In the models considered here, an all-or-nothing response will be assumed.

2. Impulses are transmitted to a set of association cells (A-units) in a "projection area" (A_I). This projection area may be omitted in some models, where the retina is connected directly to the association area (A_{II}). The cells in the projection area each receive a number of connections from the sensory points. The set of S-points transmitting impulses to a particular A-unit will be called the *origin points* of that A-unit. These origin points may be either *excitatory* or *inhibitory* in their effect on the A-unit. If the algebraic sum of excitatory and inhibitory impulse intensities is equal to or greater than the threshold (θ) of the A-unit, then the A-unit fires, again on an all-or-nothing basis (or, in some models, which will not be considered here, with a frequency which depends on the net value of the impulses received). The origin points of the A-units in the projection area tend to be clustered or focalized, about some central point, corresponding to each A-unit. The number of origin points falls off exponentially as the retinal distance from the central point for the A-unit in question increases. (Such a distribution seems to be supported by physiological evidence, and serves an important functional purpose in contour detection.)

3. Between the projection area and the association area (A_{II}), connections are assumed to be random. That is, each A-unit in the A_{II} set receives some number of fibers from origin points in the A_I set, but these origin points are scattered at random throughout the projection area. Apart from their connection distribution, the A_{II} units are identical with the A_I units, and respond under similar conditions.

4. The "responses," R_1, R_2, ..., R_n are cells (or sets of cells) which respond in much the same fashion as the A-units. Each response has a typically large number of origin points located at random in the A_{II} set. The set of A-units transmitting impulses to a particular response

will be called the source-set for that response. (The source-set of a response is identical to its set of origin points in the A-system.) The arrows in Figure 18.1 indicate the direction of transmission through the network. Note that up to A_{II} all connections are forward, and there is no feedback. When we come to the last set of connections, between A_{II} and the R-units, connections are established in both directions. The rule governing feedback connections, in most models of the perceptron, can be either of the following alternatives:

(a) Each response has excitatory feedback connections to the cells in its own source-set, or

(b) Each response has inhibitory feedback connections to the complement of its own source-set (i.e., it tends to prohibit activity in any association cells which do not transmit to it).

The first of these rules seems more plausible anatomically, since the R-units might be located in the same cortical area as their respective source-sets, making mutual excitation between the R-units and the A-units of the appropriate source-set highly probable. The alternative rule (b) leads to a more readily analyzed system, however, and will therefore be assumed for most of the systems to be evaluated here. ...

18.2   Conclusions and Evaluation

The main conclusions of the theoretical study of the perceptron can be summarized as follows:

1. In an environment of random stimuli, a system consisting of randomly connected units, subject to the parametric constraints discussed above, can learn to associate specific responses to specific stimuli. Even if many stimuli are associated to each response, they can still be recognized with a better-than-chance probability, although they may resemble one another closely and may activate many of the same sensory inputs to the system.
2. In such an "ideal environment," the probability of a correct response diminishes towards its original random level as the number of stimuli learned increases.
3. In such an environment, no basis for generalization exists.
4. In a "differentiated environment," where each response is associated to a distinct class of mutually correlated, or "similar" stimuli, the probability that a learned association of some specific stimulus will be correctly retained typically approaches a better-than-chance asymptote as the number of stimuli learned by the system increases. This asymptote can be made arbitrarily close to unity by increasing the number of association cells in the system.
5. In the differentiated environment, the probability that a stimulus which has not been seen before will be correctly recognized and associated to its appropriate class (the probability of correct generalization) approaches the same asymptote as the probability of a correct response to a previously reinforced stimulus. This asymptote will be better than chance if the inequality $P_{c12} < P_a < P_{c11}$ is met, for the stimulus classes in question.
6. The performance of the system can be improved by the use of a contour-sensitive projection area, and by the use of a binary response system, in which each response, or "bit," corresponds to some independent feature or attribute of the stimulus.

7. Trial-and-error learning is possible in bivalent reinforcement systems.

8. Temporal organizations of both stimulus patterns and responses can be learned by a system which uses only an extension of the original principles of statistical separability, without introducing any major complications in the organization of the system.

9. The memory of the perceptron is *distributed*, in the sense that any association may make use of a large proportion of the cells in the system, and the removal of a portion of the association system would not have an appreciable effect on the performance of any one discrimination or association, but would begin to show up as a general deficit in all learned associations

10. Simple cognitive sets, selective recall, and spontaneous recognition of the classes present in a given environment are possible. The recognition of relationships in space and time, however, seems to represent a limit to the perceptron's ability to form cognitive abstractions.

Psychologists, and learning theorists in particular, may now ask: "What has the present theory accomplished, beyond what has already been done in the quantitative theories of Hull, Bush and Mosteller, etc., or physiological theories such as Hebb's?" The present theory is still too primitive, of course, to be considered as a full-fledged rival of existing theories of human learning. Nonetheless, as a first approximation, its chief accomplishment might be stated as follows:

For a given mode of organization (α, β, or γ; Σ or μ; monovalent or bivalent) the fundamental phenomena of *learning, perceptual discrimination, and generalization can be predicted entirely from six basic physical parameters*, namely:

x: the number of excitatory connections per A-unit,

y: the number of inhibitory connections per A-unit,

θ: the expected threshold of an A-unit,

ω: the proportion of R-units to which an A-unit is connected,

N_A: the number of A-units in the system, and

N_R: the number of R-units in the system.

N_A (the number of sensory units) becomes important if it is very small. It is assumed that the system begins with all units in a uniform state of value; otherwise the initial value distribution would also be required. *Each of the above parameters is a clearly defined physical variable, which is measurable in is own right, independently of the behavioral and perceptual phenomena which we are trying to predict.*

As a direct consequence of its foundation on physical variables the present system goes far beyond existing learning and behavior theories in three main points: parsimony, verifiability, and explanatory power and generality. Let us consider each of these points in turn.

18.2.1   Parsimony   Essentially all of the basic variables and laws used in this system are already present in the structure of physical and biological science, so that we have found it necessary to postulate only one hypothetical variable (or construct) which we have called V, the "value" of an association cell; this is a variable which must conform to certain functional characteristics which can clearly be stated, and which is assumed to have a potentially measurable physical correlate.

18.2.2 Verifiability Previous quantitative learning theories, apparently without exception, have had one important characteristic in common: they have all been based on measurements of *behavior*, in specified situations, using these measurements (after theoretical manipulation) to predict *behavior* in other situations. Such a procedure, in the last analysis, amounts to a process of curve fitting and extrapolation, in the hope that the constants which describe one set of curves will hold good for other curves in other situations. While such extrapolation is not necessarily circular, in the strict sense, it shares many of the logical difficulties of circularity, particularly when used as an "explanation" of behavior. Such extrapolation is difficult to justify in a new situation, and it has been shown that if the basic constants and parameters are to be derived anew for any situation in which they break down empirically (such as change from white rats to humans), then the basic "theory" is essentially irrefutable, just as any successful curve-fitting equation is irrefutable. It has, in fact, been widely conceded by psychologists that there is little point in trying to "disprove" any of the major learning theories in use today, since by extension, or a change in parameters, they have all proved capable of adapting to any specific empirical data. This is epitomized in the increasingly common attitude that a choice of theoretical model is mostly a matter of personal aesthetic preference or prejudice, each scientist being entitled to a favorite model of his own. In considering this approach, one is reminded of a remark attributed to Kistiakowsky, that "given seven parameters, I could fit an elephant." This is clearly not the case with a system in which the independent variables, or parameters, can be measured independently of the predicted behavior. In such a system, it is not possible to "force" a fit to empirical data, if the parameters in current use should lead to improper results. In the current theory a failure to fit a curve in a new situation would be a clear indication that either the theory or the empirical measurements are wrong. Consequently, if such a theory *does* hold for repeated tests, we can be considerably more confident of its validity and of its generality than in the case of a theory which must be hand-tailored to meet each situation.

18.2.3   Explanatory power and generality The present theory, being derived from basic physical variables, is not specific to any one organism or learning situation. It can be generalized in principle to cover any form of behavior in any system for which the physical parameters are known. A theory of learning, constructed on these foundations, should be considerably more powerful than any which has previously been proposed. It would not only tell us what behavior might occur in any known organism, but would permit the synthesis of behaving systems, to meet special requirements. Other learning theories tend to become increasingly qualitative as they are generalized. Thus a set of equations describing the effects of reward on T-maze learning in a white rat reduces simply to a statement that rewarded behavior tends to occur with increasing probability when we attempt to generalize it from any species and any situation. The theory which has been presented here loses none of its precision through generality. . . .

19 Some Moral and Technical Consequences of Automation (1960)

Norbert Wiener

Norbert Wiener (1894–1964), the son of a Harvard Slavic instructor, was a child prodigy. When he entered Tufts as a college freshman at the age of 11, a news story described him as "the most remarkable boy in the world" (Unknown, 1906). Wiener conversed with the reporter about philosophy and spoke Latin and Greek. He graduated from Tufts in three years with a degree in mathematics, earned a PhD in philosophy from Harvard at age 18, and started teaching at MIT.

Wiener's MIT career, which lasted the rest of his life, intersected that of many other pioneers of the computer revolution. In the 1920s, he worked with Vannevar Bush on the design of a device to solve differential equations and made the prescient suggestion to build it using vacuum tubes rather than mechanical linkages. As his attention turned to commonalities between machines and living things, he cooperated with Warren McCulloch and with Walter Pitts, who became his academic protegé until the relation between the three tragically collapsed (page 80).

Wiener was the father of a field he dubbed "cybernetics," the study of "control and communication in the animal and the machine." The crucial concept was "feedback"; the word *cybernetics* derives from the Greek word for steering a boat, as with a tiller. Wiener's interest in messages passed between parts of a system to control its behavior naturally connected to the work of Claude Shannon on information theory.

Wiener's principal mathematical tools were continuous and statistical, rather than discrete and digital. His work on feedback and control was of intense military importance, for example in the guidance of missiles. After the Second World War, he became increasingly troubled by the uses to which his scientific work was being put. In 1946, in an open letter to a military contractor who had asked him for a copy of a paper, he drew a line. "The policy of the government itself during and after the war, say in the bombing of Hiroshima and Nagasaki, has made it clear that to provide scientific information is not a necessarily innocent act. ... The interchange of ideas, one of the great traditions of science, must of course receive certain limitations when the scientist becomes an arbiter of life and death. The measures taken during the war by our military agencies, in restricting the free intercourse among scientists on related projects or even on the same project, has gone so far that it is clear that if continued in time of peace this policy will lead to the total irresponsibility of the scientist, and ultimately to the death of science. Both these are disastrous for our civilization, and entail grave and immediate peril for the public." He refused to share

Reprinted from Wiener (1960), with permission from the American Association for the Advancement of Science.

his paper. He knew the paper could be obtained through other means, but he wanted to make a statement.

The letter, published in the *Atlantic* under the title "A scientist rebels," was highly publicized (Wiener, 1947). Wiener then backed out of an invitation he had accepted to speak at a major Harvard symposium on automatic computing organized by Howard Aiken with the support of the Navy. Wiener had not meant thereby to make a further public statement, but the programs had already been printed and were distributed at the conference with a line drawn through Wiener's name. The resulting publicity was intensely embarrassing to all, and Wiener wound up alienated from Aiken and under the suspicion of Senator Joseph McCarthy's anti-Communist witch hunt. But Wiener had taken a decisive step, and never again accepted any government money in support of his research. Some celebrated his moral stand, but his scientific influence began to fade as defense funding nourished the postwar scientific boom.

Many of the warnings Wiener issued, about the moral responsibilities of scientists and the danger of secret research, resonate today. He devoted his later years to the peaceful uses of cybernetics, and his warnings shifted, as in this paper, from the risks of militarization to the changes in daily life attendant on technological advances.

All of modern computer and communications technology owes a scientific debt to Wiener, but the field he defined has largely disappeared as it became diffused through its various descendants. "Cybernetics" is rarely heard, but "cyber" persists as a prefix for "crime," "security," and digital variants of other phenomena. Wiener became what a biographer calls a "dark hero," omnipresent in his influence and yet invisible (Conway, 2005).

His writings remain premonitory. For all of his stupendous learning and technical wizardry, he cautions us, as he puts in *The Human Use of Human Beings* (Wiener, 1950), against "the American worship of know-how as opposed to know-what."

SOME 13 years ago, a book of mine was published by the name of *Cybernetics* (Wiener, 1948). In it I discussed the problems of control and communication in the living organism and the machine. I made a considerable number of predictions about the development of controlled machines and about the corresponding techniques of automatization, which I foresaw as having important consequences affecting the society of the future. Now, 13 years later, it seems appropriate to take stock of the present position with respect to both cybernetic technique and the social consequences of this technique.

Before commencing on the detail of these matters, I should like to mention a certain attitude of the man in the street toward cybernetics and automatization. This attitude needs a critical discussion, and in my opinion it should be rejected in its entirety. This is the assumption that machines cannot possess any degree of originality. This frequently takes the form of a statement that nothing can come out of the machine which has not been put into it. This is often interpreted as asserting that a machine which man has made must remain continually subject to man, so that its operation is at any time open to human interference and to a change in policy. On the basis of such an attitude, many people have pooh-poohed the dangers of machine techniques, and they have flatly contradicted the early predictions of Samuel Butler that the machine might take over the control of mankind. [EDITOR: Wiener here refers to Butler (1863, 1872), originally published anonymously.]

It is true that in the time of Samuel Butler the available machines were far less hazardous than machines are today, for they involved only power, not a certain degree of thinking and communication. However, the machine techniques of the present day have invaded the latter fields as well, so that the actual machine of today is very different from the image that Butler held, and we cannot transfer to these new devices the assumptions which seemed axiomatic a generation ago. I find myself facing a public which has formed its attitude toward the machine on the basis of an imperfect understanding of the structure and mode of operation of modern machines.

It is my thesis that machines can and do transcend some of the limitations of their designers, and that in doing so they may be both effective and dangerous. It may well be that in principle we cannot make any machine the elements of whose behavior we cannot comprehend sooner or later. This does not mean in any way that we shall be able to comprehend these elements in substantially less time than the time required for operation of the machine, or even within any given number of years or generations.

As is now generally admitted, over a limited range of operation, machines act far more rapidly than human beings and are far more precise in performing the details of their operations. This being the case, even when machines do not in any way transcend man's intelligence, they very well may, and often do, transcend man in the performance of tasks. An intelligent understanding of their mode of performance may be delayed until long after the task which they have been set has been completed.

This means that though machines are theoretically subject to human criticism, such criticism may be ineffective until long after it is relevant. To be effective in warding off disastrous consequences, our understanding of our man-made machines should in general develop *pari passu* with the performance of the machine. By the very slowness of our human actions, our effective control of our machines may be nullified. By the time we are able to react to information conveyed by our senses and stop the car we are driving, it may already have run head on into a wall.

19.1   Game-Playing

I shall come back to this point later in this article. For the present, let me discuss the technique of machines for a very specific purpose: that of playing games. In this matter I shall deal more particularly with the game of checkers, for which the International Business Machines Corporation has developed very effective game-playing machines.

Let me say once for all that we are not concerned here with the machines which operate on a perfect closed theory of the game they play. The game theory of von Neumann and Morgenstern may be suggestive as to the operation of actual game-playing machines, but it does not actually describe them.

In a game as complicated as checkers, if each player tries to choose his play in view of the best move his opponent can make, against the best response he can give, against the best response his opponent can give, and so on, he will have taken upon himself an impossible task. Not only is this humanly impossible, but there is actually no reason to suppose that it is the best policy against the opponent by whom he is faced, whose limitations are equal to his own.

The von Neumann theory of games bears no very close relation to the theory by which game-playing machines operate. The latter corresponds much more closely to the methods of play used by expert but limited human chess players against other chess players. Such players depend on certain strategic evaluations, which are in essence not complete. While the von Neumann type of play is valid for games like ticktacktoe, with a complete theory, the very interest of chess and checkers lies in the fact that they do not possess a complete theory. Neither do war, nor business competition, nor any of the other forms of competitive activity in which we are really interested.

In a game like ticktacktoe, with a small number of moves, where each player is in a position to contemplate all possibilities and to establish a defense against the best possible moves of the other player, a complete theory of the von Neumann type is valid. In such a case, the game must inevitably end in a win for the first player, a win for the second player, or a draw.

I question strongly whether this concept of the perfect game is a completely realistic one in the cases of actual, nontrivial games. Great generals like Napoleon and great admirals like Nelson have proceeded in a different manner. They have been aware not only of the limitations of their opponents in such matters as materiel and personnel but equally of their limitations in experience and in military know-how. It was by a realistic appraisal of the relative inexperience in naval operations of the continental powers as compared with the highly developed tactical and strategic competence of the British fleet that Nelson was able to display the boldness which pushed the continental forces off the seas. This he could not have done had he engaged in the long, relatively indecisive, and possibly losing conflict to which his assumption of the best possible strategy on the part of his enemy would have doomed him.

In assessing not merely the materiel and personnel of his enemies but also the degree of judgment and the amount of skill in tactics and strategy to be expected of them, Nelson acted on the basis of their record in previous combats. Similarly, an important factor in Napoleon's conduct of his combat with the Austrians in Italy was his knowledge of the rigidity and mental limitations of Würmser.

This element of experience should receive adequate recognition in any realistic theory of games. It is quite legitimate for a chess player to play, not against an ideal, nonexisting, perfect antagonist, but rather against one whose habits he has been able to determine from the record. Thus, in the theory of games, at least two different intellectual efforts must be made. One is the short-term effort of playing with a determined policy for the individual game. The other is the examination of a record of many games. This record has been set by the player himself, by his opponent, or even by players with whom he has not personally played. In terms of this record, he determines the relative advantages of different policies as proved over the past.

There is even a third stage of judgment required in a chess game. This is expressed at least in part by the length of the significant past. The development of theory in chess decreases the importance of games played at a different stage of the art. On the other hand, an astute chess theoretician may estimate in advance that a certain policy currently in fashion has become of little value, and that it may be best to return to earlier modes of play to anticipate the change in policy of the people whom he is likely to find as his opponents.

Thus, in determining policy in chess there are several different levels of consideration which correspond in a certain way to the different logical types of Bertrand Russell. There is the level of tactics, the level of strategy, the level of the general considerations which should have been weighed in determining this strategy, the level in which the length of the relevant past—the past within which these considerations may be valid—is taken into account, and so on. Each new level demands a study of a much larger past than the previous one.

I have compared these levels with the logical types of Russell concerning classes, classes of classes, classes of classes of classes, and so on. It may be noted that Russell does not consider statements involving all types as significant. He brings out the futility of such questions as that concerning the barber who shaves all persons, and only those persons, who do not shave themselves. Does he shave himself? On one type he does, on the next type he does not, and so on, indefinitely. All such questions involving an infinity of types may lead to unsolvable paradoxes. Similarly, the search for the best policy under all levels of sophistication is a futile one and must lead to nothing but confusion.

These considerations arise in the determination of policy by machines as well as in the determination of policy by persons. These are the questions which arise in the programming of programming. The lowest type of game-playing machine plays in terms of a certain rigid evaluation of plays. Quantities such as the value of pieces gained or lost, the command of the pieces, their mobility, and so on, can be given numerical weights on a certain empirical basis, and a weighting may be given on this basis to each next play conforming to the rules of the game. The play with the greatest weight may be chosen. Under these circumstances, the play of the machine will seem to its antagonist—who cannot help but evaluate the chess personality of the machine—a rigid one.

19.2 Learning Machines

The next step is for the machine to take into consideration not merely the moves as they occurred in the individual game but the record of games previously played. On this basis, the machine may stop from time to time, not to play but to consider what (linear or nonlinear) weighting of the factors which it has been given to consider would correspond best to won games as opposed to lost (or drawn) games. On this basis, it continues to play with a new weighting. Such a machine would seem to its human opponent to have a far less rigid game personality, and tricks which would defeat it at an earlier stage may now fail to deceive it.

The present level of these learning machines is that they play a fair amateur game at chess but that in checkers they can show a marked superiority to the player who has programmed them after from 10 to 20 playing hours of working and indoctrination. They thus most definitely escape from the completely effective control of the man who has made them. Rigid as the repertory of factors may be which they are in a position to take into consideration, they do unquestionably— and so say those who have played with them—show originality, not merely in their tactics, which may be quite unforeseen, but even in the detailed weighting of their strategy.

As I have said, checker-playing machines which learn have developed to the point at which they can defeat the programmer. However, they appear still to have one weakness. This lies in the end game. Here the machines are somewhat clumsy in determining the best way to give the *coup de grâce*. This is due to the fact that the existing machines have for the most part adopted a program in which the identical strategy is carried out at each stage of the game. In view of the similarity of values of pieces to checkers this is quite natural for a large part of the play but ceases to be perfectly relevant when the board is relatively empty and the main problem is that of moving into position rather than that of direct attack. Within the frame of the methods I have described it is quite possible to have a second exploration to determine what the policy should be after the number of pieces of the opponent is so reduced that these new considerations become paramount.

Chess-playing machines have not, so far, been brought to the degree of perfection of checker-playing machines, although, as I have said, they can most certainly play a respectable amateur game. Probably the reason for this is similar to the reason for their relative efficiency in the end game of checkers. In chess, not only is the end game quite different in its proper strategy from the mid-game but the opening game is also. The difference between checkers and chess in this respect is that the initial play of the pieces in checkers is not very different in character from the play which arises in the mid-game, while in chess, pieces at the beginning have an arrangement of exceptionally low mobility, so that the problem of deploying them from this position is particularly difficult. This is the reason why opening play and development form a special branch of chess theory.

There are various ways in which the machine can take cognizance of these well-known facts and explore a separate waiting strategy for the opening. This does not mean that the type of game theory which I have here discussed is not applicable to chess but merely that it requires much more consideration before we can make a machine that can play master chess. Some of my friends who are engaged in these problems believe that this goal will be achieved in from 10 to 25 years. Not being a chess expert, I do not venture to make any such predictions on my own initiative.

It is quite in the cards that learning machines will be used to program the pushing of the button in a new push-button war. Here we are considering a field in which automata of a non-learning character are probably already in use. It is quite out of the question to program these machines on the basis of an actual experience in real war. For one thing a sufficient experience to give an adequate programming would probably see humanity already wiped out.

Moreover, the techniques of push-button war are bound to change so much that by the time an adequate experience could have been accumulated, the basis of the beginning would have radically changed. Therefore, the programming of such a learning machine would have to be based on some sort of war game, just as commanders and staff officials now learn an important part of the art of strategy in a similar manner. Here, however, if the rules for victory in a war game do not correspond to what we actually wish for our country, it is more than likely that such a machine may produce a policy which would win a nominal victory on points at the cost of every interest we have at heart, even that of national survival.

19.3 Man and Slave

The problem, and it is a moral problem, with which we are here faced is very close to one of the great problems of slavery. Let us grant that slavery is bad because it is cruel. It is, however, self-contradictory, and for a reason which is quite different. We wish a slave to be intelligent, to be able to assist us in the carrying out of our tasks. However, we also wish him to be subservient. Complete subservience and complete intelligence do not go together. How often in ancient times the clever Greek philosopher slave of a less intelligent Roman slaveholder must have dominated the actions of his master rather than obeyed his wishes! Similarly, if the machines become more and more efficient and operate at a higher and higher psychological level, the catastrophe foreseen by Butler of the dominance of the machine comes nearer and nearer.

The human brain is a far more efficient control apparatus than is the intelligent machine when we come to the higher areas of logic. It is a self-organizing system which depends on its capacity to modify itself into a new machine rather than on ironclad accuracy and speed in problem-solving. We have already made very successful machines of the lowest logical type, with a rigid policy. We are beginning to make machines of the second logical type, where the policy itself improves with learning. In the construction of operative machines, there is no specific foreseeable limit with respect to logical type, nor is it safe to make a pronouncement about the exact level at which the brain is superior to the machine. Yet for a long time at least there will always be some level at which the brain is better than the constructed machine, even though this level may shift upwards and upwards.

It may be seen that the result of a programming technique of automatization is to remove from the mind of the designer and operator an effective understanding of many of the stages by which the machine comes to its conclusions and of what the real tactical intentions of many of its operations may be. This is highly relevant to the problem of our being able to foresee undesired consequences outside the frame of the strategy of the game while the machine is still in action and while intervention on our part may prevent the occurrence of these consequences.

Here it is necessary to realize that human action is a feedback action. To avoid a disastrous consequence, it is not enough that some action on our part should be sufficient to change the course of the machine, because it is quite possible that we lack information on which to base consideration of such an action.

In neurophysiological language, ataxia can be quite as much of a deprivation as paralysis. A patient with locomotor ataxia may not suffer from any defect of his muscles or motor nerves, but if his muscles and tendons and organs do not tell him exactly what position he is in, and whether the tensions to which his organs are subjected will or will not lead to his falling, he will be unable to stand up. Similarly, when a machine constructed by us is capable of operating on its incoming data at a pace which we cannot keep, we may not know, until too late, when to turn it off. We all know the fable of the sorcerer's apprentice, in which the boy makes the broom carry water in his master's absence, so that it is on the point of drowning him when his master reappears. If the boy had had to seek a charm to stop the mischief in the grimoires of his master's library, he might have been drowned before he had discovered the relevant incantation. Similarly, if a bottle factory is programmed on the basis of maximum productivity, the owner may be made bankrupt by the enormous inventory of unsalable bottles manufactured before he learns he should have stopped production six months earlier.

The "Sorcerer's Apprentice" is only one of many tales based on the assumption that the agencies of magic are literal-minded. There is the story of the genie and the fisherman in the Arabian Nights, in which the fisherman breaks the seal of Solomon which has imprisoned the genie and finds the genie vowed to his own destruction; there is the tale of the "Monkey's Paw," by W. W. Jacobs, in which the sergeant major brings back from India a talisman which has the power to grant each of three people three wishes. Of the first recipient of this talisman we are told only that his third wish is for death. The sergeant major, the second person whose wishes are granted, finds his experiences too terrible to relate. His friend, who receives the talisman, wishes first for 200. Shortly thereafter, an official of the factory in which his son works comes to tell him that his son has been killed in the machinery and that, without any admission of responsibility, the company is sending him as consolation the sum of 200. His next wish is that his son should come back, and the ghost knocks at the door. His third wish is that the ghost should go away.

Disastrous results are to be expected not merely in the world of fairy tales but in the real world wherever two agencies essentially foreign to each other are coupled in the attempt to achieve a common purpose. If the communication between these two agencies as to the nature of this purpose is incomplete, it must only be expected that the results of this cooperation will be unsatisfactory. If we use, to achieve our purposes, a mechanical agency with whose operation we cannot efficiently interfere once we have started it, because the action is so fast and irrevocable that we have not the data to intervene before the action is complete, then we had better be quite sure that the purpose put into the machine is the purpose which we really desire and not merely a colorful imitation of it.

19.4   Time Scales

Up to this point I have been considering the quasi-moral problems caused by the simultaneous action of the machine and the human being in a joint enterprise. We have seen that one of the chief causes of the danger of disastrous consequences in the use of the learning machine is that man and machine operate on two distinct time scales, so that the machine is much faster than man and the two do not gear together without serious difficulties. Problems of the same sort arise whenever two control operators on very different time scales act together, irrespective of which system is the faster and which system is the slower. This leaves us the much more directly moral question: What are the moral problems when man as an individual operates in connection with the controlled process of a much slower time scale, such as a portion of political history or—our main subject of inquiry—the development of science?

Let it be noted that the development of science is a control and communication process for the long-term understanding and control of matter. In this process 50 years are as a day in the life of the individual. For this reason, the individual scientist must work as a part of a process whose time scale is so long that he himself can only contemplate a very limited sector of it. Here, too, communication between the two parts of a double machine is difficult and limited. Even when the individual believes that science contributes to the human ends which he has at heart, his belief needs a continual scanning and re-evaluation which is only partly possible. For the individual scientist, even the partial appraisal of this liaison between the man and the process requires an imaginative forward glance at history which is difficult, exacting, and only limitedly achievable. And if we adhere simply to the creed of the scientist, that an incomplete knowledge of the world and of ourselves is better than no knowledge, we can still by no means always justify the naïve assumption that the faster we rush ahead to employ the new powers for action which are opened up to us, the better it will be. We must always exert the full strength of our imagination to examine where the full use of our new modalities may lead us.

20 Man–Computer Symbiosis (1960)

J. C. R. Licklider

J. C. R. Licklider (1915–1990) is different from most of the characters in this book. He was neither an engineer, nor a mathematician, nor a philosopher. Yet through a happy coincidence of several mid-20th-century circumstances, his vision helped create the world in which we now live.

Licklider is invariably referred to only by the initials of his given names, because his nickname was just "Lick." He was trained as a psychologist and did important work on auditory perception, but began to think about what we would now call "human factors" in computing while working at MIT during the Cold War on the design of air defense systems. A human operator of an electronic computer was tasked with making split-second decisions of vast global consequence when confronted with data about incoming missiles and other military intelligence. How might the computer itself help the human make better decisions? Today's video games, virtual reality systems, and internet cat videos were born of such concerns about managing the risk of nuclear cataclysm.

When the center of psychology research moved to Harvard, Licklider left MIT for the Cambridge firm Bolt Beranek and Newman (BBN), which was famous for its acoustic expertise but would eventually receive contracts to build the earliest gateways for the ARPANET, the forerunner of the internet. While there, Licklider wrote the influential paper included here. It owes something to Vannevar Bush's vision, and to be sure Licklider knew Bush from MIT. But by the time it was written some computers were capable of being programmed to carry out interactive and dynamic graphics. From BBN, Licklider moved in 1962 to the Advanced Research Projects Agency (ARPA) of the Department of Defense, where he helped give birth to the ARPANET.

Licklider left the government for a short stint at IBM, which he found insufficiently visionary. He returned to MIT in 1966 and remained there for most of the rest of his career, with a short second tour of duty at DoD steering its advanced research projects. He was a funny, articulate, and humble man. I met him when I, working as an undergraduate on Harvard's DEC PDP-1, helped him debug some program he was writing. I was utterly unaware that he was the man whose vision had made possible the very work I was doing—I thought he might be a superannuated graduate student—and he made no attempt to clue me in.

———————⋄∘☙∘⋄———————

Reprinted from Licklider (1960), with permission from the Institute of Electrical and Electronics Engineers.

20.0   Summary

MAN-COMPUTER symbiosis is an expected development in cooperative interaction between men and electronic computers. It will involve very close coupling between the human and the electronic members of the partnership. The main aims are 1) to let computers facilitate formulative thinking as they now facilitate the solution of formulated problems, and 2) to enable men and computers to cooperate in making decisions and controlling complex situations without inflexible dependence on predetermined programs. In the anticipated symbiotic partnership, men will set the goals, formulate the hypotheses, determine the criteria, and perform the evaluations. Computing machines will do the routinizable work that must be done to prepare the way for insights and decisions in technical and scientific thinking. Preliminary analyses indicate that the symbiotic partnership will perform intellectual operations much more effectively than man alone can perform them. Prerequisites for the achievement of the effective, cooperative association include developments in computer time sharing, in memory components, in memory organization, in programming languages, and in input and output equipment.

20.1   Introduction

20.1.1   Symbiosis   The fig tree is pollinated only by the insect *Blastophaga grossorum*. The larva of the insect lives in the ovary of the fig tree, and there it gets its food. The tree and the insect are thus heavily interdependent: the tree cannot reproduce without the insect; the insect cannot eat without the tree; together, they constitute not only a viable but a productive and thriving partnership. This cooperative "living together in intimate association, or even close union, of two dissimilar organisms" is called symbiosis (Webster, 1959).

"Man–computer symbiosis" is a subclass of man–machine systems. There are many man–machine systems. At present, however, there are no man–computer symbioses. The purposes of this paper are to present the concept and, hopefully, to foster the development of man–computer symbiosis by analyzing some problems of interaction between men and computing machines, calling attention to applicable principles of man–machine engineering, and pointing out a few questions to which research answers are needed. The hope is that, in not too many years, human brains and computing machines will be coupled together very tightly, and that the resulting partnership will think as no human brain has ever thought and process data in a way not approached by the information-handling machines we know today.

20.1.2   Between "mechanically extended man" and "artificial intelligence"   As a concept, man–computer symbiosis is different in an important way from what North (1954) has called "mechanically extended man." In the man–machine systems of the past, the human operator supplied the initiative, the direction, the integration, and the criterion. The mechanical parts of the systems were mere extensions, first of the human arm, then of the human eye. These systems certainly did not consist of "dissimilar organisms living together ...." There was only one kind of organism—man—and the rest was there only to help him.

In one sense of course, any man-made system is intended to help man, to help a man or men outside the system. If we focus upon the human operator within the system, however, we see that, in some areas of technology, a fantastic change has taken place during the last few years. "Mechanical extension" has given way to replacement of men, to automation, and the men who remain are there more to help than to be helped. In some instances, particularly in large computer-centered information and control systems, the human operators are responsible mainly for functions that it proved infeasible to automate. Such systems ("humanly extended machines," North might call them) are not symbiotic systems. They are "semi-automatic" systems, systems that started out to be fully automatic but fell short of the goal.

Man–computer symbiosis is probably not the ultimate paradigm for complex technological systems. It seems entirely possible that, in due course, electronic or chemical "machines" will outdo the human brain in most of the functions we now consider exclusively within its province. Even now, Gelernter's IBM 704 program for proving theorems in plane geometry proceeds at about the same pace as Brooklyn high school students, and makes similar errors (Gelernter, 1959). There are, in fact, several theorem-proving, problem-solving, chess-playing, and pattern-recognizing programs—too many for complete reference (Bernstein and Roberts, 1958; Bledsoe and Browning, 1959; Dinneen, 1955; Farley and Clark, 1954; Friedberg, 1958; Gilmore and Savell, 1959; Newell, 1955; Newell and Shaw, 1957; Newell et al., 1958; Selfridge, 1958; Shannon, 1950; Sherman, 1959)—capable of rivaling human intellectual performance in restricted areas; and Newell, Simon, and Shaw's "general problem solver" may remove some of the restrictions. In short, it seems worthwhile to avoid argument with (other) enthusiasts for artificial intelligence by conceding dominance in the distant future of cerebration to machines alone. There will nevertheless be a fairly long interim during which the main intellectual advances will be made by men and computers working together in intimate association. A multidisciplinary study group, examining future research and development problems of the Air Force, estimated that it would be 1980 before developments in artificial intelligence make it possible for machines alone to do much thinking or problem solving of military significance. That would leave, say, five years to develop man–computer symbiosis and 15 years to use it. The 15 may be 10 or 500, but those years should be intellectually the most creative and exciting in the history of mankind.

20.2   Aims of Man–Computer Symbiosis

Present-day computers are designed primarily to solve preformulated problems or to process data according to predetermined procedures. The course of the computation may be conditional upon results obtained during the computation, but all the alternatives must be foreseen in advance. (If an unforeseen alternative arises, the whole process comes to a halt and awaits the necessary extension of the program.) The requirement for preformulation or predetermination is sometimes no great disadvantage. It is often said that programming for a computing machine forces one to think clearly, that it disciplines the thought process. If the user can think his problem through in advance, symbiotic association with a computing machine is not necessary.

However, many problems that can be thought through in advance are very difficult to think through in advance. They would be easier to solve, and they could be solved faster, through an intuitively guided trial-and-error procedure in which the computer cooperated, turning up flaws in reasoning or revealing unexpected turns in the solution. Other problems simply cannot be formulated without computing-machine aid. Poincaré anticipated the frustration of an important group of would-be computer users when he said, "The question is not, 'What is the answer?' The question is, 'What is the question?'" One of the main aims of man–computer symbiosis is to bring the computing machine effectively into the formulative parts of technical problems.

The other main aim is closely related. It is to bring computing machines effectively into processes of thinking that must go on in "real time," time that moves too fast to permit using computers in conventional ways. Imagine trying, for example, to direct a battle with the aid of a computer on such a schedule as this. You formulate your problem today. Tomorrow you spend with a programmer. Next week the computer devotes 5 minutes to assembling your program and 47 seconds to calculating the answer to your problem. You get a sheet of paper 20 feet long, full of numbers that, instead of providing a final solution, only suggest a tactic that should be explored by simulation. Obviously, the battle would be over before the second step in its planning was begun. To think in interaction with a computer in the same way that you think with a colleague whose competence supplements your own will require much tighter coupling between man and machine than is suggested by the example and than is possible today.

20.3   Need for Computer Participation in Formulative and Real-Time Thinking

The preceding paragraphs tacitly made the assumption that, if they could be introduced effectively into the thought process, the functions that can be performed by data-processing machines would improve or facilitate thinking and problem solving in an important way. That assumption may require justification.

20.3.1   A preliminary and informal time-and-motion analysis of technical thinking   Despite the fact that there is a voluminous literature on thinking and problem solving, including intensive case-history studies of the process of invention, I could find nothing comparable to a time-and-motion-study analysis of the mental work of a person engaged in a scientific or technical enterprise. In the spring and summer of 1957, therefore, I tried to keep track of what one moderately technical person actually did during the hours he regarded as devoted to work. Although I was aware of the inadequacy of the sampling, I served as my own subject.

It soon became apparent that the main thing I did was to keep records, and the project would have become an infinite regress if the keeping of records had been carried through in the detail envisaged in the initial plan. It was not. Nevertheless, I obtained a picture of my activities that gave me pause. Perhaps my spectrum is not typical—I hope it is not, but I fear it is.

About 85 per cent of my "thinking" time was spent getting into a position to think, to make a decision, to learn something I needed to know. Much more time went into finding or obtaining information than into digesting it. Hours went into the plotting of graphs, and other hours into instructing an assistant how to plot. When the graphs were finished, the relations were obvious at once, but the plotting had to be done in order to make them so. At one point, it was necessary to compare six experimental determinations of a function relating speech-intelligibility to speech-to-noise ratio. No two experimenters had used the same definition or measure of speech-to-noise ratio. Several hours of calculating were required to get the data into comparable form. When they were in comparable form, it took only a few seconds to determine what I needed to know.

Throughout the period I examined, in short, my "thinking" time was devoted mainly to activities that were essentially clerical or mechanical: searching, calculating, plotting, transforming, determining the logical or dynamic consequences of a set of assumptions or hypotheses, preparing the way for a decision or an insight. Moreover, my choices of what to attempt and what not to attempt were determined to an embarrassingly great extent by considerations of clerical feasibility, not intellectual capability.

The main suggestion conveyed by the findings just described is that the operations that fill most of the time allegedly devoted to technical thinking are operations that can be performed more effectively by machines than by men. Severe problems are posed by the fact that these operations have to be performed upon diverse variables and in unforeseen and continually changing sequences. If those problems can be solved in such a way as to create a symbiotic relation between a man and a fast information-retrieval and data-processing machine, however, it seems evident that the cooperative interaction would greatly improve the thinking process.

It may be appropriate to acknowledge, at this point, that we are using the term "computer" to cover a wide class of calculating, data-processing, and information-storage-and-retrieval machines. The capabilities of machines in this class are increasing almost daily. It is therefore hazardous to make general statements about capabilities of the class. Perhaps it is equally hazardous to make general statements about the capabilities of men. Nevertheless, certain genotypic differences in capability between men and computers do stand out, and they have a bearing on the nature of possible man–computer symbiosis and the potential value of achieving it.

As has been said in various ways, men are noisy, narrow-band devices, but their nervous systems have very many parallel and simultaneously active channels. Relative to men, computing machines are very fast and very accurate, but they are constrained to perform only one or a few elementary operations at a time. Men are flexible, capable of "programming themselves contingently" on the basis of newly received information. Computing machines are single-minded, constrained by their "pre-programming." Men naturally speak redundant languages organized around unitary objects and coherent actions and employing 20 to 60 elementary symbols. Computers "naturally" speak nonredundant languages, usually with only two elementary symbols and no inherent appreciation either of unitary objects or of coherent actions.

To be rigorously correct, those characterizations would have to include many qualifiers. Nevertheless, the picture of dissimilarity (and therefore potential supplementation) that they present is essentially valid. Computing machines can do readily, well, and rapidly many things that are difficult or impossible for man, and men can do readily and well, though not rapidly, many things that are difficult or impossible for computers. That suggests that a symbiotic cooperation, if successful in integrating the positive characteristics of men and computers, would be of great value. The differences in speed and in language, of course, pose difficulties that must be overcome.

20.4   Separable Functions of Men and Computers in the Anticipated Symbiotic Association

It seems likely that the contributions of human operators and equipment will blend together so completely in many operations that it will be difficult to separate them neatly in analysis. That would be the case if, in gathering data on which to base a decision, for example, both the man and the computer came up with relevant precedents from experience and if the computer then suggested a course of action that agreed with the man's intuitive judgment. (In theorem-proving programs, computers find precedents in experience, and in the SAGE System, they suggest courses of action. The foregoing is not a far-fetched example.) In other operations, however, the contributions of men and equipment will be to some extent separable.

Men will set the goals and supply the motivations, of course, at least in the early years. They will formulate hypotheses. They will ask questions. They will think of mechanisms, procedures, and models. They will remember that such-and-such a person did some possibly relevant work on a topic of interest back in 1947, or at any rate shortly after World War II, and they will have an idea in what journals it might have been published. In general, they will make approximate and fallible, but leading, contributions, and they will define criteria and serve as evaluators, judging the contributions of the equipment and guiding the general line of thought.

In addition, men will handle the very-low-probability situations when such situations do actually arise. (In current man–machine systems, that is one of the human operator's most important functions. The sum of the probabilities of very-low-probability alternatives is often much too large to neglect.) Men will fill in the gaps, either in the problem solution or in the computer program, when the computer has no mode or routine that is applicable in a particular circumstance.

The information-processing equipment, for its part, will convert hypotheses into testable models and then test the models against data (which the human operator may designate roughly and identify as relevant when the computer presents them for his approval). The equipment will answer questions. It will simulate the mechanisms and models, carry out the procedures, and display the results to the operator. It will transform data, plot graphs ("cutting the cake" in whatever way the human operator specifies, or in several alternative ways if the human operator is not sure what he wants). The equipment will interpolate, extrapolate, and transform. It will convert static equations or logical statements into dynamic models so the human operator can examine their behavior. In general, it will carry out the routinizable, clerical operations that fill the intervals between decisions.

In addition, the computer will serve as a statistical-inference, decision-theory, or game-theory machine to make elementary evaluations of suggested courses of action whenever there is enough basis to support a formal statistical analysis. Finally, it will do as much diagnosis, pattern-matching, and relevance-recognizing as it profitably can, but it will accept a clearly secondary status in those areas.

20.5   Prerequisites for Realization of Man–Computer Symbiosis

The data-processing equipment tacitly postulated in the preceding section is not available. The computer programs have not been written. There are in fact several hurdles that stand between the nonsymbiotic present and the anticipated symbiotic future. Let us examine some of them to see more clearly what is needed and what the chances are of achieving it.

20.5.1   Speed mismatch between men and computers   Any present-day large-scale computer is too fast and too costly for real-time cooperative thinking with one man. Clearly, for the sake of efficiency and economy, the computer must divide its time among many users. Time-sharing systems are currently under active development. There are even arrangements to keep users from "clobbering" anything but their own personal programs.

It seems reasonable to envision, for a time 10 or 15 years hence, a "thinking center" that will incorporate the functions of present-day libraries together with anticipated advances in information storage and retrieval and the symbiotic functions suggested earlier in this paper. The picture readily enlarges itself into a network of such centers, connected to one another by wide-band communication lines and to individual users by leased-wire services. In such a system, the speed of the computers would be balanced, and the cost of the gigantic memories and the sophisticated programs would be divided by the number of users.

20.5.2   Memory hardware requirements   When we start to think of storing any appreciable fraction of a technical literature in computer memory, we run into billions of bits and, unless things change markedly, billions of dollars.

The first thing to face is that we shall not store all the technical and scientific papers in computer memory. We may store the parts that can be summarized most succinctly—the quantitative parts and the reference citations—but not the whole. Books are among the most beautifully engineered, and human-engineered, components in existence, and they will continue to be functionally important within the context of man–computer symbiosis. (Hopefully, the computer will expedite the finding, delivering, and returning of books.)

The second point is that a very important section of memory will be permanent: part indelible memory and part published memory. The computer will be able to write once into indelible memory, and then read back indefinitcly, but the computer will not be able to erase indelible memory. (It may also over-write, turning all the 0s into 1s, as though marking over what was written earlier.) Published memory will be "read-only" memory. It will be introduced into the computer already structured. The computer will be able to refer to it repeatedly, but not to change it. These types of memory will become more and more important as computers grow larger. They can be made more compact than core, thin-film, or even tape memory, and they will be much less expensive. The main engineering problems will concern selection circuitry.

In so far as other aspects of memory requirement are concerned, we may count upon the continuing development of ordinary scientific and business computing machines. There is some prospect that memory elements will become as fast as processing (logic) elements. That development would have a revolutionary effect upon the design of computers.

20.5.3   Memory organization requirements   Implicit in the idea of man–computer symbiosis are the requirements that information be retrievable both by name and by pattern and that it be accessible through procedure much faster than serial search. At least half of the problem of memory organization appears to reside in the storage procedure. Most of the remainder seems to be wrapped up in the problem of pattern recognition within the storage mechanism or medium. Detailed discussion of these problems is beyond the present scope. However, a brief outline of one promising idea, "trie memory," may serve to indicate the general nature of anticipated developments.

Trie memory is so called by its originator, Fredkin (1960), because it is designed to facilitate retrieval of information and because the branching storage structure, when developed, resembles a tree. Most common memory systems store functions of arguments at locations designated by the arguments. (In one sense, they do not store the arguments at all. In another and more realistic sense, they store all the possible arguments in the framework structure of the memory.) The trie memory system, on the other hand, stores both the functions and the arguments. The argument is introduced into the memory first, one character at a time, starting at a standard initial register. Each argument register has one cell for each character of the ensemble (e.g., two for information encoded in binary form) and each character cell has within it storage space for the address of the next register. The argument is stored by writing a series of addresses, each one of which tells where to find the next. At the end of the argument is a special "end-of-argument" marker. Then follow directions to the function, which is stored in one or another of several ways, either further trie structure or "list structure" often being most effective.

The trie memory scheme is inefficient for small memories, but it becomes increasingly efficient in using available storage space as memory size increases. The attractive features of the scheme are these: 1) The retrieval process is extremely simple. Given the argument, enter the standard initial register with the first character, and pick up the address of the second. Then go to the second register, and pick up the address of the third, etc. 2) If two arguments have initial characters in common, they use the same storage space for those characters. 3) The lengths of the arguments need not be the same, and need not be specified in advance. 4) No room in storage is reserved for or used by any argument until it is actually stored. The trie structure is created as the items are introduced into the memory. 5) A function can be used as an argument for another function, and that function as an argument for the next. Thus, for example, by entering with the argument, "matrix multiplication," one might retrieve the entire program for performing a matrix multiplication on the computer. 6) By examining the storage at a given level, one can determine what thus-far similar items have been stored. For example, if there is no citation for Egan, J. P., it is but a step or two backward to pick up the trail of Egan, James . . . .

The properties just described do not include all the desired ones, but they bring computer storage into resonance with human operators and their predilection to designate things by naming or pointing.

20.5.4   The language problem   The basic dissimilarity between human languages and computer languages may be the most serious obstacle to true symbiosis. It is reassuring, however, to note what great strides have already been made, through interpretive programs and particularly through assembly or compiling programs such as FORTRAN, to adapt computers to human language forms. The "Information Processing Language" of Shaw et al. (1958) represents another line of rapprochement. And, in ALGOL and related systems, men are proving their flexibility by adopting standard formulas of representation and expression that are readily translatable into machine language.

For the purposes of real-time cooperation between men and computers, it will be necessary, however, to make use of an additional and rather different principle of communication and control. The idea may be highlighted by comparing instructions ordinarily addressed to intelligent human beings with instructions ordinarily used with computers. The latter specify precisely the individual steps to take and the sequence in which to take them. The former present or imply something about incentive or motivation, and they supply a criterion by which the human executor of the instructions will know when he has accomplished his task. In short: instructions directed to computers specify courses; instructions directed to human beings specify goals.

Men appear to think more naturally and easily in terms of goals than in terms of courses. True, they usually know something about directions in which to travel or lines along which to work, but few start out with precisely formulated itineraries. Who, for example, would depart from Boston for Los Angeles with a detailed specification of the route? Instead, to paraphrase Wiener, men bound for Los Angeles try continually to decrease the amount by which they are not yet in the smog.

Computer instruction through specification of goals is being approached along two paths. The first involves problem-solving, hill-climbing, self-organizing programs. The second involves real-time concatenation of preprogrammed segments and closed subroutines which the human operator can designate and call into action simply by name.

Along the first of these paths, there has been promising exploratory work. It is clear that, working within the loose constraints of predetermined strategies, computers will in due course be able to devise and simplify their own procedures for achieving stated goals. Thus far, the achievements have not been substantively important; they have constituted only "demonstration in principle." Nevertheless, the implications are far-reaching.

Although the second path is simpler and apparently capable of earlier realization, it has been relatively neglected. Fredkin's trie memory provides a promising paradigm. We may in due course see a serious effort to develop computer programs that can be connected together like the words and phrases of speech to do whatever computation or control is required at the moment. The consideration that holds back such an effort, apparently, is that the effort would produce nothing that would be of great value in the context of existing computers. It would be unrewarding to develop the language before there are any computing machines capable of responding meaningfully to it.

20.5.5   Input and output equipment   The department of data processing that seems least advanced, in so far as the requirements of man–computer symbiosis are concerned, is the one that deals with input and output equipment or, as it is seen from the human operator's point of view, displays and controls. Immediately after saying that, it is essential to make qualifying comments, because the engineering of equipment for high-speed introduction and extraction of information has been excellent, and because some very sophisticated display and control techniques have been developed in such research laboratories as the Lincoln Laboratory. By and large, in generally available computers, however, there is almost no provision for any more effective, immediate man–machine communication than can be achieved with an electric typewriter.

Displays seem to be in a somewhat better state than controls. Many computers plot graphs on oscilloscope screens, and a few take advantage of the remarkable capabilities, graphical and symbolic, of the charactron display tube. Nowhere, to my knowledge, however, is there anything approaching the flexibility and convenience of the pencil and doodle pad or the chalk and blackboard used by men in technical discussion.

1) Desk-Surface Display and Control: Certainly, for effective man–computer interaction, it will be necessary for the man and the computer to draw graphs and pictures and to write notes and equations to each other on the same display surface. The man should be able to present a function to the computer, in a rough but rapid fashion, by drawing a graph. The computer should read the man's writing, perhaps on the condition that it be in clear block capitals, and it should immediately post, at the location of each hand-drawn symbol, the corresponding character as interpreted and put into precise type-face. With such an input-output device, the operator would quickly learn to write or print in a manner legible to the machine. He could compose instructions and subroutines, set them into proper format, and check them over before introducing them finally into the computer's main memory. He could even define new symbols, as Gilmore and Savell (1959) have done at the Lincoln Laboratory, and present them directly to the computer. He could sketch out the format of a table roughly and let the computer shape it up with precision. He could correct the computer's data, instruct the machine via flow diagrams, and in general interact with it very much as he would with another engineer, except that the "other engineer" would be a precise draftsman, a lightning calculator, a mnemonic wizard, and many other valuable partners all in one.

2) Computer-Posted Wall Display: In some technological systems, several men share responsibility for controlling vehicles whose behaviors interact. Some information must be presented simultaneously to all the men, preferably on a common grid, to coordinate their actions. Other information is of relevance only to one or two operators. There would be only a confusion of uninterpretable clutter if all the information were presented on one display to all of them. The information must be posted by a computer, since manual plotting is too slow to keep it up to date.

The problem just outlined is even now a critical one, and it seems certain to become more and more critical as time goes by. Several designers are convinced that displays with the desired characteristics can be constructed with the aid of flashing lights and time-sharing viewing screens based on the light-valve principle.

The large display should be supplemented, according to most of those who have thought about the problem, by individual display-control units. The latter would permit the operators to modify the wall display without leaving their locations. For some purposes, it would be desirable for the operators to be able to communicate with the computer through the supplementary displays and perhaps even through the wall display. At least one scheme for providing such communication seems feasible.

The large wall display and its associated system are relevant, of course, to symbiotic coopera-tion between a computer and a team of men. Laboratory experiments have indicated repeatedly that informal, parallel arrangements of operators, coordinating their activities through reference to a large situation display, have important advantages over the arrangement, more widely used, that locates the operators at individual consoles and attempts to correlate their actions through the agency of a computer. This is one of several operator-team problems in need of careful study.

3) Automatic Speech Production and Recognition: How desirable and how feasible is speech communication between human operators and computing machines? That compound question is asked whenever sophisticated data-processing systems are discussed. Engineers who work and live with computers take a conservative attitude toward the desirability. Engineers who have had experience in the field of automatic speech recognition take a conservative attitude toward the feasibility. Yet there is continuing interest in the idea of talking with computing machines. In large part, the interest stems from realization that one can hardly take a military commander or a corporation president away from his work to teach him to type. If computing machines are ever to be used directly by top-level decision makers, it may be worthwhile to provide communication via the most natural means, even at considerable cost.

Preliminary analysis of his problems and time scales suggests that a corporation president would be interested in a symbiotic association with a computer only as an avocation. Business situations usually move slowly enough that there is time for briefings and conferences. It seems reasonable, therefore, for computer specialists to be the ones who interact directly with comput-ers in business offices.

The military commander, on the other hand, faces a greater probability of having to make critical decisions in short intervals of time. It is easy to overdramatize the notion of the ten-minute war, but it would be dangerous to count on having more than ten minutes in which to make a critical decision. As military system ground environments and control centers grow in capability and complexity, therefore, a real requirement for automatic speech production and recognition in computers seems likely to develop. Certainly, if the equipment were already developed, reliable, and available, it would be used.

In so far as feasibility is concerned, speech production poses less severe problems of a technical nature than does automatic recognition of speech sounds. A commercial electronic digital voltmeter now reads aloud its indications, digit by digit. For eight or ten years, at the Bell Telephone Laboratories, the Royal Institute of Technology (Stockholm), the Signals Research and Development Establishment (Christchurch), the Haskins Laboratory, and the Massachusetts Institute of Technology, Dunn (1950); Fant (1959); Lawrence (1956); Cooper et al. (1952); Stevens et al. (1953), and their co-workers, have demonstrated successive generations of intelligible automatic talkers. Recent work at the Haskins Laboratory has led to the development of a digital code, suitable for use by computing machines, that makes an automatic voice utter intelligible connected discourse (Liberman et al., 1959).

The feasibility of automatic speech recognition depends heavily upon the size of the vocabulary of words to be recognized and upon the diversity of talkers and accents with which it must work. Ninety-eight per cent correct recognition of naturally spoken decimal digits was demonstrated several years ago at the Bell Telephone Laboratories and at the Lincoln Laboratory (Davis et al., 1952; Forgie and Forgie, 1959), To go a step up the scale of vocabulary size, we may say that an automatic recognizer of clearly spoken alpha-numerical characters can almost surely be developed now on the basis of existing knowledge. Since untrained operators can read at least as rapidly as trained ones can type, such a device would be a convenient tool in almost any computer installation.

For real-time interaction on a truly symbiotic level, however, a vocabulary of about 2000 words, e.g., 1000 words of something like basic English and 1000 technical terms, would probably be required. That constitutes a challenging problem. In the consensus of acousticians and linguists, construction of a recognizer of 2000 words cannot be accomplished now. However, there are several organizations that would happily undertake to develop an automatic recognize for such a vocabulary on a five-year basis. They would stipulate that the speech be clear speech, dictation style, without unusual accent.

Although detailed discussion of techniques of automatic speech recognition is beyond the present scope, it is fitting to note that computing machines are playing a dominant role in the development of automatic speech recognizers. They have contributed the impetus that accounts for the present optimism, or rather for the optimism presently found in some quarters. Two or three years ago, it appeared that automatic recognition of sizable vocabularies would not be achieved for ten or fifteen years; that it would have to await much further, gradual accumulation of knowledge of acoustic, phonetic, linguistic, and psychological processes in speech communication. Now, however, many see a prospect of accelerating the acquisition of that knowledge with the aid of computer processing of speech signals, and not a few workers have the feeling that sophisticated computer programs will be able to perform well as speech-pattern recognizers even without the aid of much substantive knowledge of speech signals and processes. Putting those two considerations together brings the estimate of the time required to achieve practically significant speech recognition down to perhaps five years, the five years just mentioned.

21 Recursive Functions of Symbolic Expressions and Their Computation by Machine (1960)

John McCarthy

John McCarthy (1927–2011) studied mathematics at Cal Tech as an undergraduate and at Princeton as a PhD student. While teaching at Dartmouth College in 1956, McCarthy hosted a summer school there on what he dubbed "Artificial Intelligence." According to the proposal for the conference (McCarthy, 1960), co-authored by McCarthy, Shannon, Marvin Minsky (then a Junior Fellow at Harvard), and the IBM researcher Nathaniel Rochester, the subjects for the conference would include (1) "Automatic computers" (how to write programs to simulate "the higher functions of the human brain"); (2) "How can a computer be programmed to use a language"; (3) "Neuron nets" (citing McCulloch and Pitts); (4) "Theory of the size of a calculation" ("a theory of the complexity of functions"); (5) "Self-improvement"; (6) "Abstractions"; and (7) "Randomness and creativity." All are still active research problems today!

McCarthy moved to MIT, where he was instrumental in the birth of time-sharing (chapter 23). There he invented the LISP programming language as a tool for the sort of symbolic reasoning he anticipated would be key to progress in AI. It was an audacious move, to borrow so directly from the lambda-calculus that Alonzo Church had developed as a mathematical language for resolving Hilbert's Entscheidungsproblem. In this initial description of LISP, the language was purely interpretive; it would take years before compilers were developed. McCarthy had to develop the garbage collection technique of memory management in order to make even small programs executable on the memory-limited machines of the day. LISP has remained not only usable but influential; McCarthy was involved in the design of ALGOL 60, the first widely-used general purpose language featuring recursion, and LISP has influenced the design of every subsequent functional programming language.

In 1962 McCarthy moved to Stanford, where he started the Artificial Intelligence Laboratory (SAIL), the foundry of vast amounts of influential AI research. Not only McCarthy but fifteen other affiliates of the SAIL have been recognized with the Turing Award. Throughout his career, he almost uniquely combined a deeply rooted respect for formal, mathematical, logical foundations with the ambition to produce working code that emulated aspects of human thought.

———————

Reprinted from McCarthy (1960), with permission from the Association for Computing Machinery.

21.1   Introduction

A programming system called LISP (for LISt Processor) has been developed for the IBM 704 computer by the Artificial Intelligence group at M.I.T. The system was designed to facilitate experiments with a proposed system called the Advice Taker, whereby a machine could be instructed to handle declarative as well as imperative sentences and could exhibit "common sense" in carrying out its instructions. The original proposal (McCarthy, 1961) for the Advice Taker was made in November 1958. The main requirement was a programming system for manipulating expressions representing formalized declarative and imperative sentences so that the Advice Taker system could make deductions.

In the course of its development the LISP system went through several stages of simplification and eventually came to be based on a scheme for representing the partial recursive functions of a certain class of symbolic expressions. This representation is independent of the IBM 704 computer, or of any other electronic computer, and it now seems expedient to expound the system by starting with the class of expressions called S-expressions and the functions called S-functions.

In this article, we first describe a formalism for defining functions recursively. We believe this formalism has advantages both as a programming language and as vehicle for developing a theory of computation. Next, we describe S-expressions and S-functions, give some examples, and then describe the universal S-function *apply* which plays the theoretical role of a universal Turing machine and the practical role of an interpreter. Then we describe the representation of S-expressions in the memory of the IBM 704 by list structures similar to those used by Newell and Shaw (1957), and the representation of S-functions by program. Then we mention the main features of the LISP programming system for the IBM 704. Next comes another way of describing computations with symbolic expressions, and finally we give a recursive function interpretation of flow charts.

We hope to describe some of the symbolic computations for which LISP has been used in another paper, and also to give elsewhere some applications of our recursive function formalism to mathematical logic and to the problem of mechanical theorem proving.

21.2   Functions and Function Definitions

We shall need a number of mathematical ideas and notations concerning functions in general. Most of the ideas are well known, but the notion of *conditional expression* is believed to be new, and the use of conditional expressions permits functions to be defined recursively in a new and convenient way.

a. *Partial Functions.* A partial function is a function that is defined only on part of its domain. Partial functions necessarily arise when functions are defined by computations because for some values of the arguments the computation defining the value of the function may not terminate. However, some of our elementary functions will be defined as partial functions.

b. *Propositional Expressions and Predicates.* A propositional expression is an expression whose possible values are T (for truth) and F (for falsity). We shall assume that the reader is familiar with the propositional connectives $\wedge$ ("and"), $\vee$ ("or"), and $\sim$ ("not"), Typical propositional expressions are:

$$x < y$$

$$(x < y) \wedge (b = c)$$

$$x \text{ is prime}$$

A predicate is a function whose range consists of the truth values T and F.

c. *Conditional Expressions*. The dependence of truth values on the values of quantities of other kinds is expressed in mathematics by predicates, and the dependence of truth values on other truth values by logical connectives. However, the notations for expressing symbolically the dependence of quantities of other kinds on truth-values is inadequate, so that English words and phrases are generally used for expressing these dependences in texts that describe other dependences symbolically. For example, the function $|x|$ is usually defined in words.

Conditional expressions are a device for expressing the dependence of quantities on propositional quantities. A conditional expression has the form $(p_1 \rightarrow e_1, \cdots, p_n \rightarrow e_n)$, where the p's are propositional expressions and the e's are expressions of any kind. It may be read, "If p_1 then e_1, otherwise if p_2 then e_2, $\cdots$, otherwise if p_n then e_n," or "p_1 yields e_1, $\cdots$, p_n yields e_n."

We now give the rules for determining whether the value $(p_1 \rightarrow e_1, \cdots, p_n \rightarrow e_n)$ is defined, and if so what its value is. Examine the p's from left to right. If a p whose value is T is encountered before any p whose value is undefined is encountered, then the value of the conditional expression is the value of the corresponding e (if this is defined). If any undefined p is encountered before a true p, or if all p's are false, or if the e corresponding to the first true p is undefined, then the value of the conditional expression is undefined. We now give examples.

$$(1 < 2 \rightarrow 4, 1 \geq 2 \rightarrow 3) = 4$$

$$(2 < 1 \rightarrow 4, 2 > 1 \rightarrow 3, 2 > 1 \rightarrow 2) = 3$$

$$(2 < 1 \rightarrow 4, T \rightarrow 3) = 3$$

$$(2 < 1 \rightarrow \frac{0}{0}, T \rightarrow 3) = 3$$

$$(2 < 1 \rightarrow 3, T \rightarrow \frac{0}{0}) \text{ is undefined}$$

$$(2 < 1 \rightarrow 3, 4 < 1 \rightarrow 4) \text{ is undefined}$$

Some of the simplest applications of conditional expressions are in giving such definitions as

$$|x| = (x < 0 \rightarrow -x, T \rightarrow x)$$

$$\delta_{ij} = (i = j \rightarrow 1, T \rightarrow 0)$$

$$\text{sgn}(x) = (x < 0 \rightarrow -1, x = 0 \rightarrow 0, T \rightarrow 1)$$

d. *Recursive Function Definitions.* By using conditional expressions we can, without circularity, define functions by formulas in which the defined function occurs. For example, we write

$$n! = (n = 0 \rightarrow 1, T \rightarrow n \cdot (n - 1)!)$$

When we use this formula to evaluate 0! we get the answer 1; because of the way in which the value of a conditional expression was defined, the meaningless expression $0 \cdot (0 - 1)!$ does not arise. The evaluation of 2! according to this definition proceeds as follows:

$$2! = (2 = 0 \rightarrow 1, T \rightarrow 2 \cdot (2 - 1)!)$$
$$= 2 \cdot 1!$$
$$= 2 \cdot (1 = 0 \rightarrow 1, T \rightarrow 1 \cdot (1 - 1)!)$$
$$= 2 \cdot 1 \cdot 0!$$
$$= 2 \cdot 1 \cdot (0 = 0 \rightarrow 1, T \rightarrow 0 \cdot (0 - 1)!)$$
$$= 2 \cdot 1 \cdot 1$$
$$= 2.$$

We now give two other applications of recursive function definitions. The greatest common divisor, gcd(m, n), of two positive integers m and n is computed by means of the Euclidean algorithm. This algorithm is expressed by the recursive function definition:

$$\text{gcd}(m, n) = (m > n \rightarrow \text{gcd}(n, m),$$
$$\text{rem}(n, m) = 0 \rightarrow m,$$
$$T \rightarrow \text{gcd}(\text{rem}(n, m), m))$$

where rem(n, m) denotes the remainder left when n is divided by m.

The Newtonian algorithm for obtaining an approximate square root of a number a, starting with an initial approximation x and requiring that an acceptable approximation y satisfy $|y^2 - a| < \epsilon$, may be written

$$\text{sqrt}(a, x, \epsilon) = \left(|x^2 - a| < \epsilon \rightarrow x, T \rightarrow \text{sqrt}\left(a, \frac{1}{2}\left(x + \frac{a}{x}\right), \epsilon\right)\right).$$

The simultaneous recursive definition of several functions is also possible, and we shall use such definitions if they are required. There is no guarantee that the computation determined by a recursive definition will ever terminate and, for example, an attempt to compute $n!$ from our definition will only succeed if n is a non-negative integer. If the computation does not terminate, the function must be regarded as undefined for the given arguments.

The propositional connectives themselves can be defined by conditional expressions. We write

$$p \wedge q = (p \to q, T \to F)$$
$$p \vee q = (p \to T, T \to q)$$
$$\sim p = (p \to F, T \to T)$$
$$p \supset q = (p \to q, T \to T)$$

It is readily seen that the right-hand sides of the equations have the correct truth tables. If we consider situations in which p or q may be undefined, the connectives $\wedge$ and $\vee$ are seen to be noncommutative. For example if p is false and q is undefined, we see that according to the definitions given above $p \wedge q$ is false, but $q \wedge p$ is undefined. For our applications this noncommutativity is desirable, since $p \wedge q$ is computed by first computing p, and if p is false q is not computed. If the computation for p does not terminate, we never get around to computing q. We shall use propositional connectives in this sense hereafter.

e. *Functions and Forms.* It is usual in mathematics—outside of mathematical logic—to use the word "function" imprecisely and to apply it to forms such as $y^2 + x$. Because we shall later compute with expressions for functions, we need a distinction between functions and forms and a notation for expressing this distinction. This distinction and a notation for describing it, from which we deviate trivially, is given by Church (1941).

Let f be an expression that stands for a function of two integer variables. It should make sense to write $f(3, 4)$ and the value of this expression should be determined. The expression $y^2 + x$ does not meet this requirement; $y^2 + x(3, 4)$ is not a conventional notation, and if we attempted to define it we would be uncertain whether its value would turn out to be 13 or 19. Church calls an expression like $y^2 + x$ a form. A form can be converted into a function if we can determine the correspondence between the variables occurring in the form and the ordered list of arguments of the desired function. This is accomplished by Church's λ-notation.

If $\mathcal{E}$ is a form in variables $x_1, \cdots, x_n$, then $\lambda((x_1, \cdots, x_n), \mathcal{E})$ will be taken to be the function of n variables whose value is determined by substituting the arguments for the variables $x_1, \cdots, x_n$ in that order in $\mathcal{E}$ and evaluating the resulting expression. For example, $\lambda((x, y), y^2 + x)$ is a function of two variables, and $\lambda((x, y), y^2 + x)(3, 4) = 19$.

The variables occurring in the list of variables of a λ-expression are dummy or bound, like variables of integration in a definite integral. That is, we may change the names of the bound variables in a function expression without changing the value of the expression, provided that we make the same change for each occurrence of the variable and do not make two variables the same that previously were different. Thus $\lambda((x, y), y^2 + x)$, $\lambda((u, v), v^2 + u)$ and $\lambda((y, x), x^2 + y)$ denote the same function.

We shall frequently use expressions in which some of the variables are bound by λ's and others are not. Such an expression may be regarded as defining a function with parameters. The unbound variables are called free variables.

An adequate notation that distinguishes functions from forms allows an unambiguous treatment of functions of functions. It would involve too much of a digression to give examples here, but we shall use functions with functions as arguments later in this report. ...

21.3   Recursive Functions of Symbolic Expressions

We shall first define a class of symbolic expressions in terms of ordered pairs and lists. Then we shall define five elementary functions and predicates, and build from them by composition, conditional expressions, and recursive definitions an extensive class of functions of which we shall give a number of examples. We shall then show how these functions themselves can be expressed as symbolic expressions, and we shall define a universal function *apply* that allows us to compute from the expression for a given function its value for given arguments. Finally, we shall define some functions with functions as arguments and give some useful examples.

a. *A Class of Symbolic Expressions.* We shall now define the S-expressions (S stands for symbolic). They are formed by using the special characters

.

(

)

and an infinite set of distinguishable atomic symbols. For atomic symbols, we shall use strings of capital Latin letters and digits with single imbedded blanks. Examples of atomic symbols are

A

ABA

APPLE PIE NUMBER 3

There is a twofold reason for departing from the usual mathematical practice of using single letters for atomic symbols. First, computer programs frequently require hundreds of distinguishable symbols that must be formed from the 47 characters that are printable by the IBM 704 computer. Second, it is convenient to allow English words and phrases to stand for atomic entities for mnemonic reasons. The symbols are atomic in the sense that any substructure they may have as sequences of characters is ignored. We assume only that different symbols can be distinguished.

S-expressions are then defined as follows:

1. Atomic symbols are S-expressions.
2. If e_1 and e_2 are S-expressions, so is $(e_1 \cdot e_2)$.

Examples of S-expressions are

AB

$(A \cdot B)$

$((AB \cdot C) \cdot D)$

An S-expression is then simply an ordered pair, the terms of which may be atomic symbols or simpler S-expressions. We can represent a list of arbitrary length in terms of S-expressions as follows. The list $(m_1, m_2, \cdots, m_n)$ is represented by the S-expression

$$(m_1 \cdot (m_2 \cdot (\cdots (m_n \cdot \text{NIL}) \cdots)))$$

where NIL is an atomic symbol used to terminate lists.

Since many of the symbolic expressions with which we deal are conveniently expressed as lists, we shall introduce a list notation to abbreviate certain S-expressions. We have

1. (m) stands for $(m \cdot \text{NIL})$.
2. $(m_1, \cdots, m_n)$ stands for $(m_1 \cdot (\cdots (m_n \cdot \text{NIL}) \cdots))$.
3. $(m_1, \cdots, m_n \cdot x)$ stands for $(m_1 \cdot (\cdots (m_n \cdot x) \cdots))$.

Subexpressions can be similarly abbreviated. Some examples of these abbreviations are

$((AB, C), D)$ for $((AB \cdot (C \cdot \text{NIL})) \cdot (D \cdot \text{NIL}))$

$((A, B), C, D \cdot E)$ for $((A \cdot (B \cdot \text{NIL})) \cdot (C \cdot (D \cdot E)))$

Since we regard the expressions with commas as abbreviations for those not involving commas, we shall refer to them all as S-expressions.

b. *Functions of S-expressions and the Expressions That Represent Them.* We now define a class of functions of S-expressions. The expressions representing these functions are written in a conventional functional notation. However, in order to clearly distinguish the expressions representing functions from S-expressions, we shall use sequences of lower-case letters for function names and variables ranging over the set of S-expressions. We also use brackets and semicolons, instead of parentheses and commas, for denoting the application of functions to their arguments. Thus we write

car [x]

car [cons [(A · B); x]]

In these M-expressions (meta-expressions) any S-expressions that occur stand for themselves.

c. *The Elementary S-functions and Predicates.* We introduce the following functions and predicates:

1. atom. atom [x] has the value of T or F, accordingly as x is an atomic symbol or not. Thus

    atom [X] = T

    atom [(X · A)] = F

2. eq. eq[x; y] is defined if and only if both x and y are atomic. eq[x; y] = T if x and y are the same symbol, and eq[x; y] = F otherwise. Thus

    eq[X; X] = T

    eq[X; A] = F

    eq[X; (X · A)] is undefined.

3. car. car[x] is defined if and only if x is not atomic. $car[(e_1 \cdot e_2)] = e_1$. Thus car[X] is undefined.

$$car[(X \cdot A)] = X$$

$$car[((X \cdot A) \cdot Y)] = (X \cdot A)$$

4. cdr. cdr[x] is also defined when x is not atomic. We have $cdr[(e_1 \cdot e_2)] = e_2$. Thus cdr[X] is undefined.

$$cdr[(X \cdot A)] = A$$

$$cdr[((X \cdot A) \cdot Y)] = Y$$

5. cons. cons[x; y] is defined for any x and y. We have $cons[e_1; e_2] = (e_1 \cdot e_2)$. Thus

$$cons[X; A] = (X \cdot A)$$

$$cons[(X \cdot A) ; Y] = ((X \cdot A) \cdot Y)$$

car, cdr, and cons are easily seen to satisfy the relations

$$car[cons[x; y]] = x$$

$$cdr[cons[x; y]] = y$$

$$cons[car[x]; cdr[x]] = x, \text{ provide that x is not atomic.}$$

The names "car" and "cons" will come to have mnemonic significance only when we discuss the representation of the system in the computer. Compositions of car and cdr give the subexpressions of a given expression in a given position. Compositions of cons form expressions of a given structure out of pairs. The class of functions which can be formed in this way is quite limited and not very interesting.

d. *Recursive S-functions.* We get a much larger class of functions (in fact, all computable functions) when we allow ourselves to form new functions of S-expressions by conditional expressions and recursive definition.

We now give some examples of functions that are definable in this way.

ff[x]. The value of ff[x] is the first atomic symbol of the S-expression x with the parentheses ignored. Thus

$$ff[((A \cdot B) \cdot C)] = A$$

We have

$$ff[x] = [atom[x] \rightarrow x; t \rightarrow ff[car[x]]]$$

[EDITOR: Other function and predicate definitions and examples omitted.]

$\cdots$

f. *The Universal S-Function* apply. There is an S-function *apply* with the property that if f is an S-expression for an S-function f′ and args is a list of arguments of the form (arg1, $\cdots$, argn), where arg1, $\cdots$, argn are arbitrary S-expressions, then apply[f; args] and f′[arg1; $\cdots$; argn] are defined for the same values of arg1, $\cdots$, argn, and are equal when defined. For example,

$\lambda[[x; y]; cons[car[x]; y]][(A, B); (C, D)]$
   $= apply[(LAMBDA, (X, Y), (CONS, (CAR X), Y)) ((A, B), (C, D))]$
   $= (A, C, D)$

$\cdots$

g. *Functions with Functions as Arguments.* There are a number of useful functions some of whose arguments are functions. They are especially useful in defining other functions. One such function is maplist [x; f] with an S-expression argument x and an argument f that is a function from S-expressions to S-expressions. We define

maplist $[x; f] = [null [x] \rightarrow NIL; T \rightarrow cons [f[x]; maplist [cdr [x]; f]]]$

The usefulness of maplist is illustrated by formulas for the partial derivative with respect to x of expressions involving sums and products of x and other variables. The S-expressions that we shall differentiate are formed as follows.

1. An atomic symbol is an allowed expression.
2. If $e_1, \cdots , e_n$ are allowed expressions, (PLUS, $e_1, \cdots , e_n$) and (TIMES, $e_1, \cdots , e_n$) are also, and represent the sum and product, respectively, of $e_1, \cdots , e_n$.

This is, essentially, the Polish notation for functions except that the inclusion of parentheses and commas allows functions of variable numbers of arguments. An example of an allowed expression is (TIMES, X, (PLUS, X, A), Y), the conventional algebraic notation for which is X(X+A)Y.

Our differentiation formula, which gives the derivative of y with respect to x, is

diff[y; x] = [atom[y] $\rightarrow$ [eq[y; x] $\rightarrow$ ONE; T $\rightarrow$ ZERO];
   eq[car[y]; PLUS] $\rightarrow$ cons[PLUS; maplist[cdr[y]; λ[[z]; diff[car[z]; x]]]];
   eq[car[y]; TIMES] $\rightarrow$ cons[PLUS; maplist[cdr[y]; λ[[z]; cons[TIMES;
      maplist[cdr[y]; λ[[w]; ~eq[z; w] $\rightarrow$ car[w]; T $\rightarrow$ diff[car[[w]; x]]]]]]]]]]

The derivative of the allowed expression, as computed by this formula, is

(PLUS, (TIMES, ONE, (PLUS, X, A), Y), (TIMES, X, (PLUS, ONE, ZERO), Y),
   (TIMES, X, (PLUS, X, A), ZERO))

$\cdots$

21.4   The LISP **Programming System**

The LISP programming system is a system for using the IBM 704 computer to compute with symbolic information in the form of S-expressions. It has been or will be used for the following purposes:

1. Writing a compiler to compile LISP programs into machine language.
2. Writing a program to check proofs in a class of formal logical systems.

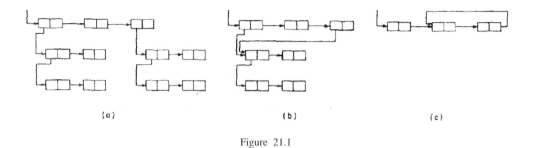

(a)   (b)   (c)

Figure 21.1

3. Writing programs for formal differentiation and integration.

4. Writing programs to realize various algorithms for generating proofs in predicate calculus.

5. Making certain engineering calculations whose results are formulas rather than numbers.

6. Programming the Advice Taker system.

The basis of the system is a way of writing computer programs to evaluate S-functions. This will be described in the following sections.

In addition to the facilities for describing S-functions, there are facilities for using S-functions in programs written as sequences of statements along the lines of FORTRAN (IBM, 1956) or ALGOL (Perlis and Samelson, 1958). These features will not be described in this article.

a. *Representation of S-Expressions by List Structure.* List structure is a collection of computer words arranged as in Figure 21.1a or 21.1b. Each word of the list structure is represented by one of the subdivided rectangles in the figure. The *left* box of a rectangle represents the *address* field of the word and the *right* box represents the *decrement* field. An arrow from a box to another rectangle means that the field corresponding to the box contains the location of the word corresponding to the other rectangle. [EDITOR: The IBM 704 provided convenient facilities for manipulating the "Contents of the Address field of the Register" (car) and the "Contents of the Decrement field of the Register" (cdr). Within each word of a list structure, early LISP implementations placed that word's two pointers (to other words of the list structure) in the right bit positions to take advantage of those facilities.]

It is permitted for a substructure to occur in more than one place in a list structure, as in Figure 21.1b, but it is not permitted for a structure to have cycles, as in Figure 21.1c.

An atomic symbol is represented in the computer by a list structure of special form called the *association list* of the symbol. The address field of the first word contains a special constant which enables the program to tell that this word represents an atomic symbol. ...

An S-expression x that is not atomic is represented by a word, the address and decrement parts of which contain the locations of the subexpressions car[x] and cdr[x], respectively. ...

The advantages of list structures for the storage of symbolic expressions are:

1. The size and even the number of expressions with which the program will have to deal cannot be predicted in advance. Therefore, it is difficult to arrange blocks of storage of fixed length to contain them.

2. Registers can be put back on the free-storage list when they are no longer needed. Even one register returned to the list is of value, but if expressions are stored linearly, it is difficult to make use of blocks of registers of odd sizes that may become available.

3. An expression that occurs as a subexpression of several expressions need be represented in storage only once.

. . .

   e. *Free-Storage List.* At any given time only a part of the memory reserved for list structures will actually be in use for storing S-expressions. The remaining registers (in our system the number, initially, is approximately 15,000) are arranged in a single list called the *free-storage list*. A certain register, FREE, in the program contains the location of the first register in this list. When a word is required to form some additional list structure, the first word on the *free-storage list* is taken and the number in register FREE is changed to become the location of the second word on the free-storage list. No provision need be made for the user to program the return of registers to the free-storage list.

   This return takes place automatically, approximately as follows (it is necessary to give a simplified description of this process in this report): There is a fixed set of base registers in the program which contains the locations of list structures that are accessible to the program. Of course, because list structures branch, an arbitrary number of registers may be involved. Each register that is accessible to the program is accessible because it can be reached from one or more of the base registers by a chain of car and cdr operations. When the contents of a base register are changed, it may happen that the register to which the base register formerly pointed cannot be reached by a car–cdr chain from any base register. Such a register may be considered abandoned by the program because its contents can no longer be found by any possible program; hence its contents are no longer of interest, and so we would like to have it back on the free-storage list. This comes about in the following way.

   Nothing happens until the program runs out of free storage. When a free register is wanted, and there is none left on the free-storage list, a reclamation cycle starts. First, the program finds all registers accessible from the base registers and makes their signs negative. This is accomplished by starting from each of the base registers and changing the sign of every register that can be reached from it by a car-cdr chain. If the program encounters a register in this process which already has a negative sign, it assumes that this register has already been reached.

   After all of the accessible registers have had their signs changed, the program goes through the area of memory reserved for the storage of list structures and puts all the registers whose signs were not changed in the previous step back on the free-storage list, and makes the signs of the accessible registers positive again.

This process, because it is entirely automatic, is more convenient for the programmer than a system in which he has to keep track of and erase unwanted lists. Its efficiency depends upon not coming close to exhausting the available memory with accessible lists. This is because the reclamation process requires several seconds to execute, and therefore must result in the addition of at least several thousand registers to the free-storage list if the program is not to spend most of its time in reclamation. . . .

22 Augmenting Human Intellect: A Conceptual Framework (1962)

Douglas C. Engelbart

Doug Engelbart (1925–2013) read Bush's "As We May Think" (chapter 11) while stationed with the Navy in the South Pacific at the end of World War II. It must have seemed like science fiction, but he spent his career trying to put flesh on the bones of Bush's vision.

Engelbart's "augmented human intellect" project was carried out mostly at SRI in Menlo Park, California (originally the Stanford Research Institute). The project encompassed collaboration between humans and interactivity between humans and computers, in order to amplify human intellectual capacity. This selection is a part of a long, early outline of the project. Engelbart's work was never considered mainstream, even at the highly innovative SRI, but it fell under the umbrella of research funding flowing from ARPA, some of it under the direction of J. C. R. Licklider. Like many daring technological investments, parts of the project never took hold (for example, a one-handed keyboard on which five fingers, each depressing a separate wand, could be placed in 31 different positions, enough to input the letters of the Roman alphabet). Others had enormous influence (such as the mouse). And others, such as the idea of distributed, collaborative workflows, greatly influenced—or were rediscovered as aspects of—later developments.

Engelbart both abstracted and concretized Licklider's vision in a famous 1968 demonstration that came to be known as "the mother of all demos." It dazzled the audience at the Fall Joint Computer Conference in San Francisco with many interactive technologies that have now become commonplace: the mouse, networking, videoconferencing, hyperlinks, collaborative text editing, and windowing, among others.

A decade later SRI sold Engelbart's laboratory to a for-profit business, where it did not flourish, in part because of Engelbart's determined idiosyncrasies, and in part because the booming personal computer and networking industries were independently changing the way computers were being used. For all his technical wizardry, Engelbart was more than anything spiritually committed to human improvement. He was a creature of the 1960s, and with the advent of the 1970s commercialization was coming. Engelbart received the Turing Award in 1997 "for an inspiring vision of the future of interactive computing and the invention of key technologies to help realize this vision."

Reprinted from Engelbart (1962), with permission from SRI International.

22.1   Introduction

B Y "augmenting human intellect" we mean increasing the capability of a man to approach a complex problem situation, to gain comprehension to suit his particular needs, and to derive solutions to problems. Increased capability in this respect is taken to mean a mixture of the following: more-rapid comprehension, better comprehension, the possibility of gaining a useful degree of comprehension in a situation that previously was too complex, speedier solutions, better solutions, and the possibility of finding solutions to problems that before seemed insoluble. And by "complex situations" we include the professional problems of diplomats, executives, social scientists, life scientists, physical scientists, attorneys, designers—whether the problem situation exists for twenty minutes or twenty years. We do not speak of isolated clever tricks that help in particular situations. We refer to a way of life in an integrated domain where hunches, cut-and-try, intangibles, and the human "feel for a situation" usefully co-exist with powerful concepts, streamlined terminology and notation, sophisticated methods, and high-powered electronic aids.

Man's population and gross product are increasing at a considerable rate, but the complexity of his problems grows still faster, and the urgency with which solutions must be found becomes steadily greater in response to the increased rate of activity and the increasingly global nature of that activity. Augmenting man's intellect, in the sense defined above, would warrant full pursuit by an enlightened society if there could be shown a reasonable approach and some plausible benefits.

This report covers the first phase of a program aimed at developing means to augment the human intellect. These "means" can include many things—all of which appear to be but extensions of means developed and used in the past to help man apply his native sensory, mental, and motor capabilities—and we consider the whole system of a human and his augmentation means as a proper field of search for practical possibilities. It is a very important system to our society, and like most systems its performance can best be improved by considering the whole as a set of interacting components rather than by considering the components in isolation.

This kind of system approach to human intellectual effectiveness does not find a ready-made conceptual framework such as exists for established disciplines. Before a research program can be designed to pursue such an approach intelligently, so that practical benefits might be derived within a reasonable time while also producing results of longrange significance, a conceptual framework must be searched out—a framework that provides orientation as to the important factors of the system, the relationships among these factors, the types of change among the system factors that offer likely improvements in performance, and the sort of research goals and methodology that seem promising.

In the first (search) phase of our program we have developed a conceptual framework that seems satisfactory for the current needs of designing a research phase. §22.2 contains the essence of this framework as derived from several different ways of looking at the system made up of a human and his intellect-augmentation means.

The process of developing this conceptual framework brought out a number of significant realizations: that the intellectual effectiveness exercised today by a given human has little likelihood of being intelligence limited—that there are dozens of disciplines in engineering, mathematics, and the social, life, and physical sciences that can contribute improvements to the system of intellect-augmentation means; that any one such improvement can be expected to trigger a chain of coordinating improvements; that until every one of these disciplines comes to a standstill and we have exhausted all the improvement possibilities we could glean from it, we can expect to continue to develop improvements in this human-intellect system; that there is no particular reason not to expect gains in personal intellectual effectiveness from a concerted system-oriented approach that compare to those made in personal geographic mobility since horseback and sailboat days. . . .

Let us consider an "augmented" architect at work. He sits at a working station that has a visual display screen some three feet on a side; this is his working surface, and is controlled by a computer (his "clerk") with which he can communicate by means of a small keyboard and various other devices.

He is designing a building. He has already dreamed up several basic layouts and structural forms, and is trying them out on the screen. The surveying data for the layout he is working on now have already been entered, and he has just coaxed the clerk to show him a perspective view of the steep hillside building site with the roadway above, symbolic representations of the various trees that are to remain on the lot, and the service tie points for the different utilities. The view occupies the left two-thirds of the screen. With a "pointer," he indicates two points of interest, moves his left hand rapidly over the keyboard, and the distance and elevation between the points indicated appear on the right-hand third of the screen.

Now he enters a reference line with his pointer, and the keyboard. Gradually the screen begins to show the work he is doing—a neat excavation appears in the hillside, revises itself slightly, and revises itself again. After a moment, the architect changes the scene on the screen to an overhead plan view of the site, still showing the excavation. A few minutes of study, and he enters on the keyboard a list of items, checking each one as it appears on the screen, to be studied later.

Ignoring the representation on the display, the architect next begins to enter a series of specifications and data—a six-inch slab floor, twelve-inch concrete walls eight feet high within the excavation, and so on. When he has finished, the revised scene appears on the screen. A structure is taking shape. He examines it, adjusts it, pauses long enough to ask for handbook or catalog information from the clerk at various points, and readjusts accordingly. He often recalls from the "clerk" his working lists of specifications and considerations to refer to them, modify them, or add to them. These lists grow into an evermore-detailed, interlinked structure, which represents the maturing thought behind the actual design.

Prescribing different planes here and there, curved surfaces occasionally, and moving the whole structure about five feet, he finally has the rough external form of the building balanced nicely with the setting and he is assured that this form is basically compatible with the materials to be used as well as with the function of the building.

Now he begins to enter detailed information about the interior. Here the capability of the clerk to show him any view he wants to examine (a slice of the interior, or how the structure would look from the roadway above) is important. He enters particular fixture designs, and examines them in a particular room. He checks to make sure that sun glare from the windows will not blind a driver on the roadway, and the "clerk" computes the information that one window will reflect strongly onto the roadway between 6 and 6:30 on midsummer mornings.

Next he begins a functional analysis. He has a list of the people who will occupy this building, and the daily sequences of their activities. The "clerk" allows him to follow each in turn, examining how doors swing, where special lighting might be needed. Finally he has the "clerk" combine all of these sequences of activity to indicate spots where traffic is heavy in the building, or where congestion might occur, and to determine what the severest drain on the utilities is likely to be.

All of this information (the building design and its associated "thought structure") can be stored on a tape to represent the design manual for the building. Loading this tape into his own clerk, another architect, a builder, or the client can maneuver within this design manual to pursue whatever details or insights are of interest to him—and can append special notes that are integrated into the design manual for his own or someone else's later benefit.

In such a future working relationship between human problem-solver and computer "clerk," the capability of the computer for executing mathematical processes would be used whenever it was needed. However, the computer has many other capabilities for manipulating and displaying information that can be of significant benefit to the human in nonmathematical processes of planning, organizing, studying, etc. Every person who does his thinking with symbolized concepts (whether in the form of the English language, pictographs, formal logic, or mathematics) should be able to benefit significantly.

22.2   Conceptual Framework

22.2.1   General   The conceptual framework we seek must orient us toward the real possibilities and problems associated with using modern technology to give direct aid to an individual in comprehending complex situations, isolating the significant factors, and solving problems. To gain this orientation, we examine how individuals achieve their present level of effectiveness, and expect that this examination will reveal possibilities for improvement. ...

Every process of thought or action is made up of sub-processes. Let us consider such examples as making a pencil stroke, writing a letter of the alphabet, or making a plan. Quite a few discrete muscle movements are organized into the making of a pencil stroke; similarly, making particular pencil strokes and making a plan for a letter are complex processes in themselves that become sub-processes to the over-all writing of an alphabetic character.

Although every sub-process is a process in its own right, in that it consists of further subprocesses, there seems to be no point here in looking for the ultimate bottom of the process-hierarchical structure. There seems to be no way of telling whether or not the apparent bottoms (processes that cannot be further subdivided) exist in the physical world or in the limitations of human understanding.

In any case, it is not necessary to begin from the bottom in discussing particular process hierarchies. No person uses a process that is completely unique every time he tackles something new. Instead, he begins from a group of basic sensory-mental-motor process capabilities, and adds to these certain of the process capabilities of his artifacts. There are only a finite number of such basic human and artifact capabilities from which to draw. Furthermore, even quite different higher order processes may have in common relatively high-order sub-processes.

When a man writes prose text (a reasonably high-order process), he makes use of many processes as sub-processes that are common to other high-order processes. For example, he makes use of planning, composing, dictating. The process of writing is utilized as a sub-process within many different processes of a still higher order, such as organizing a committee, changing a policy, and so on.

What happens, then, is that each individual develops a certain repertoire of process capabilities from which he selects and adapts those that will compose the processes that he executes. This repertoire is like a tool kit, and just as the mechanic must know what his tools can do and how to use them, so the intellectual worker must know the capabilities of his tools and have good methods, strategies, and rules of thumb for making use of them. All of the process capabilities in the individual's repertoire rest ultimately upon basic capabilities within him or his artifacts, and the entire repertoire represents an inter-knit, hierarchical structure (which we often call the repertoire hierarchy).

We find three general categories of process capabilities within a typical individual's repertoire. There are those that are executed completely within the human integument, which we call explicit-human process capabilities; there are those possessed by artifacts for executing processes without human intervention, which we call explicit-artifact process capabilities; and there are what we call the composite process capabilities, which are derived from hierarchies containing both of the other kinds.

We assume that it is our H-LAM/T system (Human using Language, Artifacts, Methodology, in which he is Trained) that has the capability and that performs the process in any instance of use of this repertoire. Let us look within the process structure for the LAM/T ingredients, to get a better "feel" for our models. Consider the process of writing an important memo. There is a particular concept associated with this process—that of putting information into a formal package and distributing it to a set of people for a certain kind of consideration—and the type of information package associated with this concept has been given the special name of memorandum. Already the system language shows the effect of this process—i.e., a concept and its name. . . .

22.2.2   The basic perspective   Individuals who operate effectively in our culture have already been considerably "augmented." Basic human capabilities for sensing stimuli, performing numerous mental operations, and for communicating with the outside world, are put to work in our society within a system—an H-LAM/T system—the individual augmented by the language, artifacts, and methodology in which he is trained. Furthermore, we suspect that improving the effectiveness of the individual as he operates in our society should be approached as a system-engineering problem—that is, the H-LAM/T system should be studied as an interacting whole from a synthesis-oriented approach.

This view of the system as an interacting whole is strongly bolstered by considering the repertoire hierarchy of process capabilities that is structured from the basic ingredients within the H-LAM/T system. The realization that any potential change in language, artifact, or methodology has importance only relative to its use within a process and that a new process capability appearing anywhere within that hierarchy can make practical a new consideration of latent change possibilities in many other parts of the hierarchy—possibilities in either language, artifacts, or methodology—brings out the strong interrelationship of these three augmentation means.

Increasing the effectiveness of the individual's use of his basic capabilities is a problem in redesigning the changeable parts of a system. The system is actively engaged in the continuous processes (among others) of developing comprehension within the individual and of solving problems; both processes are subject to human motivation, purpose, and will. To redesign the system's capability for performing these processes means redesigning all or part of the repertoire hierarchy. To redesign a structure, we must learn as much as we can of what is known about the basic materials and components as they are utilized within the structure; beyond that, we must learn how to view, to measure, to analyze, and to evaluate in terms of the functional whole and its purpose. In this particular case, no existing analytic theory is by itself adequate for the purpose of analyzing and evaluating over-all system performance; pursuit of an improved system thus demands the use of experimental methods.

It need not be just the very sophisticated or formal process capabilities that are added or modified in this redesign. Essentially any of the processes utilized by a representative human today—the processes that he thinks of when he looks ahead to his day's work—are composite processes of the sort that involve external composing and manipulating of symbols (text, sketches, diagrams, lists, etc.). Many of the external composing and manipulating (modifying, rearranging) processes serve such characteristically "human" activities as playing with forms and relationships to ask what develops, cut-and-try multiple-pass development of an idea, or listing items to reflect on and then rearranging and extending them as thoughts develop.

Existing, or near-future, technology could certainly provide our professional problem-solvers with the artifacts they need to have for duplicating and rearranging text before their eyes, quickly and with a minimum of human effort. Even so apparently minor an advance could yield total changes in an individual's repertoire hierarchy that would represent a great increase in over-all effectiveness. Normally the necessary equipment would enter the market slowly; changes from the expected would be small, people would change their ways of doing things a little at a time, and only gradually would their accumulated changes create markets for more radical versions of the equipment. Such an evolutionary process has been typical of the way our repertoire hierarchies have grown and formed.

But an active research effort, aimed at exploring and evaluating possible integrated changes throughout the repertoire hierarchy, could greatly accelerate this evolutionary process. The research effort could guide the product development of new artifacts toward taking long-range meaningful steps; simultaneously competitively minded individuals who would respond to demonstrated methods for achieving greater personal effectiveness would create a market for the more radical equipment innovations. The guided evolutionary process could be expected to be considerably more rapid than the traditional one.

The category of "more radical innovations" includes the digital computer as a tool for the personal use of an individual. Here there is not only promise of great flexibility in the composing and rearranging of text and diagrams before the individual's eyes but also promise of many other process capabilities that can be integrated into the H-LAM/T system's repertoire hierarchy.

22.2.3   Detailed discussion of the H-LAM/T system

22.2.3.1   The source of intelligence
When one looks at a computer system that is doing a very complex job, he sees on the surface a machine that can execute some extremely sophisticated processes. If he is a layman, his concept of what provides this sophisticated capability may endow the machine with a mysterious power to sweep information through perceptive and intelligent synthetic thinking devices. Actually, this sophisticated capability results from a very clever organizational hierarchy so that pursuit of the source of intelligence within this system would take one down through layers of functional and physical organization that become successively more primitive.

To be more specific, we can begin at the top and list the major levels down through which we would pass if we successively decomposed the functional elements of each level in search of the "source of intelligence." A programmer could take us down through perhaps three levels (depending upon the sophistication of the total process being executed by the computer) perhaps depicting the organization at each level with a flow chart. The first level down would organize functions corresponding to statements in a problem-oriented language (e.g., ALGOL or COBOL), to achieve the desired over-all process. The second level down would organize lesser functions into the processes represented by first-level statements. The third level would perhaps show how the basic machine commands (or rather the processes which they represent) were organized to achieve each of the functions of the second level.

Then a machine designer could take over, and with a block diagram of the computer's organization he could show us (Level 4) how the different hardware units (e.g., random-access storage, arithmetic registers, adder, arithmetic control) are organized to provide the capability of executing sequences of the commands used in Level 3. The logic designer could then give us a tour of Level 5, also using block diagrams, to show us how such hardware elements as pulse gates, flip-flops, and AND, OR, and NOT circuits can be organized into networks giving the functions utilized at Level 4. For Level 6 a circuit engineer could show us diagrams revealing how components such as transistors, resistors, capacitors, and diodes can be organized into modular networks that provide the functions needed for the elements of Level 5.

Device engineers and physicists of different kinds could take us down through more layers. But rather soon we have crossed the boundary between what is man-organized and what is nature-organized, and are ultimately discussing the way in which a given physical phenomenon is derived from the intrinsic organization of sub-atomic particles, with our ability to explain succeeding layers blocked by the exhaustion of our present human comprehension.

If we then ask ourselves where that intelligence is embodied, we are forced to concede that it is elusively distributed throughout a hierarchy of functional processes—a hierarchy whose foundation extends down into natural processes below the depth of our comprehension. If there is any one thing upon which this intelligence depends, it would seem to be *organization*. The biologists and physiologists use a term "synergism" to designate (Webster, 1959) the "... cooperative action of discrete agencies such that the total effect is greater than the sum of the two effects taken independently...." This term seems directly applicable here, where we could say that synergism is our most likely candidate for representing the actual source of intelligence

Actually, each of the social, life, or physical phenomena we observe about us would seem to derive from a supporting hierarchy of organized functions (or processes), in which the synergistic principle gives increased phenomenological sophistication to each succeedingly higher level of organization. In particular, the intelligence of a human being, derived ultimately from the characteristics of individual nerve cells, undoubtedly results from synergism.

22.2.3.2   Intelligence amplification   It has been jokingly suggested several times during the course of this study that what we are seeking is an "intelligence amplifier." (The term is attributed originally to W. Ross Ashby [1952, 1956].) At first this term was rejected on the grounds that in our view one's only hope was to make a better match between existing human intelligence and the problems to be tackled, rather than in making man more intelligent. But deriving the concepts brought out in the preceding section has shown us that indeed this term does seem applicable to our objective.

Accepting the term "intelligence amplification" does not imply any attempt to increase native human intelligence. The term "intelligence amplification" seems applicable to our goal of augmenting the human intellect in that the entity to be produced will exhibit more of what can be called intelligence than an unaided human could; we will have amplified the intelligence of the human by organizing his intellectual capabilities into higher levels of synergistic structuring. What possesses the amplified intelligence is the resulting H-LAM/T system, in which the LAM/T augmentation means represent the amplifier of the human's intelligence.

In amplifying our intelligence, we are applying the principle of synergistic structuring that was followed by natural evolution in developing the basic human capabilities. What we have done in the development of our augmentation means is to construct a superstructure that is a synthetic extension of the natural structure upon which it is built. In a very real sense, as represented by the steady evolution of our augmentation means, the development of "artificial intelligence" has been going on for centuries.

22.2.3.3 Two-domain systems   The human and the artifacts are the only physical components in the H-LAM/T system. It is upon their capabilities that the ultimate capability of the system will depend. This was implied in the earlier statement that every composite process of the system decomposes ultimately into explicit-human and explicit-artifact processes. There are thus two separate domains of activity within the H-LAM/T system: that represented by the human, in which all explicit-human processes occur; and that represented by the artifacts, in which all explicit-artifact processes occur. In any composite process, there is cooperative interaction between the two domains, requiring interchange of energy (much of it for information exchange purposes only). Figure 22.1 depicts this two-domain concept and embodies other concepts discussed below.

Where a complex machine represents the principal artifact with which a human being cooperates, the term "man–machine interface" has been used for some years to represent the boundary across which energy is exchanged between the two domains. However, the "man–artifact interface" has existed for centuries, ever since humans began using artifacts and executing composite processes.

Exchange across this "interface" occurs when an explicit-human process is coupled to an explicit-artifact

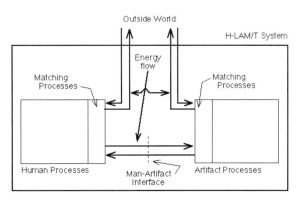

Figure 22.1: The Two Sides of the H-LAM/T System

process. Quite often these coupled processes are designed for just this exchange purpose, to provide a functional match between other explicit-human and explicit-artifact processes buried within their respective domains that do the more significant things. For instance, the finger and hand motions (explicit human processes) activate key-linkage motions in the typewriter (couple to explicit-artifact processes). But these are only part of the matching processes between the deeper human processes that direct a given word to be typed and the deeper artifact processes that actually imprint the ink marks on the paper. . . .

22.3 Examples and Discussion

22.3.2 Hypothetical description of the computer-based augmentation system   . . . Let us consider some specific possibilities for redesigning the augmentation means for an intellectually oriented, problem-solving human. We choose to present those developments of language and methodology that can capitalize upon the symbol-manipulating and portraying capabilities of computer-based equipment. The picture of the possibilities to pursue will change and grow rapidly as research gets under way, but we need to provide what pictures we can—to give substance to the generalities developed in §22.2, to try to impart our feeling of rich promise, and to introduce possible research program ....

22.3.2.1   Background   To try to give you (the reader) a specific sort of feel for our thesis in spite of this situation, we shall present the following picture of computer-based augmentation possibilities by describing what might happen if you were being given a personal discussion-demonstration by a friendly fellow (named Joe) who is a trained and experienced user of such an augmentation system within an experimental research program which is several years beyond our present stage. We assume that you approach this demonstration-interview with a background similar to what the previous portion of this report provides—that is, you will have heard or read a set of generalizations and a few rather primitive examples, but you will not yet have been given much of a feel for how a computer-based augmentation system can really help a person.

Joe understands this and explains that he will do his best to give you the valid conceptual feel that you want—trying to tread the narrow line between being too detailed and losing your over-all view and being too general and not providing you with a solid feel for what goes on. He suggests that you sit and watch him for a while as he pursues some typical work, after which he will do some explaining. You are not particularly flattered by this, since you know that he is just going to be exercising new language and methodology developments on his new artifacts—and after all, the artifacts don't look a bit different from what you expected—so why should he keep you sitting there as if you were a complete stranger to this stuff? It will just be a matter of "having the computer do some of his symbol-manipulating processes for him so that he can use more powerful concepts and concept-manipulation techniques," as you have so often been told.

Joe has two display screens side by side, but one of them he doesn't seem to use as much as the other. And the screens are almost horizontal, more like the surface of a drafting table than the near-vertical picture displays you had somehow imagined. But you see the reason easily, for he is working on the display surface as intently as a draftsman works on his drawings, and it would be awkward to reach out to a vertical surface for this kind of work. Some of the time Joe is using both hands on the keys, obviously feeding information into the computer at a great rate.

Another slight surprise, though—you see that each hand operates on a set of keys on its own side of the display frames, so that the hands are almost two feet apart. But it is plain that this arrangement allows him to remain positioned over the frames in a rather natural position, so that when he picks the light pen out of the air (which is its rest position, thanks to a system of jointed supporting arms and a controlled tension and rewind system for the attached cord) his hand is still on the way from the keyset to the display frame. When he is through with the pen at the display frame, he lets go of it, the cord rewinds, and the pen is again in position. There is thus a minimum of effort, movement, and time involved in turning to work on the frame. That is, he could easily shift back and forth from using keyset to using light pen, with either hand (one pen is positioned for each hand), without moving his head, turning, or leaning.

A good deal of Joe's time, though, seems to be spent with one hand on a keyset and the other using a light pen on the display surface. It is in this type of working mode that the images on the display frames changed most dynamically. You receive another real surprise as you realize how much activity there is on the face of these display tubes. You ask yourself why you weren't prepared for this, and you are forced to admit that the generalizations you had heard hadn't really sunk in—"new methods for manipulating symbols" had been an oft-repeated term, but it just hadn't included for you the images of the free and rapid way in which Joe could make changes in the display, and of meaningful and flexible "shaping" of ideas and work status which could take place so rapidly.

Then you realized that you couldn't make any sense at all out of the specific things he was doing, nor of the major part of what you saw on the displays. You could recognize many words, but there were a good number that were obviously special abbreviations of some sort. During the times when a given image or portion of an image remained un changed long enough for you to study it a bit, you rarely saw anything that looked like a sentence as you were used to seeing one. You were beginning to gather that there were other symbols mixed with the words that might be part of a sentence, and that the different parts of what made a full-thought statement (your feeling about what a sentence is) were not just laid out end to end as you expected. But Joe suddenly cleared the displays and turned to you with a grin that signalled the end of the passive observation period, and also that somehow told you that he knew very well that you now knew that you had needed such a period to shake out some of your limited images and to really realize that a "capability hierarchy" was a rich and vital thing.

"I guess you noticed that I was using unfamiliar notions, symbols, and processes to go about doing things that were even more unfamiliar to you?" You made a non-committal nod—you saw no reason to admit to him that you hadn't even been able to tell which of the things he had been doing were to cooperate with which other things—and he continued. "To give you a feel for what goes on, I'm going to start discussing and demonstrating some of the very basic operations and notions I've been using. You've read the stuff about process and process-capability hierarchies, I'm sure. I know from past experience in explaining radical augmentation systems to people that the new and powerful higher-level capabilities that they are interested in—because basically those are what we are all anxious to improve—can't really be explained to them without first giving them some understanding of the new and powerful capabilities upon which they are built. This holds true right on down the line to the type of low-level capability that is new and different to them all right, but that they just wouldn't ordinarily see as being 'powerful.' And yet our systems wouldn't be anywhere near as powerful without them, and a person's comprehension of the system would be rather shallow if he didn't have some understanding of these basic capabilities and of the hierarchical structure built up from them to provide the highest-level capabilities."...

22.6   Conclusions

Three principal conclusions may be drawn concerning the significance and implications of the ideas that have been presented.

First, any possibility for improving the effective utilization of the intellectual power of society's problem solvers warrants the most serious consideration. This is because man's problem-solving capability represents possibly the most important resource possessed by a society. The other contenders for first importance are all critically dependent for their development and use upon this resource. Any possibility for evolving an art or science that can couple directly and significantly to the continued development of that resource should warrant doubly serious consideration.

Second, the ideas presented are to be considered in both of the above senses: the direct-development sense and the "art of development" sense. To be sure, the possibilities have long-term implications, but their pursuit and initial rewards await us now. By our view, we do not have to wait until we learn how the human mental processes work, we do not have to wait until we learn how to make computers more intelligent or bigger or faster, we can begin developing powerful and economically feasible augmentation systems on the basis of what we now know and have. Pursuit of further basic knowledge and improved machines will continue into the unlimited future, and will want to be integrated into the "art" and its improved augmentation systems—but getting started now will provide not only orientation and stimulation for these pursuits, but will give us improved problem-solving effectiveness with which to carry out the pursuits.

Third, it becomes increasingly clear that there should be action now—the sooner the better—action in a number of research communities and on an aggressive scale. We offer a conceptual framework and a plan for action, and we recommend that these be considered carefully as a basis for action. If they be considered but found unacceptable, then at least serious and continued effort should be made toward developing a more acceptable conceptual framework within which to view the over-all approach, toward developing a more acceptable plan of action, or both.

This is an open plea to researchers and to those who ultimately motivate, finance, or direct them, to turn serious attention toward the possibility of evolving a dynamic discipline that can treat the problem of improving intellectual effectiveness in a total sense. This discipline should aim at producing a continuous cycle of improvements—increased understanding of the problem, improved means for developing new augmentation systems, and improved augmentation systems that can serve the world's problem solvers in general and this discipline's workers in particular. After all, we spend great sums for disciplines aimed at understanding and harnessing nuclear power. Why not consider developing a discipline aimed at understanding and harnessing "neural power"? In the long run, the power of the human intellect is really much the more important of the two.

23 An Experimental Time-Sharing System (1962)

Fernando Corbató, Marjorie Merwin Daggett, and Robert C. Daley

By the mid-1950s, researchers had enough experience with building and using electronic computers to begin imagining different ways computers might evolve so that more people could use them to solve more problems. In a 1954 summer school at MIT, a remarkable exchange occurred between Grace Hopper and John Backus, who would soon thereafter develop the FORTRAN programming language. "Dr. Grace Hopper raised the possibility of using several small computers in parallel. The greatest demand was for small machines. ... She foresaw a mass produced small machine, delivered with a compiler and library appropriate to the customer's needs. Mr. J. W. Backus disagreed with this philosophy on the grounds of computer speed; since increased speed costs little more, a large computer is cheaper to use than a small one. ... John Backus said that by time sharing, a big computer could be used as several small ones; there would need to be a reading station for each user" (Adams et al., 1954, pp. 16-1–16-2).

Hopper and Backus agreed to differ on the basis that Hopper was thinking more about business applications while Backus was thinking about scientific uses. But time-sharing had been imagined. A few years later, a group at MIT led by Fernando Corbató (1926–2019) fully actualized it.

Corbató had finished his PhD in physics at MIT in 1956 and was kept on to help run the Computation Center. Around 1958 John McCarthy, then on the MIT faculty, proposed expanding the capacity of the Center's IBM computer by implementing a time-sharing system, as reported by Licklider (page 207 of this volume). In 1961, after navigating some infighting within MIT and securing IBM's cooperation, Corbató, assisted by programmers Marjorie Merwin (b. 1928, later Daggett) and Robert C. Daley, cobbled together a rudimentary system. The goal was mostly, as he explained in an oral history, "to convince the skeptics that it was not an impossible task, and also, to get people to get a feel for interactive computing. It was amazing to me, and it is still amazing, that people could not imagine what the psychological difference would be to have an interactive terminal. You can talk about it on a blackboard until you are blue in the face, and people would say, 'Oh, yes, but why do you need that?' You know, we used to try to think of all these analogies, like describing it in terms of the difference between mailing a letter to your mother and getting on the telephone. To this day I can still remember people only realizing when they saw a real demo, say, 'Hey, it talks back. Wow! You just type that and you got an answer'" (Corbató and Norberg, 1989).

Reprinted from Corbató et al. (1962), with permission from the Association for Computing Machinery.

This first system was called the Compatible Time-Sharing System (CTSS); the "compatibility" was between the interactive jobs and the compute-bound jobs that were running in the background. It was the basis for, and was supplanted by, the MULTICS system (for "MULTiplexed Information and Computing Service"). MIT continued developing the system for a decade, and it was commercialized, with limited success, by GE and then Honeywell. Bell Labs was also involved in the development effort, but pulled out when the project was judged to have become bloated. Ken Thompson was among the developers there and took the lessons learned from MULTICS as the basis for the UNIX operating system (chapter 37), which he so named as a light-hearted pun.

Among the interesting aspects of this paper are its mathematical performance analysis and its retrospective on the early development of computer systems.

23.0   Summary

IT is the purpose of this paper to discuss briefly the need for time-sharing, some of the implementation problems, an experimental time-sharing system which has been developed for the contemporary IBM 7090, and finally a scheduling algorithm of one of us (FJC) that illustrates some of the techniques which may be employed to enhance and be analyzed for the performance limits of such a time-sharing system.

23.1   Introduction

The last dozen years of computer usage have seen great strides. In the early 1950s, the problems solved were largely in the construction and maintenance of hardware; in the mid-1950s, the usage languages were greatly improved with the advent of compilers; now in the early 1960s, we are in the midst of a third major modification to computer usage: the improvement of man–machine interaction by a process called time-sharing.

Much of the time-sharing philosophy, expressed in this paper, has been developed in conjunction with the work of an MIT preliminary study committee, chaired by H. Teager, which examined the long range computational needs of the Institute, and a subsequent MIT computer working committee, chaired by J. McCarthy. However, the views and conclusions expressed in this paper should be taken as solely those of the present authors.

Before proceeding further, it is best to give a more precise interpretation to time-sharing. One can mean using different parts of the hardware at the same time for different tasks, or one can mean several persons making use of the computer at the same time. The first meaning, often called multiprogramming, is oriented towards hardware efficiency in the sense of attempting to attain complete utilization of all components (Schmitt and Tonik, 1959; Codd, 1960; Heller, 1961; Leeds and Weinberg, 1961). The second meaning of time-sharing, which is meant here, is primarily concerned with the efficiency of persons trying to use a computer (Strachey, 1959;

Licklider, 1960; Brown et al., 1962). Computer efficiency should still be considered but only in the perspective of the total system utility.

The motivation for time-shared computer usage arises out of the slow man–computer interaction rate presently possible with the bigger, more advanced computers. This rate has changed little (and has become worse in some cases) in the last decade of widespread computer use (Teager and McCarthy, 1959).

In part, this effect has been due to the fact that as elementary problems become mastered on the computer, more complex problems immediately become of interest. As a result, larger and more complicated programs are written to take advantage of larger and faster computers. This process inevitably leads to more programming errors and a longer period of time required for debugging. Using current batch monitor techniques, as is done on most large computers, each program bug usually requires several hours to eliminate, if not a complete day. The only alternative presently available is for the programmer to attempt to debug directly at the computer, a process which is grossly wasteful of computer time and hampered seriously by the poor console communication usually available. Even if a typewriter is the console, there are usually lacking the sophisticated query and response programs which are vitally necessary to allow effective interaction. Thus, what is desired is to drastically increase the rate of interaction between the programmer and the computer without large economic loss and also to make each interaction more meaningful by extensive and complex system programming to assist in the man–computer communication.

To solve these interaction problems we would like to have a computer made simultaneously available to many users in a manner somewhat like a telephone exchange. Each user would be able to use a console at his own pace and without concern for the activity of others using the system. This console could at a minimum be merely a typewriter but more ideally would contain an incrementally modifiable self-sustaining display. In any case, data transmission requirements should be such that it would be no major obstacle to have remote installation from the computer proper.

The basic technique for a time-sharing system is to have many persons simultaneously using the computer through typewriter consoles with a time-sharing supervisor program sequentially running each user program in a short burst or quantum of computation. This sequence, which in the most straightforward case is a simple round-robin, should occur often enough so that each user program which is kept in the high-speed memory is run for a quantum at least once during each approximate human reaction time ($\sim$.2 seconds). In this way, each user sees a computer fully responsive to even single key strokes each of which may require only trivial computation; in the non-trivial cases, the user sees a gradual reduction of the response time which is proportional to the complexity of the response calculation, the slowness of the computer, and the total number of active users. It should be clear, however, that if there are n users actively requesting service at one time, each user will only see on the average $1/n$ of the effective computer speed. During the period of high interaction rates while debugging programs, this should not be a hindrance since ordinarily the required amount of computation needed for each debugging computer response is small compared to the ultimate production need.

Not only would such a time-sharing system improve the ability to program in the conventional manner by one or two orders of magnitude, but there would be opened up several new forms of computer usage. There would be a gradual reformulation of many scientific and engineering applications so that programs containing decision trees which currently must be specified in advance would be eliminated and instead the particular decision branches would be specified only as needed. Another important area is that of teaching machines which, although frequently trivial computationally, could naturally exploit the consoles of a time-sharing system with the additional bonus that more elaborate and adaptive teaching programs could be used. Finally, as attested by the many small business computers, there are numerous applications in business and in industry where it would be advantageous to have powerful computing facilities available at isolated locations with only the incremental capital investment of each console. But it is important to realize that even without the above and other new applications, the major advance in programming intimacy available from time-sharing would be of immediate value to computer installations in universities, research laboratories, and engineering firms where program debugging is a major problem.

23.2   Implementation Problems

As indicated, a straightforward plan for time-sharing is to execute user programs for small quantums of computation without priority in a simple round-robin; the strategy of time-sharing can be more complex as will be shown later, but the above simple scheme is an adequate solution. There are still many problems, however, some best solved by hardware, others affecting the programming conventions and practices. A few of the more obvious problems are summarized:

23.2.1   Hardware problems

1. Different user programs if simultaneously in core memory may interfere with each other or the supervisor program so some form of memory protection mode should be available when operating user programs.

2. The time-sharing supervisor may need at different times to run a particular program from several locations. (Loading relocation bits are no help since the supervisor does not know how to relocate the accumulator, etc.) Dynamic relocation of all memory accesses that pick up instructions or data words is one effective solution.

3. Input-output equipment may be initiated by a user and read words in on another user program. [EDITOR: That is, without an adequate memory protection mechanism, a user might be able to clobber another user's program by having input "read in" and then stored "on" the memory occupied by the other program.] A way to avoid this is to trap all input-output instructions issued by a user's program when operated in the memory protection mode.

4. A large random-access back-up storage is desirable for general program storage files for all users. Present large capacity disc units appear to be adequate.

5. The time-sharing supervisor must be able to interrupt a user's program after a quantum of computation. A program-initiated one-shot multivibrator which generates an interrupt a fixed time later is adequate.

6. Large core memories (e.g. a million words) would ease the system programming complications immensely since the different active user programs as well as the frequently used system programs such as compilers, query programs, etc. could remain in core memory at all times.

23.2.2 Programming problems

1. The supervisor program must do automatic user usage charge accounting. In general, the user should be charged on the basis of a system usage formula or algorithm which should include such factors as computation time, amount of high-speed memory required, rent of secondary memory storage, etc.

2. The supervisor program should coordinate all user input-output since it is not desirable to require a user program to remain constantly in memory during input-output limited operations. In addition, the supervisor must coordinate all usage of the central, shared high-speed input-output units serving all users as well as the clocks, disc units, etc.

3. The system programs available must be potent enough so that the user can think about his problem and not be hampered by coding details or typographical mistakes. Thus, compilers, query programs, post-mortem programs, loaders, and good editing programs are essential.

4. As much as possible, the users should be allowed the maximum programming flexibility both in choices of language and in the absence of restrictions.

23.2.3 Usage problems

1. Too large a computation or excessive typewriter output may be inadvertently requested so that a special termination signal should be available to the user.

2. Since real-time is not computer usage-time, the supervisor must keep each user informed so that he can use his judgment regarding loops, etc.

3. Computer processor, memory and tape malfunctions must be expected. Basic operational questions such as "Which program is running?" must be answerable and recovery procedures fully anticipated.

23.3 An Experimental Time-Sharing System for the IBM 7090

Having briefly stated a desirable time-sharing performance, it is pertinent to ask what level of performance can be achieved with existent equipment. To begin to answer this question and to explore all the programming and operational aspects, an experimental time-sharing system has been developed. This system was originally written for the IBM 709 but has since been converted for use with the 7090 computer.

The 7090 of the MIT Computation Center has, in addition to three channels with 19 tape units, a fourth channel with the standard Direct Data Connection. Attached to the Direct Data Connection is a real-time equipment buffer and control rack designed and built under the direction of H. Teager and his group. [Teager (1962) is presently using another approach in developing a time-sharing system for the MIT7090.] This rack has a variety of devices attached but the only ones required by the present systems are three flexowriter typewriters. Also installed on the 7090 are two special modifications (i.e. RPQ's): a standard 60 cycle accounting and interrupt clock, and a special mode which allows memory protection, dynamic relocation and trapping of all user attempts to initiate input-output instructions.

In the present system the time-sharing occurs between four users, three of whom are on-line each at a typewriter in a foreground system, and a fourth passive user of the background Fap-Mad-Madtran-BSS Monitor system similar to the FORTRAN-Fap-BSS Monitor System (FMS) used by most of the Center programmers and by many other 7090 installations.

Significant design features of the foreground system are:

1. It allows the user to develop programs in languages compatible with the background system,
2. Develop a private file of programs,
3. Start debugging sessions at the state of the previous session, and
4. Set his own pace with little waste of computer time.

Core storage is allocated such that all users operate in the upper 27,000 words with the time-sharing supervisor (TSS) permanently in the lower 5,000 words. To avoid memory allocation clashes, protect users from one another, and simplify the initial 709 system organization, only one user was kept in core memory at a time. However, with the special memory protection and relocation feature of the 7090, more sophisticated storage allocation procedures are being implemented. In any case, user swaps are minimized by using 2-channel overlapped magnetic tape reading and writing of the pertinent locations in the two user programs.

The foreground system is organized around commands that each user can give on his typewriter and the user's private program files which presently (for want of a disc unit) are kept on a separate magnetic tape for each user.

For convenience the format of the private tape files is such that they are card images, have title cards with name and class designators and can be written or punched using the off-line equipment. (The latter feature also offers a crude form of large-scale input-output.) The magnetic tape requirements of the system are the seven tapes required for the normal functions of the background system, a system tape for the time-sharing supervisor that contains most of the command programs, and a private file tape and dump tape for each of the three foreground users.

The commands are typed by the user to the time-sharing supervisor (not to his own program) and thus can be initiated at any time regardless of the particular user program in memory. For similar coordination reasons, the supervisor handles all input-output of the foreground system typewriters. Commands are composed of segments separated by vertical strokes; the first segment is the command name and the remaining segments are parameters pertinent to the command. Each segment consists of the last 6 characters typed (starting with an implicit 6 blanks) so that spacing is an easy way to correct a typing mistake. A carriage return is the signal which initiates action on the command. Whenever a command is received by the supervisor, "WAIT" is typed back followed by "READY." when the command is completed. (The computer responses are always in the opposite color from the user's typing.) While typing, an incomplete command line may be ignored by the "quit" sequence of a code delete signal followed by a carriage return. Similarly after a command is initiated, it may be abandoned if a "quit" sequence is given. In addition, during unwanted command typeouts, the command and output may be terminated by pushing a special "stop output" button.

The use of the foreground system is initiated whenever a typewriter user completes a command line and is placed in a waiting command queue. Upon completion of each quantum, the time-sharing supervisor gives top priority to initiating any waiting commands. The system programs corresponding to most of the commands are kept on the special supervisor command system tape so that to avoid waste of computer time, the supervisor continues to operate the last user program until the desired command program on tape is positioned for reading. At this point, the last user is read out on his dump tape, the command program read in, placed in a working status and initiated as a new user program. However, before starting the new user for a quantum of computation, the supervisor again checks for any waiting command of another user and if necessary begins the look-ahead positioning of the command system tape while operating the new user.

Whenever the waiting command queue is empty, the supervisor proceeds to execute a simple round-robin of those foreground user programs in the working status queue. Finally, if both these queues are empty, the background user program is brought in and run a quantum at a time until further foreground system actively develops.

Foreground user programs leave the working status queue by two means. If the program proceeds to completion, it can reenter the supervisor in a way which eliminates itself and places the user in dead status; alternatively, by a different entry the program can be placed in a dormant status (or be manually placed by the user executing a quit sequence). The dormant status differs from the dead status in that the user may still restart or examine his program.

User input-output is through each typewriter, and even though the supervisor has a few lines of buffer space available, it is possible to become input-output limited. Consequently, there is an additional input-output wait status, similar to the dormant, which the user is automatically placed in by the supervisor program whenever input-output delays develop. When buffers become near empty on output or near full on input, the user program is automatically returned to the working status; thus waste of computer time is avoided. ...

Although experience with the system to date is quite limited, first indications are that programmers would readily use such a system if it were generally available. It is useful to ask, now that there is some operating experience with the system, what observations can be made. [Note: Operating experience was initially gained using the system on the 709 computer; due to equipment conversion difficulties, it was not possible to use the system on the logically equivalent 7090 computer by May 3.] An immediate comment is that once a user gets accustomed to computer response, delays of even a fraction of a minute are exasperatingly long, an effect analogous to conversing with a slow-speaking person. Similarly, the requirement that a complete typewritten line rather than each character be the minimum unit of man–computer communication is an inhibiting factor in the sense that a press-to-talk radio-telephone conversation is more stilted than that of an ordinary telephone. Since maintaining a rapid computer response on a character by character basis requires at least a vestigial response program in core memory at all times, the straightforward solution within the present system is to have more core memory available. At the very least, an extra bank of memory for the time-sharing supervisor would ease compatibility problems with programs already written for 32,000 word 7090's.

For reasons of expediency, the weakest portions of the present system are the conventions for input, editing of user files, and the degree of rapid interaction and intimacy possible while debugging. Since to a large extent these areas involve the taste, habits, and psychology of the users, it is felt that proper solutions will require considerable experimentation and pragmatic evaluation; it is also clear that these areas cannot be treated in the abstract for the programming languages used will influence greatly the appropriate techniques. A greater use of symbolic referencing for locations, program names and variables is certainly desired; symbolic post-mortem programs, trace programs, and before-and-after differential dump programs should play useful roles in the debugging procedures.

In the design of the present system, great care went into making each user independent of the other users. However, it would be a useful extension of the system if this were not always the case. In particular, when several consoles are used in a computer controlled group such as in management or war games, in group behavior studies, or possibly in teaching machines, it would be desirable to have all the consoles communicating with a single program.

Another area for further improvement within the present system is that of file maintenance, since the presently used tape units are a hindrance to the easy deletion of user program files. Disc units will be of help in this area as well as with the problem of consolidating and scheduling large-scale central input-output generated by the many console users.

Finally, it is felt that it would be desirable to have the distinction between the foreground and background systems eliminated. The present-day computer operator would assume the role of a stand-in for the background users, using an operator console much like the other user consoles in the system, mounting and demounting magnetic tapes as requested by the supervisor, receiving instructions to read card decks into the central disc unit, etc. Similarly the foreground user, when satisfied with his program, would by means of his console and the supervisor program enter his program into the queue of production background work to be performed. With these procedures implemented the distinction of whether one is time-sharing or not would vanish and the computer user would be free to choose in an interchangeable way that mode of operation which he found more suitable at a particular time.

23.4 A Multi-Level Scheduling Algorithm

Regardless of whether one has a million word core memory or a 32,000 word memory as currently exists on the 7090, one is inevitably faced with the problem of system saturation where the total size of active user programs exceeds that of the high-speed memory or there are too many active user programs to maintain an adequate response at each user console. These conditions can easily arise with even a few users if some of the user programs are excessive in size or in time requirements. The predicament can be alleviated if it is assumed that a good design for the system is to have a saturation procedure which gives graceful degradation of the response time and effective real-time computation speed of the large and long-running users.

To show the general problem, Figure 23.1 qualitatively gives the user service as a function of n, the number of active users. This service parameter might be either of the two key factors: computer response time or n times the real-time computation speed. In either case there is some critical number of active users, N, representing the effective user capacity, which causes saturation. If the strategy near saturation is to execute the simple round-robin of all users, then there is an abrupt collapse of service due to the sudden onset of the large amount of time required to swap programs in-and-out of the secondary memory such as a disc or drum unit. Of course, Figure 23.1 is quite qualitative since it depends critically on the spectrum of user program sizes as well as the spectrum of user operating times.

To illustrate the strategy that can be employed to improve the saturation performance of a time-sharing system, a multi-level scheduling algorithm is presented. This algorithm also can be analyzed to give broad bounds on the system performance. The basis of the multi-level scheduling algorithm is to assign each user program as it enters the system to be run (or completes a response to a user) to an ℓth level priority queue. Programs are initially entered into a level ℓ_0, corresponding to their size such that

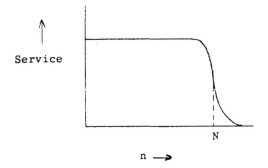

Figure 23.1: Service vs. number of active users

$$\ell_0 = \left\lceil \log_2 \left(\left\lceil \frac{w_p}{w_q} \right\rceil + 1 \right) \right\rceil$$

where w_p is the number of words in the program, w_q is the number of words which can be transmitted in *and* out of the high-speed memory from the secondary memory in the time of one quantum, q, and the bracket indicates "the integral part of." Ordinarily the time of a quantum, being the basic time unit, should be as small as possible without excessive overhead losses when the supervisor switches from one program in high-speed memory to another. The process starts with the time-sharing supervisor operating the program at the head of the lowest level occupied queue, ℓ, for up to 2^ℓ quanta of time and then if the program is not completed (i.e. has not made a response to the user) placing it at the end of the $\ell + 1$ level queue. If there are no programs entering the system at levels lower than ℓ, this process proceeds until the queue at level ℓ is exhausted; the process is then iteratively begun again at level $\ell + 1$, where now each program is run for $2^{\ell+1}$ quanta of time. If during the execution of the 2^ℓ quanta of a program at level ℓ, a lower level, ℓ', becomes occupied, the current user is replaced at the head of the ℓth queue and the process is reinitiated at level ℓ'.

Similarly, if a program of size w_p at level ℓ, during operation requests a change in memory size from the time-sharing supervisor, then the enlarged (or reduced) version of the program should be placed at the end of the ℓ'' queue where

$$\ell'' = \ell + \left\lceil \log_2 \left(\left\lceil \frac{w_p''}{w_p} \right\rceil + 1 \right) \right\rceil.$$

Again the process is re-initiated with the head-of-the-queue user at the lowest occupied level of ℓ'.

Several important conclusions can be drawn from the above algorithm which allow the performance of the system to be bounded.

1. *Computational efficiency.* Because a program is always operated for a time greater than or equal to the swap time (i.e., the time required to move the program in and out of secondary memory), it follows that the computational efficiency never falls below one-half. (Clearly, this fraction is adjustable in the formula for the initial level, ℓ_0.) An alternative way of viewing this bound is to say that the real-time computing speed available to one out of n active users is no worse than if there were $2n$ active users all of whose programs were in the high-speed memory.

2. *Response time.* If the maximum number of active users is N, then an individual user of a given program size can be guaranteed a response time,

$$t_r \leq 2Nq\left(\left\lceil \frac{w_p}{w_q} \right\rceil + 1 \right)$$

since the worst case occurs when all competing user programs are at the same level. Conversely, if t_r is a guaranteed response of arbitrary value and the largest size of program is assumed, then the maximum permissible number of active users is bounded.

3. *Long runs.* The relative swap time on long runs can be made vanishingly small. This conclusion follows since the longer a program is run, the higher the level number it cascades to with a correspondingly smaller relative swap time. It is an important feature of the algorithm that long runs must in effect prove they are long so that programs which have an unexpected demise are detected quickly. In order that there be a finite number of levels, a maximum level number, L, can be established such that the asymptotic swap overhead is

some arbitrarily small percentage, p:

$$L = \left\lceil \log_2 \left(\left\lceil \frac{w_{pmax}}{pw_q} \right\rceil + 1 \right) \right\rceil$$

where w_{pmax} is the size of the largest possible program.

4. *Multi-level vs. single-level response times.* The response time for programs of equal size, entering the system at the same time, and being run for multiple quanta, is no worse than approximately twice the response-time occurring in a single quanta round-robin procedure. If there are n equal sized programs started in a queue at level ℓ, then the worst case is that of the end-of-the-queue program which is ready to respond at the very first quantum run at the $\ell + j$ level. Using the multi-level algorithm, the total delay for the end-of-the-queue program is by virtue of the geometric series of quanta:

$$T_m \sim q2^\ell \left\{ n(2^j - 1) + (n-1)2^j \right\}.$$

Since the end-of-the-queue user has computed for a time of $2^\ell (2^j - 1)$ quanta, the equivalent single-level round-robin delay before a response is:

$$T_s \sim q2^\ell \left\{ n(2^j - 1) \right\}.$$

Hence

$$\frac{T_m}{T_s} \sim 1 + \left(\frac{n-1}{n} \right) \left(\frac{2^j}{2^j - 1} \right) \sim 2$$

and the assertion is shown. It should be noted that the above conditions, where program swap times are omitted, which are pertinent when all programs remain in high-speed memory, are the least favorable for the multi-level algorithm; if swap times are included in the above analysis, the ratio of T_m/T_s can only become smaller and may become much less than unity. By a similar analysis it is easy to show that even in the unfavorable case where there are no program swaps, head-of-the-queue programs that terminate just as the quanta are completed receive under the multi-level algorithm a response which is twice as *fast* as that under the single-level round-robin (i.e. $T_m/T_s = \frac{1}{2}$).

5. *Highest serviced level.* In the multi-level algorithm the level classification procedure for programs is entirely automatic, depending on performance and program size rather than on the declarations (or hopes) of each user. As a user taxes the system, the degradation of service occurs progressively starting with the higher level users of either large or long-running programs; however, at some level no user programs may be run because of too many active users at lower levels. To determine a bound on this cut-off point we consider N active users at level ℓ each running 2^ℓ quanta, terminating, and reentering the system again at level ℓ at a user response time, t_u, later. If there is to be no service at level $\ell + 1$, then the computing time, $Nq2^\ell$, must be greater than or equal to t_u. Thus the guaranteed active levels, are given

by the relation:

$$\ell_a \leq \left\lceil \log_2 \left(\frac{t_u}{Nq} \right) \right\rceil$$

In the limit, t_u could be as small as a minimum user reaction time ($\sim$.2 sec.), but the expected value would be several orders of magnitude greater as a result of the statistics of a large number of users.

The multi-level algorithm as formulated above makes no explicit consideration of the seek or latency time required before transmission of programs to and from disc or drum units when they are used as the secondary memory, (although formally the factor w_q could contain an average figure for these times). One simple modification to the algorithm which usually avoids wasting the seek or latency time is to continue to operate the last user program for as many quanta as are required to ready the swap of the new user with the least priority user; since ordinarily only the higher level number programs would be forced out into the secondary memory, the extended quanta of operation of the old user while seeking the new user should be but a minor distortion of the basic algorithm.

Further complexities are possible when the hardware is appropriate. In computers with input-output channels and low transmission rates to and from secondary memory, it is possible to overlap the reading and writing of the new and old users in and out of high-speed memory while operating the current user. The effect is equivalent to using a drum giving 100% multiplexor usage but there are two liabilities, namely, no individual user can utilize all the available user memory space and the look-ahead procedure breaks down whenever an unanticipated scheduling change occurs (e.g. a program terminates or a higher-priority user program is initiated).

Complexity is also possible in storage allocation but certainly an elementary procedure and a desirable one with a low-transmission rate secondary memory is to consolidate in a single block all high-priority user programs whenever sufficient fragmentary unused memory space is available to read in a new user program. Such a procedure is indicated in the flow diagram of the multi-level scheduling algorithm which is given as Figure 23.2.

It should also be noted that Figure 23.2 only accounts for the scheduling of programs in a working status and still does not take into account the storage allocation of programs which are in a dormant (or input-output wait status). One systematic method of handling this case is to modify the scheduling algorithm so that programs which become dormant at level ℓ are entered into the queue at level $\ell + 1$. The scheduling algorithm proceeds as before with the dormant programs continuing to cascade but not operating when they reached the head of a queue. Whenever a program must be removed from high-speed memory, a program is selected from the end-of-the-queue of the highest occupied level number.

Finally, it is illuminating to apply the multi-level scheduling algorithm bounds to the contemporary IBM 7090. The following approximate values are obtained:

$$q = 16 \text{ m.s. (based on 1\% switching overhead)}$$

$$w_q = 120 \text{ words (based on one IBM 1301 model 2 disk unit}$$

$$\text{without seek or latency times included)}$$

$$t_r \leq 8Nf \text{ sec. (based on programs of } (32\text{K})f \text{ words)}$$

$$\ell_a \leq \log_2(1000/N) \text{ (based on } t_u = 16 \text{ sec.)}$$

$$\ell_0 \leq 8 \text{ (based on a maximum program size of 32K words)}$$

Using the arbitrary criteria that programs up to the maximum size of 32,000 words should always get some service, which is to say that max ℓ_a = max ℓ_0, we deduce as a conservative estimate that N can be 4 and that at worst the response time for a trivial reply will be 32 seconds.

The small value of N arrived at is a direct consequence of the small value of w_q that results from the slow disc word transmission rate. This rate is only 3.3% of the maximum core memory multiplexor rate. It is of interest that using high-capacity high-speed drums of current design such as in the SAGE System or in the IBM Sabre System it would be possible to attain nearly 100% multiplexor utilization and thus multiply w_q by a factor of 30. It immediately follows that user response times equivalent to those given above with the disc unit would be given to 30 times as many persons or to 120 users; the total computational capacity, however, would not change.

In any case, considerable caution should be used with capacity and computer response time estimates since they are critically dependent upon the distribution functions for the user response time, t_u, and the user program size, and the computational capacity requested by each user. Past experience using conventional programming systems is of little assistance because these distribution functions will depend very strongly upon the programming systems made available to the time-sharing users as well as upon the user habit patterns which will gradually evolve.

23.5   Conclusions

In conclusion, it is clear that contemporary computers and hardware are sufficient to allow moderate performance time-sharing for a limited number of users. There are several problems which can be solved by careful hardware design, but there are also a large number of intricate system programs which must be written before one has an adequate time-sharing system. An important aspect of any future time-shared computer is that until the system programming is completed, especially the critical time-sharing supervisor, the computer is completely worthless. Thus, it is essential for future system design and implementation that all aspects of time-sharing system problems be explored and understood in prototype form on present computers so that major advances in computer organization and usage can be made.

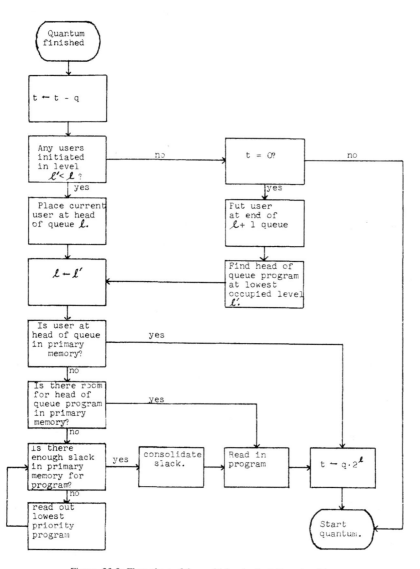

Figure 23.2: Flow chart of the multi-level scheduling algorithm

24 Sketchpad (1963)

Ivan E. Sutherland

While he was growing up, Ivan Sutherland (b. 1938) covered his school books with blueprints that his father, a civil engineer, had discarded. (His mother said that the family could not afford the college-themed book covers his schoolmates were using.) He learned the concise, elegant language of blueprints by staring at his book covers during moments of classroom boredom. When he studied engineering as an undergraduate, he had to create blueprints as well as to interpret them, and he lacked the dexterity and patience to draw them well. So when he entered MIT as a graduate student and found himself with time on the TX-2 computer and in need of a PhD thesis topic, it occurred to him to program the computer to help out with the drawing task. Sutherland was aware of the vision of both Bush (chapter 11) and Licklider (chapter 20), but nothing much like what they imagined had actually been built. This dissertation was written under the direction of Claude Shannon, and thus was born the entire field of computer graphics and interactive computing.

The TX-2 was transistorized, and at the time was the most powerful computer in the world. It had 64K of 36-bit words—twice as much memory as any other machine. It also had a primitive display—just a circular cathode ray tube, and a machine instruction that would flash a point at coordinates specified in the instruction. (Such displays were not new—they had been part of the EDVAC design. See page 210 for Licklider's analysis of the limitations of display technology in 1960.) There were no raster, line-drawing, or character displays at the time; to draw a line, the software had to stipulate the coordinates of the successive points to be displayed, and then flash each point in rapid succession, repeating the process to give the illusion that the whole line was being displayed at once. More complicated images could be painted on the screen in the same way, as long as the whole process took less than a thirtieth of a second or so, in order to avoid annoying flicker.

To create a drawing program, Sutherland also needed a graphic input device. The TX-2 had a light pen—a photocell connected to the computer by an electric wire. If the photocell was held over part of the displayed image, the program could determine where it was by correlating the time the photocell was activated to the position of the point being displayed at that moment. By displaying a small cross at that position and checking which parts of the cross were visible to the photocell from one instant to the next, the program could determine the direction in which the user was moving the light pen.

Reprinted from Sutherland (1963), with permission from the Massachusetts Institute of Technology.

All these instrumentalities were replaced by better ones in the following decade—fiber optic cables, tablets, touchscreens, raster displays, color displays, and so on. Sutherland's durable intellectual contribution was a form of human–computer symbiosis, exactly what Licklider had predicted. Sketchpad allowed the user to stipulate constraints, for example about which lines should be parallel or should meet at their endpoints. The program did its best to keep all constraints satisfied as objects were dragged and distorted. Thus it understood the topology as well as the geometry of the drawing. Sketchpad had facilities for grouping, reduplicating, rotating, and moving objects around. It was the first computer-aided design program. Even more remarkably, its use of novel programming techniques such as constraint satisfaction and object hierarchies sowed the seeds of both non-procedural programming and of object-oriented system design.

When Sutherland visited Bell Helicopter Company in Texas around 1963, he was shown a clever contraption designed to aid pilots landing at night. An infrared camera mounted on the bottom of the helicopter was automatically oriented in coordination with the pilot's head movements, and the camera image was projected through prisms into the pilot's field of view. Sutherland had the idea of substituting a computer-generated image for the infrared camera image, and thus was born the first virtual reality system, built at Harvard in 1968. A head-mounted display was tethered to the ceiling by telescoping tubes, enabling the wearer to view a wire-frame cube floating in space and to walk through and around it. Sutherland went on to build the graphic system for the first practical flight simulator at the Evans and Sutherland Computer Company in Utah. As computer graphics developed toward extraordinary verisimilitude in the next decade, Sutherland shifted his efforts to the design of very fast electronic circuits, a field in which he remains active.

One other biographical detail has proved important to the development of computer science. When J. C. R. Licklider left ARPA in 1964 to go to private industry, he was replaced by Sutherland, then fresh out of graduate school and fulfilling the military obligation he had incurred as a ROTC cadet. During the tenure of Licklider and Sutherland at ARPA, visionary funding initiatives stimulated computer science research all across the U.S. That too was part of the creation of the future.

——————◦◦◦∽◦◦——————

24.1   Abstract

THE Sketchpad system uses drawing as a novel communication medium for a computer. The system contains input, output, and computation programs which enable it to interpret information drawn directly on a computer display. It has been used to draw electrical, mechanical, scientific, mathematical, and animated drawings; it is a general purpose system. Sketchpad has shown the most usefulness as an aid to the understanding of processes, such as the notion of linkages, which can be described with pictures. Sketchpad also makes it easy to draw highly repetitive or highly accurate drawings and to change drawings previously drawn with it. The many drawings in this thesis were all made with Sketchpad.

A Sketchpad user sketches directly on a computer display with a "light pen." The light pen is used both to position parts of the drawing on the display and to point to them to change them. A set of push buttons controls the changes to be made such as "erase," or "move." Except for legends, no written language is used. Information sketched can include straight line segments and circle arcs. Arbitrary symbols may be defined from any collection of line segments, circle arcs, and previously defined symbols. A user may define and use as many symbols as he wishes. Any change in the definition of a symbol is at once seen wherever that symbol appears.

Sketchpad stores explicit information about the topology of a drawing. If the user moves one vertex of a polygon, both adjacent sides will be moved. If the user moves a symbol, all lines attached to that symbol will automatically move to stay attached to it. The topological connections of the drawing are automatically indicated by the user as he sketches. Since Sketchpad is able to accept topological information from a human being in a picture language perfectly natural to the human, it can be used as an input program for computation programs which require topological data, e.g., circuit simulators.

Sketchpad itself is able to move parts of the drawing around to meet new conditions which the user may apply to them. The user indicates conditions with the light pen and push buttons. For example, to make two lines parallel, he successively points to the lines with the light pen and presses a button. The conditions themselves are displayed on the drawing so that they may be erased or changed with the light pen language. Any combination of conditions can be defined as a composite condition and applied in one step.

It is easy to add entirely new types of conditions to Sketchpad's vocabulary. Since the conditions can involve anything computable, Sketchpad can be used for a very wide range of problems. For example, Sketchpad has been used to find the distribution of forces in the members of truss bridges drawn with it.

Sketchpad drawings are stored in the computer in a specially designed "ring" structure. The ring structure features rapid processing of topological information with no searching at all. The basic operations used in Sketchpad for manipulating the ring structure are described.

24.2 Introduction

The Sketchpad system makes it possible for a man and a computer to converse rapidly through the medium of line drawings. Heretofore, most interaction between men and computers has been slowed down by the need to reduce all communication to written statements that can be typed; in the past, we have been writing letters to rather than conferring with our computers. For many types of communication, such as describing the shape of a mechanical part or the connections of an electrical circuit, typed statements can prove cumbersome. The Sketchpad system, by eliminating typed statements (except for legends) in favor of line drawings, opens up a new area of man–machine communication.

The decision actually to implement a drawing system reflected our feeling that knowledge of the facilities which would prove useful could only be obtained by actually trying them. The decision actually to implement a drawing system did not mean, however, that brute force techniques were to be used to computerize ordinary drafting tools; it was implicit in the research nature of the work that simple new facilities should be discovered which, when implemented, should be useful in a wide range of applications, preferably including some unforeseen ones. It has turned out that the properties of a computer drawing are entirely different from a paper drawing not only because of the accuracy, ease of drawing, and speed of erasing provided by the computer, but also primarily because of the ability to move drawing parts around on a computer drawing without the need to erase them. Had a working system not been developed, our thinking would have been too strongly influenced by a lifetime of drawing on paper to discover many of the useful services that the computer can provide.

As the work has progressed, several simple and very widely applicable facilities have been discovered and implemented. They provide a subpicture capability for including arbitrary symbols on a drawing, a constraint capability for relating the parts of a drawing in any computable way, and a definition copying capability for building complex relationships from combinations of simple atomic constraints. When combined with the ability to point at picture parts given by the demonstrative light pen language, the subpicture, constraint, and definition copying capabilities produce a system of extraordinary power. As was hoped at the outset, the system is useful in a wide range of applications, and unforeseen uses are turning up.

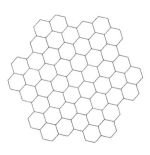

Figure 24.1: Hexagonal pattern.

To understand what is possible with the system at present let us consider using it to draw the hexagonal pattern of Figure 24.1. We will issue specific commands with a set of push buttons, turn functions on and off with switches, indicate position information and point to existing drawing parts with the light pen, rotate and magnify picture parts by turning knobs, and observe the drawing on the display system. This equipment as provided at Lincoln Laboratory's TX-2 computer (Clark et al., 1957) is shown in Figure 24.2. When our drawing is complete it may be inked on paper, as were all the drawings in the thesis, by the plotter (EAI, 1959) shown in Figure 24.3. It is our intent with this example to show what the computer can do to help us draw while leaving the details of how it performs its functions for the chapters which follow.

24.2.1   An introductory example   If we point the light pen at the display system and press a button called "draw," the computer will construct a straight line segment which stretches like a rubber band from the initial to the present location of the pen as shown in Figure 24.4. Additional presses of the button will produce additional lines until we have made six, enough for a single hexagon. To close the figure we return the light pen to near the end of the first line drawn where

Figure 24.2: TX-2 operating area—Sketchpad in use. On the display can be seen part of a bridge . . . . The Author is holding the Light pen. The push buttons used to control specific drawing functions are on the box in front of the Author. Part of the bank of toggle switches can be seen behind the Author. The size and position of the part of the total picture seen on the display is obtained through the four black knobs just above the table.

Figure 24.3: Plotter used with Sketchpad. A digital and analog control system makes the plotter draw straight lines and circles either under direct control of the TX-2 or off-line from punched paper tape.

it will "lock on" to the end exactly. A sudden flick of the pen terminates drawing, leaving the closed irregular hexagon shown in Figure 24.5A.

To make the hexagon regular, we can inscribe it in a circle. To draw the circle we place the light pen where the center is to be and press the button "circle center," leaving behind a center point. Now, choosing a point on the circle (which fixes the radius), we press the button "draw" again, this time getting a circle arc whose length only is controlled by light pen position as shown in Figure 24.4. Next we move the hexagon into the circle by pointing to a corner of the hexagon and pressing the button "move" so that the corner follows the light pen, stretching two rubber band line segments behind it. By pointing to the circle and giving the termination flick we indicate that the corner is to lie on the circle. Each corner is in this way moved onto the circle at roughly equal spacing around it as shown in Figure 24.5D.

We have indicated that the vertices of the hexagon are to lie on the circle, and they will remain on the circle throughout our further manipulations. If we also insist that the sides of the hexagon be of equal length, a regular hexagon will be constructed. This we can do by pointing to one side and pressing the "copy" button, and then to another side and giving the termination flick. The button in this case copies a definition of equal length lines and applies it to the lines indicated. We have said, in effect, make this line equal in length to that line. We indicate that all six lines are equal in length by five such statements. The computer satisfies all existing conditions (if it is possible) whenever we turn on a toggle switch. This done, we have a complete regular hexagon inscribed in a circle. We can erase the entire circle by pointing to any part of it and pressing the "delete" button. The completed hexagon is shown in Figure 24.5F.

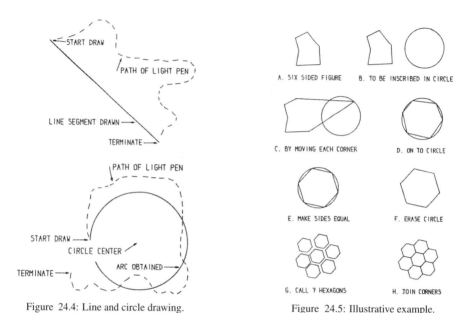

Figure 24.4: Line and circle drawing.   Figure 24.5: Illustrative example.

To make the hexagonal pattern of Figure 24.1 we wish to attach a large number of hexagons together by their corners, and so we designate the six corners of our hexagon as attachment points by pointing to each and pressing a button. We now file away the basic hexagon and begin work on a fresh "sheet of paper" by changing a switch setting. On the new sheet we assemble, by pressing a button to create each hexagon as a subpicture, six hexagons around a central seventh in approximate position as shown in Figure 24.5G. Subpictures may be positioned, each in its entirety, with the light pen, rotated or scaled with the knobs and fixed in position by the pen flick termination signal; but their internal shape is fixed. By pointing to the corner of one hexagon, pressing a button, and then pointing to the corner of another hexagon we can fasten those corners together, because these corners have been designated as attachment points. If we attach two corners of each outer hexagon to the appropriate corners of the inner hexagon, the seven are uniquely related, and the computer will reposition them as shown in Figure 24.5H. An entire group of hexagons, once assembled, can be treated as a symbol. The entire group can be called up on another "sheet of paper" as a subpicture and assembled with other groups or with single hexagons to make a very large pattern. Using Figure 24.5H seven times we get the pattern of Figure 24.1. Constructing the pattern of Figure 24.1 takes less than five minutes with the Sketchpad system.

24.2.2   Interpretation of introductory example   In the introductory example above we have seen how to draw lines and circles and how to move existing parts of the drawing around. We used the light pen both to position parts of the drawing and to point to existing parts. For example, we pointed to the circle to erase it, and while drawing the sixth line, we pointed to the end of the first line drawn to close the hexagon. We also saw in action the very general *subpicture*, *constraint*, and *definition copying* capabilities of the system.

24.2.2.1   Subpicture   The original hexagon might just as well have been anything else: a picture of a transistor, a roller bearing, an airplane wing, a letter, or an entire figure for this report. Any number of different symbols may be drawn, in terms of other simpler symbols if desired, and any symbol may be used as often as desired.

24.2.2.2   Constraint   When we asked that the vertices of the hexagon lie on the circle we were making use of a basic relationship between picture parts that is built into the system. Basic relationships (atomic constraints) to make lines vertical, horizontal, parallel, or perpendicular; to make points lie on lines or circles; to make symbols appear upright, vertically above one another or be of equal size; and to relate symbols to other drawing parts such as points and lines have been included in the system. It is so easy to program new constraint types that the set of atomic constraints was expanded from five to the seventeen listed in Appendix A in a period of about two days; specialized constraint types may be added as needed. [EDITOR: Appendix omitted.]

24.2.2.3   Definition copying   In the introductory example above we asked that the sides of the hexagon be equal in length by pressing a button while pointing to the side in question. Here we were using the definition copying capability of the system. Had we defined a composite operation such as to make two lines both parallel and equal in length, we could have applied it just as easily. The number of operations which can be defined from the basic constraints applied to various picture parts is almost unlimited. Useful new definitions are drawn regularly; they are as simple as horizontal lines and as complicated as dimension lines complete with arrowheads and a number which indicates the length of the line correctly. The definition copying capability makes using the constraint capability easy.

24.2.3   Implications of the introductory example   As we have seen in the introductory example, drawing with the Sketchpad system is different from drawing with an ordinary pencil and paper. Most important of all, the Sketchpad drawing itself is entirely different from the trail of carbon left on a piece of paper. Information about how the drawing is tied together is stored in the computer as well as the information which gives the drawing its particular appearance. Since the drawing is tied together, it will keep a useful appearance even when parts of it are moved. For example, when we moved the corners of the hexagon onto the circle, the lines next to each corner were automatically moved so that the closed topology of the hexagon was preserved. Again, since we indicated that the corners of the hexagon were to lie on the circle they remained on the circle throughout our further manipulations.

It is this ability to store information relating the parts of a drawing to each other that makes Sketchpad most useful. For example, the linkage shown in Figure 24.6 was drawn with Sketchpad in just a few minutes. Constraints were applied to the linkage to keep the length of its various members constant. Rotation of the short central link is supposed to move the left end of the dotted line vertically. Since exact information about the properties of the linkage has been stored in

Sketchpad, it is possible to observe the motion of the entire linkage when the short central link is rotated. The value of the number in Figure 24.6 was constrained to indicate the length of the dotted line, comparing the actual motion with the vertical line at the right of the linkage. One can observe that for all positions of the linkage the length of the dotted line is constant, demonstrating that this is indeed a straight line linkage. Other examples of moving drawings made with Sketchpad may be found in the final chapter.

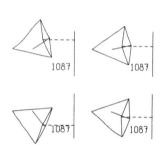

Figure 24.6: Four positions of linkage. Number shows length of dotted line.

As well as storing how the various parts of the drawing are related, Sketchpad stores the structure of the subpicture used. For example, the storage for the hexagonal pattern of Figure 24.1 indicates that this pattern is made of smaller patterns which are in turn made of smaller patterns which are composed of single hexagons. If the master hexagon is changed, the entire appearance of the hexagonal pattern will be changed. The structure of the pattern will, of course, be the same. For example, if we change the basic hexagon into a semicircle, the fish scale pattern shown in Figure 24.7 instantly results.

Since Sketchpad stores the structure of a drawing, a Sketchpad drawing explicitly indicates similarity of symbols. In an electrical drawing, for example, all transistor symbols are created from a single master transistor drawing. If some change to the basic transistor symbol is made, this change appears at once in all transistor symbols without further effort. Most important of all, the computer "knows" that a "transistor" is intended at that place in the circuit. It has no need to interpret the collection of lines which we would easily recognize as a transistor symbol. Since Sketchpad stores the topology of the drawing as we saw in closing the hexagon, one indicates both what a circuit looks like and its electrical connections when one draws it with Sketchpad. One can see that the circuit connections are stored because moving a component automatically moves any wiring on that component to maintain the correct connections. Sketchpad circuit drawings will soon be used as inputs for a circuit simulator. Having drawn a circuit one will find out its electrical properties.

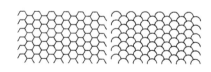

Figure 24.7: Half hexagons and semicircles on same lattice.

24.2.4   Sketchpad and the design process

Construction of a drawing with Sketchpad is itself a model of the design process. The locations of the points and lines of the drawing model the variables of a design, and the geometric constraints applied to the points and lines of the drawing model the design constraints which limit the values of design variables. The ability of Sketchpad to satisfy the geometric constraints applied to the parts of a drawing models the ability of a good designer to satisfy all the design conditions imposed by the limitations of his materials, cost, etc. In fact, since designers in many fields produce nothing themselves but a drawing of a part, design conditions may well be thought of as applying to the drawing of a part rather than to the part itself. If such design conditions were added to Sketchpad's vocabulary of constraints the computer could assist a user not only in arriving at a nice looking drawing, but also in arriving at a sound design.

24.2.5   Present usefulness   At the outset of the research no one had ever drawn engineering drawings directly on a computer display with nearly the facility now possible, and consequently no one knew what it would be like. We have now accumulated about a hundred hours of experience actually making drawings with a working system. As is shown in the final chapter, application of computer drawing techniques to a variety of problems has been made. As more and more applications have been made it has become clear that the properties of Sketchpad drawings make them most useful in four broad areas:

24.2.5.1   For making small changes to existing drawings   Each time a drawing is made, a description of that drawing is stored in the computer in a form that is readily transferred to magnetic tape. Thus, as time passes, a library of drawings will develop, parts of which may be used in other drawings at only a fraction of the investment of time that was put into the original drawing. Since a drawing stored in the computer may contain explicit representation of design conditions in its constraints, manual change of a critical part will automatically result in appropriate changes to related parts.

24.2.5.2   For gaining scientific or engineering understanding of operations that can be described graphically   The description of a drawing stored in the Sketchpad system is more than a collection of static drawing parts, lines and curves, etc. A drawing in the Sketchpad system may contain explicit statements about the relations between its parts so that as one part is changed the implications of this change become evident throughout the drawing. It is possible, as we saw in Figure 24.6, to give the property of fixed length to lines so as to study mechanical linkages, observing the path of some parts when others are moved. As we saw in Figure 24.7 any change made in the definition of a subpicture is at once reflected in the appearance of that subpicture wherever it may occur. By making such changes, understanding of the relationships of complex sets of subpictures can be gained. For example, one can study how a change in the basic element of a crystal structure is reflected throughout the crystal.

24.2.5.3   As a topological input device for circuit simulators, etc.   Since the ring structure storage of Sketchpad reflects the topology of any circuit or diagram, it can serve as an input for many network or circuit simulating programs. The additional effort required to draw a circuit completely from scratch with the Sketchpad system may well be recompensed if the properties of the circuit are obtainable through simulation of the circuit drawn.

24.2.5.4   For highly repetitive drawings   The ability of the computer to reproduce any drawn symbol anywhere at the press of a button, and to recursively include subpictures within subpictures makes it easy to produce drawings which are composed of huge numbers of parts all similar in shape. Great interest in doing this comes from people in such fields as memory development and micro logic where vast numbers of elements are to be generated at once through photographic processes. Master drawings of the repetitive patterns necessary can be easily drawn. Here again, the ability to change the individual element of the repetitive structure and have the change at once brought into all subelements makes it possible to change the elements of an array without redrawing the entire array. ...

24.3   History of Sketchpad

... Had I the work to do again, I could start afresh with the sure knowledge that generic structure, separation of subroutines into general purpose ones applying to all types of picture parts and ones specific to particular types of picture parts, and unlimited applicability of functions (e.g. anything should be moveable) would more than recompense the effort involved in achieving them. I have great admiration for those people who were able to tell me these things all along, but I, personally, had to follow the stumbling trail described in this chapter to become convinced myself. It is to be hoped that future workers can either grasp the power of generality at once and strive for it or have the courage to stumble along a trail like mine until they achieve it. ...

[T]here are possibilities for application of the system not yet even dreamed of. The richness of the possibilities of the definition copying function, and the new types of constraints which might easily be added to the system for special purposes suggest that further application will bring about a new body of knowledge of system application. For example, the bridge design examples shown at the end of this paper were not anticipated. There are, of course, limitations to the system. In the last chapter are suggested the improvements, some just minor changes, but some major additions which would change the entire character of the system. It is to be hoped that future work will far surpass my effort.

25 Cramming More Components onto Integrated Circuits (1965)

Gordon Moore

The transistor was one of the greatest inventions of the twentieth century. Small, cool, reliable, and drawing very little power, by the mid-1950s transistors were replacing vacuum tubes in many applications. The first battery-operated pocket radios appeared around 1954; they were a miraculous improvement over plug-in tabletop radios with glowing tubes. It became apparent that transistors could be used not just as amplifiers but as switches, stimulating the design of electronic computers like the TX-2.

And yet no one saw the *real* revolution coming: miniaturization. In the early 1960s it became possible to mass-produce entire electronic circuits by photolithography. At first the silicon chips accommodated only a handful of transistors, but the numbers increased rapidly. In 1965, Gordon Moore (b. 1929) was asked by *Electronics*—a trade magazine, not a scholarly journal—to predict what would happen to semiconductor engineering over the next decade. This article was his response. Moore was at the time the director of research and development at Fairchild Semiconductor, and based on his observation of the improvements in the design and manufacture of chips, he predicted that the number of a components on a chip would double yearly. (He later ramped down that prediction to doubling every two years.)

The prediction soon turned into a challenge; it certainly is not, and never has been, the "law" that it was dubbed. While it is astonishing that the prediction held true for thirty or forty generations, it was obvious from the beginning that eventually the sizes of the transistors and their interconnections would have to become comparable to the size of the molecules of which they were composed. As that point approached, the "law" was generalized to refer to increases in speed or computing capacity achievable in some way other than packing more components onto a chip.

Be that as it may, Moore's original article is remarkably prescient in calling attention to the yield of working components in the manufacturing process, to the eventual emergence of a consumer version of the electronic computer, and in other ways.

In 1968, Moore and Robert Noyce co-founded Intel Corporation, still one of the largest semiconductor companies in the world.

Reprinted from Moore (1965, 2006), with permission from the Institute of Electrical and Electronics Engineers.

THE future of integrated electronics is the future of electronics itself. The advantages of integration will bring about a proliferation of electronics, pushing this science into many new areas.

Integrated circuits will lead to such wonders as home computers—or at least terminals connected to a central computer—automatic controls for automobiles, and personal portable communications equipment. The electronic wristwatch needs only a display to be feasible today.

But the biggest potential lies in the production of large systems. In telephone communications, integrated circuits in digital filters will separate channels on multiplex equipment. Integrated circuits will also switch telephone circuits and perform data processing.

Computers will be more powerful, and will be organized in completely different ways. For example, memories built of integrated electronics may be distributed throughout the machine instead of being concentrated in a central unit. In addition, the improved reliability made possible by integrated circuits will allow the construction of larger processing units. Machines similar to those in existence today will be built at lower costs and with faster turnaround.

25.1   Present and Future

By integrated electronics, I mean all the various technologies which are referred to as microelectronics today as well as any additional ones that result in electronics functions supplied to the user as irreducible units. These technologies were first investigated in the late 1950s. The object was to miniaturize electronics equipment to include increasingly complex electronic functions in limited space with minimum weight. Several approaches evolved, including microassembly techniques for individual components, thin-film structures, and semiconductor integrated circuits.

Each approach evolved rapidly and converged so that each borrowed techniques from another. Many researchers believe the way of the future to be a combination of the various approaches.

The advocates of semiconductor integrated circuitry are already using the improved characteristics of thin-film resistors by applying such films directly to an active semiconductor substrate. Those advocating a technology based upon films are developing sophisticated techniques for the attachment of active semiconductor devices to the passive film arrays.

Both approaches have worked well and are being used in equipment today.

25.2   The Establishment

Integrated electronics is established today. Its techniques are almost mandatory for new military systems, since the reliability, size, and weight required by some of them is achievable only with integration. Such programs as Apollo, for manned moon flight, have demonstrated the reliability of integrated electronics by showing that complete circuit functions are as free from failure as the best individual transistors.

Most companies in the commercial computer field have machines in design or in early production employing integrated electronics. These machines cost less and perform better than those which use "conventional" electronics.

Instruments of various sorts, especially the rapidly increasing numbers employing digital techniques, are starting to use integration because it cuts costs of both manufacture and design.

The use of linear integrated circuitry is still restricted primarily to the military. Such integrated functions are expensive and not available in the variety required to satisfy a major fraction of linear electronics. But the first applications are beginning to appear in commercial electronics, particularly in equipment which needs low-frequency amplifiers of small size.

25.3   Reliability Counts

In almost every case, integrated electronics has demonstrated high reliability. Even at the present level of production—low compared to that of discrete components—it offers reduced systems cost, and in many systems improved performance has been realized.

Integrated electronics will make electronic techniques more generally available throughout all of society, performing many functions that presently are done inadequately by other techniques or not done at all. The principal advantages will be lower costs and greatly simplified design—payoffs from a ready supply of low-cost functional packages.

For most applications, semiconductor integrated circuits will predominate. Semiconductor devices are the only reasonable candidates presently in existence for the active elements of integrated circuits. Passive semiconductor elements look attractive too, because of their potential for low cost and high reliability, but they can be used only if precision is not a prime requisite.

Silicon is likely to remain the basic material, although others will be of use in specific applications. For example, gallium arsenide will be important in integrated microwave functions. But silicon will predominate at lower frequencies because of the technology which has already evolved around it and its oxide, and because it is an abundant and relatively inexpensive starting material.

25.4   Costs and Curves

Reduced cost is one of the big attractions of integrated electronics, and the cost advantage continues to increase as the technology evolves toward the production of larger and larger circuit functions on a single semiconductor substrate. For simple circuits, the cost per component is nearly inversely proportional to the number of components, the result of the equivalent piece of semiconductor in the equivalent package containing more components. But as components are added, decreased yields more than compensate for the increased complexity, tending to raise the cost per component. Thus there is a minimum cost at any given time in the evolution of the technology. At present, it is reached when 50 components are used per circuit. But the minimum is rising rapidly while the entire cost curve is falling (see graph). If we look ahead five years, a plot of costs suggests that the minimum cost per component might be expected in circuits with about 1000 components per circuit (providing such circuit functions can be produced in moderate quantities). In 1970, the manufacturing cost per component can be expected to be only a tenth of the present cost.

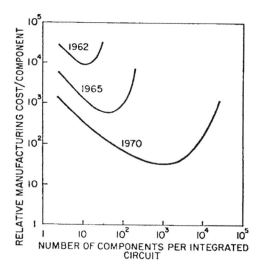

The complexity for minimum component costs has increased at a rate of roughly a factor of two per year (see graph). Certainly over the short term this rate can be expected to continue, if not to increase. Over the longer term, the rate of increase is a bit more uncertain, although there is no reason to believe it will not remain nearly constant for at least ten years. That means by 1975, the number of components per integrated circuit for minimum cost will be 65,000.

I believe that such a large circuit can be built on a single wafer.

25.5   Two-Mil Squares

With the dimensional tolerances already being employed in integrated circuits, isolated high-performance transistors can be built on centers two-thousandths of an inch apart. Such a two-mil square can also contain several kilohms of resistance or a few diodes. This allows at least 500 components per linear inch or a quarter million per square inch. Thus, 65,000 components need occupy only about one-fourth a square inch.

On the silicon wafer currently used, usually an inch or more in diameter, there is ample room for such a structure if the components can be closely packed with no space wasted for interconnection patterns. This is realistic, since efforts to achieve a level of complexity above the presently available integrated circuits are already under way using multilayer metallization patterns separated by dielectric films. Such a density of components can be achieved by present optical techniques and does not require the more exotic techniques, such as electron beam operations, which are being studied to make even smaller structures.

25.6   Increasing the Yield

There is no fundamental obstacle to achieving device yields of 100%. At present, packaging costs so far exceed the cost of the semiconductor structure itself that there is no incentive to improve yields, but they can be raised as high as is economically justified. No barrier exists comparable to the thermodynamic equilibrium considerations that often limit yields in chemical reactions; it is not even necessary to do any fundamental research or to replace present processes. Only the engineering effort is needed.

In the early days of integrated circuitry, when yields were extremely low, there was such incentive. Today ordinary integrated circuits are made with yields comparable with those obtained

for individual semiconductor devices. The same pattern will make larger arrays economical, if other considerations make such arrays desirable.

25.7 Heat Problem

Will it be possible to remove the heat generated by tens of thousands of components in a single silicon chip?

If we could shrink the volume of a standard high-speed digital computer to that required for the components themselves, we would expect it to glow brightly with present power dissipation. But it won't happen with integrated circuits. Since integrated electronic structures are two dimensional, they have a surface available for cooling close to each center of heat generation. In addition, power is needed primarily to drive the various lines and capacitances associated with the system. As long as a function is confined to a small area on a wafer, the amount of capacitance which must be driven is distinctly limited. [EDITOR: Heat became a problem because this premise ceased to be true.] In fact, shrinking dimensions on an integrated structure makes it possible to operate the structure at higher speed for the same power per unit area.

25.8 Day of Reckoning

Clearly, we will be able to build such component-crammed equipment. Next, we ask under what circumstances we should do it. The total cost of making a particular system function must be minimized. To do so, we could amortize the engineering over several identical items, or evolve flexible techniques for the engineering of large functions so that no disproportionate expense need be borne by a particular array. Perhaps newly devised design automation procedures could translate from logic diagram to technological realization without any special engineering.

It may prove to be more economical to build large systems out of smaller functions, which are separately packaged and interconnected. The availability of large functions, combined with functional design and construction, should allow the manufacturer of large systems to design and construct a considerable variety of equipment both rapidly and economically.

25.9   Linear Circuitry

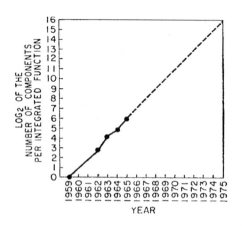

Integration will not change linear systems as radically as digital systems. Still, a considerable degree of integration will be achieved with linear circuits. The lack of large-value capacitors and inductors is the greatest fundamental limitation to integrated electronics in the linear area.

By their very nature, such elements require the storage of energy in a volume. For high Q it is necessary that the volume be large. The incompatibility of large volume and integrated electronics is obvious from the terms themselves. Certain resonance phenomena, such as those in piezoelectric crystals, can be expected to have some applications for tuning functions, but inductors and capacitors will be with us for some time.

The integrated RF amplifier of the future might well consist of integrated stages of gain, giving high performance at minimum cost, interspersed with relatively large tuning elements.

Other linear functions will be changed considerably. The matching and tracking of similar components in integrated structures will allow the design of differential amplifiers of greatly improved performance. The use of thermal feedback effects to stabilize integrated structures to a small fraction of a degree will allow the construction of oscillators with crystal stability.

Even in the microwave area, structures included in the definition of integrated electronics will become increasingly important. The ability to make and assemble components small compared with the wavelengths involved will allow the use of lumped parameter design, at least at the lower frequencies. It is difficult to predict at the present time just how extensive the invasion of the microwave area by integrated electronics will be. The successful realization of such items as phased-array antennas, for example, using a multiplicity of integrated microwave power sources, could completely revolutionize radar.

26 Solution of a Problem in Concurrent Program Control (1965)

Edsger Dijkstra

Edsger Dijkstra (1930–2002) was a brilliant and challenging figure. Even completing the sentence "Dijkstra was a Dutch ..." is a challenge. He was a devastatingly trenchant thinker and elegant writer about computer programming. But he didn't like the term "computer science," preferring "computing science" if such a term had to be used at all. He rejected the bifurcation of computing into theory and engineering; he insisted on elegance and clarity in everything he touched. "The art of programming is the art of organizing complexity, of mastering multitude and avoiding its bastard chaos as effectively as possible," he wrote (Dijkstra, 1972). And if that required more brainpower, well, not everyone was cut out for the work. "Don't blame me for the fact that competent programming, as I view it as an intellectual possibility, will be too difficult for 'the average programmer'—you must not fall into the trap of rejecting a surgical technique because it is beyond the capabilities of the barber in his shop around the corner" (Dijkstra, 1975).

Dijkstra's career was spent trying to move the focus from the machine that executed a program to the abstract thinking behind the computation. Trained as a mathematician and a physicist, he challenged the field to think methodically about programming problems, and to reason about them mathematically, before writing a line of code. He made important contributions to many aspects of the field, originally as a practicing programmer in the computer industry, and later as a professor at the Technological University in Eindhoven in the Netherlands and at the University of Texas at Austin. His name is associated with an elegant all-pairs shortest paths algorithm (Dijkstra, 1959), and he also made important contributions to the study of compilers, operating systems (see chapter 28), distributed systems, and programming methods (see chapter 29).

This selection is arguably the first scientific paper on algorithmic problems—as opposed to language constructs—in the field of concurrent programming (which others might call parallel computing or multiprogramming). The paper is a model of logical rigor, though the code is far from self-documenting. It set off the entire research field of concurrent computing. Operating systems and database systems in particular have the property that because concurrent code segments are executed so many times under so many different conditions, anything that can possibly go wrong eventually will. Dijkstra here points the way to the use of clear reasoning to preclude timing bugs. He introduces the terms "critical section" and "mutual exclusion," and proves that his code meets what would now be called safety and liveness conditions (Lamport, 2015).

Reprinted from Dijkstra (1965), with permission from the Association for Computing Machinery.

As much as Dijkstra set a standard for rigorous thinking, he was dismissive of work that did not meet his standards—including entire research programs. One can't fully appreciate his imperative for logical clarity without understanding his attitude toward work that lacked it. Asked in 1985 about the future of artificial intelligence, he replied, "Can you research something that is not science? I feel that the effort to use machines to try to mimic human reasoning is both foolish and dangerous. It is foolish because if you look at human reasoning as is, it is pretty lousy; even the most trained mathematicians are amateur thinkers. ... Any successful AI project by its very nature would castrate the machine." Asked about the huge increase in student interest in computer science, he replied, "If you ask whether there are too many or too few students: *an order of magnitude too many.* From a scientific point of view you would like to weed out the lot. Keep the brightest 2% and do business" (van Vlissingen and Dijkstra, 1985).

On the importance of making software more usable: "[T]he computer user, as functioning in the development of computer products is not a real person of flesh and blood but a literary figure .... He is stupid, education resistant if not education proof, and he hates any form of intellectual demand made on him, he cannot be delighted by something beautiful, because he lacks the education to appreciate beauty. Large sections of computer science are paralyzed by accepting this moron as their typical customer."

——————◦∘◦✐◦∘◦——————

26.1   Introduction

GIVEN in this paper is a solution to a problem for which, to the knowledge of the author, has been an open question since at least 1962, irrespective of the solvability. The paper consists of three parts: the problem, the solution, and the proof. Although the setting of the problem might seem somewhat academic at first, the author trusts that anyone familiar with the logical problems that arise in computer coupling will appreciate the significance of the fact that this problem indeed can be solved.

26.2   The Problem

To begin, consider N computers, each engaged in a process which, for our aims, can be regarded as cyclic. In each of the cycles a so-called "critical section" occurs and the computers have to be programmed in such a way that at any moment only one of these N cyclic processes is in its critical section. In order to effectuate this mutual exclusion of critical-section execution the computers can communicate with each other via a common store. Writing a word into or nondestructively reading a word from this store are undividable operations; i.e., when two or more computers try to communicate (either for reading or for writing) simultaneously with the same common location, these communications will take place one after the other, but in an unknown order.

The solution must satisfy the following requirements.

(a) The solution must be symmetrical between the N computers; as a result we are not allowed to introduce a static priority.

(b) Nothing may be assumed about the relative speeds of the N computers; we may not even assume their speeds to be constant in time.

(c) If any of the computers is stopped well outside its critical section, this is not allowed to lead to potential blocking of the others.

(d) If more than one computer is about to enter its critical section, it must be impossible to devise for them such finite speeds, that the decision to determine which one of them will enter its critical section first is postponed until eternity. In other words, constructions in which "After you"-"After you"-blocking is still possible, although improbable, are not to be regarded as valid solutions.

We beg the challenged reader to stop here for a while and have a try himself, for this seems the only way to get a feeling for the tricky consequences of the fact that each computer can only request one one-way message at a time. And only this will make the reader realize to what extent this problem is far from trivial.

26.3   The Solution

The common store consists of: "**boolean array** $b, c[1 : N]$; **integer** k".

The integer k will satisfy $1 \leq k \leq N$, $b[i]$ and $c[i]$ will only be set by the ith computer; they will be inspected by the others. It is assumed that all computers are started well outside their critical sections with all boolean arrays mentioned set to **true**; the starting value of k is immaterial.

The program for the ith computer ($1 \leq i \leq N$) is:

```
"integer j;
Li0 :   b[i] := false;
Li1 :   if k ≠ i then
Li2 :       begin
                c[i] := true;
Li3 :           if b[k] then k := i;
                go to Li1
            end
        else
Li4 :       begin
                c[i] := false;
                for j := 1 step 1 until N do
                    if j ≠ i and not c[j] then go to Li1
            end;
        critical section;
        c[i] := true; b[i] := true;
        remainder of the cycle in which stopping is allowed;
        go to Li0"
```

26.4   The Proof

We start by observing that the solution is safe in the sense that no two computers can be in their critical section simultaneously. For the only way to enter its critical section is the performance of the compound statement *Li*4 without jumping back to *Li*1, i.e., finding all other *c*'s **true** after having set its own *c* to **false**.

The second part of the proof must show that no infinite "After you"-"After you"-blocking can occur; i.e., when none of the computers is in its critical section, of the computers looping (i.e., jumping back to *Li*1) at least one—and therefore exactly one—will be allowed to enter its critical section in due time.

If the kth computer is not among the looping ones, $b[k]$ will be **true** and the looping ones will all find $k \neq i$. As a result one or more of them will find in *Li*3 the boolean $b[k]$ **true** and therefore one or more will decide to assign "$k := i$". After the first assignment "$k := i$", $b[k]$ becomes **false** and no new computers can decide again to assign a new value to k. When all decided assignments to k have been performed, k will point to one of the looping computers and will not change its value for the time being, i.e., until $b[k]$ becomes **true**, viz., until the kth computer has completed its critical section. As soon as the value of k does not change any more, the kth computer will wait (via the compound statement *Li*4) until all other *c*'s are **true**, but this situation will certainly arise, if not already present, because all other looping ones are forced to set their *c* **true**, as they will find $k \neq i$. And this, the author believes, completes the proof.

27 ELIZA—A Computer Program for the Study of Natural Language Communication between Man and Machine (1966)

Joseph Weizenbaum

Joseph Weizenbaum (1923–2008) was a German Jewish refugee who came to the United States with his family at the age of 13. After studying mathematics and computing at Wayne State University, he joined the MIT faculty in computer science. There, starting in 1964, he wrote the first example of what we would now call chatbots—programs that "know" very little but create an illusion of conversation by manipulating the discourse of their conversational partners. He was surprised that people engaged intensely with his simple program, as though it was human. Famously, his own staff assistant, who knew better than anyone that no human being was answering her musings, asked Weizenbaum to leave the room while she was using ELIZA (Weizenbaum, 1976, p. 6). It was as though she thought he was eavesdropping on a personal conversation.

ELIZA was a sensation, in part because time-sharing was new in 1966—so new that in this paper Weizenbaum felt he had to explain it to the readers of the *Communications of the ACM*. For the first time, people with no technical training were starting to use computers, and programmers started to write programs designed, in no small measure, to allow ordinary people to have some fun.

But ELIZA also touched a deep human nerve. The program is named after Eliza Doolittle, a character in George Bernard Shaw's play *Pygmalion*, which became the Broadway musical *My Fair Lady* in 1956. A film based on the musical was released in 1964. In Shaw's play, Eliza is an unschooled London flower girl who is "reprogrammed" by Professor Henry Higgins, a linguist, to feign aristocratic roots. Higgins falls in love with the (almost) perfectly transformed Eliza, in the same way that in the original Greek myth, the artist Pygmalion falls in love with the ivory statue he has sculpted of a woman.

The Greek myth of Pygmalion is in fact closer than the modern drama to the reality of ELIZA, because it involves the animation of the inanimate. In the original, Pygmalion's prayers are answered and the gods breathe life into his statue. This is only one of the Western myths of an inanimate object being brought to life in human form (see page xix).

Having witnessed as a boy the dehumanization of human beings, Weizenbaum was deeply troubled that people were so easily fooled, and skeptical of his colleagues' scientific agenda to humanize machines. He was a sharp critic of artificial intelligence throughout his life; his most important work, his attempt to separate humans and machines once and for all, was entitled *Computer Power and Human Reason* (Weizenbaum, 1976). It did not convince AI advocates,

Reprinted from Weizenbaum (1966), with permission from the Association for Computing Machinery.

and with the maturing of technologies of understanding and synthesizing speech and simulating emotion, the debate has continued about where computers *should*—as opposed to *can*—replace human interactions.

——◦○◦◦——

ELIZA is a program operating within the MAC time-sharing system at MIT which makes certain kinds of natural language conversation between man and computer possible. Input sentences are analyzed on the basis of decomposition rules which are triggered by key words appearing in the input text. Responses are generated by reassembly rules associated with selected decomposition rules. The fundamental technical problems with which ELIZA is concerned are: (1) the identification of key words, (2) the discovery of minimal context, (3) the choice of appropriate transformations, (4) generation of responses in the absence of key words, and (5) the provision of an editing capability for ELIZA "scripts." A discussion of some psychological issues relevant to the ELIZA approach as well as of future developments concludes the paper.

27.1   Introduction

It is said that to explain is to explain away. This maxim is nowhere so well fulfilled as in the area of computer programming, especially in what is called heuristic programming and artificial intelligence. For in those realms machines are made to behave in wondrous ways, often sufficient to dazzle even the most experienced observer. But once a particular program is unmasked, once its inner workings are explained in language sufficiently plain to induce understanding, its magic crumbles away; it stands revealed as a mere collection of procedures, each quite comprehensible. The observer says to himself "I could have written that." With that thought he moves the program in question from the shelf marked "intelligent," to that reserved for curios, fit to be discussed only with people less enlightened than he.

The object of this paper is to cause just such a re-evaluation of the program about to be "explained." Few programs ever needed it more.

27.2   ELIZA Program

ELIZA is a program which makes natural language conversation with a computer possible. Its present implementation is on the MAC time-sharing system at MIT. It is written in MAD-SLIP (Weizenbaum, 1963) for the IBM 7094. Its name was chosen to emphasize that it may be incrementally improved by its users, since its language abilities may be continually improved by a "teacher." Like the Eliza of Pygmalion fame, it can be made to appear even more civilized, the relation of appearance to reality, however, remaining in the domain of the playwright.

For the present purpose it is sufficient to characterize the MAC system as one which permits an individual to operate a full scale computer from a remotely located typewriter. The individual operator has the illusion that he is the sole user of the computer complex, while in fact others may be "time-sharing" the system with him. What is important here is that the computer can read messages typed on the typewriter and respond by writing on the same instrument. The time between the computer's receipt of a message and the appearance of its response is a function of the program controlling the dialogue and of such MAC system parameters as the number of users currently corresponding with the system. These latter parameters generally contribute so little to the overall response time that conversational interaction with the computer need never involve truly intolerable delays.

When in conversation with ELIZA, the user types in some statement or set of statements in natural language using normal punctuation and sentence structures. Only the question mark may not be used, because it is interpreted as a line delete character by the MAC system. The user's statement is terminated by a double carriage return which serves to turn control over to ELIZA. ELIZA then analyzes the user's statement and generates some response which it types out. Control is then again with the user. A typical conversation is the following:

Men are all alike.

IN WHAT WAY

They're always bugging us about something or other.

CAN YOU THINK OF A SPECIFIC EXAMPLE

Well, my boyfriend made me come here.

YOUR BOYFRIEND MADE YOU COME HERE

He says I'm depressed much of the time.

I AM SORRY TO HEAR YOU ARE DEPRESSED

It's true. I am unhappy.

DO YOU THINK COMING HERE WILL HELP YOU NOT TO BE UNHAPPY

I need some help, that much seems certain.

WHAT WOULD IT MEAN TO YOU IF YOU GOT SOME HELP

Perhaps I could learn to get along with my mother.

TELL ME MORE ABOUT YOUR FAMILY

My mother takes care of me.

WHO ELSE IN YOUR FAMILY TAKES CARE OF YOU

My father.

YOUR FATHER

You are like my father in some ways.

WHAT RESEMBLANCE DO YOU SEE

You are not very aggressive but I think you don't want me to notice that.

WHAT MAKES YOU THINK I AM NOT VERY AGGRESSIVE

You don't argue with me.

WHY DO YOU THINK I DON'T ARGUE WITH YOU

You are afraid of me.

DOES IT PLEASE YOU TO BELIEVE I AM AFRAID OF YOU

My father is afraid of everybody.

WHAT ELSE COMES TO MIND WHEN YOU THINK OF YOUR FATHER

Bullies.

DOES THAT HAVE ANYTHING TO DO WITH THE FACT THAT YOUR BOYFRIEND MADE YOU COME HERE

The capitalized lines are the machine responses.

The gross procedure of the program is quite simple; the text is read and inspected for the presence of a *keyword*. If such a word is found, the sentence is transformed according to a *rule* associated with the keyword, if not a content-free remark or, under certain conditions, an earlier transformation is retrieved. The text so computed or retrieved is then printed out.

In detail, of course, the procedure sketched above is considerably more complex. Keywords, for example, may have a RANK or precedence number. The procedure is sensitive to such numbers in that it will abandon a keyword already found in the left-to-right scan of the text in favor of one having a higher rank. Also, the procedure recognizes a comma or a period as a delimiter. Whenever either one is encountered and a keyword has already been found, all subsequent text is deleted from the input message. If no key had yet been found the phrase or sentence to the left of the delimiter (as well as the delimiter itself) is deleted. As a result, only single phrases or sentences are ever transformed.

Keywords and their associated transformation rules constitute the SCRIPT for a particular class of conversation. An important property of ELIZA is that a script is data; i.e., it is not part of the program itself. Hence, ELIZA is not restricted to a particular set of recognition patterns or responses, indeed not even to any specific language. ELIZA scripts exist (at this writing) in Welsh and German as well as in English.

The fundamental technical problems with which ELIZA must be preoccupied are the following:

1. The identification of the "most important" keyword in the input message.
2. The identification of some minimal context within which the chosen keyword appears; e.g., if the keyword is "you," is it followed by the word "are" (in which case an assertion is probably being made).
3. The choice of an appropriate transformation rule and, of course, the making of the transformation itself.
4. The provision of mechanism that will permit ELIZA to respond "intelligently" when the input text contained no keywords.
5. The provision of machinery that facilitates editing, particularly extension, of the script on the script writing level.

There are, of course, the usual constraints dictated by the need to be economical in the use of computer time and storage space.

The central issue is clearly one of text manipulation, and at the heart of that issue is the concept of the *transformation rule* which has been said to be associated with certain keywords. The mechanisms subsumed under the slogan "transformation rule" are a number of SLIP functions which serve to (1) decompose a data string according to certain criteria, hence to test the string as to whether it satisfies these criteria or not, and (2) to reassemble a decomposed string according to certain assembly specifications. . . .

27.3   Discussion

At this writing, the only serious ELIZA scripts which exist are some which cause ELIZA to respond roughly as would certain psychotherapists (Rogerians). ELIZA performs best when its human correspondent is initially instructed to "talk" to it, via the typewriter of course, just as one would to a psychiatrist. This mode of conversation was chosen because the psychiatric interview is one of the few examples of categorized dyadic natural language communication in which one of the participating pair is free to assume the pose of knowing almost nothing of the real world. If, for example, one were to tell a psychiatrist "I went for a long boat ride" and he responded "Tell me about boats," one would not assume that he knew nothing about boats, but that he had some purpose in so directing the subsequent conversation. It is important to note that this assumption is one made by the speaker. Whether it is realistic or not is an altogether separate question.

In any case, it has a crucial psychological utility in that it serves the speaker to maintain his sense of being heard and understood. The speaker further defends his impression (which may even be illusory) by attributing to his conversational partner all sorts of background knowledge, insights, and reasoning ability. But again, these are the *speaker's* contribution to the conversation. They manifest themselves inferentially in *interpretations* he makes of the offered responses. From the purely technical programming point of view then, the psychiatric interview form of an ELIZA script has the advantage that it eliminates the need of storing *explicit* information about the real world.

The human speaker will, as has been said, contribute much to clothe ELIZA's responses in vestments of plausibility. But he will not defend his illusion (that he is being understood) against all odds. In human conversation a speaker will make certain (perhaps generous) assumptions about his conversational partner. As long as it remains possible to interpret the latter's responses consistently with those assumptions, the speaker's image of his partner remains unchanged, in particular, undamaged. Responses which are difficult to so interpret may well result in an enhancement of the image of the partner, in additional rationalizations which then make more complicated interpretations of his responses reasonable.

When, however, such rationalizations become too massive and even self-contradictory, the entire image may crumble and be replaced by another ("He is not, after all, as smart as I thought he was"). When the conversational partner is a machine (the distinction between machine and program is here not useful) then the idea of *credibility* may well be substituted for that of *plausibility* in the above.

With ELIZA as the basic vehicle, experiments may be set up in which the subjects find it credible to believe that the responses which appear on his typewriter are generated by a human sitting at a similar instrument in another room. How must the script be written in order to maintain the credibility of this idea over a long period of time? How can the performance of ELIZA be systematically degraded in order to achieve controlled and predictable thresholds of credibility in the subject? What, in all this, is the role of the initial instruction to the subject? On the other hand, suppose the subject is told he is communicating with a machine. What is he led to believe about the machine as a result of his conversational experience with it? Some subjects have been very hard to convince that ELIZA (with its present script) is not human. This is a striking form of Turing's test. What experimental design would make it more nearly rigorous and airtight?

The whole issue of the credibility (to humans) of machine output demands investigation. Important decisions increasingly tend to be made in response to computer output. The ultimately responsible human interpreter of "What the machine says" is not unlike the correspondent with ELIZA, constantly faced with the need to make credibility judgments. ELIZA shows, if nothing else, how easy it is to create and maintain the illusion of understanding, hence perhaps, of judgment deserving of credibility. A certain danger lurks there.

The idea that the present ELIZA script contains no information about the real world is not entirely true. For example, the transformation rules which cause the input

> Everybody hates me

to be transformed to

> Can you think of anyone in particular

and other such are based on quite specific hypotheses about the world. The whole script constitutes, in a loose way, a model of certain aspects of the world. The act of writing a script is a kind of programming act and has all the advantages of programming, most particularly that it clearly shows where the programmer's understanding and command of his subject leaves off.

A large part of whatever elegance may be credited to ELIZA lies in the fact that ELIZA maintains the illusion of understanding with so little machinery. But there are bounds on the extendability of ELIZA's "understanding" power, which are a function of the ELIZA program itself and not a function of any script it may be given. The crucial test of understanding, as every teacher should know, is not the subject's ability to continue a conversation, but to draw valid conclusions from what he is being told. In order for a computer program to be able to do that, it must at least have the capacity to store selected parts of its inputs. ELIZA throws away each of its inputs, except for those few transformed by means of the MEMORY machinery. [EDITOR: A few inputs are saved in the MEMORY data structure so that things the user has mentioned earlier in the conversation can be revived when the dialog seems to have petered out.] Of course, the problem is more than one of storage. A great part of it is, in fact, subsumed under the word "selected" used just above. ELIZA in its use so far has had as one of its principal objectives the *concealment* of its lack of understanding. But to encourage its conversational partner to offer inputs from which it can select remedial information, it, must *reveal* its misunderstanding. A switch of objectives from the concealment to the revelation of misunderstanding is seen as a precondition to making an ELIZA-like program the basis for an effective natural language man–machine communication system.

One goal for an augmented ELIZA program is thus a system which already has access to a store of information about some aspects of the real world and which, by means of conversational interaction with people, can reveal both what it knows, i.e., behave as an information retrieval system, and where its knowledge ends and needs to be augmented. Hopefully the augmentation of its knowledge will also be a direct consequence of its conversational experience. It is precisely the prospect that such a program will converse with many people and learn something from each of them, which leads to the hope that it will prove an interesting and even useful conversational partner.

One way to state a slightly different intermediate goal is to say that ELIZA should be given the power to slowly build a model of the subject conversing with it. If the subject mentions that he is not married, for example, and later speaks of his wife, then ELIZA should be able make the tentative inference that he is either a widower or divorced. Of course, he could simply be confused. In the long run, ELIZA should be able to build up a belief structure (to use Abelson's phrase) of the subject and on that basis detect the subject's rationalizations, contradictions, etc. Conversations with such an ELIZA would often turn into arguments. Important steps in the realization of these goals have already been taken. Most notable among these is Abelson's and Carroll's work on simulation of belief structures (Abelson and Carroll, 1965).

The script that has formed the basis for most of this discussion happens to be one with an overwhelmingly psychological orientation. The reason for this has already been discussed. There is a danger, however, that the example will run away with what it is supposed to illustrate. It is useful to remember that the ELIZA program itself is merely a translating processor in the technical programming sense. Gorn (1964) in a paper on language systems says:

> Given a language which already possesses semantic content, then a translating processor, even if it operates only syntactically, generates corresponding expressions of another language to which we can attribute as "meanings" (possibly multiple—the translator may not be one to one) the "semantic intents" of the generating source expressions; whether we find the result consistent or useful or both is, of course, another problem. It is quite possible that by this method the same syntactic object language can be usefully assigned multiple meanings for each expression. . . .

It is striking to note how well his words fit ELIZA. The "given language" is English as is the "other," expressions of which are generated. In principle, the given language could as well be the kind of English in which "word problems" in algebra are given to high school students and the other language, a machine code allowing a particular computer to "solve" the stated problems. (See Bobrow's program STUDENT [Bobrow, 1964].)

The intent of the above remarks is to further rob ELIZA of the aura of magic to which its application to psychological subject matter has to some extent contributed. Seen in the coldest possible light, ELIZA is a translating processor in Gorn's sense; however, it is one which has been especially constructed to work well with natural language text.

28 The Structure of the "THE"-Multiprogramming System (1968)

Edsger Dijkstra

For background on the author, see chapter 26, a demonstration of Dijkstra's skill as a mathematical and logical thinker about computations. But Dijkstra was ever an engineer, a very skilled system designer and developer. This successful design and development project not only cemented Dijkstra's reputation as a computer scientist in the fullest sense of the word; it stimulated a great deal of academic research into provable, secure, reliable operating systems.

The Appendix presents semaphores, a very important control abstraction, encapsulating in a form suitable for general reasoning a variety of machine-specific techniques then in use for atomically locking and unlocking resources in concurrent programs.

———————◦○◦———————

28.1 Introduction

IN response to a call explicitly asking for papers "on timely research and development efforts," I present a progress report on the multiprogramming effort at the Department of Mathematics at the Technological University in Eindhoven.

Having very limited resources (viz. a group of six people of, on the average, half-time availability) and wishing to contribute to the art of system design—including all the stages of conception, construction, and verification, we were faced with the problem of how to get the necessary experience. To solve this problem we adopted the following three guiding principles:

1. Select a project as advanced as you can conceive, as ambitious as you can justify, in the hope that routine work can be kept to a minimum; hold out against all pressure to incorporate such system expansions that would only result into a purely quantitative increase of the total amount of work to be done.

2. Select a machine with sound basic characteristics (e.g. an interrupt system to fall in love with is certainly an inspiring feature); from then on try to keep the specific properties of the configuration for which you are preparing the system out of your considerations as long as possible.

Reprinted from Dijkstra (1968b), with permission from the Association for Computing Machinery.

3. Be aware of the fact that experience does by no means automatically lead to wisdom and understanding; in other words, make a conscious effort to learn as much as possible from your previous experiences.

Accordingly, I shall try to go beyond just reporting what we have done and how, and I shall try to formulate as well what we have learned.

I should like to end the introduction with two short remarks on working conditions, which I make for the sake of completeness. I shall not stress these points any further.

One remark is that production speed is severely slowed down if one works with half-time people who have other obligations as well. This is at least a factor of four; probably it is worse. The people themselves lose time and energy in switching over; the group as a whole loses decision speed as discussions, when needed, have often to be postponed until all people concerned are available.

The other remark is that the members of the group (mostly mathematicians) have previously enjoyed as good students a university training of five to eight years and are of Master's or Ph.D. level. I mention this explicitly because at least in my country the intellectual level needed for system design is in general grossly underestimated. I am convinced more than ever that this type of work is very difficult, and that every effort to do it with other than the best people is doomed to either failure or moderate success at enormous expense.

28.2   The Tool and the Goal

The system has been designed for a Dutch machine, the EL X8 (N.V. Electrologica, Rijswijk (ZH)). Characteristics of our configuration are:

1. core memory cycle time 2.5 μsec, 27 bits; at present 32K;
2. drum of 512K words, 1024 words per track, rev. time 40 msec;
3. an indirect addressing mechanism very well suited for stack implementation;
4. a sound system for commanding peripherals and controlling of interrupts;
5. a potentially great number of low capacity channels; ten of them are used (3 paper tape readers at 1000 char/sec; 3 paper tape punches at 150 char/sec; 2 teleprinters; a plotter; a line printer);
6. absence of a number of not unusual, awkward features.

The primary goal of the system is to process smoothly a continuous flow of user programs as a service to the University. A multiprogramming system has been chosen with the following objectives in mind: (1) a reduction of turn-around time for programs of short duration, (2) economic use of peripheral devices, (3) automatic control of backing store to be combined with economic use of the central processor, and (4) the economic feasibility to use the machine for those applications for which only the flexibility of a general purpose computer is needed, but (as a rule) not the capacity nor the processing power.

The system is not intended as a multiaccess system. There is no common data base via which independent users can communicate with each other: they only share the configuration and a procedure library (that includes a translator for ALGOL 60 extended with complex numbers). The system does not cater for user programs written in machine language. ...

28.3   A Progress Report

We have made some minor mistakes of the usual type (such as paying too much attention to eliminating what was not the real bottleneck) and two major ones.

Our first major mistake was that for too long a time we confined our attention to "a perfect installation"; by the time we considered how to make the best of it, one of the peripherals broke down, we were faced with nasty problems. Taking care of the "pathology" took more energy than we had expected, and some of our troubles were a direct consequence of our earlier ingenuity, i.e., the complexity of the situation into which the system could have maneuvered itself. Had we paid attention to the pathology at an earlier stage of the design, our management rules would certainly have been less refined.

The second major mistake has been that we conceived and programmed the major part of the system without giving more than scanty thought to the problem of debugging it. I must decline all credit for the fact that this mistake had no serious consequences—on the contrary! one might argue as an afterthought.

As captain of the crew I had had extensive experience (dating back to 1958) in making basic software dealing with real-time interrupts, and I knew by bitter experience that as a result of the irreproducibility of the interrupt moments a program error could present itself misleadingly like an occasional machine malfunctioning. As a result I was terribly afraid. Having fears regarding the possibility of debugging, we decided to be as careful as possible and, prevention being better than cure, to try to prevent nasty bugs from entering the construction.

This decision, inspired by fear, is at the bottom of what I regard as the group's main contribution to the art of system design. We have found that it is possible to design a refined multiprogramming system in such a way that its logical soundness can be proved a priori and its implementation can admit exhaustive testing. The only errors that showed up during testing were trivial coding errors (occurring with a density of one error per 500 instructions), each of them located within 10 minutes (classical) inspection by the machine and each of them correspondingly easy to remedy. At the time this was written the testing had not yet been completed, but the resulting system is guaranteed to be flawless. When the system is delivered we shall not live in the perpetual fear that a system derailment may still occur in an unlikely situation, such as might result from an unhappy "coincidence" of two or more critical occurrences, for we shall have proved the correctness of the system with a rigor and explicitness that is unusual for the great majority of mathematical proofs.

28.4   A Survey of the System Structure

28.4.1   Storage allocation   In the classical von Neumann machine, information is identified by the address of the memory location containing the information. When we started to think about the automatic control of secondary storage we were familiar with a system (viz. GIER ALGOL) in which all information was identified by its drum address (as in the classical von Neumann machine) and in which the function of the core memory was nothing more than to make the information "page-wise" accessible.

We have followed another approach and, as it turned out, to great advantage. In our terminology we made a strict distinction between memory units (we called them "pages" and had "core pages" and "drum pages") and corresponding information units (for lack of a better word we called them "segments"), a segment just fitting in a page. For segments we created a completely independent identification mechanism in which the number of possible segment identifiers is much larger than the total number of pages in primary and secondary store. The segment identifier gives fast access to a so-called "segment variable" in core whose value denotes whether the segment is still empty or not, and if not empty, in which page (or pages) it can be found.

As a consequence of this approach, if a segment of information, residing in a core page, has to be dumped onto the drum in order to make the core page available for other use, there is no need to return the segment to the same drum page from which it originally came. In fact, this freedom is exploited: among the free drum pages the one with minimum latency time is selected. A next consequence is the total absence of a drum allocation problem: there is not the slightest reason why, say, a program should occupy consecutive drum pages. In a multiprogramming environment this is very convenient.

28.4.2   Processor allocation   We have given full recognition to the fact that in a single sequential process (such as can be performed by a sequential automaton) only the time succession of the various states has a logical meaning, but not the actual speed with which the sequential process is performed. Therefore we have arranged the whole system as a society of sequential processes, progressing with undefined speed ratios. To each user program accepted by the system corresponds a sequential process, to each input peripheral corresponds a sequential process (buffering input streams in synchronism with the execution of the input commands), to each output peripheral corresponds a sequential process (unbuffering output streams in synchronism with the execution of the output commands); furthermore, we have the "segment controller" associated with the drum and the "message interpreter" associated with the console keyboard.

This enabled us to design the whole system in terms of these abstract "sequential processes." Their harmonious cooperation is regulated by means of explicit mutual synchronization statements. On the one hand, this explicit mutual synchronization is necessary, as we do not make any assumption about speed ratios; on the other hand, this mutual synchronization is possible because "delaying the progress of a process temporarily" can never be harmful to the interior logic of the process delayed. The fundamental consequence of this approach—viz. the explicit mutual synchronization—is that the harmonious cooperation of a set of such sequential processes can be established by discrete reasoning; as a further consequence the whole harmonious society of cooperating sequential processes is independent of the actual number of processors available to carry out these processes, provided the processors available can switch from process to process.

28.4.3   System hierarchy   The total system admits a strict hierarchical structure.

At level 0 we find the responsibility for processor allocation to one of the processes whose dynamic progress is logically permissible (i.e. in view of the explicit mutual synchronization). At this level the interrupt of the real-time clock is processed and introduced to prevent any process to monopolize processing power. At this level a priority rule is incorporated to achieve quick response of the system where this is needed. Our first abstraction has been achieved; above level 0 the number of processors actually shared is no longer relevant. At higher levels we find the activity of the different sequential processes, the actual processor that had lost its identity having disappeared from the picture.

At level 1 we have the so-called "segment controller," a sequential process synchronized with respect to the drum interrupt and the sequential processes on higher levels. At level 1 we find the responsibility to cater to the bookkeeping resulting from the automatic backing store. At this level our next abstraction has been achieved; at all higher levels identification of information takes place in terms of segments, the actual storage pages that had lost their identity having disappeared from the picture.

At level 2 we find the "message interpreter" taking care of the allocation of the console keyboard via which conversations between the operator and any of the higher level processes can be carried out. The message interpreter works in close synchronism with the operator. When the operator presses a key, a character is sent to the machine together with an interrupt signal to announce the next keyboard character, whereas the actual printing is done through an output command generated by the machine under control of the message interpreter. (As far as the hardware is concerned the console teleprinter is regarded as two independent peripherals: an input keyboard and an output printer.) If one of the processes opens a conversation, it identifies itself in the opening sentence of the conversation for the benefit of the operator. If, however, the operator opens a conversation, he must identify the process he is addressing, in the opening sentence of the conversation, i.e., this opening sentence must be interpreted before it is known to which of the processes the conversation is addressed! Here lies the logical reason for the introduction of a separate sequential process for the console teleprinter, a reason that is reflected in its name, "message interpreter."

Above level 2 it is as if each process had its private conversational console. The fact that they share the same physical console is translated into a resource restriction of the form "only one conversation at a time," a restriction that is satisfied via mutual synchronization. At this level the next abstraction has been implemented; at higher levels the actual console teleprinter loses its identity. (If the message interpreter had not been on a higher level than the segment controller, then the only way to implement it would have been to make a permanent reservation in core for it; as the conversational vocabulary might become large (as soon as our operators wish to be addressed in fancy messages), this would result in too heavy a permanent demand upon core storage. Therefore, the vocabulary in which the messages are expressed is stored on segments, i.e., as information units that can reside on the drum as well. For this reason the message interpreter is one level higher than the segment controller.)

At level 3 we find the sequential processes associated with buffering of input streams and unbuffering of output streams. At this level the next abstraction is effected, viz. the abstraction of the actual peripherals used that are allocated at this level to the "logical communication units" in terms of which are worked in the still higher levels. The sequential processes associated with the peripherals are of a level above the message interpreter, because they must be able to converse with the operator (e.g. in the case of detected malfunctioning). The limited number of peripherals again acts as a resource restriction for the processes at higher levels to be satisfied by mutual synchronization between them.

At level 4 we find the independent user programs and at level 5 the operator (not implemented by us).

The system structure has been described at length in order to make the next section intelligible.

28.5   Design Experience

The conception stage took a long time. During that period of time the concepts have been born in terms of which we sketched the system in the previous section. Furthermore, we learned the art of reasoning by which we could deduce from our requirements the way in which the processes should influence each other by their mutual synchronization so that these requirements would be met. (The requirements being that no information can be used before it has been produced, that no peripheral can be set to two tasks simultaneously, etc.) Finally we learned the art of reasoning by which we could prove that the society composed of processes thus mutually synchronized by each other would indeed in its time behavior satisfy all requirements.

The construction stage has been rather traditional, perhaps even old-fashioned, that is, plain machine code. Reprogramming on account of a change of specifications has been rare, a circumstance that must have contributed greatly to the feasibility of the "steam method." That the first two stages took more time than planned was somewhat compensated by a delay in the delivery of the machine.

In the verification stage we had the machine, during short shots, completely at our disposal; these were shots during which we worked with a virgin machine without any software aids for debugging. Starting at level 0 the system was tested, each time adding (a portion of) the next level only after the previous level had been thoroughly tested. Each test shot itself contained, on top of the (partial) system to be tested, a number of testing processes with a double function. First, they had to force the system into all different relevant states; second, they had to verify that the system continued to react according to specification.

I shall not deny that the construction of these testing programs has been a major intellectual effort: to convince oneself that one has not overlooked "a relevant state" and to convince oneself that the testing programs generate them all is no simple matter. The encouraging thing is that (as far as we know!) it could be done.

This fact was one of the happy consequences of the hierarchical structure.

Testing level 0 (the real-time clock and processor allocation) implied a number of testing sequential processes on top of it, inspecting together that under all circumstances processor time was divided among them according to the rules. This being established, sequential processes as such were implemented.

Testing the segment controller at level 1 meant that all "relevant states" could be formulated in terms of sequential processes making (in various combinations) demands on core pages, situations that could be provoked by explicit synchronization among the testing programs. At this stage the existence of the real-time clock—although interrupting all the time—was so immaterial that one of the testers indeed forgot its existence!

By that time we had implemented the correct reaction upon the (mutually unsynchronized) interrupts from the real-time clock and the drum. If we had not introduced the separate levels 0 and 1, and if we had not created a terminology (viz. that of the rather abstract sequential processes) in which the existence of the clock interrupt could be discarded, but had instead tried in a nonhierarchical construction, to make the central processor react directly upon any weird time succession of these two interrupts, the number of "relevant states" would have exploded to such a height that exhaustive testing would have been an illusion. (Apart from that it is doubtful whether we would have had the means to generate them all, drum and clock speed being outside our control.) ...

28.6   Conclusion

As far as program verification is concerned I present nothing essentially new. In testing a general purpose object (be it a piece of hardware, a program, a machine, or a system), one cannot subject it to all possible cases: for a computer this would imply that one feeds it with all possible programs! Therefore one must test it with a set of relevant test cases. What is, or is not, relevant cannot be decided as long as one regards the mechanism as a black box; in other words, the decision has to be based upon the internal structure of the mechanism to be tested. It seems to be the designer's responsibility to construct his mechanism in such a way—i.e. so effectively structured—that at each stage of the testing procedure the number of relevant test cases will be so small that he can try them all and that what is being tested will be so perspicuous that he will not have overlooked any situation. I have presented a survey of our system because I think it a nice example of the form that such a structure might take.

In my experience, I am sorry to say, industrial software makers tend to react to the system with mixed feelings. On the one hand, they are inclined to think that we have done a kind of model job; on the other hand, they express doubts whether the techniques used are applicable outside the sheltered atmosphere of a University and express the opinion that we were successful only because of the modest scope of the whole project. It is not my intention to underestimate the organizing ability needed to handle a much bigger job, with a lot more people, but I should like to venture the opinion that the larger the project, the more essential the structuring! A hierarchy of five logical levels might then very well turn out to be of modest depth, especially when one designs the system more consciously than we have done, with the aim that the software can be smoothly adapted to (perhaps drastic) configuration expansions. ...

28.7 Appendix

28.7.1 Synchronizing primitives   Explicit mutual synchronization of parallel sequential processes is implemented via so-called "semaphores." They are special purpose integer variables allocated in the universe in which the processes are embedded; they are initialized (with the value 0 or 1) before the parallel processes themselves are started. After this initialization the parallel processes will access the semaphores only via two very specific operations, the so-called synchronizing primitives. For historical reasons they are called the *P*-operation and the *V*-operation.

A process, "*Q*" say, that performs the operation "*P*(sem)" decreases the value of the semaphore called "sem" by 1. If the resulting value of the semaphore concerned is nonnegative, process *Q* can continue with the execution of its next statement; if, however, the resulting value is negative, process *Q* is stopped and booked on a waiting list associated with the semaphore concerned. Until further notice (i.e. a *V*-operation on this very same semaphore), dynamic progress of process *Q* is not logically permissible and no processor will be allocated to it (see above "System Hierarchy," at level 0).

A process, "*R*" say, that performs the operation "*V*(sem)" increases the value of the semaphore called "sem" by 1. If the resulting value of the semaphore concerned is positive, the *V*-operation in question has no further effect; if, however, the resulting value of the semaphore concerned is nonpositive, one of the processes booked on its waiting list is removed from this waiting list, i.e. its dynamic progress is again logically permissible and in due time a processor will be allocated to it (again, see above "System Hierarchy," at level 0).

COROLLARY 1. *If a semaphore value is nonpositive its absolute value equals the number of processes booked on its waiting list.*

COROLLARY 2. *The P-operation represents the potential delay, the complementary V-operation represents the removal of a barrier.*

Note 1. *P*- and *V*-operations are "indivisible actions"; i.e. if they occur "simultaneously" in parallel processes they are noninterfering in the sense that they can be regarded as being performed one after the other.

Note 2. If the semaphore value resulting from a *V*-operation is negative, its waiting list originally contained more than one process. It is undefined—i.e, logically immaterial—which of the waiting processes is then removed from the waiting list.

Note 3. A consequence of the mechanisms described above is that a process whose dynamic progress is permissible can only lose this status by actually progressing, i.e., by performance of a *P*-operation on a semaphore with a value that is initially nonpositive.

During system conception it transpired that we used the semaphores in two completely different ways. The difference is so marked that, looking back, one wonders whether it was really fair to present the two ways as uses of the very same primitives. On the one hand, we have the semaphores used for mutual exclusion, on the other hand, the private semaphores.

28.7.2   Mutual exclusion   In the following program we indicate two parallel, cyclic processes (between the brackets "**parbegin**" and "**parend**") that come into action after the surrounding universe has been introduced and initialized.

```
begin semaphore mutex; mutex := 1;
   parbegin
      begin
         L1 : P(mutex); critical section 1; V(mutex); remainder of cycle 1; go to L1;
      end;
      begin
         L2 : P(mutex); critical section 2; V(mutex); remainder of cycle 2; go to L2;
      end;
   parend
end
```

As a result of the *P*- and *V*-operations on "mutex" the actions, marked as "critical sections" exclude each other mutually in time; the scheme given allows straightforward extension to more than two parallel processes, the maximum value of mutex equals 1, the minimum value equals $-(n-1)$ if we have n parallel processes.

Critical sections are used always, and only for the purpose of unambiguous inspection and modification of the state variables (allocated in the surrounding universe) that describe the current state of the system (as far as needed for the regulation of the harmonious cooperation between the various processes).

28.7.3   Private semaphores   Each sequential process has associated with it a number of private semaphores and no other process will ever perform a *P*-operation on them. The universe initializes them with the value equal to 0, their maximum value equals 1, and their mininum value equals -1.

Whenever a process reaches a stage where the permission for dynamic progress depends on current values of state variables, it follows the pattern:

P(mutex) ;

"inspection and modification of state variables
      including a conditional *V*(private semaphore)";

V(mutex);

P(private semaphore).

If the inspection learns that the process in question should continue, it performs the operation "*V*(private semaphore)"—the semaphore value then changes from 0 to 1—otherwise, this *V*-operation is skipped, leaving to the other processes the obligation to perform this *V*-operation at a suitable moment. The absence or presence of this obligation is reflected in the final values of the state variables upon leaving the critical section.

Whenever a process reaches a stage where as a result of its progress possibly one (or more) blocked processes should now get permission to continue, it follows the pattern:

P(mutex);

"modification and inspection of state variables including zero or more *V*-operations on private sema-phores of other processes";

V(mutex).

By the introduction of suitable state variables and appropriate programming of the critical sections any strategy assigning peripherals, buffer areas, etc. can be implemented.

The amount of coding and reasoning can be greatly reduced by the observation that in the two complementary critical sections sketched above the same inspection can be performed by the introduction of the notion of "an unstable situation," such as a free reader and a process needing a reader. Whenever an unstable situation emerges it is removed (including one or more *V*-operations on private semaphores) in the very same critical section in which it has been created.

28.7.4   Proving the harmonious cooperation   The sequential processes in the system can all be regarded as cyclic processes in which a certain neutral point can be marked, the so-called "homing position," in which all processes are when the system is at rest.

When a cyclic process leaves its homing position "it accepts a task"; when the task has been performed and not earlier, the process returns to its homing position. Each cyclic process has a specific task processing power (e.g. the execution of a user program or unbuffering a portion of printer output, etc.).

The harmonious cooperation is mainly proved in roughly three stages.

1. It is proved that although a process performing a task may in so doing generate a finite number of tasks for other processes, a single initial task cannot give rise to an infinite number of task generations. The proof is simple as processes can only generate tasks for processes at lower levels of the hierarchy so that circularity is excluded. (If a process needing a segment from the drum has generated a task for the segment controller, special precautions have been taken to ensure that the segment asked for remains in core at least until the requesting process has effectively accessed the segment concerned. Without this precaution finite tasks could be forced to generate an infinite number of tasks for the segment controller, and the system could get stuck in an unproductive page flutter.)

2. It is proved that it is impossible that all processes have returned to their homing position while somewhere in the system there is still pending a generated but unaccepted task. (This is proved via instability of the situation just described.)

3. It is proved that after the acceptance of an initial task all processes eventually will be (again) in their homing position. Each process blocked in the course of task execution relies on the other processes for removal of the barrier. Essentially, the proof in question is a demonstration of the absence of "circular waits": process *P* waiting for process *Q* waiting for process *R* waiting for process *P*. (Our usual term for the circular wait is "the Deadly Embrace.") . . .

29 Go To Statement Considered Harmful (1968)

Edsger Dijkstra

The movement toward "structured programming" did not happen all at once. It evolved as the software industry matured: compilers got better, so programmers were less motivated to write tricky code in order to save a few compute steps or a few bytes of program memory; and systems got bigger, so teams were more motivated to write comprehensible code with easily explained modular structure. Early processors lacked stack operations. By 1968 recursion was no longer exotic and was architecturally supported, and looping structures like **while** were becoming common in programming languages (this paper was published about the time Wirth was designing the PASCAL language).

So as Edsger Dijkstra (see chapter 26) acknowledges, this article—actually a mere "Letter to the Editor"—is less a scientific contribution than a summary statement of an ongoing movement, accompanied by a call to action. Be that as it may, the piece had a profound effect on programming practice—the words "structured programming" appeared in hundreds of article and book titles over the next decade. Like other calls to orthodoxy, Dijkstra's letter drew some opposition, or at least pleas for flexibility. Donald Knuth (1974a) documented that some things really were easier to say with **go to**s and suggested that structured programming could coexist with **go to** statements. But by and large, Dijkstra's argument won the day, by shifting the way programming was taught and by setting minimum conditions on the linguistic structures in programming languages.

One textual note: The phrase "considered harmful," now widely imitated by computer scientists, was not Dijkstra's. The editor, Niklaus Wirth, supplied the title when he decided to publish this note (originally entitled "A Case Against the GOTO Statement") as a letter rather than as a research paper. And the formula was not original with Wirth either; it was already a journalistic convention when this paper was published (Laplante, 1996, p. 420).

Reprinted from Dijkstra (1968a), with permission from the Association for Computing Machinery.

E DITOR: For a number of years I have been familiar with the observation that the quality of programmers is a decreasing function of the density of **go to** statements in the programs they produce. More recently I discovered why the use of the **go to** statement has such disastrous effects, and I became convinced that the **go to** statement should be abolished from all "higher level" programming languages (i.e., everything except, perhaps, plain machine code). At that time I did not attach too much importance to this discovery; I now submit my considerations for publication because in very recent discussions in which the subject turned up, I have been urged to do so.

My first remark is that, although the programmer's activity ends when he has constructed a correct program, the process taking place under control of his program is the true subject matter of his activity, for it is this process that has to accomplish the desired effect; it is this process that in its dynamic behavior has to satisfy the desired specifications. Yet, once the program has been made, the "making" of the corresponding process is delegated to the machine.

My second remark is that our intellectual powers are rather geared to master static relations and that our powers to visualize processes evolving in time are relatively poorly developed. For that reason we should do (as wise programmers aware of our limitations) our utmost to shorten the conceptual gap between the static program and the dynamic process, to make the correspondence between the program (spread out in text space) and the process (spread out in time) as trivial as possible.

Let us now consider how we can characterize the progress of a process. (You may think about this question in a very concrete manner: suppose that a process, considered as a time succession of actions, is stopped after an arbitrary action, what data do we have to fix in order that we can redo the process until the very same point?) If the program text is a pure concatenation of, say, assignment statements (for the purpose of this discussion regarded as the descriptions of single actions) it is sufficient to point in the program text to a point between two successive action descriptions. (In the absence of **go to** statements I can permit myself the syntactic ambiguity in the last three words of the previous sentence: if we parse them as "successive (action descriptions)" we mean successive in text space; if we parse as "(successive action) descriptions" we mean successive in time.) Let us call such a pointer to a suitable place in the text a "textual index."

When we include conditional clauses (**if** B **then** A), alternative clauses (**if** B **then** $A1$ **else** $A2$), choice clauses as introduced by C. A. R. Hoare (case[i] of $(A1, A2, \ldots, An)$), or conditional expressions as introduced by J. McCarthy ($B1 \rightarrow E1, B2 \rightarrow E2, \ldots, Bn \rightarrow En$), the fact remains that the progress of the process remains characterized by a single textual index.

As soon as we include in our language procedures we must admit that a single textual index is no longer sufficient. In the case that a textual index points to the interior of a procedure body the dynamic progress is only characterized when we also give to which call of the procedure we refer. With the inclusion of procedures we can characterize the progress of the process via a sequence of textual indices, the length of this sequence being equal to the dynamic depth of procedure calling.

Let us now consider repetition clauses (like, **while** B **repeat** A or **repeat** A **until** B). Logically speaking, such clauses are now superfluous, because we can express repetition with the aid of recursive procedures. For reasons of realism I don't wish to exclude them: on the one hand, repetition clauses can be implemented quite comfortably with present day finite equipment; on the other hand, the reasoning pattern known as "induction" makes us well equipped to retain our intellectual grasp on the processes generated by repetition clauses. With the inclusion of the repetition clauses textual indices are no longer sufficient to describe the dynamic progress of the process. With each entry into a repetition clause, however, we can associate a so-called "dynamic index," inexorably counting the ordinal number of the corresponding current repetition. As repetition clauses (just as procedure calls) may be applied nestedly, we find that now the progress of the process can always be uniquely characterized by a (mixed) sequence of textual and/or dynamic indices.

The main point is that the values of these indices are outside programmer's control; they are generated (either by the write-up of his program or by the dynamic evolution of the process) whether he wishes or not. They provide independent coordinates in which to describe the progress of the process. Why do we need such independent coordinates? The reason is—and this seems to be inherent to sequential processes—that we can interpret the value of a variable only with respect to the progress of the process. If we wish to count the number, n say, of people in an initially empty room, we can achieve this by increasing n by one whenever we see someone entering the room. In the in-between moment that we have observed someone entering the room but have not yet performed the subsequent increase of n, its value equals the number of people in the room minus one!

The unbridled use of the **go to** statement has an immediate consequence that it becomes terribly hard to find a meaningful set of coordinates in which to describe the process progress. Usually, people take into account as well the values of some well chosen variables, but this is out of the question because it is relative to the progress that the meaning of these values is to be understood! With the **go to** statement one can, of course, still describe the progress uniquely by a counter counting the number of actions performed since program start (viz. a kind of normalized clock). The difficulty is that such a coordinate, although unique, is utterly unhelpful. In such a coordinate system it becomes an extremely complicated affair to define all those points of progress where, say, n equals the number of persons in the room minus one!

The **go to** statement as it stands is just too primitive; it is too much an invitation to make a mess of one's program. One can regard and appreciate the clauses considered as bridling its use. I do not claim that the clauses mentioned are exhaustive in the sense that they will satisfy all needs, but whatever clauses are suggested (e.g. abortion clauses) they should satisfy the requirement that a programmer independent coordinate system can be maintained to describe the process in a helpful and manageable way.

It is hard to end this with a fair acknowledgment. Am I to judge by whom my thinking has been influenced? It is fairly obvious that I am not uninfluenced by Peter Landis and Christopher

Strachey. Finally I should like to record (as I remember it quite distinctly) how Heinz Zemanek at the pre-ALGOL meeting in early 1959 in Copenhagen quite explicitly expressed his doubts whether the **go to** statement should be treated on equal syntactic footing with the assignment statement. To a modest extent I blame myself for not having then drawn the consequences of his remark.

The remark about the undesirability of the **go to** statement is far from new. I remember having read the explicit recommendation to restrict the use of the **go to** statement to alarm exits, but I have not been able to trace it; presumably, it has been made by C. A. R. Hoare. Wirth and Hoare (1966, §3.21) make a remark in the same direction in motivating the case construction: "Like the conditional, it mirrors the dynamic structure of a program more clearly than **go to** statements and switches, and it eliminates the need for introducing a large number of labels in the program."

Böhm and Jacopini (1966) seem to have proved the (logical) superfluousness of the **go to** statement. The exercise to translate an arbitrary flow diagram more or less mechanically into a jumpless one, however, is not to be recommended. Then the resulting flow diagram cannot be expected to be more transparent than the original one.

30 Gaussian Elimination is Not Optimal (1969)

Volker Strassen

Matrix multiplication is such a simple operation that it is hard to imagine there is anything left to learn about it. To multiply two $n \times n$ matrices A and B and get an $n \times n$ product matrix C, compute the n^2 dot products of rows of A with columns of B. Each of those dot products involves n multiplications of numbers and $n-1$ additions, for a total of n^3 number multiplications and $n^2(n-1)$ additions. What else could there be to say?

A great deal, it turns out. The German mathematician Volker Strassen (b. 1936) may have been trying to prove a lower bound, that n^3 multiplications are necessary as well as sufficient, when he discovered this algorithm. The paper entails two remarkable ideas. The first is that a divide-and-conquer, recursive algorithm might beat the conventional algorithm, if there is a way to compute the product of 2×2 matrices with fewer than 8 multiplications. Even after seeing this proved, it still seems surprising that the overhead of implementing the recursion is asymptotically repaid. The other amazing discovery is that two 2×2 matrices can be multiplied with only 7 multiplications. Any high school student might have figured that out scribbling on a pad of paper between classes; in the centuries that people have been multiplying matrices, nobody noticed because nobody had a reason to try. (An analogous algorithm for integer multiplication, due to Karatsuba and Ofman (1962), was already known. It recursively computes the product of two $2n$-bit numbers by three multiplications of n-bit numbers, thus yielding a $O(n^{\log_2 3}) \approx n^{1.58}$ time algorithm for n-bit multiplications, better than the conventional $\Theta(n^2)$ algorithm.)

Strassen's algorithm is tricky to implement both correctly and efficiently, but its utility under a good implementation is not merely theoretical. The discovery that $n \times n$ matrices can be multiplied using $n^{\log_2 7} \approx n^{2.8}$ multiplications led to the still unsolved problem of how much smaller the exponent can be. As of this writing, the answer is no more than 2.373, but no lower bound greater than 2 is known; these more exotic algorithms are not practically useful, however.

This paper, alongside Karatsuba and Ofman (1962), established the divide-and-conquer technique as a tool for a variety of algorithmic problems. The implications for efficiently solving systems of linear equations—which give the paper its title—are remarkable in their own right.

———————

Reprinted from Strassen (1969), with permission from Springer.

30.1

$\mathbf{B}$ELOW we will give an algorithm which computes the coefficients of the product of two square matrices A and B of order n from the coefficients of A and B with less than $4.7 \cdot n^{\log 7}$ arithmetical operations (all logarithms in this paper are for base 2, thus $\log 7 \approx 2.8$; the usual method requires approximately $2n^3$ arithmetical operations). The algorithm induces algorithms for inverting a matrix of order n, solving a system of n linear equations in n unknowns, computing a determinant of order n etc. all requiring less than const $n^{\log 7}$ arithmetical operations.

This fact should be compared with the result of Klyuev and Kokovkin-Shcherbak (1965) that Gaussian elimination for solving a system of linear equations is optimal if one restricts oneself to operations upon rows and columns as a whole. We also note that Winograd (1968) modifies the usual algorithms for matrix multiplication and inversion and for solving systems of linear equations, trading roughly half of the multiplications for additions and subtractions. It is a pleasure to thank D. Brillinger for inspiring discussions about the present subject and S. Cook and B. Parlett for encouraging me to write this paper.

30.2

We define algorithms $\alpha_{m,k}$ which multiply matrices of order $m2^k$, by induction on k: $\alpha_{m,0}$ is the usual algorithm for matrix multiplication (requiring m^3 multiplications and $m^2(m-1)$ additions). $\alpha_{m,k}$ already being known, define $\alpha_{m,k+1}$ as follows:

If A, B are matrices of order $m2^{k+1}$ to be multiplied, write

$$A = \begin{pmatrix} A_{11} & A_{12} \\ A_{21} & A_{22} \end{pmatrix}, \ B = \begin{pmatrix} B_{11} & B_{12} \\ B_{21} & B_{22} \end{pmatrix}, \ C = \begin{pmatrix} C_{11} & C_{12} \\ C_{21} & C_{22} \end{pmatrix},$$

where the A_{ik}, B_{ik}, C_{ik} are matrices of order $m2^k$. Then compute

$$I = (A_{11} + A_{22})(B_{11} + B_{22}),$$
$$II = (A_{21} + A_{22})B_{11},$$
$$III = A_{11}(B_{12} - B_{22}),$$
$$IV = A_{22}(-B_{11} + B_{21}),$$
$$V = (A_{11} + A_{12})B_{22},$$
$$VI = (-A_{11} + A_{21})(B_{11} + B_{12}),$$
$$VII = (A_{12} - A_{22})(B_{21} + B_{22}),$$
$$C_{11} = I + IV - V + VII,$$
$$C_{21} = II + IV,$$
$$C_{12} = III + V,$$
$$C_{22} = I + III - II + VI,$$

using α_{mk} for multiplication and the usual algorithm for addition and subtraction of matrices of order $m2^k$.

By induction on k one easily sees

Fact 1. $\alpha_{m,k}$ computes the product of two matrices of order $m2^k$ with $m^3 7^k$ multiplications and $(5+m)m^2 7^k - 6(m2^k)^2$ additions and subtractions of numbers.

Thus one may multiply two matrices of order 2^k with 7^k number multiplications and less than $6 \cdot 7^k$ additions and subtractions.

Fact 2. The product of two matrices of order n may be computed with $< 4.7n^{\log 7}$ arithmetical operations.

Proof. Put $k = \lfloor \log n - 4 \rfloor$, $m = \lfloor n2^{-k} \rfloor + 1$; then $n \le m2^k$. Imbedding matrices of order n into matrices of order $m2^k$ reduces our task to that of estimating the number of operations of $\alpha_{m,k}$. By Fact 1 this number is

$$(5 + 2m)m^2 7^k - 6(m2^k)^2$$
$$< (5 + 2(n2^{-k} + 1))(n2^{-k} + 1)^2 7^k$$
$$< 2n^3(7/8)^k + 12.03n^2(7/4)^k \quad \text{(here we have used } 16 \cdot 2^k \le n)$$
$$= (2(8/7)^{\log n - k} + 12.03(4/7)^{\log n - k})n^{\log 7}$$
$$\le \max_{4 \le t \le 5}(2(8/7)^t + 12.03(4/7)^t)n^{\log 7}$$
$$\le 4.7 \cdot n^{\log 7}$$

by a convexity argument.

We now turn to matrix inversion. To apply the algorithms below it is necessary to assume not only that the matrix is invertible but that all occurring divisions make sense (a similar assumption is of course necessary for Gaussian elimination).

We define algorithms $\beta_{m,k}$ which invert matrices of order $m2^k$, by induction on k: $\beta_{m,0}$ is the usual Gaussian elimination algorithm. $\beta_{m,k}$ already being known, define $\beta_{m,k+1}$ as follows:

If A is a matrix of order $m2^{k+1}$ to be inverted, write

$$A = \begin{pmatrix} A_{11} & A_{12} \\ A_{21} & A_{22} \end{pmatrix}, \quad A^{-1} = \begin{pmatrix} C_{11} & C_{12} \\ C_{21} & C_{22} \end{pmatrix},$$

where the A_{ik}, C_{ik} are matrices of order $m2^k$. Then compute

$$I = A_{11}^{-1},$$
$$II = A_{21} \cdot I,$$
$$III = I \cdot A_{12},$$
$$IV = A_{21} \cdot III,$$
$$V = IV - A_{22},$$
$$VI = V^{-1},$$
$$C_{12} = III \cdot VI,$$
$$C_{21} = VI \cdot II,$$
$$VII = III \cdot C_{21},$$
$$C_{11} = I - VII,$$
$$C_{22} = -VI$$

using $\alpha_{m,k}$ for multiplication, $\beta_{m,k}$ for inversion and the usual algorithm for addition or subtraction of two matrices of order $m2^k$.

By induction on k one easily sees

Fact 3. $\beta_{m,k}$ computes the inverse of a matrix of order $m2^k$ with $m2^k$ divisions, $\leq \frac{6}{5}m^3 7^k - m2^k$ multiplications and $\leq \frac{6}{5}(5 + m)m^2 7^k - 7(m2^k)^2$ additions and subtractions of numbers. The next Fact follows in the same way as Fact 2.

Fact 4. The inverse of a matrix of order n may be computed with $< 5.64 \cdot n^{\log 7}$ arithmetical operations.

Similar results hold for solving a system of linear equations or computing a determinant (use $\det A = (\det A_{11}) \det(A_{22} - A_{21}A_{11}^{-1}A_{12})$).

31 An Axiomatic Basis for Computer Programming (1969)

C. A. R. Hoare

C. A. R. "Tony" Hoare (b. 1934) was recognized with the Turing Award in 1980 "for his fundamental contributions to the definition and design of programming languages" (Hoare, 1981). This selection presents his most influential contribution: the ambition to formalize Dijkstra's insistence that computer programming was a branch of mathematical reasoning, and to fulfill the agenda of John McCarthy (1963): "Instead of debugging a program, one should prove that it meets its specifications, and this proof should be checked by a computer program."

Hoare had been educated at Oxford, where he studied modern analytic philosophy and thereby became familiar with mathematical logic. He joined the British computer company Elliott Brothers, and there led the team responsible for building a compiler for the ALGOL 60 programming language. That experience brought him in contact with Edsger Dijkstra and the importance of languages in which programming concepts could be expressed elegantly and concisely. In 1968 he took up a position as professor at Queen's University, Belfast. There he read Robert Floyd's paper "Assigning meanings to programs" (Floyd, 1967), which described a way of attaching invariant predicates to the edges of a flowchart in such a way that the behavior of a program could be subjected to rigorous analysis. Hoare determined to get rid of the flowchart notation and attach the invariants directly to the program statements, thus making a complete logical analysis imaginable.

Hoare spent the maturity of his career on difficult problems in the programming of concurrent systems, and on the design of language systems to make such programs easier to write and to verify. But his name will also be long associated with the Quicksort algorithm, an easy-to-implement sorting algorithm that uses recursion in a surprising way. This formulation of Quicksort (Hoare, 1962) was another byproduct of Hoare's ALGOL 60 experience. By making recursion easy to express, the language made apparent the structure of the algorithm.

Formal program verification has had its ups and downs since Hoare's seminal paper. It is now a standard tool in the production of low-level code, which can be all but unreadable by humans and correspondingly difficult to understand and reason about. In its more ambitious forms it has excited strong antipathy (see chapter 44). Later, still advocating for formal methods in programming, Hoare acknowledged that he had been too sanguine about the prospects for correctness proofs of large systems (Hoare, 1996). "Ten years ago, researchers into formal methods (and I was the most mistaken among them) predicted that the programming world would embrace with

Reprinted from Hoare (1969), with permission from the Association for Computing Machinery.

gratitude every assistance promised by formalisation to solve the problems of reliability that arise when programs get large and more safety-critical," he wrote. "Programs have now got very large and very critical—well beyond the scale which can be comfortably tackled by formal methods. There have been many problems and failures, but these have nearly always been attributable to inadequate analysis of requirements or inadequate management control. It has turned out that the world just does not suffer significantly from the kind of problem that our research was originally intended to solve."

Although he was at Queen's University in Belfast when he wrote this paper, Hoare spent most of his career as professor at Oxford. He was knighted in the year 2000.

——————◦◦⟨⟩◦◦——————

IN this paper an attempt is made to explore the logical foundations of computer programming by use of techniques which were first applied in the study of geometry and have later been extended to other branches of mathematics. This involves the elucidation of sets of axioms and rules of inference which can be used in proofs of the properties of computer programs. Examples are given of such axioms and rules, and a formal proof of a simple theorem is displayed. Finally, it is argued that important advantages, both theoretical and practical, may follow from a pursuance of these topics.

31.1 Introduction

Computer programming is an exact science in that all the properties of a program and all the consequences of executing it in any given environment can, in principle, be found out from the text of the program itself by means of purely deductive reasoning. Deductive reasoning involves the application of valid rules of inference to sets of valid axioms. It is therefore desirable and interesting to elucidate the axioms and rules of inference which underlie our reasoning about computer programs. The exact choice of axioms will to some extent depend on the choice of programming language. For illustrative purposes, this paper is confined to a very simple language, which is effectively a subset of all current procedure-oriented languages.

31.2 Computer Arithmetic

The first requirement in valid reasoning about a program is to know the properties of the elementary operations which it invokes, for example, addition and multiplication of integers. Unfortunately, in several respects computer arithmetic is not the same as the arithmetic familiar to mathematicians, and it is necessary to exercise some care in selecting an appropriate set of axioms. For example, the axioms displayed in Figure 31.1 are rather a small selection of axioms relevant to integers. From this incomplete set of axioms it is possible to deduce such simple

A1	$x + y = y + x$	addition is commutative	A7	$x + 0 = x$
A2	$x \times y = y \times x$	multiplication is commutative	A8	$x \times 0 = 0$
A3	$(x + y) + z = x + (y + z)$	addition is associative	A9	$x \times 1 = x$
A4	$(x \times y) \times z = x \times (y \times z)$	multiplication is associative		
A5	$x \times (y + z) = x \times y + x \times z$	multiplication distributes through addition		
A6	$y \leq x \supset (x - y) + y = x$	addition cancels subtraction		

Figure 31.1

theorems as:

$$x = x + y \times 0$$
$$y \leq r \supset r + y \times q = (r - y) + y \times (1 + q)$$

The proof of the second of these is:

$$(r - y) + y \times (1 + q) = (r - y) + (y \times 1 + y \times q) \qquad \text{(A5)}$$
$$= (r - y) + (y + y \times q) \qquad \text{(A9)}$$
$$= ((r - y) + y) + y \times q \qquad \text{(A3)}$$
$$= r + y \times q \text{ provided } y \leq r \qquad \text{(A6)}$$

The axioms A1 to A9 are, of course, true of the traditional infinite set of integers in mathematics. However, they are also true of the finite sets of "integers" which are manipulated by computers provided that they are confined to nonnegative numbers. Their truth is independent of the size of the set; furthermore, it is largely independent of the choice of technique applied in the event of "overflow"; for example:

1. Strict interpretation: the result of an overflowing operation does not exist; when overflow occurs, the offending program never completes its operation. Note that in this case, the equalities of A1 to A9 are strict, in the sense that both sides exist or fail to exist together.

2. Firm boundary: the result of an overflowing operation is taken as the maximum value represented.

3. Modulo arithmetic: the result of an overflowing operation is computed modulo the size of the set of integers represented.

These three techniques are illustrated in Figure 31.2 by addition and multiplication tables for a trivially small model in which 0, 1, 2, and 3 are the only integers represented.

It is interesting to note that the different systems satisfying axioms A1 to A9 may be rigorously distinguished from each other by choosing a particular one of a set of mutually exclusive supplementary axioms. For example, infinite arithmetic satisfies the axiom:

$$\neg \exists x \forall y \, (y \leq x), \qquad \text{(A10}_I\text{)}$$

where all finite arithmetics satisfy:

$$\forall x\,(x \le \max) \tag{A10$_F$}$$

where "max" denotes the largest integer represented.

Similarly, the three treatments of overflow may be distinguished by a choice of one of the following axioms relating to the value of max + 1:

$\neg\exists x\,(x = \max + 1)$	(strict interpretation)	(A11$_S$)
$\max + 1 = \max$	(firm boundary)	(A11$_B$)
$\max + 1 = 0$	(modulo arithmetic)	(A11$_M$)

Having selected one of these axioms, it is possible to use it in deducing the properties of programs; however, these properties will not necessarily obtain, unless the program is executed on an implementation which satisfies the chosen axiom.

31.3   Program Execution

As mentioned above, the purpose of this study is to provide a logical basis for proofs of the properties of a program. One of the most important properties of a program is whether or not it carries out its intended function. The intended function of a program, or part of a program, can be specified by making general assertions about the values which the relevant variables will take after execution of the program. These assertions will usually not ascribe particular values to each variable, but will rather specify certain general properties of the values and the relationships holding between them. We use the normal notations of mathematical logic to express these assertions, and the familiar rules of operator precedence have been used wherever possible to improve legibility.

In many cases, the validity of the results of a program (or part of a program) will depend on the values taken by the variables before that program is initiated. These initial preconditions of successful use can be specified by the same type of general assertion as is used to describe the results obtained on termination. To state the required connection between a precondition (P), a program (Q) and a description of the result of its execution (R), we introduce a new notation:

$$P\{Q\}R.$$

This may be interpreted "If the assertion P is true before initiation of a program Q, then the assertion R will be true on its completion." If there are no preconditions imposed, we write **true**$\{Q\}R$.

The treatment given below is essentially due to Floyd (1967) but is applied to texts rather than flowcharts.

31.3.1   Axiom of assignment   Assignment is undoubtedly the most characteristic feature of programming a digital computer, and one that most clearly distinguishes it from other branches of mathematics. It is surprising therefore that the axiom governing our reasoning about assignment is quite as simple as any to be found in elementary logic. Consider the assignment statement: $x := f$ where

> x is an identifier for a simple variable;
>
> f is an expression of a programming language without side effects, but possibly containing x.

Now any assertion $P(x)$ which is to be true of (the value of) x after the assignment is made must also have been true of (the value of) the expression f, taken *before* the assignment is made, i.e. with the old value of x. Thus if $P(x)$ is to be true after the assignment, then $P(f)$ must be true before the assignment. This fact may be expressed more formally:

D0 Axiom of Assignment

$$\vdash P_0\{x := f\}P$$

where

> x is a variable identifier;
>
> f is an expression;
>
> P_0 is obtained from P by substituting f for all occurrences of x.

+	0	1	2	3		×	0	1	2	3
0	0	1	2	3		0	0	0	0	0
1	1	2	3	*		1	0	1	2	3
2	2	3	*	*		2	0	2	*	*
3	3	*	*	*		3	0	3	*	*

Strict Interpretation

+	0	1	2	3		×	0	1	2	3
0	0	1	2	3		0	0	0	0	0
1	1	2	3	3		1	0	1	2	3
2	2	3	3	3		2	0	2	3	3
3	3	3	3	3		3	0	3	3	3

Firm Boundary

+	0	1	2	3		×	0	1	2	3
0	0	1	2	3		0	0	0	0	0
1	1	2	3	0		1	0	1	2	3
2	2	3	0	1		2	0	2	0	2
3	3	0	1	2		3	0	3	2	1

Modulo Arithmetic

Figure 31.2

It may be noticed that D0 is not really an axiom at all, but rather an axiom schema, describing an infinite set of axioms which share a common pattern. This pattern is described in purely syntactic terms, and it is easy to check whether any finite text conforms to the pattern, thereby qualifying as an axiom, which may validly appear in any line of a proof.

31.3.2 Rules of consequence In addition to axioms, a deductive science requires at least one rule of inference, which permits the deduction of new theorems from one or more axioms or theorems already proved. A rule of inference takes the form "If $\vdash X$ and $\vdash Y$ then $\vdash Z$," i.e. if assertions of the form X and Y have been proved as theorems, then Z also is thereby proved as a theorem. The simplest example of an inference rule states that if the execution of a program Q ensures the truth of the assertion R, then it also ensures the truth of every assertion logically implied by R. Also, if P is known to be a precondition for a program Q to produce result R, then so is any other assertion which logically implies P. These rules may be expressed more formally:

D1 Rules of Consequence

$$\text{If } \vdash P\{Q\}R \text{ and } \vdash R \supset S \text{ then } \vdash P\{Q\}S$$
$$\text{If } \vdash P\{Q\}R \text{ and } \vdash S \supset P \text{ then } \vdash S\{Q\}R$$

31.3.3   Rules of composition   A program generally consists of a sequence of statements which are executed one after another. The statements may be separated by a semicolon or equivalent symbol denoting procedural composition: $(Q_1; Q_2; \cdots ; Q_n)$. In order to avoid the awkwardness of dots, it is possible to deal initially with only two statements $(Q_1; Q_2)$, since longer sequences can be reconstructed by nesting, thus $(Q_1; (Q_2; (\cdots (Q_{n-1}; Q_n) \cdots)))$. The removal of the brackets of this nest may be regarded as convention based on the associativity of the ";-operator," in the same way as brackets are removed from an arithmetic expression $(t_1 + (t_2 + (\cdots (t_{n-1} + t_n) \cdots)))$.

The inference rule associated with composition states that if the proven result of the first part of a program is identical with the precondition under which the second part of the program produces its intended result, then the whole program will produce the intended result, provided that the precondition of the first part is satisfied.

In more formal terms:

D2 Rule of Composition

If $\vdash P\{Q_1\}R_1$ and $\vdash R_1\{Q_2\}R$ then $\vdash P\{(Q_1; Q_2)\}R$

31.3.4   Rule of iteration   The essential feature of a stored program computer is the ability to execute some portion of program (S) repeatedly until a condition (B) goes false. A simple way of expressing such an iteration is to adapt the ALGOL 60 **while** notation:

$$\textbf{while } B \textbf{ do } S$$

In executing this statement, a computer first tests the condition B. If this is false, S is omitted, and execution of the loop is complete. Otherwise, S is executed and B is tested again. This action is repeated until B is found to be false. The reasoning which leads to a formulation of an inference rule for iteration is as follows. Suppose P to be an assertion which is always true on completion of S, provided that it is also true on initiation. Then obviously P will still be true after any number of iterations of the statement S (even no iterations). Furthermore, it is known that the controlling condition B is false when the iteration finally terminates. A slightly more powerful formulation is possible in light of the fact that B may be assumed to be true on initiation of S:

D3 Rule of Iteration

$$\text{If } \vdash P \wedge B\{S\}P \text{ then } \vdash P\{\textbf{while } B \textbf{ do } S\}\neg B \wedge P$$

31.3.5   Example   The axioms quoted above are sufficient to construct the proof of properties of simple programs, for example, a routine intended to find the quotient q and remainder r obtained on dividing x by y. All variables are assumed to range over a set of nonnegative integers conforming to the axioms listed in Figure 31.1. For simplicity we use the trivial but inefficient method of successive subtraction. The proposed program is:

$$((r := x; q := 0); \; \textbf{while} \; y \le r \; \textbf{do} \; (r := r - y; q := 1 + q))$$

An important property of this program is that when it terminates, we can recover the numerator x by adding to the remainder r the product of the divisor y and the quotient q (i.e. $x = r + y \times q$). Furthermore, the remainder is less than the divisor. These properties may be expressed formally:

$$\textbf{true}\{Q\}\neg y \le r \wedge x = r + y \times q$$

where Q stands for the program displayed above. This expresses a necessary (but not sufficient) condition for the "correctness" of the program.

A formal proof of this theorem is given [EDITOR: in an omitted figure]. Like all formal proofs, it is excessively tedious, and it would be fairly easy to introduce notational conventions which would significantly shorten it. An even more powerful method of reducing the tedium of formal proofs is to derive general rules for proof construction out of the simple rules accepted as postulates. These general rules would be shown to be valid by demonstrating how every theorem proved with their assistance could equally well (if more tediously) have been proved without. Once a powerful set of supplementary rules has been developed, a "formal proof" reduces to little more than an informal indication of how a formal proof could be constructed.

31.4   General Reservations

The axioms and rules of inference quoted in this paper have implicitly assumed the absence of side effects of the evaluation of expressions and conditions. In proving properties of programs expressed in a language permitting side effects, it would be necessary to prove their absence in each case before applying the appropriate proof technique. If the main purpose of a high level programming language is to assist in the construction and verification of correct programs, it is doubtful whether the use of functional notation to call procedures with side effects is a genuine advantage. Another deficiency in the axioms and rules quoted above is that they give no basis for a proof that a program successfully terminates. Failure to terminate may be due to an infinite loop; or it may be due to violation of an implementation-defined limit, for example, the range of numeric operands, the size of storage, or an operating system time limit. Thus the notation "$P\{Q\}R$" should be interpreted "provided that the program successfully terminates, the properties of its results are described by R." It is fairly easy to adapt the axioms so that they cannot be used to predict the "results" of nonterminating programs; but the actual use of the axioms would now depend on knowledge of many implementation-dependent features, for example, the size and speed of the computer, the range of numbers, and the choice of overflow technique. Apart from proofs of the avoidance of infinite loops, it is probably better to prove the "conditional" correctness of a program and rely on an implementation to give a warning if it has had to abandon execution of the program as a result of violation of an implementation limit.

Finally it is necessary to list some of the areas which have not been covered: for example, real arithmetic, bit and character manipulation, complex arithmetic, fractional arithmetic, arrays, records, overlay definition, files, input/output, declarations, subroutines, parameters, recursion, and parallel execution. Even the characterization of integer arithmetic is far from complete. There does not appear to be any great difficulty in dealing with these points, provided that the programming language is kept simple. Areas which do present real difficulty are labels and jumps, pointers, and name parameters. Proofs of programs which made use of these features are likely to be elaborate, and it is not surprising that this should be reflected in the complexity of the underlying axioms.

31.5   Proofs of Program Correctness

The most important property of a program is whether it accomplishes the intentions of its user. If these intentions can be described rigorously by making assertions about the values of variables at the end (or at intermediate points) of the execution of the program, then the techniques described in this paper may be used to prove the correctness of the program, provided that the implementation of the programming language conforms to the axioms and rules which have been used in the proof. This fact itself might also be established by deductive reasoning, using an axiom set which describes the logical properties of the hardware circuits. When the correctness of a program, its compiler, and the hardware of the computer have all been established with mathematical certainty, it will be possible to place great reliance on the results of the program, and predict their properties with a confidence limited only by the reliability of the electronics.

The practice of supplying proofs for nontrivial programs will not become widespread until considerably more powerful proof techniques become available, and even then will not be easy. But the practical advantages of program proving will eventually outweigh the difficulties, in view of the increasing costs of programming error. At present, the method which a programmer uses to convince himself of the correctness of his program is to try it out in particular cases and to modify it if the results produced do not correspond to his intentions. After he has found a reasonably wide variety of example cases on which the program seems to work, he believes that it will always work. The time spent in this program testing is often more than half the time spent on the entire programming project; and with a realistic costing of machine time, two thirds (or more) of the cost of the project is involved in removing errors during this phase.

The cost of removing errors discovered after a program has gone into use is often greater, particularly in the case of items of computer manufacturer's software for which a large part of the expense is borne by the user. And finally, the cost of error in certain types of program may be almost incalculable—a lost spacecraft, a collapsed building, a crashed aeroplane, or a world war. Thus the practice of program proving is not only a theoretical pursuit, followed in the interests of academic respectability, but a serious recommendation for the reduction of the costs associated with programming error.

The practice of proving programs is likely to alleviate some of the other problems which afflict the computing world. For example, there is the problem of program documentation, which is essential, firstly, to inform a potential user of a subroutine how to use it and what it accomplishes, and secondly, to assist in further development when it becomes necessary to update a program to meet changing circumstances or to improve it in the light of increased knowledge. The most rigorous method of formulating the purpose of a subroutine, as well as the conditions of its proper use, is to make assertions about the values of variables before and after its execution. The proof of the correctness of these assertions can then be used as a lemma in the proof of any program which calls the subroutine. Thus, in a large program, the structure of the whole can be clearly mirrored in the structure of its proof. Furthermore, when it becomes necessary to modify a program, it will always be valid to replace any subroutine by another which satisfies the same criterion of correctness. Finally, when examining the detail of the algorithm, it seems probable that the proof will be helpful in explaining not only what is happening but *why*.

Another problem which can be solved, insofar as it is soluble, by the practice of program proofs is that of transferring programs from one design of computer to another. Even when written in a so-called machine-independent programming language, many large programs inadvertently take advantage of some machine-dependent property of a particular implementation, and unpleasant and expensive surprises can result when attempting to transfer it to another machine. However, presence of a machine-dependent feature will always be revealed in advance by the failure of an attempt to prove the program from machine-independent axioms. The programmer will then have the choice of formulating his algorithm in a machine-independent fashion, possibly with the help of environment enquiries; or if this involves too much effort or inefficiency, he can deliberately construct a machine-dependent program, and rely for his proof on some machine-dependent axiom, for example, one of the versions of A11 (page 300). In the latter case, the axiom must be explicitly quoted as one of the preconditions of successful use of the program. The program can still, with complete confidence, be transferred to any other machine which happens to satisfy the same machine-dependent axiom; but if it becomes necessary to transfer it to an implementation which does not, then all the places where changes are required will be clearly annotated by the fact that the proof at that point appeals to the truth of the offending machine-dependent axiom.

Thus the practice of proving programs would seem to lead to solution of three of the most pressing problems in software and programming, namely, reliability, documentation, and compatibility. However, program proving, certainly at present, will be difficult even for programmers of high caliber; and may be applicable only to quite simple program designs. As in other areas, reliability can be purchased only at the price of simplicity.

31.6 Formal Language Definition

A high level programming language, such as ALGOL, FORTRAN, or COBOL, is usually intended to be implemented on a variety of computers of differing size, configuration, and design. It has been found a serious problem to define these languages with sufficient rigour to ensure compatibility among all implementors. Since the purpose of compatibility is to facilitate interchange of programs expressed in the language, one way to achieve this would be to insist that all implementations of the language shall "satisfy" the axioms and rules of inference which underlie proofs of the properties of programs expressed in the language, so that all predictions based on these proofs will be fulfilled, except in the event of hardware failure. In effect, this is equivalent to accepting the axioms and rules of inference as the ultimately definitive specification of the meaning of the language.

Apart from giving an immediate and possibly even provable criterion for the correctness of an implementation, the axiomatic technique for the definition of programming language semantics appears to be like the formal syntax of the ALGOL 60 report, in that it is sufficiently simple to be understood both by the implementor and by the reasonably sophisticated user of the language. It is only by bridging this widening communication gap in a single document (perhaps even provably consistent) that the maximum advantage can be obtained from a formal language definition.

Another of the great advantages of using an axiomatic approach is that axioms offer a simple and flexible technique for leaving certain aspects of a language undefined, for example, range of integers, accuracy of floating point, and choice of overflow technique. This is absolutely essential for standardization purposes, since otherwise the language will be impossible to implement efficiently on differing hardware designs. Thus a programming language standard should consist of a set of axioms of universal applicability, together with a choice from a set of supplementary axioms describing the range of choices facing an implementor. An example of the use of axioms for this purpose was given in §31.2.

Another of the objectives of formal language definition is to assist in the design of better programming languages. The regularity, clarity, and ease of implementation of the ALGOL 60 syntax may at least in part be due to the use of an elegant formal technique for its definition. The use of axioms may lead to similar advantages in the area of "semantics," since it seems likely that a language which can be described by a few "self-evident" axioms from which proofs will be relatively easy to construct will be preferable to a language with many obscure axioms which are difficult to apply in proofs. Furthermore, axioms enable the language designer to express his general intentions quite simply and directly, without the mass of detail which usually accompanies algorithmic descriptions. Finally, axioms can be formulated in a manner largely independent of each other, so that the designer can work freely on one axiom or group of axioms without fear of unexpected interaction effects with other parts of the language. ...

32 A Relational Model of Large Shared Data Banks (1970)

Edgar F. Codd

It is common in academic circles to think that the science of computing is about algorithms. But in business, computing has always been about data. Of course the two perspectives are not opposed, but the world looks very different from a data-oriented view than from an algorithm-oriented view. A database scientist told me that data was the ocean, deep, eternal, and mysterious, and algorithms were just boats skimming its surface.

Until the 1960s, most practical applications of computers were for computing numbers—either values of mathematical functions (such as the tables generated by Aiken's Mark I) or parameters of physical phenomena (astronomical calculations, for example, or the predicted behavior of an atom bomb). Of course any calculation involving physical phenomena requires numerical data, but early computers did not have enough storage to process large amounts of it. The scientific interest in computing was driven by the need to perform numerical calculations, plus the extraordinary discovery by Church and Turing of the ontology of algorithms. Turing's remarkable codebreaking work at Bletchley Park was an exercise of logic and carefully controlled combinatorial search driven by very small amounts of data (intercepted encrypted messages).

Certainly Vannevar Bush had foreseen the importance of large-scale data manipulation ("Selection devices ... will soon be speeded up from their present rate of reviewing data at a few hundred a minute," page 115). Howard Aiken and Grace Hopper anticipated the importance of business applications, and the International Business Machines Corporation, which had grown out of companies supplying tabulating machines for the U.S. Census, came to dominate the business market for computers. Starting in the mid-1960s, IBM developed a database product to manage inventory for the Apollo space program. The data model of this system, known originally as IMS, drew ultimately on graph theory: mechanical parts had sub-parts, and the same sub-parts might be used in several different larger assemblies, so the connection between data entities resembled the links connecting nodes of a directed graph.

The quantity of data managed by such systems steadily grew, and it became clear that the way data were described and queried need not correspond to the memory structures used to store it. In much the same way as compilers had made it possible to abstract the statement of algorithms from the particulars of the machine code that executed them, there was a need to talk about data with some formal clarity, leaving to computer systems themselves the problem of optimally organizing the data in physical devices for most effective storage and retrieval.

Reprinted from Codd (1970), with permission from the Association for Computing Machinery.

For Edgar Frank Codd (1923–2003), the way to talk about data was to use a language derived from the predicate calculus. Data was to be organized as relations. A relation is a set of *n*-tuples, for example a set of ordered triples or ordered quadruples, where each position or "column" contains data of a particular type. The relation can be depicted as a table, with one *n*-tuple per row, but the order of the rows in the table is semantically irrelevant because the *n*-tuples are logically a set.

In this seminal paper Codd worked out the basics of the relational view of data, and most importantly, developed a relational algebra for combining relations. Codd spent much of his career with IBM, and this work emerged from his frustration that existing database systems entangled the database's logical structure (and thus the logic of programs accessing the database) with its internal "physical" representation. IBM welcomed Codd's innovations only tepidly, perhaps because a successful relational database system would compete with existing IBM products, so Codd left to start his own firm. Research implementations of the relational database model began to appear later in the 1970s, with IBM's System R and the Ingres system of Michael Stonebraker at Berkeley. Oracle Corporation, Tandem Computers, Stonebraker's Relational Technology Inc., and IBM all released commercial implementations between 1979 and 1981, establishing the model as a *de facto* standard. The model and the associated data management language SQL are now ubiquitous, and Codd was recognized with the Turing award for his contribution.

—◦◦◯⟋⟋◯◦◦—

32.1   Relational Model and Normal Form

THIS paper is concerned with the application of elementary relation theory to systems which provide shared access to large banks of formatted data. Except for a paper by Childs (1968), the principal application of relations to data systems has been to deductive question-answering systems. Levien and Maron (1967) provide numerous references to work in this area.

In contrast, the problems treated here are those of data *independence*—the independence of application programs and terminal activities from growth in data types and changes in data representation—and certain kinds of data *inconsistency* which are expected to become troublesome even in nondeductive systems.

The relational view (or model) of data described in §32.1 appears to be superior in several respects to the graph or network model (Bachman, 1965; McGee, 1969) presently in vogue for non-inferential systems. It provides a means of describing data with its natural structure only—that is, without superimposing any additional structure for machine representation purposes. Accordingly, it provides a basis for a high level data language which will yield maximal independence between programs on the one hand and machine representation and organization of data on the other.

A further advantage of the relational view is that it forms a sound basis for treating derivability, redundancy, and consistency of relations—these are discussed in §32.2. The network model, on the other hand, has spawned a number of confusions, not the least of which is mistaking the derivation of connections for the derivation of relations ....

Finally, the relational view permits a clearer evaluation of the scope and logical limitations of present formatted data systems, and also the relative merits (from a logical standpoint) of competing representations of data within a single system. Examples of this clearer perspective are cited in various parts of this paper. Implementations of systems to support the relational model are not discussed.

32.1.2   Data dependencies in present systems   The provision of data description tables in recently developed information systems represents a major advance toward the goal of data independence (IBM, 1965b,a; Bleier, 1967; IDS, 1968). Such tables facilitate changing certain characteristics of the data representation stored in a data bank. However, the variety of data representation characteristics which can be changed without logically impairing some application programs is still quite limited. Further, the model of data with which users interact is still cluttered with representational properties, particularly in regard to the representation of collections of data (as opposed to individual items). Three of the principal kinds of data dependencies which still need to be removed are: ordering dependence, indexing dependence, and access path dependence. In some systems these dependencies are not clearly separable from one another.

32.1.2.1   Ordering dependence   Elements of data in a data bank may be stored in a variety of ways, some involving no concern for ordering, some permitting each element to participate in one ordering only, others permitting each element to participate in several orderings. Let us consider those existing systems which either require or permit data elements to be stored in at least one total ordering which is closely associated with the hardware-determined ordering of addresses. For example, the records of a file concerning parts might be stored in ascending order by part serial number. Such systems normally permit application programs to assume that the order of presentation of records from such a file is identical to (or is a subordering of) the stored ordering. Those application programs which take advantage of the stored ordering of a file are likely to fail to operate correctly if for some reason it becomes necessary to replace that ordering by a different one. Similar remarks hold for a stored ordering implemented by means of pointers.

It is unnecessary to single out any system as an example, because all the well-known information systems that are marketed today fail to make a clear distinction between order of presentation on the one hand and stored ordering on the other. Significant implementation problems must be solved to provide this kind of independence.

32.1.2.2   Indexing dependence   In the context of formatted data, an index is usually thought of as a purely performance-oriented component of the data representation. It tends to improve response to queries and updates and, at the same time, slow down response to insertions and deletions. From an informational standpoint, an index is a redundant component of the data representation. If a system uses indices at all and if it is to perform well in an environment with changing patterns of activity on the data bank, an ability to create and destroy indices from time

File	Segment	Fields
F	PART	part #
		part name
		part description
		quantity-on-hand
		quantity-on-order
	PROJECT	project #
		project name
		project description
		quantity committed

Figure 32.1: Structure 1. Projects subordinate to parts

File	Segment	Fields
F	PROJECT	project #
		project name
		project description
	PART	part #
		part name
		part description
		quantity-on-hand
		quantity-on-order
		quantity committed

Figure 32.2: Structure 2. Parts subordinate to projects

to time will probably be necessary. The question then arises: Can application programs and terminal activities remain invariant as indices come and go?

Present formatted data systems take widely different approaches to indexing. TDMS (Bleier, 1967) unconditionally provides indexing on all attributes. The presently released version of IMS (IBM, 1965b) provides the user with a choice for each file: a choice between no indexing at all (the hierarchic sequential organization) or indexing on the primary key only (the hierarchic indexed sequential organization). In neither case is the user's application logic dependent on the existence of the unconditionally provided indices. IDS, however, permits the file designers to select attributes to be indexed and to incorporate indices into the file structure by means of additional chains. Application programs taking advantage of the performance benefit of these indexing chains must refer to those chains by name. Such programs do not operate correctly if these chains are later removed.

32.1.2.3   Access path dependence   Many of the existing formatted data systems provide users with tree-structured files or slightly more general network models of the data. Application programs developed to work with these systems tend to be logically impaired if the trees or networks are changed in structure. A simple example follows.

Suppose the data bank contains information about parts and projects. For each part, the part number, part name, part description, quantity-on-hand, and quantity-on-order are recorded. For each project, the project number, project name, project description are recorded. Whenever a project makes use of a certain part, the quantity of that part committed to the given project is also recorded. Suppose that the system requires the user or file designer to declare or define the data in terms of tree structures. Then, any one of the hierarchical structures may be adopted for the information mentioned above (see Structures 1–5, Figures 32.1–32.5).

Now, consider the problem of printing out the part number, part name, and quantity committed for every part used in the project whose project name is "alpha." The following observations may be made regardless of which available tree-oriented information system is selected to tackle this problem. If a program P is developed for this problem assuming one of the five structures above—that is, P makes no test to determine which structure is in effect—then P will fail on at least three of the remaining structures. More specifically, if P succeeds with structure 5, it will

File	Segment	Fields
F	PART	part #
		part name
		part description
		quantity-on-hand
		quantity-on-order
G	PROJECT	project #
		project name
		project description
	PART	part #
		quantity committed

Figure 32.3: Structure 3. Parts and projects as peers, commitment relationship subordinate to projects

File	Segment	Fields
F	PART	part #
		part description
		quantity-on-hand
		quantity-on-order
	PROJECT	project #
		quantity committed
G	PROJECT	project #
		project name
		project description

Figure 32.4: Structure 4. Parts and projects as peers, commitment relationship subordinate to parts

fail with all the others; if *P* succeeds with structure 3 or 4, it will fail with at least 1, 2, and 5; if *P* succeeds with 1 or 2, it will fail with at least 3, 4, and 5. The reason is simple in each case. In the absence of a test to determine which structure is in effect, *P* fails because an attempt is made to execute a reference to a nonexistent file (available systems treat this as an error) or no attempt is made to execute a reference to a file containing needed information. The reader who is not convinced should develop sample programs for this simple problem.

Since, in general, it is not practical to develop application programs which test for all tree structurings permitted by the system, these programs fail when a change in structure becomes necessary.

Systems which provide users with a network model of the data run into similar difficulties. In both the tree and network cases, the user (or his program) is required to exploit a collection of user access paths to the data. It does not matter whether these paths are in close correspondence with pointer-defined paths in the stored representation—in IDS the correspondence is extremely simple, in TDMS it is just the opposite. The consequence, regardless of the stored representation, is that terminal activities and programs become dependent on the continued existence

File	Segment	Fields
F	PART	part #
		part name
		part description
		quantity-on-hand
		quantity-on-order
G	PROJECT	project #
		project name
		project description
H	COMMIT	part #
		project #
		quantity committed

Figure 32.5: Structure 5. Parts, projects, and commitment relationship as peers

of the user access paths. One solution to this is to adopt the policy that once a user access path is defined it will not be made obsolete until all application programs using that path have become obsolete. Such a policy is not practical, because the number of access paths in the total model for the community of users of a data bank would eventually become excessively large.

32.1.3   A relational view of data   The term *relation* is used here in its accepted mathematical sense. Given sets $S_1, S_2, \ldots, S_n$ (not necessarily distinct), R is a relation on these n sets if it is a set of *n*-tuples each of which has its first element from S_1, its second element from S_2, and so on. We shall refer to S_j as the jth *domain* of R. As defined above, R is said to have *degree n*. Relations of degree 1 are often called *unary*, degree 2 *binary*, degree 3 *ternary*, and degree n *n-ary*.

For expository reasons, we shall frequently make use of an array representation of relations, but it must be remembered that this particular representation is not an essential part of the relational view being expounded. An array which represents an *n*-ary relation R has the following properties:

1. Each row represents an *n*-tuple of R.
2. The ordering of rows is immaterial.
3. All rows are distinct.
4. The ordering of columns is significant—it corresponds to the ordering S_1, S_2, ..., S_n of the domains on which R is defined (see, however, remarks below on domain-ordered and domain-unordered relations).
5. The significance of each column is partially conveyed by labeling it with the name of the corresponding domain.

The example in Figure 32.6 illustrates a relation of degree 4, called *supply*, which reflects the shipments-in-progress of parts from specified suppliers to specified projects in specified quantities.

supply	(supplier	part	project	quantity)
	1	2	5	17
	1	3	5	23
	2	3	7	9
	2	7	5	4
	4	1	1	12

Figure 32.6: A relation of degree 4

One might ask: If the columns are labeled by the name of corresponding domains, why should the ordering of columns matter? As the example in Figure 32.7 shows, two columns may have identical headings (indicating identical domains) but possess distinct meanings with respect to the relation. The relation depicted is called *component*. It is a ternary relation, whose first two domains are called part and third domain is called *quantity*. The meaning of *component* (x, y, z) is that part x is an immediate component (or subassembly) of part y, and z units of part x are needed to assemble one unit of part y. It is a relation which plays a critical role in the parts explosion problem.

It is a remarkable fact that several existing information systems (chiefly those based on tree-structured files) fail to provide data representations for relations which have two or more identical domains. The present version of IMS/360 (IBM, 1965b) is an example of such a system.

The totality of data in a data bank may be viewed as a collection of time-varying relations. These relations are of assorted degrees. As time progresses, each *n*-ary relation may be subject to insertion of additional *n*-tuples, deletion of existing ones, and alteration of components of any of its existing *n*-tuples.

In many commercial, governmental, and scientific data banks, however, some of the relations are of quite high degree (a degree of 30 is not at all uncommon). Users should not normally be burdened with remembering the domain ordering of any relation (for example, the ordering *supplier*, then *part*, then *project*, then *quantity* in the relation *supply*). Accordingly, we propose that users deal, not with relations which are domain-ordered, but with *relationships* which are their domain-unordered counterparts. (In mathematical terms, a relationship is an equivalence class of those relations that are equivalent under permutation of domains (see §32.2.1.1).) To accomplish this, domains must be uniquely identifiable at least within any given relation, without using position. Thus, where there are two or more identical domains, we require in each case that the domain name be qualified by a distinctive *role name*, which serves to identify the role played by that domain in the given relation. For example, in the relation *component* of Figure 32.7, the first domain *part* might be qualified by the role name *sub*, and the second by *super*, so that users could deal with the relationship *component* and its domains—*sub.part*, *super.part*, *quantity*—without regard to any ordering between these domains.

To sum up, it is proposed that most users should interact with a relational model of the data consisting of a collection of time-varying relationships (rather than relations). Each user need not know more about any relationship than its name together with the names of its domains (role qualified whenever necessary). (Naturally, as with any data put into and retrieved from a computer system, the user will normally make far more effective use of the data if he is aware of its meaning.) Even this information might be offered in menu style by the system (subject to security and privacy constraints) upon request by the user.

component	(*part*	*part*	*quantity*)
	1	5	9
	2	5	7
	3	5	2
	2	6	12
	3	6	3
	4	7	1
	6	7	1

Figure 32.7: A relation with two identical domains

There are usually many alternative ways in which a relational model may be established for a data bank. In order to discuss a preferred way (or normal form), we must first introduce a few additional concepts (active domain, primary key, foreign key, nonsimple domain) and establish some links with terminology currently in use in information systems programming. In the remainder of this paper, we shall not bother to distinguish between relations and relationships except where it appears advantageous to be explicit.

Consider an example of a data bank which includes relations concerning parts, projects, and suppliers. One relation called *part* is defined on the following domains:

1. part number
2. part name
3. part color
4. part weight
5. quantity on hand
6. quantity on order

and possibly other domains as well. Each of these domains is, in effect, a pool of values, some or all of which may be represented in the data bank at any instant. While it is conceivable that, at some instant, all part colors are present, it is unlikely that all possible part weights, part names, and part numbers are. We shall call the set of values represented at some instant the *active domain* at that instant.

Normally, one domain (or combination of domains) of a given relation has values which uniquely identify each element (*n*-tuple) of that relation. Such a domain (or combination) is called a *primary key*. In the example above, part number would be a primary key, while part color would not be. A primary key is *nonredundant* if it is either a simple domain (not a combination) or a combination such that none of the participating simple domains is superfluous in uniquely identifying each element. A relation may possess more than one nonredundant primary key. This would be the case in the example if different parts were always given distinct names. Whenever a relation has two or more nonredundant primary keys, one of them is arbitrarily selected and called *the* primary key of that relation.

A common requirement is for elements of a relation to cross-reference other elements of the same relation or elements of a different relation. Keys provide a user-oriented means (but not the only means) of expressing such cross-references. We shall call a domain (or domain combination) of relation *R* a *foreign key* if it is not the primary key of *R* but its elements are values of the primary key of some relation *S* (the possibility that *S* and *R* are identical is not excluded). In the relation *supply* of Figure 32.6, the combination of *supplier*, *part*, *project* is the primary key, while each of these three domains taken separately is a foreign key.

In previous work there has been a strong tendency to treat the data in a data bank as consisting of two parts, one part consisting of entity descriptions (for example, descriptions of suppliers) and the other part consisting of relations between the various entities or types of entities (for example, the *supply* relation). This distinction is difficult to maintain when one may have foreign keys in any relation whatsoever. In the user's relational model there appears to be no advantage to making such a distinction (there may be some advantage, however, when one applies relational concepts to machine representations of the user's set of relationships).

So far, we have discussed examples of relations which are defined on simple domains— domains whose elements are atomic (nondecomposable) values. Nonatomic values can be discussed within the relational framework. Thus, some domains may have relations as elements. These relations may, in turn, be defined on nonsimple domains, and so on. For example, one of the domains on which the relation *employee* is defined might be *salary history*. An element of the salary history domain is a binary relation defined on the domain *date* and the domain *salary*. The *salary history* domain is the set of all such binary relations. At any instant of time there are as many instances of the *salary history* relation in the data bank as there are employees. In contrast, there is only one instance of the *employee* relation.

The terms attribute and repeating group in present data base terminology are roughly analogous to simple domain and nonsimple domain, respectively. Much of the confusion in present

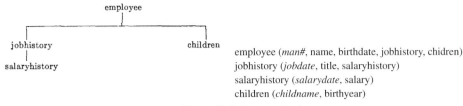

employee (*man#*, name, birthdate, jobhistory, chidren)
jobhistory (*jobdate*, title, salaryhistory)
salaryhistory (*salarydate*, salary)
children (*childname*, birthyear)

Figure 32.8: Unnormalized set

terminology is due to failure to distinguish between type and instance (as in "record") and between components of a user model of the data on the one hand and their machine representation
counterparts on the other hand (again, we cite "record" as an example).

32.1.4   Normal form   A relation whose domains are all simple can be represented in storage
by a two-dimensional column-homogeneous array of the kind discussed above. Some more complicated data structure is necessary for a relation with one or more nonsimple domains. For this
reason (and others to be cited below) the possibility of eliminating nonsimple domains appears
worth investigating. There is, in fact, a very simple elimination procedure, which we shall call
normalization.

Consider, for example, the collection of relations exhibited in Figure 32.8. *Job history* and
children are nonsimple domains of the relation *employee*. *Salary history* is a nonsimple domain
of the relation *job history*. The tree in Figure 32.8 shows just these interrelationships of the
nonsimple domains.

Normalization proceeds as follows. Starting with
the relation at the top of the tree, take its primary
key and expand each of the immediately subordinate relations by inserting this primary key domain or domain combination. The primary key of
each expanded relation consists of the primary key
before expansion augmented by the primary key

employee' (*man#*, name, birthdate)
jobhistory' (*man#*, *jobdate*, title)
salaryhistory' (*man#*, *jobdate*, *salarydate*, salary)
children' (*man#*, *childname*, birthyear)

Figure 32.9: Normalized set

copied down from the parent relation. Now, strike out from the parent relation all nonsimple
domains, remove the top node of the tree, and repeat the same sequence of operations on each
remaining subtree.

The result of normalizing the collection of relations in Figure 32.8 is the collection in Figure 32.9. The primary key of each relation is italicized to show how such keys are expanded by
the normalization.

If normalization as described above is to be applicable, the unnormalized collection of relations
must satisfy the following conditions:

1. The graph of interrelationships of the nonsimple domains is a collection of trees.
2. No primary key has a component domain which is nonsimple.

The writer knows of no application which would require any relaxation of these conditions. Further operations of a normalizing kind are possible. These are not discussed in this paper.

The simplicity of the array representation which becomes feasible when all relations are cast in normal form is not only an advantage for storage purposes but also for communication of bulk data between systems which use widely different representations of the data. The communication form would be a suitably compressed version of the array representation and would have the following advantages:

1. It would be devoid of pointers (address-valued or displacement-valued).
2. It would avoid all dependence on hash addressing schemes.
3. It would contain no indices or ordering lists.

If the user's relational model is set up in normal form, names of items of data in the data bank can take a simpler form than would otherwise be the case. A general name would take a form such as

$$R(g).r.d$$

where R is a relational name; g is a generation identifier (optional); r is a role name (optional); d is a domain name. Since g is needed only when several generations of a given relation exist, or are anticipated to exist, and r is needed only when the relation R has two or more domains named d, the simple form $R.d$ will often be adequate.

32.1.5   Some linguistic aspects   The adoption of a relational model of data, as described above, permits the development of a universal data sublanguage based on an applied predicate calculus. A first-order predicate calculus suffices if the collection of relations is in normal form. Such a language would provide a yardstick of linguistic power for all other proposed data languages, and would itself be a strong candidate for embedding (with appropriate syntactic modification) in a variety of host languages (programming, command- or problem-oriented). While it is not the purpose of this paper to describe such a language in detail, its salient features would be as follows.

Let us denote the data sublanguage by R and the host language by H. R permits the declaration of relations and their domains. Each declaration of a relation identifies the primary key for that relation. Declared relations are added to the system catalog for use by any members of the user community who have appropriate authorization. H permits supporting declarations which indicate, perhaps less permanently, how these relations are represented in storage. R permits the specification for retrieval of any subset of data from the data bank. Action on such a retrieval request is subject to security constraints.

The universality of the data sublanguage lies in its descriptive ability (not its computing ability). In a large data bank each subset of the data has a very large number of possible (and sensible) descriptions, even when we assume (as we do) that there is only a finite set of function subroutines to which the system has access for use in qualifying data for retrieval. Thus, the class of qualification expressions which can be used in a set specification must have the descriptive power of the class of well-formed formulas of an applied predicate calculus. It is well known that to preserve this descriptive power it is unnecessary to express (in whatever syntax is chosen) every formula of the selected predicate calculus. For example, just those in prenex normal form are adequate (Church, 1956).

Arithmetic functions may be needed in the qualification or other parts of retrieval statements. Such functions can be defined in H and invoked in R.

A set so specified may be fetched for query purposes only, or it may be held for possible changes. Insertions take the form of adding new elements to declared relations without regard to any ordering that may be present in their machine representation. Deletions which are effective for the community (as opposed to the individual user or sub-communities) take the form of removing elements from declared relations. Some deletions and updates may be triggered by others, if deletion and update dependencies between specified relations are declared in R.

One important effect that the view adopted toward data has on the language used to retrieve it is in the naming of data elements and sets. Some aspects of this have been discussed in the previous section. With the usual network view, users will often be burdened with coining and using more relation names than are absolutely necessary, since names are associated with paths (or path types) rather than with relations.

Once a user is aware that a certain relation is stored, he will expect to be able to exploit it using any combination of its arguments as "knowns" and the remaining arguments as "unknowns," because the information (like Everest) is there. This is a system feature (missing from many current information systems) which we shall call (logically) *symmetric exploitation* of relations. Naturally, symmetry in performance is not to be expected.

To support symmetric exploitation of a single binary relation, two directed paths are needed. For a relation of degree n, the number of paths to be named and controlled is n factorial.

Again, if a relational view is adopted in which every n-ary relation ($n > 2$) has to be expressed by the user as a nested expression involving only binary relations (see Feldman's LEAP System [Feldman and Rovner, 1968], for example) then $2n - 1$ names have to be coined instead of only $n + 1$ with direct n-ary notation as described in §32.1.2. For example, the 4-ary relation supply of Figure 32.6, which entails 5 names in n-ary notation, would be represented in the form

$$P(supplier, Q(part, R(project, quantity)))$$

in nested binary notation and, thus, employ 7 names.

A further disadvantage of this kind of expression is its asymmetry. Although this asymmetry does not prohibit symmetric exploitation, it certainly makes some bases of interrogation very awkward for the user to express (consider, for example, a query for those parts and quantities related to certain given projects via Q and R).

32.1.6   Expressible, named, and stored relations   Associated with a data bank are two collections of relations: the *named set* and the *expressible set*. The named set is the collection of all those relations that the community of users can identify by means of a simple name (or identifier). A relation R acquires membership in the named set when a suitably authorized user declares R; it loses membership when a suitably authorized user cancels the declaration of R.

The expressible set is the total collection of relations that can be designated by expressions in the data language. Such expressions are constructed from simple names of relations in the named set; names of generations, roles and domains; logical connectives; the quantifiers of the predicate calculus; and certain constant relation symbols such as =, >. The named set is a subset of the expressible set—usually a very small subset.

Since some relations in the named set may be time-independent combinations of others in that set, it is useful to consider associating with the named set a collection of statements that define these time-independent constraints. We shall postpone further discussion of this until we have introduced several operations on relations (see §32.2).

One of the major problems confronting the designer of a data system which is to support a relational model for its users is that of determining the class of stored representations to be supported. Ideally, the variety of permitted data representations should be just adequate to cover the spectrum of performance requirements of the total collection of installations. Too great a variety leads to unnecessary overhead in storage and continual reinterpretation of descriptions for the structures currently in effect.

For any selected class of stored representations the data system must provide a means of translating user requests expressed in the data language of the relational model into corresponding—and efficient—actions on the current stored representation. For a high level data language this presents a challenging design problem. Nevertheless, it is a problem which must be solved—as more users obtain concurrent access to a large data bank, responsibility for providing efficient response and throughput shifts from the individual user to the data system.

32.2   Redundancy and Consistency

32.2.1   Operations on relations   Since relations are sets, all of the usual set operations are applicable to them. Nevertheless, the result may not be a relation; for example, the union of a binary relation and a ternary relation is not a relation.

The operations discussed below are specifically for relations. These operations are introduced because of their key role in deriving relations from other relations. Their principal application is in noninferential information systems—systems which do not provide logical inference services—although their applicability is not necessarily destroyed when such services are added.

Most users would not be directly concerned with these operations. Information systems designers and people concerned with data bank control should, however, be thoroughly familiar with them.

32.2.1.1   Permutation   A binary relation has an array representation with two columns. Interchanging these columns yields the converse relation. More generally, if a permutation is applied to the columns of an n-ary relation, the resulting relation is said to be a *permutation* of the given relation. There are, for example, 4! = 24 permutations of the relation *supply* in Figure 32.6, if we include the identity permutation which leaves the ordering of columns unchanged.

Since the user's relational model consists of a collection of relationships (domain-unordered relations), permutation is not relevant to such a model considered in isolation. It is, however, relevant to the consideration of stored representations of the model. In a system which provides symmetric exploitation of relations, the set of queries answerable by a stored relation is identical to the set answerable by any permutation of that relation. Although it is logically unnecessary to store both a relation and some permutation of it, performance considerations could make it advisable.

32.2.1.2   Projection   Suppose now we select certain columns of a relation (striking out the others) and then remove from the resulting array any duplication in the rows. The final array represents a relation which is said to be a *projection* of the given relation.

A selection operator π is used to obtain any desired permutation, projection, or combination of the two operations. Thus, if L is a list of indices $L = i_1, i_2, \ldots, i_k$ and R is an n-ary relation $(n \geq k)$, then $\pi_L(R)$ is the k-ary relation whose j^{th} column is column i_j of R ($j = 1, 2, \ldots, k$) except that duplication in resulting rows is removed. Consider the relation *supply* of Figure 32.6. A permuted projection of this relation is exhibited in Figure 32.10. Note that, in this particular case, the projection has fewer n-tuples than the relation from which it is derived.

32.2.1.3   Join   Suppose we are given two binary relations, which have some domain in common. Under what circumstances can we combine these relations to form a ternary relation which preserves all of the information in the given relations?

The example in Figure 32.11 shows two relations R, S, which are joinable without loss of information, while Figure 32.12 shows a join of R with S. A binary relation R is *joinable* with a binary relation S if there exists a ternary relation U such that $\pi_{12}(U) = R$ and $\pi_{23}(U) = S$. Any such ternary relation is called a *join* of R with S. If R, S are binary relations such that $\pi_2(R) = \pi_1(S)$, then R is joinable with S. One join that always exists in such a case is the *natural join* of R with S defined by

$$R * S = \{(a, b, c) : R(a, b) \wedge S(b, c)\}$$

where $R(a, b)$ has the value *true* if (a, b) is a member of R and similarly for $S(b, c)$. It is immediate that

$$\pi_{12}(R * S) = R$$

and

$$\pi_{23}(R * S) = S.$$

Note that the join shown in Figure 32.12 is the natural join of R with S from Figure 32.11. Another join is shown in Figure 32.13.

Inspection of these relations reveals an element (element 1) of the domain *part* (the domain on which the join is to be made) with the property that it possesses more than one relative under R

$\Pi_{31}(supply)$	(*project*	*supplier*)
	5	1
	5	2
	1	4
	7	2

Figure 32.10: A permuted projection of the relation in Figure 32.6

R	(*supplier*	*part*)	S	(*part*	*project*)
	1	1		1	1
	2	1		1	2
	2	2		2	1

Figure 32.11: Two joinable relations

and also under S. It is this element which gives rise to the plurality of joins. Such an element in the joining domain is called a *point of ambiguity* with respect to the joining of R with S.

$R * S$	(*supplier*	*part*	*project*)
	1	1	1
	1	1	2
	2	1	1
	2	1	2
	2	2	1

Figure 32.12: The natural join of R with S (from Figure 32.11)

U	(*supplier*	*part*	*project*)
	1	1	2
	2	1	1
	2	2	1

Figure 32.13: Another join of R with S (from Figure 32.11)

If either $\pi_{21}(R)$ or S is a function, no point of ambiguity can occur in joining R with S. In such a case, the natural join of R with S is the only join of R with S. Note that the reiterated qualification "of R with S" is necessary, because S might be joinable with R (as well as R with S), and this join would be an entirely separate consideration. In Figure 32.11, none of the relations $R, \pi_{21}(R), S, \pi_{21}(S)$ is a function. . . .

32.2.2   Redundancy   . . .

32.2.3   Consistency   . . .

32.2.4   Summary   In §32.1 a relational model of data is proposed as a basis for protecting users of formatted data systems from the potentially disruptive changes in data representation caused by growth in the data bank and changes in traffic. A normal form for the time-varying collection of relationships is introduced.

In §32.2 operations on relations and two types of redundancy are defined and applied to the problem of maintaining the data in a consistent state. This is bound to become a serious practical problem as more and more different types of data are integrated together into common data banks. . . .

33 Managing the Development of Large Software Systems (1970)

Winston W. Royce

Winston Royce (1929–1995) was an aeronautical engineer by training and a software engineer in practice. From 1961 until 1994 he led software development projects in the aerospace industry, first at TRW and then at Lockheed. Like Fred Brooks (chapter 40), he drew on his experience developing large systems to develop practical guidance on how the process can be improved. This paper summarizes key ideas which he elaborated in later works.

Royce's ideas remain influential. Figures 33.1 and 33.2 gave rise to the term "waterfall model" for software development, referring to a protocol requiring each development stage to be completed before the next stage is begun, with no backing up and any problems discovered in later stages attributed to failed execution of earlier stages. However, Royce himself never uses the term "waterfall," and the paper plainly describes elements of what would today be called "iterative" or "agile" development methods, in which early implementations are provisional and used in order to refine the design.

Royce de-emphasizes coding and stresses design, analysis, and documentation; these ideas are resonant with Dijkstra's insistence on thinking logically and thoroughly about a program before writing any code. Royce has none of Dijkstra's mathematical stiffness; as the person responsible for delivering enormous systems to be used in critical aeronautical and aerospace systems, he could not have insisted on simplicity and elegance as the highest values. His commitment to thorough testing would not have impressed Dijkstra, who observed, correctly, that testing can only reveal errors, not establish correctness. Yet this paper is so full of useful wisdom that it has passed the test of time and remains good advice today.

33.1 Introduction

I am going to describe my personal views about managing large software developments. I have had various assignments during the past nine years, mostly concerned with the development of software packages for spacecraft mission planning, commanding and post-flight analysis. In these assignments I have experienced different degrees of success with respect to arriving at an operational state, on-time, and within costs. I have become prejudiced by my experiences and I am going to relate some of these prejudices in this presentation.

Reprinted from Royce (1970, 1987), with permission from the Institute of Electrical and Electronics Engineers.

33.2   Computer Program Development Functions

There are two essential steps common to all computer program developments, regardless of size or complexity. There is first an analysis step, followed second by a coding step as depicted in Figure 33.1. This sort of very simple implementation concept is in fact all that is required if the effort is sufficiently small and if the final product is to be operated by those who built it—as is typically done with computer programs for internal use. It is also the kind of development effort for which most customers are happy to pay, since both steps involve genuinely creative work which directly contributes to the usefulness of the final product. An implementation plan to manufacture larger software systems, and keyed only to these steps, however, is doomed to failure. Many additional development steps are required, none contribute as directly to the final product as analysis and coding, and all drive up the development costs. Customer personnel typically would rather not pay for them, and development personnel would rather not implement them. The prime function of management is to sell these concepts to both groups and then enforce compliance on the part of development personnel.

A more grandiose approach to software development is illustrated in Figure 33.2. The analysis and coding steps are still in the picture, but they are preceded by two levels of requirements analysis, are separated by a program design step, and followed by a testing step. These additions are treated separately from analysis and coding because they are distinctly different in the way they are executed. They must be planned and staffed differently for best utilization of program resources.

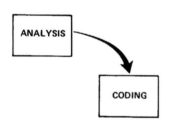

Figure 33.1: Implementation steps to deliver a small computer program for internal operations.

Figure 33.3 portrays the iterative relationship between successive development phases for this scheme. The ordering of steps is based on the following concept: that as each step progresses and the design is further detailed, there is an iteration with the preceding and succeeding steps but rarely with the more remote steps in the sequence. The virtue of all of this is that as the design proceeds the change process is scoped down to manageable limits. At any point in the design process after the requirements analysis is completed there exists a firm and closeup moving baseline to which to return in the event of unforeseen design difficulties. What we have is an effective fallback position that tends to maximize the extent of early work that is salvageable and preserved.

I believe in this concept, but the implementation described above is risky and invites failure. The problem is illustrated in Figure 33.4. The testing phase which occurs at the end of the development cycle is the first event for which timing, storage, input/output transfers, etc., are experienced as distinguished from analyzed. These phenomena are not precisely analyzable. They are not the solutions to the standard partial differential equations of mathematical physics for instance. Yet if these phenomena fail to satisfy the various external constraints, then invariably a

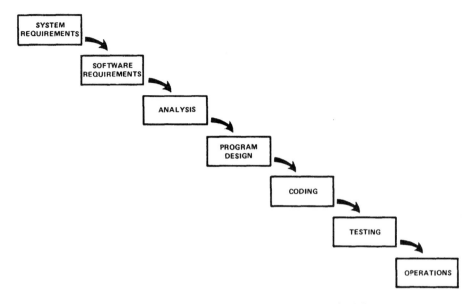

Figure 33.2: Implementation steps to develop a large computer program for delivery to a customer.

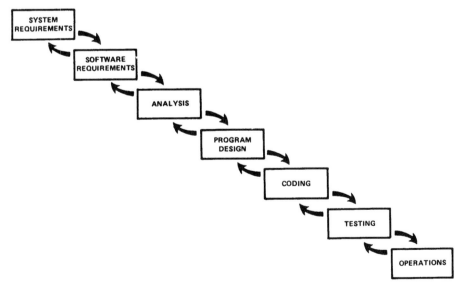

Figure 33.3: Hopefully, the iterative interaction between the various phases is confined to successive steps.

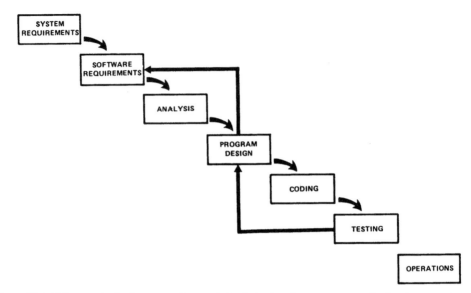

Figure 33.4: Unfortunately, for the process illustrated, the design iterations are never confined to the successive steps.

major redesign is required. A simple octal patch or redo of some isolated code will not fix these kinds of difficulties. The required design changes are likely to be so disruptive that the software requirements upon which the design is based and which provides the rationale for everything are violated. Either the requirements must be modified, or a substantial change in the design is required. In effect the development process has returned to the origin and one can expect up to a 100-percent overrun in schedule and/or costs.

One might note that there has been a skipping-over of the analysis and code phases. One cannot, of course, produce software without these steps, but generally these phases are managed with relative ease and have little impact on requirements, design, and testing. In my experience there are whole departments consumed with the analysis of orbit mechanics, spacecraft attitude determination, mathematical optimization of payload activity and so forth, but when these departments have completed their difficult and complex work, the resultant program steps involve a few lines of serial arithmetic code. If in the execution of their difficult and complex work the analysts have made a mistake, the correction is invariably implemented by a minor change in the code with no disruptive feedback into the other development bases.

However, I believe the illustrated approach to be fundamentally sound. The remainder of this discussion presents five additional features that must be added to this basic approach to eliminate most of the development risks.

33.3   Step 1: Program Design Comes First

The first step towards a fix is illustrated in Figure 33.5. A preliminary program design phase has been inserted between the software requirements generation phase and the analysis phase. This procedure can be criticized on the basis that the program designer is forced to design in the relative vacuum of initial software requirements without any existing analysis. As a result, his preliminary design may be substantially in error as compared to his design if he were to wait until the analysis was complete. This criticism is correct but it misses the point. By this technique the program designer assures that the software will not fail because of storage, timing, and data flux reasons. As the analysis proceeds in the succeeding phase the program designer must impose on the analyst the storage, timing, and operational constraints in such a way that he senses the consequences. When he justifiably requires more of this kind of resource in order to implement his equations it must be simultaneously snatched from his analyst compatriots. In this way all the analysts and all the program designers will contribute to a meaningful design process which will culminate in the proper allocation of execution time and storage resources. If the total resources to be applied are insufficient or if the embryo operational design is wrong it will be recognized at this earlier stage and the iteration with requirements and preliminary design can be redone before final design, coding and test commences. How is this procedure implemented? The following steps are required.

1. Begin the design process with program designers, not analysts or programmers.
2. Design, define and allocate the data processing modes even at the risk of being wrong. Allocate processing, functions, design the data base, define data base processing, allocate execution time, define interfaces and processing modes with the operating system, describe input and output processing, and define preliminary operating procedures.
3. Write an overview document that is understandable, informative and current. Each and every worker must have an elemental understanding of the system. At least one person must have a deep understanding of the system which comes partially from having had to write an overview document.

33.4   Step 2: Document the Design

At this point it is appropriate to raise the issue of—"how much documentation?" My own view is "quite a lot"; certainly more than most programmers, analysts, or program designers are willing to do if left to their own devices. The first rule of managing software development is ruthless enforcement of documentation requirements.

Occasionally I am called upon to review the progress of other software design efforts. My first step is to investigate the state of the documentation. If the documentation is in serious default my first recommendation is simple. Replace project management. Stop all activities not related to documentation. Bring the documentation up to acceptable standards. Management of software is simply impossible without a very high degree of documentation. As an example, let

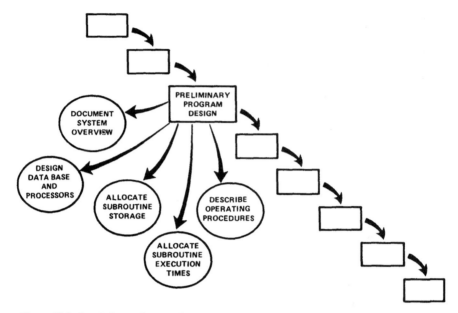

Figure 33.5: Step 1: Insure that a preliminary program design is complete before analysis begins.

me offer the following estimates for comparison. In order to procure a 5 million dollar hardware device, I would expect that a 30 page specification would provide adequate detail to control the procurement. In order to procure 5 million dollars of software I would estimate a 1500 page specification is about right in order to achieve comparable control.

Why so much documentation?

1. Each designer must communicate with interfacing designers, with his management and possibly with the customer. A verbal record is too intangible to provide an adequate basis for an interface or management decision. An acceptable written description forces the designer to take an unequivocal position and provide tangible evidence of completion. It prevents the designer from hiding behind the "I am 90-percent finished"-syndrome month after month.

2. During the early phase of software development the documentation *is* the specification and *is* the design. Until coding begins these three nouns (documentation, specification, design) denote a single thing. If the documentation is bad the design is bad. If the documentation does not yet exist there is as yet no design, only people thinking and talking about the design which is of some value, but not much.

3. The real monetary value of good documentation begins downstream in the development process during the testing phase and continues through operations and redesign. The value of documentation can be described in terms of three concrete, tangible situations that every program manager faces.

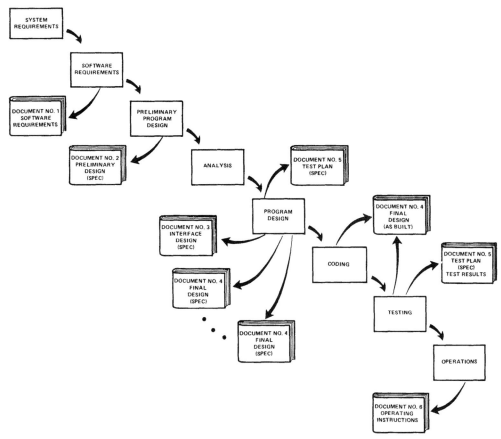

Figure 33.6: Step 2: Insure that documentation is current and complete—at least six uniquely different documents are required.

(a) During the testing phase, with good documentation the manager can concentrate personnel on the mistakes in the program. Without good documentation every mistake, large or
small, is analyzed by one man who probably made the mistake in the first place because
he is the only man who understands the program area.

(b) During the operational phase, with good documentation the manager can use operation-
oriented personnel to operate the program and to do a better job, cheaper. Without
good documentation the software must be operated by those who built it. Generally
these people are relatively disinterested in operations and do not do as effective a job
as operations-oriented personnel. It should be pointed out in this connection that in an
operational situation, if there is some hangup the software is always blamed first. In or-

der either to absolve the software or to fix the blame, the software documentation must speak clearly.

(c) Following initial operations, when system improvements are in order, good documentation permits effective redesign, updating, and retrofitting in the field. If documentation does not exist, generally the entire existing framework of operating software must be junked, even for relatively modest changes.

Figure 33.6 shows a documentation plan which is keyed to the steps previously shown. Note that six documents are produced, and at the time of delivery of the final product, Documents No. 1, No. 3, No. 4, No. 5, and No. 6 are updated and current.

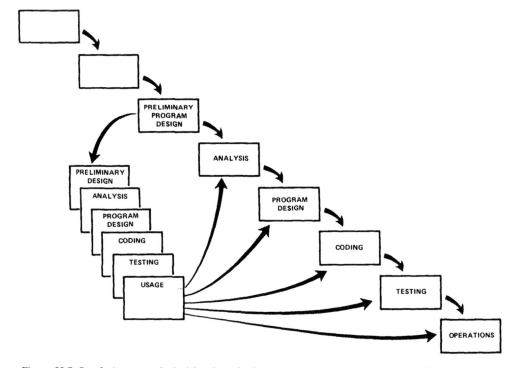

Figure 33.7: Step 3: Attempt to do the job twice—the first result provides an early simulation of the final product.

33.5   Step 3: Do It Twice

After documentation, the second most important criterion for success revolves around whether the product is totally original. If the computer program in question is being developed for the first time, arrange matters so that the version finally delivered to the customer for operational deployment is actually the second version insofar as critical design/operations areas are concerned.

Figure 33.7 illustrates how this might be carried out by means of a simulation. Note that it is simply the entire process done in miniature, to a time scale that is relatively small with respect to the overall effort. The nature of this effort can vary widely depending primarily on the overall time scale and the nature of the critical problem areas to be modeled. If the effort runs 30 months then this early development of a pilot model might be scheduled for 10 months. For this schedule, fairly formal controls, documentation procedures, etc., can be utilized. If, however, the overall effort were reduced to 12 months, then the pilot effort could be compressed to three months perhaps, in order to gain sufficient leverage on the mainline development. In this case a very special kind of broad competence is required on the part of the personnel involved. They must have an intuitive feel for analysis, coding, and program design. They must quickly sense the trouble spots in the design, model them, model their alternatives, forget the straightforward aspects of the design which aren't worth studying at this early point, and finally arrive at an error-free program. In either case the point of all this, as with a simulation, is that questions of timing, storage, etc. which are otherwise matters of judgment, can now be studied with precision. Without this simulation the project manager is at the mercy of human judgment. With the simulation he can at least perform experimental tests of some key hypotheses and scope down what remains for human judgment, which in the area of computer program design (as in the estimation of takeoff gross weight, costs to complete, or the daily double) is invariably and seriously optimistic.

33.6   Step 4. Plan, Control, and Monitor Testing

Without question the biggest user of project resources, whether it be manpower, computer time, or management judgment, is the test phase. It is the phase of greatest risk in terms of dollars and schedule. It occurs at the latest point in the schedule when backup alternatives are least available, if at all.

The previous three recommendations to design the program before beginning analysis and coding, to document it completely, and to build a pilot model are all aimed at uncovering and solving problems before entering the test phase. However, even after doing these things there is still a test phase and there are still important things to be done. Figure 33.8 lists some additional aspects to testing. In planning for testing, I would suggest the following for consideration.

1. Many parts of the test process are best handled by test specialists who did not necessarily contribute to the original design. If it is argued that only the designer can perform a thorough test because only he understands the area he built, this is a sure sign of a failure to document properly. With good documentation it is feasible to use specialists in software product assurance who will, in my judgment, do a better job of testing than the designer.

2. Most errors are of an obvious nature that can be easily spotted by visual inspection. Every bit of an analysis and every bit of code should be subjected to a simple visual scan by a second party who did not do the original analysis or code but who would spot things like dropped minus signs, missing factors of two, jumps to wrong addresses, etc., which are in

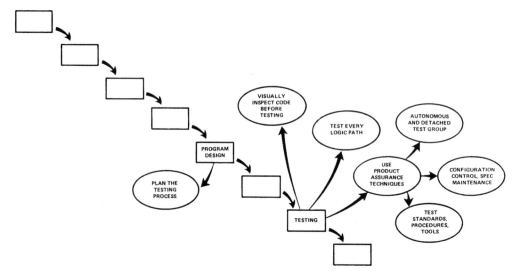

Figure 33.8: Step 4: Plan, control, and monitor computer program testing.

the nature of proofreading the analysis and code. Do not use the computer to detect this kind of thing—it is too expensive.

3. Test every logic path in the computer program at least once with some kind of numerical check. If I were a customer, I would not accept delivery until this procedure was completed and certified. This step will uncover the majority of coding errors.

    While this test procedure sounds simple, for a large, complex computer program it is relatively difficult to plow through every logic path with controlled values of input. In fact there are those who will argue that it is very nearly impossible. In spite of this I would persist in my recommendation that every logic path be subjected to at least one authentic check.

4. After the simple errors (which are in the majority, and which obscure the big mistakes) are removed, then it is time to turn over the software to the test area for checkout purposes. At the proper time during the course of development and in the hands of the proper person the computer itself is the best device for checkout. Key management decisions are: when is the time and who is the person to do final checkout?

33.7   Step 5: Involve the Customer

For some reason what a software design is going to do is subject to wide interpretation even after previous agreement. It is important to involve the customer in a formal way so that he has committed himself at earlier points before final delivery. To give the contractor free rein between requirement definition and operation is inviting trouble. Figure 33.9 indicates three

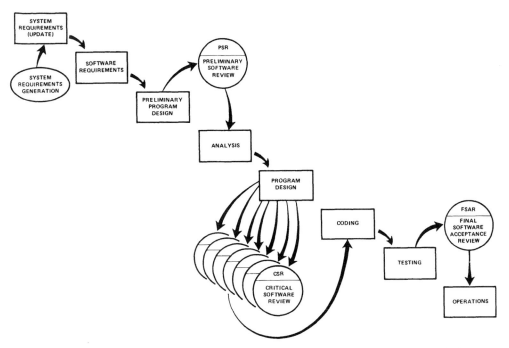

Figure 33.9: Step 5: Involve the customer—the involvement should be formal, in-depth, and continuing.

points following requirements definition where the insight, judgment, and commitment of the customer can bolster the development effort.

33.8 Summary

Figure 33.10 summarizes the five steps that I feel necessary to transform a risky development process into one that will provide the desired product. I would emphasize that each item costs some additional sum of money. If the relatively simpler process without the five complexities described here would work successfully, then of course the additional money is not well spent. In my experience, however, the simpler method has never worked on large software development efforts and the costs to recover far exceeded those required to finance the five-step process listed.

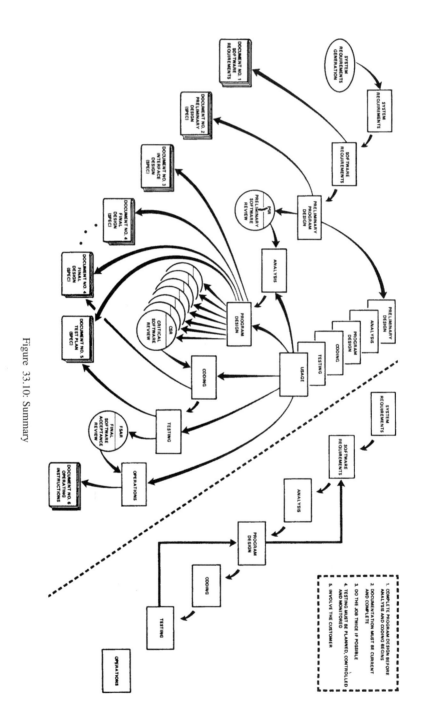

Figure 33.10: Summary

34 The Complexity of Theorem-Proving Procedures (1971)

Stephen A. Cook

While discussing maximal matchings in graphs a decade after Kruskal's unelaborated claim that his spanning tree algorithm was "practical" (chapter 17), the computer scientist Jack Edmonds paused to draw the distinction between polynomial- and exponential-time algorithms (as we now call them). A "digression" near the beginning of Edmonds (1965) states, "An explanation is due on the use of the words 'efficient algorithm.'... For practical purposes the difference between algebraic and exponential order is often more crucial than the difference between finite and non-finite." At about the same time, the mathematician Alan Cobham (1965) formulated a machine-model-independent class he called $\mathcal{L}$, the functions computable in time "bounded by polynomials in the lengths of the numbers involved" represented in digital form.

In this seminal paper, Stephen Cook (b. 1939) defines as $\mathcal{L}_*$ the class that Edmonds refers to as problems with "algebraic order" solutions and which are today known as $\mathcal{P}$ or PTIME. That is, $\mathcal{L}_*$ or $\mathcal{P}$ is the set analog of Cobham's class $\mathcal{L}$ of functions. Cook then provides the crucial definition of polynomial-time reducibility between problems, and proves that all problems accepted in polynomial time by a nondeterministic Turing machine are polynomial-time reducible to the set of satisfiable formulas of the propositional calculus in conjunctive normal form. (The $\mathcal{NP}$ notation for this class was adopted soon after publication of this paper—see chapter 36 and Knuth (1974b). Also, the theorem is stated in terms of tautologyhood, which is in co-$\mathcal{NP}$, rather than—as would be customary today—satisfiability, which is in $\mathcal{NP}$.)

Cook received his PhD in mathematics at Harvard in 1966, working under the direction of the logician Hao Wang on the complexity of multiplication and other mathematical functions. He joined the mathematics department at Berkeley as assistant professor. In what can only be considered a blunder, Cook was denied tenure at Berkeley in 1970 and moved to the University of Toronto. He presented this short paper at a major computer science theory conference, demonstrating that time-bounded nondeterministic computations could be described succinctly by boolean formulas, and therefore that a polynomial-time algorithm for boolean satisfiability would immediately result in polynomial-time algorithms for every $\mathcal{NP}$ problem. The proof is easy—the brilliant insight was to describe computations by formulas in a distant echo of Turing

Reprinted from Cook (1971b), with permission from the Association for Computing Machinery.

(1936, here page 60). Cook's result set off the still unfinished search for an answer to the question of whether or not $\mathcal{P} = \mathcal{NP}$ and hundreds of other research threads in complexity theory.

There is one more important historical aspect of the $\mathcal{P} = \mathcal{NP}$ question. Working independently and in relative isolation in the Soviet Union, Leonid Levin (b. 1948) had identified the same class of "Universal Search Problems" (Levin, 1973) that came to be known as the $\mathcal{NP}$-complete problems. The discoveries by Cook and Levin were nearly simultaneous, though Levin's publication was delayed. The existence of $\mathcal{NP}$-complete problems is now known as the Cook–Levin Theorem. Levin emigrated to the US in 1978 and is now a professor at Boston University.

34.0   Summary

$\mathbf{I}$T is shown that any recognition problem solved by a polynomial time-bounded nondeterministic Turing machine can be "reduced" to the problem of determining whether a given propositional formula is a tautology. Here "reduced" means, roughly speaking, that the first problem can be solved deterministically in polynomial time provided an oracle is available for solving the second. From this notion of reducible, polynomial degrees of difficulty are defined, and it is shown that the problem of determining tautologyhood has the same polynomial degree as the problem of determining whether the first of two given graphs is isomorphic to a subgraph of the second. Other examples are discussed. A method of measuring the complexity of proof procedures for the predicate calculus is introduced and discussed.

Throughout this paper, a *set of strings* means a set of strings on some fixed, large, finite alphabet Σ. This alphabet is large enough to include symbols for all sets described here. All Turing machines are deterministic recognition devices, unless the contrary is explicitly stated.

34.1   Tautologies and Polynomial Reducibility

Let us fix a formalism for the propositional calculus in which formulas are written as strings on Σ. Since we will require infinitely many proposition symbols (atoms), each such symbol will consist of a member of Σ followed by a number in binary notation to distinguish that symbol. Thus a formula of length n can only have about $n/\log n$ distinct function and predicate symbols. The logical connectives are $\wedge$ (and), $\vee$ (or), and $\neg$ (not).

The set of tautologies (denoted by {tautologies}) is a certain recursive set of strings on this alphabet, and we are interested in the problem of finding a good lower bound on its possible recognition times. We provide no such lower bound here, but Theorem 1 will give evidence that {tautologies} is a difficult set to recognize, since many apparently difficult problems can be reduced to determining tautologyhood. By *reduced* we mean, roughly speaking, that if tautologyhood could be decided instantly (by an "oracle") then these problems could be decided in polynomial time. In order to make this notion precise, we introduce query machines, which are like Turing machines with oracles in Kreider and Ritchie (1964).

A *query machine* is a multitape Turing machine with a distinguished tape called the *query tape*, and three distinguished states called the *query state*, *yes state*, and *no state*, respectively. If M is a query machine and T is a set of strings, then a *T-computation* of M is a computation of M in which initially M is in the initial state and has an input string w on its input tape, and each time M assumes the query state there is a string u on the query tape, and the next state M assumes is the yes state if $u \in T$ and the no state if $u \notin T$. We think of an "oracle," which knows T, placing M in the yes state or no state.

Definition. A set S of strings is *P-reducible* (P for polynomial) to a set T of strings iff there is some query machine M and a polynomial $Q(n)$ such that for each input string w, the T-computation of M with input w halts within $Q(|w|)$ steps ($|w|$ is the length of w) and ends in an accepting state iff $w \in S$.

It is not hard to see that *P*-reducibility is a transitive relation. Thus the relation E on sets of strings, given by $(S, T) \in E$ iff each of S and T is *P*-reducible to the other, is an equivalence relation. The equivalence class containing a set S will be denoted by $\deg(S)$ (the polynomial degree of difficulty of S).

Definition. We will denote $\deg(\{0\})$ by $\mathcal{L}_*$, where 0 denotes the zero function.

Thus $\mathcal{L}_*$ is the class of sets recognizable in polynomial time. $\mathcal{L}_*$ was discussed in Cook (1971a, p. 5), and is the string analog of Cobham's class $\mathcal{L}$ of functions (Cobham, 1965).

We now define the following special sets of strings.

1. *The subgraph problem* is the problem given two finite undirected graphs, determine whether the first is isomorphic to a subgraph of the second. A graph G can be represented by a string $\overline{G}$ on the alphabet $\{0, 1, *\}$ by listing the successive rows of its adjacency matrix, separated by *s. We let {subgraph pairs} denote the set of strings $\overline{G_1} ** \overline{G_2}$ such that G_1 is isomorphic to a subgraph of G_2.

2. *The graph isomorphism problem* will be represented by the set, denoted by {isomorphic graph pairs}, of all strings $\overline{G_1} ** \overline{G_2}$ such that G_1 is isomorphic to G_2.

3. The set {primes} is the set of all binary notations for prime numbers.

4. The set {DNF tautologies} is the set of strings representing tautologies in disjunctive normal form.

5. The set D_3 consists of those tautologies in disjunctive normal form in which each disjunct has at most three conjuncts (each of which is an atom or negation of an atom).

Theorem 1. If a set S of strings is accepted by some nondeterministic Turing machine within polynomial time, then S is *P*-reducible to {DNF tautologies}.

Corollary. Each of the sets in definitions 1–5 is *P*-reducible to {DNF tautologies}.

This is because each set, or its complement, is accepted in polynomial time by some nondeterministic Turing machine.

Proof of Theorem 1. Suppose a nondeterministic Turing machine M accepts a set S of strings within time $Q(n)$, where $Q(n)$ is a polynomial. Given an input w for M, we will construct a proposition formula $A(w)$ in conjunctive normal form such that $A(w)$ is satisfiable iff M accepts w.

Thus $\neg A(w)$ is easily put in disjunctive normal form (using De Morgan's laws), and $\neg A(w)$ is a tautology if and only if $w \notin S$. Since the whole construction can be carried out in time bounded by a polynomial in $|w|$ (the length of w), the theorem will be proved.

We may as well assume the Turing machine M has only one tape, which is infinite to the right but has a left-most square. Let us number the squares from left to right $1, 2, \ldots$. Let us fix an input w to M of length n, and suppose $w \in S$. Then there is a computation of M with input w that ends in an accepting state within $T = Q(n)$ steps. The formula $A(w)$ will be built from many different proposition symbols, whose intended meanings, listed below, refer to such a computation.

Suppose the tape alphabet for M is $\{\sigma_1, \ldots, \sigma_\ell\}$, and the set of states is $\{q_1, \ldots, q_r\}$. Notice that since the computation has at most $T = Q(n)$ steps, no tape square beyond T is scanned.

Proposition symbols:

$P_{s,t}^i$ for $1 \leq i \leq \ell$, $1 \leq s, t \leq T$. $P_{s,t}^i$ is true iff tape square number s at step t contains the symbol σ_i.

Q_t^i for $1 \leq i \leq r$, $1 \leq t \leq T$. Q_t^i is true iff at step t the machine is in state q_i.

$S_{s,t}$ for $1 \leq s, t \leq T$ is true iff at time t square number s is scanned by the tape head.

The formula $A(w)$ is a conjunction $B \wedge C \wedge D \wedge E \wedge F \wedge G \wedge H \wedge I$ formed as follows. Notice $A(w)$ is in conjunctive normal form.

B will assert that at each step t, one and only one square is scanned. B is a conjunction $B_1 \wedge B_2 \wedge \cdots \wedge B_T$, where B_t asserts that at time t one and only one square is scanned:

$$B_t = (S_{1,t} \vee S_{2,t} \vee \cdots \vee S_{T,t}) \wedge \left(\bigwedge_{1 \leq i < j \leq T} (\neg S_{i,t} \vee \neg S_{j,t}) \right).$$

For $1 \leq s \leq T$ and $1 \leq t \leq T$, $C_{s,t}$ asserts that at square s and time t there is one and only one symbol. C is the conjunction of all the $C_{s,t}$.

D asserts that for each t there is one and only one state.

E asserts the initial conditions are satisfied:

$$E = Q_1^0 \wedge S_{1,1} \wedge P_{1,1}^{i_1} \wedge P_{2,2}^{i_2} \wedge \cdots \wedge P_{n,1}^{i_n} \wedge P_{n+1,1}^1 \wedge \cdots \wedge P_{T,1}^1$$

where $w = \sigma_{i_1} \ldots \sigma_{i_n}$, q_0 is the initial state and σ_1 is the blank symbol.

F, G, and H assert that for each time t the values of the P's, Q's and S's are updated properly. For example, G is the conjunction over all t, i, j of $G_{i,j}^t$, where $G_{i,j}^t$ asserts that if at time t the machine is in state q_i scanning symbol σ_j, then at time $t + 1$ the machine is in state q_k, where q_k is the state given by the transition function for M. [EDITOR: The version of the original paper posted on Cook's website includes a handwritten note here: "(or states: nondeterminism)." Indeed, the construction as presented is correct only if the machine is deterministic; it needs to be done somewhat differently for nondeterministic machines.]

$$G_{i,j}^t = \bigwedge_{s=1}^{T} (\neg Q_t^i \vee \neg S_{s,t} \vee \neg P_{s,t}^j \vee Q_{t+1}^k)$$

Finally, the formula I asserts that the machine reaches an accepting state at some time. The machine M should be modified so that it continues to compute in some trivial fashion after reaching an accepting state, so that $A(w)$ will be satisfied.

It is now straightforward to verify that $A(w)$ has all the properties asserted in the first paragraph of the proof.

Theorem 2. The following sets are P-reducible to each other in pairs (and hence each has the same polynomial degree of difficulty): {tautologies}, {DNF tautologies}, D_3, {subgraph pairs}.

Remark. We have not been able to add either {primes} or {isomorphic graph pairs} to the above list. To show {tautologies} is P-reducible to {primes} would seem to require some deep results in number theory, while showing {tautologies} is P-reducible to {isomorphic graph pairs} would probably upset a conjecture of Corneil's (Corneil and Gotlieb, 1970) from which he deduces that the graph isomorphism problem can be solved in polynomial time.

Incidentally, it is not hard to see from the Davis–Putnam procedure (Davis and Putnam, 1960) that the set D_2 consisting of all DNF tautologies with at most two conjuncts per disjunct, is in $\mathcal{L}_*$. Hence D_2 cannot be added to the list in Theorem 2 (unless all sets in the list are in $\mathcal{L}_*$).

Proof of Theorem 2. By the corollary to Theorem 1, each of the sets is P-reducible to {DNF tautologies}. Since obviously {DNF tautologies} is P-reducible to {tautologies}, it remains to show {DNF tautologies} is P-reducible to D_3 and D_3 is P-reducible to {subgraph pairs}.

To show {DNF tautologies} is P-reducible to D_3, let A be a proposition formula in disjunctive normal form. Say $A = B_1 \vee B_2 \vee \cdots \vee B_k$, where $B_1 = R_1 \wedge \cdots \wedge R_s$, and each R_i is an atom or negation of an atom, and $s > 3$. Then A is a tautology if and only if A' is a tautology where

$$A' = P \wedge R_3 \wedge \cdots \wedge R_s \vee \neg P \wedge R_1 \wedge R_2 \vee B_2 \vee \cdots \vee B_k,$$

where P is a new atom. Since we have reduced the number of conjuncts in B_1, this process may be repeated until eventually a formula is found with at most three conjuncts per disjunct. Clearly the entire process is bounded in time by a polynomial in the length of A.

It remains to show that D_3 is P-reducible to {subgraph pairs}. Suppose A is a formula in disjunctive normal form with three conjuncts per disjunct. Thus $A = C_1 \vee \cdots \vee C_k$, where $C_i = R_{i1} \wedge R_{i2} \wedge R_{i3}$, and each R_{ij} is an atom or a negation of an atom. Now let G_1 be the complete graph with vertices $\{v_1, v_2, \ldots, v_k\}$, and let G_2 be the graph with vertices $\{u_{ij}\}$, $1 \leq i \leq k$, $1 \leq j \leq 3$, such that u_{ij} is connected by an edge to u_{rs} if and only if $i \neq r$ and the two literals (R_{ij}, R_{rs}) do not form an opposite pair (that is they are neither of the form $(P, \neg P)$ nor of the form $(\neg P, P)$). Thus there is a falsifying truth assignment to the formula A iff there is a graph homomorphism $\phi : G_1 \to G_2$ such that for each i, $\phi(v_i) = u_{ij}$ for some j. (The homomorphism tells for each i which of R_{i1}, R_{i2}, R_{i3} should be falsified, and the selective lack of edges in G_2 guarantees that the resulting truth assignment is consistently specified.)

In order to guarantee that a one-one homomorphism $\phi : G_1 \to G_2$ has the property that for each i, $\phi(v_i) = u_{ij}$ for some j, we modify G_1 and G_2 as follows. We select graphs $H_1, H_2, \ldots, H_k$ which are sufficiently distinct from each other that if G_1' is formed from G_1 by attaching H_i to v_i,

$1 \leq i \leq k$, and G'_2 is formed from G_2 by attaching H_i to each of u_{i1} and u_{i2} and u_{i3}, $1 \leq i \leq k$, then every one-one homomorphism $\phi : G'_1 \to G'_2$ has the property just stated. It is not hard to see such a construction can be carried out in polynomial time. Then G'_1 can be embedded in G'_2 if and only if $A \notin D_3$. This completes the proof of Theorem 2.

34.2   Discussion

Theorem 1 and its corollary give strong evidence that it is not easy to determine whether a given proposition formula is a tautology, even if the formula is in normal disjunctive form. Theorems 1 and 2 together suggest that it is fruitless to search for a polynomial decision procedure for the subgraph problem, since success would bring polynomial decision procedures to many other apparently intractable problems. Of course the same remark applies to any combinatorial problem to which tautologies is P-reducible.

Furthermore, the theorems suggest that {tautologies} is a good candidate for an interesting set not in $\mathcal{L}_*$, and I feel it is worth spending considerable effort trying to prove this conjecture. Such a proof would be a major breakthrough in complexity theory.

In view of the apparent complexity of {DNF tautologies}, it is interesting to examine the Davis–Putnam procedure (Davis and Putnam, 1960). This procedure was designed to determine whether a given formula in conjunctive normal form is satisfiable, but of course the "dual" procedure determines whether a given formula in disjunctive normal form is a tautology. I have not yet been able to find a series of examples showing the procedure (treated sympathetically to avoid certain pitfalls) must require more than polynomial time. Nor have I found an interesting upper bound for the time required.

If we let strings represent natural numbers (or k-tuples of natural numbers) using m-adic or other suitable notation, then the notions in the preceding sections can be made to apply to sets of numbers (or k-place relations on numbers). It is not hard to see that the set of relations accepted in polynomial time by some nondeterministic Turing machine is precisely the set $\mathcal{L}^+$ of relations of the form

$$(\exists y \leq g_k(\overline{x})) \, R(\overline{x}, y) \tag{34.1}$$

where $g_k(\overline{x}) = 2^{(\ell(\max \overline{x}))^k}$, $\ell(z)$ is the dyadic length of z, and $R(\overline{x}, y)$ is an $\mathcal{L}_*$ relation. ($\mathcal{L}^+$ is the class of extended positive rudimentary relations of Bennett (1962).) If we remove the bound on the quantifier in formula (34.1), the class $\mathcal{L}^+$ would become the class of recursively enumerable sets. Thus if $\mathcal{L}^+$ is the analog of the class of r.e. sets, then determining tautologyhood is the analog of the halting problem; since, according to Theorem 1, {tautologies} has the complete $\mathcal{L}^+$ degree just as the halting problem has the complete r.e. degree. Unfortunately, the diagonal argument which shows the halting problem is not recursive apparently cannot be adapted to show {tautologies} is not in $\mathcal{L}_*$. . . .

35 A Statistical Interpretation of Term Specificity and Its Application in Retrieval (1972)

Karen Spärck Jones

The World Wide Web has existed only since the early 1990s, and search engines for less time than that. But the problem of locating documents by searching for keywords has existed as long as documents have existed. What is the best way to construct an index of the terms appearing in documents to make it easy to find a document using a set of interesting terms?

In this 1972 paper, Karen Spärck Jones (1935–2007) described a simple method that is still widely used at the heart of document retrieval systems. It has two components. The more often a term appears in a document, the more relevant it probably is to the document's content. For example, a paper that uses the term "zebra" repeatedly is probably at least somewhat about zebras. But of course such a paper will also use the term "the" repeatedly, so mere frequency within a document is an unreliable indicator of a word's significance.

However, the importance of high frequency of a term within a document must be tempered if that term also appears frequently in many *other* documents. The less common a term is in a collection of documents, the more likely it is of significance for the few documents in which it does appear. This counter-weighting factor is called the "inverse document frequency" or IDF. Most web search engines today use some form of IDF as a basis for retrieving web pages.

Spärck Jones's methods, carefully tuned using mathematical statistics, proved to be remarkably useful, even though they made no attempt to extract meaning from documents, to analyze sentence structure, or to cluster similar words together. She demonstrated, that is, that simple text statistics could be extremely powerful tools in the analysis of natural language.

Though she worked at laboratories and at the University of Cambridge from the 1950s until she retired in 2002, and became president of the Association for Computational Linguistics in 1994, Spärck Jones was awarded the title of professor only in 1999 (Bowles, 2019).

⚬∘⚬

35.0 Abstract

THE exhaustivity of document descriptions and the specificity of index terms are usually regarded as independent. It is suggested that specificity should be interpreted statistically, as a function of term use rather than of term meaning. The effects on retrieval of variations in term specificity are examined, experiments with three test collections showing, in particular, that frequently-occurring terms are required for good overall performance. It is argued that terms should be weighted according to collection frequency, so that matches on less frequent, more specific, terms are of greater value than matches on frequent terms. Results for the test collections show that considerable improvements in performance are obtained with this very simple procedure.

35.1   Exhaustivity and Specificity

We are familiar with the notions of exhaustivity and specificity: exhaustivity is a property of index descriptions, and specificity one of index terms. They are most clearly illustrated by a simple keyword or descriptor system. In this case the exhaustivity of a document description is the coverage of its various topics given by the terms assigned to it; and the specificity of an individual term is the level of detail at which a given concept is represented.

These features of a document retrieval system have been discussed by Cleverdon et al. (1966) and Lancaster (1968), for example, and the effects of variation in either have been noted. For instance, if the exhaustivity of a document description is increased by the assignment of more terms, when the number of terms in the indexing vocabulary is constant, the chance of the document matching a request is increased. The idea of an optimum level of indexing exhaustivity for a given document collection then follows: the average number of descriptors per document should be adjusted so that, hopefully, the chances of requests matching relevant documents are maximized, while too many false drops are avoided. Exhaustivity obviously applies to requests too, and one function of a search strategy is to vary request exhaustivity. I will be mainly concerned here, however, with document descriptions.

Specificity as characterized above is a semantic property of index terms: a term is more or less specific as its meaning is more or less detailed and precise. This is a natural view for anyone concerned with the construction of an entire indexing vocabulary. Some decision has to be made about the discriminating power of individual terms in addition to their descriptive propriety. For example, the index term "beverage" may be as properly used for documents about tea, coffee, and cocoa as the terms "tea", "coffee", and "cocoa". Whether the more general term "beverage" only is incorporated in the vocabulary, or whether "tea", "coffee", and "cocoa" are adopted, depends on judgements about the retrieval utility of distinctions between documents made by the latter but not the former. It is also predicted that the more general term would be applied to more documents than the separate terms "tea", "coffee", and "cocoa", so the less specific term would have a larger collection distribution than the more specific ones.

It is of course assumed here that such choices when a vocabulary is constructed are exclusive: we may either have "beverage" or "tea", "coffee", and "cocoa". What happens if we have all four terms is a different matter. We may then either interpret "beverage" to mean "other beverages" or explicitly treat it as a related broader term. I will, however, disregard these alternatives here.

In setting up an index vocabulary the specificity of index terms is looked at from one point of view: we are concerned with the probable effects on document description, and hence retrieval, of choosing particular terms, or rather of adopting a certain set of terms. For our decisions will, in part, be influenced by relations between terms, and how the set of chosen terms will collectively characterize the set of documents. But throughout we assume some level of indexing exhaustivity. We are concerned with obtaining an effective vocabulary for a collection of documents of some broadly known subject matter and size, where a given level of indexing exhaustivity is believed to be sufficient to represent the content of individual documents adequately, and distinguish one document from another.

Index term specificity must, however, be looked at from another point of view. What happens when a given index vocabulary is actually used? We predict when we opt for "beverage", for example, that it will be used more than "cocoa". But we do not have much idea of how many documents there will be to which "beverage" may appropriately be assigned. This is not simply determined even when some level of exhaustivity is assumed. There will be some documents which cry out for "beverage" so to speak, and we may have some idea of what proportion of the collection this is likely to be. There will also be documents to which "beverage" cannot justifiably be assigned, and this proportion may also be estimated. But there is unfortunately liable to be some number of documents to which "beverage" may or may not be assigned, in either case quite plausibly. In general, therefore, the actual use of a descriptor may diverge considerably from the predicted use. The proportions of a collection to which a term does and does not belong can only be estimated very roughly; and there may be enough intermediate documents for the way the term is assigned to these to affect its overall distribution considerably. Over a long period the character of the collection as a whole may also change, with further effects on term distribution.

This is where the level of exhaustivity of description matters. As a collection grows maintaining a certain level of exhaustivity may mean that the descriptions of different documents are not sufficiently distinguished, while some terms are very heavily used. More generally, great variation in term distribution is likely to appear. It may thus be the case that a particular term becomes less effective as a means of retrieval, whatever its actual meaning. This is because it is not discriminating. It may be properly assigned to documents, in the sense that their content justifies the assignment; but it may no longer be sufficiently useful in itself as a device for distinguishing the typically small class of documents relevant to a request from the remainder of the collection. A frequently used term thus functions in retrieval as a nonspecific term, even though its meaning may be quite specific in the ordinary sense.

35.2   Statistical Specificity

It is not enough, in other words, to think of index term specificity solely in setting up an index vocabulary, as having to do with accuracy of concept representation. We should think of specificity as a function of term use. It should be interpreted as a statistical rather than semantic property of index terms. In general we may expect vaguer terms to be used more often, but the behaviour of individual terms will be unpredictable. We can thus redefine exhaustivity and specificity for simple term systems: the exhaustivity of a document description is the number of terms it contains, and the specificity of a term is the number of documents to which it pertains. The relation between the two is then clear, and we can see, for instance, that a change in the exhaustivity of descriptions will affect term specificity: if descriptions are longer, terms will be used more often. This is inevitable for a controlled vocabulary, but also applies if extracted keywords are used, particularly in stem form. The incidence of words new to the keyword vocabulary does not simply parallel the number of documents indexed, and the extraction of more keywords per document is more likely to increase the frequency of current keywords than to generate new ones.

Once this statistical interpretation of specificity, and the relation between it and exhaustivity, are recognized, it is natural to attempt a more formal approach to seeking an optimum level of specificity in a vocabulary and an optimum level of exhaustivity in indexing, for a given collection. Within the broad limits imposed by having sensible terms, i.e. ones which can be reached from requests and applied to documents, we may try to set up a vocabulary with the statistical properties which are hopefully optimal for retrieval. Purely formal calculations may suggest the correct number of terms, and of terms per document, for a certain degree of document discrimination. Work on these lines has been done by Zunde and Slamecka (1967), for instance. More informally, the suggestion that descriptors should be designed to have approximately the same distribution, made by Salton (1968), for example, is motivated by respect for the retrieval effects of purely statistical features of term use.

Unfortunately, abstract calculations do not select actual terms. Nor are document collections static. More importantly, it is difficult to control requests. One may characterize documents with a view to distinguishing them nicely and then find that users do not provide requests utilizing these distinctions. We may therefore be forced to accept a *de facto* non-optimal situation with terms of varying specificity and at least some disagreeably non-specific terms. There will be some terms which, whatever the original intention, retrieve a large number of documents, of which only a small proportion can be expected to be relevant to a request. Such terms are on the whole more of a nuisance than rare, over-specific terms which fail to retrieve documents.

These features of term behaviour can be illustrated by examples from three well-known test collections, obtained from the Aslib Cranfield, INSPEC, and College of Librarianship Wales projects. In fact in these the vocabulary consists of extracted keyword stems, which may be expected to show more variation than controlled terms. But there is no reason to suppose that the situation is essentially different. Full descriptions of the collections are given in Cleverdon et al. (1966), Aitchison et al. (1970), and Keen and Digger (1972). Relevant characteristics of the collections are given in Section A of Figure 35.1. The INSPEC Collection, for instance, has 541 documents indexed by 1,341 terms. In all the collections, there are some very frequently occurring terms: for example in the Cranfield collection, one term occurs in 144 out of 200 documents; in the INSPEC one term occurs in 112 out of 541, and in the Keen collection one term occurs in 199 out of 797 documents. The terms concerned do not necessarily represent concepts central to the subject areas of the collections, and they are not always general terms. In the Keen collection, which is about information science, the most frequent term is "index-", and

		Cranfield	INSPEC	Keen
A.	Number of documents	200	541	797
	Number of terms	712	1,341	939
	Number of terms per document	32	12.2	7.9
	Number of documents per term	9	4.9	6.1
B.	Number of requests	42	97	63
	Number of terms represented	166	248	183
	Number of terms per request	6.9	5.6	5.3
	Number of documents per request term	31.6	11.5	44.8
C.	Number of retrieving terms per request	5	3.2	3.3
	Number of retrieving terms per document	1.8	1.2	1.2
	Number of retrieving terms per relevant document	3.6	2	1.8
D.	Number of frequent terms	96	73	50
	Number of frequent terms per request	4	2.5	2.3

Figure 35.1

other frequent ones include "librar-", "inform-", and "comput-". In the INSPEC collection the most frequent is "theor-", followed by "measur-" and "method-". And in the Cranfield collection the most frequent is "flow-", followed by "pressur-", "distribut-" and "bound-" (boundary). The rarer terms are a fine mixed bag including "purchas-", and "xerograph-" for Keen, "parallel-" and "silver-" for INSPEC, and "logarithm-" and "seri-" (series) for Cranfield.

35.3 Specificity and Matching

How should one cope with variable term specificity, and especially with insufficiently specific terms, when these occur in requests? The untoward effects of frequent term use can in principle be dealt with very naturally, through term combinations. For instance, though the three terms "bound-", "layer-", and "flow-" occur in 73, 62, and 144 documents each in the Cranfield collection, there are only 50 documents indexed by all three terms together. Relying on term conjunction is quite straightforward. It is in particular a way of overcoming the untoward consequences of the fact that requests tend to be formulated in better known, and hence generally more frequent, terms. It is unfortunate, but not surprising, that requests tend to be presented in terms with an average frequency much above that for the indexing vocabulary as a whole. This holds for all three test collections, as appears in Section B of Figure 35.1. For the Cranfield collection, for example, the average number of postings for the terms in the vocabulary is nine, while the average for the terms used in the requests is 31.6; for Keen the figures are 6.1 and 44.8.

But relying on term combination to reduce false drops is well-known to be risky. It is true that the more terms in common between a document and a request, the more likely it is that the document is relevant to the request. Unfortunately, it just happens to be difficult to match term conjunctions. This is well exhibited by the term-matching behaviour of the three collections, as shown in Section C of Figure 35.1. The average number of starting terms per request ranges from 5.3 for Keen to 6.9 for Cranfield. But the average number of retrieving terms per request, i.e. the average of the highest matching scores, ranges from 3.2 to 5.0. More importantly, the average number of matching terms for the relevant documents retrieved ranges from only 1.8 for Keen to 3.6 for Cranfield, though fortunately the average for all documents retrieved, which are predominantly non-relevant, ranges from a mere 1.2 to 1.8.

Clearly, one solution to this problem is to provide for more matching terms in some way. This may be achieved either by providing alternative substitutes for given terms, through a classification; or by increasing the exhaustivity of document or request specifications, say by adding statistically associated terms. But either approach involves effort, perhaps considerable effort, since the sets of terms related to individual terms must be identified. The question naturally arises as to whether better use of existing term descriptions can be made which does not involve such effort.

As very frequently occurring terms are responsible for noise in retrieval, one possible course is simply to remove them from requests. The fact that this will reduce the number of terms available for conjoined matching may be offset by the fact that fewer non-relevant documents will be retrieved. Unfortunately, while frequent terms cause noise, they are also required for reasonably high recall. For all three test collections, the deletion of very frequent terms by the application of a suitable threshold leads to a decline in overall performance. For the INSPEC collection, for example, the threshold was set to delete terms occurring in 20 or more documents, so that 73 terms out of the total vocabulary of 1,341 were removed. The effect in retrieval performance is illustrated by the recall/precision graph of Figure 35.2 for the Cranfield collection. Matching is by simple term co-ordination levels, and averaging over the set of requests is by straightforward average of numbers. Precision at ten standard recall values is then interpolated. The same relationship between full term matching and this restricted matching with non-frequent terms only is exhibited by the other collections: the recall ceiling is lowered by at least 30 per cent, and indeed for the Keen collection is reduced from 75 per cent to 25 per cent, though precision is maintained.

Inspection of the requests shows why this result is obtained. Not merely is request term frequency much above average collection frequency; the comparatively small number of very frequent terms plays a large part in request formulation. "Flow-" for example, appears in twelve Cranfield requests out of 42, and in general for all three collections about half the terms in a request are very frequent ones, as shown in Section D of Figure 35.1. Throwing very frequent terms away is throwing the baby out with the bath water, since they are required for the retrieval of many relevant documents. The combination of non-frequent terms is discriminating, but no more than that of frequent and non-frequent terms. The value of the non-frequent terms is clearly seen, on the other hand, when matching using frequent terms only is compared with full matching, also shown in Figure 35.2. Matching levels for total and relevant documents are nearly as high as for all terms, but the non-frequent terms in the latter raise the relevant matching level about 1.

These features of term retrieval suggest that to improve on the initial full term performance we need to exploit the good features of very frequent and non-frequent terms, while minimizing their bad ones. We should allow some merit in frequent term matches, while allowing rather more in non-frequent ones. In any case we wish to maximize the number of matching terms.

35.4 Weighting by Specificity

This clearly suggests a weighting scheme. In normal term co-ordination matches, if a request and document have a frequent term in common, this counts for as much as a non-frequent one; so if a request and document share three common terms, the document is retrieved at the same level as another one sharing three rare terms with the request. But it seems we should treat matches on non-frequent terms as more valuable than ones on frequent terms, without disregarding the latter altogether. The natural solution is to correlate a term's matching value with its collection frequency. At this stage the division of terms into frequent and non-frequent is arbitrary and probably not optimal: the elegant and almost certainly better approach is to relate matching value more closely to relative frequency. The appropriate way of doing this is suggested by the term distribution curve for the vocabulary, which has the familiar Zipf shape. Let $f(n) = m$ such that $2^{m-1} < n \leq 2^m$. Then where there are N documents in the collection, the weight of a term which occurs n times is $f(N) - f(n) + 1$. For the Cranfield collection with 200 documents, for example, this means that a term occurring ninety times has weight 2, while one occurring three times has weight 7.

The matching value of a term is thus correlated with its specificity and the retrieval level of a document is determined by the sum of the values of its matching terms. Simple co-ordination levels are replaced by a more sophisticated quasi-ranking. The effect can be illustrated by the different retrieval levels at which two documents matching a request on the same number of relatively frequent and relatively non-frequent terms respectively. With the Cranfield range of values, a document matching on two terms with frequencies 15 and 43 will be retrieved at level $5 + 3 = 8$, while one matching on terms with frequencies 3 and 7 will be retrieved at level $7 + 6 = 13$. Clearly, as the range of levels is "stretched", more discrimination is possible.

The idea of term weighting is not new. But it is typically related to the presumed importance of a term with respect to a document in itself. For instance, if a document is mainly about paint and only mentions varnish in passing, we may utilize some simple weighting scale to assign a weight of 2 to the term "paint" and 1 to "varnish". More informally, in putting a request, we may state that during searching term x must be retained, but term y may be dropped. More systematic weighting on a statistical base may be adopted if the necessary information is available. If the actual frequency of occurrence of terms in a document (or abstract) is known, this may be used to generate weights. Artandi and Wolf (1969) report the use of frequency to select a weight from a three-point scale, while Salton and Lesk (1968) more wholeheartedly uses the frequency of occurrence as a weight. In a range of experiments Salton has demonstrated that weighting terms in this way leads to a noticeable improvement in performance over that obtained for unweighted terms.

Weighting by collection frequency as opposed to document frequency is quite different. It places greater emphasis on the value of a term as a means of distinguishing one document from another than on its value as an indication of the content of the document itself. The relation between the two forms of weighting is not obvious. In some cases a term may be common in a document and rare in the collection, so that it would be heavily weighted in both schemes. But the reverse may also apply. It is really that the emphasis is on different properties of terms.

The treatment of term collection frequency in connection with term matching does not seem to have been systematically investigated. The effect of term frequency on statistical associations has been studied, for example by Lesk, but this is a different matter. The fact that a given term is likely to retrieve a large number of documents may be informally exploited in setting up searches, in particular in the context of on-line retrieval as described by Borko (1968), for example. More whole-hearted approaches are probably hampered by the lack of the necessary information. Such a procedure as the one described is also much more suited to automatic than manual searching. It is of interest, therefore, that term frequencies have been exploited in the general manner indicated within an operational interactive retrieval system for internal reports implemented at A. D. Little (Curtice and Jones, 1968). In this system indexing keywords are extracted automatically from text, and the weighting is therefore associated with a changing vocabulary and collection. However, no systematic experiments are reported.

35.5 Experimental Results

The term weighting system described was tried on the three collections. As noted, these are very different in character, with different sizes of vocabulary, document description, and request specification, as indicated in Figure 35.1. In all cases, however, matching with term weighting led to a substantial improvement in performance over simple term matching. The results presented in the form mentioned earlier, are given in Figures 35.3, 35.4 and 35.5. A simple significance test based on the difference in area enclosed by the curves shows that the improvement given by weighted terms is fully significant, the difference being well above the required minimum.

These results are of interest for two reasons. All three collections have been used for a whole range of experiments with different index languages, search techniques, and so on: see Cleverdon et al. (1966); Salton (1968); Salton and Lesk (1968); Spärck Jones (1971); Aitchison et al. (1970); Keen and Digger (1972). The performance improvement obtained here nevertheless represents as good an improvement over simple unweighted keyword stem matching as has been obtained by any other means, including carefully constructed thesauri: Salton's iterative search methods are not comparable. The details of the way these experimental results are presented varies, so rigorous comparisons are impossible: but the general picture is clear. Indeed, insofar as anything can be called a solid result in information retrieval research, this is one. The second

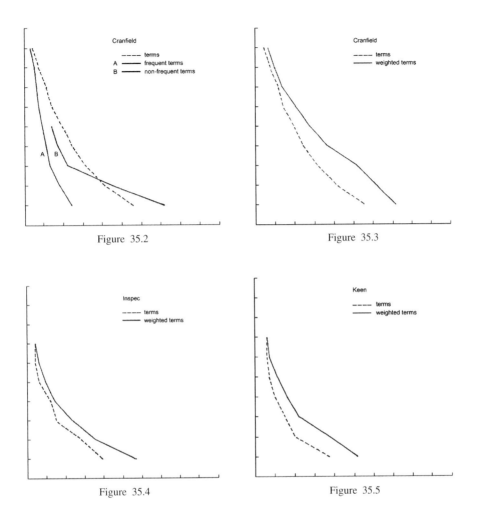

Figure 35.2

Figure 35.3

Figure 35.4

Figure 35.5

point about the present results is that the improvement in performance is obtained by extremely simple means. It is compatible with an initially plain method of indexing, namely the use of extracted keywords, which may be reduced to stems automatically; it is readily implemented given an automatic term-matching procedure, since all that is required is a term frequency list and this is easily obtained; and it has the merit that the weight assigned to terms is naturally adjusted to follow the growth of and changes in a collection. Experiments with very much larger collections than those used here are clearly desirable; they will hopefully not be long delayed.

36 Reducibility among Combinatorial Problems (1972)

Richard Karp

Richard "Dick" Karp (b. 1935) was born in the Dorchester neighborhood of Boston. His father was a school teacher who rose to be a school principal. Karp liked puzzles and games, and received an early practical lesson in combinatorial explosion helping his father arrange the school's class calendar by shuffling cards in search of a schedule that satisfied various constraints about use of classrooms, availability of teachers, and so on.

Karp studied mathematics at Harvard, and found discrete math particularly attractive because it drew on his puzzle-solving instincts and also because he was intimidated by the best pure math students in his classes, some of whom went on to win major mathematical prizes. Upon receiving his undergraduate degree in 1955, Karp joined Harvard's graduate program in digital computing, earning a PhD in 1959. From there he went to IBM Research, where he made contributions to a variety of computer algorithms, especially for combinatorial optimization. In 1968 he left IBM to become a computer science professor at Berkeley, where he has remained for most of his career.

These biographical details set the stage for Karp's reaction to Cook (1971b, here chapter 34). Karp recognized that a great many combinatorial problems had a family resemblance to boolean satisfiability, in that their solution seemed to require searching an exponentially large search space for a proof or certificate that would be relatively small, if found, and easily verified.

Karp here defines $\mathcal{P}$, $\mathcal{NP}$, polynomial-time reducibility (a version of computable reducibility that had been studied by his undergraduate advisor Hartley Rogers), and $\mathcal{NP}$-completeness. And then he lists 21 problems, all self-evidently in $\mathcal{NP}$, to which boolean satisfiability is directly or indirectly reducible, thus showing them all to be $\mathcal{NP}$-complete. Many of these problems had long histories; Karp's paper showed that they are all the same problem except for superficial variations. In short order hundreds of other problems were added to Karp's list, and the $\mathcal{P} = \mathcal{NP}$ question became one of the most important unsolved problems of modern mathematics. Garey and Johnson (1979) is the compendium to which computer scientists turn to see if a new problem is $\mathcal{NP}$-complete—in which case they stop trying to find an efficient exact solution and move on to seek approximate methods, more tractable sub-cases of the problem, etc.

Reprinted from Karp (1972), with permission from Springer.

36.0   Abstract

A large class of computational problems involve the determination of properties of graphs, digraphs, integers, arrays of integers, finite families of finite sets, boolean formulas and elements of other countable domains. Through simple encodings from such domains into the set of words over a finite alphabet these problems can be converted into language recognition problems, and we can inquire into their computational complexity. It is reasonable to consider such a problem satisfactorily solved when an algorithm for it is found which terminates within a number of steps bounded by a polynomial in the length of the input. We show that a large number of classic unsolved problems of covering, matching, packing, routing, assignment and sequencing are equivalent, in the sense that either each of them possesses a polynomial-bounded algorithm or none of them does.

36.1   Introduction

All the general methods presently known for computing the chromatic number of a graph, deciding whether a graph has a Hamilton circuit, or solving a system of linear inequalities in which the variables are constrained to be 0 or 1, require a combinatorial search for which the worst case time requirement grows exponentially with the length of the input. In this paper we give theorems which strongly suggest, but do not imply, that these problems, as well as many others, will remain intractable perpetually.

We are specifically interested in the existence of algorithms that are guaranteed to terminate in a number of steps bounded by a polynomial in the length of the input. We exhibit a class of well-known combinatorial problems, including those mentioned above, which are equivalent, in the sense that a polynomial-bounded algorithm for any one of them would effectively yield a polynomial-bounded algorithm for all. We also show that, if these problems do possess polynomial-bounded algorithms then all the problems in an unexpectedly wide class (roughly speaking, the class of problems solvable by polynomial-depth backtrack search) possess polynomial-bounded algorithms.

The following is a brief summary of the contents of the paper. For the sake of definiteness our technical development is carried out in terms of the recognition of languages by one-tape Turing machines, but any of a wide variety of other abstract models of computation would yield the same theory. Let Σ^* be the set of all finite strings of 0s and 1s. A subset of Σ^* is called a *language*. Let $\mathcal{P}$ be the class of languages recognizable in polynomial time by one-tape deterministic Turing machines, and let $\mathcal{NP}$ be the class of languages recognizable in polynomial time by one-tape nondeterministic Turing machines. Let Π be the class of functions from Σ^* into Σ^* computable in polynomial time by one-tape Turing machines. Let L and M be languages. We say that $L \leq M$ (L *is reducible to* M) if there is a function $f \in \Pi$ such that $f(x) \in M \Leftrightarrow x \in L$. If $M \in \mathcal{P}$ and $L \leq M$ then $L \in \mathcal{P}$. We call L and M *equivalent* if $L \leq M$ and $M \leq L$. Call L *(polynomial) complete* if $L \in \mathcal{NP}$ and every language in $\mathcal{NP}$ is reducible to L. Either all complete languages are in $\mathcal{P}$, or none of them are. The former alternative holds if and only if $\mathcal{P} = \mathcal{NP}$.

The main contribution of this paper is the demonstration that a large number of classic difficult computational problems, arising in fields such as mathematical programming, graph theory,
combinatorics, computational logic and switching theory, are complete (and hence equivalent)
when expressed in a natural way as language recognition problems.

This paper was stimulated by the work of Stephen Cook (1971b), and rests on an important
theorem which appears in his paper. The author also wishes to acknowledge the substantial
contributions of Eugene Lawler and Robert Tarjan.

36.2   The Class $\mathcal{P}$

There is a large class of important computational problems which involve the determination of
properties of graphs, digraphs, integers, finite families of finite sets, boolean formulas and elements of other countable domains. It is a reasonable working hypothesis, championed originally
by Jack Edmonds (1965) in connection with problems in graph theory and integer programming,
and by now widely accepted, that such a problem can be regarded as tractable if and only if there
is an algorithm for its solution whose running time is bounded by a polynomial in the size of the
input. ...

We complete this section by listing a sampling of problems which are solvable in polynomial
time. In the next section we examine a number of close relatives of these problems which are not
known to be solvable in polynomial time. Appendix 1 establishes our notation. Each problem
is specified by giving (under the heading "INPUT") a generic element of its domain of definition
and (under the heading "PROPERTY") the property which causes an input to be accepted.

SATISFIABILITY WITH AT MOST 2 LITERALS PER CLAUSE (Cook, 1971b)
INPUT: Clauses $C_1, C_2, \ldots, C_p$, each containing at most 2 literals
PROPERTY: The conjunction of the given clauses is satisfiable; i.e., there is a set

$$S \subseteq \{x_1, x_2, \ldots, x_n, \overline{x_1}, \overline{x_2}, \ldots, \overline{x_n}\}$$

such that

a) S does not contain a complementary pair of literals and

b) $S \cap C_k \neq \emptyset, k = 1, 2, \ldots, p$.

MINIMUM SPANNING TREE (Kruskal, 1956, here chapter 17)
INPUT: G, w, W
PROPERTY: There exists a spanning tree of weight $\leq W$.

SHORTEST PATH (Dijkstra, 1959)
INPUT: G, w, W, s, t
PROPERTY: There is a path between s and t of weight $\leq W$.

MINIMUM CUT (Edmonds and Karp, 1972)
INPUT: G, w, W, s, t
PROPERTY: There is an s, t cut of weight $\leq W$. ...

36.3   Nondeterministic Algorithms and Cook's Theorem

In this section we state an important theorem due to Cook (1971b) which asserts that any language in a certain wide class $\mathcal{NP}$ is reducible to a specific set S, which corresponds to the problem of deciding whether a boolean formula in conjunctive normal form is satisfiable.

Let $\mathcal{P}^{(2)}$ denote the class of subsets of $\Sigma^* \times \Sigma^*$ which are recognizable in polynomial time. Given $L^{(2)} \in \mathcal{P}^{(2)}$ and a polynomial p, we define a language L as follows:

$$L = \{x : \text{ there exists } y \text{ such that } \langle x, y \rangle \in L^{(2)} \text{ and } \lg(y) \le p(\lg(x))\}.$$

We refer to L as the language derived from $L^{(2)}$ by p-bounded existential quantification.

Definition $\mathcal{NP}$ is the set of languages derived from elements of $\mathcal{P}^{(2)}$ by polynomial-bounded existential quantification.

There is an alternative characterization of $\mathcal{NP}$ in terms of nondeterministic Turing machines.
...

The class $\mathcal{NP}$ is very extensive. Loosely, a recognition problem is in $\mathcal{NP}$ if and only if it can be solved by a backtrack search of polynomial bounded depth. A wide range of important computational problems which are not known to be in $\mathcal{P}$ are obviously in $\mathcal{NP}$. For example, consider the problem of determining whether the nodes of a graph G can be colored with k colors so that no two adjacent nodes have the color. A nondeterministic algorithm can simply guess an assignment of colors to the nodes and then check (in polynomial time) whether all pairs of adjacent nodes have distinct colors.

In view of the wide extent of $\mathcal{NP}$, the following theorem due to Cook is remarkable. We define the satisfiability problem as follows:

SATISFIABILITY

INPUT: Clauses $C_1, C_2, \ldots, C_p$

PROPERTY: The conjunction of the given clauses is satisfiable; i.e., there is a set
$S \subseteq \{x_1, x_2, \ldots, x_n, \overline{x_1}, \overline{x_2}, \ldots, \overline{x_n}\}$ such that

a) S does not contain a complementary pair of literals and

b) $S \cap C_k \ne \emptyset, k = 1, 2, \ldots, p.$

Theorem 2 (Cook). If $L \in \mathcal{NP}$ then $L \le$ SATISFIABILITY.

The theorem stated by Cook (1971b) uses a weaker notion of reducibility than the one used here, but Cook's proof supports the present statement.

Corollary 1. $\mathcal{P} = \mathcal{NP} \Leftrightarrow$ SATISFIABILITY $\in \mathcal{P}$.

Proof. If SATISFIABILITY $\in \mathcal{P}$, then for each $L \in \mathcal{NP}$, $L \in \mathcal{P}$, since $L \le$ SATISFIABILITY. If SATISFIABILITY $\notin \mathcal{P}$, then since clearly SATISFIABILITY $\in \mathcal{NP}$, $\mathcal{P} \ne \mathcal{NP}$.

Remark. If $\mathcal{P} = \mathcal{NP}$ then $\mathcal{NP}$ is closed under complementation and polynomial-bounded existential quantification. Hence it is also closed under polynomial-bounded universal quantification. It follows that a polynomial-bounded analogue of Kleene's Arithmetic Hierarchy (Rogers, 1967) becomes trivial if $\mathcal{P} = \mathcal{NP}$.

Theorem 2 shows that, if there were a polynomial-time algorithm to decide membership in SATISFIABILITY then every problem solvable by a polynomial-depth backtrack search would also be solvable by a polynomial-time algorithm. This is strong circumstantial evidence that SATISFIABILITY $\notin \mathcal{P}$.

36.4   Complete Problems

The main object of this paper is to establish that a large number of important computational problems can play the role of SATISFIABILITY in Cook's theorem. Such problems will be called complete.

Definition 5. The language L is *(polynomial) complete* if

a) $L \in \mathcal{NP}$ and

b) SATISFIABILITY $\leq L$.

Theorem 3. Either all complete languages are in $\mathcal{P}$, or none of them are. The former alternative holds if and only if $\mathcal{P} = \mathcal{NP}$. ...

The rest of the paper is mainly devoted to the proof of the following theorem.

Main theorem. All the problems on the following list are complete.

1. SATISFIABILITY

    COMMENT: By duality, this problem is equivalent to determining whether a disjunctive normal form expression is a tautology.

2. 0-1 INTEGER PROGRAMMING

    INPUT: integer matrix C and integer vector d

    PROPERTY: There exists a 0-1 vector x such that $Cx = d$.

3. CLIQUE

    INPUT: graph G, positive integer k

    PROPERTY: G has a set of k mutually adjacent nodes.

4. SET PACKING

    INPUT: Family of sets $\{S_j\}$, positive integer ℓ

    PROPERTY: $\{S_j\}$ contains ℓ mutually disjoint sets.

5. NODE COVER

    INPUT: graph G', positive integer ℓ

    PROPERTY: There is a set $R \subseteq N'$ such that $|R| \leq \ell$ and every arc is incident with some node in R.

6. SET COVERING

    INPUT: finite family of finite sets $\{S_j\}$, positive integer k

    PROPERTY: There is a subfamily $\{T_h\} \subseteq \{S_j\}$ containing $\leq k$ sets such that $\bigcup T_h = \bigcup S_j$.

7. FEEDBACK NODE SET

    INPUT: digraph H, positive integer k

PROPERTY: There is a set $R \subseteq V$ such that every (directed) cycle of H contains a node in R.

8. FEEDBACK ARC SET

   INPUT: digraph H, positive integer k

   PROPERTY: There is a set $S \subseteq E$ such that every (directed) cycle of H contains an arc in S.

9. DIRECTED HAMILTON CIRCUIT

   INPUT: digraph H

   PROPERTY: H has a directed cycle which includes each node exactly once.

10. UNDIRECTED HAMILTON CIRCUIT

    INPUT: graph G

    PROPERTY: G has a cycle which includes each node exactly once.

11. SATISFIABILITY WITH AT MOST 3 LITERALS PER CLAUSE

    INPUT: Clauses $D_1, D_2, \ldots, D_r$, each consisting of at most 3 literals from the set $\{u_1, u_2, \ldots, u_m\} \cup \{\overline{u_1}, \overline{u_2}, \ldots, \overline{u_m}\}$

    PROPERTY: The set $\{D_1, D_2, \ldots, D_r\}$ is satisfiable.

12. CHROMATIC NUMBER

    INPUT: graph G, positive integer k

    PROPERTY: There is a function $\phi : N \rightarrow Z_k$ such that, if u and v are adjacent, then $\phi(u) \neq \phi(v)$.

13. CLIQUE COVER

    INPUT: graph G', positive integer ℓ

    PROPERTY: N' is the union of ℓ or fewer cliques.

14. EXACT COVER

    INPUT: family $\{S_j\}$ of subsets of a set $\{u_i, i = 1, 2, \ldots, t\}$

    PROPERTY: There is a subfamily $\{T_h\} \subseteq \{S_j\}$ such that the sets T_h are disjoint and $\bigcup T_h = \bigcup S_j = \{u_i, i = 1, 2, \ldots, t\}$.

15. HITTING SET

    INPUT: family $\{U_i\}$ of subsets of $\{s_j, j = 1, 2, \ldots, r\}$

    PROPERTY: There is a set W such that, for each i, $|W \cap U_i| = 1$.

16. STEINER TREE

    INPUT: graph G, $R \subseteq N$, weighting function $w : A \rightarrow Z$, positive integer k

    PROPERTY: G has a subtree of weight $\leq k$ containing the set of nodes in R.

17. 3-DIMENSIONAL MATCHING

    INPUT: set $U \subseteq T \times T \times T$, where T is a finite set

    PROPERTY: There is a set $W \subseteq U$ such that $|W| = |T|$ and no two elements of W agree in any coordinate.

18. KNAPSACK

    INPUT: $(a_1, a_2, \ldots, a_n, b) \in Z^{n+1}$

PROPERTY: $\sum a_j x_j = b$ has a 0-1 solution.

19. JOB SEQUENCING

INPUT: "execution time vector" $(T_l, T_p) \in Z^p$, "deadline vector" $(D_1, \ldots, D_p) \in Z^p$, "penalty vector" $(P_1, \ldots, P_p) \in Z^p$, positive integer k

PROPERTY: There is a permutation π of $\{1, 2, \ldots, p\}$ such that

$$\left(\sum_{j=1}^{p} (\text{if } T_{\pi(1)} + \cdots + T_{\pi(j)} > D_{\pi(j)} \text{ then } P_{\pi(j)} \text{ else } 0) \right) \leq k.$$

20. PARTITION

INPUT: $(c_1, c_2, \ldots, c_s) \in Z^s$

PROPERTY: There is a set $I \subseteq \{1, 2, \ldots, s\}$ such that $\sum_{h \in I} c_h = \sum_{h \notin I} c_h$.

21. MAX CUT

INPUT: graph G, weighting function $w : A \to Z$, positive integer W

PROPERTY: There is a set $S \subseteq N$ such that

$$\sum_{\substack{\{u,v\} \in A \\ u \in S \\ v \notin S}} w(\{u, v\}) \geq W.$$

It is clear that these problems (or, more precisely, their encodings into Σ^*) are all in $\mathcal{NP}$. We proceed to give a series of explicit reductions, showing that SATISFIABILITY is reducible to each of the problems listed. Figure 36.1 shows the structure of the set of reductions. Each line in the figure indicates a reduction of the upper problem to the lower one.

To exhibit a reduction of a set $\subseteq D$ to a set $T' \subseteq D'$ we specify a function $F : D \to D'$ which satisfies the conditions of Lemma 2. In each case, the reader should have little difficulty in verifying that F does satisfy these conditions.

SATISFIABILITY $\leq$ 0-1 INTEGER PROGRAMMING

$$c_{ij} = \begin{cases} 1 & \text{if } x_j \in C_i \\ -1 & \text{if } \overline{x_j} \in C_i \\ 0 & \text{otherwise} \end{cases} \qquad i = 1, \ldots, p, j = 1, \ldots, n$$

$b_i = 1 - (\text{the number of complemented variables in } C_i), i = 1, 2, \ldots, p.$

SATISFIABILITY $\leq$ CLIQUE

$$N = \{\langle \sigma, i \rangle : \sigma \text{ is a literal and occurs in } C_i\}$$

$$A = \{\{\langle \sigma, i \rangle, \langle \delta, j \rangle\} : i \neq j \text{ and } \sigma \neq \overline{\delta}\}$$

$$k = p, \text{ the number of clauses.}$$

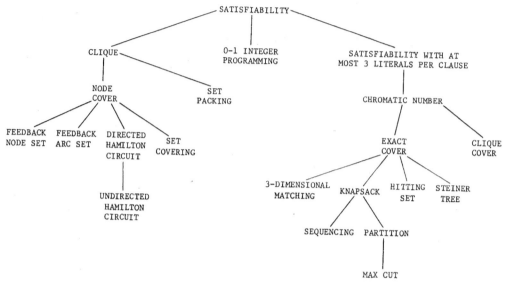

Figure 36.1: Complete problems

CLIQUE ≤ SET PACKING

Assume $N = \{1, 2, \ldots, n\}$. The elements of the sets $S_1, S_2, \ldots, S_n$ are those two-element sets of nodes $\{i, j\}$ not in A.

$$S_i = \{\{i, j\} : \{i, j\} \notin A\}, i = 1, 2, \ldots, n$$
$$\ell = k\ldots.$$

We conclude by listing the following important problems in $\mathcal{NP}$ which are not known to be complete. [EDITOR: The complexity of GRAPH ISOMORPHISM remains unknown, though László Babai (2016) has made significant progress on this problem. But it is now known that NONPRIMES ∈ $\mathcal{P}$ (Agrawal et al., 2004) and LINEAR INEQUALITIES ∈ $\mathcal{P}$ (Khachiyan, 1979).]

GRAPH ISOMORPHISM
INPUT: graphs G and G'
PROPERTY: G is isomorphic to G'.

NONPRIMES
INPUT: positive integer k
PROPERTY: k is composite.

LINEAR INEQUALITIES
INPUT: integer matrix C, integer vector d
PROPERTY: $Cx \geq d$ has a rational solution.

. . .

37 The Unix Time-Sharing System (1974)

Dennis Ritchie and Kenneth Thompson

The Compatible Time-Sharing System (chapter 23) was used only at MIT, but inspired a great deal of research and development on time-sharing systems. CTSS was succeeded by MULTICS, which MIT made some attempt to commercialize. One of the private-industry groups involved in developing MULTICS was at Bell Labs, which was building expertise in computer systems as the telephone system became automated. Ultimately Bell Labs withdrew from the MULTICS project, and a few of the researchers who had been involved in it decided to build a simpler, leaner operating system of their own, mostly to make it easier for them to write and debug code. Originally designed to run as a single-user system on a small computer (hence the name, a take-off on "MULTICS"), UNIX grew as the original developers, and their colleagues, found more uses for it at Bell Labs.

Bell Labs licensed UNIX for use outside the company, charging very low fees to universities. The effect was to make UNIX the *de facto* standard in computer science research departments. Generations of top technical talent graduated with knowledge of its structure and fondness for its modular, flexible, unencumbered design. The team working on UNIX developed the C programming language to implement it effectively (the original implementation was in assembly language), and this low-level higher-level language became a systems programming staple. UNIX's hierarchical file structure (which UNIX inherited from MULTICS) has also been widely influential. Ultimately UNIX became the basis for the Berkeley Software Distribution (BSD), Richard Stallman's GNU ("GNU's not UNIX"), Linus Torvalds's Linux, and Apple's Mac OS X.

Dennis Ritchie (1941–2011) was the son of a Bell Labs scientist. He studied physics at Harvard and computer science as a graduate student. He wrote and defended his PhD dissertation in 1968. But by then he was working at Bell Labs and failed to turn in the final version of the thesis, so he never received his PhD. Ritchie worked at Bell Labs for the remainder of his career. Ken Thompson (b. 1943), a Berkeley graduate, started at Bell Labs in 1966 and remained there until he retired in 2000, when he moved to Google. Ritchie and Thompson were recognized with the Turing Award in 1983—less than a decade after the publication of this description of UNIX.

Reprinted from Ritchie and Thompson (1974), with permission from the Association for Computing Machinery.

U NIX is a general-purpose, multi-user, interactive operating system for the Digital Equipment Corporation (DEC) PDP-11/40 and 11/45 computers. It offers a number of features
seldom found even in larger operating systems, including: (1) a hierarchical file system incorporating demountable volumes; (2) compatible file, device, and inter-process I/O; (3) the ability
to initiate asynchronous processes; (4) system command language selectable on a per-user basis;
and (5) over 100 subsystems including a dozen languages. This paper discusses the nature and
implementation of the file system and of the user command interface.

37.1   Introduction

There have been three versions of UNIX. The earliest version (circa 1969–70) ran on the Digital
Equipment Corporation PDP-7 and -9 computers. The second version ran on the unprotected
PDP-11/20 computer. [EDITOR: That is, the computer lacked memory protection mechanisms
to support time-sharing.] This paper describes only the PDP-11/40 and /45 (DEC, 1972) system
since it is more modern and many of the differences between it and older UNIX systems result
from redesign of features found to be deficient or lacking.

Since PDP-11 UNIX became operational in February 1971, about 40 installations have been put
into service; they are generally smaller than the system described here. Most of them are engaged
in applications such as the preparation and formatting of patent applications and other textual
material, the collection and processing of trouble data from various switching machines within
the Bell System, and recording and checking telephone service orders. Our own installation is
used mainly for research in operating systems, languages, computer networks, and other topics
in computer science, and also for document preparation.

Perhaps the most important achievement of UNIX is to demonstrate that a powerful operating
system for interactive use need not be expensive either in equipment or in human effort: UNIX
can run on hardware costing as little as $40,000, and less than two man years were spent on
the main system software. Yet UNIX contains a number of features seldom offered even in
much larger systems. It is hoped, however, the users of UNIX will find that the most important
characteristics of the system are its simplicity, elegance, and ease of use. . . .

37.2   Hardware and Software Environment

. . .

37.3   The File System

The most important job of UNIX is to provide a file system. From the point of view of the user,
there are three kinds of files: ordinary disk files, directories, and special files.

37.3.1   Ordinary files   A file contains whatever information the user places on it, for example
symbolic or binary (object) programs. No particular structuring is expected by the system. Files
of text consist simply of a string of characters, with lines demarcated by the new-line character.
Binary programs are sequences of words as they will appear in core memory when the program

starts executing. A few user programs manipulate files with more structure: the assembler generates and the loader expects an object file in a particular format. However, the structure of files is controlled by the programs which use them, not by the system.

37.3.2 Directories Directories provide the mapping between the names of files and the files themselves, and thus induce a structure on the file system as a whole. Each user has a directory of his own files; he may also create subdirectories to contain groups of files conveniently treated together. A directory behaves exactly like an ordinary file except that it cannot be written on by unprivileged programs, so that the system controls the contents of directories. However, anyone with appropriate permission may read a directory just like any other file.

The system maintains several directories for its own use. One of these is the *root* directory. All files in the system can be found by tracing a path through a chain of directories until the desired file is reached. The starting point for such searches is often the root. Another system directory contains all the programs provided for general use; that is, all the *commands*. As will be seen however, it is by no means necessary that a program reside in this directory for it to be executed.

Files are named by sequences of 14 or fewer characters. When the name of a file is specified to the system, it may be in the form of a *path name*, which is a sequence of directory names separated by slashes "/" and ending in a file name. If the sequence begins with a slash, the search begins in the root directory. The name */alpha/beta/gamma* causes the system to search the root for directory *alpha*, then to search *alpha* for *beta*, finally to find *gamma* in *beta*. *Gamma* may be an ordinary file, a directory, or a special file. As a limiting case, the name "/" refers to the root itself.

A path name not starting with "/" causes the system to begin the search in the user's current directory. Thus, the name *alpha/beta* specifies the file named *beta* in subdirectory *alpha* of the current directory. The simplest kind of name, for example *alpha*, refers to a file which itself is found in the current directory. As another limiting case, the null file name refers to the current directory.

The same nondirectory file may appear in several directories under possibly different names. This feature is called *linking*; a directory entry for a file is sometimes called a link. UNIX differs from other systems in which linking is permitted in that all links to a file have equal status. That is, a file does not exist within a particular directory; the directory entry for a file consists merely of its name and a pointer to the information actually describing the file. Thus a file exists independently of any directory entry, although in practice a file is made to disappear along with the last link to it.

Each directory always has at least two entries. The name "." in each directory refers to the directory itself. Thus a program may read the current directory under the name "." without knowing its complete path name. The name ".." by convention refers to the parent of the directory in which it appears, that is, to the directory in which it was created.

The directory structure is constrained to have the form of a rooted tree. Except for the special entries "." and "..", each directory must appear as an entry in exactly one other, which is its parent.

The reason for this is to simplify the writing of programs which visit subtrees of the directory structure, and more important, to avoid the separation of portions of the hierarchy. If arbitrary links to directories were permitted, it would be quite difficult to detect when the last connection from the root to a directory was severed.

37.3.3   Special files   Special files constitute the most unusual feature of the UNIX file system. Each I/O device supported by UNIX is associated with at least one such file. Special files are read and written just like ordinary disk files, but requests to read or write result in activation of the associated device. An entry for each special file resides in directory */dev*, although a link may be made to one of these files just like an ordinary file. Thus, for example, to punch paper tape, one may write on the file */dev/ppt*. Special files exist for each communication line, each disk, each tape drive, and for physical core memory. Of course, the active disks and the core special file are protected from indiscriminate access.

There is a threefold advantage in treating I/O devices this way: file and device I/O are as similar as possible; file and device names have the same syntax and meaning, so that a program expecting a file name as a parameter can be passed a device name; finally, special files are subject to the same protection mechanism as regular files.

37.3.4   Removable file systems   ...

37.3.5   Protection   Although the access control scheme in UNIX is quite simple, it has some unusual features. Each user of the system is assigned a unique user identification number. When a file is created, it is marked with the user ID of its owner. Also given for new files is a set of seven protection bits. Six of these specify independently read, write, and execute permission for the owner of the file and for all other users.

If the seventh bit is on, the system will temporarily change the user identification of the current user to that of the creator of the file whenever the file is executed as a program. This change in user ID is effective only during the execution of the program which calls for it. The set-user-ID feature provides for privileged programs which may use files inaccessible to other users. For example, a program may keep an accounting file which should neither be read nor changed except by the program itself. If the set-user-identification bit is on for the program, it may access the file although this access might be forbidden to other programs invoked by the given program's user. Since the actual user ID of the invoker of any program is always available, set-user-ID programs may take any measures desired to satisfy themselves as to their invoker's credentials. This mechanism is used to allow users to execute the carefully written commands which call privileged system entries. For example, there is a system entry invocable only by the "super-user" (below) which creates an empty directory. As indicated above, directories are expected to have entries for "." and "..". The command which creates a directory is owned by the super user and has the set-user-ID bit set. After it checks its invoker's authorization to create the specified directory, it creates it and makes the entries for "." and "..".

Since anyone may set the set-user-ID bit on one of his own files, this mechanism is generally available without administrative intervention. For example, this protection scheme easily solves the MOO accounting problem posed in Aleph-Null (1971).

The system recognizes one particular user ID (that of the "super-user") as exempt from the usual constraints on file access; thus (for example) programs may be written to dump and reload the file system without unwanted interference from the protection system.

37.3.6   I/O calls   The system calls to do I/O are designed to eliminate the differences between the various devices and styles of access. There is no distinction between "random" and sequential I/O, nor is any logical record size imposed by the system. The size of an ordinary file is determined by the highest byte written on it; no predetermination of the size of a file is necessary or possible. To illustrate the essentials of I/O in UNIX, Some of the basic calls are summarized below in an anonymous language which will indicate the required parameters without getting into the complexities of machine language programming. Each call to the system may potentially result in an error return, which for simplicity is not represented in the calling sequence. To read or write a file assumed to exist already, it must be opened by the following call:

filep = open (name, flag)

Name indicates the name of the file. An arbitrary path name may be given. The *flag* argument indicates whether the file is to be read, written, or "updated", that is read and written simultaneously.

The returned value *filep* is called a *file descriptor*. It is a small integer used to identify the file in subsequent calls to read, write, or otherwise manipulate it.

To create a new file or completely rewrite an old one, there is a *create* system call which creates the given file if it does not exist, or truncates it to zero length if it does exist. *Create* also opens the new file for writing and, like *open*, returns a file descriptor.

There are no user-visible locks in the file system, nor is there any restriction on the number of users who may have a file open for reading or writing; although it is possible for the contents of a file to become scrambled when two users write on it simultaneously, in practice, difficulties do not arise. We take the view that locks are neither necessary nor sufficient, in our environment, to prevent interference between users of the same file. They are unnecessary because we are not faced with large, single-file data bases maintained by independent processes. They are insufficient because locks in the ordinary sense, whereby one user is prevented from writing on a file which another user is reading, cannot prevent confusion when, for example, both users are editing a file with an editor which makes a copy of the file being edited. It should be said that the system has sufficient internal interlocks to maintain the logical consistency of the file system when two users engage simultaneously in such inconvenient activities as writing on the same file, creating files in the same directory or deleting each other's open files.

Except as indicated below, reading and writing are sequential. This means that if a particular byte in the file was the last byte written (or read), the next I/O call implicitly refers to the first following byte. For each open file there is a pointer, maintained by the system, which indicates the next byte to be read or written. If *n* bytes are read or written, the pointer advances by *n* bytes.

Once a file is open, the following calls may be used:

n = read(filep, buffer, count)
n = write(filep, buffer, count)

Up to *count* bytes are transmitted between the file specified by *filep* and the byte array specified by *buffer*. The returned value *n* is the number of bytes actually transmitted. In the *write* case, *n* is the same as *count* except under exceptional conditions like I/O errors or end of physical medium on special files; in a read, however, *n* may without error be less than *count*. If the read pointer is so near the end of the file that reading count characters would cause reading beyond the end, only sufficient bytes are transmitted to reach the end of the file; also, typewriter-like devices never return more than one line of input. When a *read* call returns with *n* equal to zero, it indicates the end of the file. For disk files this occurs when the read pointer becomes equal to the current size of the file. It is possible to generate an end-of-file from a typewriter by use of an escape sequence which depends on the device used.

Bytes written on a file affect only those implied by the position of the write pointer and the count; no other part of the file is changed. If the last byte lies beyond the end of the file, the file is grown as needed.

To do random (direct access) I/O, it is only necessary to move the read or write pointer to the appropriate location in the file.

location = seek(filep, base, offset)

The pointer associated with *filep* is moved to a position *offset* bytes from the beginning of the file, from the current position of the pointer, or from the end of the file, depending on *base*. *Offset* may be negative. For some devices (e.g. paper tape and typewriters) seek calls are ignored. The actual offset from the beginning of the file to which the pointer was moved is returned in *location*.

37.3.6.1   I/O calls   There are several additional system entries having to do with I/O and with the file system which will not be discussed. For example: close a file, get the status of a file, change the protection mode or the owner of a file, create a directory, make a link to an existing file, delete a file.

37.4   Implementation of the File System

As mentioned in §37.3.2 above, a directory entry contains only a name for the associated file and a pointer to the file itself. This pointer is an integer called the *i-number* (for index number) of the file. When the file is accessed, its *i-number* is used as an index into a system table (the *i-list*) stored in a known part of the device on which the directory resides. The entry thereby found (the file's *i-node*) contains the description of the file as follows.

1. Its owner.
2. Its protection bits.

3. The physical disk or tape addresses for the file contents.
4. Its size.
5. Time of last modification
6. The number of links to the file, that is, the number of times it appears in a directory.
7. A bit indicating whether the file is a directory.
8. A bit indicating whether the file is a special file.
9. A bit indicating whether the file is "large" or "small."

The purpose of an *open* or *create* system call is to turn the path name given by the user into an i-number by searching the explicitly or implicitly named directories. Once a file is open, its device, i-number, and read/write pointer are stored in a system table indexed by the file descriptor returned by the *open* or *create*. Thus the file descriptor supplied during a subsequent call to read or write the file may be easily related to the information necessary to access the file.

When a new file is created, an i-node is allocated for it and a directory entry is made which contains the name of the file and the i-node number. Making a link to an existing file involves creating a directory entry with the new name, copying the i-number from the original file entry, and incrementing the link-count field of the i-node. Removing (deleting) a file is done by decrementing the link-count of the i-node specified by its directory entry and erasing the directory entry. If the link-count drops to 0, any disk blocks in the file are freed and the i-node is deallocated.

The space on all fixed or removable disks which contain a file system is divided into a number of 512-byte blocks logically addressed from 0 up to a limit which depends on the device. There is space in the i-node of each file for eight device addresses. A *small* (nonspecial) file fits into eight or fewer blocks; in this case the addresses of the blocks themselves are stored. For *large* (nonspecial) files, each of the eight device addresses may point to an indirect block of 256 addresses of blocks constituting the file itself. These files may be as large as $8 \cdot 256 \cdot 512$, or $1,048,576$ (2^{20}) bytes.

The foregoing discussion applies to ordinary files. When an I/O request is made to a file whose i-node indicates that it is special, the last seven device address words are immaterial, and the list is interpreted as a pair of bytes which constitute an internal *device* name. These bytes specify respectively a device type and subdevice number. The device type indicates which system routine will deal with I/O on that device; the subdevice number selects, for example, a disk drive attached to a particular controller or one of several similar typewriter interfaces.

In this environment, the implementation of the *mount* system call (§37.3.4) is quite straightforward. *Mount* maintains a system table whose argument is the i-number and device name of the ordinary file specified during the *mount*, and whose corresponding value is the device name of the indicated special file. This table is searched for each (i-number, device)-pair which turns up while a path name is being scanned during an *open* or *create*; if a match is found, the i-number is replaced by 1 (which is the i-number of the root directory on all file systems), and the device name is replaced by the table value.

To the user, both reading and writing of files appear to be synchronous and unbuffered. That is immediately after return from a *read* call the data are available, and conversely after a *write* the user's workspace may be reused. In fact the system maintains a rather complicated buffering mechanism which reduces greatly the number of I/O operations required to access a file. Suppose a *write* call is made specifying transmission of a single byte.

UNIX will search its buffers to see whether the affected disk block currently resides in core memory; if not, it will be read in from the device. Then the affected byte is replaced in the buffer, and an entry is made in a list of blocks to be written. The return from the *write* call may then take place, although the actual I/O may not be completed until a later time. Conversely, if a single byte is read, the system determines whether the secondary storage block in which the byte is located is already in one of the system's buffers; if so, the byte can be returned immediately. If not, the block is read into a buffer and the byte picked out.

A program which reads or writes files in units of 512 bytes has an advantage over a program which reads or writes a single byte at a time, but the gain is not immense; it comes mainly from the avoidance of system overhead. A program which is used rarely or which does no great volume of I/O may quite reasonably read and write in units as small as it wishes.

The notion of the i-list is an unusual feature of UNIX. In practice, this method of organizing the file system has proved quite reliable and easy to deal with. To the system itself, one of its strengths is the fact that each file has a short, unambiguous name which is related in a simple way to the protection, addressing, and other information needed to access the file. It also permits a quite simple and rapid algorithm for checking the consistency of a file system, for example verification that the portions of each device containing useful information and those free to be allocated are disjoint and together exhaust the space on the device. This algorithm is independent of the directory hierarchy, since it need only scan the linearly-organized i-list. At the same time the notion of the i-list induces certain peculiarities not found in other file system organizations. For example, there is the question of who is to be charged for the space a file occupies, since all directory entries for a file have equal status. Charging the owner of a file is unfair, in general, since one user may create a file, another may link to it, and the first user may delete the file. The first user is still the owner of the file, but it should be charged to the second user. The simplest reasonably fair algorithm seems to be to spread the charges equally among users who have links to a file. The current version of UNIX avoids the issue by not charging any fees at all.

37.4.1   Efficiency of the file system   ...

37.5   Processes and Images

An *image* is a computer execution environment. It includes a core image, general register values, status of open files, current directory, and the like. An image is the current state of a pseudo computer.

A *process* is the execution of an image. While the processor is executing on behalf of a process, the image must reside in core; during the execution of other processes it remains in core unless the appearance of an active, higher-priority process forces it to be swapped out to the fixed-head disk.

The user-core part of an image is divided into three logical segments. The program text segment begins at location 0 in the virtual address space. During execution, this segment is write-protected and a single copy of it is shared among all processes executing the same program. At the first 8K byte boundary above the program text segment in the virtual address space begins a non-shared, writable data segment, the size of which may be extended by a system call. Starting at the highest address in the virtual address space is a stack segment, which automatically grows downward as the hardware's stack pointer fluctuates.

37.5.1 Processes Except while UNIX is bootstrapping itself into operation, a new process can come into existence only by use of the fork system call:

processid = fork (label)

When *fork* is executed by a process, it splits into two independently executing processes. The two processes have independent copies of the original core image, and share any open files. The new processes differ only in that one is considered the parent process: in the parent, control returns directly from the *fork*, while in the child, control is passed to location *label*. The *processid* returned by the *fork* call is the identification of the other process. Because the return points in the parent and child process are not the same, each image existing after a *fork* may determine whether it is the parent or child process.

37.5.2 Pipes Processes may communicate with related processes using the same system *read* and *write* calls that are used for file system I/O. The call

filep = pipe( )

returns a file descriptor *filep* and creates an interprocess channel called a *pipe*. This channel, like other open files, is passed from parent to child process in the image by the *fork* call. A *read* using a pipe file descriptor waits until another process writes using the file descriptor for the same pipe. At this point, data are passed between the images of the two processes. Neither process need know that a pipe, rather than an ordinary file, is involved.

Although interprocess communication via pipes is a quite valuable tool (see §37.6.2), it is not a completely general mechanism since the pipe must be set up by a common ancestor of the processes involved.

37.5.3 Execution of programs Another major system primitive is invoked by

execute(file, arg_1, arg_2, ..., arg_n)

which requests the system to read in and execute the program named by *file*, passing it string arguments $arg_1, arg_2, ..., arg_n$. Ordinarily, arg_1 should be the same string as *file*, so that the program may determine the name by which it was invoked. All the code and data in the process using *execute* is replaced from the file, but open files, current directory, and interprocess relationships are unaltered. Only if the call fails, for example because *file* could not be found or because its execute-permission bit was not set, does a return take place from the *execute* primitive; it resembles a "jump" machine instruction rather than a subroutine call.

37.5.4   Process synchronization   Another process control system call

processid = wait( )

causes its caller to suspend execution until one of its children has completed execution. Then *wait* returns the *processid* of the terminated process. An error return is taken if the calling process has no descendants. Certain status from the child process is also available. *Wait* may also present status from a grandchild or more distant ancestor; see §37.5.5.

37.5.5   Termination   Lastly,

exit (status)

terminates a process, destroys its image, closes its open files, and generally obliterates it. When the parent is notified through the *wait* primitive, the indicated *status* is available to the parent; if the parent has already terminated, the status is available to the grandparent, and so on. Processes may also terminate as a result of various illegal actions or user-generated signals (§37.7 below).

37.6   The Shell

For most users, communication with UNIX is carried on with the aid of a program called the Shell. The Shell is a command line interpreter: it reads lines typed by the user and interprets them as requests to execute other programs. In simplest form, a command line consists of the command name followed by arguments to the command, all separated by spaces:

command arg$_1$ arg$_2$ ... arg$_n$

The Shell splits up the command name and the arguments into separate strings. Then a file with name *command* is sought; *command* may be a path name including the "/" character to specify any file in the system. If *command* is found, it is brought into core and executed. The arguments collected by the Shell are accessible to the command. When the command is finished, the Shell resumes its own execution, and indicates its readiness to accept another command by typing a prompt character.

If file *command* cannot be found, the Shell prefixes the string /bin/ to command and attempts again to find the file. Directory */bin* contains all the commands intended to be generally used.

37.6.1   Standard I/O   The discussion of I/O in §37.3 above seems to imply that every file used by a program must be opened or created by the program in order to get a file descriptor for the file. Programs executed by the Shell, however, start off with two open files which have file descriptors 0 and 1. As such a program begins execution, file 1 is open for writing, and is best understood as the standard output file. Except under circumstances indicated below, this file is the user's typewriter. Thus programs which wish to write informative or diagnostic information ordinarily use file descriptor 1. Conversely, file 0 starts off open for reading, and programs which wish to read messages typed by the user usually read this file. The Shell is able to change the standard assignments of these file descriptors from the user's typewriter printer and keyboard. If one of the arguments to a command is prefixed by ">", file descriptor 1 will, for the duration of the command, refer to the file named after the ">". For example, ls

ordinarily lists, on the typewriter, the names of the files in the current directory. The command

ls >there

creates a file called there and places the listing there. Thus the argument "> there" means, "place output on there." On the other hand,

ed

ordinarily enters the editor, which takes requests from the user via his typewriter. The command

ed <script

interprets *script* as a file of editor commands; thus "<script" means, "take input from script."

Although the file name following "<" or ">" appears to be an argument to the command, in fact it is interpreted completely by the Shell and is not passed to the command at all. Thus no special coding to handle I/O redirection is needed within each command; the command need merely use the standard file descriptors 0 and 1 where appropriate.

37.6.2   Filters   An extension of the standard I/O notion is used to direct output from one command to the input of another. A sequence of commands separated by vertical bars causes the Shell to execute all the commands simultaneously and to arrange that the standard output of each command be delivered to the standard input of the next command in the sequence. Thus in the command line

ls | pr -2 | opr

ls lists the names of the files in the current directory; its output is passed to *pr*, which paginates its input with dated headings. The argument "-2" means double column. Likewise the output from *pr* is input to *opr*. This command spools its input onto a file for off-line printing.

This process could have been carried out more clumsily by

ls > temp1
pr -2 <temp1 >temp2
opr <temp2

followed by removal of the temporary files. In the absence of the ability to redirect output and input, a still clumsier method would have been to require the ls command to accept user requests to paginate its output, to print in multicolumn format, and to arrange that its output be delivered off-line. Actually it would be surprising, and in fact unwise for efficiency reasons, to expect authors of commands such as ls to provide such a wide variety of output options.

A program such as *pr* which copies its standard input to its standard output (with processing) is called a *filter*. Some filters which we have found useful perform character transliteration, sorting of the input, and encryption and decryption.

37.6.3   Command separators: multitasking   Another feature provided by the Shell is relatively straightforward. Commands need not be on different lines; instead they may be separated by semicolons.

ls; ed

will first list the contents of the current directory, then enter the editor.

A related feature is more interesting. If a command is followed by "&", the Shell will not wait for the command to finish before prompting again; instead, it is ready immediately to accept a new command. For example,

as source > output &

causes source to be assembled, with diagnostic output going to output; no matter how long the assembly takes, the Shell returns immediately. When the Shell does not wait for the completion of a command, the identification of the process running that command is printed. This identification may be used to wait for the completion of the command or to terminate it. The "&" may be used several times in a line:

as source > output & ls > files &

does both the assembly and the listing in the background. In the examples above using "&", an output file other than the typewriter was provided; if this had not been done, the outputs of the various commands would have been intermingled.

The Shell also allows parentheses in the above operations. For example,

(date; ls) > x &

prints the current date and time followed by a list of the current directory onto the file x. The Shell also returns immediately for another request.

37.6.4   The Shell as a command: command files   The Shell is itself a command, and may be called recursively. Suppose file tryout contains the lines

as source
mv a.out testprog
testprog

The *mv* command causes the file *a.out* to be renamed *testprog.a.out* is the (binary) output of the assembler, ready to be executed. Thus if the three lines above were typed on the console, *source* would be assembled, the resulting program named *testprog*, and *testprog* executed. When the lines are in *tryout*, the command

sh < tryout

would cause the Shell *sh* to execute the commands sequentially.

The Shell has further capabilities, including the ability to substitute parameters and to construct argument lists from a specified subset of the file names in a directory. It is also possible to execute commands conditionally on character string comparisons or on existence of given files and to perform transfers of control within filed command sequences.

37.6.5   Implementation of the Shell   The outline of the operation of the Shell can now be understood. Most of the time, the Shell is waiting for the user to type a command. When the new-line character ending the line is typed, the Shell's *read* call returns. The Shell analyzes the command line, putting the arguments in a form appropriate for *execute*. Then *fork* is called. The child process, whose code of course is still that of the Shell, attempts to perform an *execute* with the appropriate arguments. If successful, this will bring in and start execution of the program whose name was given. Meanwhile, the other process resulting from the *fork*, which is the parent process, *waits* for the child process to die. When this happens, the Shell knows the command is finished, so it types its prompt and reads the typewriter to obtain another command.

Given this framework, the implementation of background processes is trivial; whenever a command line contains "&", the Shell merely refrains from waiting for the process which it created to execute the command.

Happily, all of this mechanism meshes very nicely with the notion of standard input and output files. When a process is created by the *fork* primitive, it inherits not only the core image of its parent but also all the files currently open in its parent, including those with file descriptors 0 and 1. The Shell, of course, uses these files to read command lines and to write its prompts and diagnostics, and in the ordinary case its children—the command programs—inherit them automatically. When an argument with "<" or ">" is given however, the offspring process, just before it performs execute, makes the standard I/O file descriptor 0 or 1 respectively refer to the named file. This is easy because, by agreement, the smallest unused file descriptor is assigned when a new file is *open*ed (or *create*d); it is only necessary to close file 0 (or 1) and open the named file. Because the process in which the command program runs simply terminates when it is through, the association between a file specified after "<" or ">" and file descriptor 0 or 1 is ended automatically when the process dies. Therefore the Shell need not know the actual names of the files which are its own standard input and output since it need never reopen them.

Filters are straightforward extensions of standard I/O redirection with pipes used instead of files.

In ordinary circumstances, the main loop of the Shell never terminates. (The main loop includes that branch of the return from fork belonging to the parent process; that is, the branch which does a wait, then reads another command line.) The one thing which causes the Shell to terminate is discovering an end-of-file condition on its input file. Thus, when the Shell is executed as a command with a given input file, as in

sh < comfile

the commands in *comfile* will be executed until the end of *comfile* is reached; then the instance of the Shell invoked by sh will terminate. Since this Shell process is the child of another instance of the Shell, the *wait* executed in the latter will return, and another command may be processed.

37.6.6   Initialization   The instances of the Shell to which users type commands are themselves children of another process. The last step in the initialization of UNIX is the creation of a single process and the invocation (via *execute*) of a program called *init*. The role of *init* is to create one process for each typewriter channel which may be dialed up by a user. The various subinstances of init open the appropriate typewriters for input and output. Since when *init* was invoked there were no files open, in each process the typewriter keyboard will receive file descriptor 0 and the printer file descriptor 1. Each process types out a message requesting that the user log in and waits, reading the typewriter, for a reply. At the outset, no one is logged in, so each process simply hangs. Finally someone types his name or other identification. The appropriate instance of *init* wakes up, receives the log-in line, and reads a password file. If the user name is found, and if he is able to supply the correct password, *init* changes to the user's default current directory, sets the process's user ID to that of the person logging in, and performs an *execute* of the Shell. At this point the Shell is ready to receive commands and the logging-in protocol is complete.

Meanwhile, the mainstream path of *init* (the parent of all the subinstances of itself which will later become Shells) does a *wait*. If one of the child processes terminates, either because a Shell found an end of file or because a user typed an incorrect name or password, this path of *init* simply recreates the defunct process, which in turn reopens the appropriate input and output files and types another login message. Thus a user may log out simply by typing the end-of-file sequence in place of a command to the Shell.

37.6.7   Other programs as Shell   The Shell as described above is designed to allow users full access to the facilities of the system since it will invoke the execution of any program with appropriate protection mode. Sometimes, however, a different interface to the system is desirable, and this feature is easily arranged.

Recall that after a user has successfully logged in by supplying his name and password, *init* ordinarily invokes the Shell to interpret command lines. The user's entry in the password file may contain the name of a program to be invoked after login instead of the Shell. This program is free to interpret the user's messages in any way it wishes.

For example, the password file entries for users of a secretarial editing system specify that the editor *ed* is to be used instead of the Shell. Thus when editing system users log in, they are inside the editor and can begin work immediately; also, they can be prevented from invoking UNIX programs not intended for their use. In practice, it has proved desirable to allow a temporary escape from the editor to execute the formatting program and other utilities.

Several of the games (e.g. chess, blackjack, 3D tic-tac-toe) available on UNIX illustrate a much more severely restricted environment. For each of these an entry exists in the password file specifying that the appropriate game-playing program is to be invoked instead of the Shell. People who log in as a player of one of the games find themselves limited to the game and unable to investigate the presumably more interesting offerings of UNIX as a whole.

37.7   Traps

The PDP-11 hardware detects a number of program faults, such as references to nonexistent memory, unimplemented instructions, and odd addresses used where an even address is required. Such faults cause the processor to trap to a system routine. When an illegal action is caught, unless other arrangements have been made, the system terminates the process and writes the user's image on file core in the current directory. A debugger can be used to determine the state of the program at the time of the fault.

Programs which are looping, which produce unwanted output, or about which the user has second thoughts may be halted by the use of the *interrupt* signal, which is generated by typing the "delete" character. Unless special action has been taken, this signal simply causes the program to cease execution without producing a core image file.

There is also a *quit* signal which is used to force a core image to be produced. Thus programs which loop unexpectedly may be halted and the core image examined without prearrangement.

The hardware-generated faults and the interrupt and quit signals can, by request, be either ignored or caught by the process. For example, the Shell ignores quits to prevent a quit from logging the user out. The editor catches interrupts and returns to its command level. This is useful for stopping long printouts without losing work in progress (the editor manipulates a copy of the file it is editing). In systems without floating point hardware, unimplemented instructions are caught, and floating point instructions are interpreted.

37.8 Perspective

Perhaps paradoxically, the success of UNIX is largely due to the fact that it was not designed to meet any predefined objectives. The first version was written when one of us (Thompson), dissatisfied with the available computer facilities, discovered a little-used system PDP-7 and set out to create a more hospitable environment. This essentially personal effort was sufficiently successful to gain the interest of the remaining author and others, and later to justify the acquisition of the PDP-11/20, specifically to support a text editing and formatting system. Then in turn the 11/20 was outgrown, UNIX had proved useful enough to persuade management to invest in the PDP-11/45. Our goals throughout the effort, when articulated at all, have always concerned themselves with building a comfortable relationship with the machine and with exploring ideas and inventions in operating systems. We have not been faced with the need to satisfy someone else's requirements, and for this freedom we are grateful. Three considerations which influenced the design of UNIX are visible in retrospect.

First, since we are programmers, we naturally designed the system to make it easy to write, test, and run programs. The most important expression of our desire for programming convenience was that the system was arranged for interactive use, even though the original version only supported one user. We believe that a properly designed interactive system is much more productive and satisfying to use than a "batch" system. Moreover such a system is rather easily adaptable to noninteractive use, while the converse is not true. Second there have always been fairly severe size constraints on the system and its software. Given the partiality antagonistic desires for reasonable efficiency and expressive power, the size constraint has encouraged not only economy but a certain elegance of design. This may be a thinly disguised version of the "salvation through suffering" philosophy, but in our case it worked.

Third, nearly from the start, the system was able to, and did, maintain itself. This fact is more important than it might seem. If designers of a system are forced to use that system, they quickly become aware of its functional and superficial deficiencies and are strongly motivated to correct them before it is too late. Since all source programs were always available and easily modified on-line, we were willing to revise and rewrite the system and its software when new ideas were invented, discovered, or suggested by others.

The aspects of UNIX discussed in this paper exhibit clearly at least the first two of these design considerations. The interface to the file system, for example, is extremely convenient from a programming standpoint. The lowest possible interface level is designed to eliminate distinctions between the various devices and files and between direct and sequential access. No large "access method" routines are required to insulate the programmer from the system calls; in fact, all user programs either call the system directly or use a small library program, only tens of instructions long, which buffers a number of characters and reads or writes them all at once.

Another important aspect of programming convenience is that there are no "control blocks" with a complicated structure partially maintained by and depended on by the file system or other system calls. Generally speaking, the contents of a program's address space are the property of the program, and we have tried to avoid placing restrictions on the data structures within that address space.

Given the requirement that all programs should be usable with any file or device as input or output, it is also desirable from a space-efficiency standpoint to push device-dependent considerations into the operating system itself. The only alternatives seem to be to load routines for dealing with each device with all programs, which is expensive in space, or to depend on some means of dynamically linking to the routine appropriate to each device when it is actually needed, which is expensive either in overhead or in hardware.

Likewise, the process control scheme and command interface have proved both convenient and efficient. Since the Shell operates as an ordinary, swappable user program, it consumes no wired-down space in the system proper, and it may be made as powerful as desired at little cost, In particular, given the framework in which the Shell executes as a process which spawns other processes to perform commands, the notions of I/O redirection, background processes, command files, and user-selectable system interfaces all become essentially trivial to implement.

. . .

38 A Protocol for Packet Network Intercommunication (1974)

Vinton Cerf and Robert Kahn

Computer networking responded to several needs and took shape under the influence of commercial, governmental, and scientific initiatives. The launch of the Soviet space satellite *Sputnik* in 1957 resulted in the formation of the Advanced Research Projects Agency (ARPA) in the U.S. Department of Defense, essentially tasked with fostering research that would avoid such shocking surprises in the future. As early as 1960, Paul Baran, a researcher at the RAND Corporation with funding from the Air Force, was proposing that a redundant, distributed, packet-switched network could survive a nuclear attack that might cripple the U.S. telecommunications grid (Baran, 1964). Meanwhile J. C. R. Licklider, after publishing *Man-Computer Symbiosis* (chapter 20), began speculating about an "Intergalactic Computer Network," and when he became the head of the Information Processing Technology Office (IPTO) within ARPA in 1964, started generously funding computer networking research, an initiative that was continued by his successor at IPTO, Robert Taylor. Taylor started what would become the ARPANET, which became the internet, by using a million dollars of his budget to enable remote access to ARPA-funded computers. Taylor tasked Lawrence "Larry" Roberts with designing the network, and Roberts, after connecting with Baran and the British researcher Donald Davies (who was developing related ideas), settled on the packet-switched design and, in 1968, issued the request for proposals to build the ARPANET hardware and software. Roberts succeeded Taylor as head of IPTO, providing continuity to the networking initiatives.

Meanwhile, IBM, DEC, and other computer manufacturers were developing their own networks so to share data and peripheral devices, but the manufacturers had no incentive to agree on a networking standard that would enable competitors' machines to join a network of their machines. Vinton Cerf (b. 1943) and Robert Kahn (b. 1938) turned the ARPANET into the internet by developing a set of protocols for connecting networks together.

Cerf and Kahn had both worked on the early ARPANET project, Cerf at UCLA and Kahn at Bolt Beranek and Newman (BBN), the firm that had won the initial ARPANET contract. In 1973, Cerf and Kahn began to collaborate on the design of standards and protocols for internetworking, which yielded this seminal paper. The basic design it describes remains in place, with one major revision. What the paper calls TCP was in 1978 split into a set of two protocols, TCP/IP—the host protocol TCP and the separate Internet Protocol IP. TCP provides reliable end-to-end service between hosts, relying on IP, a simpler and unreliable protocol running on gateways.

Reprinted from Cerf and Kahn (1974), with permission from the Institute of Electrical and Electronics Engineers.

Cerf and Kahn have both played major roles in promoting not just internet technology but the spirit of the internet as a global information sharing resource. Their Turing Award citation (ACM, 2004) recognizes them both for their technical contributions and for "inspired leadership in networking."

—————————————⋙⋘—————————————

A protocol that supports the sharing of resources that exist in different packet switching networks is presented. The protocol provides for variation in individual network packet sizes, transmission failures, sequencing, flow control, end-to-end error checking, and the creation and destruction of logical process-to-process connections. Some implementation issues are considered, and problems such as internetwork routing, accounting, and timeouts are exposed.

38.1   Introduction

In the last few years considerable effort has been expended on the design and implementation of packet switching networks (Roberts and Wessler, 1970a; Pouzin, 1973b; Dell, 1971; Scantlebury and Wilkinson, 1971; Barber, 1972; Despres, 1972; Kahn and Crowther, 1972). A principal reason for developing such networks has been to facilitate the sharing of computer resources. A packet communication network includes a transportation mechanism for delivering data between computers or between computers and terminals. To make the data meaningful, computer and terminals share a common protocol (i.e., a set of agreed upon conventions). Several protocols have already been developed for this purpose (Chambon et al., 1973; Carr et al., 1970; McKenzie, 1972; Pouzin, 1973a; Walden, 1972; McKenzie, 1973). However, these protocols have addressed only the problem of communication on the same network. In this paper we present a protocol design and philosophy that supports the sharing of resources that exist in different packet switching networks.

After a brief introduction to internetwork protocol issues, we describe the function of a GATEWAY as an interface between networks and discuss its role in the protocol. We then consider the various details of the protocol, including addressing, formatting, buffering, sequencing, flow control, error control, and so forth. We close with a description of an interprocess communication mechanism and show how it can be supported by the internetwork protocol.

Even though many different and complex problems must be solved in the design of an individual packet switching network, these problems are manifestly compounded when dissimilar networks are interconnected. Issues arise which may have no direct counterpart in an individual network and which strongly influence the way in which internetwork communication can take place.

A typical packet switching network is composed of a set of computer resources called HOSTS, a set of one or more *packet switches*, and a collection of communication media that interconnect the packet switches. Within each HOST, we assume that there exist *processes* which must communicate with processes in their own or other HOSTS. Any current definition of a process will be adequate for our purposes (Lampson, 1968). These processes are generally the ultimate source and destination of data in the network. Typically, within an individual network, there exists a protocol for communication between any source and destination process. Only the source and destination processes require knowledge of this convention for communication to take place. Processes in two distinct networks would ordinarily use different protocols for this purpose. The ensemble of packet switches and communication media is called the *packet switching subnet*. Figure 38.1 illustrates these ideas.

In a typical packet switching subnet, data of a fixed maximum size are accepted from a source HOST, together with a formatted destination address which is used to route the data in a store and forward fashion. The transmit time for this data is usually dependent upon internal network parameters such as communication media data rates, buffering and signaling strategies, routing, propagation delays, etc. In addition, some mechanism is generally present for error handling and determination of status of the network's components.

Individual packet switching networks may differ in their implementations as follows.

1. Each network may have distinct ways of addressing the receiver, thus requiring that a uniform addressing scheme be created which can be understood by each individual network.

2. Each network may accept data of different maximum size, thus requiring networks to deal in units of the smallest maximum size (which may be impractically small) or requiring procedures which allow data crossing a network boundary to be reformatted into smaller pieces.

3. The success or failure of a transmission and its performance in each network is governed by different time delays in accepting, delivering, and transporting the data. This requires careful development of internetwork timing procedures to insure that data can be successfully delivered through the various networks.

4. Within each network, communication may be disrupted due to unrecoverable mutation of the data or missing data. End-to-end restoration procedures are desirable to allow complete recovery from these conditions.

5. Status information, routing, fault detection, and isolation are typically different in each network. Thus, to obtain verification of certain conditions, such as an inaccessible or dead destination, various kinds of coordination must be invoked between the communicating networks.

It would be extremely convenient if all the differences between networks could be economically resolved by suitable interfacing at the network boundaries. For many of the differences, this objective can be achieved. However, both economic and technical considerations lead us to prefer that the interface be as simple and reliable as possible and deal primarily with passing data between networks that use different packet switching strategies.

The question now arises as to whether the interface ought to account for differences in HOST or process level protocols by transforming the source conventions into the corresponding destination conventions. We obviously want to allow conversion between packet switching strategies at the interface, to permit interconnection of existing and planned networks. However, the complexity and dissimilarity of the HOST or process level protocols makes it desirable to avoid having to transform between them at the interface, even if this transformation were always possible. Rather, compatible HOST and process level protocols must be developed to achieve effective internetwork resource sharing. The unacceptable alternative is for every HOST or process to implement every protocol (a potentially unbounded number) that may be needed to communicate with other networks. We therefore assume that a common protocol is to be used between HOSTS or processes in different networks and that the interface between networks should take as small a role as possible in this protocol.

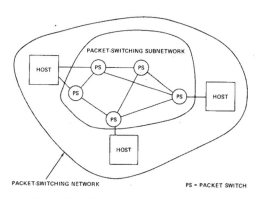

Figure 38.1: Typical packet switching network

To allow networks under different ownership to interconnect, some accounting will undoubtedly be needed for traffic that passes across the interface. In its simplest terms, this involves an accounting of packets handled by each net for which charges are passed from net to net until the buck finally stops at the user or his representative. Furthermore, the interconnection must preserve intact the internal operation of each individual network. This is easily achieved if two networks interconnect as if each were a HOST to the other network, but without utilising or indeed incorporating any elaborate HOST protocol transformations. It is thus apparent that the interface between networks must play a central role in the development of any network interconnection strategy. We give a special name to this interface that performs these functions and call it a GATEWAY.

38.2   The Gateway Notion

In Figure 38.2 we illustrate three individual networks labelled *A*, *B*, and *C* which are joined by GATEWAYS *M* and *N*. GATEWAY *M* interfaces network *A* with network *B*, and GATEWAY *N* interfaces network *B* to network *C*. We assume that an individual network may have more than one GATEWAY (e.g., network *B*) and that there may be more than one GATEWAY path to use in going between a pair of networks. The responsibility for properly routing data resides in the GATEWAY.

In practice, a GATEWAY between two networks may be composed of two halves, each associated with its own network. It is possible to implement each half of a GATEWAY so it need only embed internetwork packets in local packet format or extract them. We propose that the GATE-

WAY handle internetwork packets in a standard format, but we are not proposing any particular transmission procedure between GATEWAY halves.

Let us now trace the flow of data through the interconnected networks. We assume a packet of data from process *X* enters network *A* destined for process *Y* in network *C*. The address of *Y* is initially specified by pro-

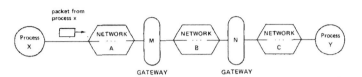

Figure 38.2: Three networks interconnected by two GATEWAYS

cess *X* and the address of GATEWAY *M* is derived from the address of process *Y*. We make no attempt to specify whether the choice of GATEWAY is made by process *X*, its HOST, or one of the packet switches in network *A*. The packet traverses network *A* until it reaches GATEWAY *M*. At the GATEWAY, the packet is reformatted to meet the requirements of network *B*, account is taken of this unit of flow between *A* and *B*, and the GATEWAY delivers the packet to network *B*. Again the derivation of the next GATEWAY address is accomplished based on the address of the destination *Y*. In this case, GATEWAY *N* is the next one. The packet traverses network *B* until it finally reaches GATEWAY *N* where it is formatted to meet the requirements of network *C*. Account is again taken of this unit of flow between networks *B* and *C*. Upon entering network *C*, the packet is routed to the HOST in which process *Y* resides and there it is delivered to its ultimate destination.

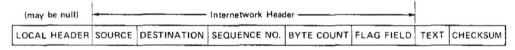

Figure 38.3: Internetwork packet format (fields not shown to scale)

Since the GATEWAY must understand the address of the source and destination HOSTS, this information must be available in a standard format in every packet which arrives at the GATEWAY. This information is contained in an internetwork header prefixed to the packet by the source HOST. The packet format, including the internetwork header, is illustrated in Figure 38.3. The source and destination entries uniformly and uniquely identify the address of every HOST in the composite network. Addressing is a subject of considerable complexity which is discussed in greater detail in the next section. The next two entries in the header provide a sequence number and a byte count that may be used to properly sequence the packets upon delivery to the destination and may also enable the GATEWAYS to detect fault conditions affecting the packet. The flag field is used to convey specific control information and is discussed in the section on retransmission and duplicate detection later. The remainder of the packet consists of text for delivery to the destination and a trailing check sum used for end-to-end software verification. The GATEWAY does not modify the text and merely forwards the check sum along without computing or recomputing it.

Each network may need to augment the packet format before it can pass through the individual network. We have indicated a *local header* in the figure which is prefixed to the beginning of the packet. This local header is introduced merely to illustrate the concept of embedding an internetwork packet in the format of the individual network through which the packet must pass. It will obviously vary in its exact form from network to network and may even be unnecessary in some cases. Although not explicitly indicated in the figure, it is also possible that a local trailer may be appended to the end of the packet. Unless all transmitted packets are legislatively restricted to be small enough to be accepted by every individual network, the GATEWAY may be forced to split a packet into two or more smaller packets. This action is called fragmentation and must be done in such a way that the destination is able to piece together the fragmented packet. It is clear that the internetwork header format imposes a minimum packet size which all networks must carry (obviously all networks will want to carry packets larger than this minimum). We believe the long range growth and development of internetwork communication would be seriously inhibited by specifying how much larger than the minimum a packet size can be, for the following reasons.

1. If a maximum permitted packet size is specified then it becomes impossible to completely isolate the internal packet size parameters of one network from the internal packet size parameters of all other networks.

2. It would be very difficult to increase the maximum permitted packet size in response to new technology (e.g. large memory systems, higher data rate communication facilities, etc.) since this would require the agreement and then implementation by all participating networks.

3. Associative addressing and packet encryption may require the size of a particular packet to expand during transit for incorporation of new information.

Provision for fragmentation (regardless of where it is performed) permits packet size variations to be handled on an individual network basis without global administration and also permits HOSTS and processes to be insulated from changes in the packet sizes permitted in any networks through which their data must pass.

If fragmentation must be done, it appears best to do it upon entering the next network at the GATEWAY since only this GATEWAY (and not the other networks) must be aware of the internal packet size parameters which made the fragmentation necessary.

If a GATEWAY fragments an incoming packet into two or more packets, they must eventually be passed along to the destination HOST as fragments or reassembled for the HOST. It is conceivable that one might desire the GATEWAY to perform the reassembly to simplify the task of the destination HOST (or process) and/or to take advantage of the larger packet size. We take the position that GATEWAYS should not perform this function since GATEWAY reassembly can lead to serious buffering problems, potential deadlocks, the necessity for all fragments of a packet to pass through the same GATEWAY, and increased delay in transmission. Furthermore, it is not sufficient for the GATEWAY to provide this function since the final GATEWAY may also have to fragment a packet for transmission. Thus the destination HOST must be prepared to do this task.

Let us now turn briefly to the somewhat unusual accounting effect which arises when a packet may be fragmented by one or more GATEWAY. We assume, for simplicity, that each network initially charges a fixed rate per packet transmitted, regardless of distance, and if one network can handle a larger packet size than another, it charges a proportionally larger price per packet. We also assume that a subsequent increase in any network's packet size does not result in additional cost per packet to its users. The charge to a user thus remains basically constant through any net which must fragment a packet. The unusual effect occurs when a packet is fragmented into smaller packets which must individually pass through a subsequent network with a larger packet size than the original unfragmented packet. We expect that most networks will naturally select packet sizes close to one another, but in any case, an increase in packet size in one net, even when it causes fragmentation, will not increase the cost of transmission and may actually decrease it. In the event that any other packet charging policies (than the one we suggest) are adopted, differences in cost can be used as an economic lever toward optimization of individual network performance.

38.3   Process Level Communication

We suppose that processes wish to communicate in full duplex with their correspondents using unbounded but finite length messages. A single character might constitute the text of a message from a process to a terminal or vice versa. An entire page of characters might constitute the text of a message from a file to a process. A data stream (e.g. a continuously generated bit string) can be represented as a sequence of finite length messages.

Within a HOST we assume that existence of a transmission control program (TCP) which handles the transmission and acceptance of messages on behalf of the processes it serves. The TCP is in turn served by one or more packet switches connected to the HOST in which the TCP resides. Processes that want to communicate present messages to the TCP for transmission, and TCP's deliver incoming messages to the appropriate destination processes. We allow the TCP to break up messages into segments because the destination may restrict the amount of data that may arrive, because the local network may limit the maximum transmission size, or because the TCP may need to share its resources among many processes concurrently. Furthermore, we constrain the length of a segment to an integral number of 8-bit bytes. This uniformity is most helpful in simplifying the software needed with HOST machines of different natural word lengths. Provision at the process level can be made for padding a message that is not an integral number of bytes and for identifying which of the arriving bytes of text contain information of interest to the receiving process.

Mutliplexing and demultiplexing of segments among processes are fundamental tasks of the TCP. On transmission, a TCP must multiplex together segments from different source processes and produce internetwork packets for delivery to one of its serving packet switches. On reception, a TCP will accept a sequence of packets from its serving packet switch(es). From this sequence of arriving packets (generally from different HOSTS), the TCP must be able to reconstruct and deliver messages to the proper destination processes.

We assume that every segment is augmented with additional information that allows transmitting and receiving TCP's to identify destination and source processes, respectively. At this point, we must face a major issue. How should the source TCP format segments destined for the same destination TCP? We consider two cases.

Case 1) If we take the position that segment boundaries are immaterial and that a byte stream can be formed of segments destined for the same TCP, then we may gain improved transmission efficiency and resource sharing by arbitrarily parceling the stream into packets, permitting many segments to share a single internetwork packet header. However, this position results in the need to reconstruct exactly, and in order, the stream of text bytes produced by the source TCP. At the destination, this stream must first be parsed into segments and these in turn must be used to reconstruct messages for delivery to the appropriate processes. There are fundamental problems associated with this strategy due to the possible arrival of packets out of order at the destination. The most critical problem appears to be the amount of interference that processes sharing the same TCP–TCP byte stream may cause among themselves. This is especially so at the receiving end. First, the TCP may be put to some trouble to parse the stream back into segments and then distribute them to buffers where messages are reassembled. If it is not readily apparent that all of a segment has arrived (remember, it may come as several packets), the receiving TCP may have to suspend parsing temporarily until more packets have arrived. Second, if a packet is missing, it may not be clear whether succeeding segments, even if they are identifiable, can be passed on to the receiving process, unless the TCP has knowledge of some process level sequencing scheme. Such knowledge would permit the TCP to decide whether a succeeding segment could be delivered to its waiting process. Finding the beginning of a segment when there are gaps in the byte stream may also be hard.

Case 2) Alternatively, we might take the position that the destination TCP should be able to determine, upon its arrival and without additional information, for which process or processes a received packet is intended, and if so, whether it should be delivered then.

If the TCP is to determine for which process an arriving packet is intended, every packet must contain a *process header* (distinct from the internetwork header) that completely identifies the destination process. For simplicity, we assume that each packet contains text from a single process which is destined for a single process. Thus each packet need contain only one process header. To decide whether the arriving data is deliverable to the destination process, the TCP must be able to determine whether the data is in the proper sequence (we can make provision for the destination process to instruct its TCP to ignore sequencing, but this is considered a special case). With the assumption that each arriving packet contains a process header, the necessary sequencing and destination process identification is immediately available to the destination TCP.

Both Cases 1) and 2) provide for the demultiplexing
and delivery of segments to destination processes, but
only Case 2) does so without the introduction of potential interprocess interference. Furthermore, Case 1)
introduces extra machinery to handle flow control on
a HOST-to-HOST basis, since there must also be some
provision for process level control, and this machinery is little used since the probability is small
that within a given HOST, two processes will be coincidentally scheduled to send messages to
the same destination HOST. For this reason, we select the method of Case 2) as a part of the
internetwork transmission protocol.

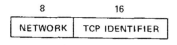

Figure 38.4: TCP address

38.4   Address Formats

The selection of address formats is a problem between networks because the local network addresses of TCP's may vary substantially in format and size. A uniform internetwork TCP address
space, understood by each GATEWAY and TCP, is essential to routing and delivery of internetwork packets. Similar troubles are encountered when we deal with process addressing and, more
generally, port addressing. We introduce the notion of ports in order to permit a process to distinguish between multiple message streams. The port is simply a designator of one such message
stream associated with a process. The means for identifying a port are generally different in
different operating systems, and therefore, to obtain uniform addressing, a standard port address
format is also required. A port address designates a full duplex message stream.

38.5   TCP Addressing

TCP addressing is intimately bound up in routing issues, since a HOST or GATEWAY must choose
a suitable destination HOST or GATEWAY for an outgoing internetwork packet. Let us postulate
the following address format for the TCP address (Figure 38.4). The choice for network identification (8 bits) allows up to 256 distinct networks. This size seems sufficient for the foreseeable
future. Similarly, the TCP identifier field permits up to 65,536 distinct TCP's to be addressed,
which seems more than sufficient for any given network.

As each packet passes through a GATEWAY, the GATEWAY observes the destination network ID
to determine how to route the packet. If the destination network is connected to the GATEWAY,
the lower 16 bits of the TCP address are used to produce a local TCP address in the destination
network. If the destination network is not connected to the GATEWAY, the upper 8 bits are used
to select a subsequent GATEWAY. We make no effort to specify how each individual network
shall associate the internetwork TCP identifier with its local TCP address. We also do not rule
out the possibility that the local network understands the internetwork addressing scheme and
thus alleviates the GATEWAY of the routing responsibility.

38.6   Port Addressing

A receiving TCP is faced with the task of demultiplexing the stream of internetwork packets it receives and reconstructing the original messages for each destination process. Each operating system has its own internal means of identifying processes and ports. We assume that 16 bits are sufficient to serve as internetwork port identifiers. A sending process need not know how the destination port identification will be used. The destination TCP will be able to parse this number appropriately to find the proper buffer into which it will place arriving packets. We permit a large port number field to support processes which want to distinguish between many different message streams concurrently. In reality, we do not care how the 16 bits are sliced up by the TCP's involved.

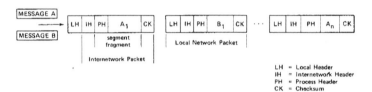

Figure 38.5: Creation of segments and packets from messages

Even though the transmitted port name field is large, it is still a compact external name for the internal representation of the port. The use of short names for port identifiers is often desirable to reduce transmission overhead and possibly reduce packet processing time at the destination TCP. Assigning short names to each port, however, requires an initial negotiation between source and destination to agree on a suitable short name assignment, the subsequent maintenance of conversion tables at both the source and the destination, and a final transaction to release the short name. For dynamic assignment of port names, this negotiation is generally necessary in any case.

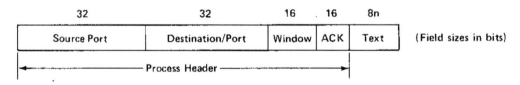

Figure 38.6: Segment format (process header and text)

38.7   Segment and Packet Formats

As shown in Figure 38.5, messages are broken by the TCP into segments whose format is shown in more detail in Figure 38.6. The field lengths illustrated are merely suggestive. The first two fields (source port and destination port in the figure) have already been discussed in the preceding section on addressing. The uses of the third and fourth fields (window and acknowledgement in the figure) will be discussed later in the section on retransmission and duplicate detection. We recall from Figure 38.3 that an internetwork header contains both a sequence number and a byte count, as well as a flag field and a check sum. The uses of these fields are explained in the following section.

38.8   Reassembly and Sequencing

The reconstruction of a message at the receiving TCP clearly requires that each internetwork packet carry a sequence number which is unique to its particular destination port message stream. The sequence numbers must be monotonic increasing (or decreasing) since they are used to reorder and reassemble arriving packets into a message. If the space of sequence numbers were infinite, we could simply assign the next one to each new packet. Clearly, this space cannot be infinite, and we will consider what problems a finite sequence number space will cause when we discuss retransmission and duplicate detection in the next section. We propose the following scheme for performing the sequencing of packets and hence the reconstruction of messages by the destination TCP.

A pair of ports will exchange one or more messages over a period of time. We could view the sequence of messages produced by one port as if it were embedded in an infinitely long stream of bytes. Each byte of the message has a unique sequence number which we take to be its byte location relative to the beginning of the stream. When a segment is ex-

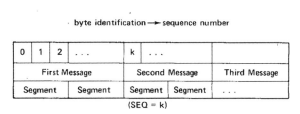

Figure 38.7: Assignment of sequence numbers

tracted from the message by the source TCP and formatted for internetwork transmission, the relative location of the first byte of segment text is used as the sequence number for the packet. The byte count field in the internetwork header accounts for all the text in the segment (but does not include the check-sum bytes or the bytes in either internetwork or process header). We emphasize that the sequence number associated with a given packet is unique only to the pair of ports that are communicating (see Figure 38.7). Arriving packets are examined to determine for which port they are intended. The sequence numbers on each arriving packet are then used to determine the relative location of the packet text in the messages under reconstruction. We note that this allows the exact position of the data in the reconstructed message to be determined even when pieces are still missing.

Every segment produced by a source TCP is packaged in a single internetwork packet and a check sum is computed over the text and process header associated with the segment. The splitting of messages into segments by the TCP and the potential splitting of segments into smaller pieces by GATEWAYS creates the necessity for indicating to the destination TCP when the end of a segment (ES) has arrived and when the end of a message (EM) has arrived. The flag field of the internetwork header is used for this purpose (see Figure 38.8).

The ES flag is set by the source TCP each time it prepares a segment for transmission. If it should happen that the message is completely contained in the segment, then the EM flag would also be set. The EM flag is also set on the last segment of a message, if the message could not be contained in one segment. These two flags are used by the destination TCP, respectively, to discover the presence of a check sum for a given segment and to discover that a complete message has arrived.

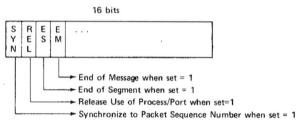

Figure 38.8: Internetwork header flag field

The ES and EM flags in the internetwork header are known to the GATEWAY and are of special importance when packets must be split apart from propagation through the next local network. We illustrate their use with an example in Figure 38.9.

The original message A in Figure 38.9 is shown split into two segments A_1 and A_2 and formatted by the TCP into a pair of internetwork packets. Packets A_1 and A_2 have their ES bits set, and A_2 has its EM bit set as well. When packet A_1 passes through the GATEWAY, it is split into two pieces: packet A_{11} for which neither EM nor ES bits are set, and packet A_{12} whose ES bit is set. Similarly, packet A_2 is split such that the first piece, packet A_{21}, has neither bit set, but packet A_{22} has both bits set. The sequence number field (SEQ) and the byte count field (CT) of each packet is modified by the GATEWAY to properly identify the text bytes of each packet. The GATEWAY need only examine the internetwork header to do fragmentation.

The destination TCP, upon reassembling segment A_1, will detect the ES flag and will verify the check sum it knows is contained in packet A_{12}. Upon receipt of packet A_{22}, assuming all other packets have arrived, the destination TCP detects that it has reassembled a complete message and can now advise the destination process of its receipt.

No transmission can be 100 percent reliable. We propose a timeout and positive acknowledgement mechanism which will allow TCP's to recover from packet losses from one HOST to another. A TCP transmits packets and waits for replies (acknowledgements) that are carried in the reverse packet stream. If no acknowledgement for a particular packet is received, the TCP will retransmit. It is our expectation that the HOST level retransmission mechanism, which is described in the following paragraphs, will not be called upon very often in practice. Evidence already exists (Pouzin, 1973b) that individual networks can be effectively constructed without this feature. However, the inclusion of a HOST retransmission capability makes it possible to recover from occasional network problems and allows a wide range of HOST protocol strategies

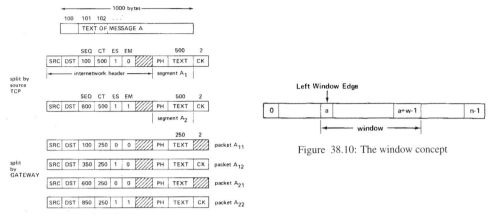

Figure 38.9: Message splitting and packet splitting

Figure 38.10: The window concept

to be incorporated. We envision it will occasionally be invoked to allow HOST accommodation to infrequent overdemands for limited buffer resources, and otherwise not used much.

Any retransmission policy requires some means by which the receiver can detect duplicate arrivals. Even if an infinite number of distinct packet sequence numbers were available, the receiver would still have the problem of knowing how long to remember previously received packets in order to detect duplicates. Matters are complicated by the fact that only a finite number of distinct sequence numbers are in fact available, and if they are reused, the receiver must be able to distinguish between new transmissions and retransmissions.

A *window* strategy, similar to that used by the French CYCLADES system (*voie virtuelle* transmission mode [Chambon et al., 1973]) and the ARPANET very distant HOST connection (BBN, 1973), is proposed here (see Figure 38.10).

1	Source Address	
2	Destination Address	
3	Next Packet Seq.	
4	Current Buffer Size	
5	Next Write Position	
6	Next Read Position	
7	End Read Position	
8	No. Retrans.	Max Retrans.
9	Timeout	Flags
10	Curr. Ack	Window

Figure 38.11: Conceptual TCB format
[EDITOR: "TCB" = transmit control block.]

Suppose that the sequence number field in the internetwork header permits sequence numbers to range from 0 to $n - 1$. We assume that the sender will not transmit more than w bytes without receiving an acknowledgment. The w bytes serve as the window (see Figure 38.11). Clearly, w must be less than n. The rules for sender and receiver are as follows.

Sender: Let L be the sequence number associated with the left window edge.

1. The sender transmits bytes from segments whose text lies between L and up to $L + w - 1$.

2. On timeout (duration unspecified), the sender retransmits unacknowledged bytes.

3. On receipt of acknowledgment consisting of the receiver's current left window edge, the sender's left window edge is advanced over the acknowledged bytes (advancing the right window edge implicitly).

Receiver:

1. Arriving packets whose sequence numbers coincide with the receiver's current left window edge are acknowledged by sending to the source the next sequence number expected. This effectively acknowledges bytes in between. The left window edge is advanced to the next sequence number expected.

2. Packets arriving with a sequence number to the left of the window edge (or, in fact, outside of the window) are discarded, and the current left window edge is returned as acknowledgement.

3. Packets whose sequence numbers lie within the receiver's window but do not coincide with the receiver's left window edge are optionally kept or discarded, but are now acknowledged. This is the case when packets arrive out of order. ...

38.9 Flow Control

Every segment that arrives at the destination TCP is ultimately acknowledged by returning the sequence number of the next segment which must be passed to the process (it may not yet have arrived).

Earlier we described the use of a sequence number space and window to aid in duplicate detection. Acknowledgments are carried in the process header (see Figure 38.6) and along with them there is provision for a "suggested window" which the receiver can use to control the flow of data from the sender. This is intended to be the main component of the process flow control mechanism. The receiver is free to vary the window size according to any algorithm it desires so long as the window size never exceeds half the sequence number space.

This flow control mechanism is exceedingly powerful and flexible and does not suffer from synchronization troubles that may be encountered by incremental buffer allocation schemes (Carr et al., 1970; McKenzie, 1972). However, it relies heavily on an effective retransmission strategy. The receiver can reduce the window even while packets are en route from the sender whose window is presently larger. The net effect of this reduction will be that the receiver may discard incoming packets (they may be outside the window) and reiterate the current window size along with a current window edge as acknowledgment. By the same token, the sender can, upon occasion, choose to send more than a window's worth of data on the possibility that the receiver will expand the window to accept it (of course, the sender must not send more than half the sequence number space at any time). Normally, we would expect the sender to abide by the window limitation. Expansion of the window by the receiver merely allows more data to be accepted. ...

39 Programming with Abstract Data Types (1974)

Barbara Liskov and Stephen Zilles

From the mid-1960s through the 1970s, as the ambition of computer scientists became more extravagant, software projects became larger, bugs became more subtle, and more than once a software system costing millions of dollars didn't work at all and had to be discarded. A "software crisis" was declared, and initiatives were spawned to manage complexity by constraining programmers' freedom of expression. Language features were adopted, and others omitted, in order to encourage (or coerce) programmers to hide the complexity of the machine code that implemented their higher-level programming abstractions. These efforts followed two paths, one on control of program flow and the other on the manipulation of data. On the control side, software was to be modularized and control structures limited to a few looping and subroutining primitives (see chapter 29 for Dijkstra's attack on the "**go to**" statement, and Dijkstra (1972) for a full articulation of the structured programming philosophy). The other path, of which this paper is an early exemplar, was to adopt language conventions that allow expression only of the minimum necessary functional operations on data, not the internal structure of the data. This sort of "very high level" programming language has now become fairly standard; the object-oriented programming paradigm traces its roots to here.

Barbara Liskov (b. 1939) received her PhD from Stanford under the direction of John McCarthy in 1968; she was one of the first female PhDs in the field. She has spent most of her career since then at MIT, where she is Institute Professor, MIT's highest faculty rank. She received the Turing Award in 2008, in part for her work on data abstraction, though she has also worked extensively on problems in distributed computing and fault-tolerant computing. Stephen Zilles, a graduate student at MIT when this paper was written, is now retired from a career at IBM and Adobe.

———— ⊸০⊂⧫ঌ০⊷ ————

39.0 Abstract

THE motivation behind the work in very-high-level languages is to ease the programming task by providing the programmer with a language containing primitives or abstractions suitable to his problem area. The programmer is then able to spend his effort in the right place; he concentrates on solving his problem, and the resulting program will be more reliable as a result. Clearly, this is a worthwhile goal.

Reprinted from Liskov and Zilles (1974), with permission from the Association for Computing Machinery.

Unfortunately, it is very difficult for a designer to select in advance all the abstractions which the users of his language might need. If a language is to be used at all, it is likely to be used to solve problems which its designer did not envision, and for which the abstractions embedded in the language are not sufficient.

This paper presents an approach which allows the set of built-in abstractions to be augmented when the need for a new data abstraction is discovered. This approach to the handling of abstraction is an outgrowth of work on designing a language for structured programming. Relevant aspects of this language are described, and examples of the use and definitions of abstractions are given.

39.1   Introduction

This paper describes an approach to computer representation of abstraction. The approach, developed while designing a language to support structured programming, is also relevant to work in very-high-level languages. We begin by explaining its relevance and by comparing work in structured programming and very-high-level languages.

The purpose of structured programming is to enhance the reliability and understandability of programs. Very-high-level languages, while primarily intended to increase programmer productivity by easing the programmer's task, can also be expected to enhance the reliability and understandability of code. Thus, similar benefits can be expected from work in the two areas.

Work in the two areas, however, proceeds along different lines. A very-high-level language attempts to present the user with the abstractions (operations, data structures, and control structures) useful to his application area. The user can use these abstractions without being concerned with how they are implemented—he is only concerned with what they do. He is thus able to ignore details not relevant to his application area, and to concentrate on solving his problem.

Structured programming attempts to impose a discipline on the programming task so that the resulting programs are "well-structured." In this discipline, a problem is solved by means of a process of successive decomposition. The first step is to write a program which solves the problem but which runs on an abstract machine, one which provides just those data objects and operations which are ideally suited to solving the problem. Some or all of those data objects and operations are truly abstract, i.e., not present as primitives in the programming language being used. We will, for the present, group them loosely together under the term "abstraction."

The programmer is initially concerned with satisfying himself (or proving) that his program correctly solves the problem. In this analysis he is concerned with the way his program makes use of the abstractions, but not with any details of how those abstractions may be realized. When he is satisfied with the correctness of his program, he turns his attention to the abstractions it uses. Each abstraction represents a new problem, requiring additional programs for its solution. The new program may also be written to run on an abstract machine, introducing further abstractions. The original problem is completely solved when all abstractions generated in the course of constructing the program have been realized by further programs.

It is clear now that the approaches of very-high-level languages and structured programming are related to one another: each is based on the idea of making use of those abstractions which are correct for the problem being solved. Furthermore, the rationale for using the abstractions is the same in both approaches: to free the programmer from concern with details not relevant to the problem he is solving.

In very-high-level languages, the designers attempt to identify the set of useful abstractions in advance. A structured programming language, on the other hand, contains no preconceived notions about the particular set of useful abstractions, but, instead, must provide a mechanism whereby the language can be extended to contain the abstractions which the user requires. A language containing such a mechanism can be viewed as a general-purpose, indefinitely-high-level language.

In this paper we describe an approach to abstraction which permits the set of built-in abstractions to be augmented when the need for new abstractions is discovered. We begin by analyzing the abstractions used in writing programs, and identify the need for data abstractions. A language supporting the use and definition of data abstractions is informally described, and some example programs are given. Remaining sections of the paper discuss the relationship of the approach to previous work, and some aspects of the implementation of the language.

39.2   The Meaning of Abstraction

The description of structured programming given in the preceding section is vague because it is couched in such undefined terms as "abstraction" and "abstract machine." In this section we analyze the meaning of "abstraction" to determine what kinds of abstraction a programmer requires, and how a structured programming language can support these requirements.

What we desire from an abstraction is a mechanism which permits the expression of relevant details and the suppression of irrelevant details. In the case of programming, the use which may be made of an abstraction is relevant; the way in which the abstraction is implemented is irrelevant. If we consider conventional programming languages, we discover that they offer a powerful aid to abstraction: the function or procedure. When a programmer makes use of a procedure, he is (or should be) concerned only with what it does—what function it provides for him. He is not concerned with the algorithm executed by the procedure. In addition, procedures provide a means of decomposing a problem—performing part of the programming task inside a procedure, and another part in the program which calls the procedure. Thus, the existence of procedures goes quite far toward capturing the meaning of abstraction.

Unfortunately, procedures alone do not provide a sufficiently rich vocabulary of abstractions. The abstract data objects and control structures of the abstract machine mentioned above are not accurately represented by independent procedures. Because we are considering abstraction in the context of structured programming, we will omit discussion of control abstractions.

This leads us to the concept of abstract data type which is central to the design of the language. An *abstract data type* defines a class of abstract objects which is completely characterized by the operations available on those objects. This means that an abstract data type can be defined by defining the characterizing operations for that type.

We believe that the above concept captures the fundamental properties of abstract objects. When a programmer makes use of an abstract data object, he is concerned only with the behavior which that object exhibits but not with any details of how that behavior is achieved by means of an implementation. The behavior of an object is captured by the set of characterizing operations. Implementation information, such as how the object is represented in storage, is only needed when defining how the characterizing operations are to be implemented. The user of the object is not required to know or supply this information.

Abstract types are intended to be very much like the built-in types provided by a programming language. The user of a built-in type, such as **integer** or **integer array**, is only concerned with creating objects of that type and then performing operations on them. He is not (usually) concerned with how the data objects are represented, and he views the operations on the objects as indivisible and atomic when in fact several machine instructions may be required to perform them. In addition, he is not (in general) permitted to decompose the objects. Consider, for example, the built-in type **integer**. A programmer wants to declare objects of type **integer** and to perform the usual arithmetic operations on them. He is usually not interested in an integer object as a bit string, and cannot make use of the format of the bits within a computer word. Also, he would like the language to protect him from foolish misuses of types (e.g., adding an integer to a character) either by treating such a thing as an error (strong typing), or by some sort of automatic type conversion.

In the case of a built-in data type, the programmer is making use of a concept or abstraction which is realized at a lower level of detail—the programming language itself and its compiler. Similarly, an abstract data type is used at one level and realized at a lower level, but the lower level does not come into existence automatically by being part of the language, instead, an abstract data type is realized by writing a special kind of program, called an *operation cluster*, or cluster for short, which defines the type in terms of the operations which can be performed on it. The language facilitates this activity by allowing the use of an abstract data type without requiring its on-the-spot definition. The language processor supports abstract data types by building links between the use of a type and its definition (which may be provided either earlier or later), and by enforcing the view of a data type as equivalent to a set of operations by a very strong form of data typing.

We observe that a consequence of the concept of abstract data types is that most of the abstract operations in a program will belong to the sets of operations characterizing abstract types. We will use the term *functional abstraction* to denote those abstract operations which do not belong to any characterizing set. A functional abstraction will be implemented as a composition of the characterizing operations of one or more data types, and will be supported in the usual way by a procedure. A sine routine might be an example of such a functional abstraction. The implementation of the sine routine could be a Taylor series expansion expressed in terms of characterizing operations of the type **real**.

39.3   The Programming Language

We now give an informal description of a programming language which permits the use and definition of abstract data types. This language is a simplified version of a structured programming language that is under development at M.I.T. It is derived primarily from PASCAL (Wirth, 1971) and is conventional in many respects, but it differs from conventional languages in several important ways.

The language provides *two* forms of modules corresponding to the two forms of abstraction: procedures, which support functional abstractions, and operation clusters, which support abstract data types. Each module is translated (compiled) by itself.

The language has no free variables in the conventional sense. Within a module, the only names that are free, and therefore are defined externally, are the names of other modules; that is, cluster names and procedure names. These names are bound at translation time by means of a directory of module names created by the programmer expressly for this purpose. No names remain to be bound in the translated module.

The language has only structured control. There are no **goto**'s or labels, but merely variants of concatenation, selection (**if**, **case**) and iteration (**while**) constructions. A structured error-handling mechanism is under development. In this paper, it is represented only by the presence of the reserved word **error**.

The way in which the language permits the use and definition of abstract data types can best be illustrated by an example. We have chosen the following problem: Write a program, Polish_gen, which will translate from an infix language to a Polish post-fix language. Polish_gen is to be a general-purpose program which makes no assumptions about input or output devices (or files). It makes only the following assumptions about the input language:

1. The input language has an operator precedence grammar.
2. A symbol of the input language is either an arbitrary string of letters and numbers, or a single, non-alphanumeric character; blanks terminate symbols but are otherwise ignored.

For example, if Polish_gen received the string $a + b * (c + d)$ as input, it would produce the string $a\,b\,c\,d + * +$ as output. We have chosen this problem as our example because the problem and its solution are familiar to people interested in programming languages, and the problem is sufficiently complex to illustrate the use of many abstractions.

39.4   Using Abstract Data Types

The procedure Polish_gen, shown in Figure 39.1, performs the translation described above. It takes three arguments: input, an object of abstract type infile which holds the sentence of the input language; output, an object of abstract type outfile which will accept a sentence of the output language; and g, an object of abstract type grammar which can be used to recognize symbols of the input language and determine their precedence relations. In addition, Polish_gen makes use of local variables of abstract types stack and token. Note that all the data-type-names appear free in Polish_gen, as does "scan," which names the single functional abstraction used by Polish_gen.

The language uses the same syntax to declare variables of abstract data type as to declare variables of primitive type. The syntax distinguishes between declarations which involve the creation of an object and those which do not. For example,

t: token

states that t is the name of a variable which holds an object of abstract type token, but that no token object is to be created, so that the value of t is initially undefined. Thus the variable t is being declared in the same way as mustscan in

mustscan: **boolean**

The presence of parentheses following the type name signals creation of an object. For example,

s: stack(token)

states that s is the name of a variable which holds an object of abstract type stack, and a stack object is to be created and stored in s. Information required for creating the object is passed in a parameter list; in the example, the only parameter, token, defines the type of element which may be placed on the stack s. The declaration of a stack is similar to an array declaration, such as "**array**[1..10] **of characters**," in that they both require the type of elements to be specified.

The language is strongly typed; thus there are only three ways in which an abstract object can be used:

1. An abstract object may be operated upon by the operations which define its abstract type.
2. An abstract object may be passed as a parameter to a procedure. In this case, the type of the actual argument passed by the calling procedure must be identical to the type of the corresponding formal parameter in the called procedure.

```
Polish_gen: procedure(input: infile,
                      output: outfile, g: grammar);

    t : token;
    mustscan: boolean;
    s: stack(token) ;

    mustscan := true;
    stack$push (s, token (g, grammar$eof (g)));
    while ¬stack$empty (s) do
       if mustscan
          then t := scan(input, g)
          else mustscan := true;
       if token$is_op(t)
          then
             case token$prec_rel(stack$top(s), t) of
                "<":: stack$push(s, t);
                "=":: stack$erasetop(s);
                ">"::
                    begin
                       outfile$out_str(output,
                          token$symbol(stack$pop(s)));
                       mustscan := false;
                    end
                otherwise error;
          else outfile$out_str(output, token$symbol(t));
    end
    outfile$close(output);
    return;
end Polish_gen
```

Figure 39.1

3 An abstract object may be assigned to a variable, but only if the variable is declared to hold
   objects of that type.

Application of a defining operation to an abstract object is indicated by an *operation call* in which
a compound name is used: for example,

grammar$eof(g)
stack$push(s, t)
token$is_op(t)

The first part of the compound name identifies the abstract type to which the operation belongs
while the second component identifies the operation. An operation call will always have at least
one parameter—an object of the abstract type to which the operation belongs.

There are several reasons why the type-name is included in the operation call. First, since an
operation call may have several parameters of different abstract types, the absence of the type-
name may lead to an ambiguity as to which object is actually being operated on. Second, use of
the compound name permits different data types to use the same names for operations without
any clash of identifiers arising. Third, we believe that the type-name prefix will enhance the
understandability of programs, once the reader is used to the notation. Not only is the type of
the operation immediately apparent, but operation calls are clearly distinguished from procedure
calls.

The statement

t := scan(input, g)

illustrates both passing abstract objects as parameters, and assigning an abstract object to a variable. The procedure scan, shown in Figure 39.2, expects objects of type infile and grammar as
its arguments, and returns an object of type token, which is then stored in the token variable r.

We have explained that objects can be created in conjunction with variable declaration. It is
also possible for objects to be created independently of variable declaration. Object creation is
specified (whether inside a declaration or not) by the appearance of the typename followed by
parentheses. For example, in the last line of scan

token(g, newsymb)

states that a token object, representing the symbol just scanned, is to be created; the information
required to create the object (the grammar and the symbol just scanned) is passed in a parameter
list.

A brief description of the logic of Polish_gen can now be given. Polish_gen uses the functional
abstraction scan to obtain a symbol of the grammar from the input string. Scan returns the
symbol in the form of a token—a type introduced to provide efficient execution without revealing
information about how the grammar represents symbols.

Polish_gen stores the token containing the newly scanned symbol in variable t. If t holds a
token representing an identifier (like "a") rather than an operator (like "+"), that identifier is put
in the output file immediately. Otherwise, the token on top of the stack is compared with t to

determine the precedence relation between them. If the relation is "<", t is pushed on the stack (e.g., "+" < "*"). If the relation is "=", both t and the top-of-stack token are discarded (e.g., "(" = ")"). If the relation is ">", the operator held in the top-of-stack token is appended to the output file, exposing a new top-of-stack token. Since that operator token may have a higher precedence than t, the boolean variable mustscan is used to prevent a new symbol from being scanned and to insure the next comparison is with the current value of t. Because a grammar-dependent representation of the end of file symbol (grammar$eof(g)) is initially pushed onto the stack, the stack will become empty causing Polish_gen to complete only when a matching of token is generated by exhausting the input. (We have made the simplifying assumption that the input is a legitimate sentence of the infix language.)

```
scan: procedure(input: infile, g: grammar) returns token;
   newsymb: string;
   ch: char;
   ch := infile$get(input)
   while ch = " " do ch := infile$get(input); end
   if infile$eof(input)
      then return token(g, grammar$eof(g));
   newsymb := unit_string(ch);
   if alphanumeric(ch) then
      while alphanumeric(infile$peek(input)) do
         newsymb := newsymb concat infile$get(input);
      end
   return token(g, newsymb);
end scan
```

Figure 39.2

The scan procedure obtains characters from the input file via the operations defining the abstract type infile. It makes use of the data types **char** and **string**, and operations on objects of these types. Although these types are shown as built-in, they could easily have been abstract types instead. In that case, the built-in predicate **alphanumeric**, for example, would have been expressed as char$alphanumeric. Only the syntax would change; the meaning and use of the types would be the same in either case.

To sum up, Polish_gen makes use of five data abstractions, infile, outfile, grammar, token and stack, plus one functional abstraction, scan. The power of the data abstractions is illustrated by the types infile and outfile, which are used to shield Polish_gen from any physical facts concerning its input and output, respectively. Polish_gen does not know what input and output devices are being used, when the I/O actually takes place, nor does it know how characters are represented on the devices. What it does know is just enough for its needs: For parameter output it knows how to add a string of characters (outfile$out_str) and how to signify that the output is complete (outfile$close). For parameter input, it knows how to obtain the next character (infile$get), how to look at the next character without removing it from input (infile$peek), and how to recognize the end of input (infile$eof). (Note that for scan to operate correctly, infile must provide a non-blank, non-alphanumeric character on any call on infile$get or infile$peek after the end of file has been reached.) In every case its knowledge consists of the names of the operations which provide these services.

39.5   Defining Abstract Data Types

In this section, we describe the programming object—the operation cluster—whose translation provides an implementation of a type. The cluster contains code implementing each of the characterizing operations and thereby embodies the idea that a data type is defined by a set of operations.

As an example, consider the abstract data type stack used by Polish_gen. A cluster supporting stacks is shown in Figure 39.3. This cluster implements a very general kind of stack object in which the type of the stack elements is not known in advance. The cluster parameter element_type indicates the type of element a particular stack object is to contain. The first part of a cluster definition provides a very brief description of the interface which the cluster presents to its users. The cluster interface defines the name of the cluster, the parameters required to create an instance of the cluster (an object of the abstract type which the cluster implements), and a list of the operations defining the type which the cluster implements, e.g.,

> stack: **cluster**(element_type: **type**)
>
> **is** push, pop, top, erasetop, empty

The use of the reserved word **is** underlines the idea of a data type being characterized by a group of operations.

The remainder of the cluster definition, describing how the abstract type is actually supported, contains three parts: the object representation, the code to create objects and the operation definitions.

39.5.1   Object representation   Users of the abstract data type view objects of that type as indivisible entities. Inside the cluster, however, objects are viewed as decomposable into elements of more primitive type. The **rep** *description*

> **rep**[(⟨rep-parameters⟩)] = ⟨type-definition⟩

defines a new type, denoted by the reserved word **rep**, which is accessible only within the cluster and describes how objects are viewed there. The ⟨type-definition⟩ defines a template which permits objects of that type to be built and decomposed. In general, it will make use of the data structuring methods provided by the language: arrays (possibly unbounded) or PASCAL records. The optional ("[ ]") ⟨rep-parameters⟩ make it possible to delay specifying some aspects of the ⟨type definition⟩ until an instance of the rep is created. Consider the **rep** description of the stack cluster:

> rep(type_param: **type**) = (tp: **integer**; e_type: **type**; stk: **array**[1..] **of** type_param)

The ⟨type-definition⟩ specifies that a stack object is represented by a record containing three components named tp, stk, and e_type. The parameter, type_param, specifies the type of element which may be stored in the unbounded array named stk which will hold the elements pushed onto a stack object. This same type will also be stored in the e_type component, and is used for type checking as will be described below. The tp component holds the index of the topmost element of the stack.

39.5.2   Object creation   The reserved word **create** marks the create_code—the code to be executed when an object of the abstract type is created. The cluster may be viewed as a procedure whose procedure body is the create-code. When a user indicates that an object of abstract type is to be created, for example,

   s: stack(token)

one thing that happens (at execution time) is a call on the create-code, causing that procedure body to be executed. The parameters of the cluster are actually parameters of the create-code. Since free variables, other than references to externally defined modules, are not provided, these parameters are not accessible either to the operations or to the ⟨type definition⟩ in the **rep**. Therefore, any information about the parameters that is to be saved must be explicitly inserted into each instance of the **rep**.

   The code shown in the stack cluster is typical of create-code. First, an object of type rep is created; that is, space is allocated to hold the object as defined by the **rep**. Then, some initial values are stored in the object. Finally, the object is returned to the caller. When the object is returned, its type is changed from type **rep** to the abstract type defined by the cluster.

39.5.3   Operations   The remainder of the cluster consists of a group of *operation definitions*, which provide implementations of the permissible operations on the data type. Operation definitions are like ordinary procedure definitions except that they have access to the rep of the cluster, which permits them to decompose objects of the cluster type. Operations are not themselves modules; they will be accepted by the translator only as part of a cluster.

   Operations always have at least one parameter—of type **rep**. Because the cluster may simultaneously support many objects of its defined type, this parameter tells the operation the particular object on which to operate. Note that the type of this parameter will change from the abstract type to type **rep** as it is passed between the caller and the operation.

   Because the language is strongly typed, the type of objects pushed on a given stack must be checked for consistency with the type of elements the stack can hold. This consistency requirement is specified syntactically by declaring that the type of the second argument of push is to be the same as the e_type component of the **rep** of the stack object which is the first argument of push. The translator can generate code to verify that the types match at run time and to raise an error if they don't.

39.6   Controlling the Use of Information

Abstract data types were introduced as a way of freeing a programmer from concern about irrelevant details in his use of data abstractions. But in fact we have gone further than that. Because the language is strongly typed, the user is unable to make use of any implementation details. In this section we discuss the benefits that accrue from this limitation: the programs which result are more modular, and easier to understand, modify, maintain and prove correct.

Token is a good example of a type created to control access to implementation details. Instead of introducing a new type, Polish_gen could have been written to accept strings from scan, to store strings on the stack, and to compare strings to determine the precedence relation (via an appropriate operation grammar$prec_rel). Such a solution would be inefficient. Since the precedence matrix can be indexed by the positions of the operators in the reserved word table of the grammar, an efficient implementation would look up the character string only once to find out if it is an operator symbol and, if so, use the index of the operator in Polish_gen.

This, however, exposes information about the representation of the grammar. If Polish_gen or some other module which uses the grammar makes use of this information, normal maintenance and modification of the grammar cluster can introduce errors which are difficult to track down (Parnas, 1971). Therefore, the new type, token, is introduced to limit the distribution of information about how the grammar is represented. Now a redefinition of the grammar cluster can affect only the token cluster— -which makes no assumptions about the index it receives from grammar. If an error occurs while looking up a precedence relation (like an index out of bounds), the error can only have been caused by something in the token or grammar cluster.

Actually, the selection of an implementation of tokens—for example, whether a token is represented by an integer or a character string— involves a design decision. This decision can be delayed until the cluster for tokens is defined and need not be made during the coding of Polish_gen. Therefore, the programming of Polish_gen can be done according to one of Dijkstra's programming principles: build the program one decision at a time (Dijkstra, 1972). Following this principle leads to a simplified logic for Polish_gen, making it easier to understand and maintain.

```
stack: cluster(element_type: type)
                    is push, pop, top, erasetop, empty ;
    rep(type_param: type) = (tp: integer;
        e_type: type; stk: array[1..10] of type_param);
    create
        s: rep(element_type);
        s.tp := 0;
        s.e_type := element_type;
        return s;
    end
    push: operation(s: rep, v: s.e_type);
        s.tp := s.tp+1;
        s.stk[s.tp] := v;
        return;
    end
    pop: operation(s: rep) returns s.e_type;
        if s.tp = 0 then error;
        s.tp := s.tp−1;
        return s.stk[s.tp+1];
    end
    top: operation(s: rep) returns s.e_type;
        if s.tp = 0 then error;
        return s.stk[s.tp];
    end
    erasetop: operation(s: rep);
        if s.tp = 0 then error;
        s.tp := s.tp−1;
        return;
    end
    empty: operation(s: rep) returns boolean;
        return s.tp = 0;
    end
end stack
```

Figure 39.3

Making the representation inaccessible also results in a program which is easier to prove correct. The proof of a program is divided into two parts: a proof that the cluster correctly implements the type, and a proof that the program using the type is correct. Only in the former proof need details of the implementation of type objects be considered; the latter proof is based only on the abstract properties of the types, which may be expressed in terms of relations among the characterizing operations for each type.

...

40 The Mythical Man-Month (1975)

Frederick C. Brooks

As computer systems grew larger and more complicated, an unhappy fact became evident. Software was hard to write, and it was even harder to judge how long it would take to write. The protocols that had been developed for the management of engineering projects didn't seem applicable to software. Computer scientist Tom Cheatham used to say, "The difference between civil engineering and software engineering is that when someone tells you that a bridge is half built, you can walk out onto it and see." (Cf. Royce's 90%-finished syndrome, page 326.)

Frederick C. "Fred" Brooks (b. 1931) was a PhD student of Howard Aiken at Harvard and wrote his PhD thesis (Brooks, 1956) analyzing a problem in business data processing. He joined IBM in 1956 as the company was producing a series of increasingly powerful computers, each incompatible with its predecessor. Recognizing (as Hopper had predicted) that software costs would be unsustainable if customers had to rewrite their programs to move up to newer machines, he designed the System/360 line so that software that ran on one machine in the line could easily be ported to run on a newer and more powerful model, even one with a different underlying hardware implementation (microprogramming helped; see page 165). Brooks coined the term "computer architecture" to refer to the structure of a computer system as the software saw it.

When he left IBM in 1964, Thomas Watson Jr. asked him why software projects are so hard to manage. "The Mythical Man-Month" is part of Brooks's answer. This essay is one of several in a volume of the same name; all are worth reading, but this one has acquired iconic status. Remarkably, it is still not unusual to hear proposals to add labor to a project in order to speed up its completion, taking into account neither the time for the new workers to come up to the needed knowledge level, nor the problems of coordinating the activities of a larger number of contributors.

Brooks went from IBM to found the computer science department at the University of North Carolina, where he spent the rest of his career. His group has made significant contributions to computer graphics, but his most enduring legacy is his wisdom on software engineering. ("All programmers are optimists" still.) A decade later he published another trenchant analysis of the "tar pit" of software engineering, "No Silver Bullet: Essence and Accident in Software Engineering" (Brooks, 1987), in which he sought to explain why—despite intense effort and grandiose promises—none of the technologies that had been developed to speed the software production process seemed to have made it significantly simpler and faster, or to have greatly improved the

Reprinted from Brooks (1995), with permission from Pearson Education, Inc.

quality of the result. Modularization, re-use, and open source libraries have helped in recent years, but have by no means invalidated the humble wisdom of this essay.

[EDITOR: The text at the top of the menu says, "Good cuisine takes time. If we make you wait, it's to serve you better and please you."]

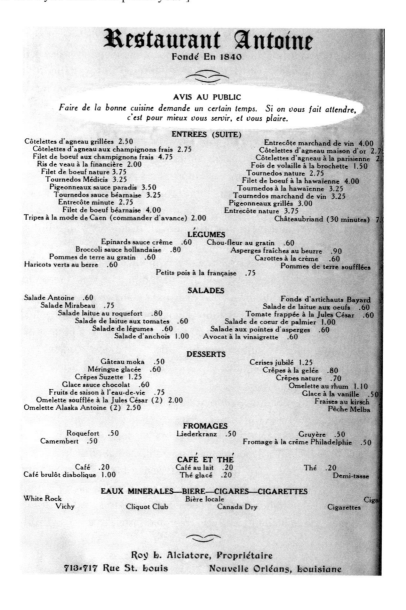

MORE software projects have gone awry for lack of calendar time than for all other causes combined. Why is this cause of disaster so common?

First, our techniques of estimating are poorly developed. More seriously, they reflect an unvoiced assumption which is quite untrue, i.e., that all will go well.

Second, our estimating techniques fallaciously confuse effort with progress, hiding the assumption that men and months are interchangeable.

Third, because we are uncertain of our estimates, software managers often lack the courteous stubbornness of Antoine's chef.

Fourth, schedule progress is poorly monitored. Techniques proven and routine in other engineering disciplines are considered radical innovations in software engineering.

Fifth, when schedule slippage is recognized, the natural (and traditional) response is to add manpower. Like dousing a fire with gasoline, this makes matters worse, much worse. More fire requires more gasoline, and thus begins a regenerative cycle which ends in disaster.

Schedule monitoring will be the subject of a separate essay. Let us consider other aspects of the problem in more detail.

40.1   Optimism

All programmers are optimists. Perhaps this modern sorcery especially attracts those who believe in happy endings and fairy godmothers. Perhaps the hundreds of nitty frustrations drive away all but those who habitually focus on the end goal. Perhaps it is merely that computers are young, programmers are younger, and the young are always optimists. But however the selection process works, the result is indisputable: "This time it will surely run," or "I just found the last bug."

So the first false assumption that underlies the scheduling of systems programming is that *all will go well*, i.e., that *each task will take only as long as it "ought" to take*.

The pervasiveness of optimism among programmers deserves more than a flip analysis. Dorothy Sayers, in her excellent book, *The Mind of the Maker*, divides creative activity into three stages: the idea, the implementation, and the interaction. A book, then, or a computer, or a program comes into existence first as an ideal construct, built outside time and space, but complete in the mind of the author. It is realized in time and space, by pen, ink, and paper, or by wire, silicon, and ferrite. The creation is complete when someone reads the book, uses the computer, or runs the program, thereby interacting with the mind of the maker.

This description, which Miss Sayers uses to illuminate not only human creative activity but also the Christian doctrine of the Trinity, will help us in our present task. For the human makers of things, the incompletenesses and inconsistencies of our ideas become clear only during implementation. Thus it is that writing, experimentation, "working out" are essential disciplines for the theoretician.

In many creative activities the medium of execution is intractable. Lumber splits; paints smear; electrical circuits ring. These physical limitations of the medium constrain the ideas that may be expressed, and they also create unexpected difficulties in the implementation.

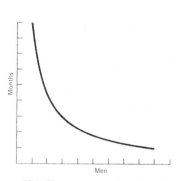

Figure 40.1: Time versus number of workers—
perfectly partitionable task.

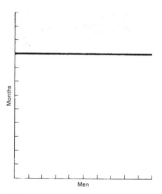

Figure 40.2: Time versus number of workers—
unpartitionable task.

Implementation, then, takes time and sweat both because of the physical media and because of the inadequacies of the underlying ideas. We tend to blame the physical media for most of our implementation difficulties; for the media are not "ours" in the way the ideas are, and our pride colors our judgment.

Computer programming, however, creates with an exceedingly tractable medium. The programmer builds from pure thought-stuff: concepts and very flexible representations thereof. Because the medium is tractable, we expect few difficulties in implementation; hence our pervasive optimism. Because our ideas are faulty, we have bugs; hence our optimism is unjustified.

In a single task, the assumption that all will go well has a probabilistic effect on the schedule. It might indeed go as planned, for there is a probability distribution for the delay that will be encountered, and "no delay" has a finite probability. A large programming effort, however, consists of many tasks, some chained end-to-end. The probability that each will go well becomes vanishingly small.

40.2   The Man-Month

The second fallacious thought mode is expressed in the very unit of effort used in estimating and scheduling: the man-month. Cost does indeed vary as the product of the number of men and the number of months. Progress does not. *Hence the man-month as a unit for measuring the size of a job is a dangerous and deceptive myth.* It implies that men and months are interchangeable.

Men and months are interchangeable commodities only when a task can be partitioned among many workers with no communication among them (Figure 40.1). This is true of reaping wheat or picking cotton; it is not even approximately true of systems programming.

When a task cannot be partitioned because of sequential constraints, the application of more effort has no effect on the schedule (Figure 40.2). The bearing of a child takes nine months, no matter how many women are assigned. Many software tasks have this characteristic because of the sequential nature of debugging. In tasks that can be partitioned but which require communi-

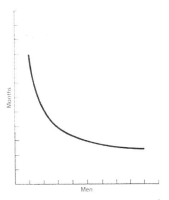

Figure   40.3:   Time versus number
of workers—partitionable task requiring
communication.

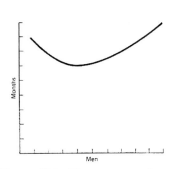

Figure   40.4:   Time versus number of
workers—task with complex interrelationships.

cation among the subtasks, the effort of communication must be added to the amount of work to
be done. Therefore the best that can be done is somewhat poorer than an even trade of men for
months (Figure 40.3).

The added burden of communication is made up of two parts, training and intercommunication.
Each worker must be trained in the technology, the goals of the effort, the overall strategy, and the
plan of work. This training cannot be partitioned, so this part of the added effort varies linearly
with the number of workers.

Intercommunication is worse. If each part of the task must be separately coordinated with each
other part, the effort increases as $n(n-1)/2$. Three workers require three times as much pairwise
intercommunication as two; four require six times as much as two. If, moreover, there need to be
conferences among three, four, etc., workers to resolve things jointly, matters get worse yet. The
added effort of communicating may fully counteract the division of the original task and bring
us to the situation of Figure 40.4.

Since software construction is inherently a systems effort—an exercise in complex interrelationships—communication effort is great, and it quickly dominates the decrease in individual
task time brought about by partitioning. Adding more men then lengthens, not shortens, the
schedule.

40.3   Systems Test

No parts of the schedule are so thoroughly affected by sequential constraints as component debugging and system test. Furthermore, the time required depends on the number and subtlety of
the errors encountered. Theoretically this number should be zero. Because of optimism, we usually expect the number of bugs to be smaller than it turns out to be. Therefore testing is usually
the most mis-scheduled part of programming.

For some years I have been successfully using the following rule of thumb for scheduling a
software task:

1/3 planning
1/6 coding
1/4 component test and early system test
1/4 system test, all components in hand.

This differs from conventional scheduling in several important ways:

1. The fraction devoted to planning is larger than normal. Even so, it is barely enough to produce a detailed and solid specification, and not enough to include research or exploration of totally new techniques.
2. The half of the schedule devoted to debugging of completed code is much larger than normal.
3. The part that is easy to estimate, i.e., coding, is given only one-sixth of the schedule.

In examining conventionally scheduled projects, I have found that few allowed one-half of the projected schedule for testing, but that most did indeed spend half of the actual schedule for that purpose. Many of these were on schedule until and except in system testing.

Failure to allow enough time for system test, in particular, is peculiarly disastrous. Since the delay comes at the end of the schedule, no one is aware of schedule trouble until almost the delivery date. Bad news, late and without warning, is unsettling to customers and to managers.

Furthermore, delay at this point has unusually severe financial, as well as psychological, repercussions. The project is fully staffed, and cost-per-day is maximum. More seriously, the software is to support other business effort (shipping of computers, operation of new facilities, etc.) and the secondary costs of delaying these are very high, for it is almost time for software shipment. Indeed, these secondary costs may far outweigh all others. It is therefore very important to allow enough system test time in the original schedule.

40.4   Gutless Estimating

Observe that for the programmer, as for the chef, the urgency of the patron may govern the scheduled completion of the task, but it cannot govern the actual completion. An omelette, promised in two minutes, may appear to be progressing nicely. But when it has not set in two minutes, the customer has two choices—wait or eat it raw. Software customers have had the same choices. The cook has another choice; he can turn up the heat. The result is often an omelette nothing can save—burned in one part, raw in another.

Now I do not think software managers have less inherent courage and firmness than chefs, nor than other engineering managers. But false scheduling to match the patron's desired date is much more common in our discipline than elsewhere in engineering. It is very difficult to make a vigorous, plausible, and job-risking defense of an estimate that is derived by no quantitative method, supported by little data, and certified chiefly by the hunches of the managers.

Clearly two solutions are needed. We need to develop and publicize productivity figures, bug-incidence figures, estimating rules, and so on. The whole profession can only profit from sharing such data.

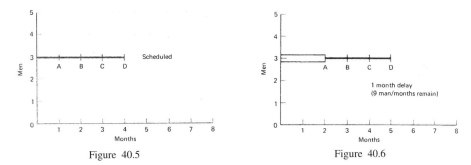

Figure 40.5   Figure 40.6

Until estimating is on a sounder basis, individual managers will need to stiffen their backbones and defend their estimates with the assurance that their poor hunches are better than wish-derived estimates.

40.5   Regenerative Schedule Disaster

What does one do when an essential software project is behind schedule? Add manpower, naturally. As Figures 40.1 through 40.4 suggest, this may or may not help.

Let us consider an example. Suppose a task is estimated at 12 man-months and assigned to three men for four months, and that there are measurable mileposts A, B, C, D, which are scheduled to fall at the end of each month (Figure 40.5).

Now suppose the first milepost is not reached until two months have elapsed (Figure 40.6). What are the alternatives facing the manager?

1. Assume that the task must be done on time. Assume that only the first part of the task was misestimated, so Figure 40.6 tells the story accurately. Then 9 man-months of effort remain, and two months, so $4\frac{1}{2}$ men will be needed. Add 2 men to the 3 assigned.
2. Assume that the task must be done on time. Assume that the whole estimate was uniformly low, so that Figure 40.7 really describes the situation. Then 18 man-months of effort remain, and two months, so 9 men will be needed. Add 6 men to the 3 assigned.
3. Reschedule. I like the advice given by P. Fagg, an experienced hardware engineer, "Take no small slips." That is, allow enough time in the new schedule to ensure that the work can be carefully and thoroughly done, and that rescheduling will not have to be done again.
4. Trim the task. In practice this tends to happen anyway, once the team observes schedule slippage. Where the secondary costs of delay are very high, this is the only feasible action. The manager's only alternatives are to trim it formally and carefully, to reschedule, or to watch the task get silently trimmed by hasty design and incomplete testing.

In the first two cases, insisting that the unaltered task be completed in four months is disastrous. Consider the regenerative effects, for example, for the first alternative (Figure 40.7). The two new men, however competent and however quickly recruited, will require training in the task by one of the experienced men. If this takes a month, *3 man-months will have been devoted to work*

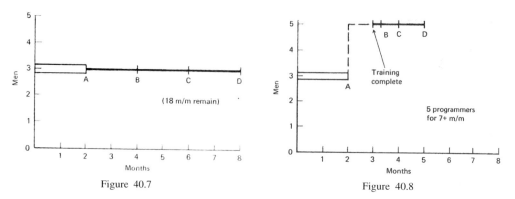

Figure 40.7   Figure 40.8

not in the original estimate. Furthermore, the task, originally partitioned three ways, must be repartitioned into five parts; hence some work already done will be lost, and system testing must be lengthened. So at the end of the third month, substantially more than 7 man-months of effort remain, and 5 trained people and one month are available. As Figure 40.8 suggests, the product is just as late as if no one had been added (Figure 40.6).

To hope to get done in four months, considering only training time and not repartitioning and extra systems test, would require adding 4 men, not 2, at the end of the second month. To cover repartitioning and system test effects, one would have to add still other men. Now, however, one has at least a 7-man team, not a 3-man one; thus such aspects as team organization and task division are different in kind, not merely in degree.

Notice that by the end of the third month things look very black. The March 1 milestone has not been reached in spite of all the managerial effort. The temptation is very strong to repeat the cycle, adding yet more manpower. Therein lies madness.

The foregoing assumed that only the first milestone was misestimated. If on March 1 one makes the conservative assumption that the whole schedule was optimistic, as Figure 40.7 depicts, one wants to add 6 men just to the original task. Calculation of the training, repartitioning, system testing effects is left as an exercise for the reader. Without a doubt, the regenerative disaster will yield a poorer product, later, than would rescheduling with the original three men, unaugmented.

Oversimplifying outrageously, we state Brooks's Law:

Adding manpower to a late software project makes it later.

This then is the demythologizing of the man-month. The number of months of a project depends upon its sequential constraints. The maximum number of men depends upon the number of independent subtasks. From these two quantities one can derive schedules using fewer men and more months. (The only risk is product obsolescence.) One cannot, however, get workable schedules using more men and fewer months. More software projects have gone awry for lack of calendar time than for all other causes combined.

41 Ethernet: Distributed Packet Switching for Local Computer Networks (1976)

Robert Metcalfe and David R. Boggs

Networking is tricky. To ensure flawless message delivery over failure-prone links connecting potentially hostile nodes, protocols have to anticipate hard-to-imagine circumstances. Time dependencies must be treated skeptically, and the implementation, which may rely on special purpose hardware, may be hard to verify. The difficulties compounded as computers became smaller and businesses started to install local networks with hardware from disparate manufacturers.

Robert "Bob" Metcalfe (b. 1946) earned undergraduate degrees from MIT in 1969, and then started graduate school at Harvard, just when universities were first connecting to the ARPANET. Harvard resisted Metcalfe's offer to take charge of its ARPANET connection, so he took a similar job at MIT. While the experience ignited Metcalfe's passion for networking, it disconnected him from Harvard's then skeletal computer science faculty, and he suffered the rare indignity of failing his PhD defense. He took a position at the Xerox Palo Alto Research Center (PARC), where the Alto, the first networked personal computer, was under development. (He later submitted a revised thesis to Harvard and was awarded the degree.)

At PARC Metcalfe learned about the wireless packet Aloha Network connecting the Hawaiian islands and realized that the solution to the subtleties of interconnecting computers with wires was to relax control. Computers would be networked by connecting them to a common coaxial cable using a physical "tap"—a spike driven into the copper core at any convenient spot along the cable. Computers would communicate by dumping data packets onto the passive network, where the messages would spread out in both directions, and by listening to the network for packets meant for them. David Boggs (b. 1950), a young radio engineer also at PARC, applied his wireless engineering expertise to Metcalfe's idea. Since the networked computers were not synchronized, packets would inevitably overlap or collide, a circumstance that could be handled by retransmission. So a coaxial cable was analogous to the "ether" that had in the seventeenth century been hypothesized to explain the wave nature of light in a vacuum. The name stuck, and because the idea of a passive network was backed up by low licensing fees from Xerox, Ethernet became a ubiquitous standard. Both Metcalfe and Boggs went on to entrepreneurial success.

Reprinted from Metcalfe and Boggs (1976), with permission from the Association for Computing Machinery.

41.1   Background

ONE can characterize distributed computing as a spectrum of activities varying in their degree of decentralization, with one extreme being remote computer networking and the other extreme being multiprocessing. Remote computer networking is the loose interconnection of previously isolated, widely separated, and rather large computing systems. Multiprocessing is the construction of previously monolithic and serial computing systems from increasingly numerous and smaller pieces computing in parallel. Near the middle of this spectrum is local networking, the interconnection of computers to gain the resource sharing of computer networking and the parallelism of multiprocessing.

The separation between computers and the associated bit rate of their communication can be used to divide the distributed computing spectrum into broad activities. The product of separation and bit rate, now about 1 gigabit-meter per second (1 Gbmps), is an indication of the limit of current communication technology and can be expected to increase with time (Figure 41.1).

Activity	Separation	Bit rate
Remote networks	> 10 km	< .1 Mbps
Local networks	10–.1 km	.1–10 Mbps
Multiprocessors	< .1 km	> 10 Mbps

Figure 41.1

41.1.1   Remote computer networking   Computer networking evolved from telecommunications *terminal-computer* communication, where the object was to connect remote terminals to a central computing facility. As the need for *computer-computer* interconnection grew, computers themselves were used to provide communication (Abramson, 1970; Baran, 1964; Rustin, 1970). Communication using computers as packet switches (Heart et al., 1970, 1972; Kahn, 1975; Metcalfe, 1972b,c, 1973; Roberts and Wessler, 1970b) and communications *among* computers for resource sharing (Crocker et al., 1972; Farber, 1973) were both advanced by the development of the ARPA Computer Network.

The Aloha Network at the University of Hawaii was originally developed to apply packet radio techniques for communication between a central computer and its terminals scattered among the Hawaiian Islands. Many of the terminals are now minicomputers communicating among themselves using the Aloha Network's Menehune as a packet switch. The Menehune and an ARPANET Imp are now connected, providing terminals on the Aloha Network access to computing resources on the U.S. mainland.

Just as computer networks have grown across continents and oceans to interconnect major computing facilities around the world, they are now growing down corridors and between buildings to interconnect minicomputers in offices and laboratories (Ashenhurst and Vonderohe, 1975; Farber, 1973, 1975a,b; Willard, 1973).

41.1.2   Multiprocessing   Multiprocessing first took the form of connecting an I/O controller to a large central computer; IBM's ASP is a classic example (Rustin, 1970). Next, multiple central processors were connected to a common memory to provide more power for compute-bound applications (Thornton, 1970). For certain of these applications, more exotic multiprocessor architectures such as Illiac IV were introduced (Barnes et al., 1968).

More recently minicomputers have been connected in multiprocessor configurations for economy, reliability, and increased system modularity (Ornstein et al., 1975; Wulf and Levin, 1972). The trend has been toward decentralization for reliability; loosely coupled multiprocessor systems depend less on shared central memory and more on *thin wires* for interprocess communication with increased component isolation (Metcalfe, 1972b; Roberts and Wessler, 1970b). With the continued thinning of interprocessor communication for reliability and the development of distributable applications, multiprocessing is gradually approaching a local form of distributed computing.

41.1.3   Local computer networking   Ethernet shares many objectives with other local networks such as Mitre's Mitrix, Bell Telephone Laboratory's Spider, and U. C. Irvine's Distributed Computing System (DCS) (Farber, 1973, 1975a,b; Willard, 1973). Prototypes of all four local networking schemes operate at bit rates between one and three megabits per second. Mitrix and Spider have a central minicomputer for switching and bandwidth allocation while DCS and Ethernet use distributed control. Spider and DCS use a ring communication path, Mitrix uses off-the-shelf CATV technology to implement two one-way busses, and our experimental Ethernet uses a branching two-way passive bus. Differences among these systems are due to differences among their intended applications, differences among the cost constraints under which trade-offs were made, and differences of opinion among researchers.

Before going into a detailed description of Ethernet, we offer the following overview (see Figure 41.2).

41.2   System Summary

Ethernet is a system for local communication among computing stations. Our experimental Ethernet uses tapped coaxial cables to carry variable-length digital data packets among, for example, personal minicomputers, printing facilities, large file storage devices, magnetic tape backup stations, larger central computers, and longer-haul communication equipment.

The shared communication facility, a branching Ether, is passive. A station's Ethernet interface connects bit-serially through an interface cable to a transceiver which in turn taps into the passing Ether. A packet is broadcast onto the Ether, is heard by all stations, and is copied from the Ether by destinations which select it according to the packet's leading address bits. This is broadcast packet switching and should be distinguished from store-and-forward packet switching in which routing is performed by intermediate processing elements. To handle the demands of growth, an Ethernet can be extended using packet repeaters for signal regeneration, packet filters for traffic localization, and packet gateways for internetwork address extension.

Control is completely distributed among stations with packet transmissions coordinated through statistical arbitration. Transmissions initiated by a station defer to any which may already be in progress. Once started, if interference with other packets is detected, a transmission is aborted and rescheduled by its source station. After a certain period of interference-free transmission, a packet is heard by all stations and will run to completion without interference. Ethernet controllers in colliding stations each generate random retransmission intervals to avoid repeated collisions. The mean of a packet's retransmission intervals is adjusted as a function of collision history to keep Ether utilization near the optimum with changing network load.

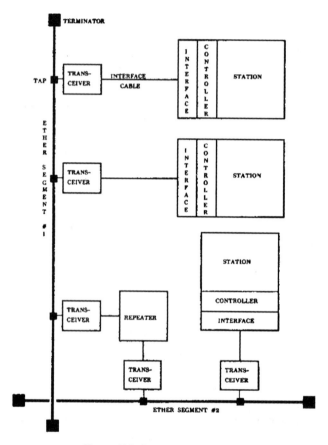

Figure 41.2: A two-segment Ethernet

Even when transmitted without source-detected interference, a packet may still not reach its destination without error; thus, packets are delivered only with high probability. Stations requiring a residual error rate lower than that provided by the bare Ethernet packet transport mechanism must follow mutually agreed upon packet protocols.

41.3   Design Principles

Our object is to design a communication system which can grow smoothly to accommodate several buildings full of personal computers and the facilities needed for their support.

Like the computing stations to be connected, the communication system must be inexpensive. We choose to distribute control of the communications facility among the communicating computers to eliminate the reliability problems of an active central controller, to avoid creating a bottleneck in a system rich in parallelism, and to reduce the fixed costs which make small systems uneconomical.

Ethernet design started with the basic idea of packet collision and retransmission developed in the Aloha Network (Abramson, 1970). We expected that, like the Aloha Network, Ethernets would carry bursty traffic so that conventional, synchronous time-division multiplexing (STDM) would be inefficient (Abramson, 1970, 1973; Metcalfe, 1973; Roberts and Wessler, 1970a). We saw promise in the Aloha approach to distributed control of radio channel multiplexing and hoped that it could be applied effectively with media suited to local computer communication. With several innovations of our own, the promise is realized.

Ethernet is named for the historical *luminiferous ether* through which electromagnetic radiations were once alleged to propagate. Like an Aloha radio transmitter, an Ethernet transmitter broadcasts completely-addressed transmitter-synchronous bit sequences called packets onto the Ether and hopes that they are heard by the intended receivers. The Ether is a logically passive medium for the propagation of digital signals and can be constructed using any number of media including coaxial cables, twisted pairs, and optical fibers.

41.3.1 Topology We cannot afford the redundant connections and dynamic routing of store-and-forward packet switching to assure reliable communication, so we choose to achieve reliability through simplicity. We choose to make the shared communication facility passive so that the failure of an active element will tend to affect the communications of only a single station. The layout and changing needs of office and laboratory buildings leads us to pick a network topology with the potential for convenient incremental extension and reconfiguration with minimal service disruption.

The topology of the Ethernet is that of an unrooted tree. It is a *tree* so that the Ether can branch at the entrance to a building's corridor, yet avoid multipath interference. There must be only one path through the Ether between any source and destination; if more than one path were to exist, a transmission would interfere with itself: repeatedly arriving at its intended destination having travelled by paths of different length. The Ether is *unrooted* because it can be extended from any of its points in any direction. Any station wishing to join an Ethernet taps into the Ether at the nearest convenient point.

Looking at the relationship of interconnection and control, we see that Ethernet is the dual of a star network. Rather than *distributed* interconnection through many separate links and *central* control in a switching node, as in a star network, the Ethernet has *central* interconnection through the Ether and *distributed* control among its stations.

Unlike an Aloha Network which is a star network with an outgoing broadcast channel and an incoming multi-access channel, an Ethernet supports many-to-many communication with a single broadcast multi-access channel.

41.3.2 Control Sharing of the Ether is controlled in such a way that it is not only possible but probable that two or more stations will attempt to transmit a packet at roughly the same time. Packets which overlap in time on the Ether are said to *collide*; they interfere so as to be unrecognizable by a receiver. A station recovers from a detected collision by abandoning the attempt and retransmitting the packet after some dynamically-chosen random time period. Arbitration of conflicting transmission demands is both distributed and statistical.

When the Ether is largely unused; a station transmits its packets at will, the packets are received without error, and all is well. As more stations begin to transmit, the rate of packet interference increases. Ethernet controllers in each station are built to adjust the mean retransmission interval in proportion to the frequency of collisions; sharing of the Ether among competing station-station transmissions is thereby kept near the optimum.

A degree of cooperation among the stations is required to share the Ether equitably. In demanding applications certain stations might usefully take transmission priority through some systematic violation of equity rules. A station could usurp the Ether by not adjusting its retransmission interval with increasing traffic or by sending very large packets. Both practices are now prohibited by low level software in each station.

41.3.3   Addressing   Each packet has a source and destination, both of which are identified in the packet's header. A packet placed on the Ether eventually propagates to all stations. Any station can copy a packet from the Ether into its local memory, but normally only an active destination station matching its address in the packet's header will do so as the packet passes. By convention, a zero destination address is a wildcard and matches all addresses; a packet with a destination of zero is called a *broadcast packet*.

41.3.4   Reliability   An Ethernet is probabilistic. Packets may be lost due to interference with other packets, impulse noise on the Ether, an inactive receiver at a packet's intended destination, or purposeful discard. Protocols used to communicate through an Ethernet must assume that packets will be received correctly at intended destinations *only with high probability*.

An Ethernet gives its *best efforts* to transmit packets successfully, but it is the responsibility of processes in the source and destination stations to take the precautions necessary to assure reliable communication of the quality they themselves desire (Metcalfe, 1972b, 1973). Recognizing the costliness and dangers of promising "error-free" communication, we refrain from guaranteeing reliable delivery of any single packet to get both economy of transmission and high reliability averaged over many packets (Metcalfe, 1973). Removing the responsibility for reliable communication from the packet transport mechanism allows us to tailor reliability to the application and to place error recovery where it will do the most good. This policy becomes more important as Ethernets are interconnected in a hierarchy of networks through which packets must travel farther and suffer greater risks.

41.3.5   Mechanisms   A station connects to the Ether with a *tap* and a *transceiver*. A tap is a device for physically connecting to the Ether while disturbing its transmission characteristics as little as possible. The design of the transceiver must be an exercise in paranoia. Precautions must be taken to insure that likely failures in the transceiver or station do not result in pollution of the Ether. In particular, removing power from the transceiver should cause it to disconnect from the Ether.

Five mechanisms are provided in our experimental Ethernet for reducing the probability and cost of losing a packet. These are (1) carrier detection, (2) interference detection, (3) packet error detection, (4) truncated packet filtering, and (5) collision consensus enforcement.

41.3.5.1   Carrier detection   As a packet's bits are placed on the Ether by a station, they are phase encoded (like bits on a magnetic tape), which guarantees that there is at least one transition on the Ether during each bit time. The passing of a packet on the Ether can therefore be detected by listening for its transitions. To use a radio analogy, we speak of the presence of *carrier* as a packet passes a transceiver. Because a station can sense the carrier of a passing packet, it can delay sending one of its own until the detected packet passes safely. The Aloha Network does not have carrier detection and consequently suffers a substantially higher collision rate. Without carrier detection, efficient use of the Ether would decrease with increasing packet length. In §41.6 below, we show that with carrier detection, Ether efficiency increases with increasing packet length.

With carrier detection we are able to implement *deference*: no station will start transmitting while hearing carrier. With deference comes *acquisition*: once a packet transmission has been in progress for an Ether end-to-end propagation time, all stations are hearing carrier and are deferring; the Ether has been acquired and the transmission will complete without an interfering collision. With carrier detection, collisions should occur only when two or more stations find the Ether silent and begin transmitting simultaneously: within an Ether end-to-end propagation time. This will almost always happen immediately after a packet transmission during which two or more stations were deferring. Because stations do not now randomize after deferring, when the transmission terminates, the waiting stations pile on together, collide, randomize, and retransmit.

41.3.5.2 Interference detection Each transceiver has an interference detector. Interference is indicated when the transceiver notices a difference between the value of the bit it is receiving from the Ether and the value of the bit it is attempting to transmit.

Interference detection has three advantages. First, a station detecting a collision knows that its packet has been damaged. The packet can be scheduled for retransmission immediately, avoiding a long acknowledgement timeout. Second, interference periods on the Ether are limited to a maximum of one round trip time. Colliding packets in the Aloha Network run to completion, but the truncated packets resulting from Ethernet collisions waste only a small fraction of a packet time on the Ether. Third, the frequency of detected interference is used to estimate Ether traffic for adjusting retransmission intervals and optimizing channel efficiency.

41.3.5.3 Packet error detection As a packet is placed on the Ether, a checksum is computed and appended. As the packet is read from the Ether, the checksum is recomputed. Packets which do not carry a consistent checksum are discarded. In this way transmission errors, impulse noise errors and errors due to undetected interference are caught at a packet's destination.

41.3.5.4 Truncated packet filtering Interference detection and deference cause most collisions to result in *truncated packets* of only a few bits; colliding stations detect interference and abort transmission within an Ether round-trip time. To reduce the processing load that the rejection of such obviously damaged packets would place on listening station software, truncated packets are filtered out in hardware.

41.3.5.5 Collision consensus enforcement When a station determines that its transmission is experiencing interference, it momentarily jams the Ether to insure that all other participants in the collision will detect interference and, because of deference, will be forced to abort. Without this *collision consensus enforcement* mechanism, it is possible that the transmitting station which would otherwise be the last to detect a collision might not do so as the other interfering transmissions successively abort and stop interfering. Although the packet may look good to that last transmitter, different path lengths between the colliding transmitters and the intended receiver will cause the packet to arrive damaged.

41.4   Implementation

Our choices of 1 kilometer, 3 megabits per second, and 256 stations for the parameters of an experimental Ethernet were based on characteristics of the locally-distributed computer communication environment and our assessments of what would be marginally achievable; they were certainly not hard restrictions essential to the Ethernet concept.

We expected that a reasonable maximum network size would be on the order of 1 kilometer of cable. We used this working number to choose among Ethers of varying signal attenuation and to design transceivers with appropriate power and sensitivity.

The dominant station on our experimental Ethernet is a minicomputer for which 3 megabits per second is a convenient data transfer rate. By keeping the peak rate well below that of the computer's path to main memory, we reduce the need for expensive special-purpose packet buffering in our Ethernet interfaces. By keeping the peak rate as high as is convenient, we provide for larger numbers of stations and more ambitious multiprocessing communications applications.

To expedite low-level packet handling among 256 stations, we allocate the first 8-bit byte of the packet to be the destination address field and the second byte to be the source address field (see Figure 41.3). 256 is a number small enough to allow each station to get an adequate share of the available bandwidth and approaches the limit of what we can achieve with current techniques for tapping cables. 256 is only a convenient number for the lowest level of protocol; higher levels can accommodate extended address spaces with additional fields inside the packet and software to interpret them.

Our experimental Ethernet implementation has four major parts: the Ether, transceivers, interfaces, and controllers (see Figure 41.2).

41.4.1   Ether   We chose to implement our experimental Ether using low-loss coaxial cable with off-the-shelf CATV taps and connectors. It is possible to mix Ethers on a single Ethernet; we use a smaller-diameter coax for convenient connection within station clusters and a larger-diameter coax for low-loss runs between clusters. The cost of coaxial cable Ether is insignificant relative to the cost of the distributed computing systems supported by Ethernet.

41.4.2   Transceivers   Our experimental transceivers can drive a kilometer of coaxial cable Ether tapped by 256 stations transmitting at 3 megabits per second. The transceivers can *endure* (i.e., work after) sustained direct shorting, improper termination of the Ether, and simultaneous drive by all 256 stations; they can *tolerate* (i.e., work during) ground differentials and everyday electrical noise, from typewriters or electric drills, encountered when stations are separated by as much as a kilometer.

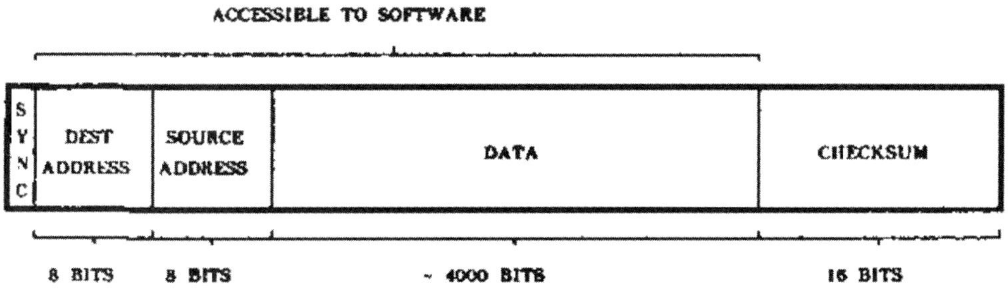

ACCESSIBLE TO SOFTWARE

S Y N C	DEST ADDRESS	SOURCE ADDRESS	DATA	CHECKSUM
	8 BITS	8 BITS	~ 4000 BITS	16 BITS

Figure 41.3: Ethernet packet layout

An Ethernet transceiver attaches directly to the Ether which passes by in the ceiling or under the floor. It is powered and controlled through 5 twisted pairs in an interface cable carrying transmit data, receive data, interference detect, and power supply voltages. When unpowered, the transceiver disconnects itself electrically from the Ether. Here is where our fight for reliability is won or lost; a broken transceiver can, but should not, bring down an entire Ethernet. A watchdog timer circuit in each transceiver attempts to prevent pollution of the Ether by shutting down the output stage if it acts suspiciously. For transceiver simplicity we use the Ether's base frequency band, but an Ethernet could be built to use any suitably sized band of a frequency division multiplexed Ether. . . .

41.4.3   Interface   An Ethernet interface serializes and deserializes the parallel data used by its station. There are a number of different stations on our Ethernet; an interface must be built for each kind.

A transmitting interface uses a packet buffer address and word count to serialize and phase encode a variable number of 16-bit words which are taken from the station's memory and passed to the transceiver, preceded by a start bit (called SYNC in Figure 41.3) and followed by the CRC. A receiving interface uses the appearance of carrier to detect the start of a packet and uses the SYNC bit to acquire bit phase. As long as carrier stays on, the interface decodes and deserializes the incoming bit stream depositing 16-bit words in a packet buffer in the station's main memory. When carrier goes away, the interface checks that an integral number of 16-bit words has been received and that the CRC is correct. The last word received is assumed to be the CRC and is not copied into the packet buffer.

These interfaces ordinarily include hardware for accepting only those packets with appropriate addresses in their headers. Hardware address filtering helps a station avoid burdensome software packet processing when the Ether is very busy carrying traffic intended for other stations.

41.4.4   Controller   An Ethernet controller is the station-specific low-level firmware or software for getting packets onto and out of the Ether. When a source-detected collision occurs, it is the source controller's responsibility to generate a new random retransmission interval based on the updated, collision count. We have studied a number of algorithms for controlling retransmission rates in stations to maintain Ether efficiency (Metcalfe, 1972a). The more practical of these algorithms estimate traffic load using recent collision history.

Retransmission intervals are multiples of a slot, the maximum time between starting a transmission and detecting a collision, one end-to-end round trip delay. An Ethernet controller begins transmission of each new packet with a mean retransmission interval of one slot. Each time a transmission attempt ends in collision, the controller delays for an interval of random length with a mean twice that of the previous interval, defers to any passing packet, and then attempts retransmission. This heuristic approximates an algorithm we have called Binary Exponential Backoff (see Figure 41.4).

When the network is unloaded and collisions are rare, the mean seldom departs from one and retransmissions are prompt. As the traffic load increases, more collisions are experienced, a backlog of packets builds up in the stations, retransmission intervals increase, and retransmission traffic backs off to sustain channel efficiency.

41.5   Growth

41.5.1   Signal cover   One can expand an Ethernet just so far by adding transceivers and Ether. At some point, the transceivers and Ether will be unable to carry the required signals. The *signal cover* can be extended with a simple unbuffered *packet repeater*. In our experimental Ethernet where, because of transceiver simplicity the Ether cannot be branched passively, a simple repeater may join any number of Ether *segments* to enrich the topology while extending the signal cover.

We operate an experimental two-segment packet repeater, but hope to avoid relying on them. In branching the Ether and extending its signal cover, there is a trade-off between using sophisticated transceivers and using repeaters. With increased power and sensitivity, transceivers become more expensive and less reliable. The introduction of repeaters into an Ethernet makes the centrally interconnecting Ether active. The failure of a transceiver will sever the communications of its owner; the failure of a repeater partitions the Ether severing many communications.

41.5.2   Traffic cover   One can expand an Ethernet just so far by adding Ether and packet repeaters. At some point the Ether will be so busy that additional stations will just divide more finely the already inadequate bandwidth: The *traffic cover* can be extended with an unbuffered repeater or *packet filter*, which passes packets from one Ether segment to another only if the destination station is located on the new segment. A packet filter also extends the signal cover.

41.5.3   Address cover   One can expand an Ethernet just so far by adding Ether, repeaters, and traffic filters. At some point there will be too many stations to be addressed with the Ethernet's 8-bit addresses. The *address cover* can be extended with packet gateways and the software addressing conventions they implement (Cerf and Kahn, 1974, here chapter 38). Addresses can be expanded in two directions: down into the station by adding fields to identify destination ports or processes within a station, and up into the internetwork by adding fields to identify destination stations on remote networks. A gateway also extends the traffic and signal covers.

There can be only one repeater or packet filter connecting two Ether segments; a packet repeated onto a segment by multiple repeaters would interfere with itself. However, there is no limit to the number of gateways connecting two segments; a gateway only repeats packets addressed to itself as an intermediary. Failure of the single repeater connecting two segments partitions the network; failure of a gateway need not partition the net if there are paths through other gateways between the segments.

41.6   Performance

... We develop a simple model of the performance of a loaded Ethernet by examining alternating Ether time periods. The first, called a transmission interval, is that during which the Ether has been acquired for a successful packet transmission. The second, called a contention interval, is that composed of the retransmission slots of §41.4.4, during which stations attempt to acquire control of the Ether. Because the model's Ethernets are loaded and because stations defer to passing packets before starting transmission, the slots are synchronized by the tail of the preceding acquisition interval. A slot will be empty when no station chooses to attempt transmission in it and it will contain a collision if more than one station attempts to transmit. When a slot contains only one attempted transmission, then the Ether has been acquired for the duration of a packet, the contention interval ends, and a transmission interval begins.

Let P be the number of bits in an Ethernet packet. Let C be the peak capacity in bits per second, carried on the Ether. Let T be the time in seconds of a slot, the number of seconds it takes to detect a collision after starting a transmission. Let us assume that there are Q stations continuously queued to transmit a packet; either the acquiring station has a new packet immediately after a successful acquisition or another station comes ready. Note that Q also happens to give the total offered load on the network which for this analysis is always 1 or greater. We assume that a queued station attempts to transmit in the current slot with probability $1/Q$, or delays with probability $1 - (1/Q)$; this is known to be the optimum statistical decision rule, approximated in Ethernet stations by means of our load-estimating retransmission control algorithms.

41.6.1   Acquisition probability   We now compute A, the probability that exactly one station attempts a transmission in a slot and therefore acquires the Ether. A is $Q \cdot (1/Q) \cdot ((1-(1/Q))^{Q-1})$: there are Q ways in which one station can choose to transmit (with probability $(1/Q)$) while $Q-1$ stations choose to wait (with probability $1 - (1/Q)$). Simplifying, $A = (1 - (1/Q))^{Q-1}$.

41.6.2   Waiting time   We now compute W, the mean number of slots of *waiting* in a contention interval before a successful acquisition of the Ether by a station's transmission. The probability of waiting no time at all is just A, the probability that one and only one station chooses to transmit in the first slot following a transmission. The probability of waiting 1 slot is $A(1 - A)$; the probability of waiting i slots is $A(1 - A)^i$. The mean of this geometric distribution is $W = (1 - A)/A$.

41.6.3   Efficiency   We now compute E, that fraction of time the Ether is carrying good packets, the efficiency. The Ether's time is divided between transmission intervals and contention intervals. A packet transmission takes P/C seconds. The mean time to acquisition is WT. Therefore, by our simple model, $E = (P/C)/((P/C) + (WT))$. ...

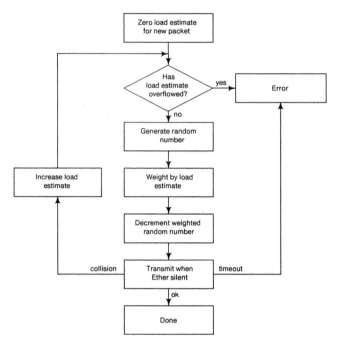

Figure 41.4: Collision control algorithm

For packets whose size is above 4000 bits, the efficiency of our experimental Ethernet stays well above 95 percent. For packets with a size approximating that of a slot, Ethernet efficiency approaches $1/e$, the asymptotic efficiency of a slotted Aloha Network (Roberts, 1973).

41.7 Protocol

There is more to the construction of a viable packet communication system than simply providing the mechanisms for packet transport. Methods for error correction, flow control, process naming, security, and accounting must also be provided through higher level protocols implemented on top of the Ether control protocol described in §§41.3 and 41.4 above (Cerf and Kahn, 1974; Crocker et al., 1972; Farber, 1973; Metcalfe, 1973; Rowe, 1975; Walden, 1972). Ether control includes packet framing, error detection, addressing and multi-access control; like other line control procedures, Ethernet is used to support numerous network and multiprocessor architectures (IBM, 1974, 1975).

Here is a brief description of one simple error-controlling packet protocol. The EFTP (Ethernet File Transfer Protocol) is of interest both because it is relatively easy to understand and implement correctly and because it has dutifully carried many valuable files during the development of more general and efficient protocols.

41.7.1 General terminology In discussing packet protocols we use the following generally useful terminology. A packet is said to have a *source* and a *destination*. A flow of data is said to have a *sender* and a *receiver*, recognizing that to support a flow of data some packets (typically acknowledgments) will be sourced at the receiver and destined for the sender. A connection is said to have a *listener* and an *initiator* and a service is said to have a *server* and a *user*. It is very useful to treat these as orthogonal descriptors of the participants in a communication. Of course, a server is usually a listener and the source of data-bearing packets is usually the sender.

41.7.2 EFTP The first 16 bits of all Ethernet packets contain its interface-interpretable destination and source station addresses, a byte each, in that order (see Figure 41.3). By software convention, the second 16 bits of all Ethernet packets contain the packet type. Different protocols use disjoint sets of packet types. The EFTP uses 5 packet types: data, ack, abort, end, and endreply. Following the 16-bit type word of an EFTP packet are 16 bits of sequence number, 16 bits of length, optionally some 16-bit data words, and finally a 16-bit software checksum word (see Figure 41.5). The Ethernet's hardware checksum is present only on the Ether and is not counted at this level of protocol.

It should be obvious that little care has been taken to cram certain fields into just the right number of bits. The emphasis here is on simplicity and ease of programming. Despite this disclaimer, we do feel that it is more advisable to err on the side of spacious fields; try as you may, one field or another will always turn out to be too small.

The software checksum word is used to lower the probability of an undetected error. It serves not only as a backup for the experimental Ethernet's serial hardware 16-bit cyclic redundancy checksum (in Figure 41.3), but also for protection against failures in parallel data paths within stations which are not checked by the CRC. The checksum used by the EFTP is a 1's complement add and cycle over the entire packet, including header and content data. The checksum can be ignored at the user's peril at either end; the sender may put all 1's (an impossible value) into the checksum word to indicate to the receiver that no checksum was computed.

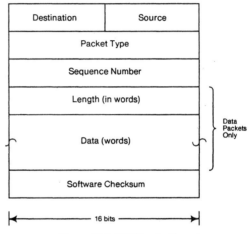

Figure 41.5: EFTP packet layout

41.7.2.1 Data transfer The 16-bit words of a file are carried from sending station to receiving station in data packets consecutively numbered from 0. Each data packet is retransmitted periodically by the sender until an ack packet with a matching sequence number is returned from the receiver. The receiver ignores all damaged packets, packets from a station other than the sender, and packets whose sequence number does not match either the expected one or the one preceding. When a packet has the expected sequence number, the packet is acked, its data is accepted as part of the file, and the sequence number is incremented. When a packet arrives with a sequence number one less than that expected, it is acknowledged and discarded; the presumption is that its ack was lost and needs retransmission.

41.7.2.2   End   When all the data has been transmitted, an end packet is sent with the next consecutive sequence number and then the sender waits for a matching endreply. Having accepted an end packet in sequence, the data receiver responds with a matching endreply and then *dallys* for some reasonably long period of time (10 seconds). Upon getting the endreply, the sending station transmits an echoing endreply and is free to go off with the assurance that the file has been transferred successfully. The dallying receiver then gets the echoed endreply and it too goes off assured.

The comparatively complex end-dally sequence is intended to make it practically certain that the sender and receiver of a file will agree on whether the file has been transmitted correctly. If the end packet is lost, the data sender simply retransmits it as it would any packet with an overdue acknowledgement. If the endreply from the data receiver is lost, the data sender will time out in the same way and retransmit the end packet which will in turn be acknowledged by the dallying receiver. If the echoed endreply is lost, the dallying receiver will be inconvenienced having to wait for it, but when it has timed out, the receiver can nevertheless be assured of successful transfer of the file because the end packet has been received.

At any time during all of this, either side is free to decide communication has failed and just give up; it is considered polite to send an abort packet to end the communication promptly in the event of, say, a user-initiated abort or a file system error.

41.7.2.3   EFTP shortcomings   The EFTP has been very useful, but its shortcomings are many. First, the protocol provides only for file transfer from station to station in a single network and specifically not from process to process within stations either on the same network or through a gateway. Second, process rendezvous is degenerate in that there are no mechanisms for finding processes by name or for convenient handling of multiple users by a single server. Third, there is no real flow control. If data arrives at a receiver unable to accept it into its buffers, the data can simply be thrown away with complete assurance that it will be retransmitted eventually. There is no way for a receiver to quench the flow of such wasted transmissions or to expedite retransmission. Fourth, data is transmitted in integral numbers of 16-bit words belonging to unnamed files and thus the EFTP is either terribly restrictive or demands some nested file transfer formats internal to its data words. And fifth, functional generality is lost because the receiver is also the listener and server.

41.8   Conclusion

Our experience with an operating Ethernet leads us to conclude that our emphasis on distributed control was well placed. By keeping the shared components of the communication system to a minimum and passive, we have achieved a very high level of reliability. Installation and maintenance of our experimental Ethernet have been more than satisfactory. The flexibility of station interconnection provided by broadcast packet switching has encouraged the development of numerous computer networking and multiprocessing applications. . . .

42 New Directions in Cryptography (1976)

Whitfield Diffie and Martin Hellman

Many important papers did not seem important when they were first published. Even Alan Turing felt unappreciated a few months after publishing his resolution of Hilbert's Entscheidungsproblem. He wrote his mother in February of 1937 that the greats were ignoring him and that he had gotten only two requests for reprints, one from a Cambridge colleague who already knew the proof (Hodges, 1983, p. 124). Even fewer papers announce as boldly as "New Directions in Cryptography" that they are reporting from "the brink of a revolution."

The problems discussed by Whitfield Diffie (b. 1944) and Martin Hellman (b. 1945) are easy to state. The first is key distribution. Since time immemorial, people have been sending coded messages to each other. One party encodes the message with the aid of an encryption key, and the other party, having received the message, uses the same key to decrypt it. Anyone who intercepts the message in transit can't decipher it without the key. The problem is that it is fundamentally no easier to transmit the key securely from one party to the other than it would have been to send securely the unencoded message itself. The key may be shorter and therefore easier to hide, or perhaps the two parties can meet up ahead of time to settle on a key before they go their separate ways. But the net effect of the fundamental problem of sharing encryption keys was to make secure encryption a monopoly of the powerful and the wealthy—only entities with the capacity to protect the keys could reliably exchange secret messages.

The second problem is digital signatures: how to distribute an unforgeable digital message or document so the recipient can be confident that no one has impersonated the sender.

Diffie and Hellman address the key distribution problem with an idea for enabling parties at a distance to agree on a key over an insecure channel without transmitting the key itself—something even Shannon, in his unifying treatment of secrecy theory, seemed to dismiss as impossible without considering it carefully: "The key must be transmitted by non-interceptible means from transmitting to receiving points" (Shannon, 1949, p. 670). The digital signature problem turned out to be related, though the particular proposals offered in this paper for digital signatures are mathematically different from those offered for key distribution. Diffie and Hellman hoped for a unitary solution to both problems, but that would have to wait (see chapter 45).

As stunning as "New Directions" was—and it was quickly recognized in academic circles as raising a variety of important challenges—it was related to a variety of earlier work, not all of it known to the authors at the time. Diffie (1988) credits Ralph Merkle with coming up with the

Reprinted from Diffie and Hellman (1976a), with permission from the Institute of Electrical and Electronics Engineers.

basic public-key idea as an undergraduate at Berkeley in 1974—but being unable to get anyone to listen to him. And some of the public key cryptography ideas had been discovered during the 1970s by scientists at GCHQ, the British intelligence agency, work that long remained classified and therefore unknown in academic or industrial circles.

But details matter, and Diffie and Hellman furnished not just the framework but the details, including the proposal to use modular exponentiation as the basis for their encryption function. If the discrete logarithm problem—the inverse of modular exponentiation—is easy to solve, then the Diffie–Helman protocol can be cracked. Hence the search was on for a fast algorithm for discrete logarithms. Suddenly, cryptography research became mainstream, and number theory, which the eminent mathematician G. H. Hardy had proudly proclaimed would never be of practical use to anyone, became the most relevant field of mathematics. (No one has yet found a fast algorithm for discrete logarithms, but in the 1980s Adi Shamir [1984] discovered that the proposal in this paper to use the knapsack problem as the basis for a one-way digital signature algorithm was fatally flawed.)

Government and commerce were much slower than academia to acknowledge the importance of public-key cryptography. The significance of this paper, indeed, is as much for opening a new sociopolitical world as for its technical importance. Cryptography had been an intellectual backwater for centuries, because it was widely assumed that whatever was known was being kept under wraps by government agencies. Diffie and Hellman's paper marked the beginning of the open exchange of ideas about cryptography.

And it started to put encryption tools into the hands of ordinary citizens—an essential development once the internet was used for commerce and banking—and thereby set off government attempts to control the technology by imposing export controls on encryption software and requiring back-doors to communications systems and cell phones. Without public key cryptography, we would not today be debating so intensely the balance between the freedom of communication of ordinary citizens and the need for governments to protect those citizens against hostile actors.

42.1   Introduction

WE stand today on the brink of a revolution in cryptography. The development of cheap digital hardware has freed it from the design limitations of mechanical computing and brought the cost of high grade cryptographic devices down to where they can be used in such commercial applications as remote cash dispensers and computer terminals. In turn, such applications create a need for new types of cryptographic systems which minimize the necessity of secure key distribution channels and supply the equivalent of a written signature. At the same time, theoretical developments in information theory and computer science show promise of providing provably secure cryptosystems, changing this ancient art into a science.

The development of computer controlled communication networks proposes effortless and inexpensive contact between people or computers on opposite sides of the world, replacing most mail and many excursions with telecommunications. For many applications these contacts must be made secure against both eavesdropping and the injection of illegitimate messages. At present, however, the solution of security problems lags well behind other areas of communications technology. Contemporary cryptography is unable to meet the requirements, in that its use would impose such severe inconveniences on the system users, as to eliminate many of the benefits of teleprocessing.

The best known cryptographic problem is that of privacy: preventing the unauthorized extraction of information from communications over an insecure channel. In order to use cryptography to insure privacy, however, it is currently necessary for the communicating parties to share a key which is known to no one else. This is done by sending the key in advance over some secure channel such as private courier or registered mail. A private conversation between two people with no prior acquaintance is a common occurrence in business, however, and it is unrealistic to expect initial business contacts to be postponed long enough for keys to be transmitted by some physical means. The cost and delay imposed by this key distribution problem is a major barrier to the transfer of business communications to large teleprocessing networks.

§42.3 proposes two approaches to transmitting keying information over public (i.e., insecure) channels without compromising the security of the system. In a *public key cryptosystem* enciphering and deciphering are governed by distinct keys, E and D, such that computing D from E is computationally infeasible (e.g., requiring 10^{100} instructions). The enciphering key E can thus be publicly disclosed without compromising the deciphering key D. Each user of the network can, therefore, place his enciphering key in a public directory. This enables any user of the system to send a message to any other user enciphered in such a way that only the intended receiver is able to decipher it. As such, a public key cryptosystem is a multiple access cipher. A private conversation can therefore be held between any two individuals regardless of whether they have ever communicated before. Each one sends messages to the other enciphered in the receiver's public enciphering key and deciphers the messages he receives using his own secret deciphering key.

We propose some techniques for developing public key cryptosystems, but the problem is still largely open.

Public key distribution systems offer a different approach to eliminating the need for a secure key distribution channel. In such a system, two users who wish to exchange a key communicate back and forth until they arrive at a key in common. A third party eavesdropping on this exchange must find it computationally infeasible to compute the key from the information overheard. A possible solution to the public key distribution problem is given in §42.3, and Merkle (1978) has a partial solution of a different form.

A second problem, amenable to cryptographic solution, which stands in the way of replacing contemporary business communications by teleprocessing systems is authentication. In current business, the validity of contracts is guaranteed by signatures. A signed contract serves as legal evidence of an agreement which the holder can present in court if necessary. The use of signatures, however, requires the transmission and storage of written contracts. In order to have a purely digital replacement for this paper instrument, each user must be able to produce a message whose authenticity can be checked by anyone, but which could not have been produced by anyone else, even the recipient. Since only one person can originate messages but many people can receive messages, this can be viewed as a broadcast cipher. Current electronic authentication techniques cannot meet this need.

§42.4 discusses the problem of providing a true, digital, message dependent signature. For reasons brought out there, we refer to this as the one-way authentication problem. Some partial solutions are given, and it is shown how any public key cryptosystem can be transformed into a one-way authentication system.

§42.5 will consider the interrelation of various cryptographic problems and introduce the even more difficult problem of trap doors.

At the same time that communications and computation have given rise to new cryptographic problems, their offspring, information theory, and the theory of computation have begun to supply tools for the solution of important problems in classical cryptography.

The search for unbreakable codes is one of the oldest themes of cryptographic research, but until this century all proposed systems have ultimately been broken. In the nineteen twenties, however, the "one time pad" was invented, and shown to be unbreakable (Kahn, 1967, pp. 398–400). The theoretical basis underlying this and related systems was put on a firm foundation a quarter century later by information theory (Shannon, 1949). One time pads require extremely long keys and are therefore prohibitively expensive in most applications.

In contrast, the security of most cryptographic systems resides in the computational difficulty to the cryptanalyst of discovering the plaintext without knowledge of the key. This problem falls within the domains of computational complexity and analysis of algorithms, two recent disciplines which study the difficulty of solving computational problems. Using the results of these theories, it may be possible to extend proofs of security to more useful classes of systems in the foreseeable future. §42.6 explores this possibility.

Before proceeding to newer developments, we introduce terminology and define threat environments in the next section.

42.2   Conventional Cryptography

Cryptography is the study of "mathematical" systems for solving two kinds of security problems: privacy and authentication. A privacy system prevents the extraction by unauthorized parties from messages transmitted over a public channel, thus assuring the sender of a message that it is being read only by the intended recipient. An authentication system prevents the unauthorized injection of messages into a public channel, assuring the receiver of a message of the legitimacy of its sender.

A channel is considered public if its security is inadequate for the needs of its users. A channel such as a telephone line may therefore be considered private by some users and public by others. Any channel may be threatened with eavesdropping or injection or both, depending on its use. In telephone communication, the threat of injection is paramount, since the called party cannot determine which phone is calling. Eavesdropping, which requires the use of a wiretap, is technically more difficult and legally hazardous. In radio, by comparison, the situation is reversed. Eavesdropping is passive and involves no legal hazard, while injection exposes the illegitimate transmitter to discovery and prosecution.

Having divided our problems into those of privacy and authentication we will sometimes further subdivide authentication into message authentication, which is the problem defined above, and user authentication, in which the only task of the system is to verify that an individual is who he claims to be. For example, the identity of an individual who presents a credit card must be verified, but there is no message which he wishes to transmit. In spite of this apparent absence of a message in user authentication, the two problems are largely equivalent. In user authentication, there is an implicit message "I AM USER X," while message authentication is just verification of the identity of the party sending the message. Differences in the threat environments and other aspects of these two subproblems, however, sometimes make it convenient to distinguish between them.

Figure 42.1 illustrates the flow of information in a conventional cryptographic system used for privacy of communications. There are three parties: a transmitter, a receiver, and an eavesdropper. The transmitter generates a plaintext or unenciphered message P to be communicated over an insecure channel to the legitimate receiver. In order to prevent the eavesdropper from learning P, the transmitter operates on P with an invertible transformation

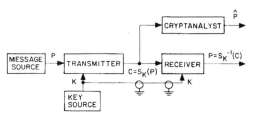

Figure 42.1: Flow of information in conventional cryptographic system

S_K to produce the ciphertext or cryptogram $C = S_K(P)$. The key K is transmitted only to the legitimate receiver via a secure channel, indicated by a shielded path in Figure 42.1. Since the legitimate receiver knows K, he can decipher C by operating with S_K^{-1} to obtain $S_K^{-1}(C) = S_K^{-1}(S_K(P)) = P$, the original plaintext message. The secure channel cannot be used to transmit P itself for reasons of capacity or delay. For example, the secure channel might be a weekly courier and the insecure channel a telephone line.

A *cryptographic system* is a single parameter family $\{S_K\}_{K \in \{K\}}$ of invertible transformations $S_K : \{P\} \to \{C\}$ from a space $\{P\}$ of plaintext messages to a space $\{C\}$ of ciphertext messages. The parameter K is called the key and is selected from a finite set $\{K\}$ called the keyspace. If the message spaces $\{P\}$ and $\{C\}$ are equal, we will denote them both by $\{M\}$. When discussing individual cryptographic transformations S_K, we will sometimes omit mention of the system and merely refer to the transformation K.

The goal in designing the cryptosystem $\{S_K\}$ is to make the enciphering and deciphering operations inexpensive, but to ensure that any successful cryptanalytic operation is too complex to be economical. There are two approaches to this problem. A system which is secure due to the computational cost of cryptanalysis, but which would succumb to an attack with unlimited computation, is called *computationally secure*; while a system which can resist any cryptanalytic attack, no matter how much computation is allowed, is called *unconditionally secure*. Unconditionally secure systems are discussed in Shannon (1949) and Hellman (1977) and belong to that portion of information theory, called the Shannon theory, which is concerned with optimal performance obtainable with unlimited computation.

Unconditional security results from the existence of multiple meaningful solutions to a cryptogram. For example, the simple substitution cryptogram XMD resulting from English text can represent the plaintext messages: now, and, the, etc. A computationally secure cryptogram, in contrast, contains sufficient information to uniquely determine the plaintext and the key. Its security resides solely in the cost of computing them.

The only unconditionally secure system in common use is the *one time pad*, in which the plaintext is combined with a randomly chosen key of the same length. While such a system is provably secure, the large amount of key required makes it impractical for most applications. Except as otherwise noted, this paper deals with computationally secure systems since these are more generally applicable. When we talk about the need to develop provably secure cryptosystems we exclude those, such as the one time pad, which are unwieldy to use. Rather, we have in mind systems using only a few hundred bits of key and implementable in either a small amount of digital hardware or a few hundred lines of software.

We will call a task *computationally infeasible* if its cost as measured by either the amount of memory used or the runtime is finite but impossibly large.

Much as error correcting codes are divided into convolutional and block codes, cryptographic systems can be divided into two broad classes: *stream ciphers* and *block ciphers*. Stream ciphers process the plaintext in small chunks (bits or characters), usually producing a pseudorandom sequence of bits which is added modulo 2 to the bits of the plaintext. Block ciphers act in a purely combinatorial fashion on large blocks of text, in such a way that a small change in the input block produces a major change in the resulting output. This paper deals primarily with block ciphers, because this *error propagation* property is valuable in many authentication applications.

In an authentication system, cryptography is used to guarantee the authenticity of the message to the receiver. Not only must a meddler be prevented from injecting totally new, authentic looking messages into a channel, but he must be prevented from creating apparently authentic messages by combining, or merely repeating, old messages which he has copied in the past. A cryptographic system intended to guarantee privacy will not, in general, prevent this latter form of mischief.

To guarantee the authenticity of a message, information is added which is a function not only of the message and a secret key, but of the date and time as well; for example, by attaching the date and time to each message and encrypting the entire sequence. This assures that only someone who possesses the key can generate a message which, when decrypted, will contain the proper date and time. Care must be taken, however, to use a system in which small changes in the ciphertext result in large changes in the deciphered plaintext. This intentional error propagation ensures that if the deliberate injection of noise on the channel changes a message such as "erase file 7" into a different message such as "erase file 8," it will also corrupt the authentication information. The message will then be rejected as inauthentic.

The first step in assessing the adequacy of cryptographic systems is to classify the threats to which they are to be subjected. The following threats may occur to cryptographic systems employed for either privacy or authentication.

A *ciphertext only attack* is a cryptanalytic attack in which the cryptanalyst possesses only ciphertext.

A *known plaintext attack* is a cryptanalytic attack in which the cryptanalyst possesses a substantial quantity of corresponding plaintext and ciphertext.

A *chosen plaintext attack* is a cryptanalytic attack in which the cryptanalyst can submit an unlimited number of plaintext messages of his own choosing and examine the resulting cryptograms.

In all cases it is assumed that the opponent knows the general system $\{S_K\}$ in use since this information can be obtained by studying a cryptographic device. [EDITOR: This assumption is known as Kerckhoffs's principle and dates to 1883, though it has often unwisely been ignored.] While many users of cryptography attempt to keep their equipment secret, many commercial applications require not only that the general system be public but that it be standard.

A ciphertext only attack occurs frequently in practice. The cryptanalyst uses only knowledge of the statistical properties of the language in use (e.g., in English, the letter e occurs 13 percent of the time) and knowledge of certain "probable" words (e.g., a letter probably begins "Dear Sir:"). It is the weakest threat to which a system can be subjected, and any system which succumbs to it is considered totally insecure.

A system which is secure against a known plaintext attack frees its users from the need to keep their past messages secret, or to paraphrase them prior to declassification. This is an unreasonable burden to place on the system's users, particularly in commercial situations where product announcements or press releases may be sent in encrypted form for later public disclosure. Similar situations in diplomatic correspondence have led to the cracking of many supposedly secure systems. While a known plaintext attack is not always possible, its occurrence is frequent enough that a system which cannot resist it is not considered secure.

A chosen plaintext attack is difficult to achieve in practice, but can be approximated. For example, submitting a proposal to a competitor may result in his enciphering it for transmission to his headquarters. A cipher which is secure against a chosen plaintext attack thus frees its users from concern over whether their opponents can plant messages in their system.

For the purpose of certifying systems as secure, it is appropriate to consider the more formidable cryptanalytic threats as these not only give more realistic models of the working environment of a cryptographic system, but make the assessment of the system's strength easier. Many systems which are difficult to analyze using a ciphertext only attack can be ruled out immediately under known plaintext or chosen plaintext attacks.

As is clear from these definitions, cryptanalysis is a system identification problem. The known plaintext and chosen plaintext attacks correspond to passive and active system identification problems, respectively. Unlike many subjects in which system identification is considered, such as automatic fault diagnosis, the goal in cryptography is to build systems which are difficult, rather than easy, to identify.

The chosen plaintext attack is often called an IFF attack, terminology which descends from its origin in the development of cryptographic "identification friend or foe" systems after World War II. An IFF system enables military radars to distinguish between friendly and enemy planes automatically. The radar sends a time-varying challenge to the airplane which receives the challenge, encrypts it under the appropriate key, and sends it back to the radar. By comparing this response with a correctly encrypted version of the challenge, the radar can recognize a friendly aircraft. While the aircraft are over enemy territory, enemy cryptanalysts can send challenges and examine the encrypted responses in an attempt to determine the authentication key in use, thus mounting a chosen plaintext attack on the system. In practice, this threat is countered by restricting the form of the challenges, which need not be unpredictable, but only nonrepeating.

There are other threats to authentication systems which cannot be treated by conventional cryptography, and which require recourse to the new ideas and techniques introduced in this paper. The *threat of compromise of the receiver's authentication data* is motivated by the situation in multiuser networks where the receiver is often the system itself. The receiver's password tables and other authentication data are then more vulnerable to theft than those of the transmitter (an individual user). As shown later, some techniques for protecting against this threat also protect against the *threat of dispute*. That is, a message may be sent but later repudiated by either the transmitter or the receiver. Or, it may be alleged by either party that a message was sent when in fact none was. Unforgeable digital signatures and receipts are needed. For example, a dishonest stockbroker might try to cover up unauthorized buying and selling for personal gain by forging orders from clients, or a client might disclaim an order actually authorized by him but which he later sees will cause a loss. We will introduce concepts which allow the receiver to verify the authenticity of a message, but prevent him from generating apparently authentic messages, thereby protecting against both the threat of compromise of the receiver's authentication data and the threat of dispute.

42.3   Public Key Cryptography

As shown in Figure 42.1, cryptography has been a derivative security measure. Once a secure channel exists along which keys can be transmitted, the security can be extended to other channels of higher bandwidth or smaller delay by encrypting the messages sent on them. The effect has been to limit the use of cryptography to communications among people who have made prior preparation for cryptographic security.

In order to develop large, secure, telecommunications systems, this must be changed. A large number of users n results in an even larger number, $(n^2 - n)/2$ potential pairs who may wish to communicate privately from all others. It is unrealistic to assume either that a pair of users with no prior acquaintance will be able to wait for a key to be sent by some secure physical means, or that keys for all $(n^2-n)/2$ pairs can be arranged in advance. In another paper (Diffie and Hellman, 1976b), the authors have considered a conservative approach requiring no new development in cryptography itself, but this involves diminished security, inconvenience, and restriction of the network to a starlike configuration with respect to initial connection protocol.

We propose that it is possible to develop systems of the type shown in Figure 42.2, in which two parties communicating solely over a public channel and using only publicly known techniques can create a secure connection. We examine two approaches to this problem, called public key cryptosystems and public key distribution systems, respectively. The first are more powerful, lending themselves to the solution of the authentica-

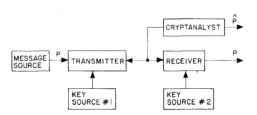

Figure 42.2: Flow of information in public key system

tion problems treated in the next section, while the second are much closer to realization.

A *public key cryptosystem* is a pair of families $\{E_K\}_{K\in\{K\}}$ and $\{D_K\}_{K\in\{K\}}$ of algorithms representing invertible transformations,

$$E_K : \{M\} \to \{M\}$$
$$D_K : \{M\} \to \{M\}$$

on a finite message space $\{M\}$, such that

1. for every $K \in \{K\}$, E_K is the inverse of D_K,
2. for every $K \in \{K\}$ and $M \in \{M\}$, the algorithms E_K and D_K are easy to compute,
3. for almost every $K \in \{K\}$, each easily computed algorithm equivalent to D_K is computationally infeasible to derive from E_K,
4. for every $K \in \{K\}$, it is feasible to compute inverse pairs E_K and D_K from K.

Because of the third property, a user's enciphering key E_K can be made public without compromising the security of his secret deciphering key D_K. The cryptographic system is therefore split into two parts, a family of enciphering transformations and a family of deciphering transformations in such a way that, given a member of one family, it is infeasible to find the corresponding member of the other.

The fourth property guarantees that there is a feasible way of computing corresponding pairs of inverse transformations when no constraint is placed on what either the enciphering or deciphering transformation is to be. In practice, the cryptoequipment must contain a true random number generator (e.g., a noisy diode) for generating K, together with an algorithm for generating the E_K–D_K pair from its outputs.

Given a system of this kind, the problem of key distribution is vastly simplified. Each user generates a pair of inverse transformations, E and D, at his terminal. The deciphering transformation D must be kept secret, but need never be communicated on any channel. The enciphering key E can be made public by placing it in a public directory along with the user's name and address. Anyone can then encrypt messages and send them to the user, but no one else can decipher messages intended for him. Public key cryptosystems can thus be regarded as *multiple access ciphers*.

It is crucial that the public file of enciphering keys be protected from unauthorized modification. This task is made easier by the public nature of the file. Read protection is unnecessary and, since the file is modified infrequently, elaborate write protection mechanisms can be economically employed.

A suggestive, although unfortunately useless, example of a public key cryptosystem is to encipher the plaintext, represented as a binary n-vector **m**, by multiplying it by an invertible binary $n \times n$ matrix E. The cryptogram thus equals $E\mathbf{m}$. Letting $D = E^{-1}$ we have $\mathbf{m} = D\mathbf{c}$. Thus, both enciphering and deciphering require about n^2 operations. Calculation of D from E, however, involves a matrix inversion which is a harder problem. And it is at least conceptually simpler to obtain an arbitrary pair of inverse matrices than it is to invert a given matrix. Start with the identity matrix I and do elementary row and column operations to obtain an arbitrary invertible matrix E. Then starting with I do the inverses of these same elementary operations in reverse order to obtain $D = E^{-1}$. The sequence of elementary operations could be easily determined from a random bit string.

Unfortunately, matrix inversion takes only about n^3 operations. The ratio of "cryptanalytic" time (i.e., computing D from E) to enciphering or deciphering time is thus at most n, and enormous block sizes would be required to obtain ratios of 10^6 or greater. Also, it does not appear that knowledge of the elementary operations used to obtain E from I greatly reduces the time for computing D. And, since there is no round-off error in binary arithmetic, numerical stability is unimportant in the matrix inversion. In spite of its lack of practical utility, this matrix example is still useful for clarifying the relationships necessary in a public key cryptosystem.

A more practical approach to finding a pair of easily computed inverse algorithms E and D; such that D is hard to infer from E, makes use of the difficulty of analyzing programs in low level languages. Anyone who has tried to determine what operation is accomplished by someone else's machine language program knows that E itself (i.e., what E does) can be hard to infer from an algorithm for E. If the program were to be made purposefully confusing through addition of unneeded variables and statements, then determining an inverse algorithm could be made very difficult. Of course, E must be complicated enough to prevent its identification from input-output pairs.

Essentially what is required is a one-way compiler: one which takes an easily understood program written in a high level language and translates it into an incomprehensible program in some machine language. The compiler is one-way because it must be feasible to do the compilation, but infeasible to reverse the process. Since efficiency in size of program and run time are not crucial in this application, such compilers may be possible if the structure of the machine language can be optimized to assist in the confusion.

Merkle (1978) has independently studied the problem of distributing keys over an insecure channel. His approach is different from that of the public key cryptosystems suggested above, and will be termed a *public key distribution* system. The goal is for two users, A and B, to securely exchange a key over an insecure channel. This key is then used by both users in a normal cryptosystem for both enciphering and deciphering. Merkle has a solution whose cryptanalytic cost grows as n^2 where n is the cost to the legitimate users. Unfortunately the cost to the legitimate users of the system is as much in transmission time as in computation, because Merkle's protocol requires n potential keys to be transmitted before one key can be decided on. Merkle notes that this high transmission overhead prevents the system from being very useful in practice. If a one megabit limit is placed on the setup protocol's overhead, his technique can achieve cost ratios of approximately 10,000 to 1, which are too small for most applications. If inexpensive, high bandwidth data links become available, ratios of a million to one or greater could be achieved and the system would be of substantial practical value.

We now suggest a new public key distribution system which has several advantages. First, it requires only one "key" to be exchanged. Second, the cryptanalytic effort appears to grow exponentially in the effort of the legitimate users. And, third, its use can be tied to a public file of user information which serves to authenticate user A to user B and vice versa. By making the public file essentially a read only memory, one personal appearance allows a user to authenticate his identity many times to many users. Merkle's technique requires A and B to verify each other's identities through other means.

The new technique makes use of the apparent difficulty of computing logarithms over a finite field $GF(q)$ with a prime number q of elements. Let

$$Y = \alpha^X \bmod q, \text{ for } 1 \leq X \leq q - 1,$$

where α is a fixed primitive element of $GF(q)$, then X is referred to as the logarithm of Y to the base α, mod q:

$$X = \log_\alpha Y \bmod q, \text{ for } 1 \leq Y \leq q - 1.$$

Calculation of Y from X is easy, taking at most $2\log_2 q$ multiplications (Knuth, 1969, pp. 398–400). For example, for $X = 18$,

$$Y = \alpha^{18} = (((\alpha^2)^2)^2)^2 \times \alpha^2.$$

Computing X from Y, on the other hand can be much more difficult and, for certain carefully chosen values of q, requires on the order of $q^{1/2}$ operations, using the best known algorithm (Pohlig and Hellman, 1978; Knuth, 1973, pp. 9, 575–576).

The security of our technique depends crucially on the difficulty of computing logarithms mod q, and if an algorithm whose complexity grew as $\log_2 q$ were to be found, our system would be broken. While the simplicity of the problem statement might allow such simple algorithms, it might instead allow a proof of the problem's difficulty. For now we assume that the best known algorithm for computing logs mod q is in fact close to optimal and hence that $q^{1/2}$ is a good measure of the problem's complexity, for a properly chosen q.

Each user generates an independent random number X_i chosen uniformly from the set of integers $\{1, 2, \ldots, q-1\}$. Each keeps X_i secret, but places $Y_i = \alpha^{X_i} \bmod q$ in a public file with his name and address. When users i and j wish to communicate privately, they use $K_{ij} = \alpha^{X_i X_j} \bmod q$ as their key. User i obtains K_{ij} by obtaining Y_j from the public file and letting

$$K_{ij} = Y_j^{X_i} \bmod q$$
$$= (\alpha^{X_j})^{X_i} \bmod q$$
$$= \alpha^{X_j X_i} = \alpha^{X_i X_j} \bmod q.$$

User j obtains K_{ij} in the similar fashion, $K_{ij} = Y_i^{X_j} \bmod q$. Another user must compute K_{ij} from Y_i and Y_j, for example, by computing $K_{ij} = Y_i^{(\log_\alpha Y_j)} \bmod q$.

We thus see that if logs mod q are easily computed the system can be broken. While we do not currently have a proof of the converse (i.e., that the system is secure if logs mod q are difficult to compute), neither do we see any way to compute K_{ij} from Y_i and Y_j without first obtaining either X_i or X_j.

If q is a prime slightly less than 2^b, then all quantities are representable as b bit numbers. Exponentiation then takes at most $2b$ multiplications mod q, while by hypothesis taking logs requires $q^{1/2} = 2^{b/2}$ operations. The cryptanalytic effort therefore grows exponentially relative to legitimate efforts. If $b = 200$, then at most 400 multiplications are required to compute Y_i from X_i, or K_{ij} from Y_i and X_j, yet taking logs mod q requires 2^{100} or approximately 10^{30} operations.

42.4   One-Way Authentication

The problem of authentication is perhaps an even more serious barrier to the universal adoption of telecommunications for business transactions than the problem of key distribution. Authentication is at the heart of any system involving contracts and billing. Without it, business cannot function. Current electronic authentication systems cannot meet the need for a purely digital, unforgeable, message dependent signature. They provide protection against third party forgeries, but do not protect against disputes between transmitter and receiver.

In order to develop a system capable of replacing the current written contract with some purely electronic form of communication, we must discover a digital phenomenon with the same properties as a written signature. It must be easy for anyone to recognize the signature as authentic, but impossible for anyone other than the legitimate signer to produce it. We will call any such technique *one-way authentication*. Since any digital signal can be copied precisely, a true digital signature must be recognizable without being known.

Consider the "login" problem in a multiuser computer system. When setting up his account, the user chooses a password which is entered into the system's password directory. Each time he logs in, the user is again asked to provide his password. By keeping this password secret from all other users, forged logins are prevented. This, however, makes it vital to preserve the security of the password directory since the information it contains would allow perfect impersonation of any user. The problem is further compounded if system operators have legitimate reasons for accessing the directory. Allowing such legitimate accesses, but preventing all others, is next to impossible.

This leads to the apparently impossible requirement for a new login procedure capable of judging the authenticity of passwords without actually knowing them. While appearing to be a logical impossibility, this proposal is easily satisfied. When the user first enters his password PW, the computer automatically and transparently computes a function $f(PW)$ and stores this, not PW, in the password directory. At each successive login, the computer calculates $f(X)$, where X is the proffered password, and compares $f(X)$ with the stored value $f(PW)$. If and only if they are equal, the user is accepted as being authentic. Since the function f must be calculated once per login, its computation time must be small. A million instructions (costing approximately $0.10 at bicentennial prices) seems to be a reasonable limit on this computation. If we could ensure, however, that calculation of f^{-1} required 10^{30} or more instructions, someone who had subverted the system to obtain the password directory could not in practice obtain PW from $f(PW)$, and could thus not perform an unauthorized login. Note that $f(PW)$ is not accepted as a password by the login program since it will automatically compute $f(f(PW))$ which will not match the entry $f(PW)$ in the password directory.

We assume that the function f is public information, so that it is not ignorance of f which makes calculation of f^{-1} difficult. Such functions are called one-way functions and were first employed for use in login procedures by R. M. Needham (Wilkes, 1972, p. 91). They are also discussed in two recent papers (Evans et al., 1974; Purdy, 1974) which suggest interesting approaches to the design of one-way functions.

More precisely, a function f is a *one-way function* if, for any argument x in the domain of f, it is easy to compute the corresponding value $f(x)$, yet, for almost all y in the range of f, it is computationally infeasible to solve the equation $y = f(x)$ for any suitable argument x.

It is important to note that we are defining a function which is not invertible from a computational point of view, but whose noninvertibility is entirely different from that normally encountered in mathematics. A function f is normally called "noninvertible" when the inverse of a point y is not unique (i.e., there exist distinct points x_1 and x_2 such that $f(x_1) = y = f(x_2)$). We emphasize that this is not the sort of inversion difficulty that is required. Rather, it must be overwhelmingly difficult, given a value y and knowledge of f, to calculate any x whatsoever with the property that $f(x) = y$. Indeed, if f is noninvertible in the usual sense, it may make the task of finding an inverse image easier. In the extreme, if $f(x) = y_0$ for all x in the domain, then the range of f is $\{y_0\}$, and we can take any x as $f^{-1}(y_0)$. It is therefore necessary that f not be too degenerate. A small degree of degeneracy is tolerable and, as discussed later, is probably present in the most promising class of one-way functions.

Polynomials offer an elementary example of one-way functions. It is much harder to find a root x_0 of the polynomial equation $p(x) = y$ than it is to evaluate the polynomial $p(x)$ at $x = x_0$. Purdy (1974) has suggested the use of sparse polynomials of very high degree over finite fields, which appear to have very high ratios of solution to evaluation time. The theoretical basis for one-way functions is discussed at greater length in §42.6. And, as shown in §42.5, one-way functions are easy to devise in practice.

The one-way function login protocol solves only some of the problems arising in a multiuser system. It protects against compromise of the system's authentication data when it is not in use, but still requires the user to send the true password to the system. Protection against eavesdropping must be provided by additional encryption, and protection against the threat of dispute is absent altogether.

A public key cryptosystem can be used to produce a true one-way authentication system as follows. If user A wishes to send a message M to user B, he "deciphers" it in his secret deciphering key and sends $D_A(M)$. When user B receives it, he can read it, and be assured of its authenticity by "enciphering" it with user A's public enciphering key E_A. B also saves $D_A(M)$ as proof that the message came from A. Anyone can check this claim by operating on $D_A(M)$ with the publicly known operation E_A to recover M. Since only A could have generated a message with this property, the solution to the one-way authentication problem would follow immediately from the development of public key cryptosystems.

One-way message authentication has a partial solution suggested to the authors by Leslie Lamport of Massachusetts Computer Associates. This technique employs a one-way function f mapping k-dimensional binary space into itself for k on the order of 100. If the transmitter wishes to send an N bit message he generates $2N$, randomly chosen, k-dimensional binary vectors x_1, X_1, x_2, X_2, ..., x_N, X_N which he keeps secret. The receiver is given the corresponding images under f, namely y_1, Y_1, y_2, Y_2, ..., y_N, Y_N. Later, when the message $\mathbf{m} = (m_1, m_2, \ldots, m_N)$ is to be sent, the transmitter sends x_1 or X_1 depending on whether $m_1 = 0$ or 1. He sends x_2 or X_2 depending on whether $m_2 = 0$ or 1, etc. The receiver operates with f on the first received block and sees whether it yields y_1 or Y_1 as its image and thus learns whether it was x_1 or X_1, and whether $m_1 = 0$ or 1. In a similar manner the receiver is able to determine $m_2, m_3, \ldots, m_N$. But the receiver is incapable of forging a change in even one bit of **m**.

This is only a partial solution because of the approximately 100-fold data expansion required. There is, however, a modification which eliminates the expansion problem when N is roughly a megabit or more. Let g be a one-way mapping from binary N-space to binary n-space where n is approximately 50. Take the N bit message **m** and operate on it with g to obtain the n bit vector **m′**. Then use the previous scheme to send **m′**. If $N = 10^6$, $n = 50$, and $k = 100$, this adds $kn = 5000$ authentication bits to the message. It thus entails only a 5 percent data expansion during transmission (or 15 percent if the initial exchange of $y_1, Y_1, \ldots, y_N, Y_N$ is included). Even though there are a large number of other messages (2^{N-n} on the average) with the same authentication sequence, the one-wayness of g makes them computationally infeasible to find and thus to forge. Actually g must be somewhat stronger than a normal one-way function, since an opponent has not only **m′** but also one of its inverse images **m**. It must be hard even given **m** to find a different inverse image of **m′**. Finding such functions appears to offer little trouble (see §42.5).

There is another partial solution to the one-way user authentication problem. The user generates a password X which he keeps secret. He gives the system $f^T(X)$, where f is a one-way function. At time t the appropriate authenticator is $f^{T-t}(X)$, which can be checked by the system by applying $f^t(X)$. Because of the one-wayness of f, past responses are of no value in forging a new response. The problem with this solution is that it can require a fair amount of computation for legitimate login (although many orders of magnitude less than for forgery). If for example t is incremented every second and the system must work for one month on each password then $T = 2.6$ million. Both the user and the system must then iterate f an average of 1.3 million times per login. While not insurmountable, this problem obviously limits use of the technique. The problem could be overcome if a simple method for calculating $f^{(2^n)}$, for $n = 1, ,2, \ldots$ could be found, much as $X^8 = ((X^2)^2)^2$. For then binary decompositions of $T - t$ and t would allow rapid computation of f^{T-t} and f^t. It may be, however, that rapid computation of f^n precludes f from being one-way.

42.5   Problem Interrelations and Trap Doors

In this section, we will show that some of the cryptographic problems presented thus far can be reduced to others, thereby defining a loose ordering according to difficulty. We also introduce the more difficult problem of trap doors.

In §42.2 we showed that a cryptographic system intended for privacy can also be used to provide authentication against third party forgeries. Such a system can be used to create other cryptographic objects, as well.

A cryptosystem which is secure against a known plaintext attack can be used to produce a one-way function.

As indicated in Figure 42.3, take the cryptosystem $\{S_K : \{P\} \to \{C\}\}_{K\in\{K\}}$ which is secure against a known plaintext attack, fix $P = P_0$ and consider the map $f : \{K\} \to \{C\}$ defined by $f(X) = S_X(P_0)$.

This function is one-way because solving for X given $f(X)$ is equivalent to the cryptanalytic problem of finding the key from a single known plaintext-cryptogram pair. Public knowledge of f is now equivalent to public knowledge of $\{S_K\}$ and P_0.

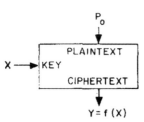

P_0

PLAINTEXT

X ⟶ KEY

CIPHERTEXT

Y = f (X)

Figure 42.3: Secure cryptosystem used as one-way function

While the converse of this result is not necessarily true, it is possible for a function originally found in the search for one-way functions to yield a good cryptosystem. This actually happened with the discrete exponential function discussed in §42.3 (Pohlig and Hellman, 1978).

One-way functions are basic to both block ciphers and key generators. A key generator is a pseudorandom bit generator whose output, the keystream, is added modulo 2 to a message represented in binary form, in imitation of a one-time pad. The key is used as a "seed" which determines the pseudorandom keystream sequence. A known plaintext attack thus reduces to the problem of determining the key from the keystream. For the system to be secure, computation of the key from the keystream must be computationally infeasible. While, for the system to be usable, calculation of the keystream from the key must be computationally simple. Thus a good key generator is, almost by definition, a one-way function.

Use of either type of cryptosystem as a one way function suffers from a minor problem. As noted earlier, if the function f is not uniquely invertible, it is not necessary (or possible) to find the actual value of X used. Rather any X with the same image will suffice. And, while each mapping S_K in a cryptosystem must be bijective, there is no such restriction on the function f from key to cryptogram defined above. Indeed, guaranteeing that a cryptosystem has this property appears quite difficult. In a good cryptosystem the mapping f can be expected to have the characteristics of a randomly chosen mapping (i.e., $f(X_i)$ is chosen uniformly from all possible Y, and successive choices are independent). In this case, if X is chosen uniformly and there are an equal number of keys and messages (X and Y), then the probability that the resultant Y has $k + 1$ inverses is approximately $e^{-1}/k!$ for $k = 0, 1, 2, 3, \ldots$. This is a Poisson distribution with mean $\lambda = 1$, shifted by 1 unit. The expected number of inverses is thus only 2. While it is possible for f to be more degenerate, a good cryptosystem will not be too degenerate since then the key is not being well used. In the worst case, if $f(X) \equiv Y_0$ for some Y_0, we have $S_K(P_0) = C_0$, and encipherment of P_0 would not depend on the key at all!

While we are usually interested in functions whose domain and range are of comparable size, there are exceptions. In the previous section we required a one-way function mapping long strings onto much shorter ones. By using a block cipher whose key length is larger than the blocksize, such functions can be obtained using the above technique.

Evans et al. (1974) have a different approach to the problem of constructing a one-way function from a block cipher. Rather than selecting a fixed P_0 as the input, they use the function $f(X) = S_X(X)$. This is an attractive approach because equations of this form are generally difficult to solve, even when the family S is comparatively simple. This added complexity, however, destroys the equivalence between the security of the system S under a known plaintext attack and the onewayness of f.

Another relationship has already been shown in §42.4.

A public key cryptosystem can be used to generate a one-way authentication system.

The converse does not appear to hold, making the construction of a public key cryptosystem a strictly more difficult problem than one-way authentication. Similarly, a public key cryptosystem can be used as a public key distribution system, but not conversely.

Since in a public key cryptosystem the general system in which E and D are used must be public, specifying E specifies a complete algorithm for transforming input messages into output cryptograms. As such a public key system is really a set of *trap-door one-way functions*. These are functions which are not really one-way in that simply computed inverses exist. But given an algorithm for the forward function it is computationally infeasible to find a simply computed inverse. Only through knowledge of certain *trap-door information* (e.g., the random bit string which produced the *E-D* pair) can one easily find the easily computed inverse.

Trap doors have already been seen in the previous paragraph in the form of *trap-door one-way functions*, but other variations exist. A *trap-door cipher* is one which strongly resists cryptanalysis by anyone not in possession of *trap-door information* used in the design of the cipher. This allows the designer to break the system after he has sold it to a client and yet falsely to maintain his reputation as a builder of secure systems. It is important to note that it is not greater cleverness or knowledge of cryptography which allows the designer to do what others cannot. If he were to lose the trap-door information he would be no better off than anyone else. The situation is precisely analogous to a combination lock. Anyone who knows the combination can do in seconds what even a skilled locksmith would require hours to accomplish. And yet, if he forgets the combination, he has no advantage.

A trap-door cryptosystem can be used to produce a public key distribution system.

For A and B to establish a common private key, A chooses a key at random and sends an arbitrary plaintext-cryptogram pair to B. B, who made the trap-door cipher public, but kept the trap-door information secret, uses the plaintext-cryptogram pair to solve for the key. A and B now have a key in common.

There is currently little evidence for the existence of trap-door ciphers. However they are a distinct possibility and should be remembered when accepting a cryptosystem from a possible opponent (Diffie and Hellman, 1977).

By definition, we will require that a trap-door problem be one in which it is computationally feasible to devise the trap door. This leaves room for yet a third type of entity for which we shall use the prefix "quasi." For example a *quasi one-way function* is not one-way in that an easily computed inverse exists. However, it is computationally infeasible, even for the designer, to find the easily computed inverse. Therefore a quasi one-way function can be used in place of a one-way function with essentially no loss in security.

Losing the trap-door information to a trap-door one-way function makes it into a quasi one-way function, but there may also be one-way functions not obtainable in this manner.

It is entirely a matter of definition that quasi one-way functions are excluded from the class of one-way functions. One could instead talk of one-way functions in the wide sense or in the strict sense.

Similarly, a quasi secure cipher is a cipher which will successfully resist cryptanalysis, even by its designer, and yet for which there exists a computationally efficient cryptanalytic algorithm (which is of course computationally infeasible to find). Again, from a practical point of view, there is essentially no difference between a secure cipher and a quasi secure one.

We have already seen that public key cryptosystems imply the existence of trap-door one-way functions. However the converse is not true. For a trap-door one-way function to be usable as a public key cryptosystem, it must be invertible (i.e., have a unique inverse).

42.6   Computational Complexity

Cryptography differs from all other fields of endeavor in the ease with which its requirements may appear to be satisfied. Simple transformations will convert a legible text into an apparently meaningless jumble. The critic, who wishes to claim that meaning might yet be recovered by cryptanalysis, is then faced with an arduous demonstration if he is to prove his point of view correct. Experience has shown, however, that few systems can resist the concerted attack of skillful cryptanalysts, and many supposedly secure systems have subsequently been broken.

In consequence of this, judging the worth of new systems has always been a central concern of cryptographers. During the sixteenth and seventeenth centuries, mathematical arguments were often invoked to argue the strength of cryptographic methods, usually relying on counting methods which showed the astronomical number of possible keys. Though the problem is far too difficult to be laid to rest by such simple methods, even the noted algebraist Cardano fell into this trap (Kahn, 1967, p. 145). As systems whose strength had been so argued were repeatedly broken, the notion of giving mathematical proofs for the security of systems fell into disrepute and was replaced by certification via crypanalytic assault.

During this century, however, the pendulum has begun to swing back in the other direction. In a paper intimately connected with the birth of information theory, Shannon (1949) showed that the one time pad system, which had been in use since the late twenties offered "perfect secrecy" (a form of unconditional security). The provably secure systems investigated by Shannon rely on the use of either a key whose length grows linearly with the length of the message or on perfect source coding and are therefore too unwieldy for most purposes. We note that neither public key cryptosystems nor one-way authentication systems can be unconditionally secure because the public information always determines the secret information uniquely among the members of a finite set. With unlimited computation, the problem could therefore be solved by a straightforward search.

The past decade has seen the rise of two closely related disciplines devoted to the study of the costs of computation: computational complexity theory and the analysis of algorithms. The former has classified known problems in computing into broad classes by difficulty, while the latter has concentrated on finding better algorithms and studying the resources they consume. After a brief digression into complexity theory, we will examine its application to cryptography, particularly the analysis of one-way functions.

A function is said to belong to the complexity class $\mathcal{P}$ (for polynomial) if it can be computed by a deterministic Turing Machine in a time which is bounded above by some polynomial function of the length of its input. One might think of this as the class of easily computed functions, but it is more accurate to say that a function not in this class must be hard to compute for at least some inputs. There are problems which are known not to be in the class $\mathcal{P}$ (Aho et al., 1974, pp. 405–425).

There are many problems which arise in engineering which cannot be solved in polynomial time by any known techniques, unless they are run on a computer with an unlimited degree of parallelism. These problems may or may not belong to the class $\mathcal{P}$, but belong to the class $\mathcal{NP}$ (for nondeterministic, polynomial) of problems solvable in polynomial time on a "nondeterministic" computer (i.e., one with an unlimited degree of parallelism). Clearly the class $\mathcal{NP}$ includes the class $\mathcal{P}$, and one of the great open questions in complexity theory is whether the class $\mathcal{NP}$ is strictly larger.

Among the problems known to be solvable in $\mathcal{NP}$ time, but not known to be solvable in $\mathcal{P}$ time, are versions of the traveling salesman problem, the satisfiability problem for propositional calculus, the knapsack problem, the graph coloring problem, and many scheduling and minimization problems (Karp, 1972; Aho et al., 1974, pp. 363–404). We see that it is not lack of interest or effort which has prevented people from finding solutions in $\mathcal{P}$ time for these problems. It is thus strongly believed that at least one of these problems must not be in the class $\mathcal{P}$, and that therefore the class $\mathcal{NP}$ is strictly larger.

Karp has identified a subclass of the $\mathcal{NP}$ problems, called $\mathcal{NP}$ complete, with the property that if any one of them is in $\mathcal{P}$, then all $\mathcal{NP}$ problems are in $\mathcal{P}$. Karp lists 21 problems which are $\mathcal{NP}$ complete, including all of the problems mentioned above (Karp, 1972, here chapter 36).

While the $\mathcal{NP}$ complete problems show promise for cryptographic use, current understanding of their difficulty includes only worst case analysis. For cryptographic purposes, typical computational costs must be considered. If, however, we replace worst case computation time with average or typical computation time as our complexity measure, the current proofs of the equivalences among the $\mathcal{NP}$ complete problems are no longer valid. This suggests several interesting topics for research. The ensemble and typicality concepts familiar to information theorists have an obvious role to play.

We can now identify the position of the general cryptanalytic problem among all computational problems. *The cryptanalytic difficulty of a system whose encryption and decryption operations can be done in $\mathcal{P}$ time cannot be greater than $\mathcal{NP}$.*

To see this, observe that any cryptanalytic problem can be solved by finding a key, inverse image, etc., chosen from a finite set. Choose the key nondeterministically and verify in $\mathcal{P}$ time that it is the correct one. If there are M possible keys to choose from, an M-fold parallelism must be employed. For example in a known plaintext attack, the plaintext is encrypted simultaneously under each of the keys and compared with the cryptogram. Since, by assumption, encryption takes only $\mathcal{P}$ time, the cryptanalysis takes only $\mathcal{NP}$ time.

We also observe that the general cryptanalytic problem is $\mathcal{NP}$ complete. This follows from the breadth of our definition of cryptographic problems. A one-way function with an $\mathcal{NP}$ complete inverse will be discussed next.

Cryptography can draw directly from the theory of $\mathcal{NP}$ complexity by examining the way in which $\mathcal{NP}$ complete problems can be adapted to cryptographic use. In particular, there is an $\mathcal{NP}$ complete problem known as the knapsack problem which lends itself readily to the construction of a one-way function.

Let $y = f(x) = \mathbf{a} \cdot \mathbf{x}$ where $\mathbf{a}$ is a known vector of n integers $(a_1, a_2, \ldots, a_n)$ and $\mathbf{x}$ is a binary n-vector. Calculation of y is simple, involving a sum of at most n integers. The problem of inverting f is known as the knapsack problem and requires finding a subset of the $\{a_i\}$ which sum to y.

Exhaustive search of all 2^n subsets grows exponentially and is computationally infeasible for n greater than 100 or so. Care must be exercised, however, in selecting the parameters of the problem to ensure that shortcuts are not possible. For example if $n = 100$ and each a_i is 32 bits long, y is at most 39 bits long, and f is highly degenerate; requiring on the average only 2^{38} tries to find a solution. Somewhat more trivially, if $a_i = 2^{i-1}$ then inverting f is equivalent to finding the binary decomposition of y. ...

Another potential one-way function, of interest in the analysis of algorithms, is exponentiation mod q, which was suggested to the authors by Prof. John Gill of Stanford University. The one-wayness of this functions has already been discussed in §42.3.

42.7   Historical Perspective

... The last characteristic which we note in the history of cryptography is the division between amateur and professional cryptographers. Skill in production cryptanalysis has always been heavily on the side of the professionals, but innovation, particularly in the design of new types of cryptographic systems, has come primarily from the amateurs. Thomas Jefferson, a cryptographic amateur, invented a system which was still in use in World War II (Kahn, 1967, pp. 192–195), while the most noted cryptographic system of the twentieth century, the rotor machine, was invented simultaneously by four separate people, all amateurs (Kahn, 1967, pp. 415, 420, 422–424). We hope this will inspire others to work in this fascinating area in which participation has been discouraged in the recent past by a nearly total government monopoly.

43 Big Omicron and Big Omega and Big Theta (1976)

Donald E. Knuth

Were I to assert that Donald Knuth (b. 1938, pronounced "Ka-NOOTH") is the greatest computer scientist of all time, I might get an argument, just as someone might protest that Willie Mays is a greater baseball player than the immortal Babe Ruth. But nobody would say I was crazy for putting Knuth first. Over his long and unique career, Knuth has made Ruthian contributions to the field.

It started conventionally enough, with a PhD in 1963 from Cal Tech, where Knuth then started on the faculty. His notes on hashing with linear probing constitute one of the first mathematical analyses of an algorithm (Knuth, 1963), but were never published. The market for such mathematical musings was limited at the time; the action was in programming systems and languages. A 1965 paper on a class of linear-time parsers known as LR parsers (Knuth, 1965) was an important contribution to that field. (And Ruth started out as a pretty good pitcher.) Knuth began working on a book on parsers and compilers. But, dissatisfied with the available background texts laying out the foundations of the field, he agreed to write a one-volume survey of computer science called *The Art of Computer Programming*, or *TAOCP* for short. It was at first to be six chapters, then seven, but by the time the first chapter was finished, it had grown to book length— in no small part due to the fact that many of the basic algorithms described in the literature were not backed up by a proper mathematical analysis until Knuth provided it. Volume 1 of *TAOCP* appeared in 1968 and is now in its third edition (Knuth, 1997a). Knuth moved to Stanford (just as Ruth moved to New York). Since then, Volumes 2 and 3 have been published and revised (Knuth, 1998, 1997b), Volume 4 has itself grown to be more than one book, and Volume 4A has been published (Knuth, 2011). "Fascicles" are being issued in anticipation of later volumes and editions.

Knuth and his students were creating the field of algorithm analysis as Knuth was writing it up. Questions he could not answer as he was systematically going through the mathematics and algorithms of computer science became challenges to the community, then thesis topics, and then entire subfields. The scholarly output of his PhD students and their PhD students, and their influence on academic departments of computer science, is staggering.

TAOCP was delayed also because after the appearance of the first volume, publishing technology changed, with the result that later editions and volumes would not be uniform in appearance with the earlier. Rather than accept this aesthetic offense, Knuth turned his attention to the prob-

Reprinted from Knuth (1976), with permission from Donald E. Knuth.

lem of typesetting, and then of font design and rendering. The results were the TEX (Knuth, 1986b) and METAFONT (Knuth, 1986a) systems used to typeset this book and much of the mathematical literature being published today.

TAOCP can't easily be summarized or extracted. Rather than choosing one of Knuth's journal papers for this volume, I have selected instead this short note, printed originally in typescript form in the newsletter of the theory community within the Association for Computing Machinery (SIGACT originally meant the Special Interest Group on Automata and Computability Theory). Like Leibniz (page 5), Knuth has profoundly influenced the propagation of good mathematical notation—here for the emerging field of algorithm analysis, and earlier in standardizing the usage of "$\mathcal{P}$" and "$\mathcal{NP}$" (see page 333). In spite of its impish title ("omicron" and "omega" literally mean "little o" and "big o"), this short note shows the depth of the scholarly standard to which the field of computer science can be held, and paints a vivid picture of the man at work, making repeated trips to Stanford's library, scolding the ghosts of great figures of the previous century for getting their definitions wrong, and finally suggesting in a conversational tone that he can't think of anything else to say, so let's all do it his way. Which is exactly what happened; these notations are now the world's standards.

MOST of us have gotten accustomed to the idea of using the notation $O(f(n))$ to stand for any function whose magnitude is upper-bounded by a constant times $f(n)$, for all large n. Sometimes we also need a corresponding notation for lower-bounded functions, i.e., those functions which are *at least* as large as a constant times $f(n)$ for all large n. Unfortunately, people have occasionally been using the O-notation for lower bounds, for example when they reject a particular sorting method "because its running time is $O(n^2)$." I have seen instances of this in print quite often, and finally it has prompted me to sit down and write a Letter to the Editor about the situation.

The classical literature does have a notation for functions that are bounded below, namely $\Omega(f(n))$. The most prominent appearance of this notation is in Titchmarsh's magnum opus on Riemann's zeta function (Titchmarsh, 1951), where he defines $\Omega(f(n))$ on p. 152 and devotes his entire Chapter 8 to "Ω-theorems." See also Prachar (1957, p. 245).

The Ω notation has not become very common, although I have noticed its use in a few places, most recently in some Russian publications I consulted about the theory of equidistributed sequences. Once I had suggested to someone in a letter that he use Ω-notation "since it had been used by number theorists for years"; but later, when challenged to show explicit references, I spent a surprisingly fruitless hour searching in the library without being able to turn up a single reference. I have recently asked several prominent mathematicians if they knew what $\Omega(n^2)$ meant, and more than half of them had never seen the notation before.

Before writing this letter, I decided to search more carefully, and to study the history of O-notation and o-notation as well. Cajori's two-volume work on history of mathematical notations does not mention any of these. While looking for definitions of Ω I came across dozens of books from the early part of this century which defined O and o but not Ω. I found Landau's remark (Landau, 1909, p. 883) that the first appearance of O known to him was in Bachmann (1894, p. 401). In the same place, Landau said that he had personally invented the o-notation while writing his handbook about the distribution of primes; his original discussion of O and o is in Landau (1909, pp. 59–62).

I could not find any appearances of Ω-notation in Landau's publications; this was confirmed later when I discussed the question with George Pólya, who told me that he was a student of Landau's and was quite familiar with his writings. Pólya knew what Ω-notation meant, but never had used it in his own work. (Like teacher, like pupil, he said.)

Since Ω notation is so rarely used, my first three trips to the library bore little fruit, but on my fourth visit I was finally able to pinpoint its probable origin: Hardy and Littlewood introduced Ω in their classic 1914 memoir (Hardy and Littlewood, 1914, p. 225), calling it a "new" notation. They used it also in their major paper on distribution of primes (Hardy and Littlewood, 1916, pp. 125ff.), but they apparently found little subsequent need for it in later works.

Unfortunately, Hardy and Littlewood didn't define $\Omega(f(n))$ as I wanted them to; their definition was a negation of $o(f(n))$, namely a function whose absolute value exceeds $Cf(n)$ for infinitely many n, when C is a sufficiently small positive constant. For all the applications I have seen so far in computer science, a stronger requirement (replacing "infinitely many n" by "all large n") is much more appropriate.

After discussing this problem with people for several years, I have come to the conclusion that the following definitions will prove to be most useful for computer scientists:

- $O(f(n))$ denotes the set of all $g(n)$ such that there exist positive constants C and n_0 with $|g(n)| \leq Cf(n)$ for all $n \geq n_0$.
- $\Omega(f(n))$ denotes the set of all $g(n)$ such that there exist positive constants C and n_0 with $g(n) \geq Cf(n)$ for all $n \geq n_0$.
- $\Theta(f(n))$ denotes the set of all $g(n)$ such that there exist positive constants C, C', and n_0 with $Cf(n) \leq g(n) < C'f(n)$ for all $n \geq n_0$.

Verbally, $O(f(n))$ can be read as "order at most $f(n)$"; $\Omega(f(n))$ as "order at least $f(n)$"; $\Theta(f(n))$ as "order exactly $f(n)$." Of course, these definitions apply only to behavior as $n \to \infty$; when dealing with $f(x)$ as $x \to 0$ we would substitute a neighborhood of zero for the neighborhood of infinity, i.e., $|x| \leq x_0$ instead of $n \geq n_0$.

Although I have changed Hardy and Littlewood's definition of Ω, I feel justified in doing so because their definition is by no means in wide use, and because there are other ways to say what they want to say in the comparatively rare cases when their definition applies. I like the mnemonic appearance of Ω by analogy with O, and it is easy to typeset. Furthermore, these two notations as defined above are nicely complemented by the Θ-notation, which was suggested to me independently by Bob Tarjan and by Mike Paterson.

The definitions above refer to "the set of all $g(n)$ such that ...", rather than to "an arbitrary function $g(n)$ with the property that ...""; I believe that this definition in terms of sets, which was suggested to me many years ago by Ron Rivest as an improvement over the definition in the first printing of my volume 1, is the best way to define O-notation. Under this interpretation, when the O-notation and its relatives are used in formulas, we are actually speaking about sets of functions rather than single functions. When A and B are sets of functions, $A + B$ denotes the set $\{a + b : a \in A \text{ and } b \in B\}$, etc.; and "$1 + O(n^{-1})$" can be taken to mean the set of all functions of the form $1 + g(n)$, where $|g(n)| \leq Cn^{-1}$ for some C and all large n. The phenomenon of *one-way equalities* arises in this connection, i.e., we write $1 + O(n^{-1}) = O(1)$ but not $O(1) = 1 + O(n^{-1})$. The equal sign here really means $\subseteq$ (set inclusion), and this has bothered many people who propose that we not be allowed to use the $=$ sign in this context. My feeling is that we should continue to use one-way equality together with O-notations, since it has been common practice of thousands of mathematicians for so many years now, and since we understand the meaning of our existing notation sufficiently well.

We could also define $\omega(f(n))$ as the set of all functions whose ratio to $f(n)$ is unbounded, by analogy to $o(f(n))$. Personally I have felt little need for these o-notations; on the contrary, I have found it a good discipline to obtain O-estimates at all times, since it has taught me about more powerful mathematical methods. However, I expect someday I may have to break down and use o-notation when faced with a function for which I can't prove anything stronger.

Note that there is a slight lack of symmetry in the above definitions of O, Ω, and Θ, since absolute value signs are used on $g(n)$ only in the case of O. This is not really an anomaly, since O refers to a neighborhood of zero while Ω refers to a neighborhood of infinity. (Hardy's book on divergent series uses O_L and O_R when a one-sided O-result is needed. Hardy and Littlewood used Ω_L and Ω_R for functions respectively $< -Cf(n)$ and $> Cf(n)$ infinitely often. Neither of these has become widespread.)

The above notations are intended to be useful in the vast majority of applications, but they are not intended to meet all conceivable needs. For example, if you are dealing with a function like $(\log \log n)^{\cos n}$ you might want a notation for "all functions which oscillate between $\log \log n$ and $1/\log \log n$ where these limits are best possible." In such a case, a local notation for the purpose, confined to the pages of whatever paper you are writing at the time, should suffice; it isn't necessary to worry about standard notations for a concept unless that concept arises frequently.

I would like to close this letter by discussing a competing way to denote the order of function growth. My library research turned up the surprising fact that this alternative approach actually antedates the O-notation itself. Paul du Bois-Reymond (1870) used the relational notations

$$g(n) \prec f(n) \, , \; f(n) \succ g(n)$$

already in 1871, for positive functions $f(n)$ and $g(n)$, with the meaning we can now describe as $g(n) = o(f(n))$ (or as $f(n) = \omega(g(n))$). Hardy's interesting tract on "Orders of Infinity" (Hardy,

1924) extends this by using also the relations

$$g(n) \le f(n) , \ f(n) \ge g(n)$$

to mean $g(n) = O(f(n))$ (or, equivalently, $f(n) = \Omega(g(n))$), since we are assuming that f and g are positive). Hardy also wrote

$$f(n) \asymp g(n)$$

when $g(n) = \Theta(f(n))$, and

$$f(n) \asymp\!\!\!\ast\ g(n)$$

when $\lim_{n\to\infty} f(n)/g(n)$ exists and is neither 0 nor ∞; and he wrote

$$f(n) \sim g(n)$$

when $\lim_{n\to\infty} f(n)/g(n) = 1$. (Hardy's $\asymp\!\!\!\ast$ notation may seem peculiar at first, until you realize what he did with it; for example, he proved the following nice theorem: "If $f(n)$ and $g(n)$ are any functions built up recursively from the ordinary arithmetic operations and the exp and log functions, we have exactly one of the three relations $f(n) \prec g(n)$, $f(n) \asymp\!\!\!\ast\ g(n)$, or $f(n) \succ g(n)$.")

Hardy's excellent notation has become somewhat distorted over the years. For example, Vinogradov (1954) writes $f(n) \ll g(n)$ instead of $f(n) \le g(n)$; thus, Vinogradov is comfortable with the formula

$$200^2 \ll \binom{n}{2},$$

while I am not. In any event such relational notations have intuitively clear transitive properties, and they avoid the use of one-way equalities which bother some people. Why, then, should they not replace O and the new symbols Ω and Θ?

The main reason why O is so handy is that we can use it right in the middle of formulas (and in the middle of English sentences, and in tables which show the running times for a family of related algorithms, etc.). The relational notations require us to transpose everything but the function we are estimating to one side of an equation. (Cf. Prachar [1957, p. 191].) Simple derivations like

$$
\begin{aligned}
\left(1 + \frac{H_n}{n}\right)^{H_n} &= \exp\left(H_n \ln(1 + H_n/n)\right) \\
&= \exp\left(H_n(H_n/n + O(\log n/n)^2)\right) \\
&= \exp\left(H_n^2/n + O((\log n)^3/n^2)\right) \\
&= \exp\left((\ln n + \gamma)^2/n + O((\log n)^3/n^2)\right) \\
&= \left(1 + O\left((\log n)^3/n^2\right)\right) e^{(\ln n + \gamma)^2/n}
\end{aligned}
$$

would be extremely cumbersome in relational notation.

When I am working on a problem, my scratch paper notes often contain *ad hoc* notations, and I have been using an expression like "$(\le 5n^2)$" to stand for the set of all functions which are

$\leq 5n^2$. Similarly, I can write "$(\sim 5n^2)$" to stand for functions which are asymptotic to $5n^2$, etc.; and "$(\leq n^2)$" would therefore be equivalent to $O(n^2)$, if I made appropriate extensions of the $\leq$ relation to functions which may be negative. This would provide a uniform notational convention for all sorts of things, for use in the middle of expressions, giving more than just the O and Ω and Θ proposed above.

In spite of this, I much prefer to publish papers with the O, Ω, and Θ notations; I would use other notations like "$(\sim 5n^2)$" only when faced with a situation that needed it. Why? The main reason is that O-notation is so universally established and accepted, I would not feel right replacing it by a notation "$(\leq f(n))$" of my own invention, however logically conceived; the O-notation has now assumed important mnemonic significance, and we are comfortable with it. For similar reasons, I am not abandoning decimal notation although I find that octal (say) is more logical. And I like the Ω and Θ notations because they now have mnemonic significance inherited from O.

Well, I think I have beat this issue to death, knowing of no other arguments pro or con the introduction of Ω and Θ. On the basis of the issues discussed here, I propose that members of SIGACT, and editors of computer science and mathematics journals, adopt the O, Ω, and Θ notations as defined above, unless a better alternative can be found reasonably soon. Furthermore I propose that the relational notations of Hardy be adopted in those situations where a relational notation is more appropriate.

44 Social Processes and Proofs of Theorems and Programs (1977)

Richard DeMillo, Richard Lipton, and Alan Perlis

A valued colleague believes this paper displays such polemical overreach that it should not appear in this collection. When published, originally in a conference proceedings, it caused such controversy that the flow of program verification funding slowed significantly. Though verification techniques are widely used today for hardware designs, formal verification of large software systems is still a rarity, for reasons even Hoare seems to have acknowledged (see page 298).

The paper hit a nerve because it demanded introspection about the ways in which computer science resembles, and differs from, mathematics—and indeed about the entire formalist program for mathematics and the way mathematics works in practice. The fact that some computer scientists still bristle when this paper is mentioned is testament to its dialectical force—and to the fact that the field had matured enough to be divided by deep resentments. The dispute continued for quite a while; a decade later, James Fetzer (1988) offended both sides by declaring that DeMillo, Lipton, and Perlis had offered "some bad arguments for some positions that need further elaboration and deserve better support." There is little doubt today that, even if Hoare's goals were excessively ambitious, the formal verification of hardware design and low-level code is not only useful but essential. The 2007 Turing Award went to Edmund Clarke, Allen Emerson, and Joseph Sifakis for harnessing formal model-checking as a tool for the verification of both hardware and software.

Alan Perlis (1922–1990) was a programming language pioneer. In 1957 he chaired the joint U.S.–European committee to design an algorithmic language, which ultimately became ALGOL 60, the precursor of all block-structured, imperative algorithmic languages. He was the first recipient of the Turing Award, in 1966. Perlis is also remembered for his role in establishing computer science as an academic discipline.

Perlis founded the computer science department at what is now Carnegie Mellon University; it became one of the nation's leading departments. In 1971 he joined the new computer science department at Yale and as chair led its growth in the late 1970s. The lead he set in positioning computer science as an intellectually independent discipline in these two institutions provided widely influential models for other colleges and universities.

Reprinted from DeMillo et al. (1977, 1979), with permission from the Association for Computing Machinery.

Richard DeMillo (b. 1947) and Richard Lipton (b. 1948) are longtime scientific collaborators. At the time the paper was written, Lipton was at Yale, with Perlis; DeMillo and Lipton are both now at Georgia Tech, where DeMillo is leading a center on the future of higher education.

⎯⎯⎯⎯∘◦◌∼◌◦∘⎯⎯⎯⎯

I should like to ask the same question that Descartes asked. You are proposing to give a precise definition of logical correctness which is to be the same as my vague intuitive feeling for logical correctness. How do you intend to show that they are the same? ... The average mathematician should not forget that intuition is the final authority.
—J. Barkley Rosser

MANY people have argued that computer programming should strive to become more like mathematics. Maybe so, but not in the way they seem to think. The aim of program verification, an attempt to make programming more mathematics-like, is to increase dramatically one's confidence in the correct functioning of a piece of software, and the device that verifiers use to achieve this goal is a long chain of formal, deductive logic. In mathematics, the aim is to increase one's confidence in the correctness of a theorem, and it's true that one of the devices mathematicians *could* in theory use to achieve this goal is a long chain of formal logic. But in fact they don't. What they use is a proof, a very different animal. Nor does the proof settle the matter; contrary to what its name suggests, a proof is only one step in the direction of confidence. We believe that, in the end, it is a social process that determines whether mathematicians feel confident about a theorem—and we believe that, because no comparable social process can take place among program verifiers, program verification is bound to fail. We can't see how it's going to be able to affect anyone's confidence about programs.

Outsiders see mathematics as a cold, formal, logical, mechanical, monolithic process of sheer intellection; we argue that insofar as it is successful, mathematics is a social, informal, intuitive, organic, human process, a community project. Within the mathematical community, the view of mathematics as logical and formal was elaborated by Bertrand Russell and David Hilbert in the first years of this century. They saw mathematics as proceeding in principle from axioms or hypotheses to theorems by steps, each step easily justifiable from its predecessors by a strict rule of transformation, the rules of transformation being few and fixed. The *Principia Mathematica* was the crowning achievement of the formalists. It was also the deathblow for the formalist view. There is no contradiction here: Russell did succeed in showing that ordinary working proofs can be reduced to formal, symbolic deductions. But he failed, in three enormous, taxing volumes, to get beyond the elementary facts of arithmetic. He showed what can be done in principle and what cannot be done in practice. If the mathematical process were really one of strict, logical progression, we would still be counting on our fingers.

44.1   Believing Theorems and Proofs

Indeed every mathematician knows that a proof has not been "understood" if one has done nothing more than verify step by step the correctness of the deductions of which it is composed and has not tried to gain a clear insight into the ideas which have led to the construction of this particular chain of deductions in preference to every other one.
—N. Bourbaki

Agree with me if I seem to speak the truth. —Socrates

Stanislaw Ulam estimates that mathematicians publish 200,000 theorems every year. A number of these are subsequently contradicted or otherwise disallowed, others are thrown into doubt, and most are ignored. Only a tiny fraction come to be understood and believed by any sizable group of mathematicians.

The theorems that get ignored or discredited are seldom the work of crackpots or incompetents. Kempe (1879) published a proof of the four-color conjecture that stood for eleven years before Heawood (1890) uncovered a fatal flaw in the reasoning. The first collaboration between Hardy and Littlewood resulted in a paper they delivered at the June 1911 meeting of the London Mathematical Society; the paper was never published because they subsequently discovered that their proof was wrong (Bateman and Diamond, 1978). Cauchy, Lamr, and Kummer all thought at one time or another that they had proved Fermat's Last Theorem (Davis, 1972). In 1945, Rademacher thought he had solved the Riemann Hypothesis; his results not only circulated in the mathematical world but were announced in *Time* magazine (Davis, 1972).

Recently we found the following group of footnotes appended to a brief historical sketch of some independence results in set theory (Jech, 1973):

1. The result of Problem 11 contradicts the results announced by Levy. Unfortunately, the construction presented there cannot be completed.

2. The transfer to ZF was also claimed by Marek but the outlined method appears to be unsatisfactory and has not been published.

3. A contradicting result was announced and later withdrawn by Truss.

4. The example in Problem 22 is a counterexample to another condition of Mostowski, who conjectured its sufficiency and singled out this example as a test case.

5. The independence result contradicts the claim of Feigner that the Cofinality Principle implies the Axiom of Choice. An error has been found by Morris (see Feigner's corrections to [1969]).

The author has no axe to grind; he has probably never even heard of the current controversy in programming; and it is clearly no part of his concern to hold his friends and colleagues up to scorn. There is simply no way to describe the history of mathematical ideas without describing the successive social processes at work in proofs. The point is not that mathematicians make mistakes; that goes without saying. The point is that mathematicians' errors are corrected, not by formal symbolic logic, but by other mathematicians.

Just increasing the number of mathematicians working on a given problem does not necessarily insure believable proofs. Recently, two independent groups of topologists, one American, the other Japanese, independently announced results concerning the same kind of topological object, a thing called a homotopy group. The results turned out to be contradictory, and since both proofs involved complex symbolic and numerical calculation, it was not at all evident who had goofed. But the stakes were sufficiently high to justify pressing the issue, so the Japanese and American proofs were exchanged. Obviously, each group was highly motivated to discover an error in the other's proof; obviously, one proof or the other was incorrect. But neither the Japanese nor the American proof could be discredited. Subsequently, a third group of researchers obtained yet another proof, this time supporting the American result. The weight of the evidence now being against their proof, the Japanese have retired to consider the matter further.

There are actually two morals to this story. First, a proof does not in itself significantly raise our confidence in the probable truth of the theorem it purports to prove. Indeed, for the theorem about the homotopy group, the horribleness of all the proffered proofs suggests that the theorem itself requires rethinking. A second point to be made is that proofs consisting entirely of calculations are not necessarily correct.

Even simplicity, clarity, and ease provide no guarantee that a proof is correct. The history of attempts to prove the Parallel Postulate is a particularly rich source of lovely, trim proofs that turned out to be false. From Ptolemy to Legendre (who tried time and time again), the greatest geometricians of every age kept ramming their heads against Euclid's fifth postulate. What's worse, even though we now know that the postulate is indemonstrable, many of the faulty proofs are still so beguiling that in Heath's definitive commentary on Euclid (Euclid, 1956) they are not allowed to stand alone; Heath marks them up with italics, footnotes, and explanatory marginalia, lest some young mathematician, thumbing through the volume, be misled.

The idea that a proof can, at best, only probably express truth makes an interesting connection with a recent mathematical controversy. In a recent issue of *Science*, Kolata (1976) suggested that the apparently secure notion of mathematical proof may be due for revision. Here the central question is not "How do theorems get believed?" but "What is it that we believe when we believe a theorem?" There are two relevant views, which can be roughly labeled classical and probabilistic.

The classicists say that when one believes mathematical statement *A*, one believes that in *principle* there is a correct, formal, valid, step by step, syntactically checkable deduction leading to *A* in a suitable logical calculus such as Zermelo-Fraenkel set theory or Peano arithmetic, a deduction of *A à la* the *Principia*, a deduction that completely formalizes the truth of *A* in the binary, Aristotelian notion of truth: "A proposition is true if it says of what is, that it is, and if it says of what is not, that it is not." [EDITOR: "To say that what is is not, or that what is not is, is false; but to say that what is is, and what is not is not, is true" (Aristotle, 1933, IV.7).] This formal chain of reasoning is by no means the same thing as an everyday, ordinary mathematical proof. The classical view does not require that an ordinary proof be accompanied by its formal counterpart; on the contrary, there are mathematically sound reasons for allowing the gods to formalize most of our arguments. One theoretician estimates, for instance, that a formal demonstration of one of Ramanujan's conjectures assuming set theory and elementary analysis would take about two thousand pages; the length of a deduction from first principles is nearly inconceivable (Manin, 1977). But the classicist believes that the formalization is in principle a possibility and that the truth it expresses is binary, either so or not so.

The probabilists argue that since any very long proof can at best be viewed as only probably correct, why not state theorems probabilistically and give probabilistic proofs? The probabilistic proof may have the dual advantage of being technically easier than the classical, bivalent one, and may allow mathematicians to isolate the critical ideas that give rise to uncertainty in traditional, binary proofs. This process may even lead to a more plausible classical proof. An illustration of the probabilist approach is Michael Rabin's algorithm for testing probable primality (Rabin, 1976). For very large integers N, all of the classical techniques for determining whether N is composite become unworkable. Using even the most clever programming, the calculations required to determine whether numbers larger than 10^{10^4} are prime require staggering amounts of computing time. Rabin's insight was that if you are willing to settle for a very good probability that N is prime (or not prime), then you can get it within a reasonable amount of time—and with vanishingly small probability of error.

In view of these uncertainties over what constitutes an acceptable proof, which is after all a fairly basic element of the mathematical process, how is it that mathematics has survived and been so successful? If proofs bear little resemblance to formal deductive reasoning, if they can stand for generations and then fall, if they can contain flaws that defy detection, if they can express only the probability of truth within certain error bounds–if they are, in fact, not able to prove theorems in the sense of guaranteeing them beyond probability and, if necessary, beyond insight, well, then, how does mathematics work? How does it succeed in developing theorems that are significant and that compel belief?

First of all, the proof of a theorem is a message. A proof is not a beautiful abstract object with an independent existence. No mathematician grasps a proof, sits back, and sighs happily at the knowledge that he can now be certain of the truth of his theorem. He runs out into the hall and looks for someone to listen to it. He bursts into a colleague's office and commandeers the blackboard. He throws aside his scheduled topic and regales a seminar with his new idea. He drags his graduate students away from their dissertations to listen. He gets onto the phone and tells his colleagues in Texas and Toronto. In its first incarnation, a proof is a spoken message, or at most a sketch on a chalkboard or a paper napkin.

That spoken stage is the first filter for a proof. If it generates no excitement or belief among his friends, the wise mathematician reconsiders it. But if they find it tolerably interesting and believable, he writes it up. After it has circulated in draft for a while, if it still seems plausible, he does a polished version and submits it for publication. If the referees also find it attractive and convincing, it gets published so that it can be read by a wider audience. If enough members of that larger audience believe it and like it, then after a suitable cooling-off period the reviewing publications take a more leisurely look, to see whether the proof is really as pleasing as it first appeared and whether, on calm consideration, they really believe it.

And what happens to a proof when it is believed? The most immediate process is probably an internalization of the result. That is, the mathematician who reads and believes a proof will attempt to paraphrase it, to put it in his own terms, to fit it into his own personal view of mathematical knowledge. No two mathematicians are likely to internalize a mathematical concept in exactly the same way, so this process leads usually to multiple versions of the same theorem, each reinforcing belief, each adding to the feeling of the mathematical community that the original statement is likely to be true. Gauss, for example, obtained at least half a dozen independent proofs of his "law of quadratic reciprocity"; to date over fifty proofs of this law are known. Imre Lakatos gives, in his *Proofs and Refutations* (Lakatos, 1976), historically accurate discussions of the transformations that several famous theorems underwent from initial conception to general acceptance. Lakatos demonstrates that Euler's formula $V - E + F = 2$ was reformulated again and again for almost two hundred years after its first statement, until it finally reached its current stable form. The most compelling transformation that can take place is generalization. If, by the same social process that works on the original theorem, the generalized theorem comes to be believed, then the original statement gains greatly in plausibility.

A believable theorem gets used. It may appear as a lemma in larger proofs; if it does not lead to contradictions, then we are all the more inclined to believe it. Or engineers may use it by plugging physical values into it. We have fairly high confidence in classical stress equations because we see bridges that stand; we have some confidence in the basic theorems of fluid mechanics because we see airplanes that fly.

Believable results sometimes make contact with other areas of mathematics—important ones invariably do. The successful transfer of a theorem or a proof technique from one branch of mathematics to another increases our feeling of confidence in it. In 1964, for example, Paul Cohen used a technique called forcing to prove a theorem in set theory (Cohen, 1963); at that time, his notions were so radical that the proof was hardly understood. But subsequently other investigators interpreted the notion of forcing in an algebraic context, connected it with more familiar ideas in logic, generalized the concepts, and found the generalizations useful. All of these connections (along with the other normal social processes that lead to acceptance) made the idea of forcing a good deal more compelling, and today forcing is routinely studied by graduate students in set theory.

After enough internalization, enough transformation, enough generalization, enough use, and enough connection, the mathematical community eventually decides that the central concepts in the original theorem, now perhaps greatly changed, have an ultimate stability. If the various proofs feel right and the results are examined from enough angles, then the truth of the theorem is eventually considered to be established. The theorem is thought to be true in the classical sense—that is, in the sense that it could be demonstrated by formal, deductive logic, although for almost all theorems no such deduction ever took place or ever will.

44.2   The Role of Simplicity

For what is clear and easily comprehended attracts; the complicated repels. —David Hilbert

Sometimes one has to say difficult things, but one ought to say them as simply as one knows how. —G. H. Hardy

As a rule, the most important mathematical problems are clean and easy to state. An important theorem is much more likely to take form *A* than form *B*.

A   Every — — is a — —.
B   If — — and — — and — — and — — and — — except for special cases

   a   — —
   b   — —
   c   — —,

  then unless

    i   — — or
   ii   — — or
  iii   — —,

  every — — that satisfies — — is a — —.

The problems that have most fascinated and tormented and delighted mathematicians over the centuries have been the simplest ones to state. Einstein held that the maturity of a scientific theory could be judged by how well it could be explained to the man on the street. The four-color theorem rests on such slender foundations that it can be stated with complete precision to a child. If the child has learned his multiplication tables, he can understand the problem of the location and distribution of the prime numbers. And the deep fascination of the problem of defining the concept of "number" might turn him into a mathematician.

The correlation between importance and simplicity is no accident. Simple, attractive theorems are the ones most likely to be heard, read, internalized, and used. Mathematicians use simplicity as the first test for a proof. Only if it looks interesting at first glance will they consider it in detail. Mathematicians are not altruistic masochists. On the contrary, the history of mathematics is one long search for ease and pleasure and elegance—in the realm of symbols, of course.

Even if they didn't want to, mathematicians would have to use the criterion of simplicity; it is a psychological impossibility to choose any but the simplest and most attractive of 200,000 candidates for one's attention. If there are important, fundamental concepts in mathematics that are not simple, mathematicians will probably never discover them. Messy, ugly mathematical propositions that apply only to paltry classes of structures, idiosyncratic propositions, propositions that rely on inordinately expensive mathematical machinery, propositions that require five blackboards or a roll of paper towels to sketch—these are unlikely ever to be assimilated into the body of mathematics. And yet it is only by such assimilation that proofs gain believability. The proof by itself is nothing; only when it has been subjected to the social processes of the mathematical community does it become believable.

In this paper, we have tended to stress simplicity above all else because that is the first filter for any proof. But we do not wish to paint ourselves and our fellow mathematicians as philistines or brutes. Once an idea has met the criterion of simplicity, other standards help determine its place among the ideas that make mathematicians gaze off abstractly into the distance. Yuri Manin has put it best: A good proof is one that makes us wiser.

44.3 Disbelieving Verifications

On the contrary, I find nothing in logistic for the discoverer but shackles. It does not help us at all in the direction of conciseness, far from it; and if it requires twenty-seven equations to establish that 1 is a number, how many will it require to demonstrate a real theorem? —Henri Poincaré

One of the chief duties of the mathematician in acting as an advisor to scientists ... is to discourage them from expecting too much from mathematics. —Norbert Wiener

Mathematical proofs increase our confidence in the truth of mathematical statements only after they have been subjected to the social mechanisms of the mathematical community. These same mechanisms doom the so-called proofs of software, the long formal verifications that correspond, not to the working mathematical proof, but to the imaginary logical structure that the mathematician conjures up to describe his feeling of belief. Verifications are not messages; a person who ran out into the hall to communicate his latest verification would rapidly find himself a social pariah. Verifications cannot really be read; a reader can flay himself through one of the shorter ones by dint of heroic effort, but that's not reading. Being unreadable and—literally—unspeakable, verifications cannot be internalized, transformed, generalized, used, connected to other disciplines, and eventually incorporated into a community consciousness. They cannot acquire credibility gradually, as a mathematical theorem does; one either believes them blindly, as a pure act of faith, or not at all.

Mathematics		*Programming*
theorem	⋯	program
proof	⋯	verification

Figure 44.1: The verifiers' original analogy

At this point, some adherents of verification admit that the analogy to mathematics fails. Having argued that *A*, programming, resembles *B*, mathematics, and having subsequently learned that *B* is nothing like what they imagined, they wish to argue instead that *A* is like *B'*, their mythical version of *B*. We then find ourselves in the peculiar position of putting across the argument that was originally theirs, asserting that yes, indeed, *A* does resemble *B*; our argument, however, matches the terms up differently from theirs. (See Figures 44.1 and 44.2.)

Verifiers who wish to abandon the simile and substitute *B'* should as an aid to understanding abandon the language of *B* as well—in particular, it would help if they did not call their verifications "proofs." As for ourselves, we will continue to argue that programming is like mathematics, and that the same social processes that work in mathematical proofs doom verifications.

There is a fundamental logical objection to verification, an objection on its own ground of formalistic rigor. Since the requirement for a program is informal and the program is formal, there must be a transition, and the transition itself must necessarily be informal. We have been distressed to learn that this proposition, which seems self-evident to us, is controversial. So we should emphasize that as antiformalists, we would not object to verification on these grounds; we only wonder how this inherently informal step fits into the formalist view. Have the adherents of verification lost sight of the informal origins of the formal objects they deal with? Is it their assertion that their formalizations are somehow incontrovertible? We must confess our confusion and dismay.

Then there is another logical difficulty, nearly as basic, and by no means so hair-splitting as the one above:
The formal demonstration that a program is consistent
with its specifications has value only if the specifications and the program are independently derived. In
the toy-program atmosphere of experimental verification, this criterion is easily met. But in real life, if during the design process a program fails, it is changed,

Mathematics		*Programming*
theorem	$\cdots$	specification
proof	$\cdots$	program
imaginary formal demonstration	$\cdots$	verification

Figure 44.2: Our analogy

and the changes are based on knowledge of its specifications; or the specifications are changed,
and those changes are based on knowledge of the program gained through the failure. In either
case, the requirement of having independent criteria to check against each other is no longer met.
Again, we hope that no one would suggest that programs and specifications should not be repeatedly modified during the design process. That would be a position of incredible poverty—the
sort of poverty that does, we fear, result from infatuation with formal logic.

Back in the real world, the kinds of input/output specifications that accompany production
software are seldom simple. They tend to be long and complex and peculiar. To cite an extreme
case, computing the payroll for the French National Railroad requires more than 3,000 pay rates
(one uphill, one downhill, and so on). The specifications for any reasonable compiler or operating
system fill volumes—and no one believes that they are complete. There are even some cases of
black-box code, numerical algorithms that can be shown to work in the sense that they are used
to build real airplanes or drill real oil wells, but work for no reason that anyone knows; the input
assertions for these algorithms are not even formulable, let alone formalizable. To take just one
example, an important algorithm with the rather jaunty name of Reverse Cuthill-McKee was
known for years to be far better than plain Cuthill-McKee, known empirically, in laboratory tests
and field trials and in production. Only recently, however, has its superiority been theoretically
demonstrable (George, 1971), and even then only with the usual informal mathematical proof,
not with a formal deduction. During all of the years when Reverse Cuthill-McKee was unproved,
even though it automatically made any program in which it appeared unverifiable, programmers
perversely went on using it.

It might be countered that while real-life specifications are lengthy and complicated, they are
not deep. Their verifications are, in fact, nothing more than extremely long chains of substitutions
to be checked with the aid of simple algebraic identities.

All we can say in response to this is: Precisely. Verifications are long and involved but shallow;
that's what's wrong with them. The verification of even a puny program can run into dozens of
pages, and there's not a light moment or a spark of wit on any of those pages. Nobody is going
to run into a friend's office with a program verification. Nobody is going to sketch a verification
out on a paper napkin. Nobody is going to buttonhole a colleague into listening to a verification.
Nobody is ever going to read it. One can feel one's eyes glaze over at the very thought. It
has been suggested that very high level languages, which can deal directly with a broad range

of mathematical objects or functional languages, which it is said can be concisely axiomatized, might be used to insure that a verification would be interesting and therefore responsive to a social process like the social process of mathematics. In theory this idea sounds hopeful; in practice, it doesn't work out. . . .

Some verifiers will concede that verification is simply unworkable for the vast majority of programs but argue that for a few crucial applications the agony is worthwhile. They point to air-traffic control, missile systems, and the exploration of space as areas in which the risks are so high that any expenditure of time and effort can be justified.

Even if this were so, we would still insist that verification renounce its claim on all other areas of programming; to teach students in introductory programming courses how to do verification, for instance, ought to be as farfetched as teaching students in introductory biology how to do open-heart surgery. But the stakes do not affect our belief in the basic impossibility of verifying any system large enough and flexible enough to do any real-world task. No matter how high the payoff, no one will ever be able to force himself to read the incredibly long, tedious verifications of real-life systems, and unless they can be read, understood, and refined, the verifications are worthless.

Now, it might be argued that all these references to readability and internalization are irrelevant, that the aim of verification is eventually to construct an automatic verifying system.

Unfortunately, there is a wealth of evidence that fully automated verifying systems are out of the question. The lower bounds on the length of formal demonstrations for mathematical theorems are immense (Stockmeyer, 1974), and there is no reason to believe that such demonstrations for programs would be any shorter or cleaner—quite the contrary. In fact, even the strong adherents of program verification do not take seriously the possibility of totally automated verifiers. Ralph London, a proponent of verification, speaks of an out-to-lunch system, one that could be left unsupervised to grind out verifications; but he doubts that such a system can be built to work with reasonable reliability. One group, despairing of automation in the foreseeable future, has proposed that verifications should be performed by teams of "grunt mathematicians," low level mathematical teams who will check verification conditions. The sensibilities of people who could make such a proposal seem odd, but they do serve to indicate how remote the possibility of automated verification must be.

Suppose, however, that an automatic verifier could somehow be built. Suppose further that programmers did somehow come to have faith in its verifications. In the absence of any real-world basis for such belief, it would have to be blind faith, but no matter. Suppose that the philosopher's stone had been found, that lead could be changed to gold, and that programmers were convinced of the merits of feeding their programs into the gaping jaws of a verifier. It seems to us that the scenario envisioned by the proponents of verification goes something like this: The programmer inserts his 300-line input/output package into the verifier. Several hours later, he returns. There is his 20,000-line verification and the message "VERIFIED."

There is a tendency, as we begin to feel that a structure is logically, provably right, to remove from it whatever redundancies we originally built in because of lack of understanding. Taken to its extreme, this tendency brings on the so-called Titanic effect; when failure does occur, it is massive and uncontrolled. To put it another way, the severity with which a system fails is directly proportional to the intensity of the designer's belief that it cannot fail. Programs designed to be clean and tidy merely so that they can be verified will be particularly susceptible to the Titanic effect. Already we see signs of this phenomenon. In their notes on Euclid (Popek et al., 1977), a language designed for program verification, several of the foremost verification adherents say, "Because we expect all Euclid programs to be verified, we have not made special provisions for exception handling .... Runtime software errors should not occur in verified programs." Errors should not occur? Shades of the ship that shouldn't be sunk.

So, having for the moment suspended all rational disbelief, let us suppose that the programmer gets the message "VERIFIED." And let us suppose further that the message does not result from a failure on the part of the verifying system. What does the programmer know? He knows that his program is formally, logically, provably, certifiably correct. He does not know, however, to what extent it is reliable, dependable, trustworthy, safe; he does not know within what limits it will work; he does not know what happens when it exceeds those limits. And yet he has that mystical stamp of approval: "VERIFIED." We can almost see the iceberg looming in the background over the unsinkable ship. Luckily, there is little reason to fear such a future. Picture the same programmer returning to find the same 20,000 lines. What message would he really find, supposing that an automatic verifier could really be built? Of course, the message would be "NOT VERIFIED." The programmer would make a change, feed the program in again, return again. "NOT VERIFIED." Again he would make a change, again he would feed the program to the verifier, again "NOT VERIFIED." A program is a human artifact; a real-life program is a complex human artifact; and any human artifact of sufficient size and complexity is imperfect. The message will never read "VERIFIED."

44.4   The Role of Continuity

We may say, roughly, that a mathematical idea is "significant" if it can be connected, in a natural and illuminating way, with a large complex of other mathematical ideas. —G. H. Hardy

The only really fetching defense ever offered for verification is the scaling-up argument. As best we can reproduce it, here is how it goes:

1. Verification is now in its infancy. At the moment, the largest tasks it can handle are verifications of algorithms like FIND and model programs like GCD. It will in time be able to tackle more and more complicated algorithms and trickier and trickier model programs. These verifications are comparable to mathematical proofs. They are read. They generate the same kinds of interest and excitement that theorems do. They are subject to the ordinary social processes that work on mathematical reasoning, or on reasoning in any other discipline, for that matter.

2. Big production systems are made up of nothing more than algorithms and model programs. Once verified, algorithms and model programs can make up large, workaday production systems, and the (admittedly unreadable) verification of a big system will be the sum of the many small, attractive, interesting verifications of its components.

With (1) we have no quarrel. Actually, algorithms were proved and the proofs read and discussed and assimilated long before the invention of computers—and with a striking lack of formal machinery. Our guess is that the study of algorithms and model programs will develop like any other mathematical activity, chiefly by informal, social mechanisms, very little if at all by formal mechanisms.

It is with (2) that we have our fundamental disagreement. We argue that there is no continuity between the world of FIND or GCD and the world of production software, billing systems that write real bills, scheduling systems that schedule real events, ticketing systems that issue real tickets. And we argue that the world of production software is itself discontinuous.

No programmer would agree that large production systems are composed of nothing more than algorithms and small programs. Patches, ad hoc constructions, bandaids and tourniquets, bells and whistles, glue, spit and polish, signature code, blood-sweat-and-tears, and, of course, the kitchen sink—the colorful jargon of the practicing programmer seems to be saying something about the nature of the structures he works with; maybe theoreticians ought to be listening to him. It has been estimated that more than half the code in any real production system consists of user interfaces and error messages—ad hoc, informal structures that are by definition unverifiable. Even the verifiers themselves sometimes seem to realize the unverifiable nature of most real software. C. A. R. Hoare has been quoted as saying, "In many applications, algorithm plays almost no role, and certainly presents almost no problem." (We wish we could report that he thereupon threw up his hands and abandoned verification, but no such luck.)

Or look at the difference between the world of GCD and the world of production software in another way: The specifications for algorithms are concise and tidy, while the specifications for real-world systems are immense, frequently of the same order of magnitude as the systems themselves. The specifications for algorithms are highly stable, stable over decades or even centuries; the specifications for real systems vary daily or hourly (as any programmer can testify). The specifications for algorithms are exportable, general; the specifications for real systems are idiosyncratic and ad hoc. These are not differences in degree. They are differences in kind. Babysitting for a sleeping child for one hour does not scale up to raising a family of ten—the problems are essentially, fundamentally different.

And within the world of real production software there is no continuity either. The scaling-up argument seems to be based on the fuzzy notion that the world of programming is like the world of Newtonian physics—made up of smooth, continuous functions. But, in fact, programs are jagged and full of holes and caverns. Every programmer knows that altering a line or sometimes even a bit can utterly destroy a program or mutilate it in ways that we do not understand and cannot predict. And yet at other times fairly substantial changes seem to alter nothing; the folklore is filled with stories of pranks and acts of vandalism that frustrated the perpetrators by remaining forever undetected.

There is a classic science-fiction story about a time traveler who goes back to the primeval jungles to watch dinosaurs and then returns to find his own time altered almost beyond recognition. Politics, architecture, language—even the plants and animals seem wrong, distorted. Only when he removes his time-travel suit does he understand what has happened. On the heel of his boot, carried away from the past and therefore unable to perform its function in the evolution of the world, is crushed the wing of a butterfly. Every programmer knows the sensation: A trivial, minute change wreaks havoc in a massive system. Until we know more about programming, we had better for all practical purposes think of systems as composed, not of sturdy structures like algorithms and smaller programs, but of butterflies' wings.

The discontinuous nature of programming sounds the death knell for verification. A sufficiently fanatical researcher might be willing to devote two or three years to verifying a significant piece of software if he could be assured that the software would remain stable. But real-life programs need to be maintained and modified. There is no reason to believe that verifying a modified program is any easier than verifying the original the first time around. There is no reason to believe that a big verification can be the sum of many small verifications. There is no reason to believe that a verification can transfer to any other program—not even to a program only one single line different from the original.

And it is this discontinuity that obviates the possibility of refining verifications by the sorts of social processes that refine mathematical proofs. The lone fanatic might construct his own verification, but he would never have any reason to read anyone else's, nor would anyone else ever be willing to read his. No community could develop. Even the most zealous verifier could be induced to read a verification only if he thought he might be able to use or borrow or swipe something from it. Nothing could force him to read someone else's verification once he had grasped the point that no verification bears any necessary connection to any other verification.

44.5   Believing Software

The program itself is the only complete description of what the program will do. —P. J. Davis

Since computers can write symbols and move them about with negligible expenditure of energy, it is tempting to leap to the conclusion that anything is possible in the symbolic realm. But reality does not yield so easily; physics does not suddenly break down. It is no more possible to construct symbolic structures without using resources than it is to construct material structures without using them. For even the most trivial mathematical theories, there are simple statements whose formal demonstrations would be impossibly long. Albert Meyer's outstanding lecture on the history of such research concludes with a striking interpretation of how hard it may be to deduce even fairly simple mathematical statements. Suppose that we encode logical formulas as binary strings and set out to build a computer that will decide the truth of a simple set of formulas of length, say, at most a thousand bits. Suppose that we even allow ourselves the luxury of a technology that will produce proton-size electronic components connected by infinitely thin wires. Even so, the computer we design must densely fill the entire observable universe. This precise observation about the length of formal deductions agrees with our intuition about the amount of detail embedded in ordinary, workaday mathematical proofs. We often use "Let us assume, without loss of generality ..." or "Therefore, by renumbering, if necessary ..." to replace enormous amounts of formal detail. To insist on the formal detail would be a silly waste of resources. Both symbolic and material structures must be engineered with a very cautious eye. Resources are limited; time is limited; energy is limited. Not even the computer can change the finite nature of the universe.

We assume that these constraints have prevented the adherents of verification from offering what might be fairly convincing evidence in support of their methods. The lack at this late date of even a single verification of a working system has sometimes been attributed to the youth of the field. The verifiers argue, for instance, that they are only now beginning to understand loop invariants. At first blush, this sounds like another variant of the scaling-up argument. But in fact there are large classes of real-life systems with virtually no loops—they scarcely ever occur in commercial programming applications. And yet there has never been a verification of, say, a COBOL system that prints real checks; lacking even one makes it seem doubtful that there could at some time in the future be many. Resources, and time, and energy are just as limited for verifiers as they are for all the rest of us.

We must therefore come to grips with two problems that have occupied engineers for many generations: First, people must plunge into activities that they do not understand. Second, people cannot create perfect mechanisms.

How then do engineers manage to create reliable structures? First, they use social processes very like the social processes of mathematics to achieve successive approximations at understanding. Second, they have a mature and realistic view of what "reliable" means; in particular, the one thing it never means is "perfect." There is no way to deduce logically that bridges stand, or that airplanes fly, or that power stations deliver electricity. True, no bridges would fall, no airplanes would crash, no electrical systems black out if engineers would first demonstrate their perfection before building them—true because they would never be built at all.

The analogy in programming is any functioning, useful, real-world system. Take for instance an organic-chemical synthesizer called SYNCHEM (Gelernter et al., 1973). For this program, the criterion of reliability is particularly straightforward—if it synthesizes a chemical, it works; if it doesn't, it doesn't work. No amount of correctness could ever hope to improve on this standard; indeed, it is not at all clear how one could even begin to formalize such a standard in a way that would lend itself to verification. But it is a useful and continuing enterprise to try to increase the number of chemicals the program can synthesize.

It is nothing but symbol chauvinism that makes computer scientists think that our structures are so much more important than material structures that (a) they should be perfect, and (b) the energy necessary to make them perfect should be expended. We argue rather that (a) they cannot be perfect, and (b) energy should not be wasted in the futile attempt to make them perfect. It is no accident that the probabilistic view of mathematical truth is closely allied to the engineering notion of reliability. Perhaps we should make a sharp distinction between program reliability and program perfection—and concentrate our efforts on reliability.

The desire to make programs correct is constructive and valuable. But the monolithic view of verification is blind to the benefits that could result from accepting a standard of correctness like the standard of correctness for real mathematical proofs, or a standard of reliability like the standard for real engineering structures. The quest for workability within economic limits, the willingness to channel innovation by recycling successful design, the trust in the functioning of a community of peers—all the mechanisms that make engineering and mathematics really work are obscured in the fruitless search for perfect verifiability.

What elements could contribute to making programming more like engineering and mathematics? One mechanism that can be exploited is the creation of general structures whose specific instances become more reliable as the reliability of the general structure increases. This notion has appeared in several incarnations, of which Knuth's insistence on creating and understanding generally useful algorithms is one of the most important and encouraging. Baker's team-programming methodology (Baker, 1972) is an explicit attempt to expose software to social processes. If reusability becomes a criterion for effective design, a wider and wider community will examine the most common programming tools.

The concept of verifiable software has been with us too long to be easily displaced. For the practice of programming, however, verifiability must not be allowed to overshadow reliability. Scientists should not confuse mathematical models with reality—and verification is nothing but a model of believability. Verifiability is not and cannot be a dominating concern in software design. Economics, deadlines, cost-benefit ratios, personal and group style, the limits of acceptable error—all these carry immensely much more weight in design than verifiability or nonverifiability.

So far, there has been little philosophical discussion of making software reliable rather than verifiable. If verification adherents could redefine their efforts and reorient themselves to this goal, or if another view of software could arise that would draw on the social processes of mathematics and the modest expectations of engineering, the interests of real-life programming and theoretical computer science might both be better served.

Even if, for some reason that we are not now able to understand, we should be proved wholly wrong and the verifiers wholly right, this is not the moment to restrict research on programming. We know too little now to sense what directions will be most fruitful. If our reasoning convinces no one, if verification still seems an avenue worth exploring, so be it; we three can only try to argue against verification, not blast it off the face of the earth. But we implore our friends and colleagues not to narrow their vision to this one view no matter how promising it may seem. Let it not be the only view, the only avenue. Jacob Bronowski has an important insight about a time in the history of another discipline that may be similar to our own time in the development of computing: "A science which orders its thought too early is stifled .... The hope of the medieval alchemists that the elements might be changed was not as fanciful as we once thought. But it was merely damaging to a chemistry which did not yet understand the composition of water and common salt."

45 A Method for Obtaining Digital Signatures and Public-Key Cryptosystems (1978)

Ronald Rivest, Adi Shamir, and Len Adleman

A copy of Diffie and Hellman (1976a, here chapter 42) quickly reached MIT, where Ronald Rivest (b. 1947), Leonard Adleman (b. 1945), and Adi Shamir (b. 1952) set to work on the problem of finding a public-key cryptosystem suitable for both the key distribution and digital signature problems. Eventually the three figured out how to use the factoring problem as the basis for such a system. The RSA algorithm became widely deployed in internet security software in the late 1990s when the World Wide Web began to be used commercially. Today, every banking transaction, e-commerce purchase, and rideshare summons involves an unspoken key exchange worked out between the user's browser or app and the computers offering the service.

The paper is a remarkable testament to the beauty of algorithms and to the utility of even the purest mathematics. No one preparing to be a computer scientist when the authors were young could have decided to study number theory in the expectation that it would be important in building computer systems, but these three knew the subject well enough to brainstorm, challenge, and correct each other's ideas of how to use it. The algorithm is elegant and easy to describe—if you know a bit of eighteenth-century mathematics about the properties of integers. Yet it depends on an unproven premise: that there is no fast algorithm for finding factors of large numbers.

The apparent difficulty of factoring was already well known. In 1801 Carl Friedrich Gauss observed that the best methods devised by both "ancient and modern" mathematicians "try the patience of even the practiced calculator," and urged that "every possible means be explored for the solution of a problem so elegant and so celebrated" (Gauss, 1986, pages 396f.)—thus foreshadowing the agenda urged in the penultimate paragraph of this paper. William Jevons, inventor of the logic piano (page 27 of this volume), noted that factorization seemed to be only one of what we would now call one-way functions. "There are many cases in which we can easily and infallibly do a certain thing but may have much trouble in undoing it. ... Given any two numbers, we may by a simple and infallible process obtain their product; but when a large number is given it is quite another matter to determine its factors" (Jevons, 1874, page 122). That factoring is exponentially costly has often been asserted (including by Jevons) but never proved, in spite of strenuous efforts since the widespread adoption of the RSA algorithm.

Fast factoring would break the RSA cryptosystem, and the system remains unbroken—as far as we know; there is always the possibility that some government agency or criminal has developed a secret technique for factoring large numbers. But as technology advanced, the key lengths

Reprinted from Rivest et al. (1978), with permission from the Association for Computing Machinery.

suggested in this paper have been increased in actual practice. And while public-key systems based on other mathematical objects (for example, elliptic curves) have been developed, they too suffer from not, as yet, having been proved secure.

Though the authors suggest that readers familiar with Diffie and Hellman (1976a) can skip the first few sections of this paper, we include them because they straightforwardly lay out the context—and, notably, introduce "Alice" and "Bob," who in much of the subsequent literature play the roles of the communicating parties.

Rivest remains on the faculty at MIT, while Adleman is at the University of Southern California and Shamir is at the Weizmann Institute in Israel. All three have contributed significantly to other areas of computer science (see chapter 46 in particular). In 1983 they founded a company to commercialize the discovery presented in this paper (RSA Security, which was acquired by Security Dynamics, which in turn was acquired by EMC, which was then acquired by Dell). In 2002 they were jointly recognized with the Turing Award.

⟶◦◦◦◦◦⟵

45.0   Abstract

A N encryption method is presented with the novel property that publicly revealing an encryption key does not thereby reveal the corresponding decryption key. This has two important consequences.

1. Couriers or other secure means are not needed to transmit keys, since a message can be enciphered using an encryption key publicly revealed by the intended recipient. Only he can decipher the message, since only he knows the corresponding decryption key.

2. A message can be "signed" using a privately held decryption key. Anyone can verify this signature using the corresponding publicly revealed encryption key. Signatures cannot be forged, and a signer cannot later deny the validity of his signature. This has obvious applications in "electronic mail" and "electronic funds transfer" systems. A message is encrypted by representing it as a number M, raising M to a publicly specified power e and then taking the remainder when the result is divided by the publicly specified product n of two large secret prime numbers p and q. Decryption is similar, only a different, secret, power d is used, where $e \cdot d \equiv 1 \pmod{(p-1) \cdot (q-1)}$. The security of the system rests in part on the difficulty of factoring the published divisor, n.

45.1   Introduction

The era of "electronic mail" (Potter, 1977) may soon be upon us; we must ensure that two important properties of the current "paper mail" system are preserved: (a) messages are *private*, and (b) messages can be *signed*. We demonstrate in this paper how to build these capabilities into an electronic mail system.

At the heart of our proposal is a new encryption method. This method provides an implementation of a "public-key cryptosystem," an elegant concept invented by Diffie and Hellman
(1976a, here chapter 42). Their article motivated our research, since they presented the concept
but not any practical implementation of such a system. Readers familiar with Diffie and Hellman
(1976a) may wish to skip directly to §45.5 for a description of our method.

45.2   Public-Key Cryptosystems

In a "public-key cryptosystem" each user places in a public file an encryption procedure E. That
is, the public file is a directory giving the encryption procedure of each user. The user keeps secret
the details of his corresponding decryption procedure D. These procedures have the following
four properties:

(a)   Deciphering the enciphered form of a message M yields M. Formally,

$$D(E(M)) = M. \tag{45.1}$$

(b)   Both E and D are easy to compute.

(c)   By publicly revealing E the user does not reveal an easy way to compute D. This means that
      in practice only he can decrypt messages encrypted with E, or compute D efficiently.

(d)   If a message M is first deciphered and then enciphered, M is the result. Formally,

$$E(D(M)) = M. \tag{45.2}$$

An encryption (or decryption) procedure typically consists of a *general method* and an *encryption key*. The general method, under control of the key, enciphers a message M to obtain the
enciphered form of the message, called the *ciphertext C*. Everyone can use the same general
method; the security of a given procedure will rest on the security of the key. Revealing an
encryption algorithm then means revealing the key.

When the user reveals E he reveals a very *inefficient* method of computing $D(C)$: testing all
possible messages M until one such that $E(M) = C$ is found. If property (c) is satisfied the
number of such messages to test will be so large that this approach is impractical.

A function E satisfying (a)–(c) is a "trap-door one-way function"; if it also satisfies (d) it is
a "trap-door one-way permutation." Diffie and Hellman (1976a, here chapter 42) introduced
the concept of trap-door one-way functions but did not present any examples. These functions
are called "one-way" because they are easy to compute in one direction but (apparently) very
difficult to compute in the other direction. They are called "trap-door" functions since the inverse
functions are in fact easy to compute once certain private "trap-door" information is known. A
trap-door one-way function which also satisfies (d) must be a permutation: every message is the
ciphertext for some other message and every ciphertext is itself a permissible message. (The
mapping is "one-to-one" and "onto.") Property (d) is needed only to implement "signatures."

The reader is encouraged to read Diffie and Hellman's excellent article for further background,
for elaboration of the concept of a public-key cryptosystem, and for a discussion of other prob-

lems in the area of cryptography. The ways in which a public-key cryptosystem can ensure privacy and enable "signatures" (described in §§45.3 and 45.4 below) are also due to Diffie and Hellman.

For our scenarios we suppose that A and B (also known as Alice and Bob) are two users of a public-key cryptosystem. We will distinguish their encryption and decryption procedures with subscripts: E_A, D_A, E_B, D_B.

45.3   Privacy

Encryption is the standard means of rendering a communication private. The sender enciphers each message before transmitting it to the receiver. The receiver (but no unauthorized person) knows the appropriate deciphering function to apply to the received message to obtain the original message. An eavesdropper who hears the transmitted message hears only "garbage" (the ciphertext) which makes no sense to him since he does not know how to decrypt it.

The large volume of personal and sensitive information currently held in computerized data banks and transmitted over telephone lines makes encryption increasingly important. In recognition of the fact that efficient, high-quality encryption techniques are very much needed but are in short supply, the National Bureau of Standards has recently adopted a "Data Encryption Standard," developed at IBM (*Federal Register*: Vol. 40, No. 42, March 17, 1975; Vol. 40, No. 149, August 1, 1975). The new standard does not have property (c), needed to implement a public-key cryptosystem.

All classical encryption methods (including the NBS standard) suffer from the "key distribution problem." The problem is that before a private communication can begin, another private transaction is necessary to distribute corresponding encryption and decryption keys to the sender and receiver, respectively. Typically a private courier is used to carry a key from the sender to the receiver. Such a practice is not feasible if an electronic mail system is to be rapid and inexpensive. A public-key cryptosystem needs no private couriers; the keys can be distributed over the insecure communications channel.

How can Bob send a private message M to Alice in a public-key cryptosystem? First, he retrieves E_A from the public file. Then he sends her the enciphered message $E_A(M)$. Alice deciphers the message by computing $D_A(E_A(M)) = M$. By property (c) of the public-key cryptosystem only she can decipher $E_A(M)$. She can encipher a private response with E_B, also available in the public file.

Observe that no private transactions between Alice and Bob are needed to establish private communication. The only "setup" required is that each user who wishes to receive private communications must place his enciphering algorithm in the public file.

Two users can also establish private communication over an insecure communications channel without consulting a public file. Each user sends his encryption key to the other. Afterwards all messages are enciphered with the encryption key of the recipient, as in the public-key system. An intruder listening in on the channel cannot decipher any messages, since it is not possible to derive the decryption keys from the encryption keys. (We assume that the intruder cannot modify or insert messages into the channel.) Ralph Merkle (1978) has developed another solution to this problem.

A public-key cryptosystem can be used to "bootstrap" into a standard encryption scheme such as the NBS method. Once secure communications have been established, the first message transmitted can be a key to use in the NBS scheme to encode all following messages. This may be desirable if encryption with our method is slower than with the standard scheme. (The NBS scheme is probably somewhat faster if special-purpose hardware encryption devices are used; our scheme may be faster on a general-purpose computer since multiprecision arithmetic operations are simpler to implement than complicated bit manipulations.)

45.4   Signatures

If electronic mail systems are to replace the existing paper mail system for business transactions, "signing" an electronic message must be possible. The recipient of a signed message has proof that the message originated from the sender. This quality is stronger than mere authentication (where the recipient can verify that the message came from the sender); the recipient can convince a "judge" that the signer sent the message. To do so, he must convince the judge that he did not forge the signed message himself! In an authentication problem the recipient does not worry about this possibility, since he only wants to satisfy himself that the message came from the sender.

An electronic signature must be message-dependent, as well as signer-dependent. Otherwise the recipient could modify the message before showing the message-signature pair to a judge. Or he could attach the signature to any message whatsoever, since it is impossible to detect electronic "cutting and pasting."

To implement signatures the public-key cryptosystem must be implemented with trap-door one-way permutations (i.e. have property (d)), since the decryption algorithm will be applied to unenciphered messages.

How can user Bob send Alice a "signed" message M in a public-key cryptosystem? He first computes his "signature" S for the message M using D_B: $S = D_B(M)$. (Deciphering an unenciphered message "makes sense" by property (d) of a public-key cryptosystem: each message is the ciphertext for some other message.) He then encrypts S using E_A (for privacy), and sends the result $E_A(S)$ to Alice. He need not send M as well; it can be computed from S.

Alice first decrypts the ciphertext with D_A to obtain S. She knows who is the presumed sender of the signature (in this case, Bob); this can be given if necessary in plain text attached to S. She then extracts the message with the encryption procedure of the sender, in this case E_B (available on the public file): $M = E_B(S)$. She now possesses a message-signature pair (M, S) with properties similar to those of a signed paper document.

Bob cannot later deny having sent Alice this message, since no one else could have created $S = D_B(M)$. Alice can convince a "judge" that $E_B(S) = M$, so she has proof that Bob signed the document.

Clearly Alice cannot modify M to a different version M', since then she would have to create the corresponding signature $S' = D_B(M')$ as well.

Therefore Alice has received a message "signed" by Bob, which she can "prove" that he sent, but which she cannot modify. (Nor can she forge his signature for any other message.)

An electronic checking system could be based on a signature system such as the above. It is easy to imagine an encryption device in your home terminal allowing you to sign checks that get sent by electronic mail to the payee. It would only be necessary to include a unique check number in each check so that even if the payee copies the check the bank will only honor the first version it sees.

Another possibility arises if encryption devices can be made fast enough: it will be possible to have a telephone conversation in which every word spoken is signed by the encryption device before transmission.

When encryption is used for signatures as above, it is important that the encryption device not be "wired in" between the terminal (or computer) and the communications channel, since a message may have to be successively enciphered with several keys. It is perhaps more natural to view the encryption device as a "hardware subroutine" that can be executed as needed.

We have assumed above that each user can always access the public file reliably. In a "computer network" this might be difficult; an "intruder" might forge messages purporting to be from the public file. The user would like to be sure that he actually obtains the encryption procedure of his desired correspondent and not, say, the encryption procedure of the intruder. This danger disappears if the public file "signs" each message it sends to a user. The user can check the signature with the public file's encryption algorithm E_{PF}. The problem of "looking up" E_{PF} itself in the public file is avoided by giving each user a description of E_{PF} when he first shows up (in person) to join the public-key cryptosystem and to deposit his public encryption procedure. He then stores this description rather than ever looking it up again. The need for a courier between every pair of users has thus been replaced by the requirement for a single secure meeting between each user and the public-file manager when the user joins the system. Another solution is to give each user, when he signs up, a book (like a telephone directory) containing all the encryption keys of users in the system.

45.5   Our Encryption and Decryption Methods

To encrypt a message M with our method, using a public encryption key (e, n), proceed as follows. (Here e and n are a pair of positive integers.)

First, represent the message as an integer between 0 and $n - 1$. (Break a long message into a series of blocks, and represent each block as such an integer.) Use any standard representation.

The purpose here is not to encrypt the message but only to get it into the numeric form necessary for encryption.

Then, encrypt the message by raising it to the eth power modulo n. That is, the result (the ciphertext C) is the remainder when M^e is divided by n.

To decrypt the ciphertext, raise it to another power d, again modulo n. The encryption and decryption algorithms E and D are thus:

$$C \equiv E(M) \equiv M^e \pmod{n}, \text{ for a message } M.$$

$$D(C) \equiv C^d \pmod{n}, \text{ for a ciphertext } C.$$

Note that encryption does not increase the size of a message; both the message and the ciphertext are integers in the range 0 to $n - 1$.

The *encryption key* is thus the pair of positive integers (e, n). Similarly, the *decryption key* is the pair of positive integers (d, n). Each user makes his encryption key public, and keeps the corresponding decryption key private. (These integers should properly be subscripted as in n_A, e_A, and d_A, since each user has his own set. However, we will only consider a typical set, and will omit the subscripts.)

How should you choose your encryption and decryption keys, if you want to use our method?

You first compute n as the product of two primes p and q: $n = p \cdot q$. These primes are very large, "random" primes. Although you will make n public, the factors p and q will be effectively hidden from everyone else due to the enormous difficulty of factoring n. This also hides the way d can be derived from e.

You then pick the integer d to be a large, random integer which is relatively prime to $(p - 1) \cdot (q - 1)$. That is, check that d satisfies $\gcd(d, (p - 1) \cdot (q - 1)) = 1$ ("gcd" means "greatest common divisor").

The integer e is finally computed from p, q, and d to be the "multiplicative inverse" of d, modulo $(p - 1) \cdot (q - 1)$. Thus we have $e \cdot d \equiv 1 \pmod{(p - 1) \cdot (q - 1)}$.

We prove in the next section that this guarantees that (45.1) and (45.2) hold, i.e. that E and D are inverse permutations. §45.7 shows how each of the above operations can be done efficiently.

The aforementioned method should not be confused with the "exponentiation" technique presented by Diffie and Hellman (1976a, here chapter 42) to solve the key distribution problem. Their technique permits two users to determine a key in common to be used in a normal cryptographic system. It is not based on a trap-door one-way permutation. Pohlig and Hellman (1978) study a scheme related to ours, where exponentiation is done modulo a prime number.

45.6   The Underlying Mathematics

We demonstrate the correctness of the deciphering algorithm using an identity due to Euler and Fermat (Niven, 1972): for any integer (message) M which is relatively prime to n,

$$M^{\phi(n)} \equiv 1 \pmod{n}. \tag{45.3}$$

Here $\phi(n)$ is the Euler totient function giving the number of positive integers less than n which are relatively prime to n. For prime numbers p, $\phi(p) = p - 1$. In our case, we have by elementary properties of the totient function:

$$\begin{aligned}
\phi(n) &= \phi(p) \cdot \phi(q) \\
&= (p - 1) \cdot (q - 1) \\
&= n - (p + q) + 1.
\end{aligned}$$

Since d is relatively prime to $\phi(n)$, it has a multiplicative inverse e in the ring of integers modulo $\phi(n)$:

$$e \cdot d \equiv 1 \pmod{\phi(n)}. \tag{45.4}$$

We now prove that equations (45.1) and (45.2) hold (that is, that deciphering works correctly if e and d are chosen as above). Now

$$D(E(M)) \equiv (E(M))^d \equiv (M^e)^d \equiv M^{e \cdot d} \pmod{n}$$
$$E(D(M)) \equiv (D(M))^e \equiv (M^d)^e \equiv M^{e \cdot d} \pmod{n}$$

and

$$M^{e \cdot d} \equiv M^{k \cdot \phi(n) + 1} \pmod{n} \qquad \text{(for some integer } k\text{)}.$$

From (45.3) we see that for all M such that p does not divide M, $M^{p-1} \equiv 1 \pmod{p}$, and since $(p - 1)$ divides $\phi(n)$,

$$M^{k \cdot \phi(n) + 1} \equiv M \pmod{p}.$$

This is trivially true when $M \equiv 0 \pmod{p}$, so that this equality actually holds for *all* M. Arguing similarly for q yields

$$M^{k \cdot \phi(n) + 1} \equiv M \pmod{q}.$$

Together these last two equations imply that for all M,

$$M^{e \cdot d} \equiv M^{k \cdot \phi(n) + 1} \equiv M \pmod{n}.$$

This implies (45.1) and (45.2) for all M, $0 \le M < n$. Therefore E and D are inverse permutations. (We thank Rich Schroeppel for suggesting the above improved version of the authors' previous proof.)

45.7 Algorithms

To show that our method is practical, we describe an efficient algorithm for each required operation.

45.7.1 How to encrypt and decrypt efficiently Computing $M^e \pmod{n}$ requires at most $2 \log_2(e)$ multiplications and $2 \log_2(e)$ divisions using the following procedure (decryption can be performed similarly using d instead of e):

1. Let $e_k e_{k-1} \ldots e_1 e_0$ be the binary representation of e.

2. Set the variable C to 1.

3. Repeat steps 3a and 3b for $i = k, k-1, \ldots, 0$:

   3a. Set C to the remainder of C^2 when divided by n.

   3b. If $e_i = 1$, then set C to the remainder of $C \cdot M$ when divided by n.

4. Halt. Now C is the encrypted form of M.

This procedure is called "exponentiation by repeated squaring and multiplication." This procedure is half as good as the best; more efficient procedures are known. Knuth (1969) studies this problem in detail.

The fact that the enciphering and deciphering are identical leads to a simple implementation. (The whole operation can be implemented on a few special-purpose integrated circuit chips.)

A high-speed computer can encrypt a 200-digit message M in a few seconds; special-purpose hardware would be much faster. The encryption time per block increases no faster than the cube of the number of digits in n.

45.7.2 How to find large prime numbers Each user must (privately) choose two large random prime numbers p and q to create his own encryption and decryption keys. These numbers must be large so that it is not computationally feasible for anyone to factor $n = p \cdot q$. (Remember that n, but not p or q, will be in the public file.) We recommend using 100-digit (decimal) prime numbers p and q, so that n has 200 digits.

To find a 100-digit "random" prime number, generate (odd) 100-digit random numbers until a prime number is found. By the prime number theorem (Niven, 1972), about $(\ln 10^{100})/2 = 115$ numbers will be tested before a prime is found.

To test a large number b for primality we recommend the elegant "probabilistic" algorithm due to Solovay and Strassen (1977). It picks a random number a from a uniform distribution on $\{1, \ldots, b-1\}$, and tests whether

$$\gcd(a, b) = 1 \text{ and } J(a, b) \equiv a^{(b-1)/2} \pmod{b}, \tag{45.5}$$

where $J(a, b)$ is the Jacobi symbol (Niven, 1972). If b is prime (45.5) is always true. If b is composite (45.5) will be false with probability at least $\frac{1}{2}$. If (45.5) holds for 100 randomly chosen values of a then b is almost certainly prime; there is a (negligible) chance of one in 2^{100} that b is composite. Even if a composite were accidentally used in our system, the receiver would probably detect this by noticing that decryption didn't work correctly. When b is odd, $a \leq b$, and $\gcd(a, b) = 1$, the Jacobi symbol $J(a, b)$ has a value in $\{-1, 1\}$ and can be efficiently computed by the program:

$$J(a, b) = \textbf{if } a = 1 \textbf{ then } 1 \textbf{ else}$$
$$\textbf{if } a \text{ is even } \textbf{then } J(a/2, b) \cdot (-1)^{(b^2-1)/8}$$
$$\textbf{else } J(b \bmod a, a) \cdot (-1)^{(a-1)\cdot(b-1)/4}$$

(The computations of $J(a, b)$ and $\gcd(a, b)$ can be nicely combined, too.) Note that this algorithm does *not* test a number for primality by trying to factor it. Other efficient procedures for testing a large number for primality are given in Miller (1976); Pollard (1974); Rabin (1976).

To gain additional protection against sophisticated factoring algorithms, p and q should differ in length by a few digits, both $(p - 1)$ and $(q - 1)$ should contain large prime factors, and $\gcd(p - 1, q - 1)$ should be small. The latter condition is easily checked.

To find a prime number p such that $(p - 1)$ has a large prime factor, generate a large random prime number u, then let p be the first prime in the sequence $i \cdot u + 1$, for $i = 2, 4, 6, \ldots$. (This shouldn't take too long.) Additional security is provided by ensuring that $(u - 1)$ also has a large prime factor.

A high-speed computer can determine in several seconds whether a 100-digit number is prime, and can find the first prime after a given point in a minute or two.

Another approach to finding large prime numbers is to take a number of known factorization, add one to it, and test the result for primality. If a prime p is found it is possible to prove that it really is prime by using the factorization of $p - 1$. We omit a discussion of this since the probabilistic method is adequate.

45.7.3   How to choose d It is very easy to choose a number d which is relatively prime to $\phi(n)$. For example, any prime number greater than $\max(p, q)$ will do. It is important that d should be chosen from a large enough set so that a cryptanalyst cannot find it by direct search.

45.7.4   How to compute e **from** d **and** $\phi(n)$ To compute e, use the following variation of Euclid's algorithm for computing the greatest common divisor of $\phi(n)$ and d. (See exercise 4.5.2.15 in Knuth (1969).) Calculate $\gcd(\phi(n), d)$ by computing a series $x_0, x_1, x_2, \ldots$, where $x_0 = \phi(n)$, $x_1 = d$, and $x_{i+1} = x_{i-1} \pmod{x_i}$, until an x_k equal to 0 is found. Then $\gcd(x_0, x_1) = x_{k-1}$. Compute for each x_i numbers a_i and b_i such that $x_i = a_i \cdot x_0 + b_i \cdot x_1$. If $x_{k-1} = 1$ then b_{k-1} is the multiplicative inverse of $x_1 \pmod{x_0}$. Since k will be less than $2 \cdot \log_2(n)$, this computation is very rapid.

If e turns out to be less than $\log_2(n)$, start over by choosing another value of d. This guarantees that every encrypted message (except $M = 0$ or $M = 1$) undergoes some "wrap-around" (reduction modulo n). ...

45.8   A Small Example ...

45.9   Security of the Method: Cryptanalytic approaches

Since no techniques exist to *prove* that an encryption scheme is secure, the only test available is to see whether anyone can think of a way to break it. The NBS standard was "certified" this way; seventeen man-years at IBM were spent fruitlessly trying to break that scheme. Once a method has successfully resisted such a concerted attack it may for practical purposes be considered secure. (Actually there is some controversy concerning the security of the NBS method [Diffie and Hellman, 1977].)

We show in the next sections that all the obvious approaches for breaking our system are at least as difficult as factoring n. While factoring large numbers is not provably difficult, it is a well-known problem that has been worked on for the last three hundred years by many famous mathematicians. Fermat (1601?–1665) and Legendre (1752–1833) developed factoring algorithms; some of today's more efficient algorithms are based on the work of Legendre. As we shall see in the next section, however, no one has yet found an algorithm which can factor a 200-digit number in a reasonable amount of time. We conclude that our system has already been partially "certified" by these previous efforts to find efficient factoring algorithms.

In the following sections we consider ways a cryptanalyst might try to determine the secret decryption key from the publicly revealed encryption key. We do not consider ways of protecting the decryption key from theft; the usual physical security methods should suffice. (For example, the encryption device could be a separate device which could also be used to *generate* the encryption and decryption keys, such that the decryption key is never printed out (even for its owner) but only used to decrypt messages. The device could erase the decryption key if it was tampered with.)

45.9.1   Factoring n   Factoring n would enable an enemy cryptanalyst to "break" our method. The factors of n enable him to compute $\phi(n)$ and thus d. Fortunately, factoring a number seems to be much more difficult than determining whether it is prime or composite. ... [EDITOR: Discussion of factoring algorithms omitted]

45.9.2   Computing $\phi(n)$ without factoring n   If a cryptanalyst could compute $\phi(n)$ then he could break the system by computing d as the multiplicative inverse of e modulo $\phi(n)$ (using the procedure of §45.7.4).

We argue that this approach is no easier than factoring n since it enables the cryptanalyst to easily factor n using $\phi(n)$. This approach to factoring n has not turned out to be practical.

How can n be factored using $\phi(n)$? First, $(p+q)$ is obtained from n and $\phi(n) = n - (p+q) + 1$. Then $(p-q)$ is the square root of $(p+q)^2 - 4n$. Finally, q is half the difference of $(p+q)$ and $(p-q)$.

Therefore breaking our system by computing $\phi(n)$ is no easier than breaking our system by factoring n. (This is why n must be composite; $\phi(n)$ is trivial to compute if n is prime.)

45.9.3   Determining d without factoring n or computing $\phi(n)$ Of course, d should be chosen from a large enough set so that a direct search for it is unfeasible.

We argue that computing d is no easier for a cryptanalyst than factoring n, since once d is known n could be factored easily. This approach to factoring has also not turned out to be fruitful.

A knowledge of d enables n to be factored as follows. Once a cryptanalyst knows d he can calculate $e \cdot d - 1$, which is a multiple of $\phi(n)$. Miller has shown that n can be factored using any multiple of $\phi(n)$. Therefore if n is large a cryptanalyst should not be able to determine d any easier than he can factor n.

A cryptanalyst may hope to find a d' which is equivalent to the d secretly held by a user of the public-key cryptosystem. If such values d' were common then a brute-force search could break the system. However, all such d' differ by the least common multiple of $(p - 1)$ and

$(q - 1)$, and finding one enables n to be factored. (In (45.3) and (45.4) , $\phi(n)$ can be replaced by lcm$(p - 1, q - 1)$.) Finding any such d' is therefore as difficult as factoring n.

45.9.4   Computing d in some other way   Although this problem of "computing e^{th} roots modulo n without factoring n" is not a well-known difficult problem like factoring, we feel reasonably confident that it is computationally intractable. It may be possible to prove that any general method of breaking our scheme yields an efficient factoring algorithm. This would establish that any way of breaking our scheme must be as difficult as factoring. We have not been able to prove this conjecture, however.

Our method should be certified by having the above conjecture of intractability withstand a concerted attempt to disprove it. The reader is challenged to find a way to "break" our method.

45.10   Avoiding "Reblocking" When Encrypting a Signed Message

A signed message may have to be "reblocked" for encryption since the signature n may be larger than the encryption n (every user has his own n). This can be avoided as follows. A threshold value h is chosen (say $h = 10^{199}$) for the public-key cryptosystem. Every user maintains two public (e, n) pairs, one for enciphering and one for signature-verification, where every signature n is less than h, and every enciphering n is greater than h. Reblocking to encipher a signed message is then unnecessary; the message is blocked according to the transmitter's signature n.

Another solution uses a technique given in Levine and Brawley (1977). Each user has a single (e, n) pair where n is between h and $2h$, where h is a threshold as above. A message is encoded as a number less than h and enciphered as before, except that if the ciphertext is greater than h, it is repeatedly re-enciphered until it is less than h. Similarly for decryption the ciphertext is repeatedly deciphered to obtain a value less than h. If n is near h re-enciphering will be infrequent. (Infinite looping is not possible, since at worst a message is enciphered as itself.)

45.11   Conclusions

We have proposed a method for implementing a public-key cryptosystem whose security rests in part on the difficulty of factoring large numbers. If the security of our method proves to be adequate, it permits secure communications to be established without the use of couriers to carry keys, and it also permits one to "sign" digitized documents.

The security of this system needs to be examined in more detail. In particular, the difficulty of factoring large numbers should be examined very closely. The reader is urged to find a way to "break" the system. Once the method has withstood all attacks for a sufficient length of time it may be used with a reasonable amount of confidence.

Our encryption function is the only candidate for a "trap-door one-way permutation" known to the authors. It might be desirable to find other examples, to provide alternative implementations should the security of our system turn out someday to be inadequate. There are surely also many new applications to be discovered for these functions.

46 How to Share a Secret (1979)

Adi Shamir

As computers were networked and information was spread around and communicated, secrecy and privacy began to assume dimensions that had not been significant in a world of stored paper documents and centralized data banks. Playful metaphors—this paper is based on a problem posed in a 1968 mathematics book—assumed grave significance in the world of networked information. Advances in cryptography (chapters 42 and 45) held out the promise (not yet mathematically verified) that ordinary people might communicate confidentially at a distance, confident that their secret communication could not be compromised without an unrealistically large level of computational effort. This paper, by contrast, describes a protocol for sharing a secret among parties who must, to a degree that can be stipulated, cooperate in order to recover it—in such a way that it is *provably impossible* for a smaller cabal of the parties to expose the secret, even by devoting *unlimited* resources to the effort. The field of secret sharing initiated with this one short contribution has now grown to include many thousands of papers.

We met Adi Shamir (b. 1952) in chapter 45 as one of the authors of the RSA public-key cryptosystem. This paper starts by posing an apparently impossible challenge, and lays out a beautiful, short solution using only high school mathematics. It is practically a problem about distributed computer systems, yet mentions nothing about computer technology itself. Computer science exploded in the 1980s, and the field remains full of simply stated problems like this one, begging for elegant solutions.

46.1 Introduction

L IU (1968) considers the following problem: Eleven scientists are working on a secret project. They wish to lock up the documents in a cabinet so that the cabinet can be opened if and only if six or more of the scientists are present. What is the smallest number of locks needed? What is the smallest number of keys to the locks each scientist must carry?

It is not hard to show that the minimal solution uses 462 locks and 252 keys per scientist. These numbers are clearly impractical, and they become exponentially worse when the number of scientists increases. In this paper we generalize the problem to one in which the secret is some

Reprinted from Shamir (1979), with permission from the Association for Computing Machinery.

data D (e.g., the safe combination) and in which nonmechanical solutions (which manipulate this data) are also allowed. Our goal is to divide D into n pieces $D_1, \ldots, D_n$ in such a way that:

1. knowledge of any k or more D_i pieces makes D easily computable;
2. knowledge of any $k - 1$ or fewer D_i pieces leaves D completely undetermined (in the sense that all its possible values are equally likely).

Such a scheme is called a (k, n) *threshold scheme*. Efficient threshold schemes can be very helpful in the management of cryptographic keys. In order to protect data we can encrypt it, but in order to protect the encryption key we need a different method (further encryptions change the problem rather than solve it). The most secure key management scheme keeps the key in a single, well-guarded location (a computer, a human brain, or a safe). This scheme is highly unreliable since a single misfortune (a computer breakdown, sudden death, or sabotage) can make the information inaccessible. An obvious solution is to store multiple copies of the key at different locations, but this increases the danger of security breaches (computer penetration, betrayal, or human errors). By using a (k, n) threshold scheme with $n = 2k - 1$ we get a very robust key management scheme: We can recover the original key even when $\lfloor n/2 \rfloor = k - 1$ of the n pieces are destroyed, but our opponents cannot reconstruct the key even when security breaches expose $\lfloor n/2 \rfloor = k - 1$ of the remaining k pieces.

In other applications the tradeoff is not between secrecy and reliability, but between safety and convenience of use. Consider, for example, a company that digitally signs all its checks (Rivest et al., 1978). If each executive is given a copy of the company's secret signature key, the system is convenient but easy to misuse. If the cooperation of all the company's executives is necessary in order to sign each check, the system is safe but inconvenient. The standard solution requires at least three signatures per check, and it is easy to implement with a $(3, n)$ threshold scheme. Each executive is given a small magnetic card with one D_i piece, and the company's signature generating device accepts any three of them in order to generate (and later destroy) a temporary copy of the actual signature key D. The device does not contain any secret information and thus it need not be protected against inspection. An unfaithful executive must have at least two accomplices in order to forge the company's signature in this scheme.

Threshold schemes are ideally suited to applications in which a group of mutually suspicious individuals with conflicting interests must cooperate. Ideally we would like the cooperation to be based on mutual consent, but the veto power this mechanism gives to each member can paralyze the activities of the group. By properly choosing the k and n parameters we can give any sufficiently large majority the authority to take some action while giving any sufficiently large minority the power to block it.

46.2   A Simple (k, n) Threshold Scheme

Our scheme is based on polynomial interpolation: given k points in the 2-dimensional plane $(x_1, y_1), \ldots, (x_k, y_k)$ with distinct x_i's, there is one and only one polynomial $q(x)$ of degree $k - 1$ such that $q(x_i) = y_i$ for all i. Without loss of generality, we can assume that the data D is (or can be made) a number. To divide it into pieces D_i, we pick a random $k - 1$ degree polynomial $q(x) = a_0 + a_1 x + \ldots a_{k-1} x^{k-1}$ in which $a_0 = D$, and evaluate:

$$D_1 = q(1), \ldots, D_i = q(i), \ldots, D_n = q(n).$$

Given any subset of k of these D_i values (together with their identifying indices), we can find the coefficients of $q(x)$ by interpolation, and then evaluate $D = q(0)$. Knowledge of just $k - 1$ of these values, on the other hand, does not suffice in order to calculate D.

To make this claim more precise, we use modular arithmetic instead of real arithmetic. The set of integers modulo a prime number p forms a field in which interpolation is possible. Given an integer valued data D, we pick a prime p which is bigger than both D and n. The coefficients a_1, $\ldots$, a_{k-1} in $q(x)$ are randomly chosen from a uniform distribution over the integers in $[0, p)$, and the values $D_1, \ldots, D_n$ are computed modulo p.

Let us now assume that $k - 1$ of these n pieces are revealed to an opponent. For each candidate value D' in $[0, p)$ he can construct one and only one polynomial $q'(x)$ of degree $k - 1$ such that $q'(0) = D'$ and $q'(i) = D_i$ for the $k - 1$ given arguments. By construction, these p possible polynomials are equally likely, and thus there is absolutely nothing the opponent can deduce about the real value of D.

Efficient $O(n \log^2 n)$ algorithms for polynomial evaluation and interpolation are discussed in Aho et al. (1974) and Knuth (1997b), but even the straightforward quadratic algorithms are fast enough for practical key management schemes. If the number D is long, it is advisable to break it into shorter blocks of bits (which are handled separately) in order to avoid multiprecision arithmetic operations. The blocks cannot be arbitrarily short, since the smallest usable value of p is $n + 1$ (there must be at least $n + 1$ distinct arguments in $[0, p)$ to evaluate $q(x)$ at). However, this is not a severe limitation since sixteen bit modulus (which can be handled by a cheap sixteen bit arithmetic unit) suffices for applications with up to 64,000 D_i pieces.

Some of the useful properties of this (k, n) threshold scheme (when compared to the mechanical locks and keys solutions) are:

1. The size of each piece does not exceed the size of the original data.

2. When k is kept fixed, D_i pieces can be dynamically added or deleted (e.g., when executives join or leave the company) without affecting the other D_i pieces. (A piece is deleted only when a leaving executive makes it completely inaccessible, even to himself.)

3. It is easy to change the D_i pieces without changing the original data D—all we need is a new polynomial $q(x)$ with the same free term. A frequent change of this type can greatly enhance security since the pieces exposed by security breaches cannot be accumulated unless all of them are values of the same edition of the $q(x)$ polynomial.

4. By using tuples of polynomial values as D_i pieces, we can get a hierarchical scheme in which the number of pieces needed to determine D depends on their importance. For example, if we give the company's president three values of $q(x)$, each vice-president two values of $q(x)$, and each executive one value of $q(x)$, then a $(3, n)$ threshold scheme enables checks

to be signed either by any three executives, or by any two executives one of whom is a vice-president, or by the president alone.

The polynomials can be replaced by any other collection of functions which are easy to evaluate and to interpolate. A different (and somewhat less efficient) threshold scheme was recently developed by G. R. Blakley (1979).

Bibliography

Abelson, R., and J. Carroll. 1965. Computer simulation of individual belief systems. *Amer. Behav. Scientist* 8 (9): 24–30.

Abramson, Norman. 1970. The Aloha system. In *AFIPS conf. prof.*, Vol. 37, 281–285. Montvale, NJ: AFIPS Press.

Abramson, Norman. 1973. *Computer-communication networks. Computer applications in electrical engineering series.* Englewood Cliffs, NJ: Prentice-Hall.

ACM. 1968. Richard W. Hamming (ACM Turing award citation). https://amturing.acm.org/info/hamming_1000652.cfm.

ACM. 2004. Vinton Cerf and Robert Kahn (ACM Turing award citation). https://amturing.acm.org/award_winners/cerf_1083211.cfm.

Adams, C. W., S. Gill, and D. Combalic, eds. 1954. *Notes from a special summer program in digital computers: Advanced coding techniques.* Cambridge, MA: Massachusetts Institute of Technology, Department of Electrical Engineering, Digital Computer Laboratory.

Agrawal, Manindra, Neeraj Kayal, and Nitin Saxena. 2004. PRIMES is in P. *Annals of Mathematics* 160 (2): 781–793.

Aho, Alfred V., J. E. Hopcroft, and J. D. Ullman. 1974. *The design and analysis of computer algorithms.* Boston: Addison-Wesley.

Aiken, Howard, A. G. Oettinger, and T. C. Bartee. 1964. Proposed automatic calculating machine. *IEEE Spectrum* 1 (8): 62–69.

Aitchison, T. M., et al. 1970. Comparative evaluation of index languages, Technical report, Institution of Electrical Engineers, London.

al Khwārizmī, Muḥammad Ibn Mūsā. 1915. *Robert of Chester's Latin translation of the algebra of al-Khowarizmi. University of Michigan studies. Humanistic series; 11.* New York; London: Macmillan.

Aleph-Null. 1971. Computer recreations. *Software Practice and Experience* 1 (2): 201–204.

Alt, Franz L. 1948a. A Bell Telephone Laboratories' computing machine. I. *Mathematics of Computation* 3 (21): 1–13.

Alt, Franz L. 1948b. A Bell Telephone Laboratories' computing machine. II. *Mathematics of Computation* 3 (22): 69–84.

Aristotle. 1933. *The metaphysics. Loeb classical library.* Cambridge, MA: Harvard University Press.

Aristotle. 1989. *Prior analytics.* Indianapolis: Hackett Pub. Co..

Artandi, Susan, and Edward H. Wolf. 1969. The effectiveness of automatically generated weights and links in mechanical indexing. *American Documentation* 20 (3): 198–202.

Ash, R., E. Broadwin, V. Della Valle, M. Greene, A. Jenny, C. Katz, and L. Yu. 1957. Preliminary manual for MATH-MATIC and ARITH-MATIC systems for algebraic translation and compilation for UNIVAC I and II. *Automatic program development, Remington Rand UNIVAC.* http://archive.computerhistory.org/resources/text/Knuth_Don_X4100/PDF_index/k-7-pdf/k-7-u2310-UNIVAC-MATH-MATIC-ARITH-MATIC.pdf.

Ashby, W. Ross. 1952. *Design for a brain.* New York: J. Wiley.

Ashby, W. Ross. 1956. Design for an intelligence-amplifier. In *Automata studies*, eds. Claude E. Shannon and J. McCarthy, 215–234. Princeton, NJ: Princeton University Press.

Ashenhurst, R. L., and R. H. Vonderohe. 1975. A hierarchical network. *Datamation* 21 (2): 40–44.

Atchison, William F., Samuel D. Conte, John W. Hamblen, Thomas E. Hull, Thomas A. Keenan, William B. Kehl, Edward J. McCluskey, Silvio O. Navarro, Werner C. Rheinboldt, Earl J. Schweppe, William Viavant, and David M. Young Jr. 1968. Curriculum 68: Recommendations for academic programs in computer science: A report of the acm curriculum committee on computer science. *Commun. ACM* 11 (3): 151–197. doi:10.1145/362929.362976. http://doi.acm.org/10.1145/362929.362976.

Babai, László. 2016. Graph isomorphism in quasipolynomial time. *arXiv.org.* https://arxiv.org/abs/1512.03547.

Babbage, Charles. 1843. Letter from Babbage to Prince Albert. https://www.instagram.com/p/ButJtIMnBrV/.

Babbage, Charles. 1989. *Science and reform: Selected works of Charles Babbage.* Cambridge; New York: Cambridge University Press.

Bachman, C. W. 1965. Software for random access processing. *Datamation.*

Bachmann, Paul. 1894. *Die analytische zahlentheorie. Zahlentheorie. versuch einer gesammtdarstellung dieser wissenschaft in ihren haupttheilen. 2. th.* Leipzig: Teubner.

Baker, F. T. 1972. Chief programmer team management of production programming. *IBM Systems Journal* 11 (1): 56–73.

Baran, Paul. 1964. On distributed communications networks (all-digital data distributed communications network with connected adjacent stations for increased survivability if nodes and links are destroyed). *IEEE Transactions on Communications Systems* cs-12: 1–9.

Barber, D. L. A. 1972. The European computer network project. In *Computer communications: Impacts and implications*, ed. S. Winkler, 192–200. Washington, DC.

Barnes, G. H., R. M. Brown, M. Kato, D. J. Kuck, D. L. Slotnick, and R. A. Stokes. 1968. The ILLIAC IV computer. *IEEE Transactions on Computers* C-17 (8): 746–757.

Bateman, P., and D. Diamond. 1978. John E. Littlewood (1885–1977): An informal obituary. *The Math. Intelligencer* 1 (1): 28–33.

BBN. 1973. Specification for the interconnection of a host and an IMP, Technical Report BBN 1822 (revised), Bolt Beranek and Newman Inc., Cambridge, MA.

Bennett, James. 1962. *On spectra.* Princeton, NJ: Princeton University Press.

Bernstein, Alex, and Michael de V. Roberts. 1958. Computer v. chess-player. *Scientific American* 198 (6): 96–106.

Blakley, G. R. 1979. Safeguarding cryptographic keys. In *1979 international workshop on managing requirements knowledge (MARK)*, 313–318.

Bledsoe, W. W., and I. Browning. 1959. Pattern recognition and reading by machine. In *IRE-AIEE-ACM '59 (Eastern): Papers presented at the December 1–3, 1959, Eastern Joint IRE-AIEE-ACM Computer Conference*, ed. F. Heart. New York: ACM.

Bleier, Robert. 1967. Treating hierarchical data structures in the SDC Time-Shared Data Management System (TDMS). In *ACM annual conference/annual meeting: Proceedings of the 1967 22nd national conference*, 41–49. ACM.

Bobrow, Daniel G. 1964. *Natural language input for a computer problem solving system.* http://hdl.handle.net/2027/pst.000008813244.

Böhm, Corrado, and Giuseppe Jacopini. 1966. Flow diagrams, Turing machines and languages with only two formation rules. *Comm. ACM* 9 (5): 366–371.

Boole, George. 1854. *An investigation of the laws of thought, on which are founded the mathematical theories of logic and probabilities.* London: Walton and Maberly.

Borko, H. 1968. Interactive document storage and retrieval systems—design concepts. In *Mechanised information storage, retrieval and dissemination*, ed. K. Samuelson, 591–599. Amsterdam: North-Holland Publishing.

Borůvka, Otakar. 1926. On a minimal problem. *Práce Moravské Pridovedecké Spolecnosti* 3.

Bowles, Nellie. 2019. Overlooked no more: Karen Spärck Jones, who established the basis for search engines. *New York Times,* 2 January 2019: D6.

Brooks, Frederick P. 1956. The analytic design of automatic data processing systems. PhD diss., Harvard University).

Brooks, Frederick P. 1987. No silver bullet: Essence and accidents of software engineering. *Computer* 20 (4): 10–19.

Brooks, Frederick P. 1995. *The mythical man-month: essays on software engineering*, Anniversary edn. Boston: Addison-Wesley.

Brown, G., J. C. R. Licklider, J. McCarthy, and A. Perlis. 1962. *Management and the computer of the future.* MIT Press.

Burks, Arthur W., Herman H. Goldstine, and John von Neumann. 1947. *Preliminary discussion of the logical design of an electronic computing instrument. planning and coding of problems for an electronic computing instrument.* Princeton, NJ: Institute for Advanced Study.

Bush, Vannevar. 1945a. As we may think. *Atlantic Monthly* 176: 101–108.

Bush, Vannevar. 1945b. As we may think. *Life,* 10 September 1945: 112–124.

Bush, Vannevar. 1945c. *Science, the endless frontier.* U. S. Government Printing Office. https://www.nsf.gov/od/lpa/nsf50/vbush1945.htm.

Butler, Samuel. 1863. Darwin among the machines (letter to the editor). *The Press* (Christchurch NZ) June 13 1863. http://www.nzetc.org/tm/scholarly/tei-ButFir-t1-g1-t1-g1-t4-body.html.

Butler, Samuel. 1872. *Erewhon: or, Over the range.* London: Trübner.

Cantor, Georg. 1996. On an elementary question in the theory of manifolds. In *From Kant to Hilbert: A source book in the foundations of mathematics*, ed. William B. Ewald Jr. *Oxford science publications*, 920–922. Oxford: Clarendon Press.

Carnap, Rudolf. 1937. *The logical syntax of language. International library of psychology, philosophy, and scientific method*. London: K. Paul, Trench, Trubner.

Carr, S., S. Crocker, and V. Cerf. 1970. HOST-HOST communication protocol in the ARPA network. In *Spring Joint Computer Conferemce, AFIPS Conf. Proc.*, Vol. 36, 539–597. Montvale, NJ: AFIPS Press.

Cerf, V., and R. Kahn. 1974. A protocol for packet network intercommunication. *IEEE Transactions on Communications* 22 (5): 637–648.

Chambon, J. F., M. Elie, J. Le Bihan, G. LeLann, and H. Zimmerman. 1973. Functional specification of transmission station in the CYCLADES network. ST-ST protocol, Technical Report SCH502.3, I.R.I.A.

Chandrasekhar, S. 1943. Stochastic problems in physics and astronomy. *Reviews of Modern Physics* 15 (1): 1–89.

Childs, D. L. 1968. Feasibility of a set-theoretical da.ta structure—a general structure based on a reconstituted definition of relation. In *Proceedings IFIP Cong*, 162–172. Amsterdam: North Holland Publishing.

Church, Alonzo. 1936a. A note on the Entscheidungsproblem. *J. Symbolic Logic* 1 (1): 40–41.

Church, Alonzo. 1936b. An unsolvable problem of elementary number theory. *American Journal of Mathematics* 58 (2): 345–363.

Church, Alonzo. 1941. *The calculi of lambda-conversion. Annals of mathematics studies ; Number 6*. Princeton, NJ: Princeton University Press.

Church, Alonzo. 1956. *Introduction to mathematical logic. Princeton mathematical series; 17*. Princeton, NJ: Princeton University Press.

Clark, W. A., J. M. Frankovich, H. P. Peterson, J. W. Forgie, R. L Best, and K. H. Olsen. 1957. The Lincoln TX-2 computer. In *Proc. Wstrn. Jt. Computer Conf.*

Clay Mathematics Institute. 2000. Millennium Prize Problems. https://www.claymath.org/millennium-problems.

Cleverdon, C. W., J. Mills, and E. M. Keen. 1966. *Factors determining the performance of indexing systems*. Cranfield, Engand: ASLIB-Cranfield Research Project.

Cobham, Alan. 1965. The intrinsic computational difficulty of functions. In *Logic, methodology and philosophy of science: Proceedings of the 1964 International Congress (Studies in Logic and the Foundations of Mathematics)*, ed. Yehoshua Bar-Hillel, 24–30. Amsterdam: North-Holland Publishing.

Codd, E. 1960. Multiprogram scheduling: parts 1 and 2. Introduction and theory. *Comm. ACM* 3 (6): 347–350.

Codd, E. 1970. A relational model of data for large shared data banks. *Comm. ACM* 13 (6): 377–387. https://doi.org/10.1145/362384.362685.

Cohen, I. Bernard. 1999. *Howard Aiken: portrait of a computer pioneer. History of computing*. Cambridge, MA: MIT Press.

Cohen, Paul J. 1963. The independence of the continuum hypothesis. *Proceedings of the National Academy of Sciences of the United States of America* 50 (6): 1143–1148.

Conway, Flo. 2005. *Dark hero of the information age: in search of Norbert Wiener, the father of cybernetics*. New York: Basic Books.

Cook, Stephen. 1971a. Characterizations of pushdown machines in terms of time-bounded computers. *J. ACM* 18 (1): 4–18.

Cook, Stephen. 1971b. The complexity of theorem-proving procedures. *Symposium on Theory of Computing (STOC)*, 151–158. New York: Association for Computing Machinery. https://doi.org/10.1145/800157.805047.

Cooper, Franklin S., Pierre C. Delattre, Alvin M. Liberman, John M. Borst, and Louis J. Gerstman. 1952. Some experiments on the perception of synthetic speech sounds. *J. Acoustical Society of America* 24 (6): 597–606.

Corbató, Fernando J., and Arthur L. Norberg. 1989. OH 162: An interview with Fernando J. Corbató on 18 April 1989 and 14 November 1990. The Charles Babbage Institute, University of Minnesota.

Corbató, Fernando J., Marjorie Merwin Daggett, and Robert C. Daley. 1962. An experimental time-sharing system. In *Proceedings of Spring Joint Computer Conference sponsored by the American Federation of Information Processing Societies*. New York: Association for Computing Machinery. https://doi.org/10.1145/1460833.1460871.

Corneil, D., and C. Gotlieb. 1970. An efficient algorithm for graph isomorphism. *J. ACM* 17 (1): 51–64.

Crocker, S. D., J. F. Heafner, R. M. Metcalfe, and J. B. Postel. 1972. Function-oriented protocols for the ARPA computer network. In *AFIPS conf. proc., Spring Joint Computer Conference*, Vol. 40, 271–279. Montvale, NJ: AFIPS Press.

Culbertson, James T. 1950. *Consciousness and behavior; a neural analysis of behavior and of consciousness*. Dubuque, IA: W. C. Brown.

Culbertson, James T. 1956. Some uneconomical robots. In *Automata studies*, eds. Claude E. Shannon and J. McCarthy, 99–116. Princeton, NJ: Princeton University Press.

Curtice, P. M., and P. E. Jones. 1968. *An operational interactive retrieval system*. Paris: Arthur D. Little.

Davis, K. H., R. Biddulph, and S. Balashek. 1952. Automatic recognition of spoken digits. *J. Acoustical Society of America* 24 (6): 637–642.

Davis, Martin. 1965. *The undecidable; Basic papers on undecidable propositions, unsolvable problems and computable functions.* Hewlett, NY: Raven Press.

Davis, Martin, and Hilary Putnam. 1960. A computing procedure for quantification theory. *J. ACM* 7 (3): 201–215.

Davis, P. J. 1972. Fidelity in mathematical discourse: Is one and one really two? *The American Mathematical Monthly* 79 (3): 252–263.

DEC. 1972. *Digital Equipment Corporation PDP-11/40 processor handbook, 1972, and PDP-11/45 processor handbook, 1971.* Maynard, MA: Digital Equipment Corporation.

Dell, F. R. E. 1971. Features of a proposed synchronous data network. In *Proc. 2nd symp. problems in the optimization of data communications systems,* 50–57.

DeMillo, Richard, Richard Lipton, and Alan Perlis. 1977. Social processes and proofs of theorems and programs. In *Annual symposium on principles of programming languages: Proceedings of the 4th ACM SIGACT-SIGPLAN symposium on principles of programming languages: Los Angeles, California; 17-19 Jan. 1977,* 206–214.

DeMillo, Richard, Richard Lipton, and Alan Perlis. 1979. Social processes and proofs of theorems and programs. *Comm. ACM* 22 (5): 271–280.

Despres, R. 1972. A packet switching network with graceful saturated operation. In *First international conference on computer communication: Computer communications: Impacts and implications, October 24–26,* 345–351. Washington, DC.

Dewey, Godfrey. 1923. *Relative frequency of English speech sounds.* Cambridge, MA: Harvard University Press.

Diffie, W. 1988. The first ten years of public-key cryptography. *Proceedings of the IEEE* 76 (5): 560–577.

Diffie, W., and M. Hellman. 1976a. New directions in cryptography. *IEEE Transactions on Information Theory* 22 (6): 644–654.

Diffie, W., and M. E. Hellman. 1976b. Multiuser cryptographic techniques. In *Proceedings of the June 7-10, 1976, national computer conference and exposition.* New York: ACM.

Diffie, W., and M. E. Hellman. 1977. Exhaustive cryptanalysis of the nbs data encryption standard. *Computer* 10 (6): 74–84.

Dijkstra, Edsger W. 1959. A note on two problems in connexion with graphs. *Numerische Mathematik* 1 (1): 269–271.

Dijkstra, Edsger W. 1965. Solution of a problem in concurrent programming control. *Comm. ACM* 8 (9): 569. https://doi.org/10.1145/365559.365617.

Dijkstra, Edsger W. 1968a. Go to statement considered harmful [letter to the editor]. *Comm. ACM* 11 (3): 147–148. https://doi.org/10.1145/362929.362947.

Dijkstra, Edsger W. 1968b. The structure of the "THE"-multiprogramming system. *Comm. ACM* 11 (5): 341–346. https://doi.org/10.1145/363095.363143.

Dijkstra, Edsger W. 1972. Notes on structured programming. In *Structured programming,* eds. O. J. Dahl, E. W. Dijkstra, and C. A. R. Hoare, 1–81.

Dijkstra, Edsger W. 1975. Comments at a symposium. http://www.cs.utexas.edu/users/EWD/transcriptions/EWD05xx/EWD512.html.

Dinneen, G. P. 1955. Programming pattern recognition. In *Proc. Western Joint Computer Conference,* 94–100.

Diophantus. 1910. *Diophantus of Alexandria, a study in the history of Greek algebra.* Cambridge: Cambridge University Press.

du Bois-Reymond, Paul. 1870. Sur la grandeur relative des infinis des fonctions. *Annali di Matematica Pura ed Applicata (1867-1897)* 4 (1): 338–353.

Dunn, H. K. 1950. The calculation of vowel resonances, and an electrical vocal tract. *J. Acoustical Society of America* 22 (6): 740–753.

EAI. 1959. *Handbook for Variplotter Models 205S and 205T, PACE.* Long Branch, NJ: Electronic Associates Incorporated.

Eccles, John C. 1953. *The neurophysiological basis of mind; the principles of neurophysiology.* Oxford: Clarendon Press.

Edmonds, Jack. 1965. Paths, trees, and flowers. *Canadian Journal of Mathematics* 17: 449–467.

Edmonds, Jack, and Richard Karp. 1972. Theoretical improvements in algorithmic efficiency for network flow problems. *J. ACM* 19 (2): 248–264.

Engelbart, D. C. 1962. Augmenting human intellect: A conceptual framework. Prepared for: Director of Information Sciences, Air Force Office of Scientific Research, Washington DC, Contract AF 49(638)-1024, Technical Report SRI 3678, AFOSR 3223, Stanford Research Institute, Menlo Park, CA.

Euclid. 1956. *The thirteen books of Euclid's elements,* Revised 2nd edn. New York: Dover Publications.

Evans Jr., Arthur, William Kantrowitz, and Edwin Weiss. 1974. A user authentication scheme not requiring secrecy in the computer. *Comm. ACM* 17 (8): 437–442.

Fant, G. 1959. On the acoustics of speech. In *Third international congress on acoustics*. Stuttgart, Germany.

Farber, D. J. 1973. The distributed computing system. In *Proc. 7th ann. IEEE Computer Soc. International Conf.*, 31–34.

Farber, D. J. 1975a. A ring network. *Datamation* 21 (2): 44–46.

Farber, D. J. 1975b. A virtual channel network. *Datamation* 21 (2): 51–53.

Farley, B. G., and W. Clark. 1954. Simulation of self-organizing systems by digital computer. *IEEE Transactions on Information Theory* 4 (4): 76–84.

Feldman, J. A., and P. D. Rovner. 1968. An Algol-based associative language, Technical report, Stanford Artificial Intelligence Laboratory, Stanford, CA.

Fetzer, James. 1988. Program verification: the very idea. *Comm. ACM* 31 (9): 1048–1063.

Floyd, Robert. 1962. Algorithm 97: Shortest path. *Comm. ACM* 5 (6): 345.

Floyd, Robert W. 1967. Assigning meanings to programs. *Mathematical Aspects of Computer Science, Proceedings of Symposia in Applied Mathematics* 19. doi:10.1090/psapm/019/0235771.

Forgie, James W., and Carma D. Forgie. 1959. Results obtained from a vowel recognition computer program. *J. Acoustical Society of America* 31 (6): 1480–1489.

Frechet, M. 1938. *Methode des fonctions arbitraires. theorie des evenements en chaine dans le cas d'un nombre fini d'etats possibles*. Paris: Gauthier-Villars.

Fredkin, Edward. 1960. Trie memory. *Comm. ACM* 3 (9): 490–499.

Frege, Gottlob. 1879. *Begriffsschrift, eine der arithmetischen nachgebildete formelsprache des reinen denkens*. Halle an der Saale: L. Nebert.

Friedberg, R. M. 1958. A learning machine: Part I. *IBM J. Research and Development* 2 (1): 2–13.

Garey, Michael R., and David S. Johnson. 1979. *Computers and intractability: a guide to the theory of np-completeness. A series of books in the mathematical sciences*. San Francisco: W. H. Freeman.

Gauss, Carl Friedrich. 1986. *Disquisitiones arithmeticae*, English edn. New York: Springer.

Gefter, Amanda. 2015. The man who tried to redeem the world with logic. *Nautilus* 21: 95–103. http://nautil.us/issue/21/information/the-man-who-tried-to-redeem-the-world-with-logic.

Gelernter, H. 1959. Realization of a geometry theorem proving machine. In *International conference on information processing*. Paris: UNESCO, NS, ICIP, 1.6.6.

Gelernter, H., N. S. Sridharan, A. J. Hart, S. C. Yen, F. W. Fowler, and H. J. Shue. 1973. Cheminform abstract: The discovery of organic synthetic routes by computer. *Chemischer Informationsdienst* 4 (52).

George, J. Alan. 1971. Computer implementation of the finite element method. PhD diss, Stanford University.

Gilmore, T., and R. E. Savell. 1959. A program for the production of proofs for theorems derivable within the first order predicate calculus from axioms. In *International conference on information processing*. Paris: UNESCO, NS, ICIP, 1.6.14.

Gorn, S. 1964. Semiotic relationships in unambiguously stratified language systems. In *Int. colloq. algebraic linguistics and automatic theory*. Jerusalem: Hebrew University of Jerusalem.

Gödel, Kurt. 1931. Über formal unentscheidbare Sätze der Principia Mathematica und verwandter Systeme I. *Monatshefte für Mathematik und Physik* 38 (1): 173–198.

Hamming, R. W. 1950. Error detecting and error correcting codes. *The Bell System Technical Journal* 29 (2): 147–160.

Hardy, G. H. 1924. *Orders of infinity*, 2d edn. *Cambridge tracts in mathematics and mathematical physics*. Cambridge: Cambridge University Press.

Hardy, G. H., and J. Littlewood. 1914. Some problems of diophantine approximation. *Acta Mathematica* 37 (1): 155–191.

Hardy, G. H., and J. Littlewood. 1916. Contributions to the theory of the Riemann zeta-function and the theory of the distribution of primes. *Acta Mathematica* 41 (1): 119–196.

Hartley, R. V. L. 1928. Transmission of information. *The Bell System Technical Journal* 7 (3): 535–563.

Hartree, Douglas R. 1949. *Calculating instruments and machines*. Urbana: University of Illinois Press.

Hayek, Friedrich A. von. 1952. *The sensory order; An inquiry into the foundations of theoretical psychology*. Chicago: University of Chicago Press.

Heart, F. E., R. E. Kahn, S. Ornstein, W. Crowther, and D. Walden. 1970. The interface message processor for the ARPA computer network. In *1970 Spring Joint Computer Conference, AFIPS Conf. Proceedings*, Vol. 36. Montvale, NJ: AFIPS Press.

Heart, F. E., S. M. Ornstein, W. R. Crowther, and W. B. Barker. 1972. A new minicomputer-multiprocessor for the ARPA network. In *AFIPS conf. proc., 1972 SJCC*, Vol. 42, 529–537. Montvale, NJ: AFIPS Press.

Heawood, P. J. 1890. Map colouring theorems. *Quarterly J. Math., Oxford Series* 24: 322–339.

Hebb, D. O. 1949. *The organization of behavior: a neuropsychological theory. Wiley book in clinical psychology.* New York: Wiley.

Heller, J. 1961. Sequencing aspects of multiprogramming. *J. ACM* 8 (3): 426–439.

Hellman, M. 1977. An extension of the Shannon theory approach to cryptography. *IEEE Transactions on Information Theory* 23 (3): 289–294.

Hilbert, David. 1902. Mathematical problems. *Bulletin of the American Mathematical Society* 8 (10): 437–479.

Hilbert, David. 1928. Die grundlagen der mathematik. *Abhandlungen aus dem Mathematischen Seminar der Hamburgischen Universität* 6.

Hoare, C. A. R. 1962. Quicksort. *The Computer Journal* 5 (1): 10–16.

Hoare, C. A. R. 1969. An axiomatic basis for computer programming. *Comm. ACM* 12 (10): 576–580. https://doi.org/10.1145/363235.363259.

Hoare, C. A. R. 1981. Emperor's old clothes. *Comm. ACM* 24 (2): 75–83.

Hoare, C. A. R. 1996. Unification of theories: A challenge for computing science. *Recent Trends In Data Type Specification* 1130: 49–57.

Hobbes, Thomas. 1655. *Elementorum philosophiæ sectio prima De corpore authore Thoma Hobbes Malmesburiensi. Early english books online.* Londini: excusum sumptibus Andreæ Crook sub signo Draconis viridis in Cœmeterio B. Pauli.

Hobson, Ernest William. 1921. *The theory of functions of a real variable and the theory of Fourier's series*, 2nd edn. Cambridge: Cambridge University Press.

Hodges, Andrew. 1983. *Alan Turing: the enigma.* New York: Simon and Schuster.

Homer. 1962. *The Iliad.* Chicago: University of Chicago Press.

Hopper, Grace. 1952. The education of a computer. In *ACM Annual Conference/Annual Meeting: Proceedings of the 1952 ACM national meeting (Pittsburgh): Pittsburgh, Pennsylvania*, 243–249.

Huffman, David A. 1952. A method for the construction of minimum-redundancy codes. *Proceedings of the IRE* 40 (9): 1098–1101.

IBM. 1956. *FORTRAN programmer's reference manual.* White Plains, NY: IBM.

IBM. 1965a. *GIS (Generalized Information System), application description manual H20-0574.* White Plains, NY: IBM.

IBM. 1965b. *Information Management System/360, application description manual H20-0524-1.* White Plains, NY: IBM.

IBM. 1974. *IBM synchronous data link control—general information.* Research Triangle Park, NC: IBM Systems Development Division.

IBM. 1975. *IBM system network architecture—general information.* Research Triangle Park, NC: IBM Systems Development Division.

IDS. 1968. *IDS reference manual ge 625/635, CPB 1093B.* Phoenix, AZ: GE Information Systems Division.

Jarník, V. 1930. O jistém problému minimálním. *Práce Moravské Přírodovědecké Společnosti* 6 (4): 57–63.

Jech, Thomas J. 1973. *The axiom of choice.* Amsterdam: North-Holland Publishing. http://hdl.handle.net/2027/coo.31924000209357.

Jefferson, Geoffrey. 1949. The mind of mechanical man. *British Medical Journal* 1 (4616). http://bmj.com/content/1/4616/1105.full.pdf.

Jevons, William Stanley. 1874. *The principles of science: A treatise on logic and scientific method.* London: Macmillan.

Jones, Matthew L. 2016. *Reckoning with matter: calculating machines, innovation, and thinking about thinking from pascal to babbage.* Chicago: University of Chicago Press.

Kahn, David. 1967. *The codebreakers: The story of secret writing.* New York: Macmillan.

Kahn, R., and W. Crowther. 1972. Flow control in a resource-sharing computer network. *IEEE Transactions on Communications* 20 (3): 539–546.

Kahn, R. R. 1975. The organization of computer resources into a packet radio network. In *Proc. 1975 NCC*, Vol. 44, 177–186. Montvale, NJ: AFIPS Press.

Karatsuba, A., and Yuri Ofman. 1962. Multiplication of many-digital numbers by automatic computers. *Proc. USSR Academy of Sciences* 142: 293–294.

Karp, R. M. 1972. Reducibility among combinatorial problems. In *Complexity of computer computations*, eds. R. E. Miller, J. W. Thatcher, and J. D. Bohlinger. *The IBM research symposia series.* Boston: Springer. https://doi.org/10.1007/978-1-4684-2001-2_9.

Keen, E., and J. Digger. 1972. Report of an information science index languages test. *Aberystwyth, Department of Information Retrieval Studies, College of Librarianship Wales, June 72, (2v) 173p.*

Kempe, A. B. 1879. On the geographical problem of the four colours. *American Journal of Mathematics* 2 (3): 193–200.

Kendall, Maurice G. 1939. *Tables of random sampling numbers. Tracts of computers.* Cambridge: Cambridge University Press.

Khachiyan, L. G. 1979. A polynomial algorithm for linear programming (in Russian). *Doklady Akadmiia Nauk USSR* 244: 1093–1096.

Kleene, S. C. 1935a. A theory of positive integers in formal logic, Part I. *American Journal of Mathematics* 57 (1): 153–173.

Kleene, S. C. 1935b. A theory of positive integers in formal logic, Part II. *American Journal of Mathematics* 57 (2): 219–244.

Kleene, S. C. 1951. Representation of events in nerve nets and finite automata, Technical report, RAND Project Air Force, Santa Monica, CA.

Klyuev, V. V., and H. I. Kokovkin-Shcherbak. 1965. Minimization of the number of arithmetic operations in the solution of linear algebraic systems of equations. *USSR Computational Mathematics and Mathematical Physics* 5 (1): 25–43.

Knuth, Donald Ervin. 1963. Notes On "Open" Addressing. http://jeffe.cs.illinois.edu/teaching/datastructures/2011/notes/knuth-OALP.pdf.

Knuth, Donald Ervin. 1965. On the translation of languages from left to right. *Information and Control* 8 (6): 607–639.

Knuth, Donald Ervin. 1969. *The art of computer programming, Volume 2: Seminumerical algorithms.* Boston: Addison-Wesley.

Knuth, Donald Ervin. 1973. *The art of computer programming, Vol. 3: Sorting and searching.* Boston: Addison-Wesley.

Knuth, Donald Ervin. 1974a. Structured programming with go to statements. *ACM Computing Surveys (CSUR)* 6 (4): 261–301.

Knuth, Donald Ervin. 1974b. A terminological proposal. *SIGACT News* 6 (1): 12–18. doi:10.1145/1811129.1811130.

Knuth, Donald Ervin. 1976. Big omicron and big omega and big theta. *ACM SIGACT News* 8 (2): 18–24.

Knuth, Donald Ervin. 1986a. *The METAFONTbook.* Boston: Addison-Wesley.

Knuth, Donald Ervin. 1986b. *The TeXbook.* Boston: Addison-Wesley.

Knuth, Donald Ervin. 1997a. *The art of computer programming. Volume 1, Fundamental algorithms*, 3rd edn. Boston: Addison Wesley.

Knuth, Donald Ervin. 1997b. *The art of computer programming, Volume 2: Seminumerical algorithms*, 3rd edn. Boston: Addison-Wesley.

Knuth, Donald Ervin. 1998. *The art of computer programming. Volume 3, Sorting and searching*, 2nd edn. Boston: Addison-Wesley.

Knuth, Donald Ervin. 2011. *The art of computer programming. Volume 4A, Combinatorial algorithms, part 1.* Boston: Addison Wesley.

Köhler, W. 1951. Relational determination in perception. In *Cerebral mechanisms in behavior*, ed. Lloyd A. Jeffress, 200–243. New York: Wiley.

Kolata, Gina Bari. 1976. Mathematical proofs: The genesis of reasonable doubt. *Science* 192 (4243): 989–990.

Kreider, D. L., and R. W. Ritchie. 1964. Predictably computable functionals and definition by recursion. *Mathematical Logic Quarterly* 10 (5): 65–80.

Kruskal, Joseph B. 1956. On the shortest spanning subtree of a graph and the traveling salesman problem. *Proc. American Mathematical Society* 7 (1): 48–50.

Lakatos, Imre. 1976. *Proofs and refutations: The logic of mathematical discovery.* Cambridge: Cambridge University Press.

Lamport, Leslie. 2015. The computer science of concurrency: the early years. https://lamport.azurewebsites.net/pubs/turing.pdf.

Lampson, Butler. 1968. A scheduling philosophy for multiprocessing systems. *Comm. ACM* 11 (5): 347–360.

Lancaster, F. Wilfrid. 1968. *Information retrieval systems; characteristics, testing, and evaluation. Information sciences series.* New York: Wiley.

Landau, Edmund. 1909. *Handbuch der lehre von der verteilung der primzahlen.* Leipzig, Germany: B. G. Teubner.

Laplante, Phillip. 1996. *Great papers in computer science.* Eagan, MN: West Publishing Company.

Lawrence, W. 1956. Methods and purposes of speech synthesis, Technical Report 56/1457, Signals Res. and Dev. Estab., Ministry of Supply, Christchurch, Hants., England.

Leeds, H. D., and G. M. Weinberg. 1961. Multiprogramming. In *Computer programming fundamentals*, ed. Herbert D. Leeds, 356–359. New York: McGraw-Hill.

Leibniz, G. W. 1666. *Dissertatio de arte combinatorica.* Leipzig, Germany: Fickium and Seuboldum.

Leibniz, G. W. 2020. The true method. Translated by Lloyd Strickland from the original 1677 manuscript.

Lettvin, J. Y., H. R. Maturana, W. S. McCulloch, and W. H. Pitts. 1959. What the frog's eye tells the frog's brain. *Proceedings of the IRE* 47 (11): 1940–1951.

Levien, R., and M. Maron. 1967. A computer system for inference execution and data retrieval. *Comm. ACM* 10 (11): 715–721.

Levin, Leonid A. 1973. Universal search problems (in Russian). *Problems of Information Transmission* 9 (3).

Levine, Jack, and J. V. Brawley. 1977. Some cryptographic applications of permutation polynomials. *Cryptologia* 1 (1): 76–92.

Liberman, A. M., Frances Ingemann, Leigh Lisker, and F. S. Cooper. 1959. Minimal rules for synthesizing speech. *J. Acoustical Soc. America* 31 (1): 1490–1499.

Licklider, J. C. R. 1960. Man-computer symbiosis. *IRE Transactions on Human Factors in Electronics* HFE-1 (1): 4–11.

Liskov, Barbara, and Stephen Zilles. 1974. Programming with abstract data types. *ACM SIGPLAN Notices* 9 (4): 50–59. https://doi.org/10.1145/942572.807045.

Ludolph van Ceulen. 1596. *Vanden circkel.* Delft, Netherlands: Jan Andriesz.

MacHale, Des. 2014. *The life and work of George Boole: A prelude to the digital age*, New edn. Cork, Ireland: Cork University Press.

Manin, I. 1977. *A course in mathematical logic. Graduate texts in mathematics; 53.* New York: Springer.

Matiyasevich, Yuri. 1993. *Hilbert's tenth problem. Foundations of computing.* Cambridge, MA: MIT Press.

McCarthy, John. 1960. Recursive functions of symbolic expressions and their computation by machine, Part I. *Comm. ACM* 3 (4): 184–195. https://doi.org/10.1145/367177.367199.

McCarthy, John. 1961. Programs with common sense. In *Mechanisation of thought processes: proceedings of a symposium held at the National Physical Laboratory on 24th, 25th, 26th and 27th November 1958.* London: H. M. Stationery Office. National Physical Laboratory (Great Britain).

McCarthy, John. 1963. Towards a mathematical science of computation. In *Information processing 1962: proceedings of IFIP congress 62, convened with the financial assistance of UNESCO, Munich [Germany], 27 August–1 September 1962*, ed. Cicely Popplewell, 21–28.

McCulloch, W. S. 1951. Why the mind is in the head. In *Cerebral mechanisms in behavior*, ed. Lloyd A. Jeffress, 42–111. New York: Wiley.

McCulloch, W. S., and W. Pitts. 1943. A logical calculus of the ideas immanent in nervous activity. *Bulletin of mathematical biophysics* 5 (4): 115–133.

McGee, W. C. 1969. Generalized file processing. In *Annual review in automatic programming*, Vol. 5. New York: Pergamon Press.

McKenzie, A. 1972. HOST-HOST protocol for the ARPA network, Technical Report NIC 8246, Network Information Center, Menlo Park, CA.

McKenzie, A. 1973. HOST-HOST protocol design considerations, Technical Report INWG 16, NIC 13879, Network Information Center, Menlo Park, CA.

Menabrea, Luigi Federico. 1843. *Sketch of the analytical engine invented by Charles Babbage, Esq.* London: Taylor and Francis.

Merkle, Ralph C. 1978. Secure communications over insecure channels. *Comm. ACM* 21 (4): 294–299. http://doi.acm.org/10.1145/359460.359473.

Metcalfe, R. M. 1972a. Steady-state analysis of a slotted and controlled alhoa system with blocking. In *Proc. 6th Hawaii Conf. on System Sci.*, 278–281.

Metcalfe, R. M. 1972b. Strategies for interprocess communication in a distributed computing system. In *Proc. symp. on computer communication networks and teletraffic.* New York: Polytechnic Press.

Metcalfe, R. M. 1972c. Strategies for operating systems in computer networks. In *Proc. ACM National Conf.* New York: ACM.

Metcalfe, R. M. 1973. Packet communication. PhD diss., Harvard University, Technical Report TR-114, Project MAC.

Metcalfe, Robert, and David Boggs. 1976. Ethernet: Distributed packet switching for local computer networks. *Comm. ACM* 19 (7): 395–404. https://doi.org/10.1145/360248.360253.

Miller, Gary L. 1976. Riemann's hypothesis and tests for primality. *J. Computer and System Sciences* 13 (3): 300–317.

Milner, P. 1957. The cell assembly: Mark II. *Psychological Review* 64.

Minsky, M. L. 1956. Some universal elements for finite automata. In *Automata studies*, eds. Claude E. Shannon and J. McCarthy, 117–128. Princeton, NJ: Princeton University Press.

Minsky, Marvin, and Seymour Papert. 1969. *Perceptrons: an introduction to computational geometry.* Cambridge, MA: MIT Press.

Moore, G. E. 1965. Cramming more components onto integrated circuits. *Electronics* 38: 114–117.

Moore, G. E. 2006. Cramming more components onto integrated circuits. *IEEE Solid-State Circuits Society Newsletter* 11 (3): 33–35.

Morland, Samuel. 1673. *The description and use of two arithmetick instruments.* London: Moses Pitt.

Newell, A. 1955. The chess machine: an example of dealing with a complex task by adaptation. In *Proc. Western Joint Computer Conference*, 101–108.

Newell, A., and J. C. Shaw. 1957. Programming the logic theory machine. In *Proc. Western Joint Computer Conference*, 230–240.

Newell, Allen, J. C. Shaw, and H. A. Simon. 1958. Chessplaying programs and the problem of complexity. *IBM J. Research and Development* 2 (4): 320–335.

Niven, Ivan Morton. 1972. *An introduction to the theory of numbers.* Hoboken, NJ: Wiley. http://hdl.handle.net/2027/umn.319510004761203.

North, J. D. 1954. The rational behavior of mechanically extended man, Technical report, Boulton Paul Aircraft, Wolverhampton, UK.

Nyquist, H. 1924. Certain factors affecting telegraph speed. *Bell System Technical Journal* 3 (2): 324–346.

Nyquist, H. 1928. Certain topics in telegraph transmission theory. *Transactions of the American Institute of Electrical Engineers* 47 (2): 617–644.

Ornstein, S. M., W. R. Crowther, M. F. Kraley, R. D. Bressler, A. Michel, and F. E. Heart. 1975. Pluribus—a reliable multiprocessor. In *AFIPS Conf. Proc., 1975 NCC*, Vol. 44, 551–559. Montvale, NJ.

Parnas, D. L. 1971. Information distribution aspects of design methodology, Technical report, Carnegie-Mellon Univ., Dept. of Computer Science, Pittsburgh.

Peacock, George. 1830. *A treatise on algebra.* Cambridge: Cambridge University Press.

Perlis, A., and K. Samelson. 1958. Preliminary report: international algebraic language. *Comm. ACM* 1 (12): 8–22.

Péter, Rózsa. 1951. *Rekursive funktionen.* Budapest: Akadémiai Kiadó.

Pohlig, S., and M. Hellman. 1978. An improved algorithm for computing logarithms over GF(p) and its cryptographic significance (corresp.). *IEEE Transactions on Information Theory* 24 (1): 106–110.

Pollard, J. M. 1974. Theorems on factorization and primality testing. *Mathematical Proceedings of the Cambridge Philosophical Society* 76 (3): 521–528.

Popek, G., J. Horning, B. Lampson, J. Mitchell, and R. London. 1977. Notes on the design of Euclid. *ACM SIGPLAN Notices* 12 (3): 11–18.

Potter, Robert J. 1977. Electronic mail. *Science* 195 (4283): 1160.

Pouzin, L. 1973a. Address format in Mitranet, Technical Report INWF 20, NIC 14497, Network Information Center.

Pouzin, L. 1973b. Presentation and major design aspects of the CYCLADES computer network. In *Proc. 3rd Data Communications Symposium.*

Prachar, Karl. 1957. *Primzahlverteilung. Die grundlehren der mathematischen wissenschaften.* Berlin: Springer.

Pratt, Fletcher. 1939. *Secret and urgent.* Garden City, NY: Blue Ribbon Books.

Pratt, Vernon. 1987. *Thinking machines: The evolution of artificial intelligence.* Oxford, UK: B. Blackwell.

Priestley, Mark. 2011. *A science of operations: Machines, logic and the invention of programming. History of computing.* London: Springer.

Prim, R. C. 1957. Shortest connection networks and some generalizations. *The Bell System Technical Journal* 36 (6): 1389–1401.

Purdy, George. 1974. A high security log-in procedure. *Comm. ACM* 17 (8): 442–445.

Rabin, Michael O. 1976. Probabilistic algorithms. In *Algorithms and complexity: Proceedings of a symposium on new directions and recent results in algorithms and complexity held by the Computer Science Department, Carnegie-Mellon University, April 7-9, 1976*, ed. Joseph Traub. Cambridge, MA: Academic Press.

Rashevsky, Nicolas. 1938. *Mathematical biophysics; physicomathematical foundations of biology.* Chicago: Univ. of Chicago Press.

Raymo, Chet. 1996. A giant of logic lost to the irrational. *Boston Globe,* 25 November 1996: D2.

Ritchie, Dennis, and Ken Thompson. 1974. The UNIX time-sharing system. *Comm. ACM* 17 (7): 365–375. https://doi.org/10.1145/361011.361061.

Rivest, R., A. Shamir, and L. Adleman. 1978. A method for obtaining digital signatures and public-key cryptosystems. *Comm. ACM* 21 (2): 120–126. https://doi.org/10.1145/359340.359342.

Roberts, L. 1973. Capture effects on Aloha channels. In *Proc. 6th Hawaii Conf. on System Sci.*

Roberts, L., and B. Wessler. 1970a. Computer network development to achieve resource sharing. In *1970 spring joint computer conference, AFIPS conf. proceedings*, Vol. 36. Montvale, NJ: AFIPS Press.

Roberts, L., and B. Wessler. 1970b. Computer network development to achieve resource sharing. In *AFIPS conf.*

proc., 1970 Spring Joint Computer Conference, Vol. 36, 543–549. Montvale, NJ: AFIPS Press.

Rogers, Hartley. 1967. *Theory of recursive functions and effective computability. McGraw-Hill series in higher mathematics.* New York: McGraw-Hill.

Rosenblatt, F. 1958a. The perceptron: A probabilistic model for information storage and organization in the brain. *Psychological Review* 65 (6): 386–408. https://doi.org/10.1037/h0042519.

Rosenblatt, F. 1958b. The perceptron: A theory of statistical separability in cognitive systems, Technical Report VG-1196-G-1, Cornell Aeronautical Lab., Buffalo, NY.

Rowe, L. A. 1975. The distributed computing operating system, Technical Report 66, Dep. of Information and Computer Sci., University of California, Irvine.

Royce, Winston. 1970. Managing the development of large software systems. In *Proceedings, IEEE WESCON*, 1–9. Los Angeles, CA: IEEE Computer Society Press.

Royce, Winston. 1987. Managing the development of large software systems. In *ICSE '87, proceedings of the 9th international conference on Software Engineering*, 328–338. Los Angeles, CA: IEEE Computer Society Press.

Rustin, R., ed. 1970. *Computer networks (Proc. Courant Computer Sci. Symp. 3, December, 1970).* Englewood Cliffs, NJ: Prentice-Hall.

Salton, G., and M. Lesk. 1968. Computer evaluation of indexing and text processing. *J. ACM* 15 (1): 8–36.

Salton, Gerard. 1968. *Automatic information organization and retrieval. McGraw-Hill computer science series.* New York: McGraw-Hill.

Sammet, Jean. 1972. Programming languages: history and future. *Comm. ACM* 15 (7): 601–610.

Scantlebury, R. A., and P. T. Wilkinson. 1971. The design of a switching system to allow remote access to computer services by other computers and terminal devices. In *Proc. 2nd symp. problems in the optimization of data communications systems*, 160–167.

Schmitt, W. F., and A. B. Tonik. 1959. Sympathetically programmed computers. In *International conference on information processing.* Paris: UNESCO, NS, ICIP, 8.2.18.

Searle, John. 1980. Minds, brains and programs. *Behavioral and Brain Sciences* 3: 417–424. http://cogprints.org/7150/.

Selfridge, O. 1958. Pandemonium, a paradigm for learning. In *Proc. symp. mechanisation of thought processes.* Teddington, England: Natl. Physical Lab..

Shamir, Adi. 1979. How to share a secret. *Comm. ACM* 22 (11): 612–613. https://doi.org/10.1145/359168.359176.

Shamir, Adi. 1984. A polynomial-time algorithm for breaking the basic Merkle-Hellman cryptosystem. *IEEE Trans. on Information Theory* 30 (5): 699–704.

Shannon, Claude E. 1938. A symbolic analysis of relay and switching circuits. *Transactions of the American Institute of Electrical Engineers* 57 (12): 713–723.

Shannon, Claude E. 1948. A mathematical theory of communication. *Bell System Technical Journal* 27 (4): 623–656.

Shannon, Claude E. 1949. Communication theory of secrecy systems. *Bell System Technical Journal* 28 (4): 656–715.

Shannon, Claude E. 1950. Programming a computer for playing chess. *Philosophical Magazine* 41 (314).

Shaw, J. C., A. Newell, H. A. Simon, and T. O. Ellis. 1958. A command structure for complex information processing. In *Proc. Western Joint Computer Conference*, 119–128.

Sherman, H. 1959. A quasi-topological method for recognition of line patterns. In *International conference on information processing.* Paris: UNESCO, NS, ICIP, H.L.5.

Shieber, Stuart, ed. 2004. *The Turing test: Verbal behavior as the hallmark of intelligence.* Cambridge, MA: MIT Press.

Shor, Peter W. 1999. Polynomial-time algorithms for prime factorization and discrete logarithms on a quantum computer. *SIAM Review* 41 (2): 303–332.

Simon, Herbert A. 1996. *The sciences of the artificial*, 3rd edn. Cambridge, MA: MIT Press.

Smith, Jane I., and Yvonne Y. Haddad. 1975. Women in the afterlife. *Journal of the American Academy of Religion* 43 (1): 39–50.

Solovay, R., and V. Strassen. 1977. A fast Monte-Carlo test for primality. *SIAM Journal on Computing* 6 (1): 84–85.

Spärck Jones, Karen. 1971. *Automatic keyword classification for information retrieval.* Hamden, CT: Archon Books. http://hdl.handle.net/2027/uc1.b4333044.

Spärck Jones, Karen. 1972. A statistical interpretation of term specificity and its application in retrieval. *Journal of Documentation* 28 (1): 11–21.

Sparks, S., and R. G. Kreer. 1947. Tape relay system for radio telegraph operation. *R.C.A. Review* 8: 393–426.

Stevens, K. N., S. Kasowski, and C. Gunnar M. Fant. 1953. An electrical analog of the vocal tract. *J. Acoustical Society of America* 25 (4): 734–742.

Stockmeyer, L. 1974. The complexity of decision problems in automata theory and logic. PhD diss, MIT, Cambridge, MA.

Strachey, C. 1959. Time sharing in large fast computers. In *International conference on information processing*. Paris: UNESCO, NS, ICIP, 8.2.19.

Strassen, Volker. 1969. Gaussian elimination is not optimal. *Numerische Mathematik* 13 (4): 354–356.

Struik, Dirk J. 1969. *A source book in mathematics, 1200-1800*. Cambridge, MA: Harvard University Press.

Sutherland, Ivan Edward. 1963. Sketchpad: a manmachine graphical communication system, Technical Report 296, MIT Lincoln Laboratory, Lexington, MA.

Tarjan, Robert. 1975. Efficiency of a good but not linear set union algorithm. *J. ACM* 22 (2): 215–225.

Teager, Herbert. 1962. Real-time, time-shared computer project. *Comm. ACM* 5 (1).

Teager, Herbert, and John McCarthy. 1959. Time-shared program testing. In *ACM annual conference/annual meeting: Preprints of papers presented at the 14th national meeting of the Association for Computing Machinery: Cambridge, Massachusetts; 01-03 Sept. 1959*, 1–2.

Thornton, J. E. 1970. *Design of a computer: the Control Data 6600*. Glenview, IL: Scott, Foresman.

Titchmarsh, E. C. 1951. *The theory of the Riemann zeta-function*. Oxford: Clarendon Press.

Turing, Alan M. 1936. On computable numbers, with an application to the Entscheidungsproblem. *Proceedings of the London Mathematical Society* s2-42 (1): 230–265. http://doi.org/10.1112/plms/s2-42.1.230.

Turing, Alan M. 1938. On computable numbers, with an application to the Entscheidungsproblem. A correction. *Proceedings of the London Mathematical Society* 43 (1): 544–546.

Turing, Alan M. 1945. Proposed electronic calculator, Technical report, National Physical Laboratory. http://www.alanturing.net/turing_archive/archive/p/p01/p01.php.

Turing, Alan M. 1950. Computing machinery and intelligence. *Mind* 59 (236): 433–460. https://doi.org/10.1093/mind/LIX.236.433.

Unknown. 1906. The most remarkable boy in the world. *World Magazine,* 7 October 1906: 1–3.

Uttley, A. M. 1956. Conditional probability machines and conditional reflexes. In *Automata studies*, eds. Claude E. Shannon and J. McCarthy, 253–275. Princeton, NJ: Princeton University Press.

Van Heijenoort, Jean. 1967. *From Frege to Gödel; a source book in mathematical logic, 1879-1931*. Cambridge, MA: Harvard University Press.

van Vlissingen, Rogier F., and Edsger W. Dijkstra. 1985. Interview with Prof. Dr. Edsger W. Dijkstra. https://www.cs.utexas.edu/users/EWD/misc/vanVlissingenInterview.html.

Vinogradov, I. M. 1954. *The method of trigonometrical sums in the theory of numbers*. Geneva: Interscience Publishers. http://hdl.handle.net/2027/mdp.39015000961329.

von Neumann, J. 1951. The general and logical theory of automata. In *Cerebral mechanisms in behavior; the Hixon symposium*, ed. Lloyd A. Jeffress, 1–41. New York: Wiley.

von Neumann, J. 1956. Probabilistic logics and the synthesis of reliable organisms from unreliable components. In *Automata studies*, eds. Claude E. Shannon and John McCarthy, 43–98. Princeton, NJ: Princeton University Press.

von Neumann, J. 1993. First draft of a report on the EDVAC. *IEEE Annals of the History of Computing* 15 (4): 27–75.

von Neumann, J. 2000. *The computer and the brain*, 2nd edn. *Mrs. Hepsa Ely Silliman memorial lectures*. New Haven, CT: Yale University Press.

Walden, David. 1972. A system for interprocess communication in a resource sharing computer network. *Comm. ACM* 15 (4): 221–230.

Warshall, Stephen. 1962. A theorem on boolean matrices. *J. ACM* 9 (1): 11–12.

Webster, Noah. 1959. *New international dictionary of the English language*, 2nd edn. Springfield, MA: G. & C. Merriam.

Weizenbaum, J. 1963. Symmetric list processor. *Comm. ACM* 6 (9): 524–536.

Weizenbaum, J. 1966. ELIZA—A computer program for the study of natural language communication between man and machine. *Comm. ACM* 9 (1): 36–45. https://doi.org/10.1145/365153.365168.

Weizenbaum, J. 1976. *Computer power and human reason: from judgment to calculation*. San Francisco: W. H. Freeman.

Wells, H. G. 1938. *World brain*. London: Methuen.

Whitehead, Alfred North, and Bertrand Russell. 1910. *Principia mathematica,*. Cambridge: Cambridge University Press.

Wiener, Norbert. 1947. A scientist rebels. *Atlantic* 179: 31.

Wiener, Norbert. 1948. *Cybernetics: or, control and communication in the animal and the machine*. New York: J. Wiley.

Wiener, Norbert. 1950. *The human use of human beings: cybernetics and society*. Boston: Houghton Mifflin.

Wiener, Norbert. 1960. Some moral and technical consequences of automation. *Science* 131 (3410): 1355–1358.

Wilkes, Maurice V. 1972. *Time-sharing computer systems*, 2nd edn. *Computer monographs; 5*. New York: Elsevier.

Wilkes, Maurice V. 1981. The best way to design an automatic calculating machine. *Microprocessing and Microprogramming* 8.

Wilkes, Maurice V. 1986. The genesis of microprogramming. *Annals of the History of Computing* 8 (2): 116–126.

Willard, D. G. 1973. A sophisticated digital cable communications system. In *Proc. National Telecommunications Conference*.

Winograd, S. 1968. A new algorithm for inner product. *IEEE Transactions on Computers* C-17 (7): 693–694.

Wirth, N. 1971. The programming language Pascal. *Acta Informatica* 1 (1): 35–63.

Wirth, Niklaus, and C. Hoare. 1966. A contribution to the development of ALGOL. *Comm. ACM* 9 (6): 413–432.

Wulf, W., and R. Levin. 1972. C.mmp—a multi-miniprocessor. In *AFIPS Conf. Proc., 1972 NCC*, Vol. 41, 551–559. Montvale, NJ.

Zunde, Pranas, and Vladimir Slamecka. 1967. Distribution of indexing terms for maximum efficiency of information transmission. *American Documentation* 18 (2): 104–108.

Index